JERUSALEM

CHRONICLES FROM THE HOLY CITY

THANK YOU MICHAEL, LOUISE, ISAAC, ASAF, IMRI, BRIGITTE, LEWIS, JUL, HUBERT, CÉCILE, NICOLAI, CHARLOTTE, AMER, ATTAR, SÉBASTIEN AND NADÈGE.

TRANSLATED BY HELGE DASCHER. WITH SPECIAL THANKS TO DAG DASCHER AND MARK LANG.

ALSO BY GUY DELISLE:
BURMA CHRONICLES
PYONGYANG: A JOURNEY IN NORTH KOREA
SHENZHEN: A TRAVELOGUE FROM CHINA
ALBERT & THE OTHERS
ALINE & THE OTHERS

ORIGINALLY PUBLISHED IN FRENCH BY EDITIONS DELCOURT.

WWW.GUYDELISLE.COM

DRAWN & QUARTERLY
POST OFFICE BOX 48056
MONTREAL, QUEBEC
CANADA H2V 4S8

WWW.DRAWNANDQUARTERLY.COM

FIRST HARDCOVER EDITION: APRIL 2012.
ISBN 978-1-77046-071-3.
PRINTED IN CHINA.
10 9 8 7 6 5 4 3 2 1

LIBRARY AND ARCHIVES CANADA CATALOGUING IN PUBLICATION:
DELISLE, GUY
       JERUSALEM: CHRONICLES FROM THE HOLY CITY / GUY DELISLE.
ISBN 978-1-77046-071-3
       1. DELISLE, GUY—TRAVEL—ISRAEL—COMICS BOOKS, STRIPS, ETC.
2. ISRAEL—DESCRIPTION AND TRAVEL—COMIC BOOKS, STRIPS, ETC.
3. GRAPHIC NOVELS. I. TITLE. DS107.5.D44 2012   915.69404'54   C2011-907513-X

DRAWN & QUARTERLY ACKNOWLEDGES THE FINANCIAL CONTRIBUTION OF THE GOVERNMENT OF CANADA THROUGH THE CANADA BOOK FUND, THE CANADA COUNCIL FOR THE ARTS, AND THE NATIONAL TRANSLATION PROGRAM FOR BOOK PUBLISHING FOR OUR PUBLISHING ACTIVITIES AND FOR SUPPORT OF THIS EDITION.

Liberté • Égalité • Fraternité
RÉPUBLIQUE FRANÇAISE

THIS BOOK HAS BEEN SUPPORTED BY THE FRENCH MINISTRY OF FOREIGN AND EUROPEAN AFFAIRS, AS PART OF THE TRANSLATION GRANT PROGRAM.

DISTRIBUTED IN THE U.S. BY:
FARRAR, STRAUS AND GIROUX
18 WEST 18TH STREET
NEW YORK, NY 10011
ORDERS: 888.330.8477

DISTRIBUTED IN CANADA BY:
RAINCOAST BOOKS
2440 VIKING WAY
RICHMOND, BC V6V 1N2
ORDERS: 800.663.5714

JERUSALEM

CHRONICLES FROM THE HOLY CITY

GUY DELISLE

COLOURED BY LUCIE FIROUD & GUY DELISLE
TRANSLATED BY HELGE DASCHER

DRAWN & QUARTERLY

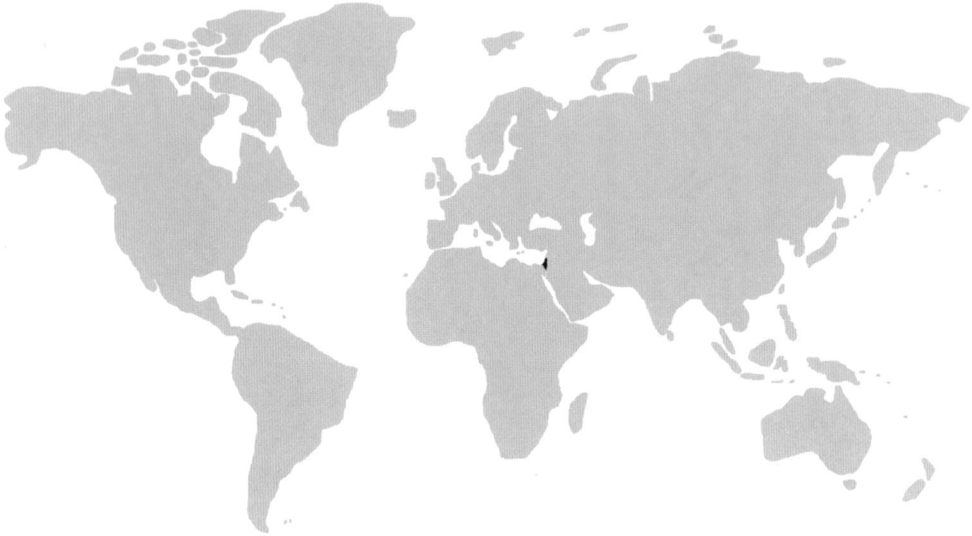

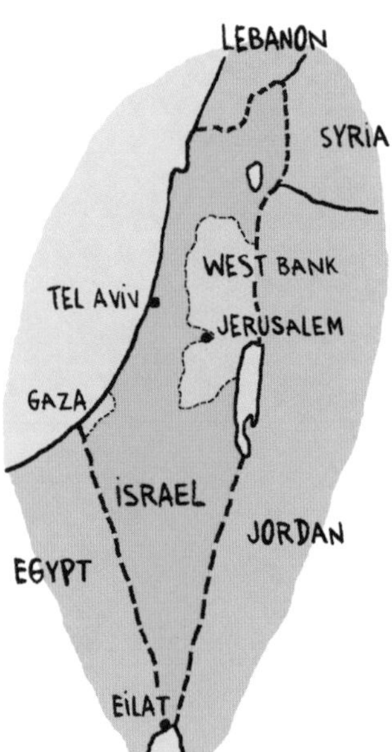
LEBANON
SYRIA
WEST BANK
TEL AVIV
JERUSALEM
GAZA
ISRAEL
JORDAN
EGYPT
EILAT

AUGUST

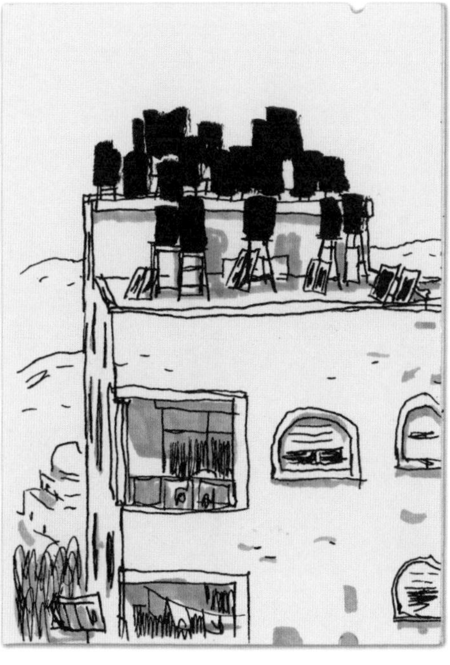

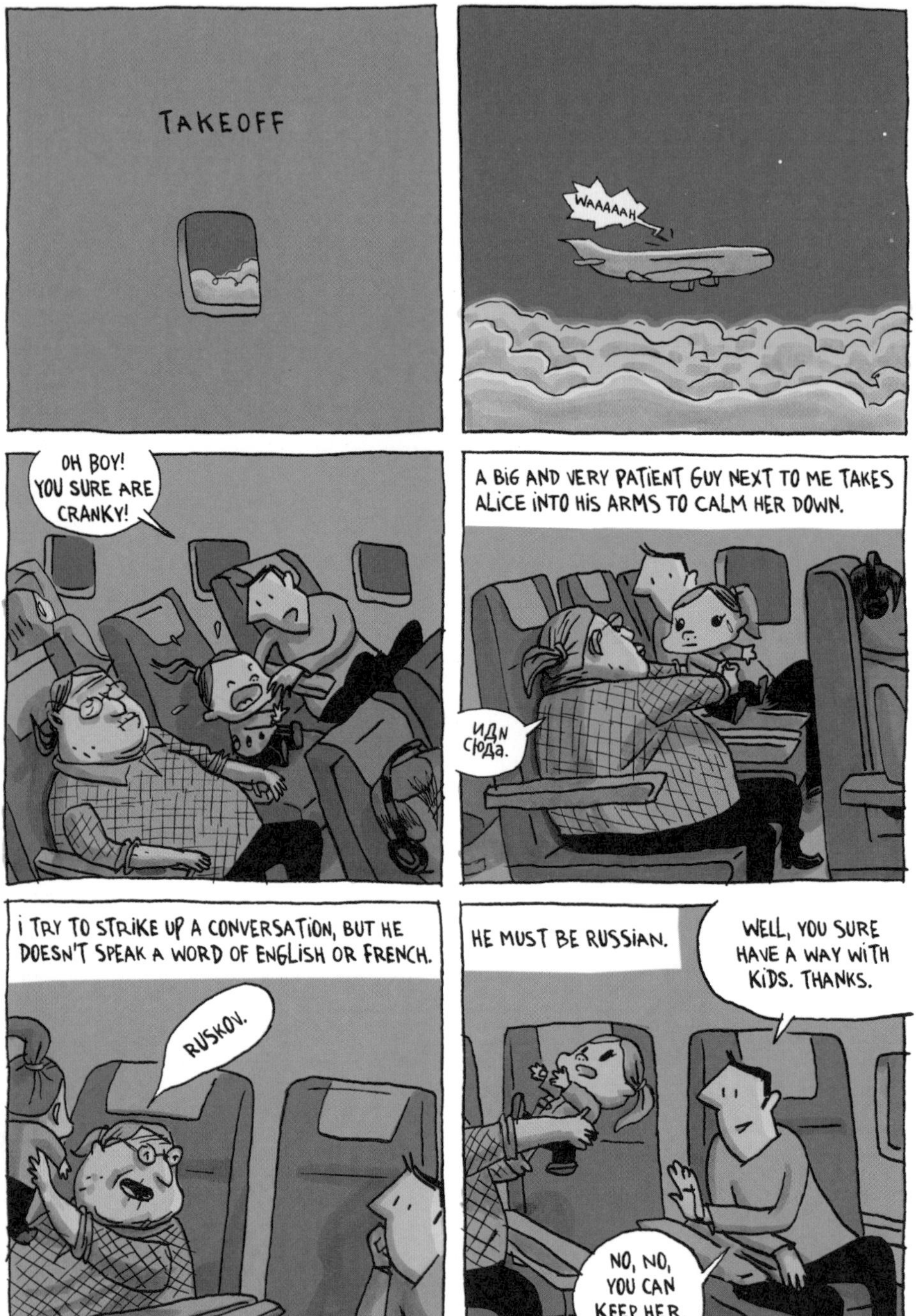
TAKEOFF
WAAAAAH
OH BOY! YOU SURE ARE CRANKY!
A BIG AND VERY PATIENT GUY NEXT TO ME TAKES ALICE INTO HIS ARMS TO CALM HER DOWN.
ИДИ сюда.
I TRY TO STRIKE UP A CONVERSATION, BUT HE DOESN'T SPEAK A WORD OF ENGLISH OR FRENCH.
RUSKOV.
HE MUST BE RUSSIAN.
WELL, YOU SURE HAVE A WAY WITH KIDS. THANKS.
NO, NO, YOU CAN KEEP HER.

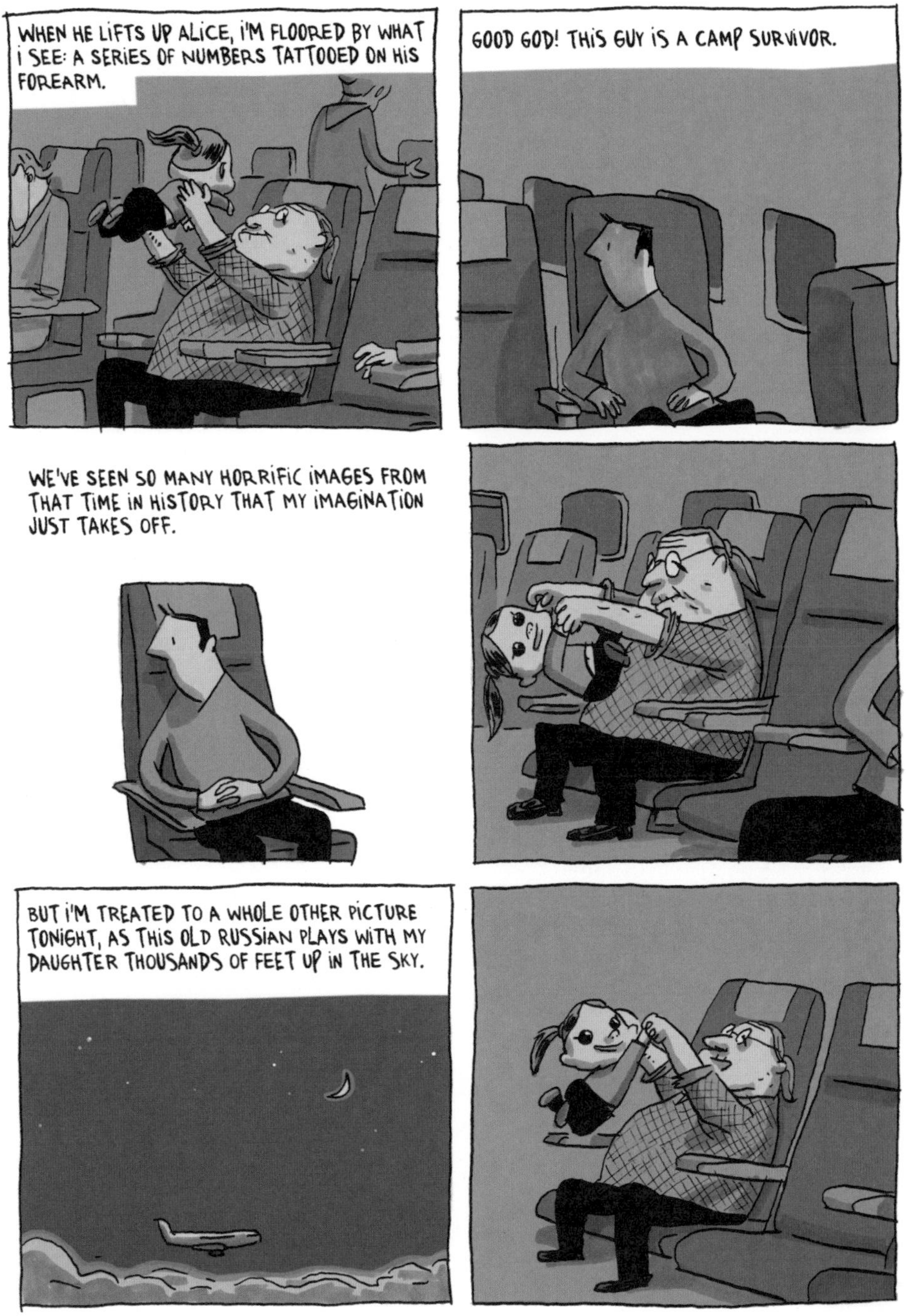
WHEN HE LIFTS UP ALICE, I'M FLOORED BY WHAT I SEE: A SERIES OF NUMBERS TATTOOED ON HIS FOREARM.
GOOD GOD! THIS GUY IS A CAMP SURVIVOR.
WE'VE SEEN SO MANY HORRIFIC IMAGES FROM THAT TIME IN HISTORY THAT MY IMAGINATION JUST TAKES OFF.
BUT I'M TREATED TO A WHOLE OTHER PICTURE TONIGHT, AS THIS OLD RUSSIAN PLAYS WITH MY DAUGHTER THOUSANDS OF FEET UP IN THE SKY.

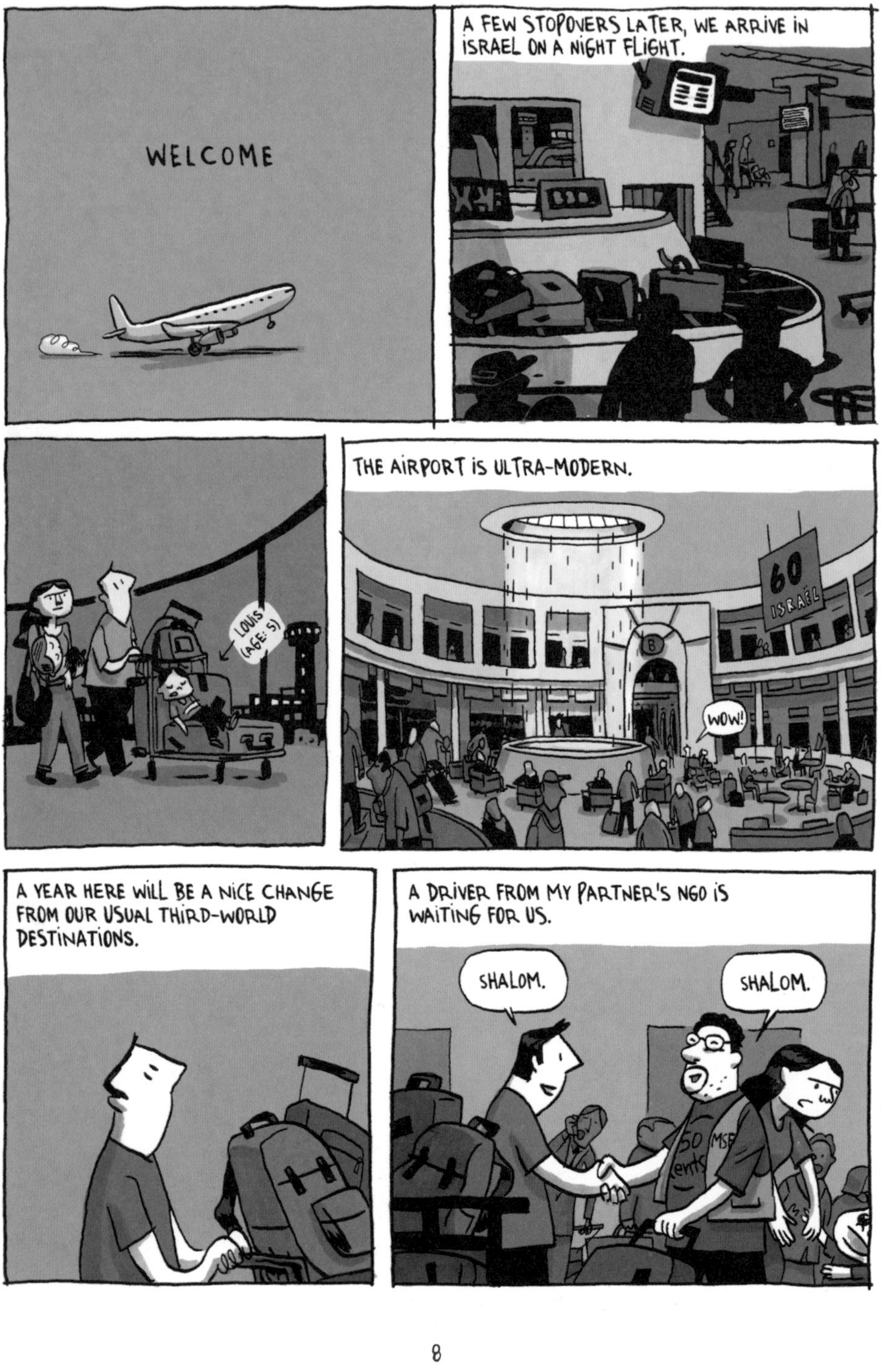
WELCOME
A FEW STOPOVERS LATER, WE ARRIVE IN ISRAEL ON A NIGHT FLIGHT.
LOUIS (AGE: 5)
THE AIRPORT IS ULTRA-MODERN.
60 ISRAEL
WOW!
A YEAR HERE WILL BE A NICE CHANGE FROM OUR USUAL THIRD-WORLD DESTINATIONS.
A DRIVER FROM MY PARTNER'S NGO IS WAITING FOR US.
SHALOM.
SHALOM.

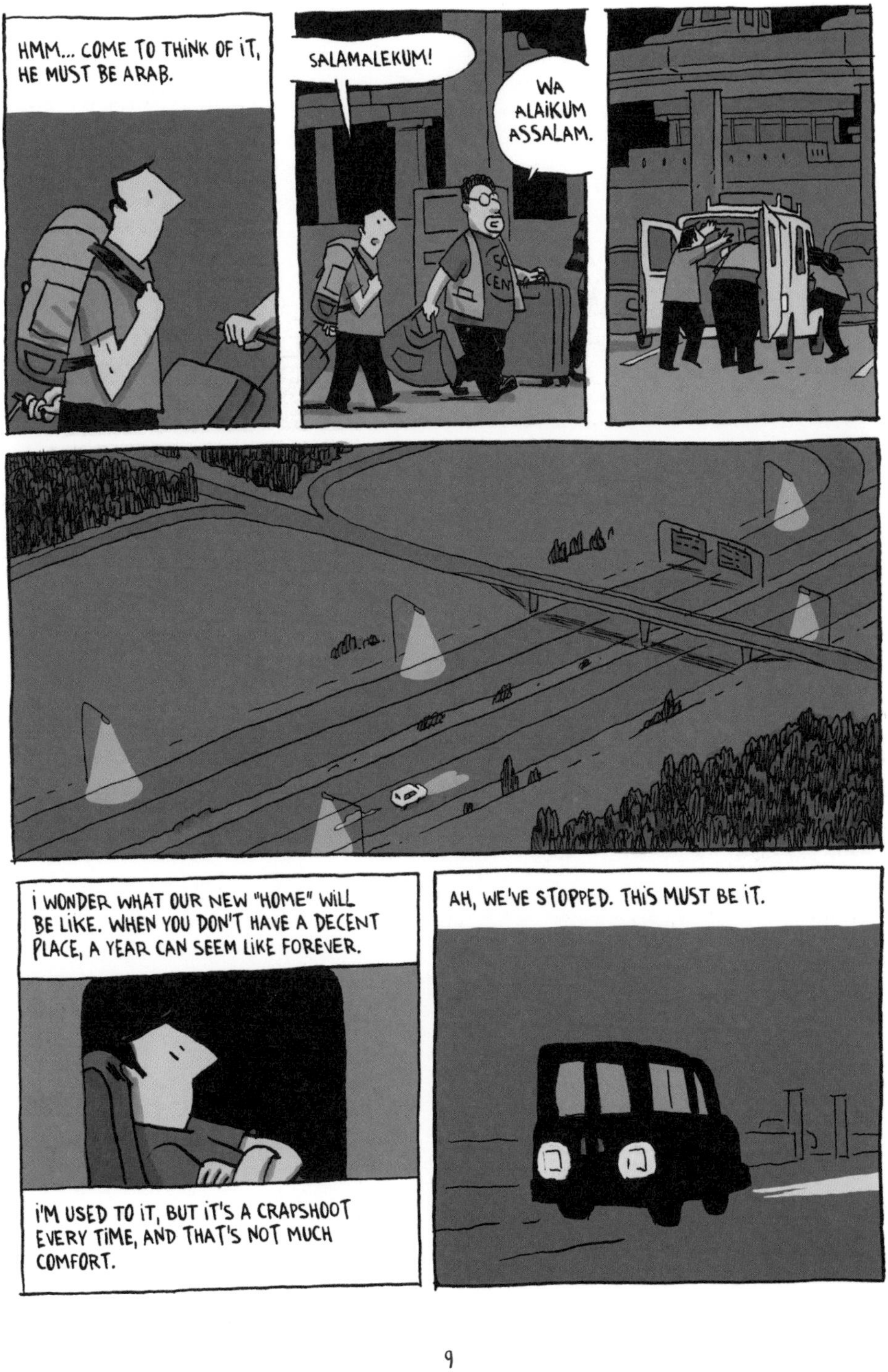
HMM... COME TO THINK OF IT, HE MUST BE ARAB.
SALAMALEKUM!
WA ALAIKUM ASSALAM.
I WONDER WHAT OUR NEW "HOME" WILL BE LIKE. WHEN YOU DON'T HAVE A DECENT PLACE, A YEAR CAN SEEM LIKE FOREVER.
I'M USED TO IT, BUT IT'S A CRAPSHOOT EVERY TIME, AND THAT'S NOT MUCH COMFORT.
AH, WE'VE STOPPED. THIS MUST BE IT.

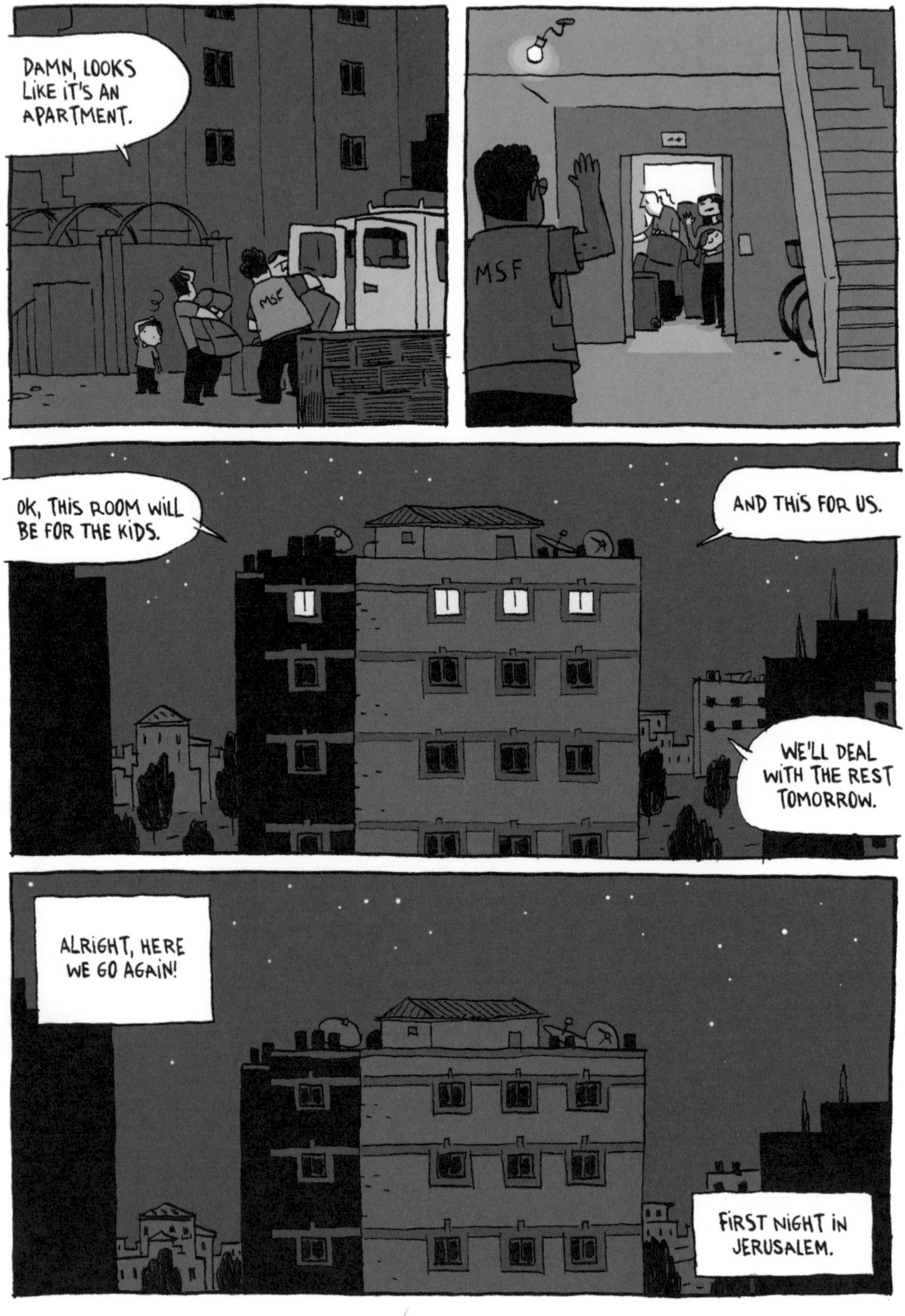
DAMN, LOOKS LIKE IT'S AN APARTMENT.
MSF
MSF
MSF
OK, THIS ROOM WILL BE FOR THE KIDS.
AND THIS FOR US.
WE'LL DEAL WITH THE REST TOMORROW.
ALRIGHT, HERE WE GO AGAIN!
FIRST NIGHT IN JERUSALEM.

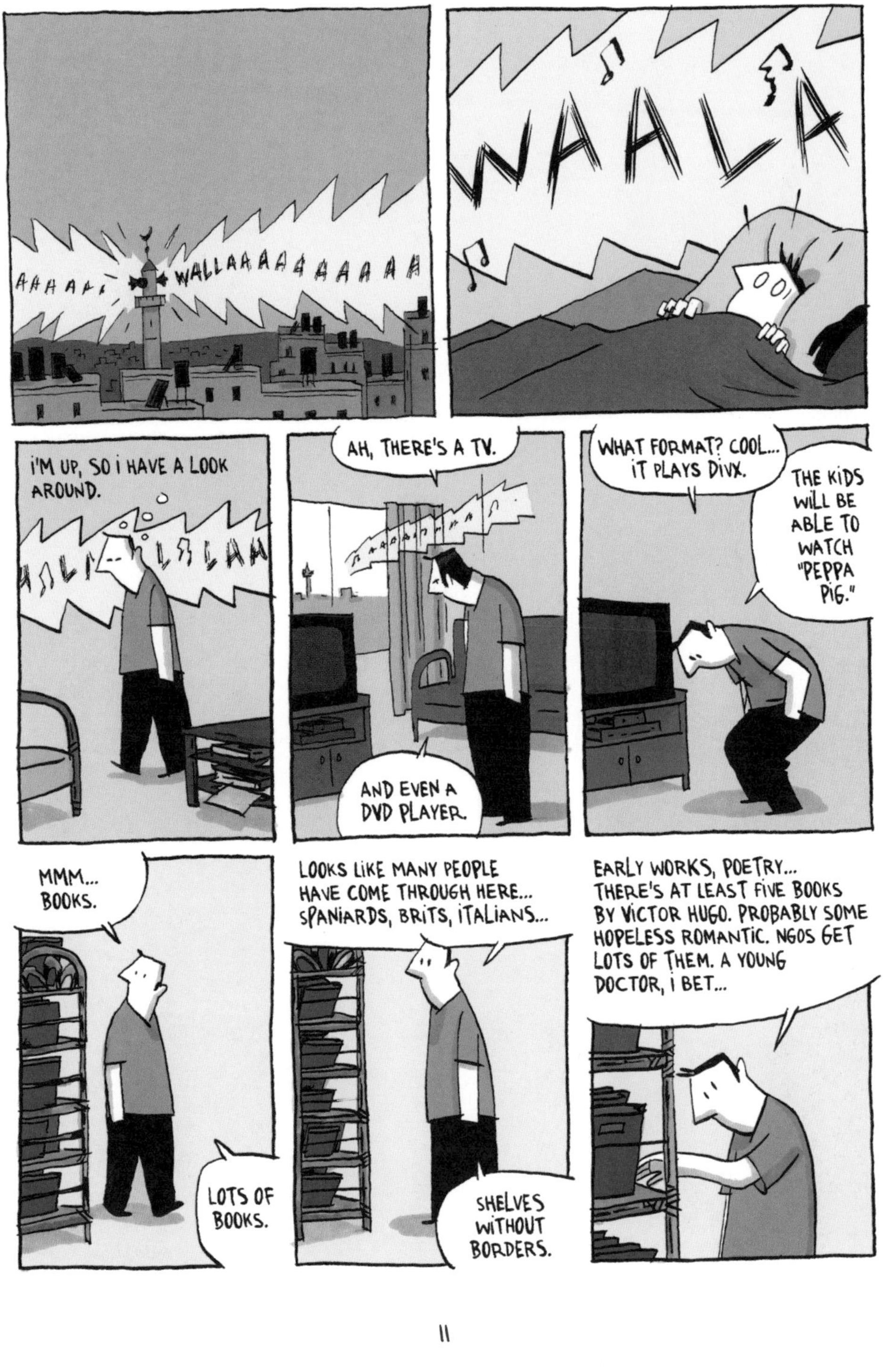
AAAAA
WALLAAAAAAAAAAA
WAALA
I'M UP, SO I HAVE A LOOK AROUND.
AH, THERE'S A TV.
AND EVEN A DVD PLAYER.
WHAT FORMAT? COOL... IT PLAYS DIVX.
THE KIDS WILL BE ABLE TO WATCH "PEPPA PIG."
MMM... BOOKS.
LOTS OF BOOKS.
LOOKS LIKE MANY PEOPLE HAVE COME THROUGH HERE... SPANIARDS, BRITS, ITALIANS...
SHELVES WITHOUT BORDERS.
EARLY WORKS, POETRY... THERE'S AT LEAST FIVE BOOKS BY VICTOR HUGO. PROBABLY SOME HOPELESS ROMANTIC. NGOS GET LOTS OF THEM. A YOUNG DOCTOR, I BET...

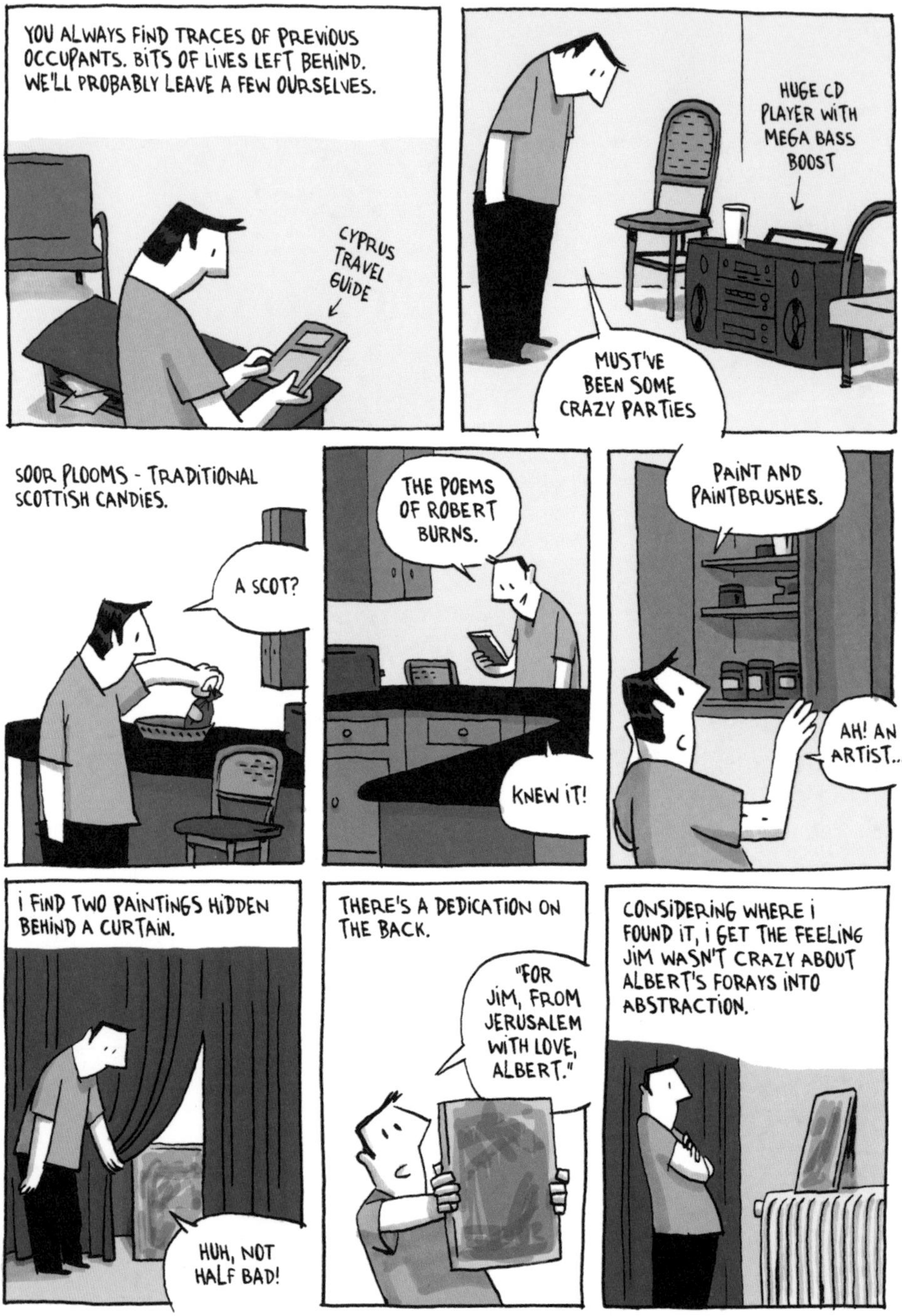
YOU ALWAYS FIND TRACES OF PREVIOUS OCCUPANTS. BITS OF LIVES LEFT BEHIND. WE'LL PROBABLY LEAVE A FEW OURSELVES.
CYPRUS TRAVEL GUIDE
HUGE CD PLAYER WITH MEGA BASS BOOST
MUST'VE BEEN SOME CRAZY PARTIES
SOOR PLOOMS - TRADITIONAL SCOTTISH CANDIES.
A SCOT?
THE POEMS OF ROBERT BURNS.
KNEW IT!
PAINT AND PAINTBRUSHES.
AH! AN ARTIST...
I FIND TWO PAINTINGS HIDDEN BEHIND A CURTAIN.
HUH, NOT HALF BAD!
THERE'S A DEDICATION ON THE BACK.
"FOR JIM, FROM JERUSALEM WITH LOVE, ALBERT."
CONSIDERING WHERE I FOUND IT, I GET THE FEELING JIM WASN'T CRAZY ABOUT ALBERT'S FORAYS INTO ABSTRACTION.

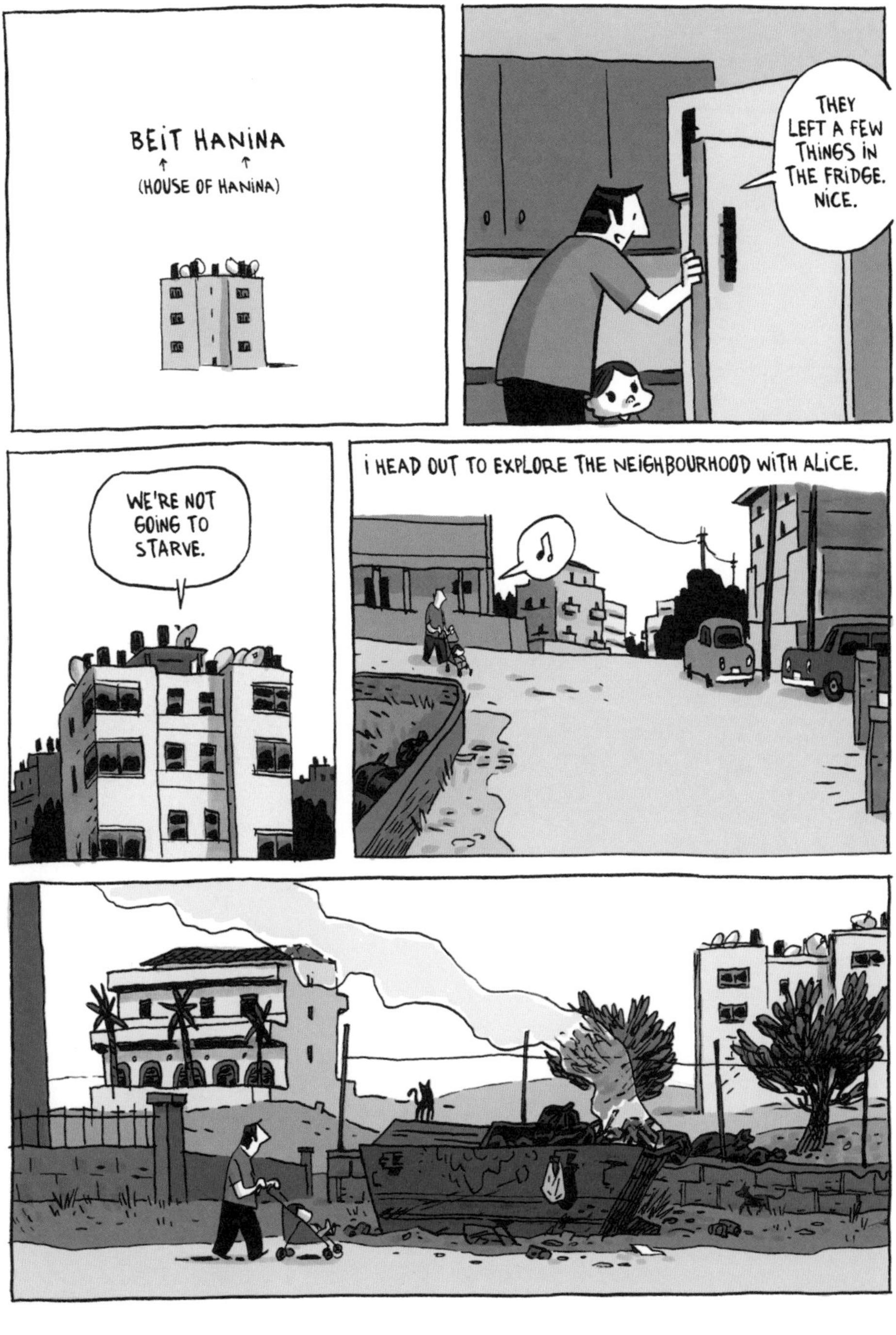
BEIT HANINA
(HOUSE OF HANINA)
THEY LEFT A FEW THINGS IN THE FRIDGE. NICE.
WE'RE NOT GOING TO STARVE.
I HEAD OUT TO EXPLORE THE NEIGHBOURHOOD WITH ALICE.
♪

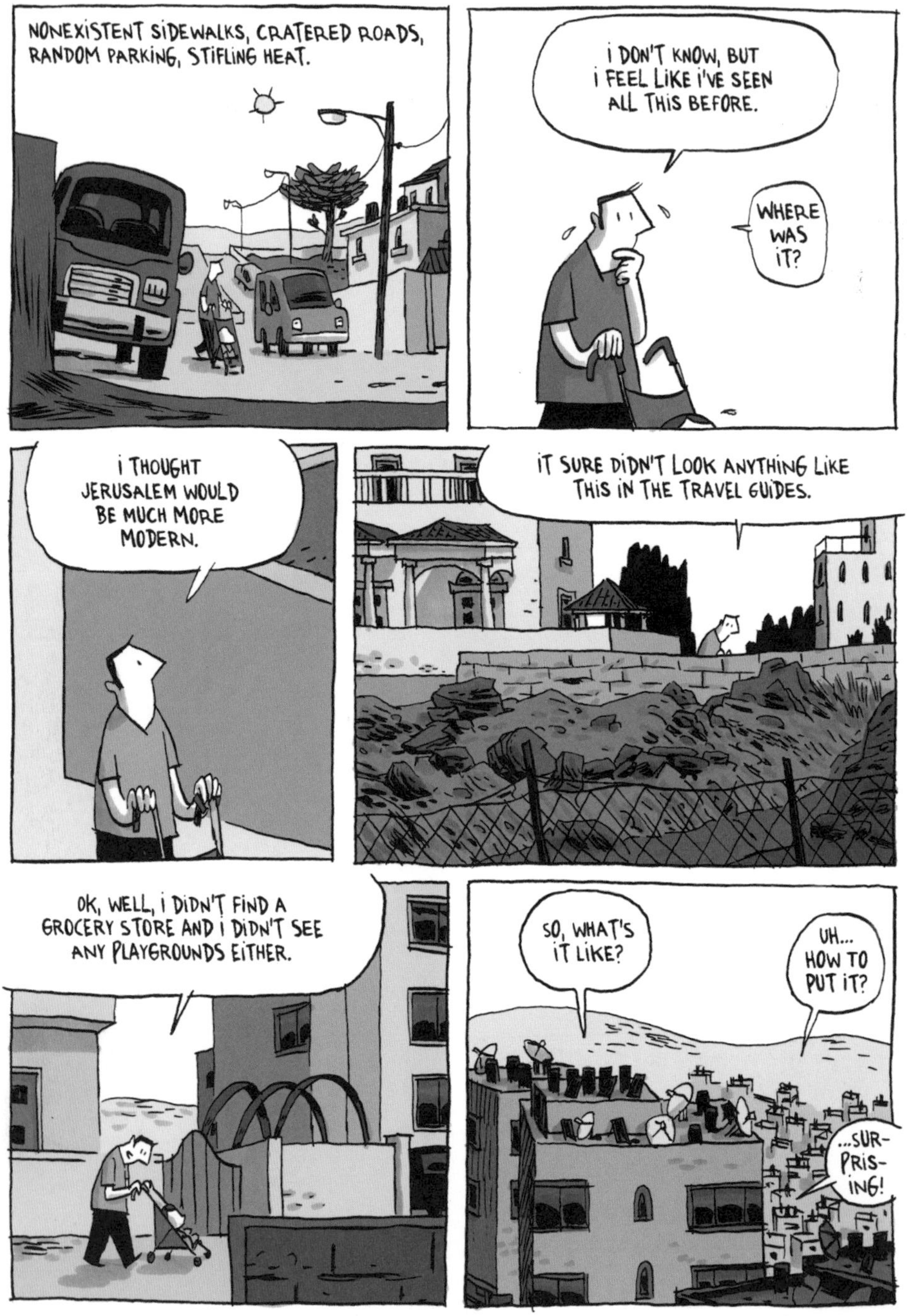
NONEXISTENT SIDEWALKS, CRATERED ROADS, RANDOM PARKING, STIFLING HEAT.
I DON'T KNOW, BUT I FEEL LIKE I'VE SEEN ALL THIS BEFORE.
WHERE WAS IT?
I THOUGHT JERUSALEM WOULD BE MUCH MORE MODERN.
IT SURE DIDN'T LOOK ANYTHING LIKE THIS IN THE TRAVEL GUIDES.
OK, WELL, I DIDN'T FIND A GROCERY STORE AND I DIDN'T SEE ANY PLAYGROUNDS EITHER.
SO, WHAT'S IT LIKE?
UH... HOW TO PUT IT?
...SUR-PRIS-ING!

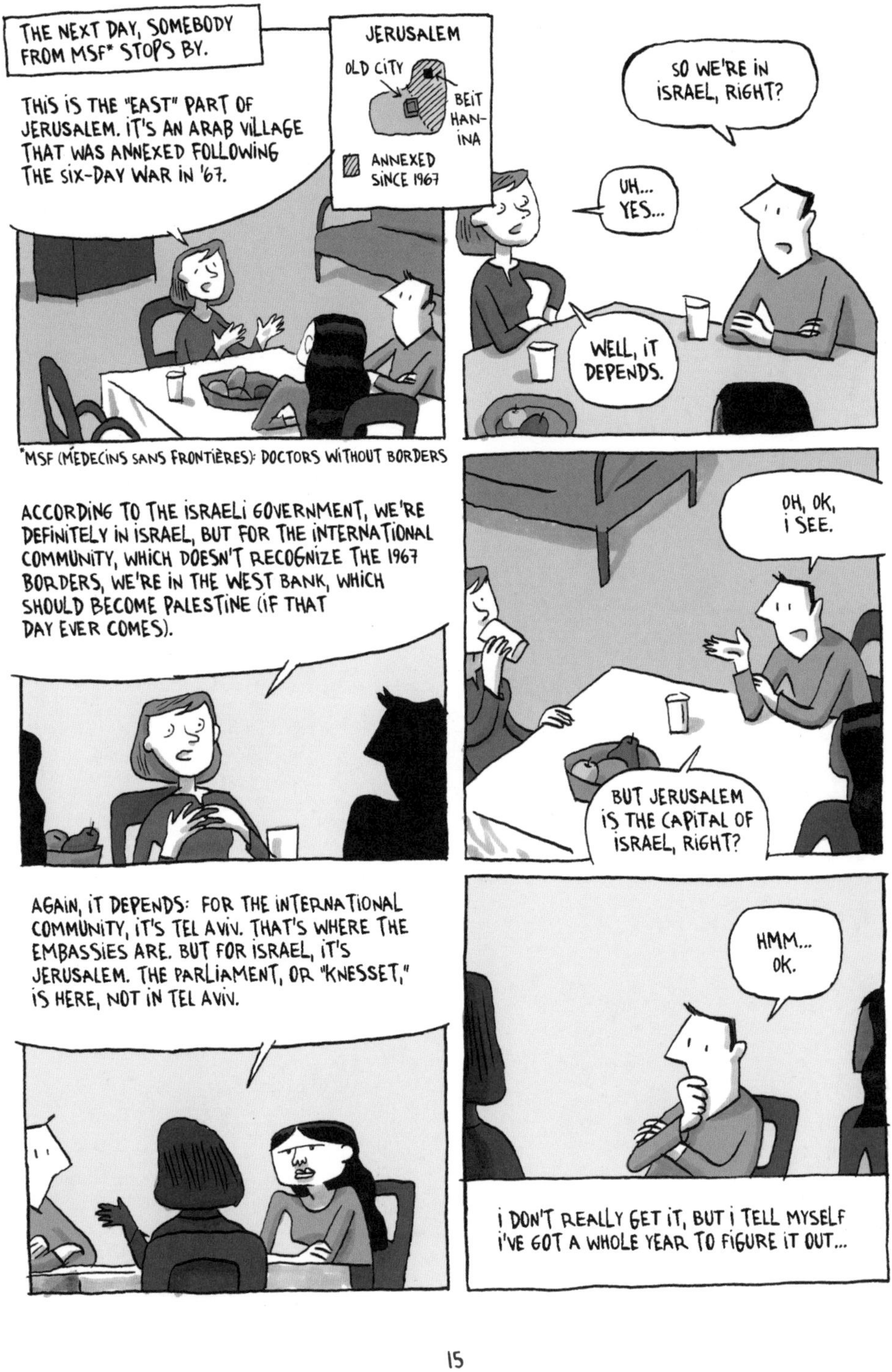
THE NEXT DAY, SOMEBODY FROM MSF* STOPS BY.
THIS IS THE "EAST" PART OF JERUSALEM. IT'S AN ARAB VILLAGE THAT WAS ANNEXED FOLLOWING THE SIX-DAY WAR IN '67.
JERUSALEM
OLD CITY
BEIT HAN-INA
ANNEXED SINCE 1967
SO WE'RE IN ISRAEL, RIGHT?
UH... YES...
WELL, IT DEPENDS.
*MSF (MÉDECINS SANS FRONTIÈRES): DOCTORS WITHOUT BORDERS
ACCORDING TO THE ISRAELI GOVERNMENT, WE'RE DEFINITELY IN ISRAEL, BUT FOR THE INTERNATIONAL COMMUNITY, WHICH DOESN'T RECOGNIZE THE 1967 BORDERS, WE'RE IN THE WEST BANK, WHICH SHOULD BECOME PALESTINE (IF THAT DAY EVER COMES).
OH, OK, I SEE.
BUT JERUSALEM IS THE CAPITAL OF ISRAEL, RIGHT?
AGAIN, IT DEPENDS: FOR THE INTERNATIONAL COMMUNITY, IT'S TEL AVIV. THAT'S WHERE THE EMBASSIES ARE. BUT FOR ISRAEL, IT'S JERUSALEM. THE PARLIAMENT, OR "KNESSET," IS HERE, NOT IN TEL AVIV.
HMM... OK.
I DON'T REALLY GET IT, BUT I TELL MYSELF I'VE GOT A WHOLE YEAR TO FIGURE IT OUT...

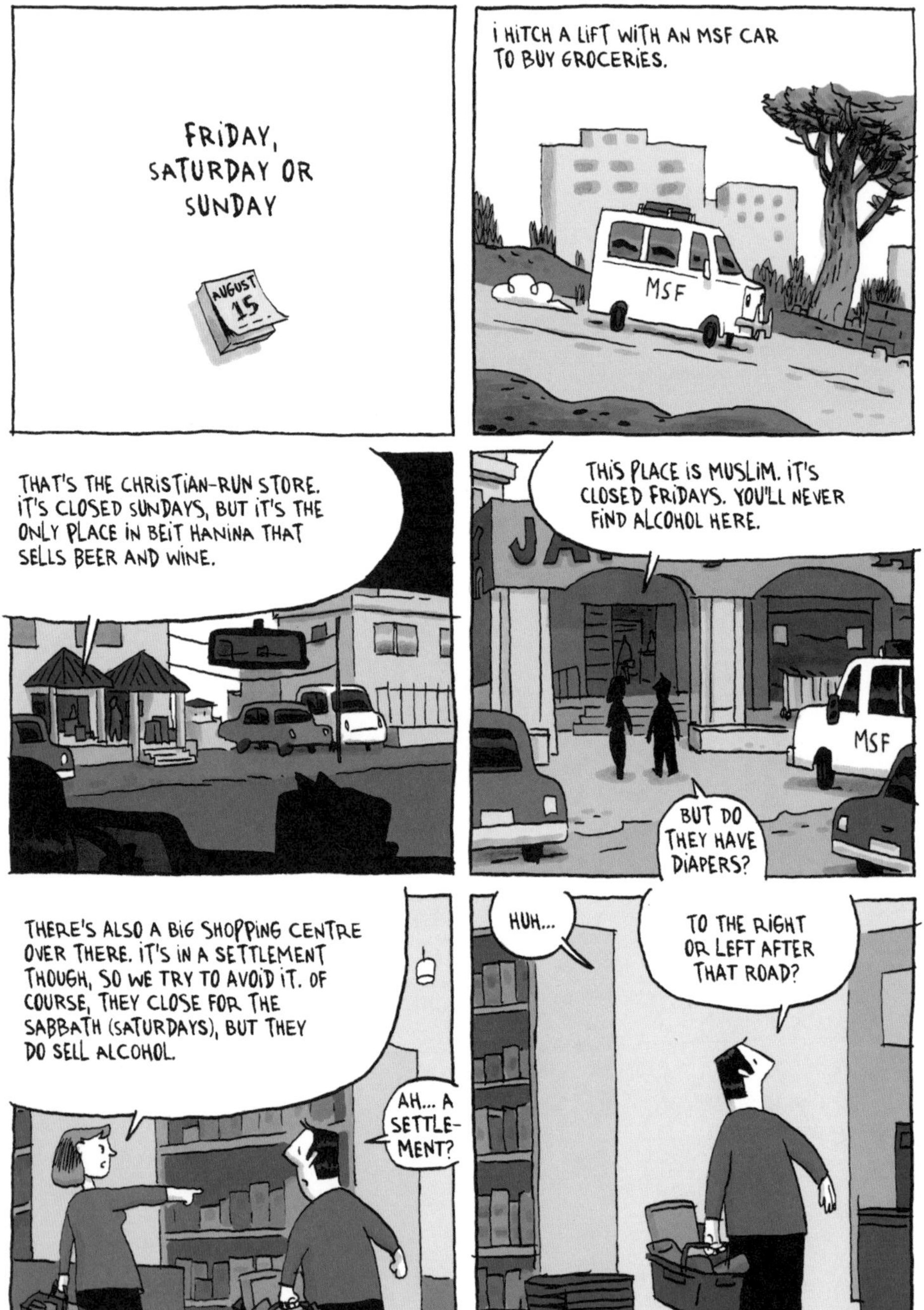
FRIDAY, SATURDAY OR SUNDAY
AUGUST 15
I HITCH A LIFT WITH AN MSF CAR TO BUY GROCERIES.
MSF
THAT'S THE CHRISTIAN-RUN STORE. IT'S CLOSED SUNDAYS, BUT IT'S THE ONLY PLACE IN BEIT HANINA THAT SELLS BEER AND WINE.
THIS PLACE IS MUSLIM. IT'S CLOSED FRIDAYS. YOU'LL NEVER FIND ALCOHOL HERE.
MSF
BUT DO THEY HAVE DIAPERS?
THERE'S ALSO A BIG SHOPPING CENTRE OVER THERE. IT'S IN A SETTLEMENT THOUGH, SO WE TRY TO AVOID IT. OF COURSE, THEY CLOSE FOR THE SABBATH (SATURDAYS), BUT THEY DO SELL ALCOHOL.
AH... A SETTLE-MENT?
HUH...
TO THE RIGHT OR LEFT AFTER THAT ROAD?

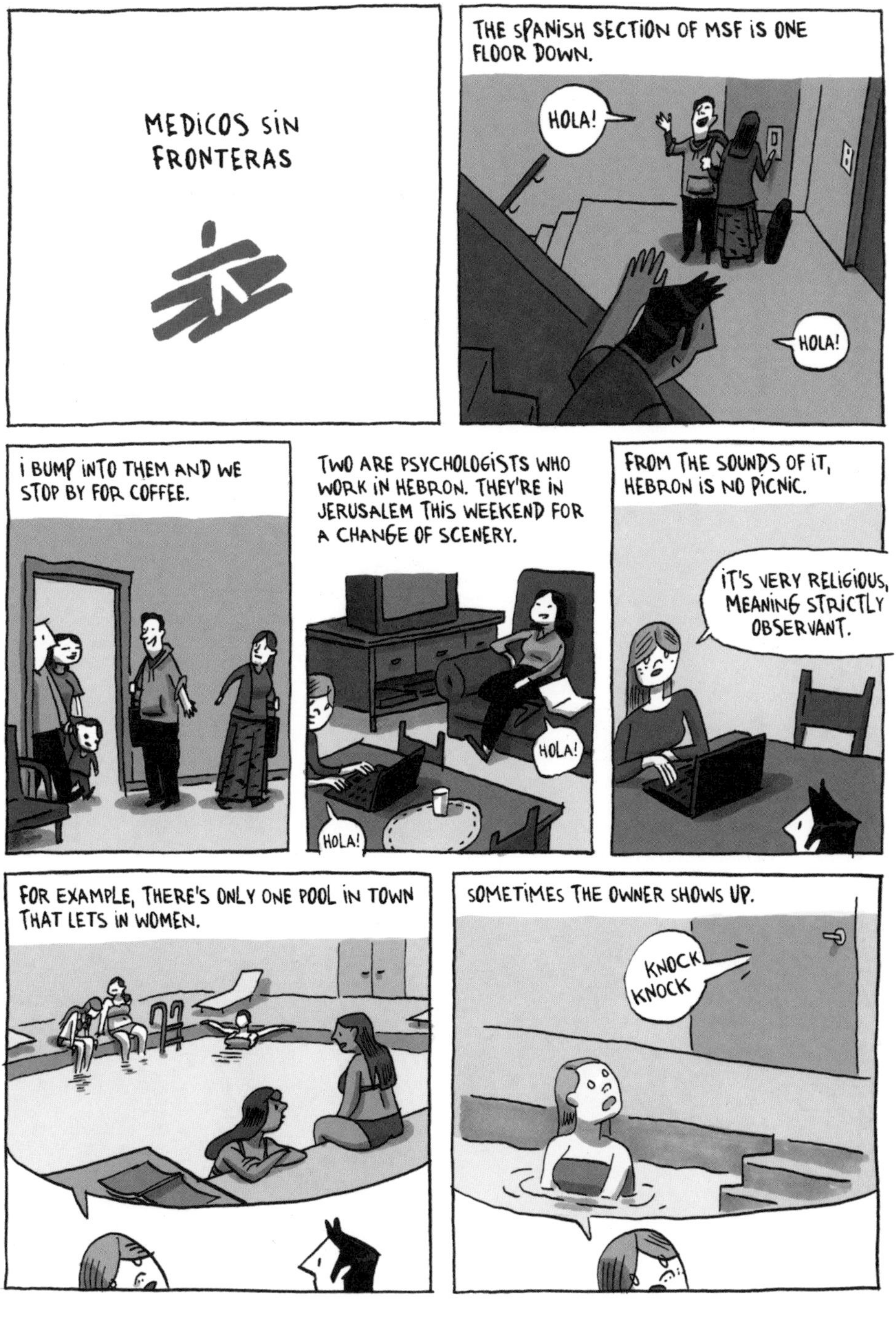

MEDICOS SIN FRONTERAS
THE SPANISH SECTION OF MSF IS ONE FLOOR DOWN.
HOLA!
HOLA!
I BUMP INTO THEM AND WE STOP BY FOR COFFEE.
TWO ARE PSYCHOLOGISTS WHO WORK IN HEBRON. THEY'RE IN JERUSALEM THIS WEEKEND FOR A CHANGE OF SCENERY.
HOLA!
HOLA!
FROM THE SOUNDS OF IT, HEBRON IS NO PICNIC.
IT'S VERY RELIGIOUS, MEANING STRICTLY OBSERVANT.
FOR EXAMPLE, THERE'S ONLY ONE POOL IN TOWN THAT LETS IN WOMEN.
SOMETIMES THE OWNER SHOWS UP.
KNOCK KNOCK

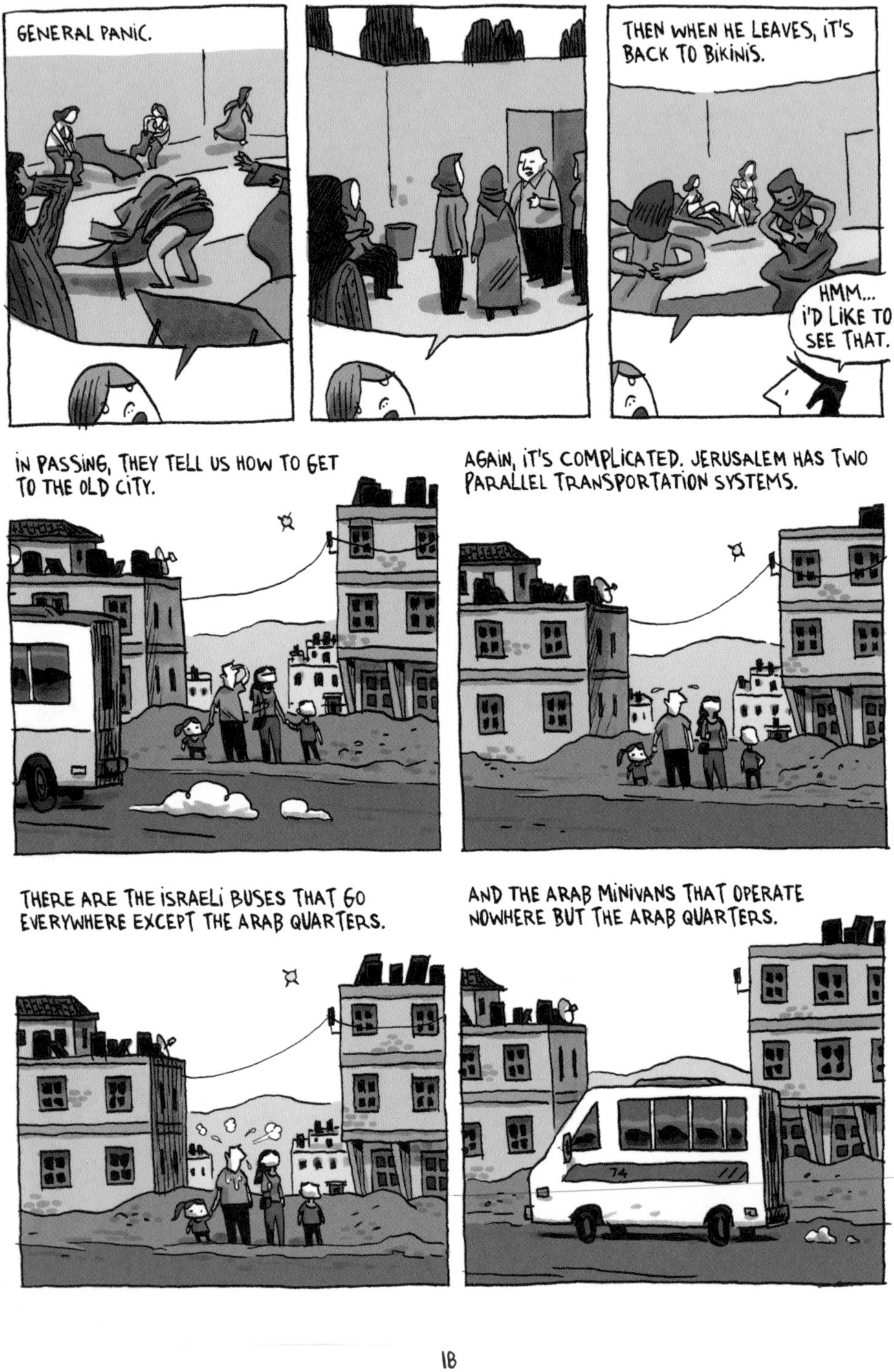
GENERAL PANIC.
THEN WHEN HE LEAVES, IT'S BACK TO BIKINIS.
HMM... I'D LIKE TO SEE THAT.
IN PASSING, THEY TELL US HOW TO GET TO THE OLD CITY.
AGAIN, IT'S COMPLICATED. JERUSALEM HAS TWO PARALLEL TRANSPORTATION SYSTEMS.
THERE ARE THE ISRAELI BUSES THAT GO EVERYWHERE EXCEPT THE ARAB QUARTERS.
AND THE ARAB MINIVANS THAT OPERATE NOWHERE BUT THE ARAB QUARTERS.
74

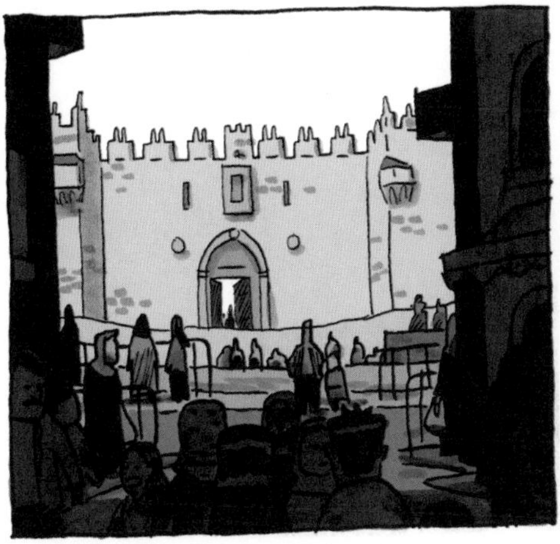

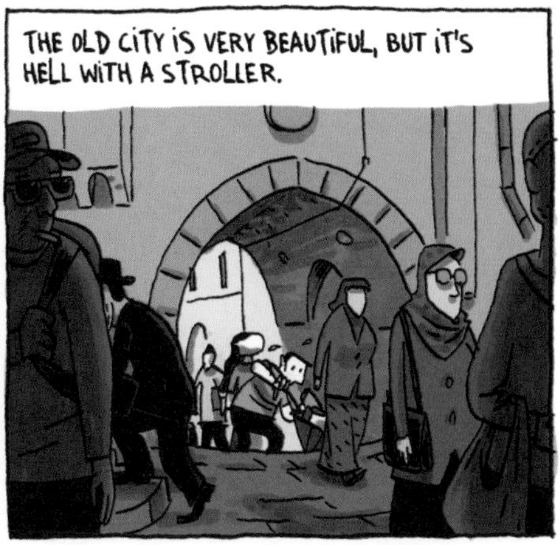
THE OLD CITY IS VERY BEAUTIFUL, BUT IT'S HELL WITH A STROLLER.

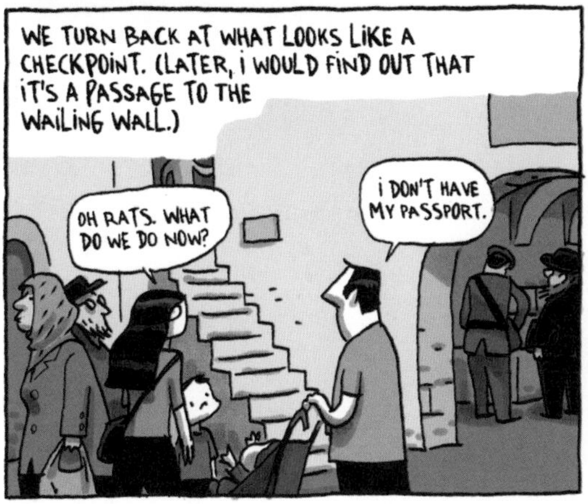
WE TURN BACK AT WHAT LOOKS LIKE A CHECKPOINT. (LATER, I WOULD FIND OUT THAT IT'S A PASSAGE TO THE WAILING WALL.)
OH RATS. WHAT DO WE DO NOW?
I DON'T HAVE MY PASSPORT.

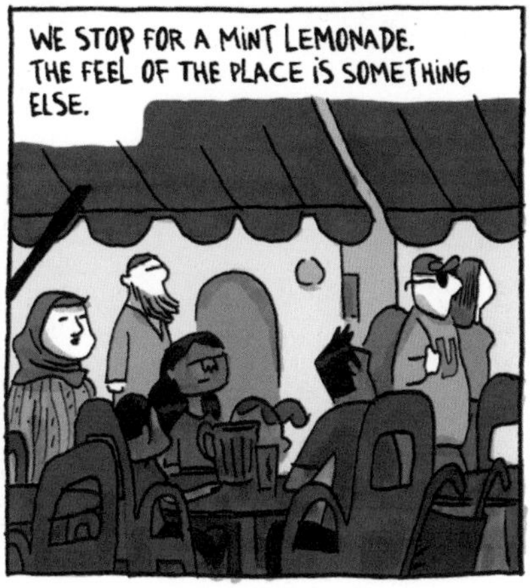
WE STOP FOR A MINT LEMONADE. THE FEEL OF THE PLACE IS SOMETHING ELSE.

TO THE LEFT, POLICE AND SOLDIERS ARE FILLING OUT A REPORT. PEOPLE CLAMOUR AROUND WITH THEIR VERSION OF EVENTS.

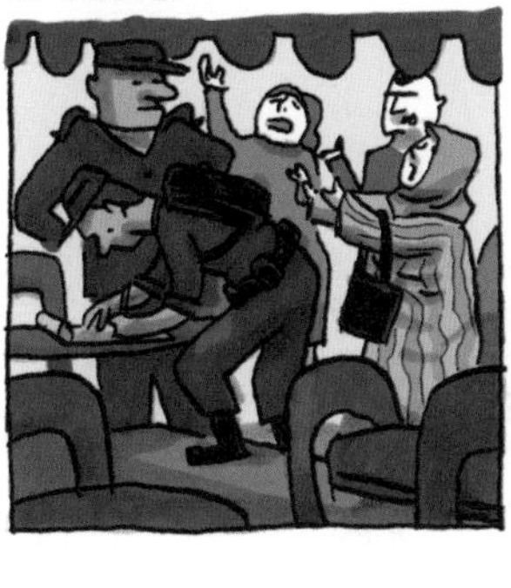

IN THE MEANTIME, A LINE OF TOURISTS CLEARS A PATH THROUGH THE TABLES TO REACH AN ATM.

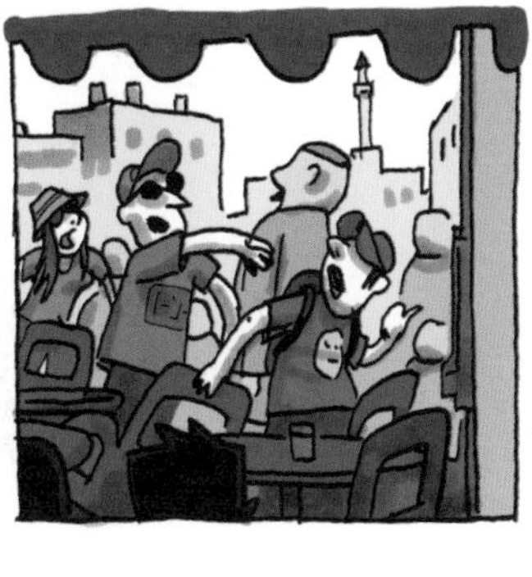

AND OPPOSITE, A GROUP OF ITALIANS STOP TO PRAY IN FRONT OF A SMALL CHAPEL.

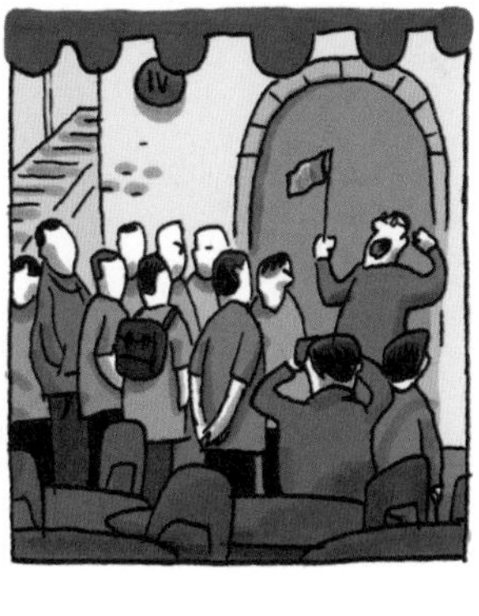

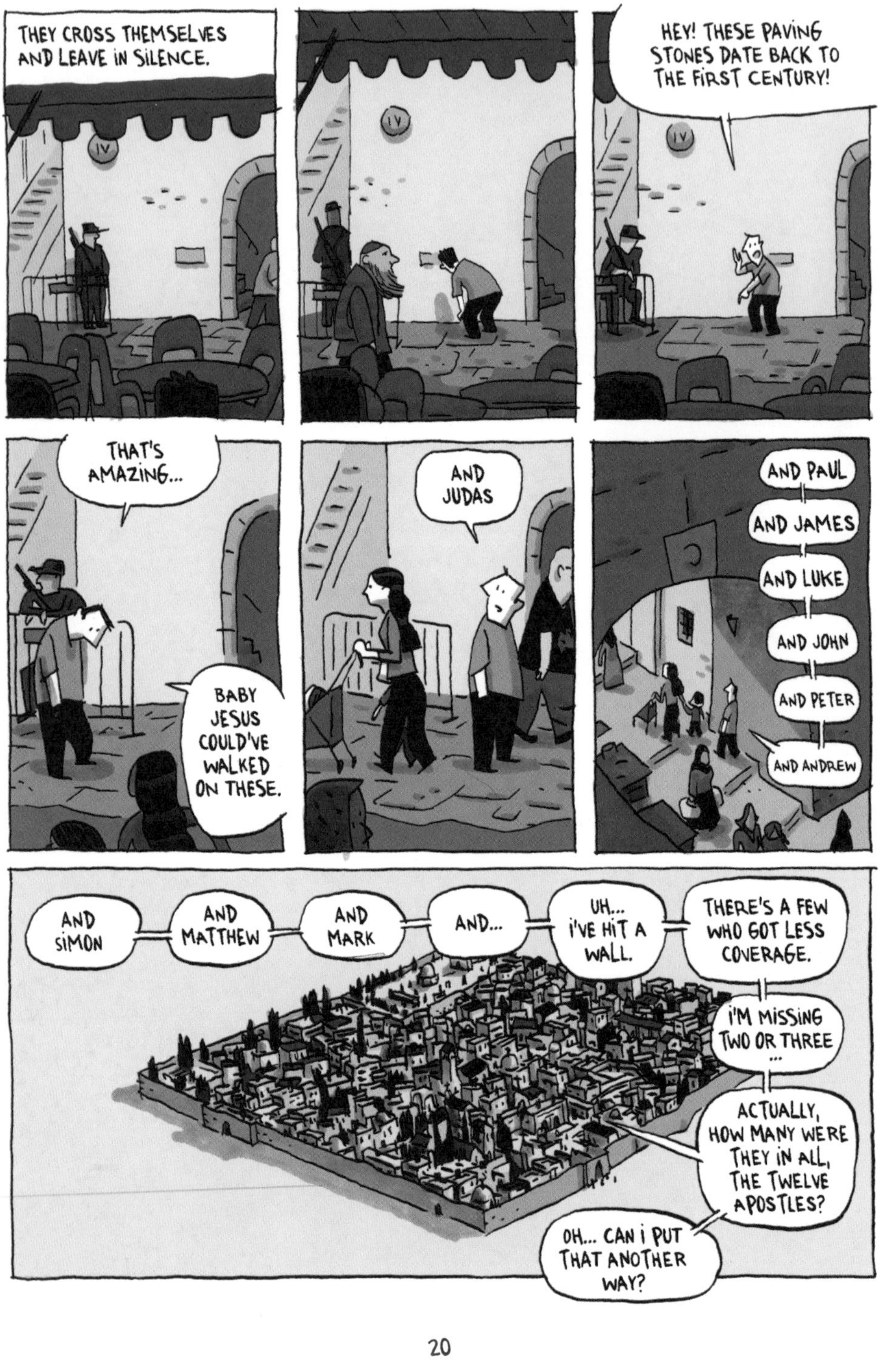
THEY CROSS THEMSELVES AND LEAVE IN SILENCE.
HEY! THESE PAVING STONES DATE BACK TO THE FIRST CENTURY!
THAT'S AMAZING...
BABY JESUS COULD'VE WALKED ON THESE.
AND JUDAS
AND PAUL
AND JAMES
AND LUKE
AND JOHN
AND PETER
AND ANDREW
AND SIMON
AND MATTHEW
AND MARK
AND...
UH... I'VE HIT A WALL.
THERE'S A FEW WHO GOT LESS COVERAGE.
I'M MISSING TWO OR THREE ...
ACTUALLY, HOW MANY WERE THEY IN ALL, THE TWELVE APOSTLES?
OH... CAN I PUT THAT ANOTHER WAY?

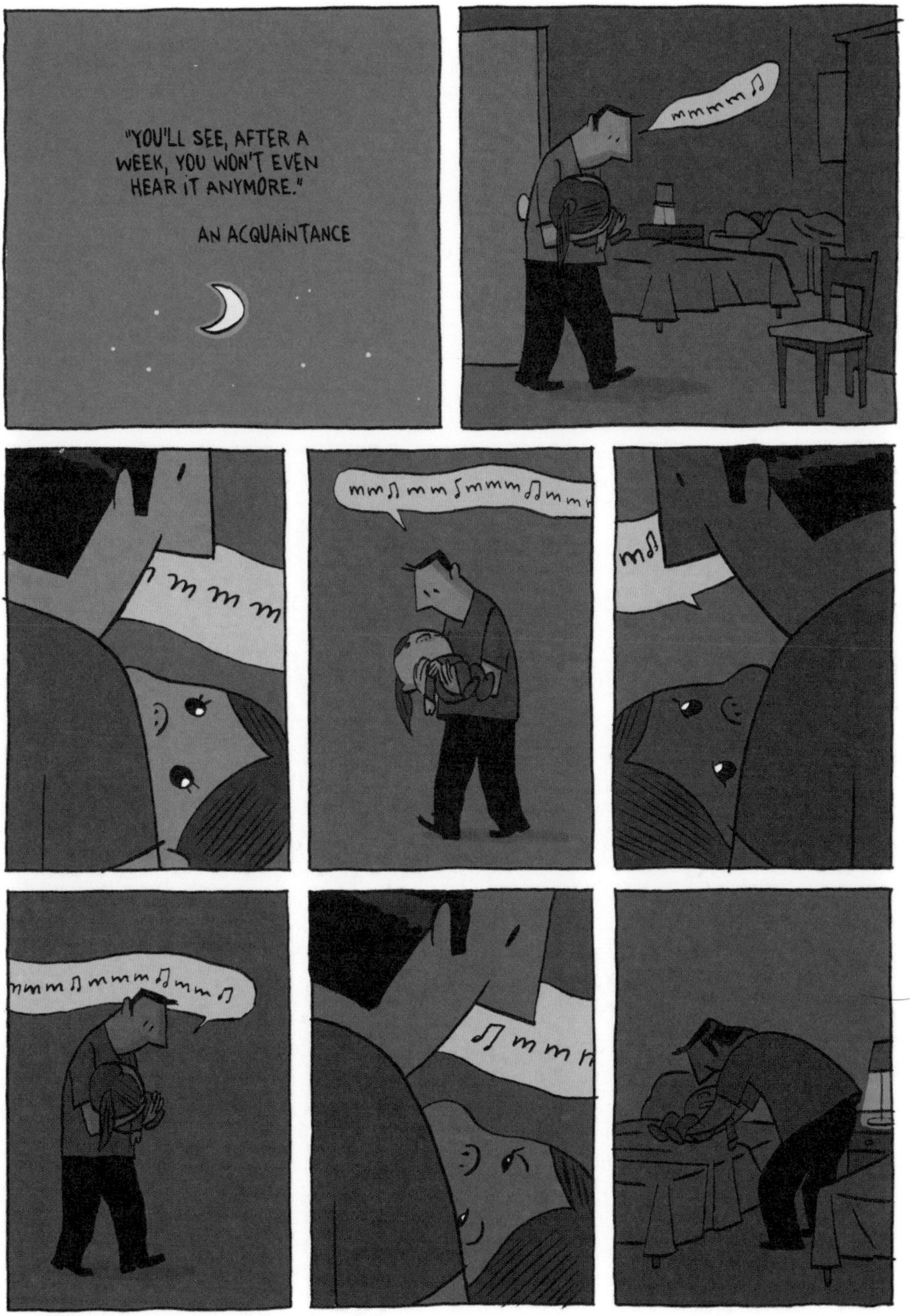
"YOU'LL SEE, AFTER A WEEK, YOU WON'T EVEN HEAR IT ANYMORE."
AN ACQUAINTANCE
mmmm ♫
mmm
mm♫ mm ♩mmm ♫mmm
m♫
mmm♫ mmm ♫mm♫
♫mmm

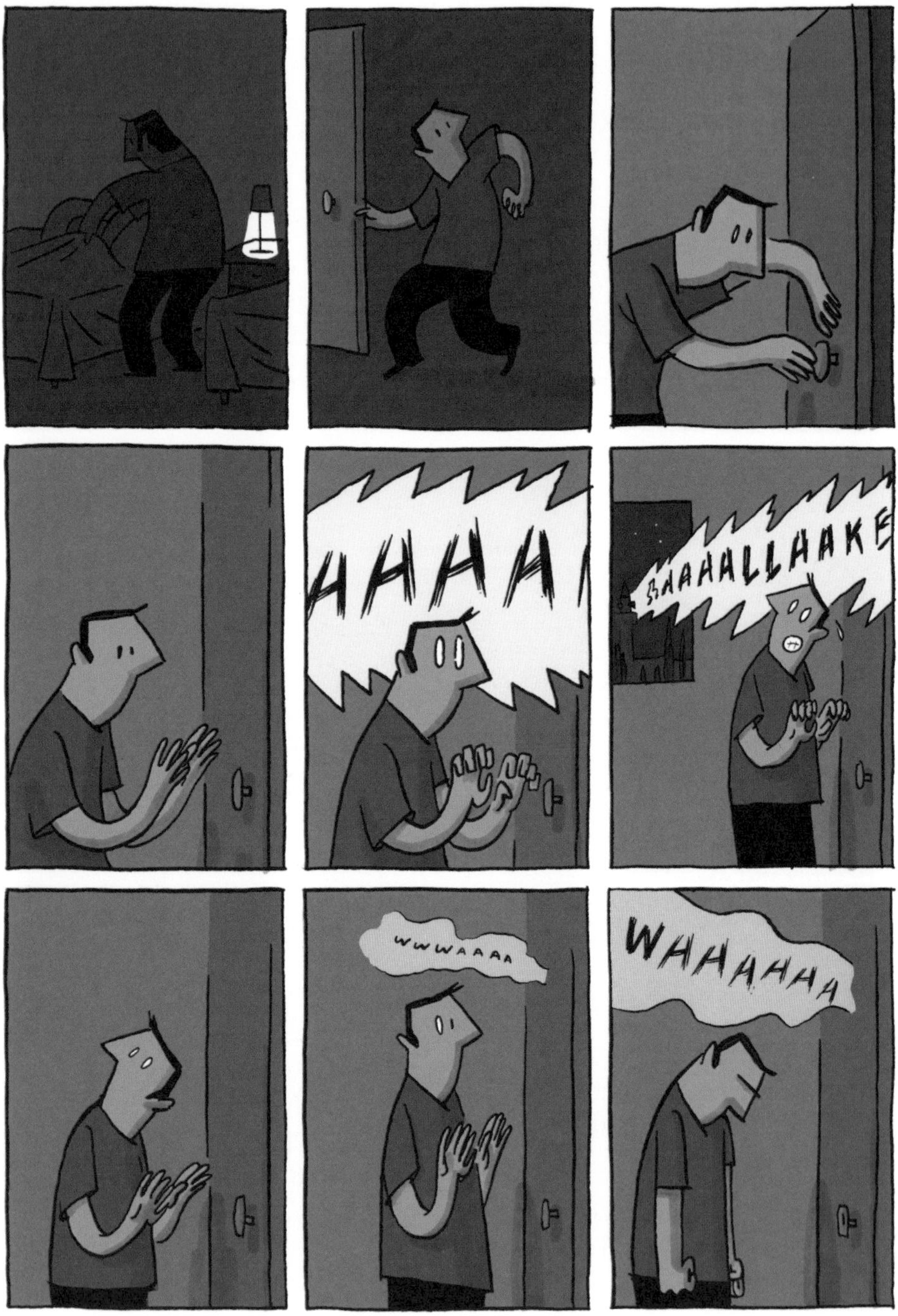
HHHHA
BAAAALLAAKE
WWWAAAA
WHHAAHHA

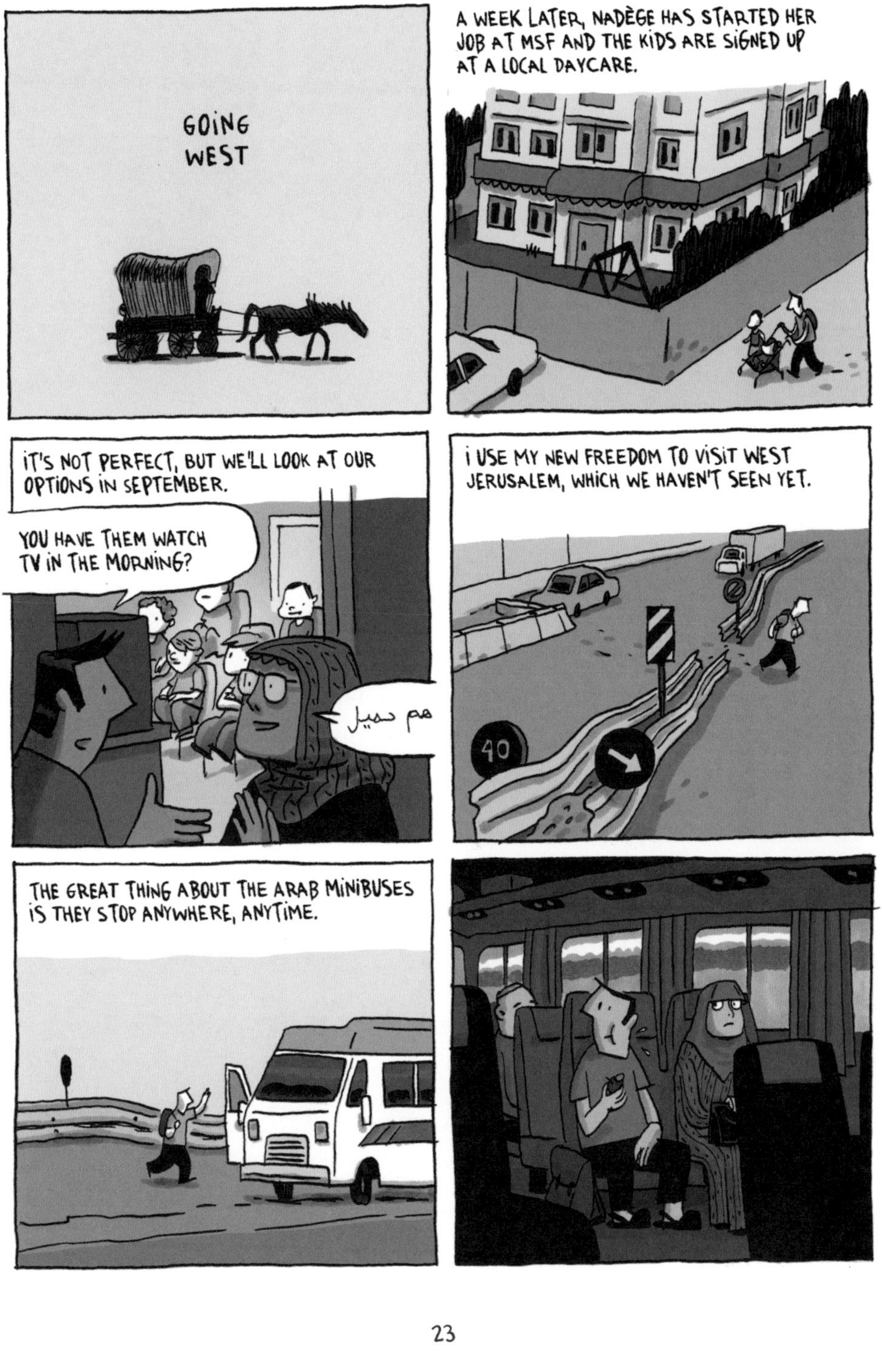
GOING WEST
A WEEK LATER, NADÈGE HAS STARTED HER JOB AT MSF AND THE KIDS ARE SIGNED UP AT A LOCAL DAYCARE.
IT'S NOT PERFECT, BUT WE'LL LOOK AT OUR OPTIONS IN SEPTEMBER.
YOU HAVE THEM WATCH TV IN THE MORNING?
I USE MY NEW FREEDOM TO VISIT WEST JERUSALEM, WHICH WE HAVEN'T SEEN YET.
40
THE GREAT THING ABOUT THE ARAB MINIBUSES IS THEY STOP ANYWHERE, ANYTIME.

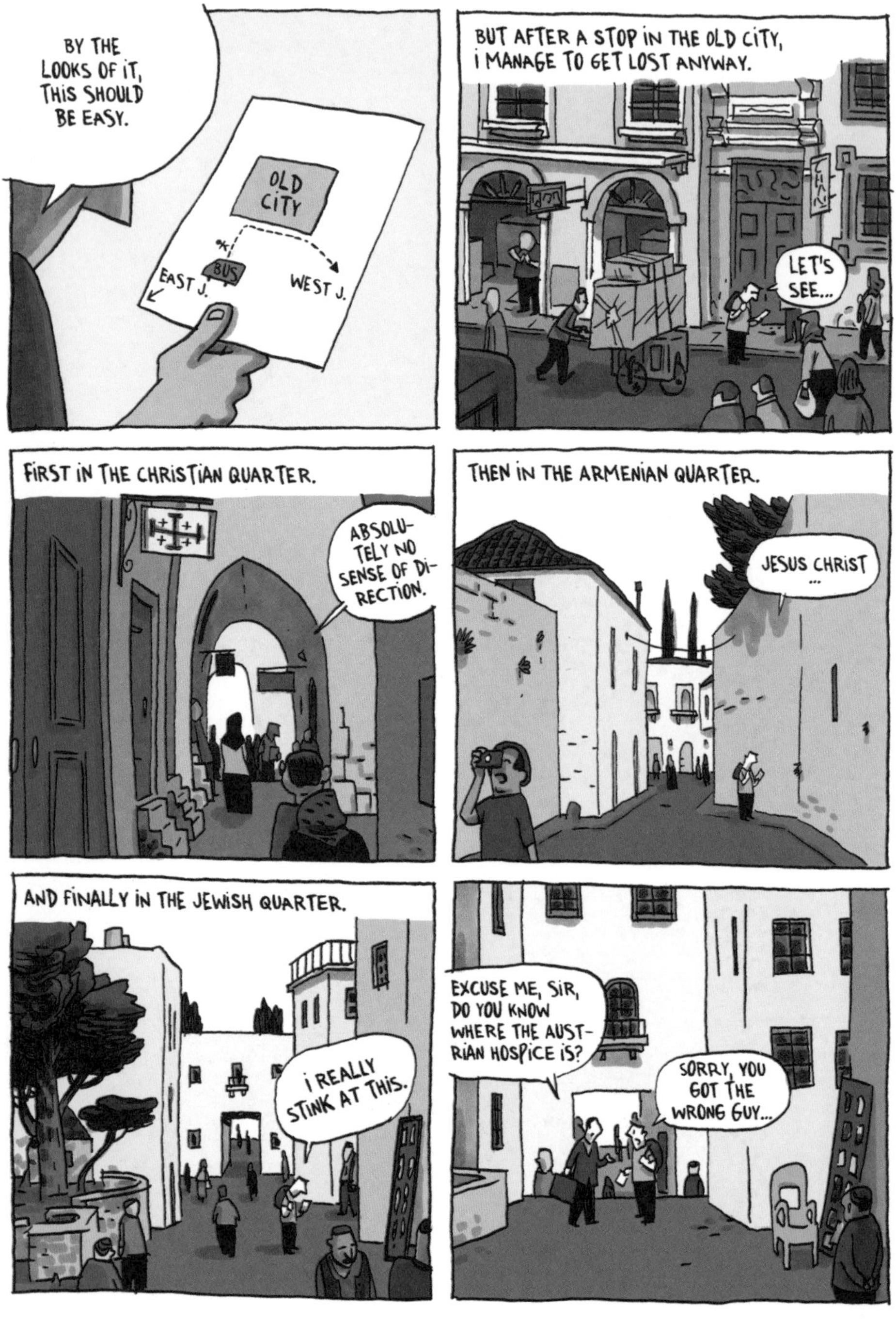
BY THE LOOKS OF IT, THIS SHOULD BE EASY.
OLD CITY
BUS
EAST J.
WEST J.
BUT AFTER A STOP IN THE OLD CITY, I MANAGE TO GET LOST ANYWAY.
LET'S SEE...
FIRST IN THE CHRISTIAN QUARTER.
ABSOLUTELY NO SENSE OF DIRECTION.
THEN IN THE ARMENIAN QUARTER.
JESUS CHRIST ...
AND FINALLY IN THE JEWISH QUARTER.
I REALLY STINK AT THIS.
EXCUSE ME, SIR, DO YOU KNOW WHERE THE AUSTRIAN HOSPICE IS?
SORRY, YOU GOT THE WRONG GUY...

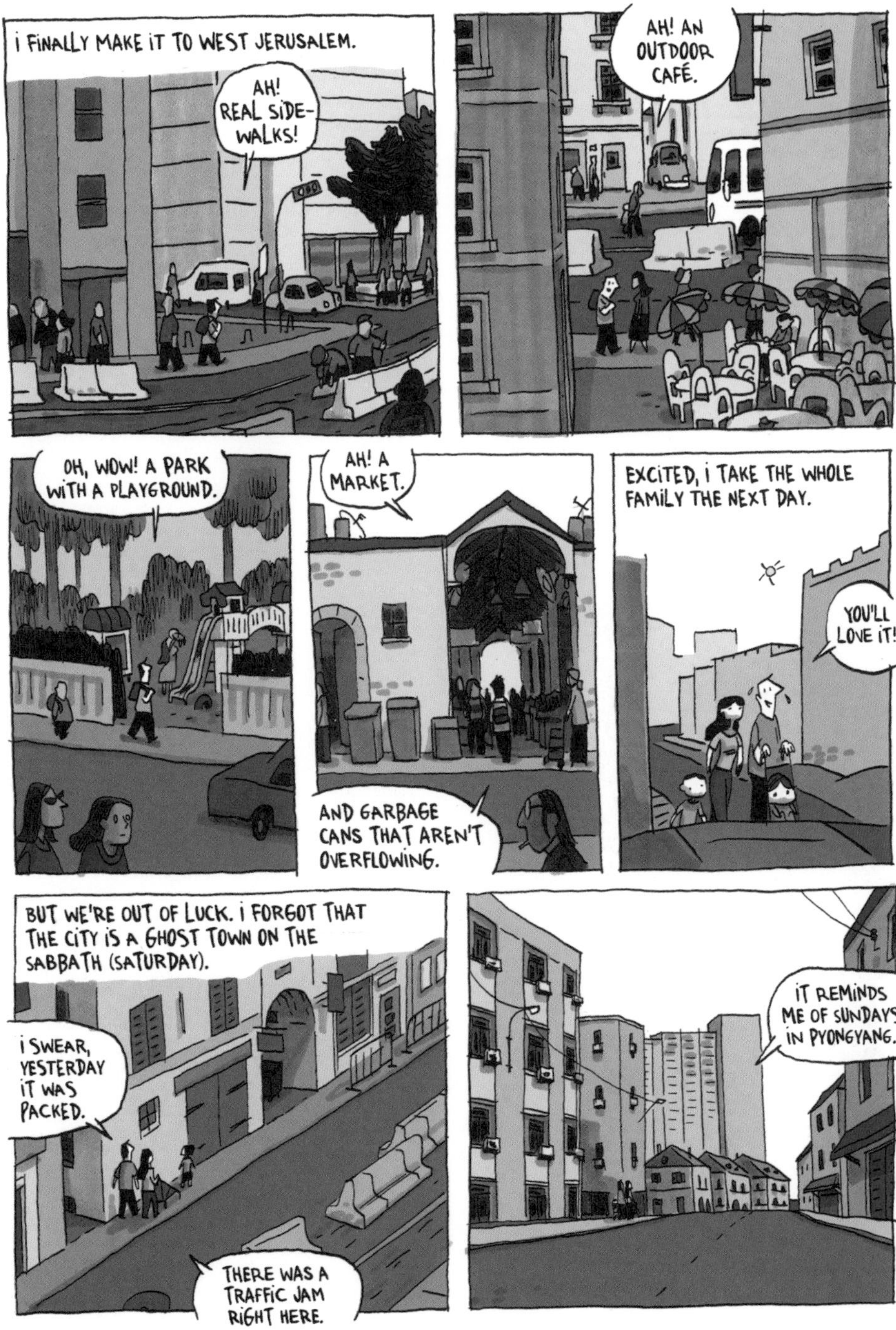
I FINALLY MAKE IT TO WEST JERUSALEM.
AH! REAL SIDE-WALKS!
AH! AN OUTDOOR CAFÉ.
OH, WOW! A PARK WITH A PLAYGROUND.
AH! A MARKET.
AND GARBAGE CANS THAT AREN'T OVERFLOWING.
EXCITED, I TAKE THE WHOLE FAMILY THE NEXT DAY.
YOU'LL LOVE IT!
BUT WE'RE OUT OF LUCK. I FORGOT THAT THE CITY IS A GHOST TOWN ON THE SABBATH (SATURDAY).
I SWEAR, YESTERDAY IT WAS PACKED.
THERE WAS A TRAFFIC JAM RIGHT HERE.
IT REMINDS ME OF SUNDAYS IN PYONGYANG.

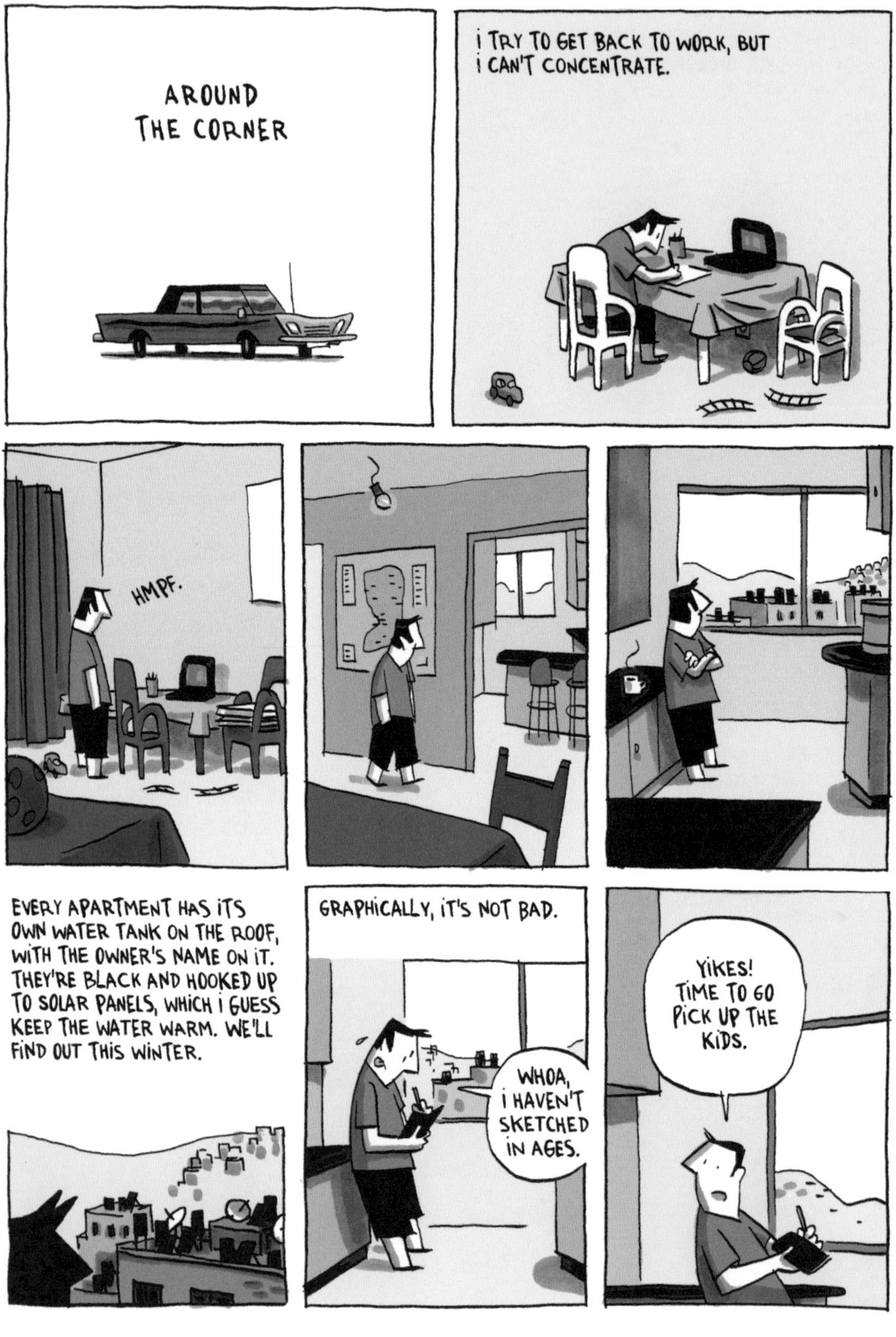
AROUND
THE CORNER
i TRY TO GET BACK TO WORK, BUT i CAN'T CONCENTRATE.
HMPF.
EVERY APARTMENT HAS iTS OWN WATER TANK ON THE ROOF, WiTH THE OWNER'S NAME ON iT. THEY'RE BLACK AND HOOKED UP TO SOLAR PANELS, WHiCH i GUESS KEEP THE WATER WARM. WE'LL FiND OUT THiS WiNTER.
GRAPHiCALLY, iT'S NOT BAD.
WHOA, i HAVEN'T SKETCHED iN AGES.
YiKES! TiME TO GO PiCK UP THE KiDS.

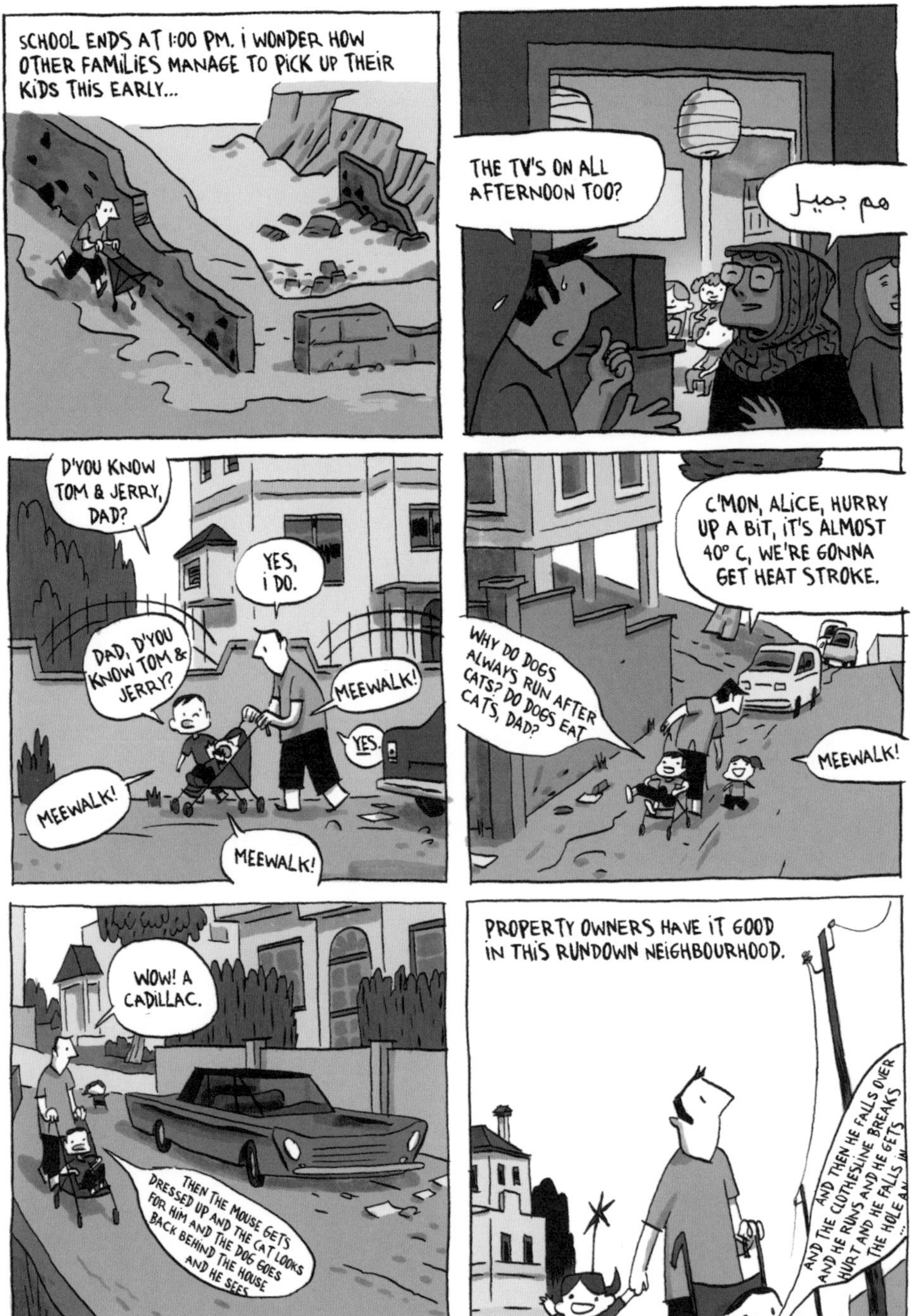
SCHOOL ENDS AT 1:00 PM. I WONDER HOW OTHER FAMILIES MANAGE TO PICK UP THEIR KIDS THIS EARLY...
THE TV'S ON ALL AFTERNOON TOO?
هم جميل
D'YOU KNOW TOM & JERRY, DAD?
YES, I DO.
DAD, D'YOU KNOW TOM & JERRY?
MEEWALK!
YES.
MEEWALK!
MEEWALK!
C'MON, ALICE, HURRY UP A BIT, IT'S ALMOST 40° C, WE'RE GONNA GET HEAT STROKE.
WHY DO DOGS ALWAYS RUN AFTER CATS? DO DOGS EAT CATS, DAD?
MEEWALK!
WOW! A CADILLAC.
THEN THE MOUSE GETS DRESSED UP AND THE CAT LOOKS FOR HIM AND THE DOG GOES BACK BEHIND THE HOUSE AND HE SEES
PROPERTY OWNERS HAVE IT GOOD IN THIS RUNDOWN NEIGHBOURHOOD.
AND THEN HE FALLS OVER AND THE CLOTHESLINE BREAKS AND HE RUNS AND HE GETS HURT AND HE FALLS IN THE HOLE

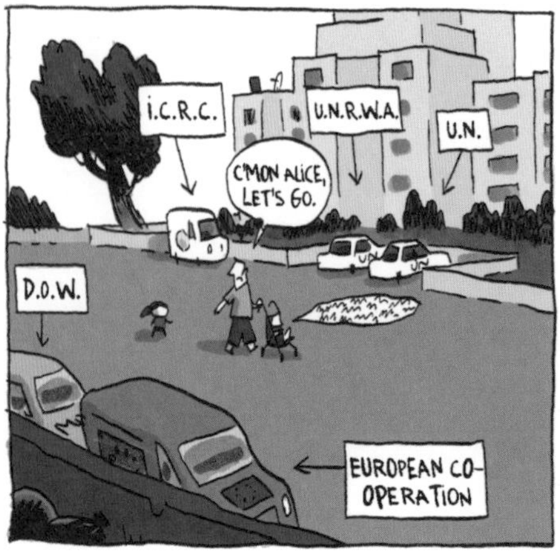
I.C.R.C.
U.N.R.W.A.
U.N.
C'MON ALICE, LET'S GO.
D.O.W.
EUROPEAN CO-OPERATION

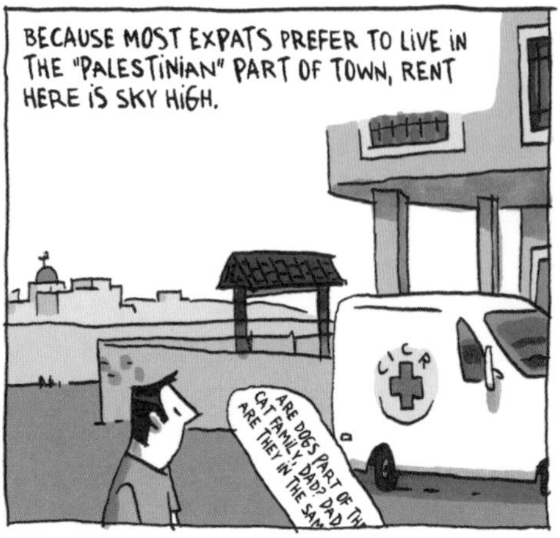
BECAUSE MOST EXPATS PREFER TO LIVE IN THE "PALESTINIAN" PART OF TOWN, RENT HERE IS SKY HIGH.
ARE DOGS PART OF THE CAT FAMILY, DAD? DAD ARE THEY IN THE SAM
CICR

AND SO YOU GET THIS STRANGE MIX OF PALATIAL HOMES SET IN THE MIDST OF GARBAGE AND DEBRIS.

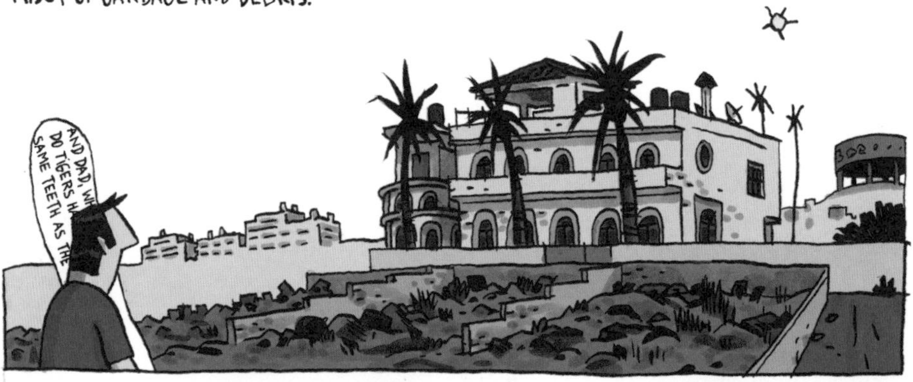
AND DAD, WH
DO TIGERS HA
SAME TEETH AS THE

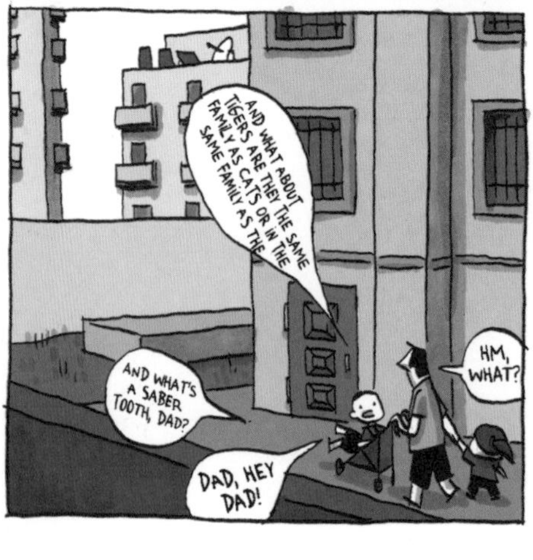
AND WHAT ABOUT TIGERS ARE THEY THE SAME FAMILY AS CATS OR IN THE SAME FAMILY AS THE
HM, WHAT?
AND WHAT'S A SABER TOOTH, DAD?
DAD, HEY DAD!

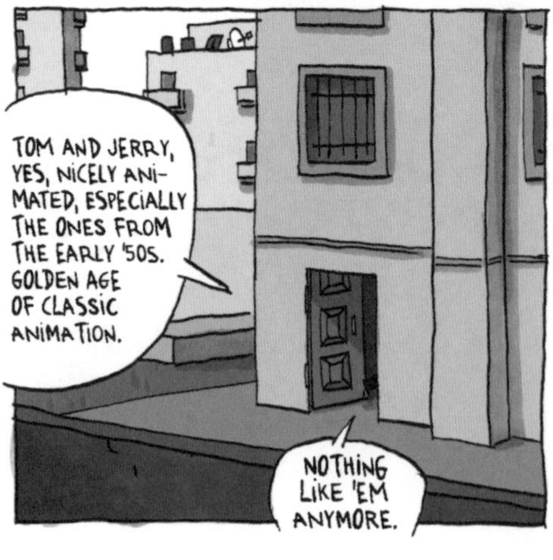
TOM AND JERRY, YES, NICELY ANI-MATED, ESPECIALLY THE ONES FROM THE EARLY '50S. GOLDEN AGE OF CLASSIC ANIMATION.
NOTHING LIKE 'EM ANYMORE.

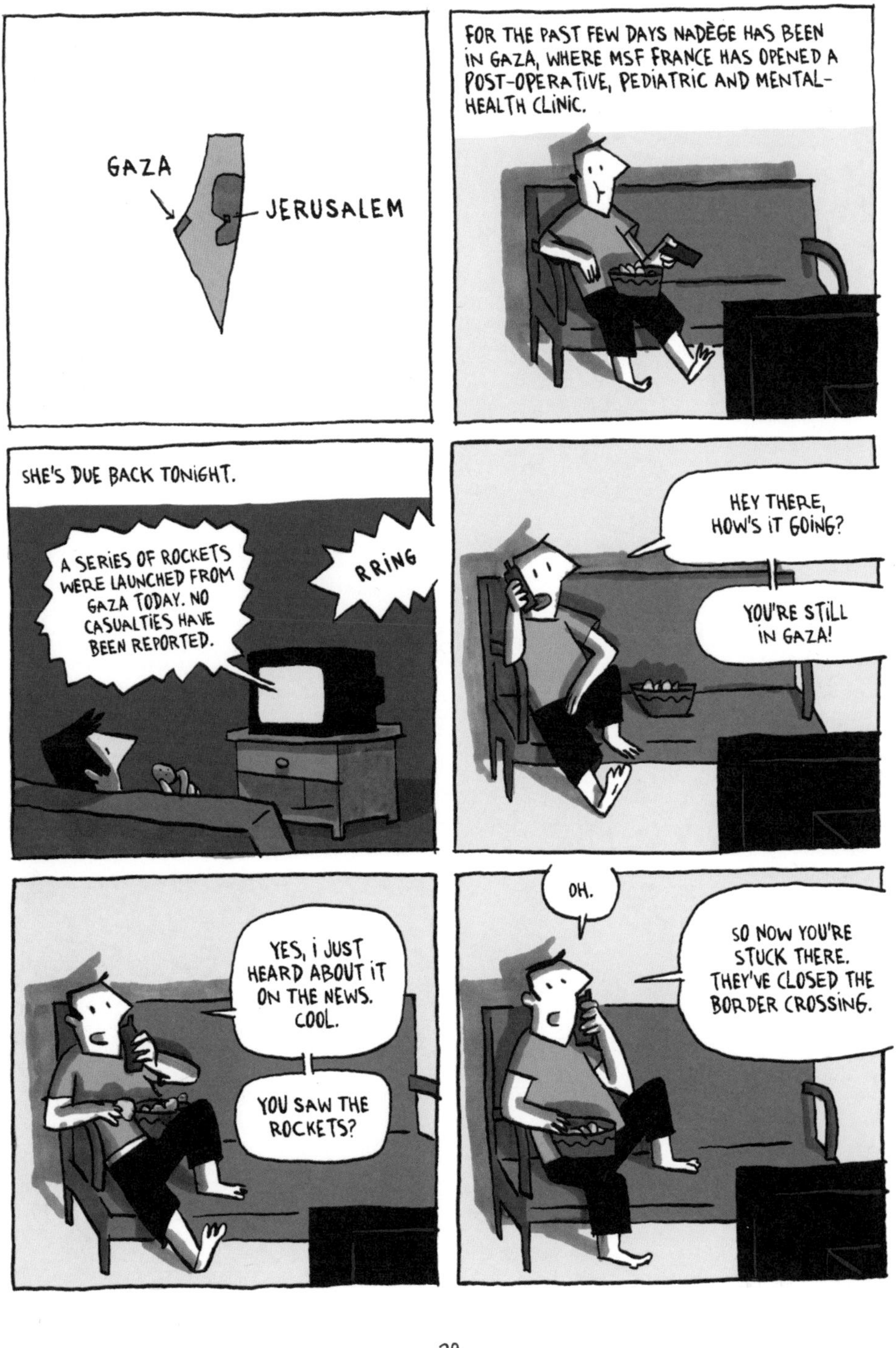
GAZA
JERUSALEM
FOR THE PAST FEW DAYS NADÈGE HAS BEEN IN GAZA, WHERE MSF FRANCE HAS OPENED A POST-OPERATIVE, PEDIATRIC AND MENTAL-HEALTH CLINIC.
SHE'S DUE BACK TONIGHT.
A SERIES OF ROCKETS WERE LAUNCHED FROM GAZA TODAY. NO CASUALTIES HAVE BEEN REPORTED.
RRING
HEY THERE, HOW'S IT GOING?
YOU'RE STILL IN GAZA!
YES, I JUST HEARD ABOUT IT ON THE NEWS. COOL.
YOU SAW THE ROCKETS?
OH.
SO NOW YOU'RE STUCK THERE. THEY'VE CLOSED THE BORDER CROSSING.

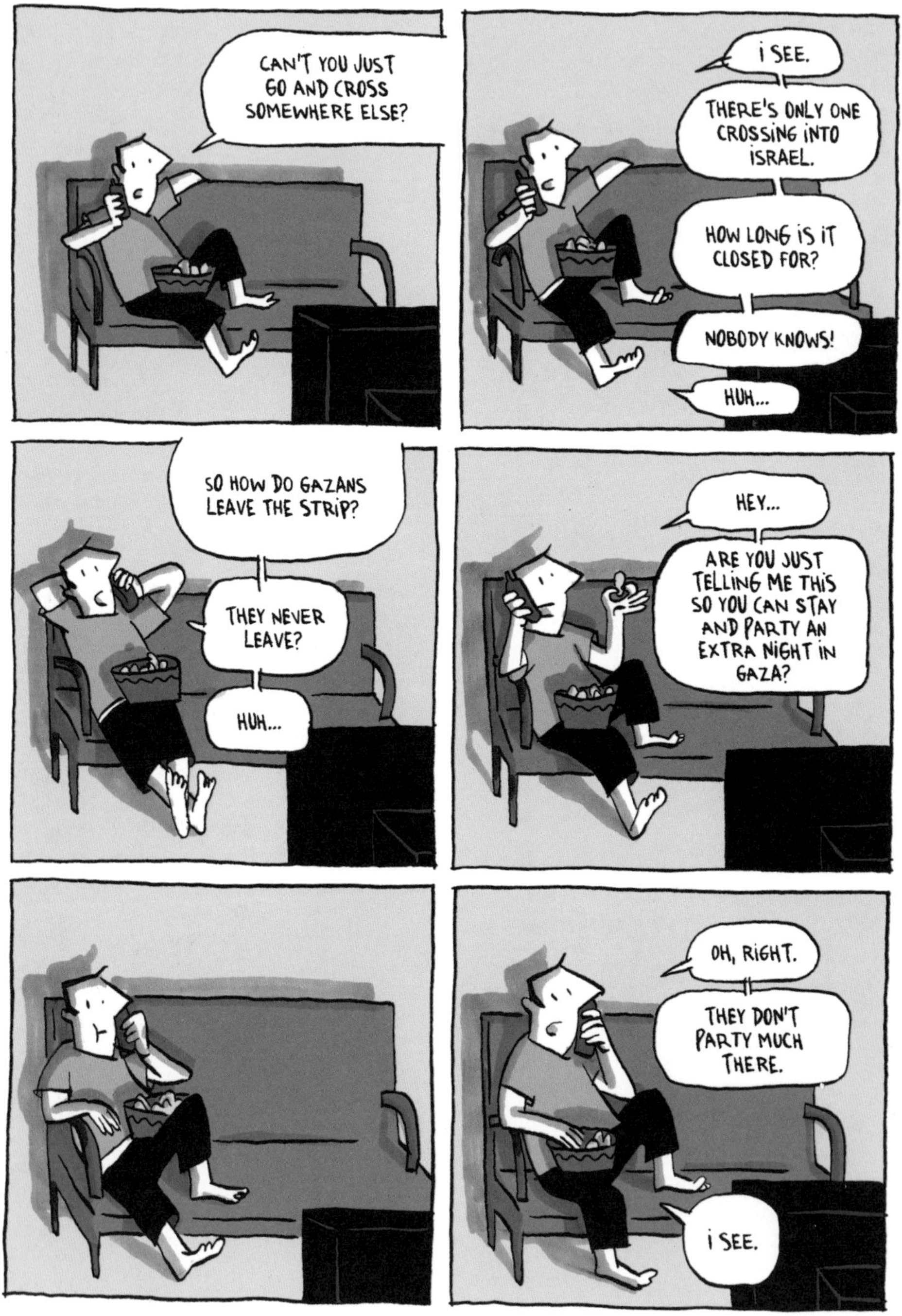
CAN'T YOU JUST GO AND CROSS SOMEWHERE ELSE?
I SEE.
THERE'S ONLY ONE CROSSING INTO ISRAEL.
HOW LONG IS IT CLOSED FOR?
NOBODY KNOWS!
HUH...
SO HOW DO GAZANS LEAVE THE STRIP?
THEY NEVER LEAVE?
HUH...
HEY...
ARE YOU JUST TELLING ME THIS SO YOU CAN STAY AND PARTY AN EXTRA NIGHT IN GAZA?
OH, RIGHT.
THEY DON'T PARTY MUCH THERE.
I SEE.

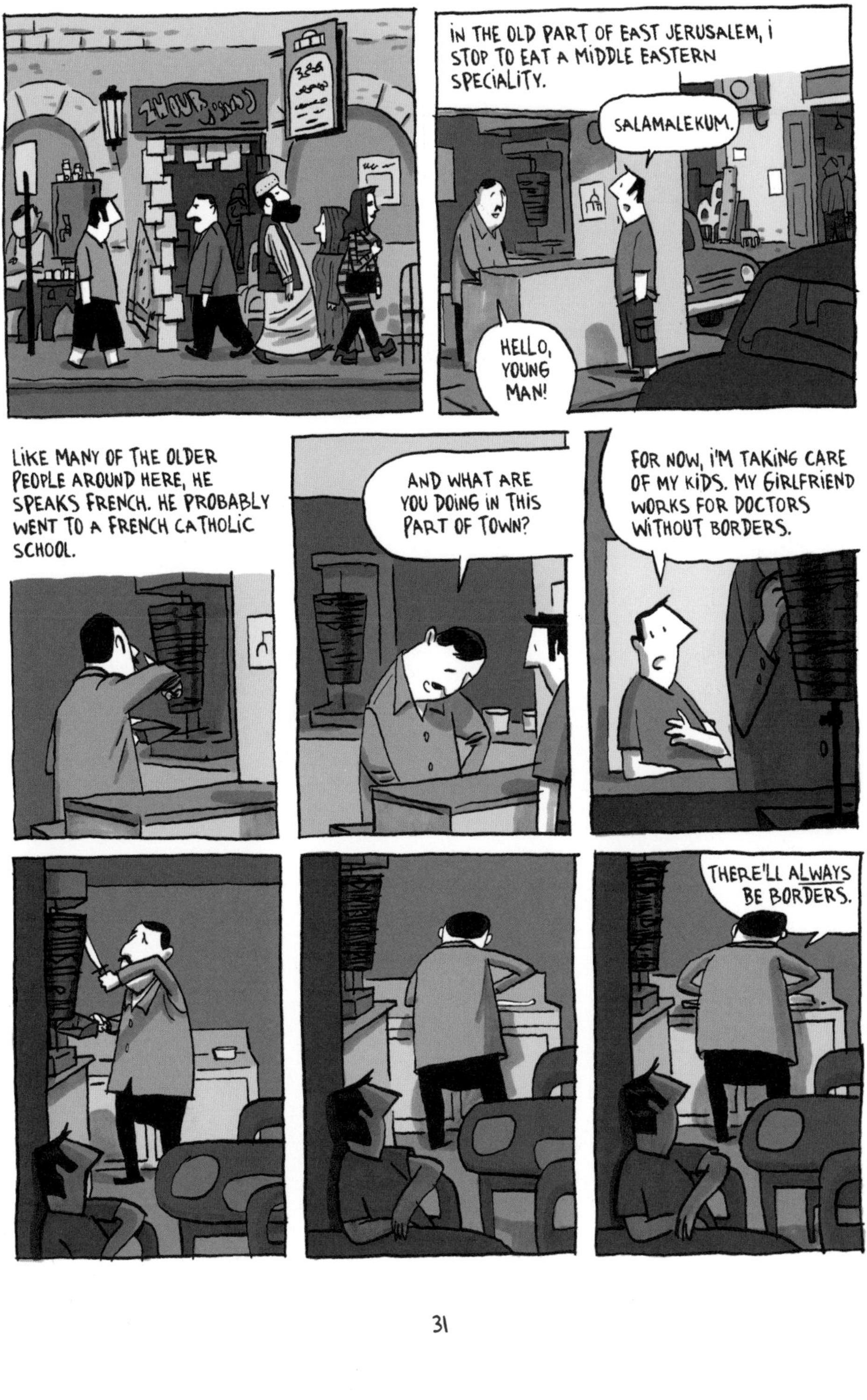
IN THE OLD PART OF EAST JERUSALEM, I STOP TO EAT A MIDDLE EASTERN SPECIALITY.
SALAMALEKUM.
HELLO, YOUNG MAN!
LIKE MANY OF THE OLDER PEOPLE AROUND HERE, HE SPEAKS FRENCH. HE PROBABLY WENT TO A FRENCH CATHOLIC SCHOOL.
AND WHAT ARE YOU DOING IN THIS PART OF TOWN?
FOR NOW, I'M TAKING CARE OF MY KIDS. MY GIRLFRIEND WORKS FOR DOCTORS WITHOUT BORDERS.
THERE'LL ALWAYS BE BORDERS.

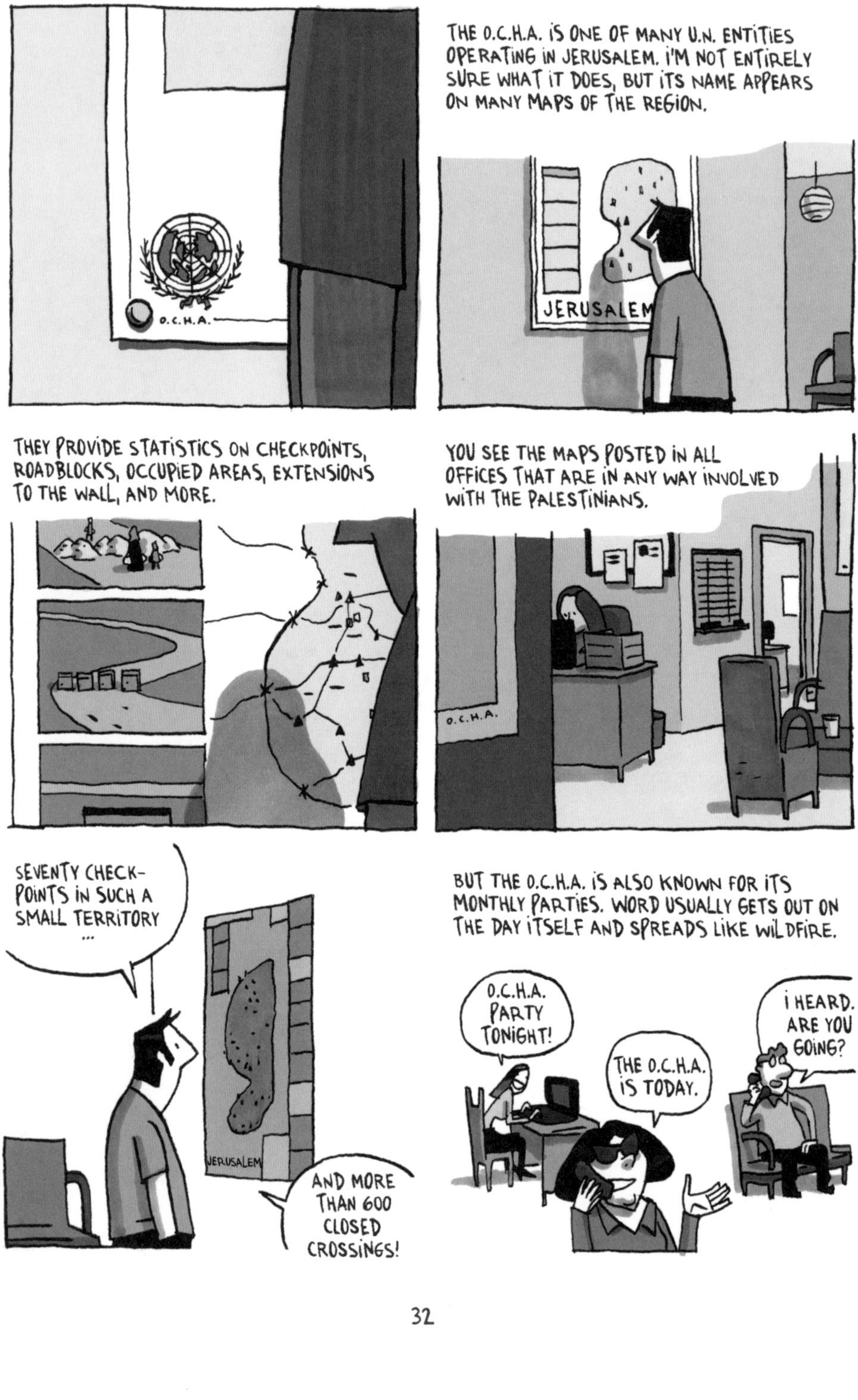
O.C.H.A.
THE O.C.H.A. IS ONE OF MANY U.N. ENTITIES OPERATING IN JERUSALEM. I'M NOT ENTIRELY SURE WHAT IT DOES, BUT ITS NAME APPEARS ON MANY MAPS OF THE REGION.
JERUSALEM
THEY PROVIDE STATISTICS ON CHECKPOINTS, ROADBLOCKS, OCCUPIED AREAS, EXTENSIONS TO THE WALL, AND MORE.
YOU SEE THE MAPS POSTED IN ALL OFFICES THAT ARE IN ANY WAY INVOLVED WITH THE PALESTINIANS.
O.C.H.A.
SEVENTY CHECK-POINTS IN SUCH A SMALL TERRITORY ...
JERUSALEM
AND MORE THAN 600 CLOSED CROSSINGS!
BUT THE O.C.H.A. IS ALSO KNOWN FOR ITS MONTHLY PARTIES. WORD USUALLY GETS OUT ON THE DAY ITSELF AND SPREADS LIKE WILDFIRE.
O.C.H.A. PARTY TONIGHT!
THE O.C.H.A. IS TODAY.
I HEARD. ARE YOU GOING?

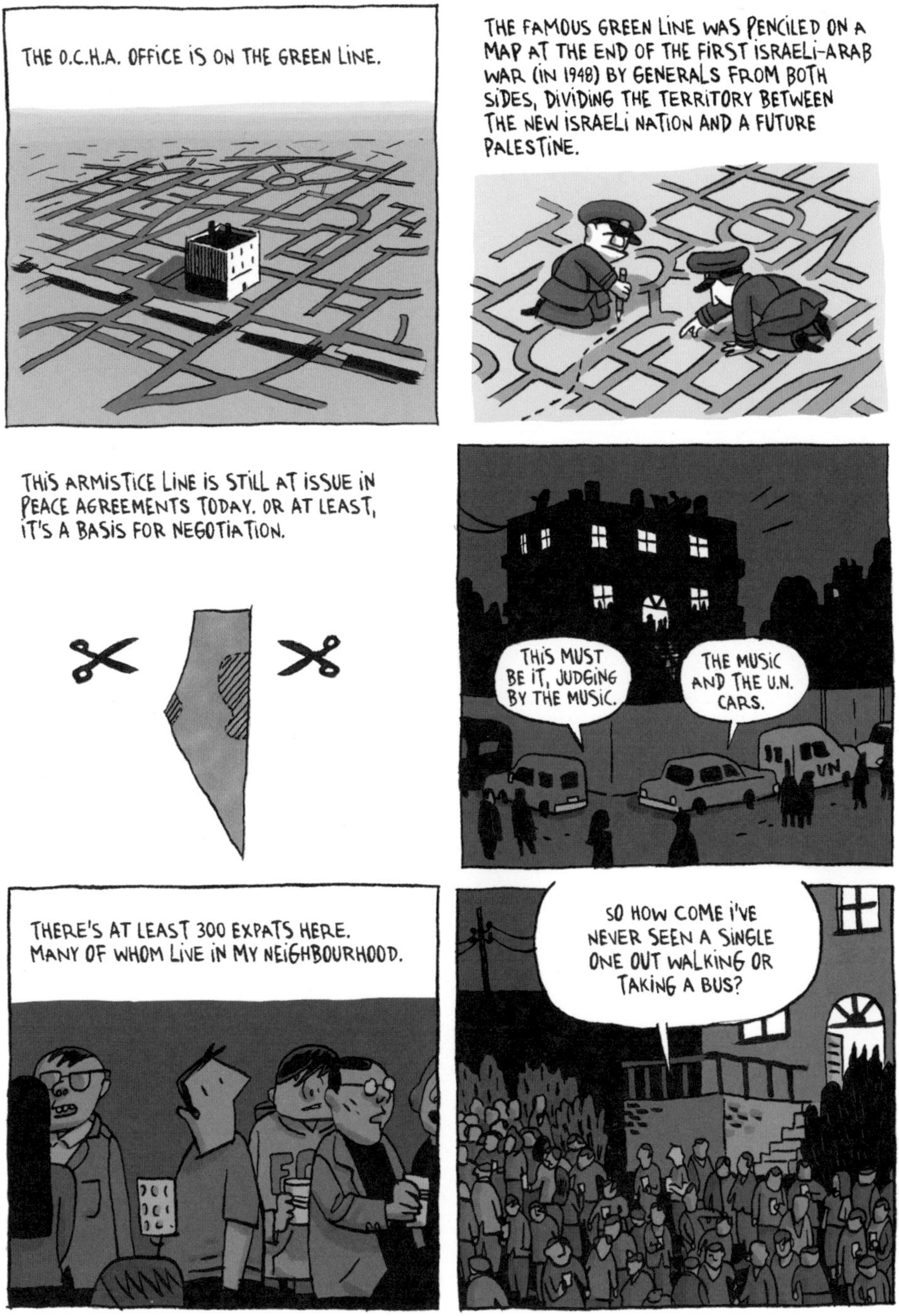
THE O.C.H.A. OFFICE IS ON THE GREEN LINE.
THE FAMOUS GREEN LINE WAS PENCILED ON A MAP AT THE END OF THE FIRST ISRAELI-ARAB WAR (IN 1948) BY GENERALS FROM BOTH SIDES, DIVIDING THE TERRITORY BETWEEN THE NEW ISRAELI NATION AND A FUTURE PALESTINE.
THIS ARMISTICE LINE IS STILL AT ISSUE IN PEACE AGREEMENTS TODAY. OR AT LEAST, IT'S A BASIS FOR NEGOTIATION.
THIS MUST BE IT, JUDGING BY THE MUSIC.
THE MUSIC AND THE U.N. CARS.
UN
THERE'S AT LEAST 300 EXPATS HERE. MANY OF WHOM LIVE IN MY NEIGHBOURHOOD.
SO HOW COME I'VE NEVER SEEN A SINGLE ONE OUT WALKING OR TAKING A BUS?

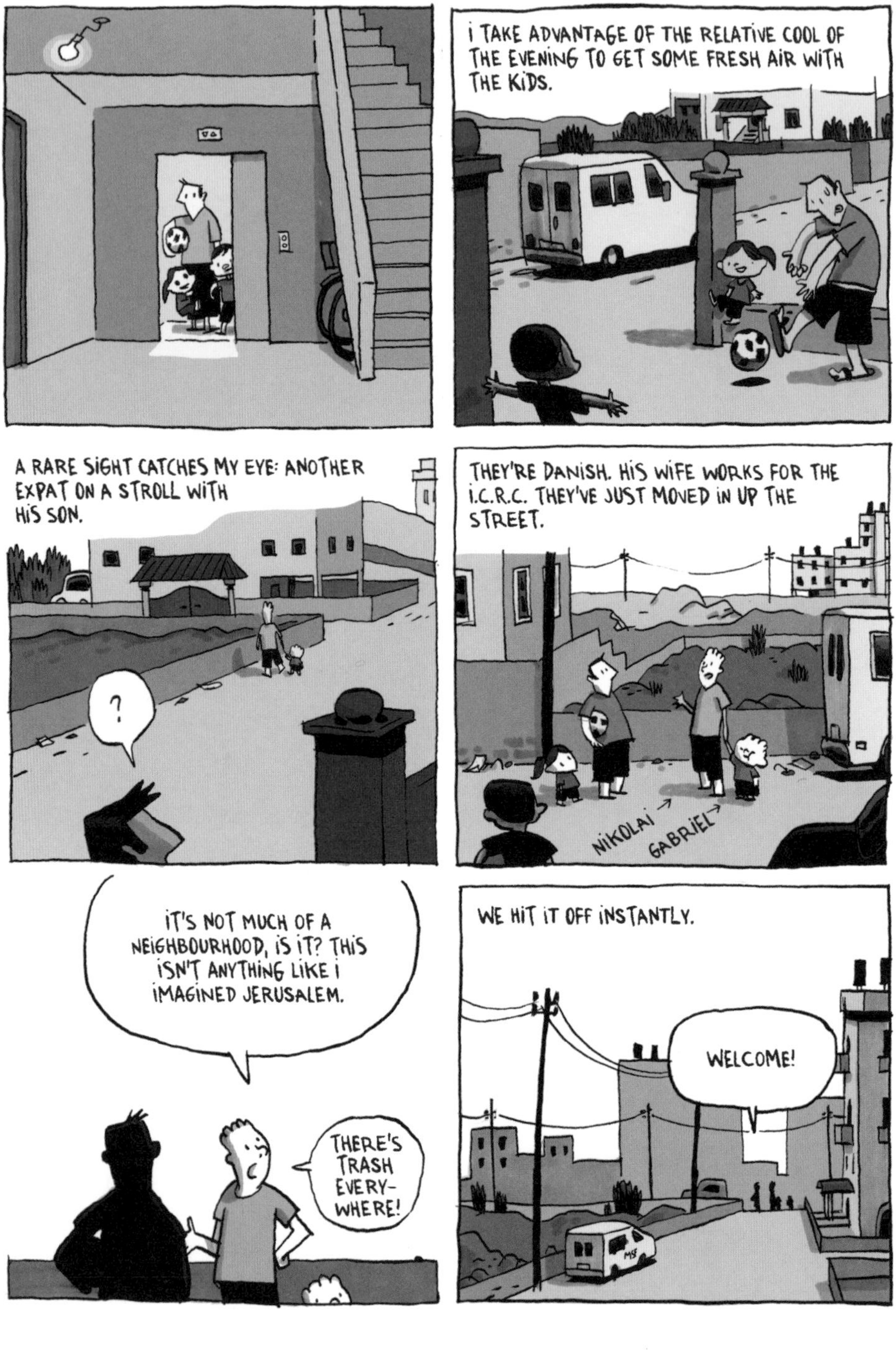
I TAKE ADVANTAGE OF THE RELATIVE COOL OF THE EVENING TO GET SOME FRESH AIR WITH THE KIDS.
A RARE SIGHT CATCHES MY EYE: ANOTHER EXPAT ON A STROLL WITH HIS SON.
?
THEY'RE DANISH. HIS WIFE WORKS FOR THE I.C.R.C. THEY'VE JUST MOVED IN UP THE STREET.
NIKOLAI →
GABRIEL →
IT'S NOT MUCH OF A NEIGHBOURHOOD, IS IT? THIS ISN'T ANYTHING LIKE I IMAGINED JERUSALEM.
THERE'S TRASH EVERY-WHERE!
WE HIT IT OFF INSTANTLY.
WELCOME!
MSF

SEPTEMBER

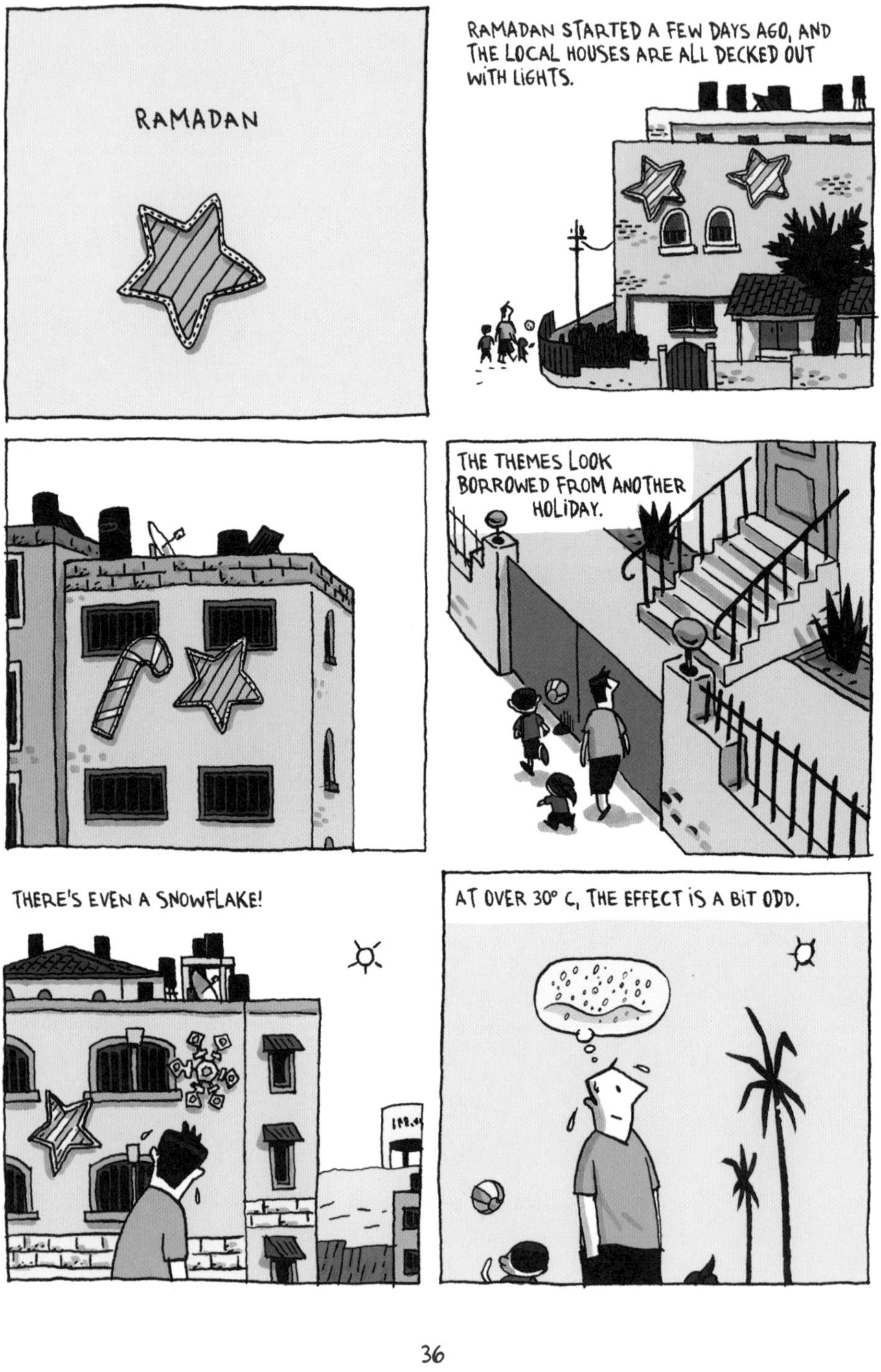
RAMADAN
RAMADAN STARTED A FEW DAYS AGO, AND THE LOCAL HOUSES ARE ALL DECKED OUT WITH LIGHTS.
THE THEMES LOOK BORROWED FROM ANOTHER HOLIDAY.
THERE'S EVEN A SNOWFLAKE!
AT OVER 30° C, THE EFFECT IS A BIT ODD.

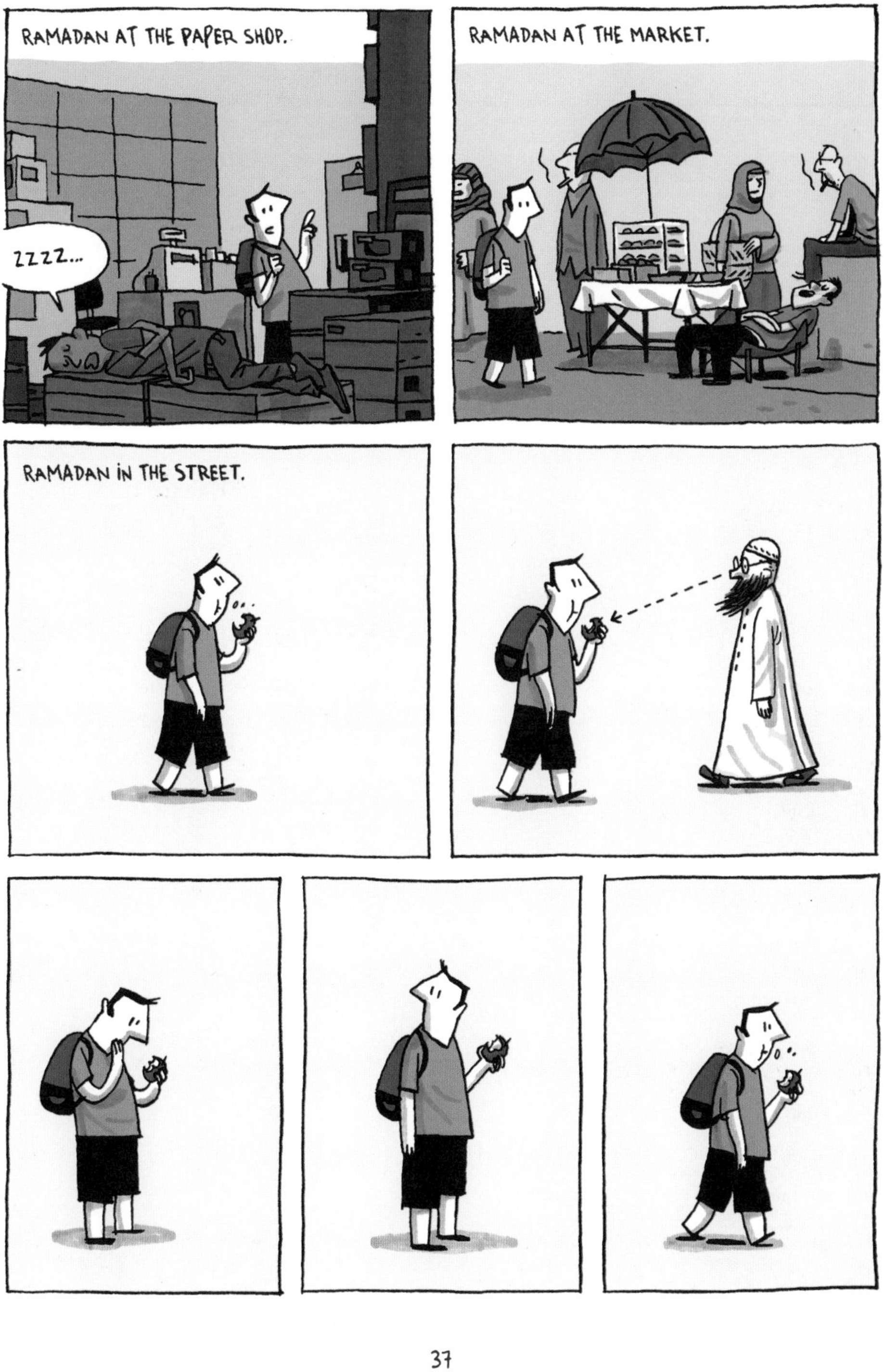
RAMADAN AT THE PAPER SHOP.
ZZZZ...
RAMADAN AT THE MARKET.
RAMADAN IN THE STREET.

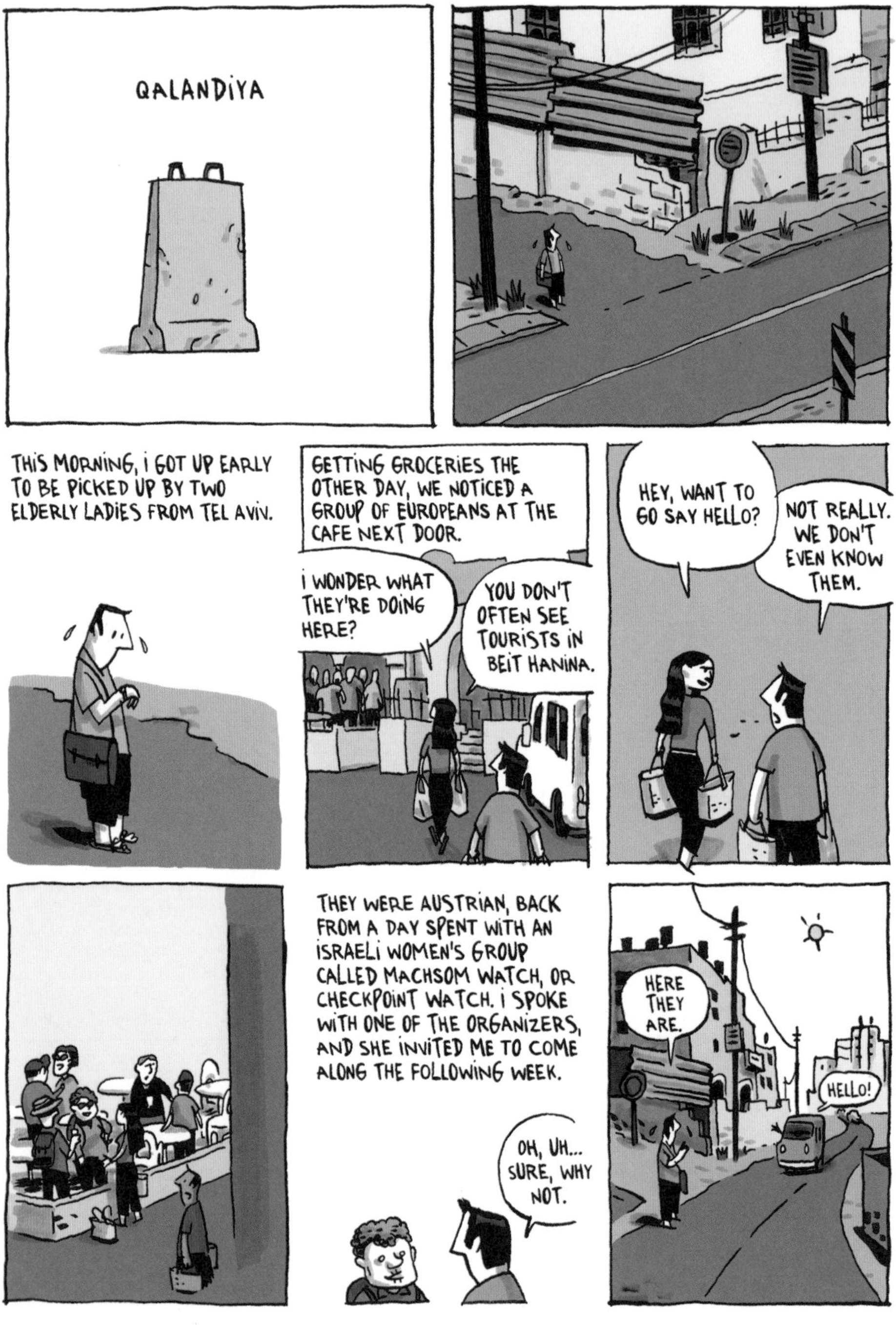
QALANDIYA
THIS MORNING, I GOT UP EARLY TO BE PICKED UP BY TWO ELDERLY LADIES FROM TEL AVIV.
GETTING GROCERIES THE OTHER DAY, WE NOTICED A GROUP OF EUROPEANS AT THE CAFE NEXT DOOR.
I WONDER WHAT THEY'RE DOING HERE?
YOU DON'T OFTEN SEE TOURISTS IN BEIT HANINA.
HEY, WANT TO GO SAY HELLO?
NOT REALLY. WE DON'T EVEN KNOW THEM.
THEY WERE AUSTRIAN, BACK FROM A DAY SPENT WITH AN ISRAELI WOMEN'S GROUP CALLED MACHSOM WATCH, OR CHECKPOINT WATCH. I SPOKE WITH ONE OF THE ORGANIZERS, AND SHE INVITED ME TO COME ALONG THE FOLLOWING WEEK.
OH, UH... SURE, WHY NOT.
HERE THEY ARE.
HELLO!

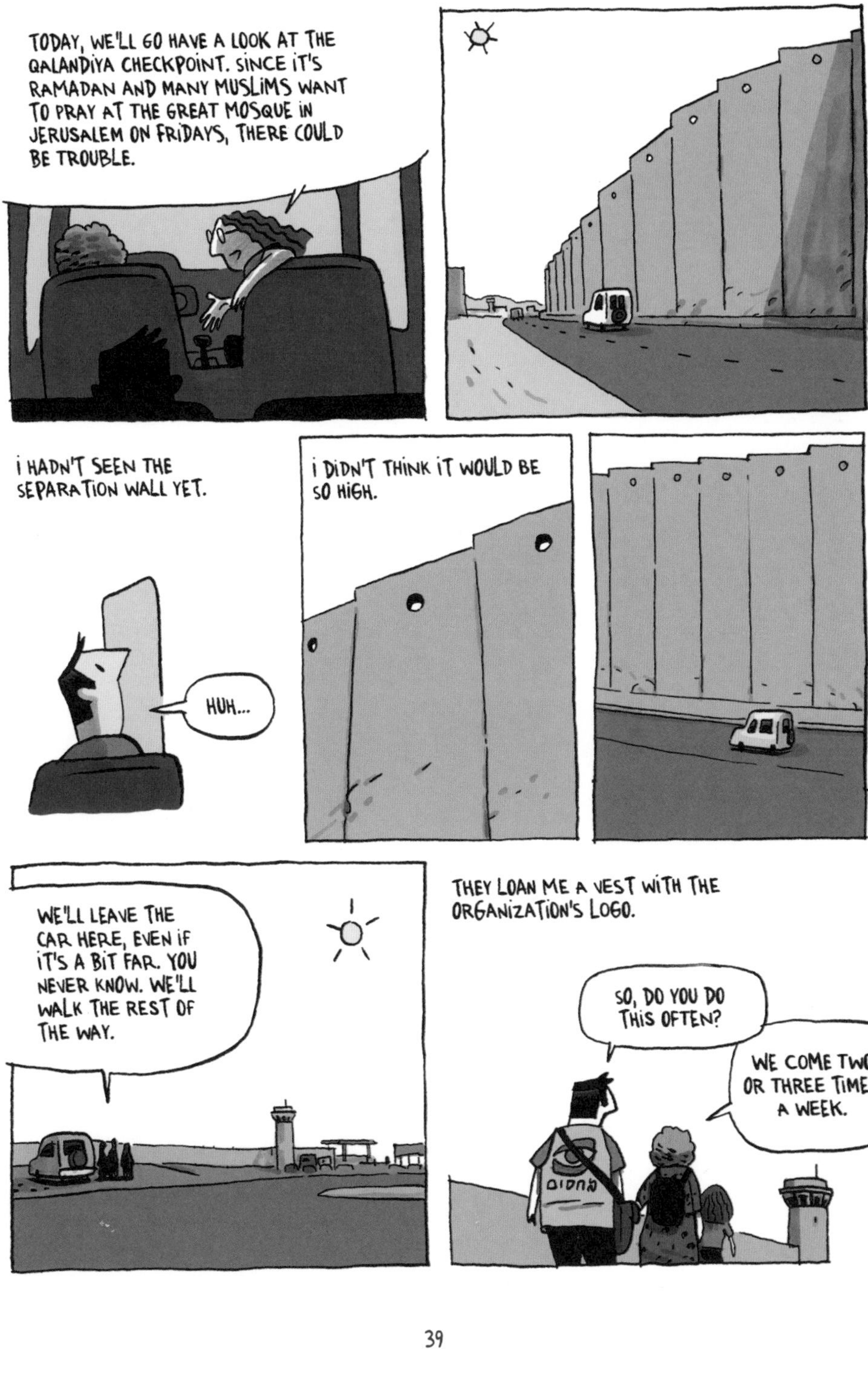
TODAY, WE'LL GO HAVE A LOOK AT THE QALANDIYA CHECKPOINT. SINCE IT'S RAMADAN AND MANY MUSLIMS WANT TO PRAY AT THE GREAT MOSQUE IN JERUSALEM ON FRIDAYS, THERE COULD BE TROUBLE.
I HADN'T SEEN THE SEPARATION WALL YET.
HUH...
I DIDN'T THINK IT WOULD BE SO HIGH.
WE'LL LEAVE THE CAR HERE, EVEN IF IT'S A BIT FAR. YOU NEVER KNOW. WE'LL WALK THE REST OF THE WAY.
THEY LOAN ME A VEST WITH THE ORGANIZATION'S LOGO.
SO, DO YOU DO THIS OFTEN?
WE COME TWO OR THREE TIMES A WEEK.

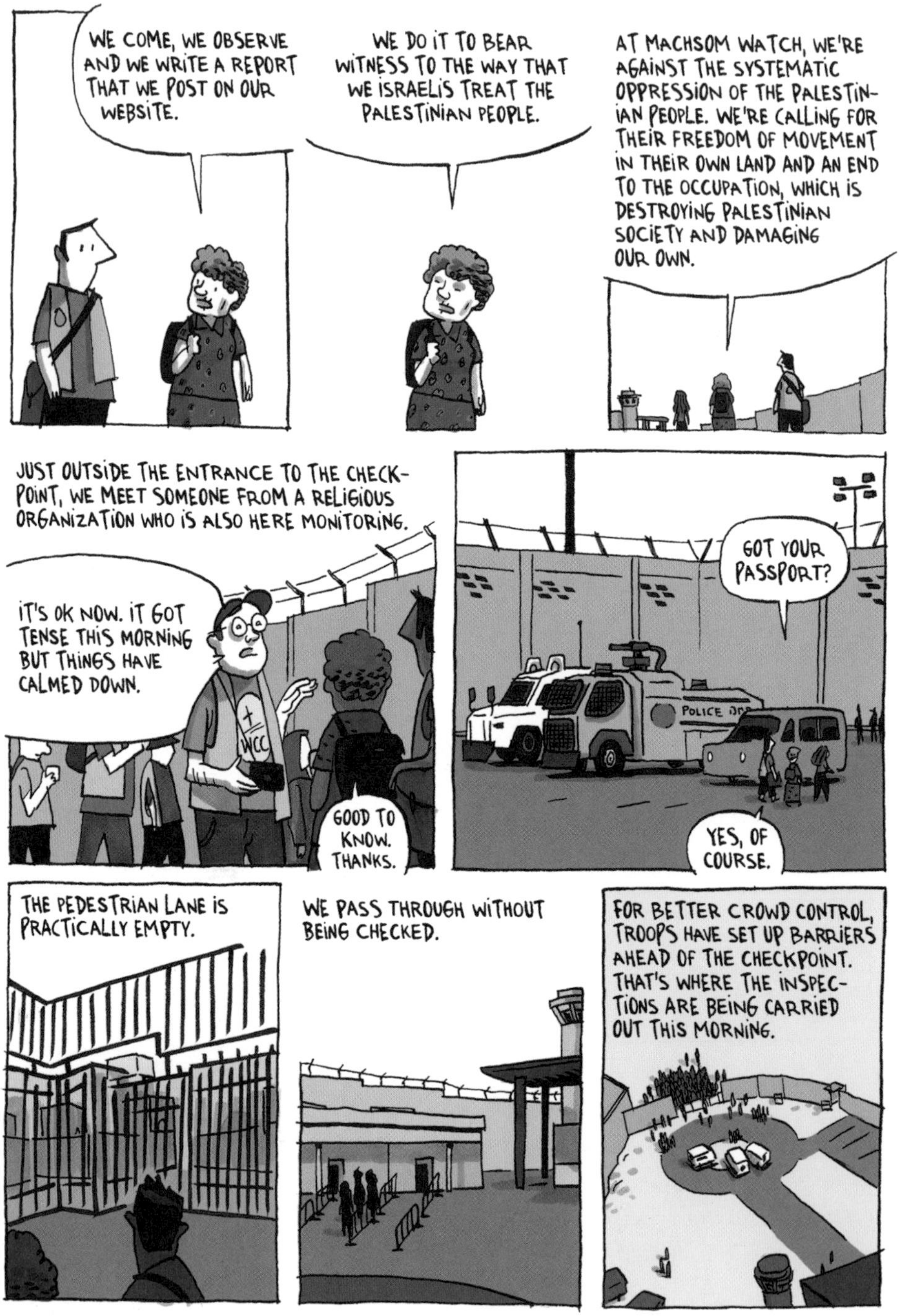
WE COME, WE OBSERVE AND WE WRITE A REPORT THAT WE POST ON OUR WEBSITE.
WE DO IT TO BEAR WITNESS TO THE WAY THAT WE ISRAELIS TREAT THE PALESTINIAN PEOPLE.
AT MACHSOM WATCH, WE'RE AGAINST THE SYSTEMATIC OPPRESSION OF THE PALESTINIAN PEOPLE. WE'RE CALLING FOR THEIR FREEDOM OF MOVEMENT IN THEIR OWN LAND AND AN END TO THE OCCUPATION, WHICH IS DESTROYING PALESTINIAN SOCIETY AND DAMAGING OUR OWN.
JUST OUTSIDE THE ENTRANCE TO THE CHECKPOINT, WE MEET SOMEONE FROM A RELIGIOUS ORGANIZATION WHO IS ALSO HERE MONITORING.
IT'S OK NOW. IT GOT TENSE THIS MORNING BUT THINGS HAVE CALMED DOWN.
WCC
GOOD TO KNOW. THANKS.
GOT YOUR PASSPORT?
POLICE
YES, OF COURSE.
THE PEDESTRIAN LANE IS PRACTICALLY EMPTY.
WE PASS THROUGH WITHOUT BEING CHECKED.
FOR BETTER CROWD CONTROL, TROOPS HAVE SET UP BARRIERS AHEAD OF THE CHECKPOINT. THAT'S WHERE THE INSPECTIONS ARE BEING CARRIED OUT THIS MORNING.

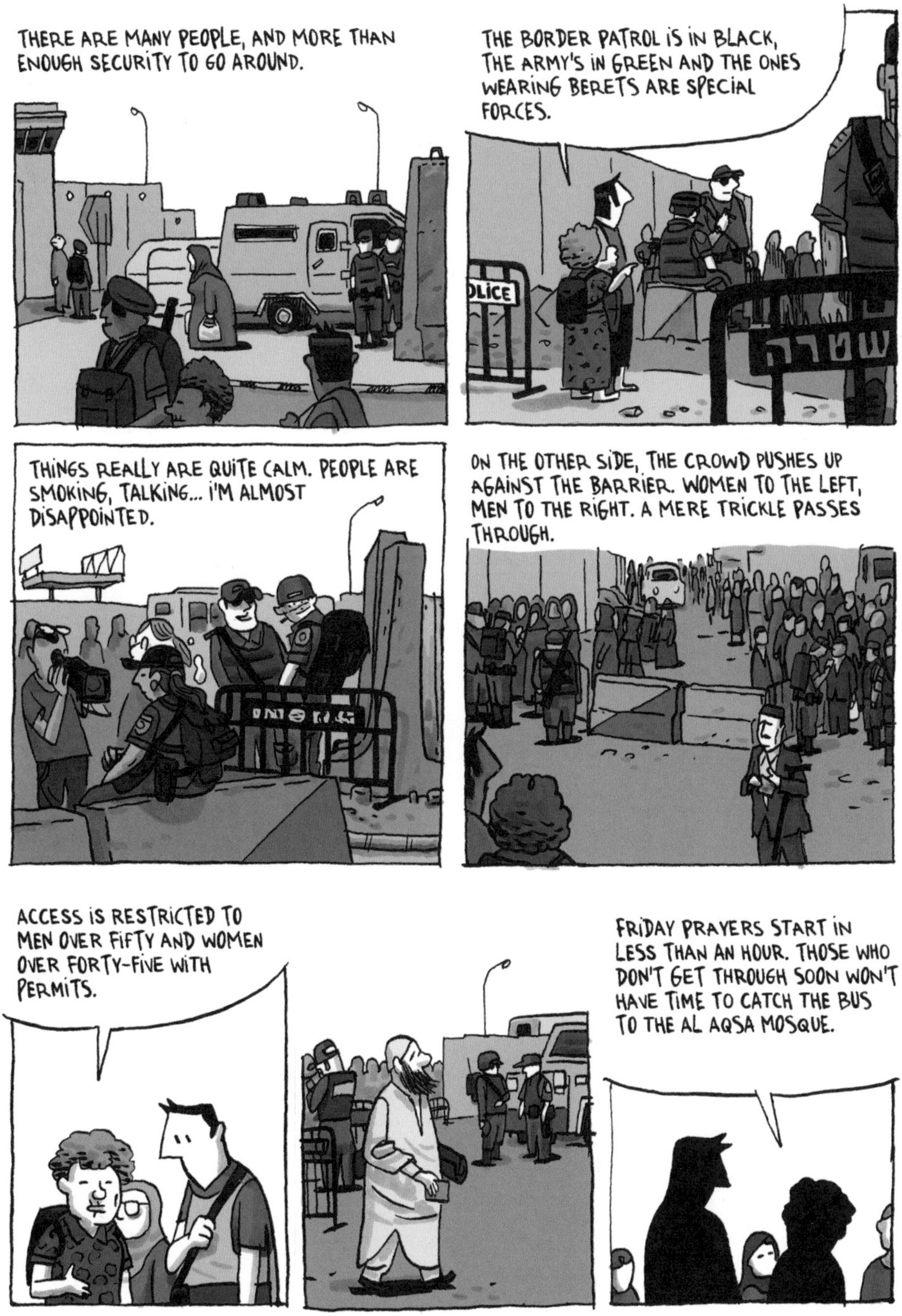
THERE ARE MANY PEOPLE, AND MORE THAN ENOUGH SECURITY TO GO AROUND.
THE BORDER PATROL IS IN BLACK, THE ARMY'S IN GREEN AND THE ONES WEARING BERETS ARE SPECIAL FORCES.
THINGS REALLY ARE QUITE CALM. PEOPLE ARE SMOKING, TALKING... I'M ALMOST DISAPPOINTED.
ON THE OTHER SIDE, THE CROWD PUSHES UP AGAINST THE BARRIER. WOMEN TO THE LEFT, MEN TO THE RIGHT. A MERE TRICKLE PASSES THROUGH.
ACCESS IS RESTRICTED TO MEN OVER FIFTY AND WOMEN OVER FORTY-FIVE WITH PERMITS.
FRIDAY PRAYERS START IN LESS THAN AN HOUR. THOSE WHO DON'T GET THROUGH SOON WON'T HAVE TIME TO CATCH THE BUS TO THE AL AQSA MOSQUE.

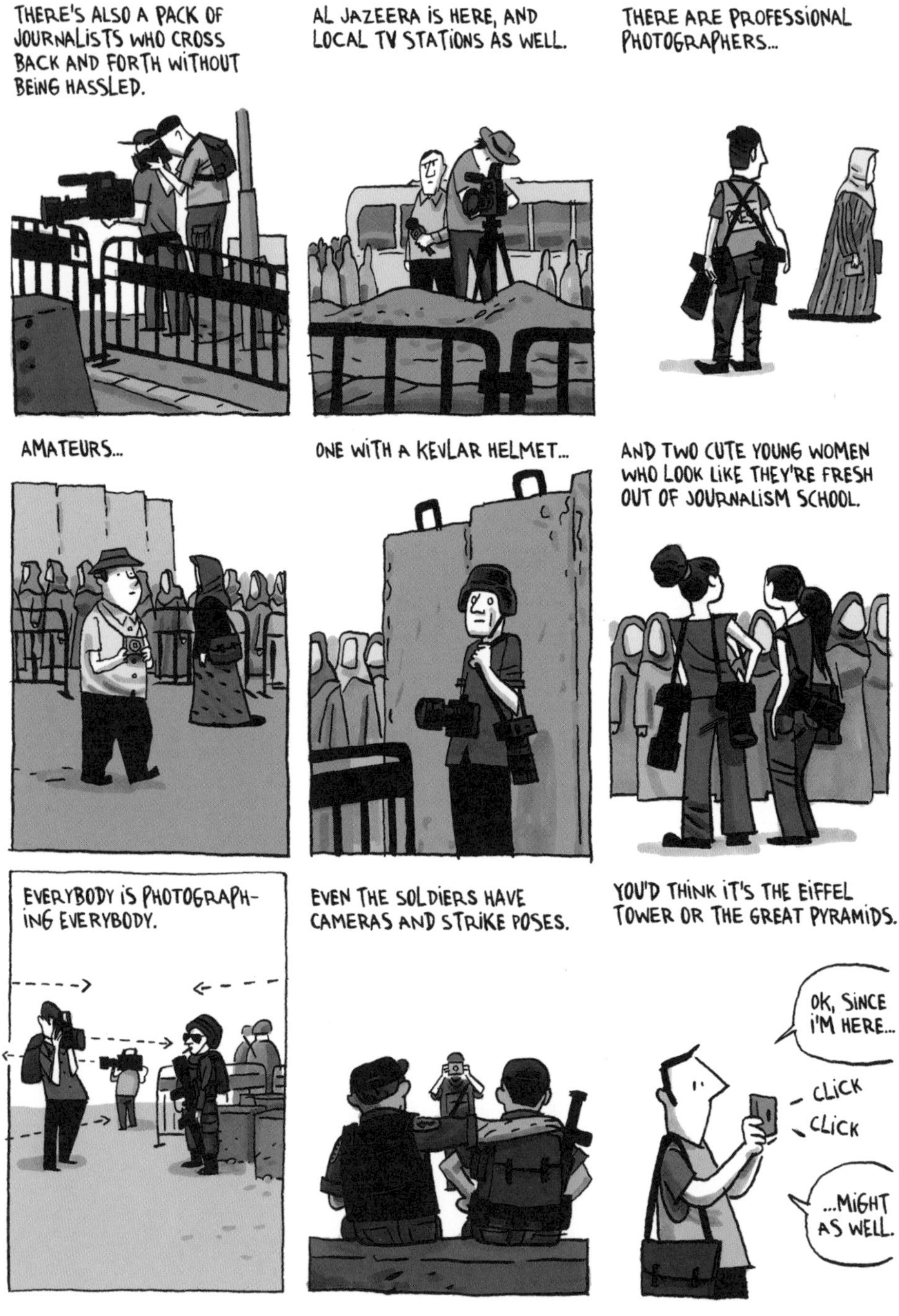
THERE'S ALSO A PACK OF JOURNALISTS WHO CROSS BACK AND FORTH WITHOUT BEING HASSLED.
AL JAZEERA IS HERE, AND LOCAL TV STATIONS AS WELL.
THERE ARE PROFESSIONAL PHOTOGRAPHERS...
AMATEURS...
ONE WITH A KEVLAR HELMET...
AND TWO CUTE YOUNG WOMEN WHO LOOK LIKE THEY'RE FRESH OUT OF JOURNALISM SCHOOL.
EVERYBODY IS PHOTOGRAPHING EVERYBODY.
EVEN THE SOLDIERS HAVE CAMERAS AND STRIKE POSES.
YOU'D THINK IT'S THE EIFFEL TOWER OR THE GREAT PYRAMIDS.
OK, SINCE I'M HERE...
CLICK
CLICK
...MIGHT AS WELL.

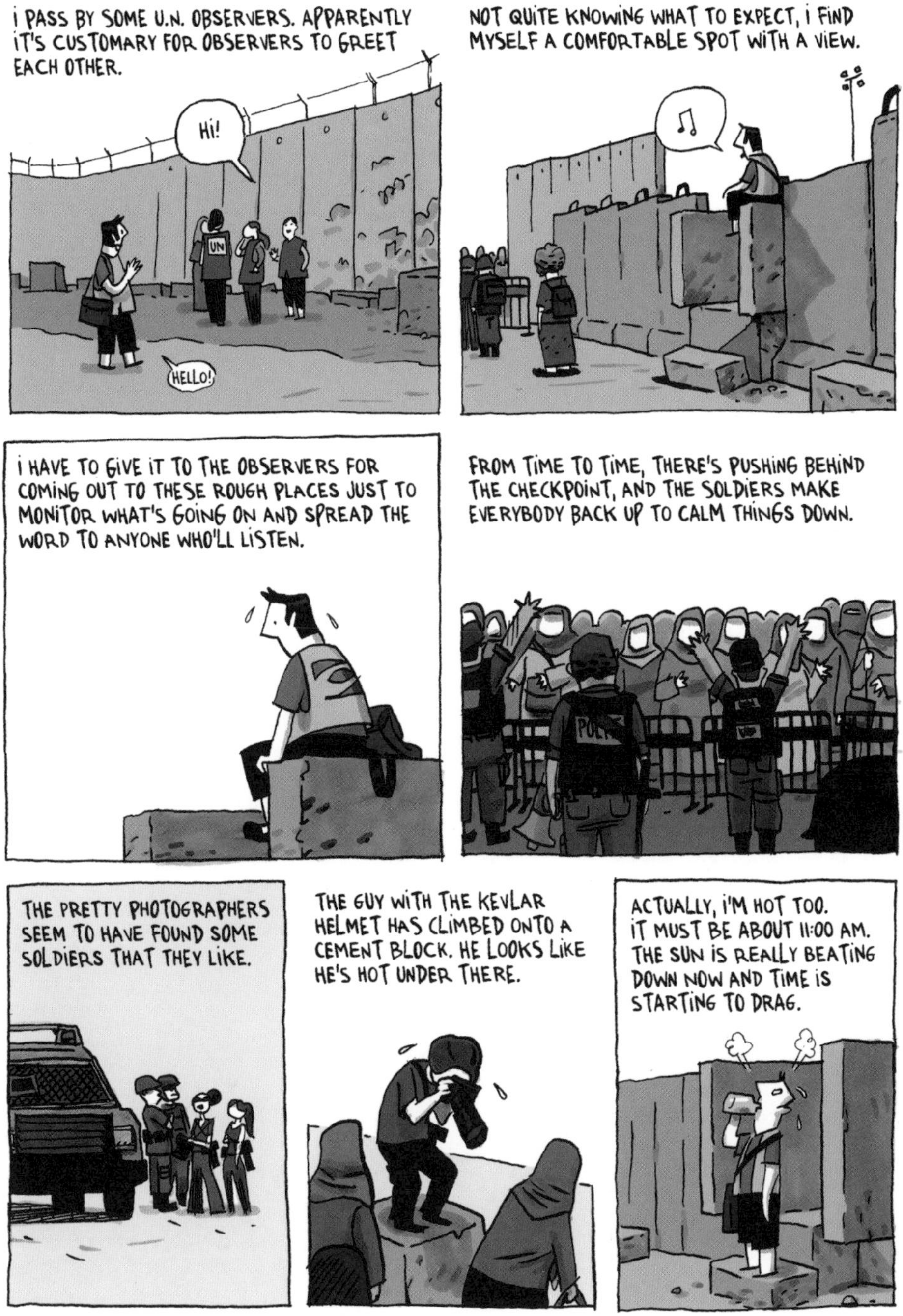
I PASS BY SOME U.N. OBSERVERS. APPARENTLY IT'S CUSTOMARY FOR OBSERVERS TO GREET EACH OTHER.
HI!
UN
HELLO!
NOT QUITE KNOWING WHAT TO EXPECT, I FIND MYSELF A COMFORTABLE SPOT WITH A VIEW.
♫
I HAVE TO GIVE IT TO THE OBSERVERS FOR COMING OUT TO THESE ROUGH PLACES JUST TO MONITOR WHAT'S GOING ON AND SPREAD THE WORD TO ANYONE WHO'LL LISTEN.
FROM TIME TO TIME, THERE'S PUSHING BEHIND THE CHECKPOINT, AND THE SOLDIERS MAKE EVERYBODY BACK UP TO CALM THINGS DOWN.
THE PRETTY PHOTOGRAPHERS SEEM TO HAVE FOUND SOME SOLDIERS THAT THEY LIKE.
THE GUY WITH THE KEVLAR HELMET HAS CLIMBED ONTO A CEMENT BLOCK. HE LOOKS LIKE HE'S HOT UNDER THERE.
ACTUALLY, I'M HOT TOO. IT MUST BE ABOUT 11:00 AM. THE SUN IS REALLY BEATING DOWN NOW AND TIME IS STARTING TO DRAG.

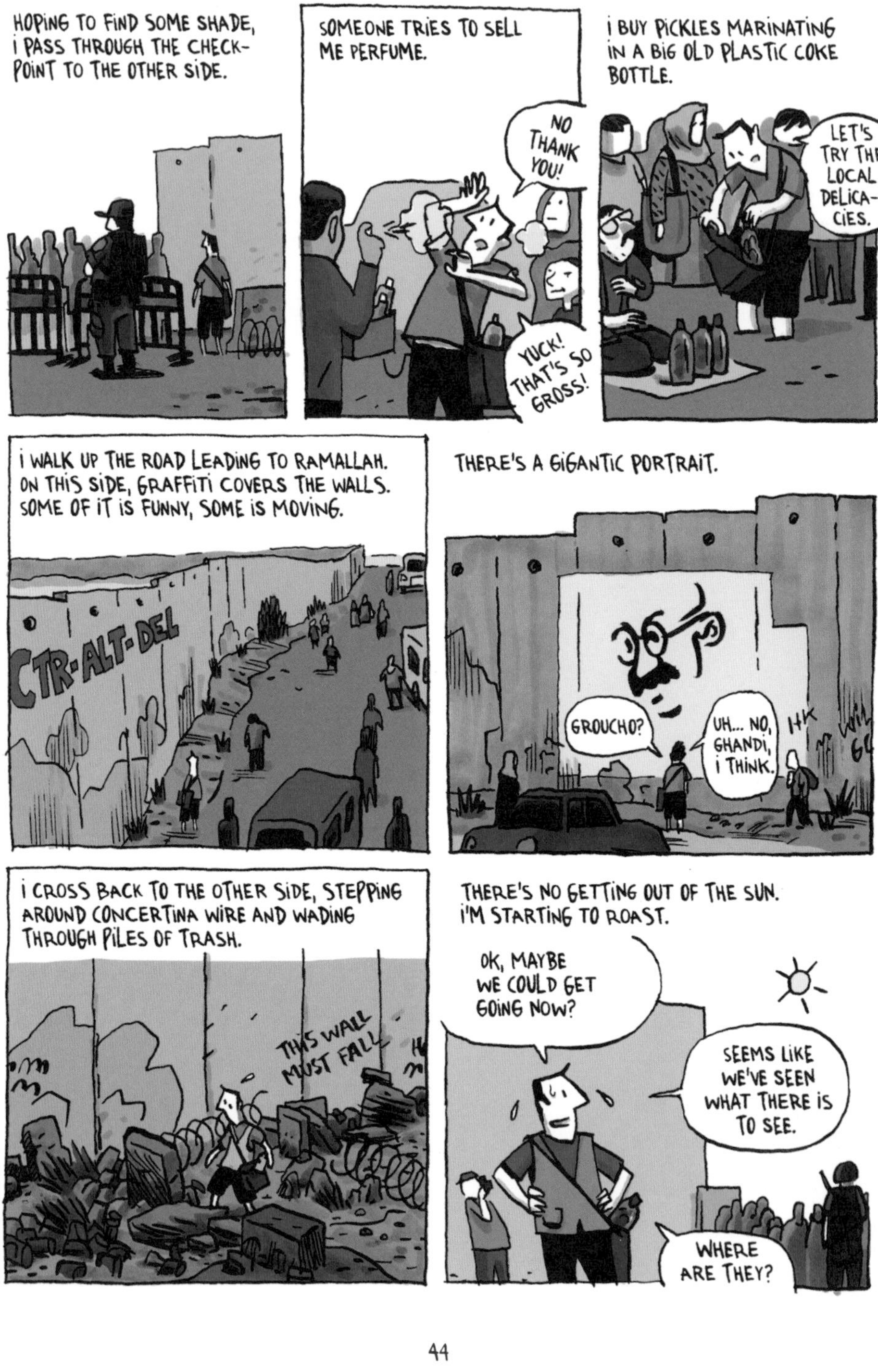
HOPING TO FIND SOME SHADE, I PASS THROUGH THE CHECK-POINT TO THE OTHER SIDE.
SOMEONE TRIES TO SELL ME PERFUME.
NO THANK YOU!
YUCK! THAT'S SO GROSS!
I BUY PICKLES MARINATING IN A BIG OLD PLASTIC COKE BOTTLE.
LET'S TRY THE LOCAL DELICA-CIES.
I WALK UP THE ROAD LEADING TO RAMALLAH. ON THIS SIDE, GRAFFITI COVERS THE WALLS. SOME OF IT IS FUNNY, SOME IS MOVING.
CTR-ALT-DEL
THERE'S A GIGANTIC PORTRAIT.
GROUCHO?
UH... NO, GHANDI, I THINK.
I CROSS BACK TO THE OTHER SIDE, STEPPING AROUND CONCERTINA WIRE AND WADING THROUGH PILES OF TRASH.
THIS WALL MUST FALL
THERE'S NO GETTING OUT OF THE SUN. I'M STARTING TO ROAST.
OK, MAYBE WE COULD GET GOING NOW?
SEEMS LIKE WE'VE SEEN WHAT THERE IS TO SEE.
WHERE ARE THEY?

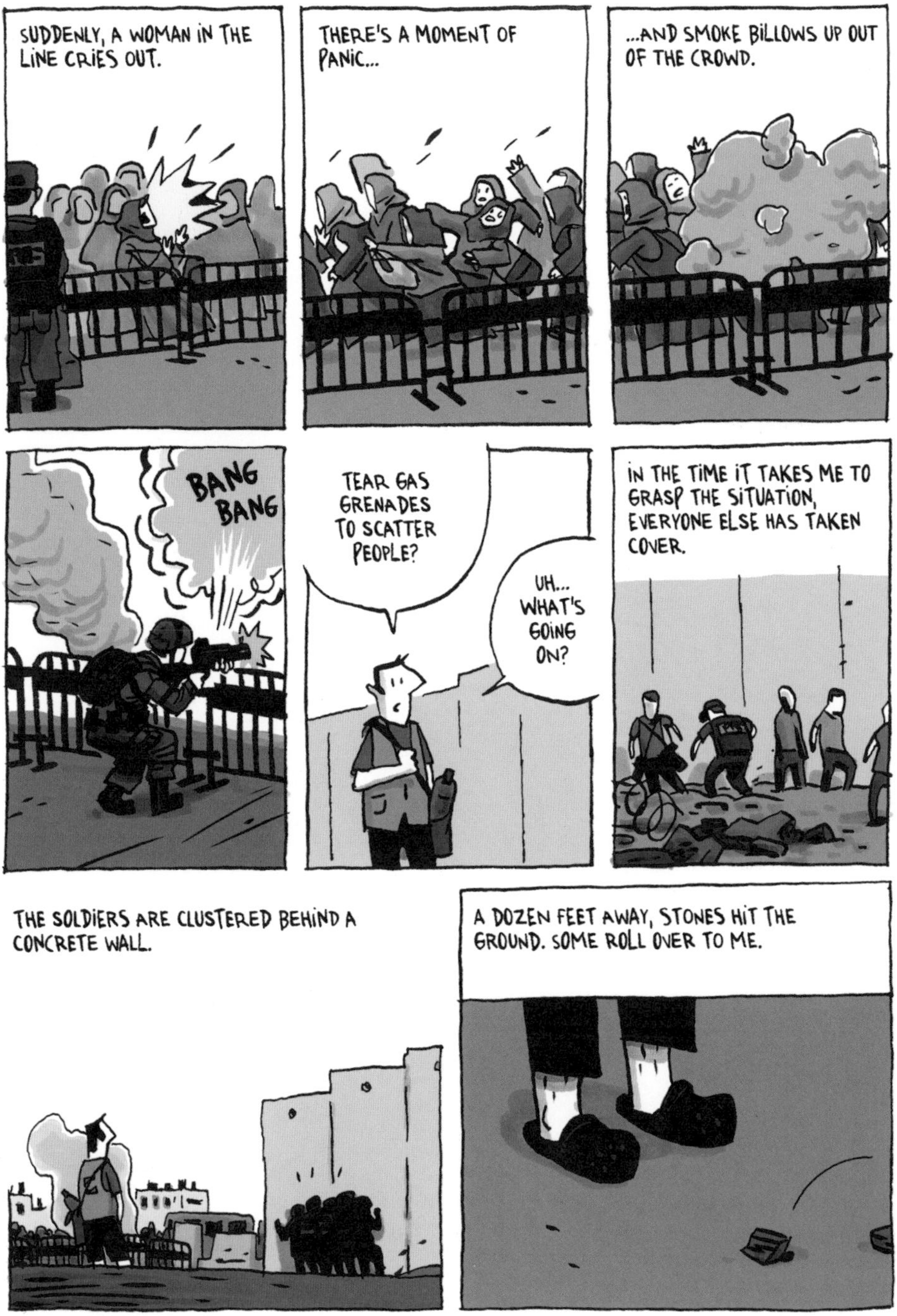
SUDDENLY, A WOMAN IN THE LINE CRIES OUT.
THERE'S A MOMENT OF PANIC...
...AND SMOKE BILLOWS UP OUT OF THE CROWD.
BANG
BANG
TEAR GAS GRENADES TO SCATTER PEOPLE?
UH... WHAT'S GOING ON?
IN THE TIME IT TAKES ME TO GRASP THE SITUATION, EVERYONE ELSE HAS TAKEN COVER.
THE SOLDIERS ARE CLUSTERED BEHIND A CONCRETE WALL.
A DOZEN FEET AWAY, STONES HIT THE GROUND. SOME ROLL OVER TO ME.

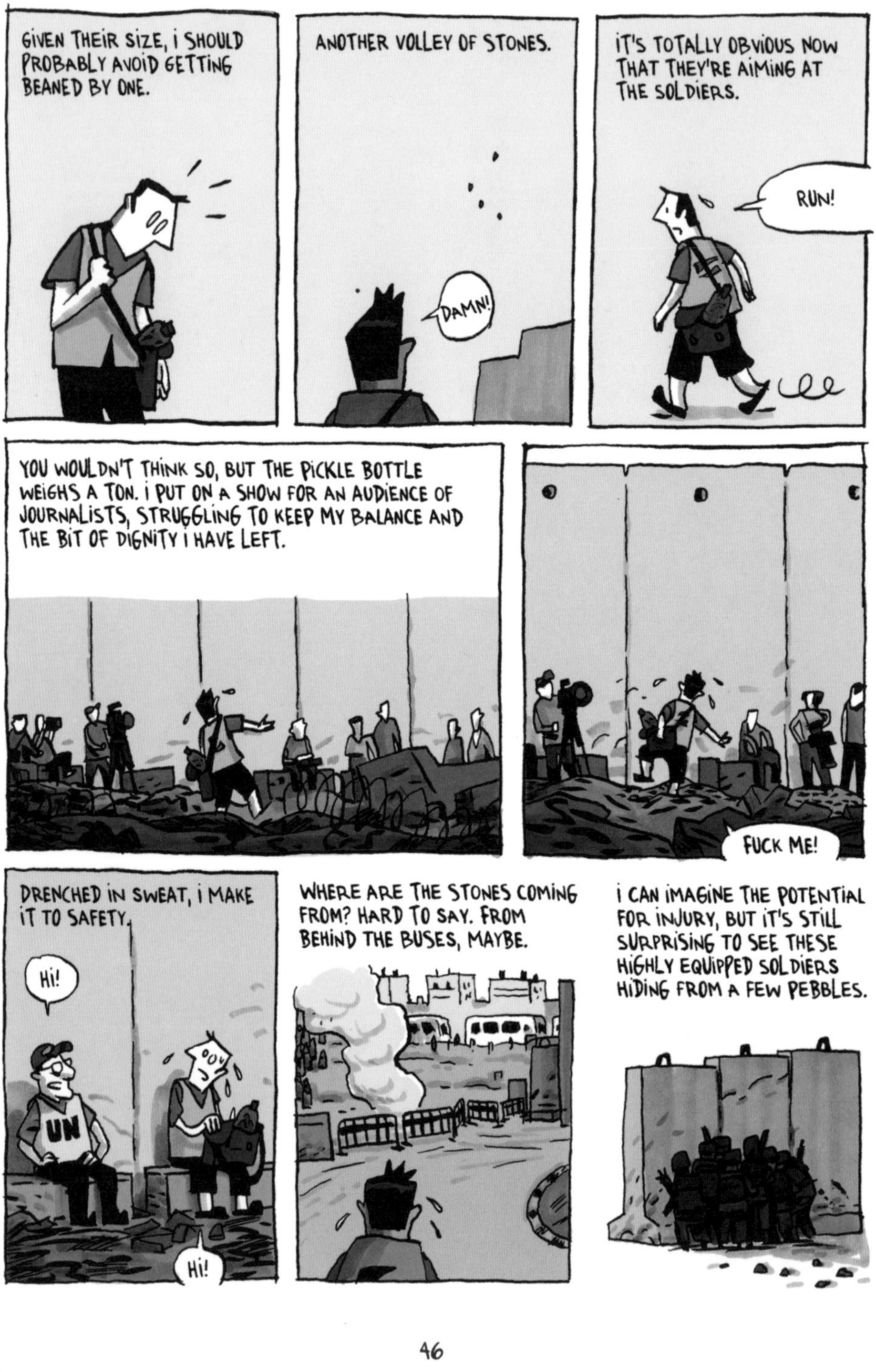
GIVEN THEIR SIZE, I SHOULD PROBABLY AVOID GETTING BEANED BY ONE.
ANOTHER VOLLEY OF STONES.
DAMN!
IT'S TOTALLY OBVIOUS NOW THAT THEY'RE AIMING AT THE SOLDIERS.
RUN!
YOU WOULDN'T THINK SO, BUT THE PICKLE BOTTLE WEIGHS A TON. I PUT ON A SHOW FOR AN AUDIENCE OF JOURNALISTS, STRUGGLING TO KEEP MY BALANCE AND THE BIT OF DIGNITY I HAVE LEFT.
FUCK ME!
DRENCHED IN SWEAT, I MAKE IT TO SAFETY.
HI!
HI!
WHERE ARE THE STONES COMING FROM? HARD TO SAY. FROM BEHIND THE BUSES, MAYBE.
I CAN IMAGINE THE POTENTIAL FOR INJURY, BUT IT'S STILL SURPRISING TO SEE THESE HIGHLY EQUIPPED SOLDIERS HIDING FROM A FEW PEBBLES.

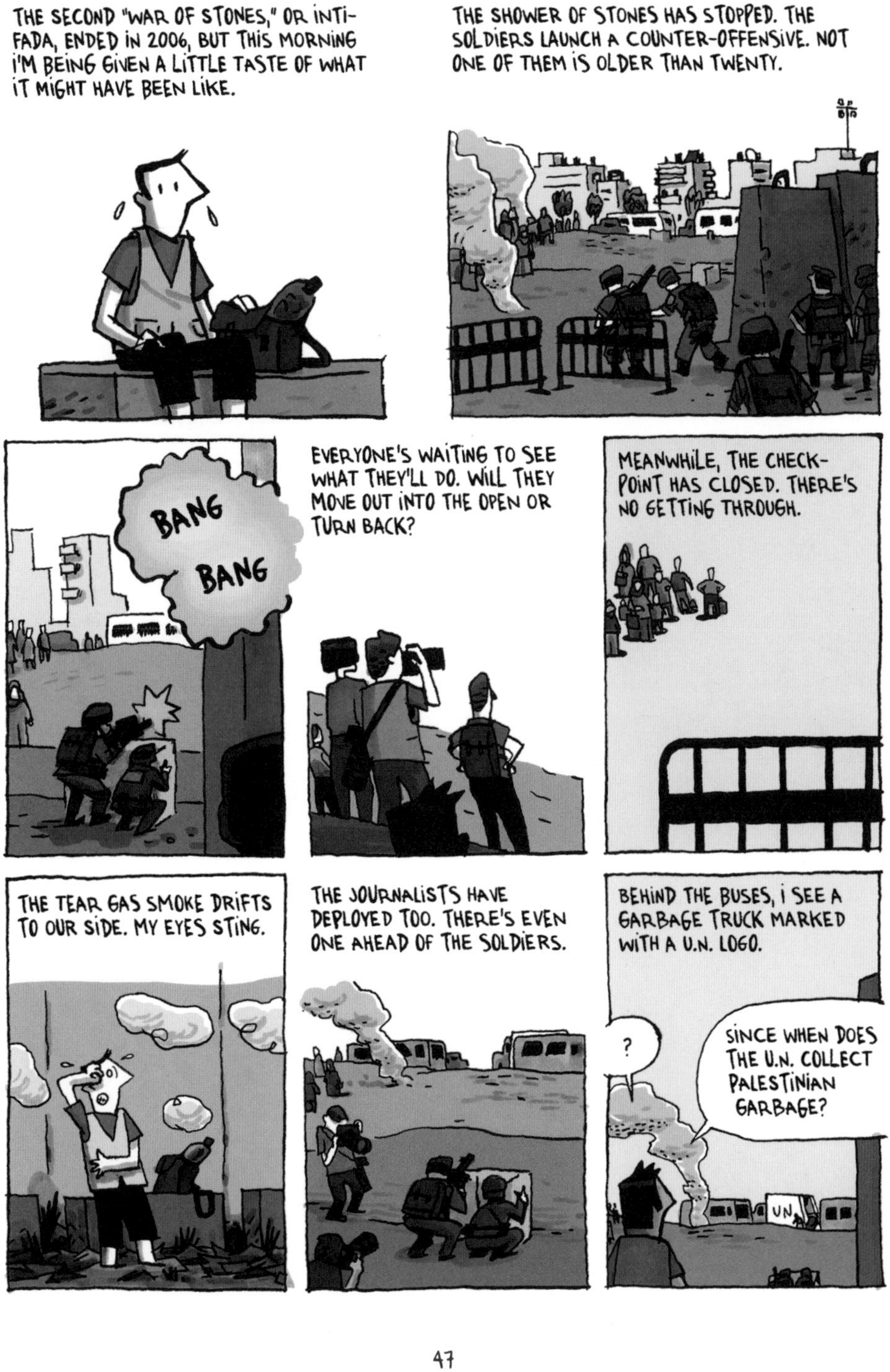
THE SECOND "WAR OF STONES," OR INTIFADA, ENDED IN 2006, BUT THIS MORNING I'M BEING GIVEN A LITTLE TASTE OF WHAT IT MIGHT HAVE BEEN LIKE.
THE SHOWER OF STONES HAS STOPPED. THE SOLDIERS LAUNCH A COUNTER-OFFENSIVE. NOT ONE OF THEM IS OLDER THAN TWENTY.
BANG
BANG
EVERYONE'S WAITING TO SEE WHAT THEY'LL DO. WILL THEY MOVE OUT INTO THE OPEN OR TURN BACK?
MEANWHILE, THE CHECKPOINT HAS CLOSED. THERE'S NO GETTING THROUGH.
THE TEAR GAS SMOKE DRIFTS TO OUR SIDE. MY EYES STING.
THE JOURNALISTS HAVE DEPLOYED TOO. THERE'S EVEN ONE AHEAD OF THE SOLDIERS.
BEHIND THE BUSES, I SEE A GARBAGE TRUCK MARKED WITH A U.N. LOGO.
?
SINCE WHEN DOES THE U.N. COLLECT PALESTINIAN GARBAGE?
UN

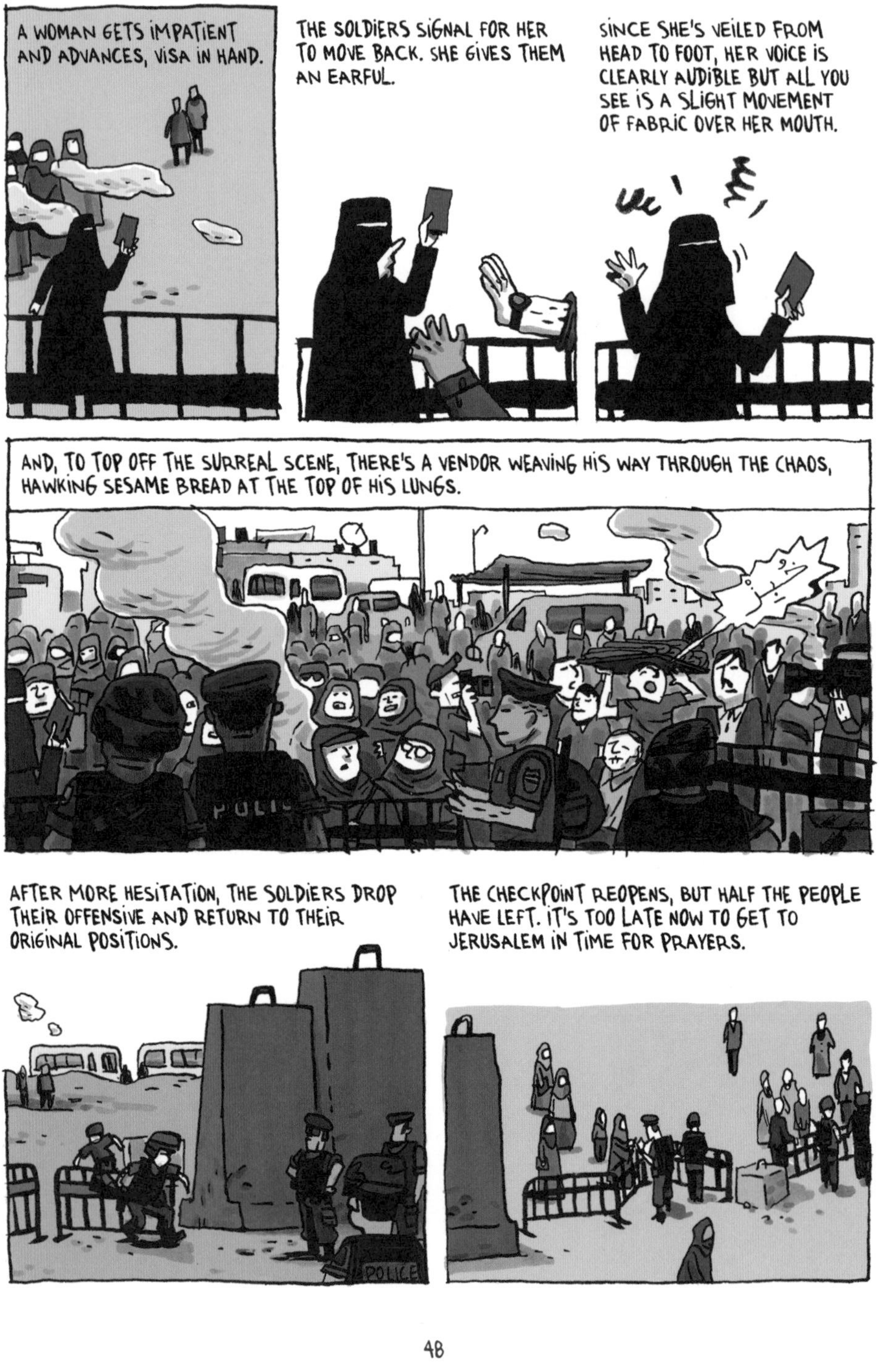
A WOMAN GETS IMPATIENT AND ADVANCES, VISA IN HAND.
THE SOLDIERS SIGNAL FOR HER TO MOVE BACK. SHE GIVES THEM AN EARFUL.
SINCE SHE'S VEILED FROM HEAD TO FOOT, HER VOICE IS CLEARLY AUDIBLE BUT ALL YOU SEE IS A SLIGHT MOVEMENT OF FABRIC OVER HER MOUTH.
AND, TO TOP OFF THE SURREAL SCENE, THERE'S A VENDOR WEAVING HIS WAY THROUGH THE CHAOS, HAWKING SESAME BREAD AT THE TOP OF HIS LUNGS.
AFTER MORE HESITATION, THE SOLDIERS DROP THEIR OFFENSIVE AND RETURN TO THEIR ORIGINAL POSITIONS.
POLICE
THE CHECKPOINT REOPENS, BUT HALF THE PEOPLE HAVE LEFT. IT'S TOO LATE NOW TO GET TO JERUSALEM IN TIME FOR PRAYERS.

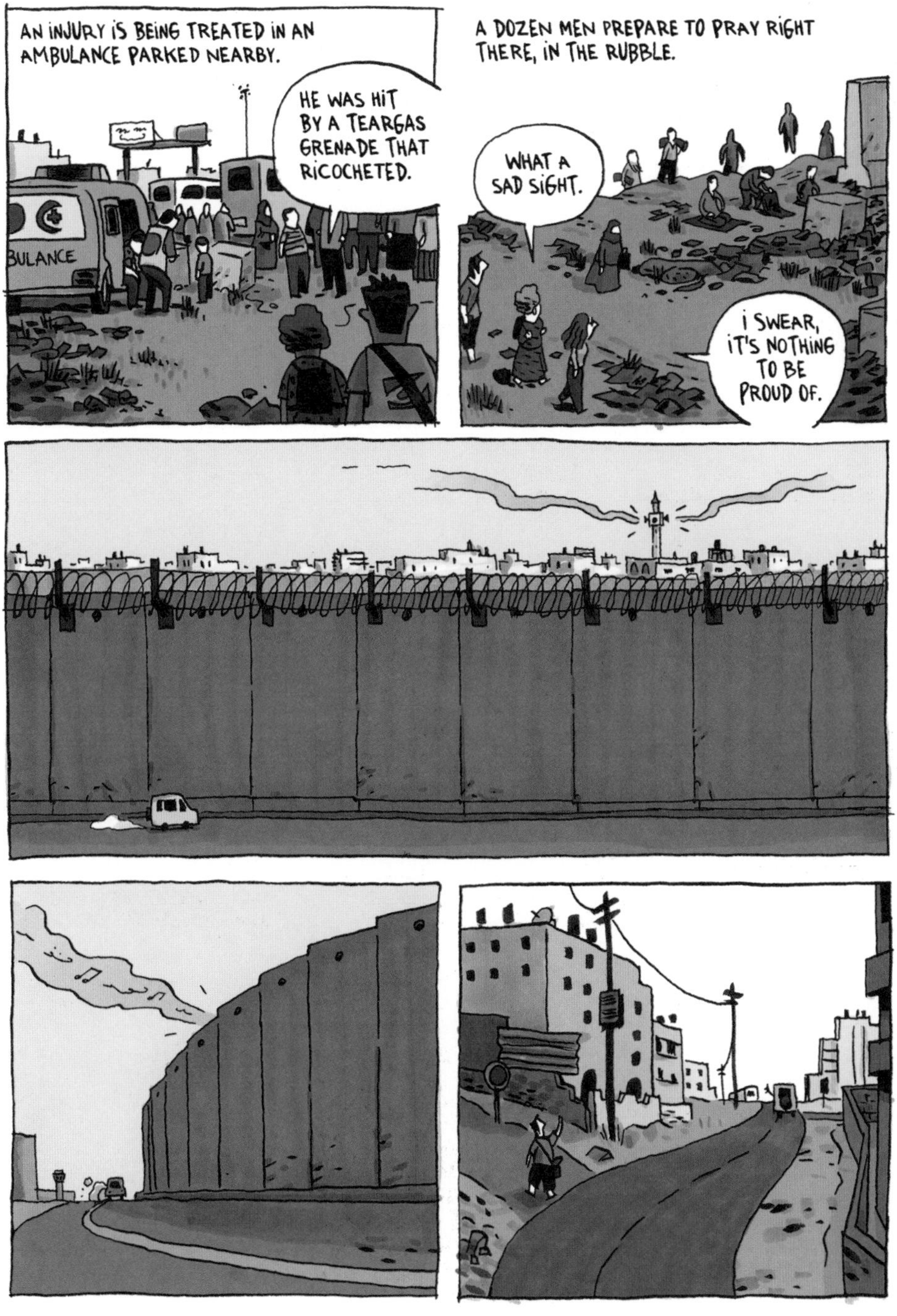
AN INJURY IS BEING TREATED IN AN AMBULANCE PARKED NEARBY.
HE WAS HIT BY A TEARGAS GRENADE THAT RICOCHETED.
BULANCE
A DOZEN MEN PREPARE TO PRAY RIGHT THERE, IN THE RUBBLE.
WHAT A SAD SIGHT.
I SWEAR, IT'S NOTHING TO BE PROUD OF.

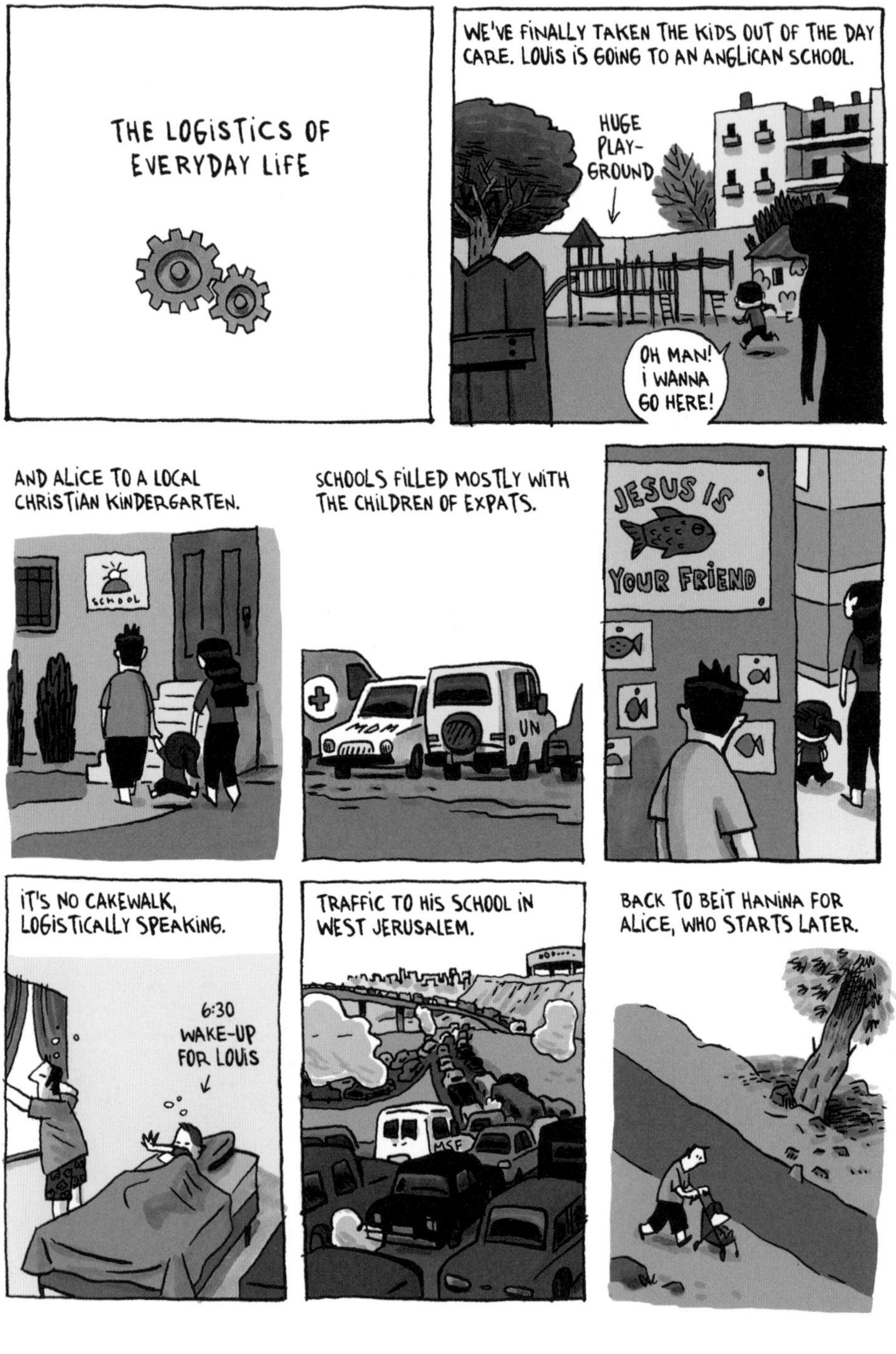

THE LOGISTICS OF EVERYDAY LIFE
WE'VE FINALLY TAKEN THE KIDS OUT OF THE DAY CARE. LOUIS IS GOING TO AN ANGLICAN SCHOOL.
HUGE PLAY-GROUND
OH MAN! I WANNA GO HERE!
AND ALICE TO A LOCAL CHRISTIAN KINDERGARTEN.
SCHOOL
SCHOOLS FILLED MOSTLY WITH THE CHILDREN OF EXPATS.
MOM
UN
JESUS IS YOUR FRIEND
IT'S NO CAKEWALK, LOGISTICALLY SPEAKING.
6:30 WAKE-UP FOR LOUIS
TRAFFIC TO HIS SCHOOL IN WEST JERUSALEM.
MSF
BACK TO BEIT HANINA FOR ALICE, WHO STARTS LATER.

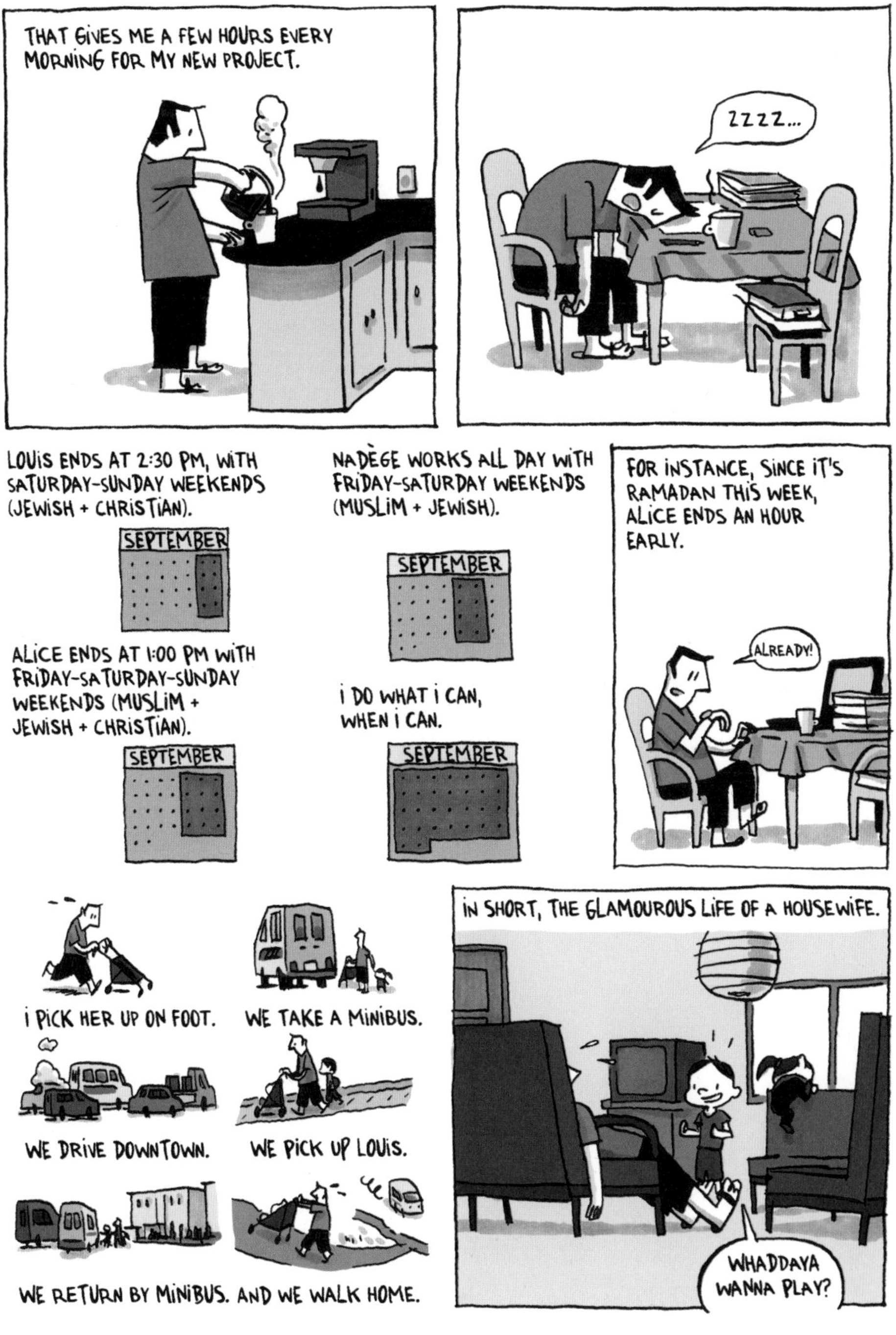

THAT GIVES ME A FEW HOURS EVERY MORNING FOR MY NEW PROJECT.
ZZZZ...
LOUIS ENDS AT 2:30 PM, WITH SATURDAY-SUNDAY WEEKENDS (JEWISH + CHRISTIAN).
SEPTEMBER
ALICE ENDS AT 1:00 PM WITH FRIDAY-SATURDAY-SUNDAY WEEKENDS (MUSLIM + JEWISH + CHRISTIAN).
SEPTEMBER
NADÈGE WORKS ALL DAY WITH FRIDAY-SATURDAY WEEKENDS (MUSLIM + JEWISH).
SEPTEMBER
I DO WHAT I CAN, WHEN I CAN.
SEPTEMBER
FOR INSTANCE, SINCE IT'S RAMADAN THIS WEEK, ALICE ENDS AN HOUR EARLY.
ALREADY!
I PICK HER UP ON FOOT.
WE TAKE A MINIBUS.
WE DRIVE DOWNTOWN.
WE PICK UP LOUIS.
WE RETURN BY MINIBUS.
AND WE WALK HOME.
IN SHORT, THE GLAMOUROUS LIFE OF A HOUSEWIFE.
WHADDAYA WANNA PLAY?

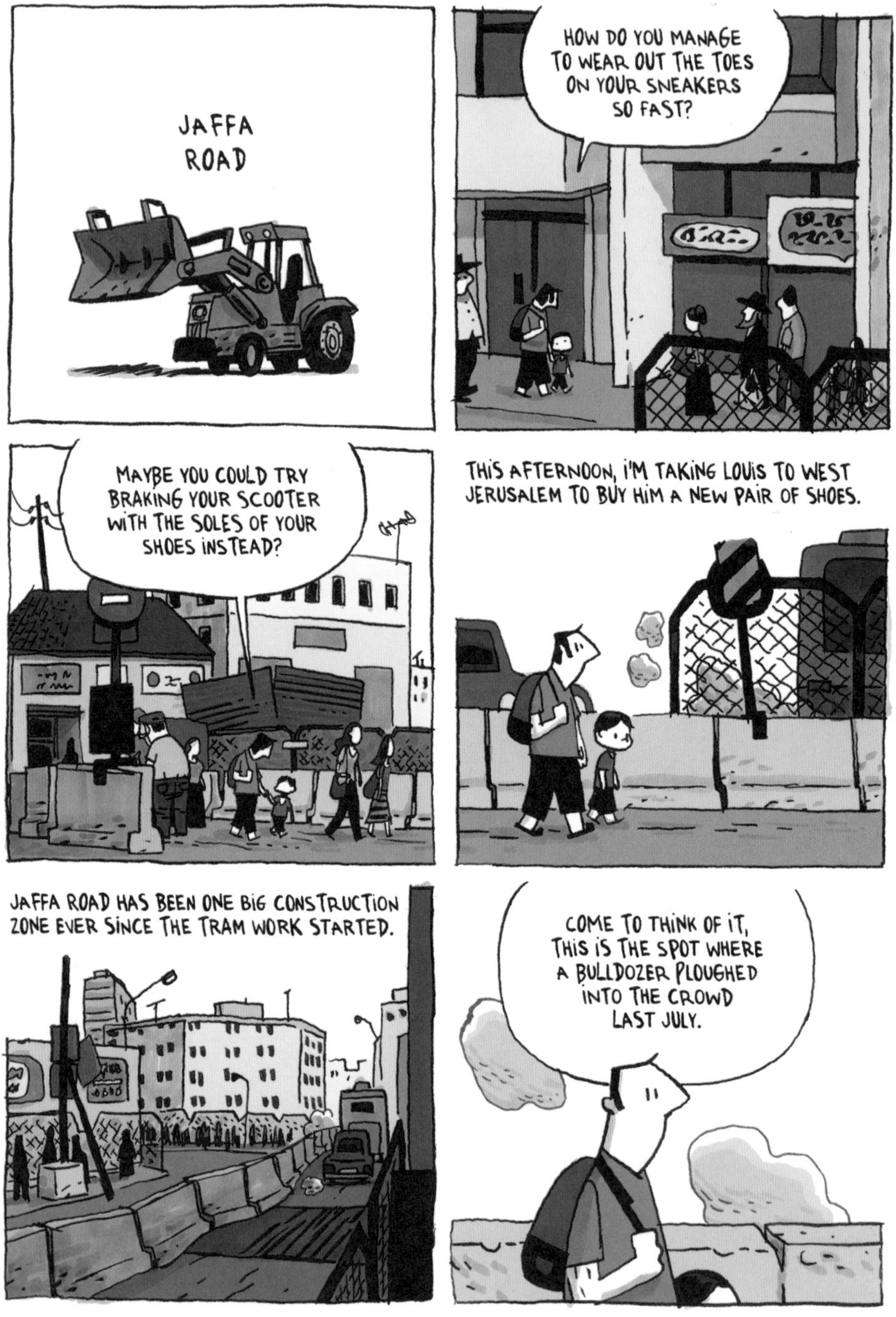
JAFFA ROAD
HOW DO YOU MANAGE TO WEAR OUT THE TOES ON YOUR SNEAKERS SO FAST?
MAYBE YOU COULD TRY BRAKING YOUR SCOOTER WITH THE SOLES OF YOUR SHOES INSTEAD?
THIS AFTERNOON, I'M TAKING LOUIS TO WEST JERUSALEM TO BUY HIM A NEW PAIR OF SHOES.
JAFFA ROAD HAS BEEN ONE BIG CONSTRUCTION ZONE EVER SINCE THE TRAM WORK STARTED.
COME TO THINK OF IT, THIS IS THE SPOT WHERE A BULLDOZER PLOUGHED INTO THE CROWD LAST JULY.

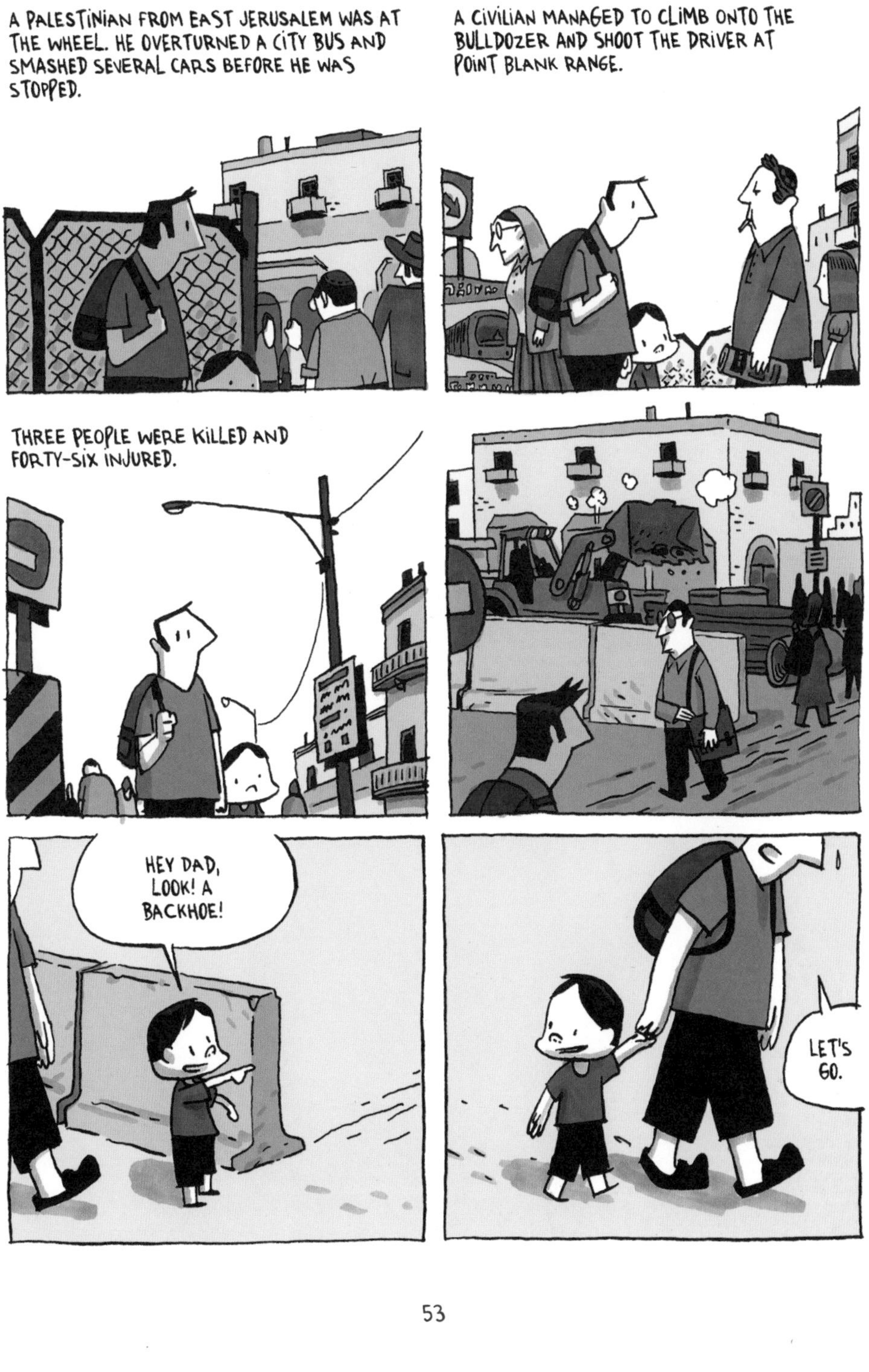
A PALESTINIAN FROM EAST JERUSALEM WAS AT THE WHEEL. HE OVERTURNED A CITY BUS AND SMASHED SEVERAL CARS BEFORE HE WAS STOPPED.
A CIVILIAN MANAGED TO CLIMB ONTO THE BULLDOZER AND SHOOT THE DRIVER AT POINT BLANK RANGE.
THREE PEOPLE WERE KILLED AND FORTY-SIX INJURED.
HEY DAD, LOOK! A BACKHOE!
LET'S GO.

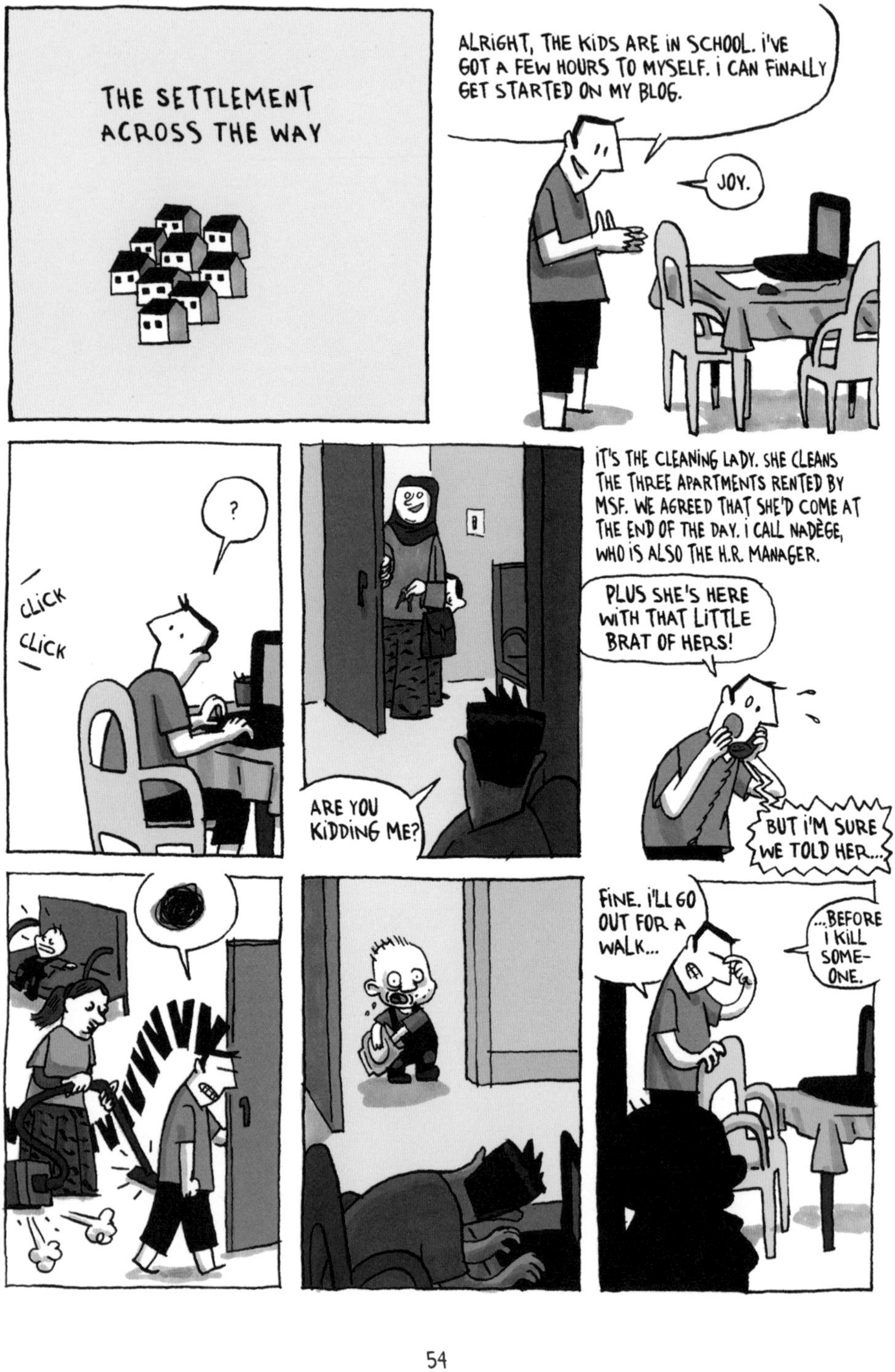
THE SETTLEMENT ACROSS THE WAY
ALRIGHT, THE KIDS ARE IN SCHOOL. I'VE GOT A FEW HOURS TO MYSELF. I CAN FINALLY GET STARTED ON MY BLOG.
JOY.
CLICK
CLICK
?
ARE YOU KIDDING ME?
IT'S THE CLEANING LADY. SHE CLEANS THE THREE APARTMENTS RENTED BY MSF. WE AGREED THAT SHE'D COME AT THE END OF THE DAY. I CALL NADÈGE, WHO IS ALSO THE H.R. MANAGER.
PLUS SHE'S HERE WITH THAT LITTLE BRAT OF HERS!
BUT I'M SURE WE TOLD HER...
FINE. I'LL GO OUT FOR A WALK...
...BEFORE I KILL SOME-ONE.

HEY, WHY NOT VISIT THE SETTLEMENT ACROSS THE STREET? MAYBE I'LL FIND A PLAYGROUND THERE?

IT'LL LET ME CLEAR MY HEAD.

ON FOOT, IT'S TEN MINUTES AWAY. YOU JUST CROSS THE EXPRESSWAY TO GET FROM THE ARAB QUARTER TO THE JEWISH SETTLEMENT.

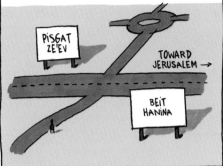

PISGAT ZE'EV

TOWARD JERUSALEM →

BEIT HANINA

THE SETTLEMENTS ARE NOTHING LIKE I THOUGHT THEY WOULD BE. I HAD PICTURED TWO OR THREE SHACKS ON A HILL WITH A DOG.

PISGAT ZE'EV HAS 50,000 RESIDENTS.

MANY OF THE PEOPLE WHO LIVE HERE ARE ORIGINALLY FROM RUSSIA OR ETHIOPIA. MOST HAVE MOVED IN BECAUSE IT'S CHEAP.* SOME WOULD BE SURPRISED TO LEARN THAT THEY'RE LIVING IN PALESTINIAN TERRITORY, AND THAT THEY'RE ILLEGAL UNDER INTERNATIONAL LAW (THOUGH NOT UNDER ISRAELI LAW).

*WHICH MAKES THIS A SO-CALLED "ECONOMIC" SETTLEMENT.

HEY, GET A LOAD OF THAT HUGE SHOPPING MALL!

HMM... SHOULD I GO?

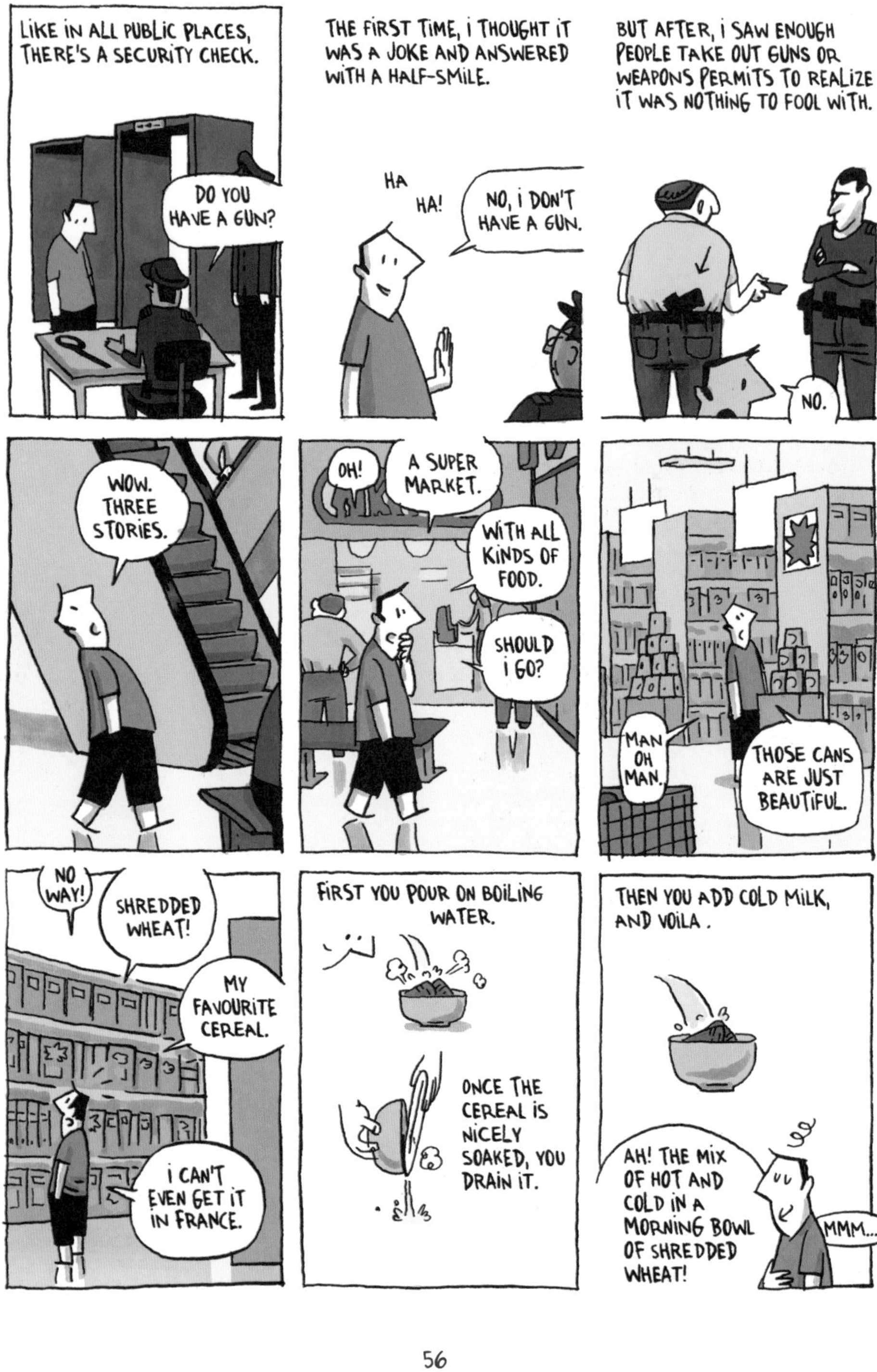
LIKE IN ALL PUBLIC PLACES, THERE'S A SECURITY CHECK.
DO YOU HAVE A GUN?
THE FIRST TIME, I THOUGHT IT WAS A JOKE AND ANSWERED WITH A HALF-SMILE.
HA
HA!
NO, I DON'T HAVE A GUN.
BUT AFTER, I SAW ENOUGH PEOPLE TAKE OUT GUNS OR WEAPONS PERMITS TO REALIZE IT WAS NOTHING TO FOOL WITH.
NO.
WOW. THREE STORIES.
OH!
A SUPER MARKET.
WITH ALL KINDS OF FOOD.
SHOULD I GO?
MAN OH MAN.
THOSE CANS ARE JUST BEAUTIFUL.
NO WAY!
SHREDDED WHEAT!
MY FAVOURITE CEREAL.
I CAN'T EVEN GET IT IN FRANCE.
FIRST YOU POUR ON BOILING WATER.
ONCE THE CEREAL IS NICELY SOAKED, YOU DRAIN IT.
THEN YOU ADD COLD MILK, AND VOILA .
AH! THE MIX OF HOT AND COLD IN A MORNING BOWL OF SHREDDED WHEAT!
MMM...

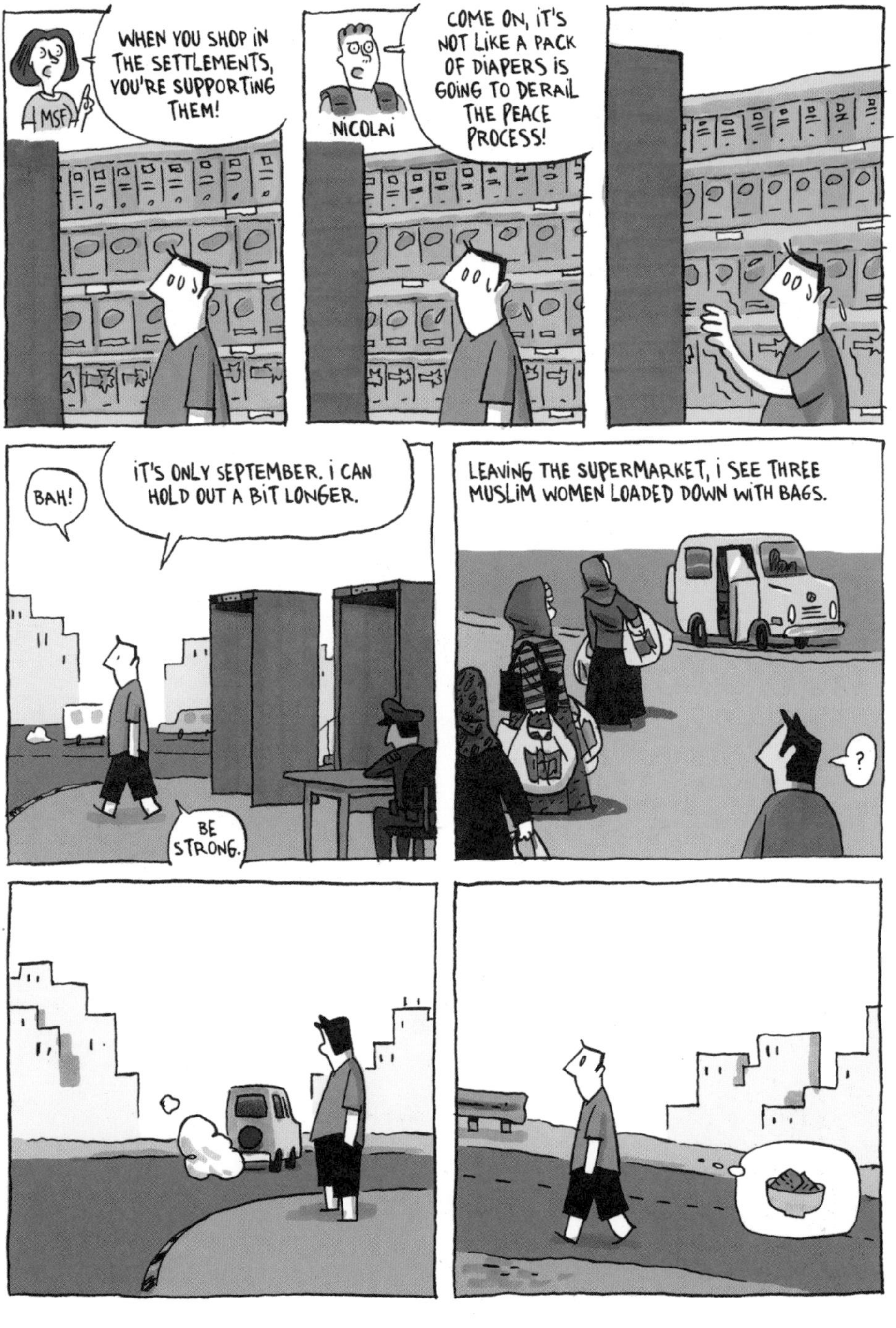

WHEN YOU SHOP IN THE SETTLEMENTS, YOU'RE SUPPORTING THEM!
MSF
NICOLAI
COME ON, IT'S NOT LIKE A PACK OF DIAPERS IS GOING TO DERAIL THE PEACE PROCESS!
BAH!
IT'S ONLY SEPTEMBER. I CAN HOLD OUT A BIT LONGER.
BE STRONG.
LEAVING THE SUPERMARKET, I SEE THREE MUSLIM WOMEN LOADED DOWN WITH BAGS.
?

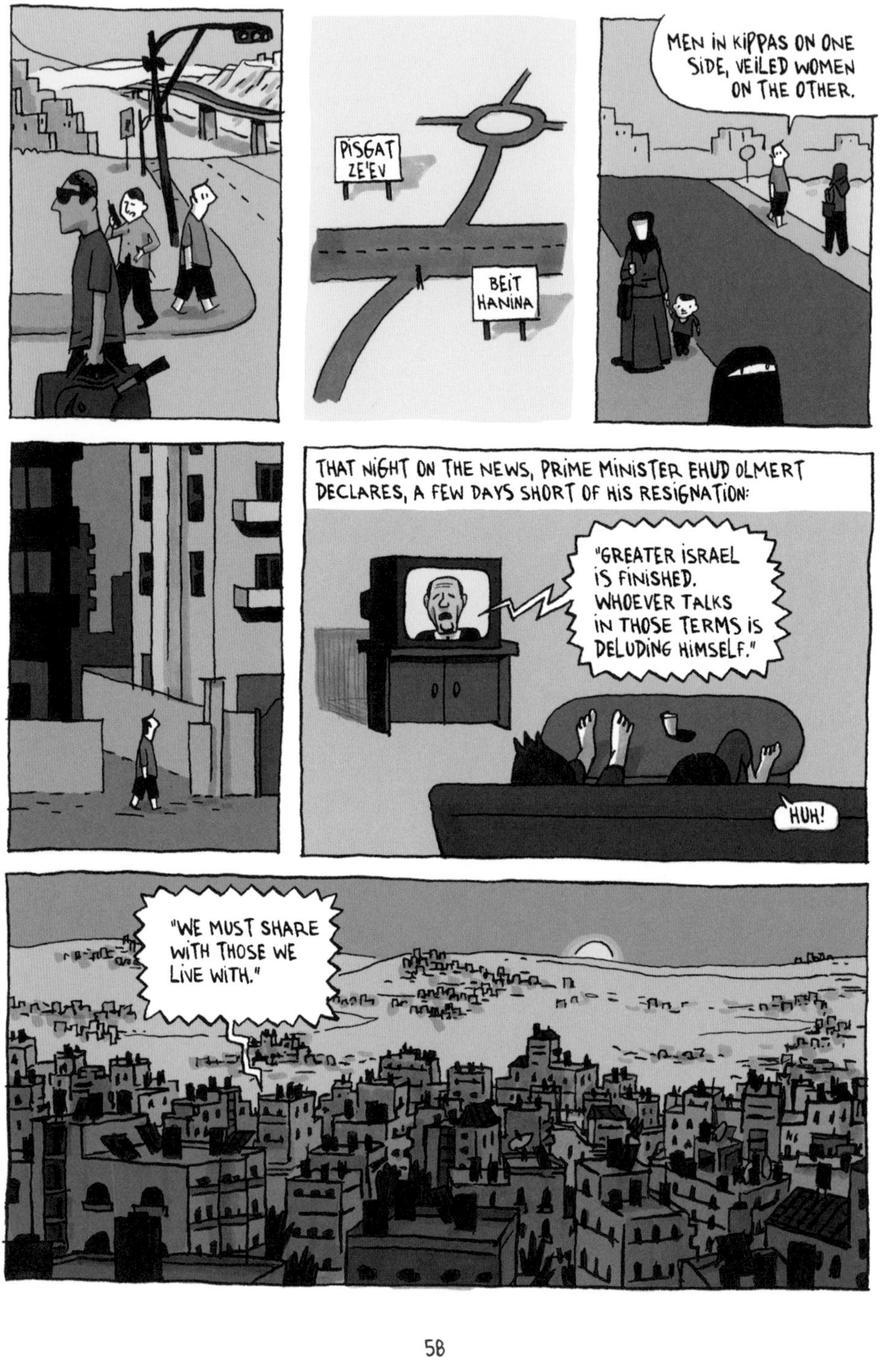
PISGAT ZE'EV
BEIT HANINA
MEN IN KIPPAS ON ONE SIDE, VEILED WOMEN ON THE OTHER.
THAT NIGHT ON THE NEWS, PRIME MINISTER EHUD OLMERT DECLARES, A FEW DAYS SHORT OF HIS RESIGNATION:
"GREATER ISRAEL IS FINISHED. WHOEVER TALKS IN THOSE TERMS IS DELUDING HIMSELF."
HUH!
"WE MUST SHARE WITH THOSE WE LIVE WITH."

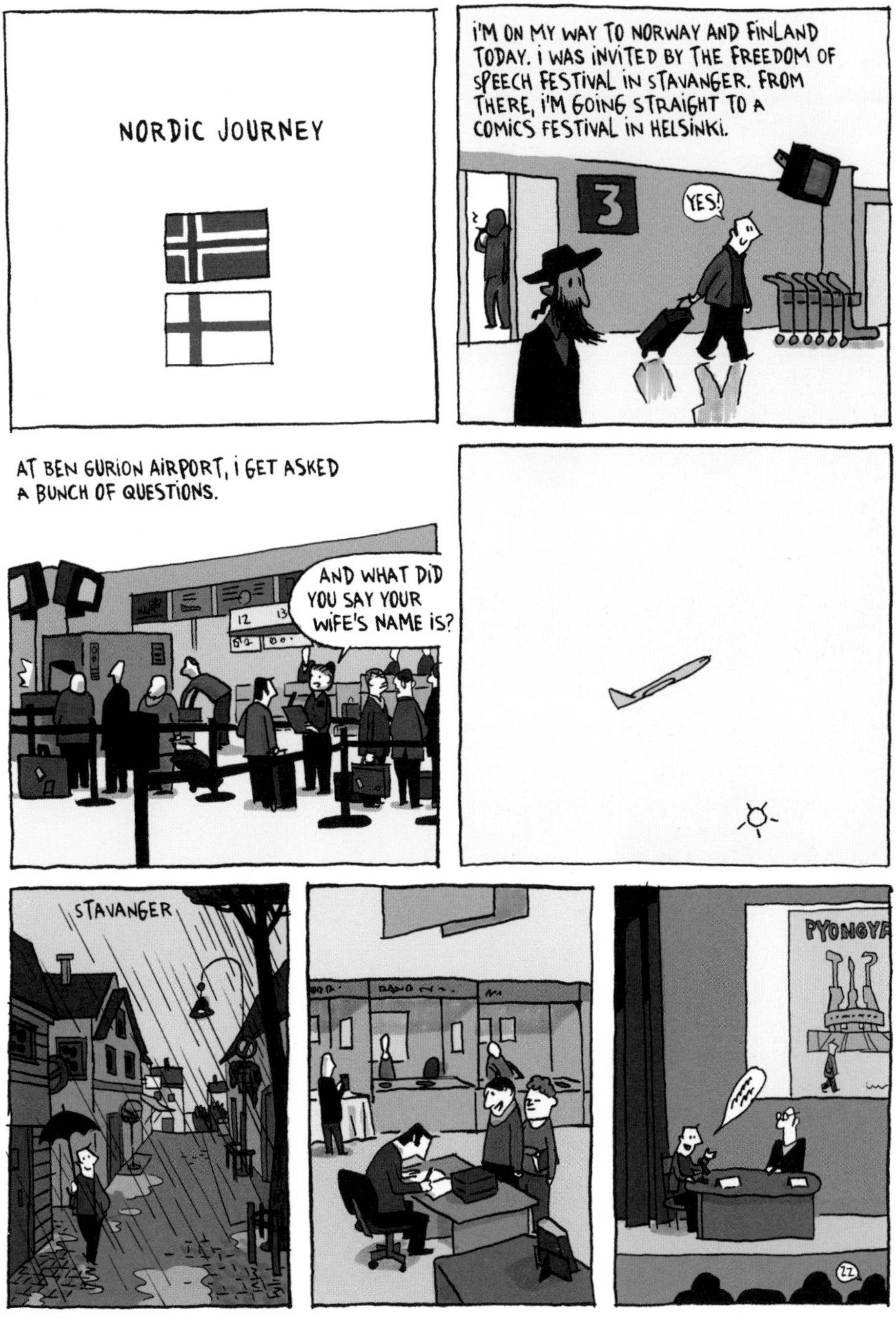
NORDIC JOURNEY
I'M ON MY WAY TO NORWAY AND FINLAND TODAY. I WAS INVITED BY THE FREEDOM OF SPEECH FESTIVAL IN STAVANGER. FROM THERE, I'M GOING STRAIGHT TO A COMICS FESTIVAL IN HELSINKI.
3
YES!
AT BEN GURION AIRPORT, I GET ASKED A BUNCH OF QUESTIONS.
AND WHAT DID YOU SAY YOUR WIFE'S NAME IS?
STAVANGER
PYONGYA

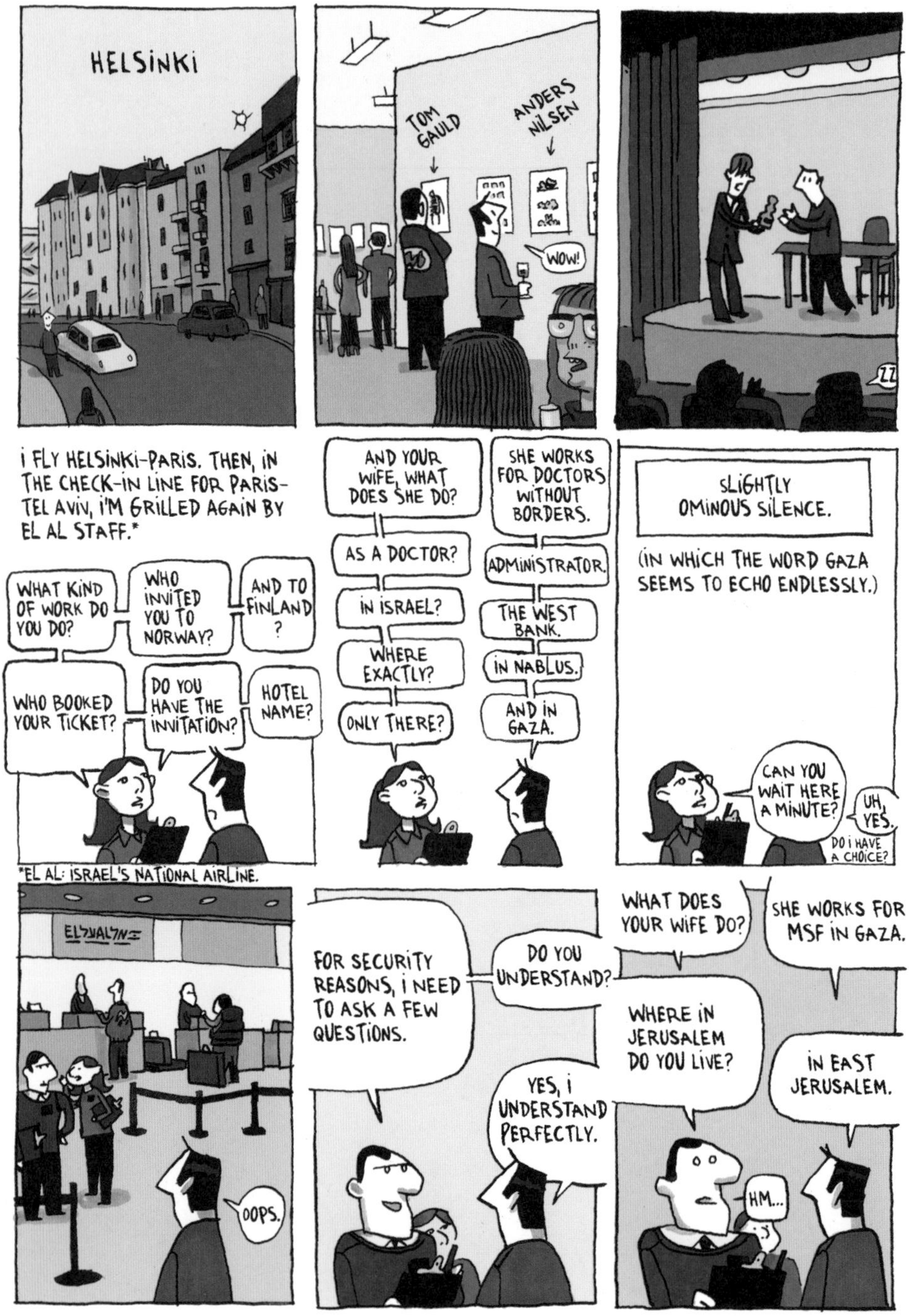

HELSINKI
TOM GAULD
ANDERS NILSEN
WOW!
ZZ
I FLY HELSINKI-PARIS. THEN, IN THE CHECK-IN LINE FOR PARIS-TEL AVIV, I'M GRILLED AGAIN BY EL AL STAFF.*
WHAT KIND OF WORK DO YOU DO?
WHO INVITED YOU TO NORWAY?
AND TO FINLAND?
WHO BOOKED YOUR TICKET?
DO YOU HAVE THE INVITATION?
HOTEL NAME?
AND YOUR WIFE, WHAT DOES SHE DO?
SHE WORKS FOR DOCTORS WITHOUT BORDERS.
AS A DOCTOR?
ADMINISTRATOR.
IN ISRAEL?
THE WEST BANK.
WHERE EXACTLY?
IN NABLUS.
ONLY THERE?
AND IN GAZA.
SLIGHTLY OMINOUS SILENCE.
(IN WHICH THE WORD GAZA SEEMS TO ECHO ENDLESSLY.)
CAN YOU WAIT HERE A MINUTE?
UH, YES.
DO I HAVE A CHOICE?
*EL AL: ISRAEL'S NATIONAL AIRLINE.
OOPS.
FOR SECURITY REASONS, I NEED TO ASK A FEW QUESTIONS.
DO YOU UNDERSTAND?
YES, I UNDERSTAND PERFECTLY.
WHAT DOES YOUR WIFE DO?
SHE WORKS FOR MSF IN GAZA.
WHERE IN JERUSALEM DO YOU LIVE?
IN EAST JERUSALEM.
HM...

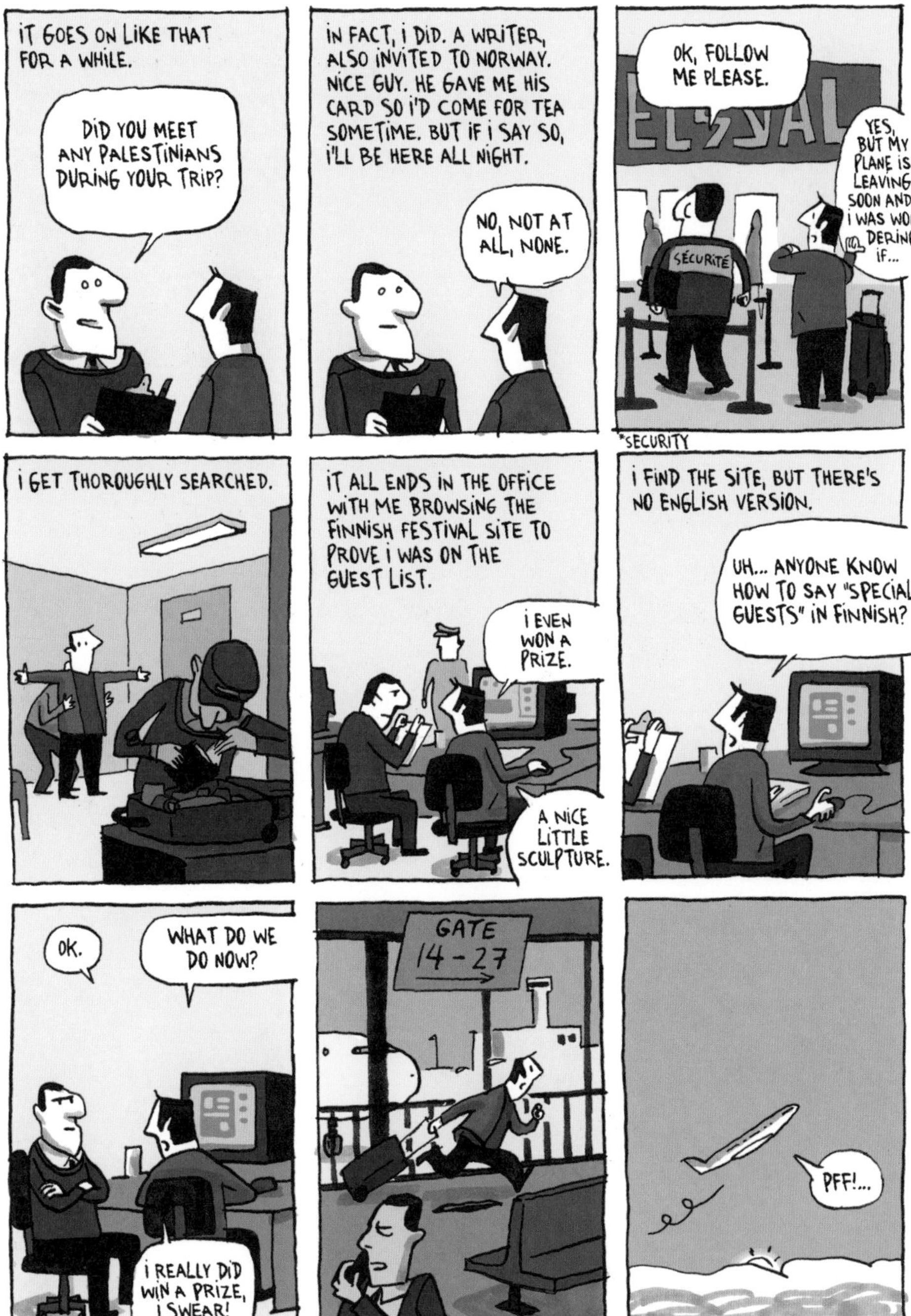
IT GOES ON LIKE THAT FOR A WHILE.
DID YOU MEET ANY PALESTINIANS DURING YOUR TRIP?
IN FACT, I DID. A WRITER, ALSO INVITED TO NORWAY. NICE GUY. HE GAVE ME HIS CARD SO I'D COME FOR TEA SOMETIME. BUT IF I SAY SO, I'LL BE HERE ALL NIGHT.
NO, NOT AT ALL, NONE.
OK, FOLLOW ME PLEASE.
YES, BUT MY PLANE IS LEAVING SOON AND I WAS WONDERING IF...
SÉCURITÉ
*SECURITY
I GET THOROUGHLY SEARCHED.
IT ALL ENDS IN THE OFFICE WITH ME BROWSING THE FINNISH FESTIVAL SITE TO PROVE I WAS ON THE GUEST LIST.
I EVEN WON A PRIZE.
A NICE LITTLE SCULPTURE.
I FIND THE SITE, BUT THERE'S NO ENGLISH VERSION.
UH... ANYONE KNOW HOW TO SAY "SPECIAL GUESTS" IN FINNISH?
OK.
WHAT DO WE DO NOW?
I REALLY DID WIN A PRIZE, I SWEAR!
GATE 14 - 27
PFF!...

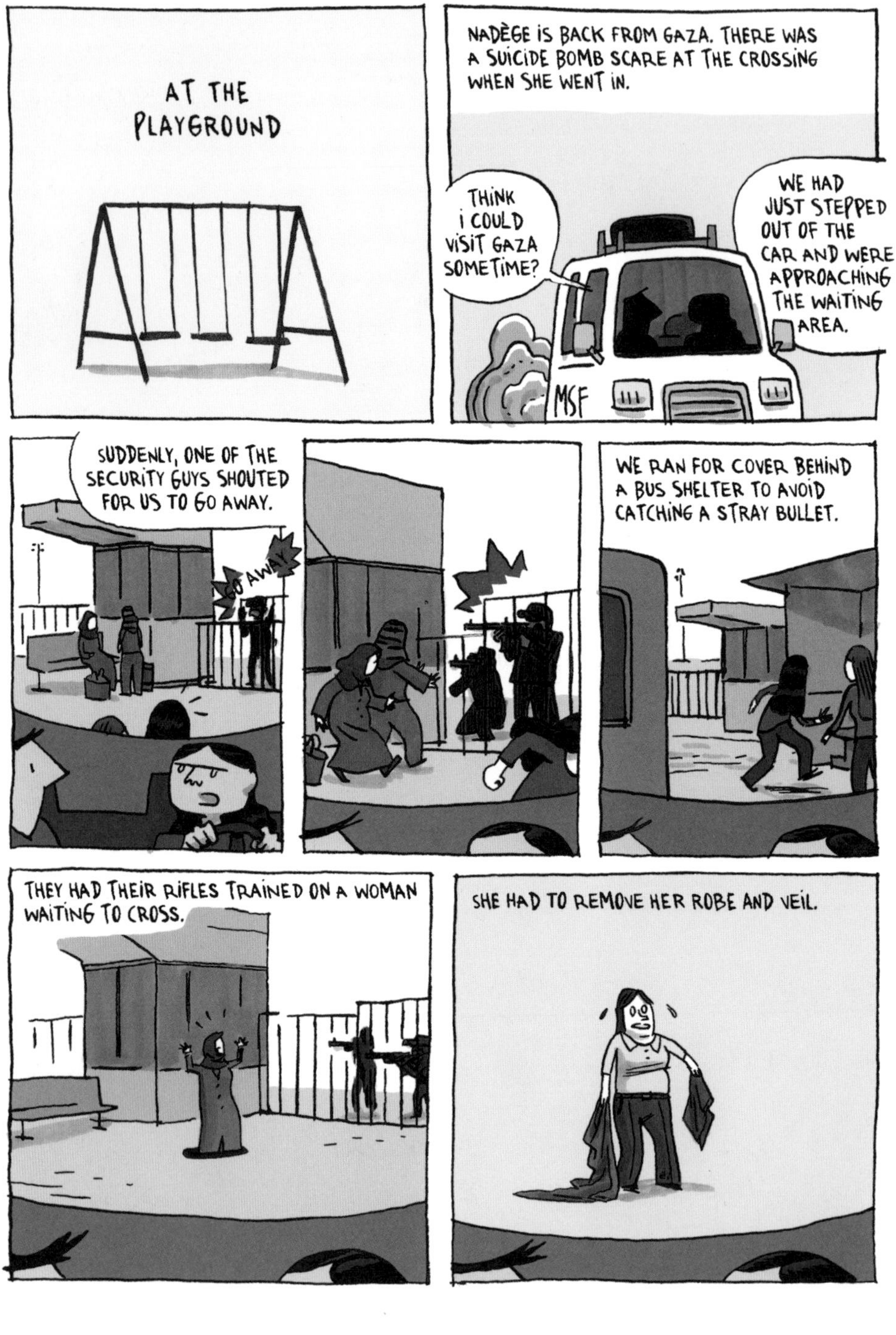
AT THE PLAYGROUND
NADÈGE IS BACK FROM GAZA. THERE WAS A SUICIDE BOMB SCARE AT THE CROSSING WHEN SHE WENT IN.
THINK I COULD VISIT GAZA SOMETIME?
WE HAD JUST STEPPED OUT OF THE CAR AND WERE APPROACHING THE WAITING AREA.
MSF
SUDDENLY, ONE OF THE SECURITY GUYS SHOUTED FOR US TO GO AWAY.
GO AWAY
WE RAN FOR COVER BEHIND A BUS SHELTER TO AVOID CATCHING A STRAY BULLET.
THEY HAD THEIR RIFLES TRAINED ON A WOMAN WAITING TO CROSS.
SHE HAD TO REMOVE HER ROBE AND VEIL.

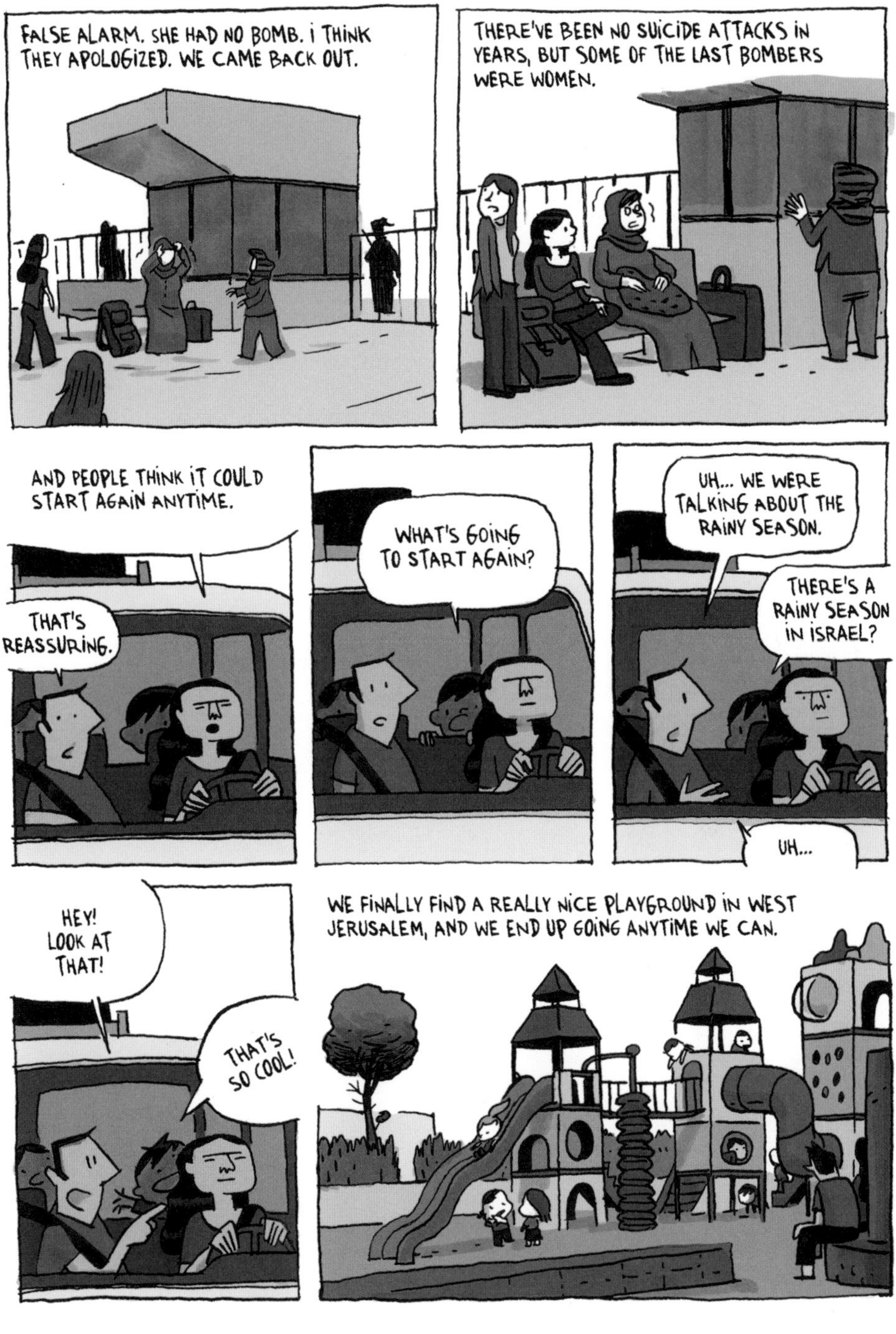
FALSE ALARM. SHE HAD NO BOMB. I THINK THEY APOLOGIZED. WE CAME BACK OUT.
THERE'VE BEEN NO SUICIDE ATTACKS IN YEARS, BUT SOME OF THE LAST BOMBERS WERE WOMEN.
AND PEOPLE THINK IT COULD START AGAIN ANYTIME.
THAT'S REASSURING.
WHAT'S GOING TO START AGAIN?
UH... WE WERE TALKING ABOUT THE RAINY SEASON.
THERE'S A RAINY SEASON IN ISRAEL?
UH...
HEY! LOOK AT THAT!
THAT'S SO COOL!
WE FINALLY FIND A REALLY NICE PLAYGROUND IN WEST JERUSALEM, AND WE END UP GOING ANYTIME WE CAN.

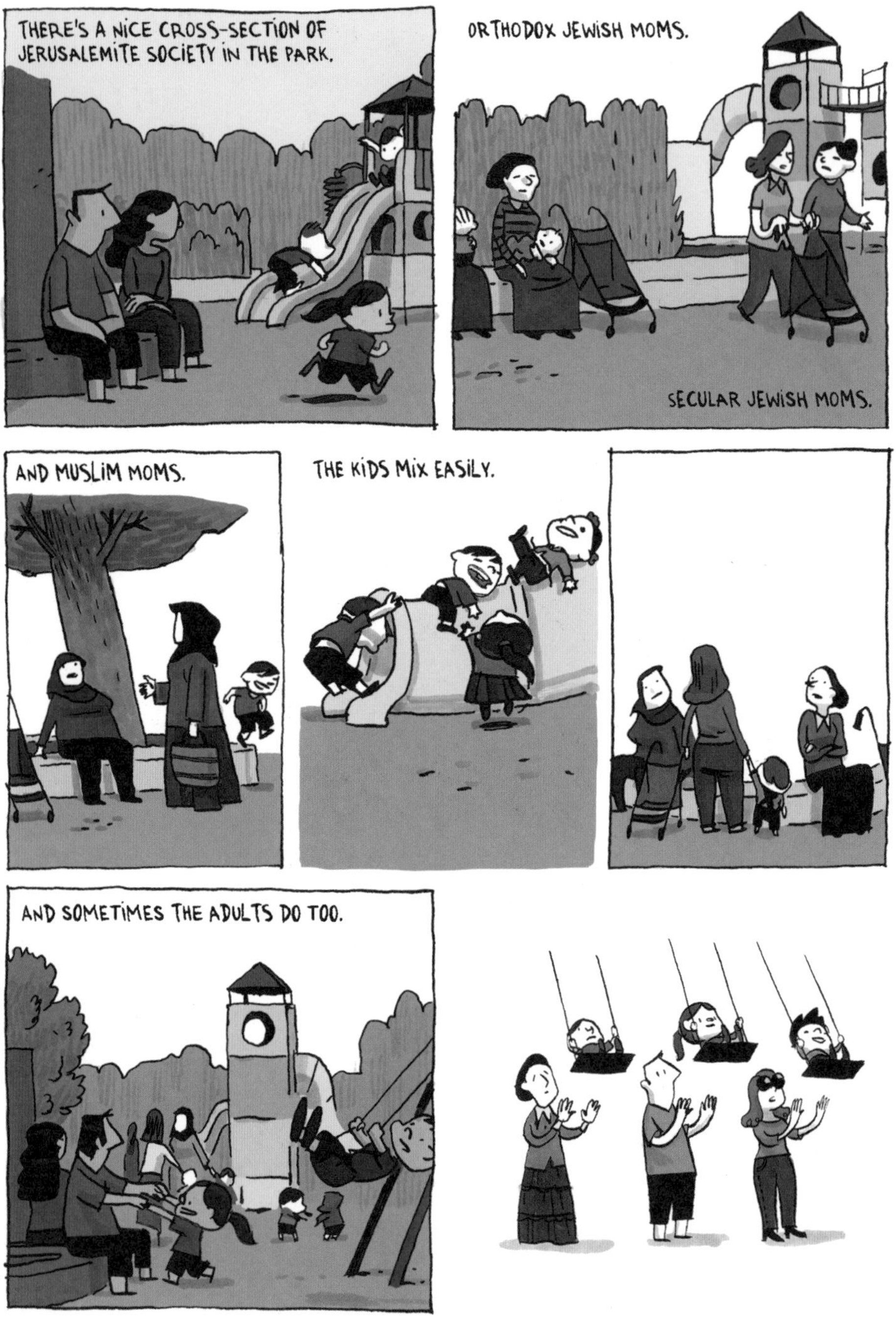
THERE'S A NICE CROSS-SECTION OF JERUSALEMITE SOCIETY IN THE PARK.
ORTHODOX JEWISH MOMS.
SECULAR JEWISH MOMS.
AND MUSLIM MOMS.
THE KIDS MIX EASILY.
AND SOMETIMES THE ADULTS DO TOO.

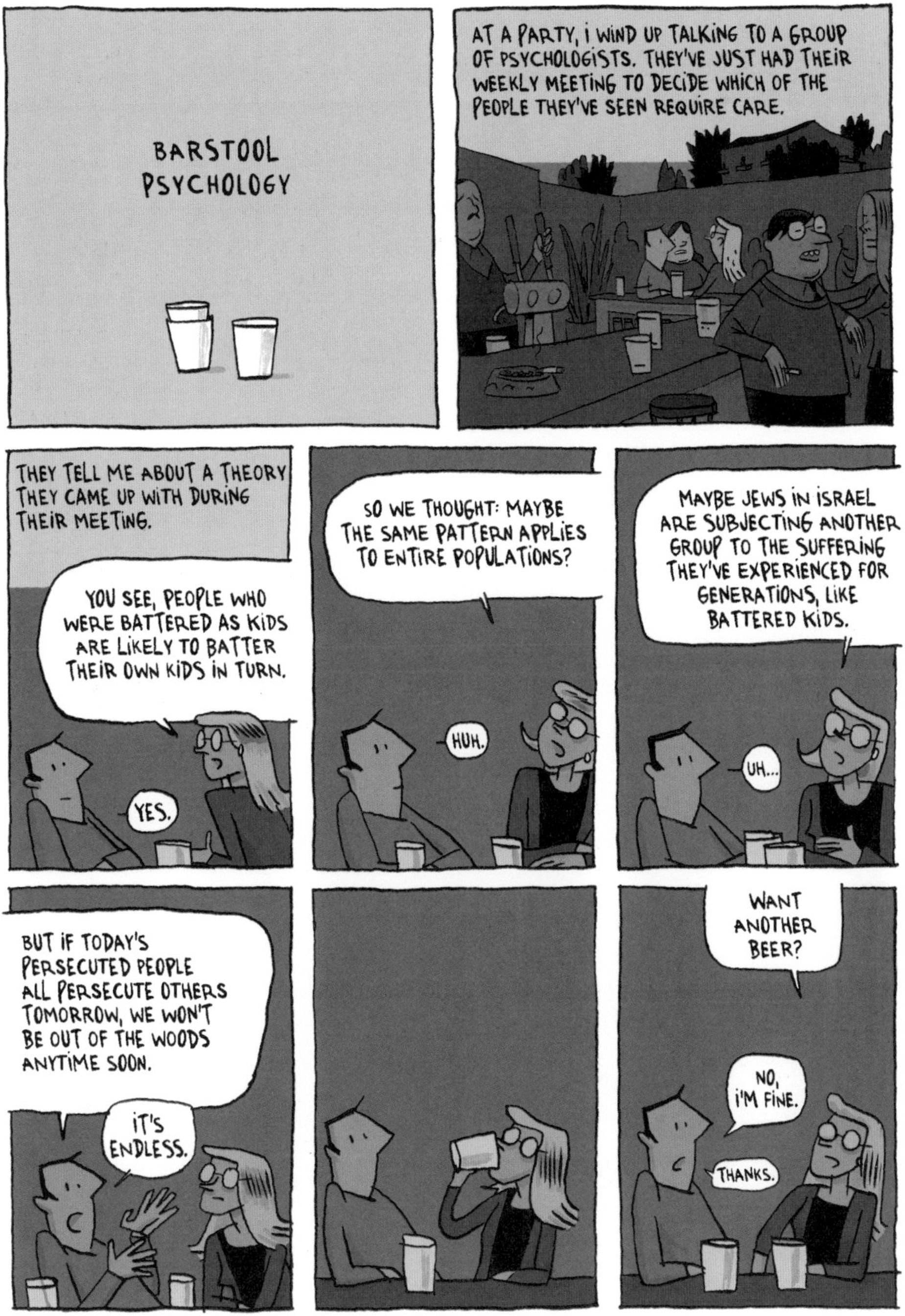
BARSTOOL PSYCHOLOGY
AT A PARTY, I WIND UP TALKING TO A GROUP OF PSYCHOLOGISTS. THEY'VE JUST HAD THEIR WEEKLY MEETING TO DECIDE WHICH OF THE PEOPLE THEY'VE SEEN REQUIRE CARE.
THEY TELL ME ABOUT A THEORY THEY CAME UP WITH DURING THEIR MEETING.
YOU SEE, PEOPLE WHO WERE BATTERED AS KIDS ARE LIKELY TO BATTER THEIR OWN KIDS IN TURN.
YES.
SO WE THOUGHT: MAYBE THE SAME PATTERN APPLIES TO ENTIRE POPULATIONS?
HUH.
MAYBE JEWS IN ISRAEL ARE SUBJECTING ANOTHER GROUP TO THE SUFFERING THEY'VE EXPERIENCED FOR GENERATIONS, LIKE BATTERED KIDS.
UH...
BUT IF TODAY'S PERSECUTED PEOPLE ALL PERSECUTE OTHERS TOMORROW, WE WON'T BE OUT OF THE WOODS ANYTIME SOON.
IT'S ENDLESS.
WANT ANOTHER BEER?
NO, I'M FINE.
THANKS.

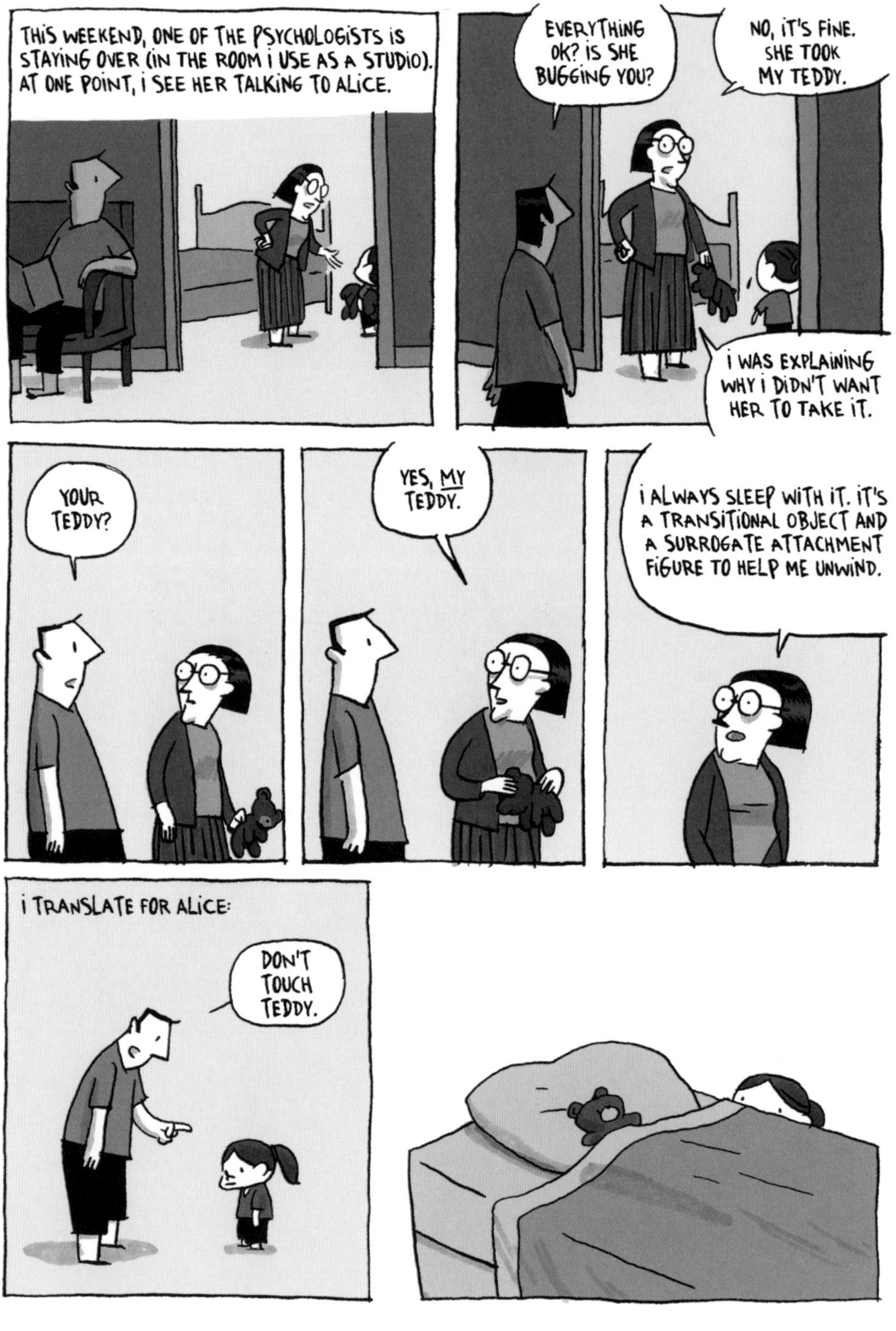
THIS WEEKEND, ONE OF THE PSYCHOLOGISTS IS STAYING OVER (IN THE ROOM I USE AS A STUDIO). AT ONE POINT, I SEE HER TALKING TO ALICE.
EVERYTHING OK? IS SHE BUGGING YOU?
NO, IT'S FINE. SHE TOOK MY TEDDY.
I WAS EXPLAINING WHY I DIDN'T WANT HER TO TAKE IT.
YOUR TEDDY?
YES, MY TEDDY.
I ALWAYS SLEEP WITH IT. IT'S A TRANSITIONAL OBJECT AND A SURROGATE ATTACHMENT FIGURE TO HELP ME UNWIND.
I TRANSLATE FOR ALICE:
DON'T TOUCH TEDDY.

OCTOBER

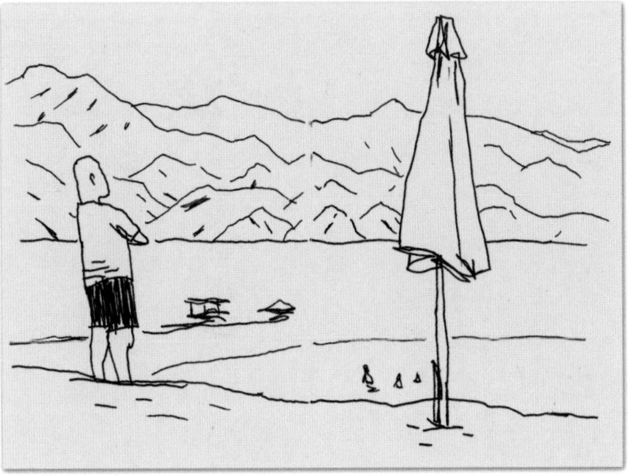

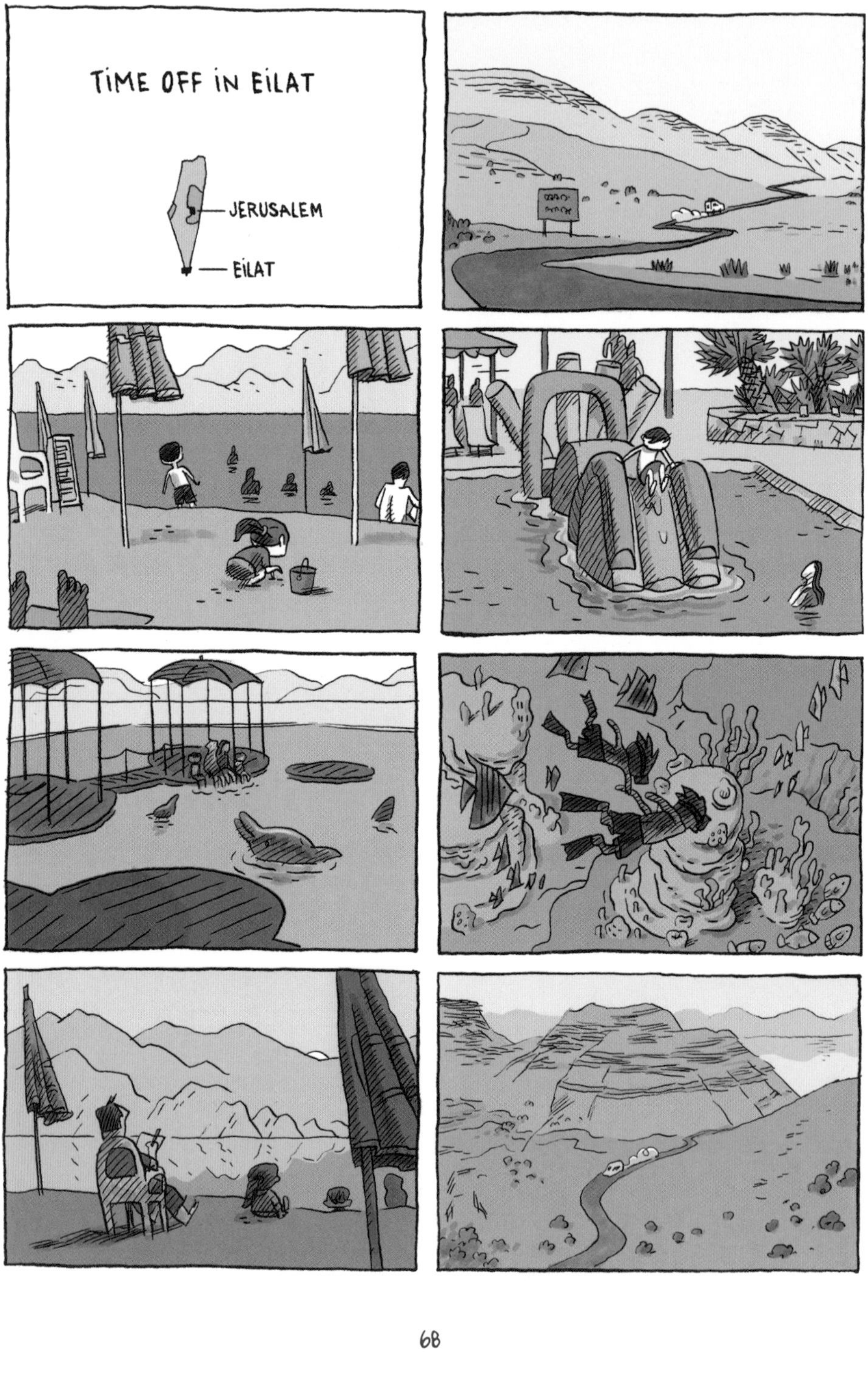
TIME OFF IN EILAT
JERUSALEM
EILAT

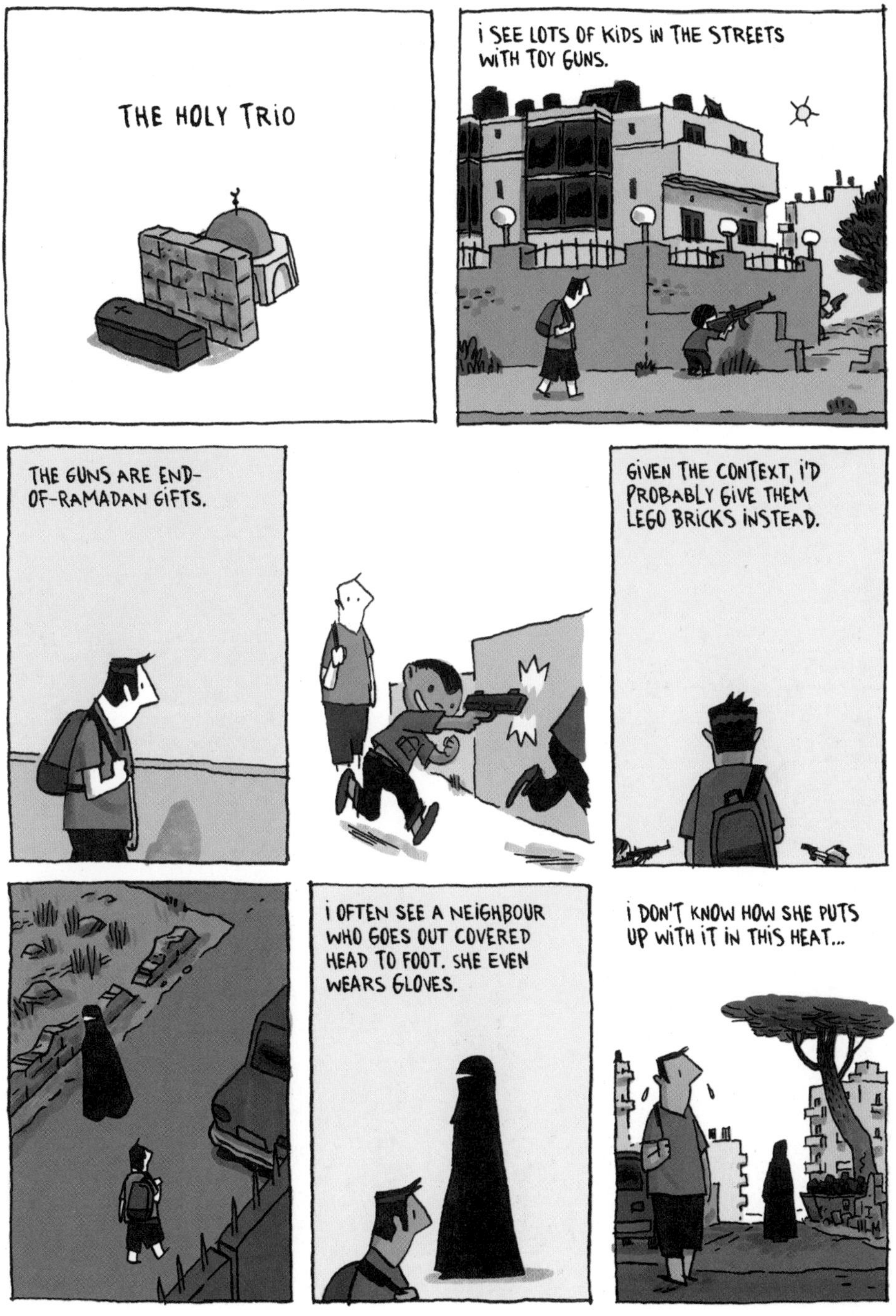
THE HOLY TRIO
I SEE LOTS OF KIDS IN THE STREETS WITH TOY GUNS.
THE GUNS ARE END-OF-RAMADAN GIFTS.
GIVEN THE CONTEXT, I'D PROBABLY GIVE THEM LEGO BRICKS INSTEAD.
I OFTEN SEE A NEIGHBOUR WHO GOES OUT COVERED HEAD TO FOOT. SHE EVEN WEARS GLOVES.
I DON'T KNOW HOW SHE PUTS UP WITH IT IN THIS HEAT...

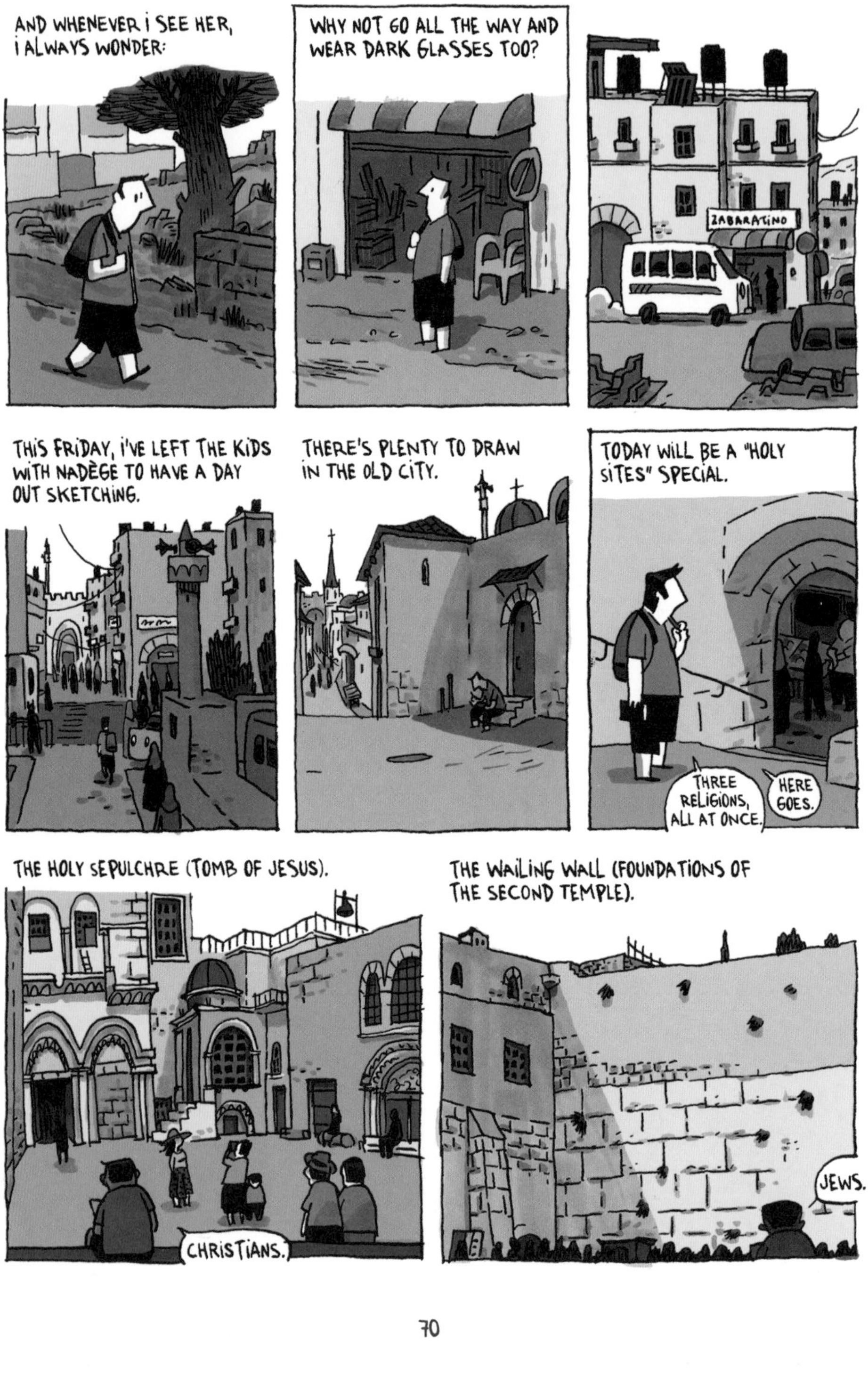
AND WHENEVER I SEE HER, I ALWAYS WONDER:
WHY NOT GO ALL THE WAY AND WEAR DARK GLASSES TOO?
ZABARATINO
THIS FRIDAY, I'VE LEFT THE KIDS WITH NADÈGE TO HAVE A DAY OUT SKETCHING.
THERE'S PLENTY TO DRAW IN THE OLD CITY.
TODAY WILL BE A "HOLY SITES" SPECIAL.
THREE RELIGIONS, ALL AT ONCE.
HERE GOES.
THE HOLY SEPULCHRE (TOMB OF JESUS).
CHRISTIANS.
THE WAILING WALL (FOUNDATIONS OF THE SECOND TEMPLE).
JEWS.

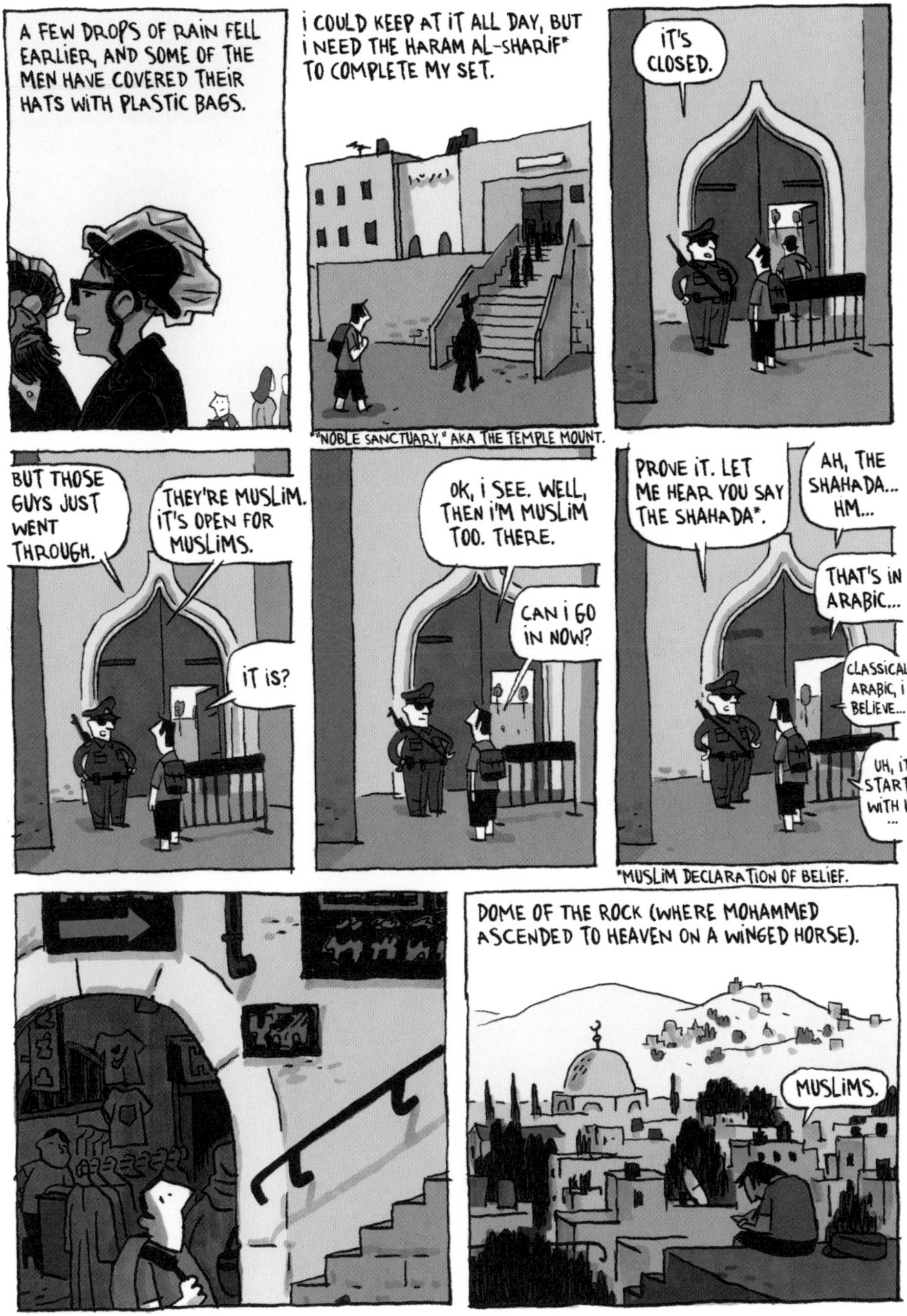
A FEW DROPS OF RAIN FELL EARLIER, AND SOME OF THE MEN HAVE COVERED THEIR HATS WITH PLASTIC BAGS.
I COULD KEEP AT IT ALL DAY, BUT I NEED THE HARAM AL-SHARIF* TO COMPLETE MY SET.
*"NOBLE SANCTUARY," AKA THE TEMPLE MOUNT.
IT'S CLOSED.
BUT THOSE GUYS JUST WENT THROUGH.
THEY'RE MUSLIM. IT'S OPEN FOR MUSLIMS.
IT IS?
OK, I SEE. WELL, THEN I'M MUSLIM TOO. THERE.
CAN I GO IN NOW?
PROVE IT. LET ME HEAR YOU SAY THE SHAHADA*.
AH, THE SHAHADA... HM...
THAT'S IN ARABIC...
CLASSICAL ARABIC, I BELIEVE...
UH, IT STARTS WITH UH ...
*MUSLIM DECLARATION OF BELIEF.
DOME OF THE ROCK (WHERE MOHAMMED ASCENDED TO HEAVEN ON A WINGED HORSE).
MUSLIMS.

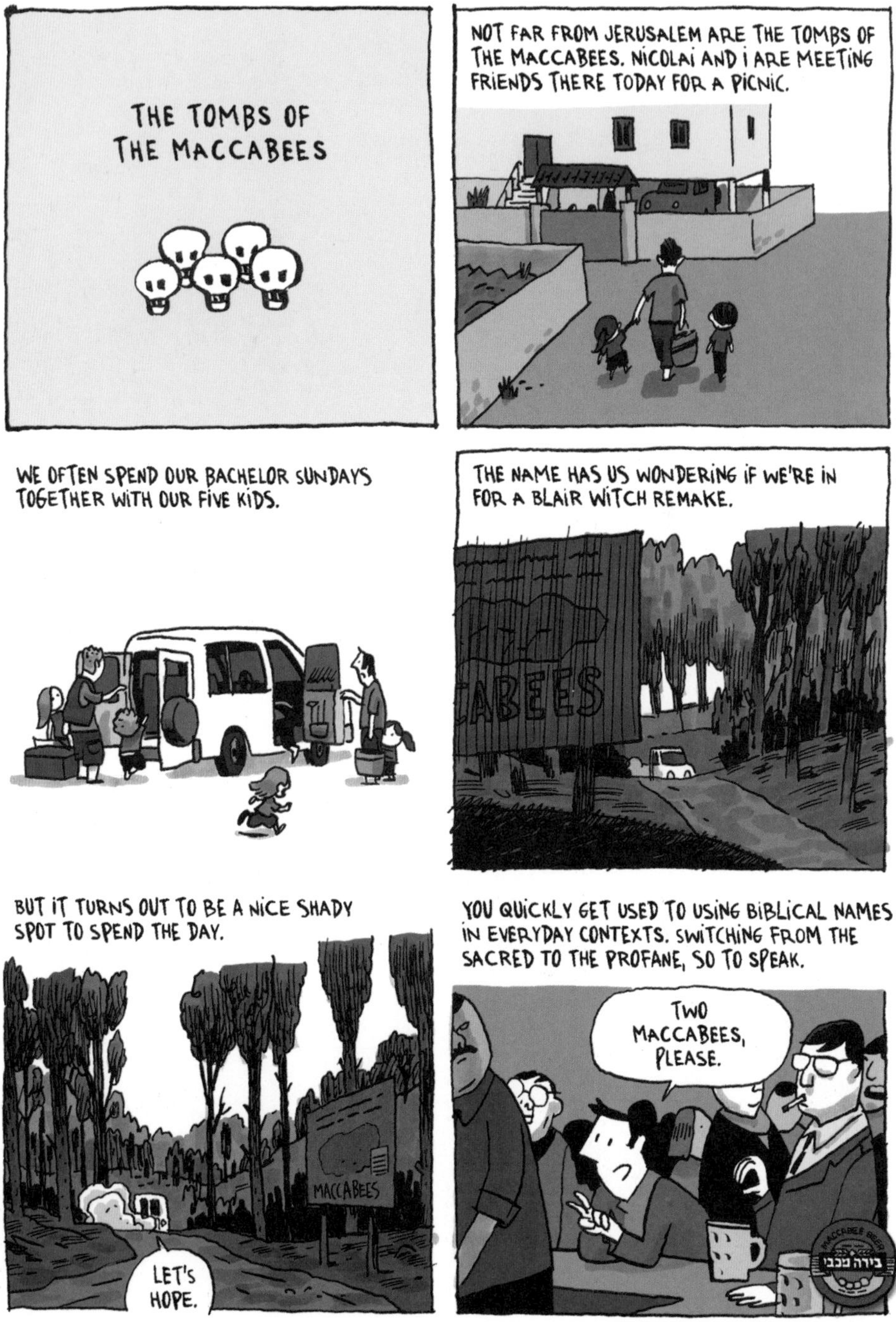
THE TOMBS OF THE MACCABEES
NOT FAR FROM JERUSALEM ARE THE TOMBS OF THE MACCABEES. NICOLAI AND I ARE MEETING FRIENDS THERE TODAY FOR A PICNIC.
WE OFTEN SPEND OUR BACHELOR SUNDAYS TOGETHER WITH OUR FIVE KIDS.
THE NAME HAS US WONDERING IF WE'RE IN FOR A BLAIR WITCH REMAKE.
CABEES
BUT IT TURNS OUT TO BE A NICE SHADY SPOT TO SPEND THE DAY.
MACCABEES
LET'S HOPE.
YOU QUICKLY GET USED TO USING BIBLICAL NAMES IN EVERYDAY CONTEXTS. SWITCHING FROM THE SACRED TO THE PROFANE, SO TO SPEAK.
TWO MACCABEES, PLEASE.
בירה מכבי

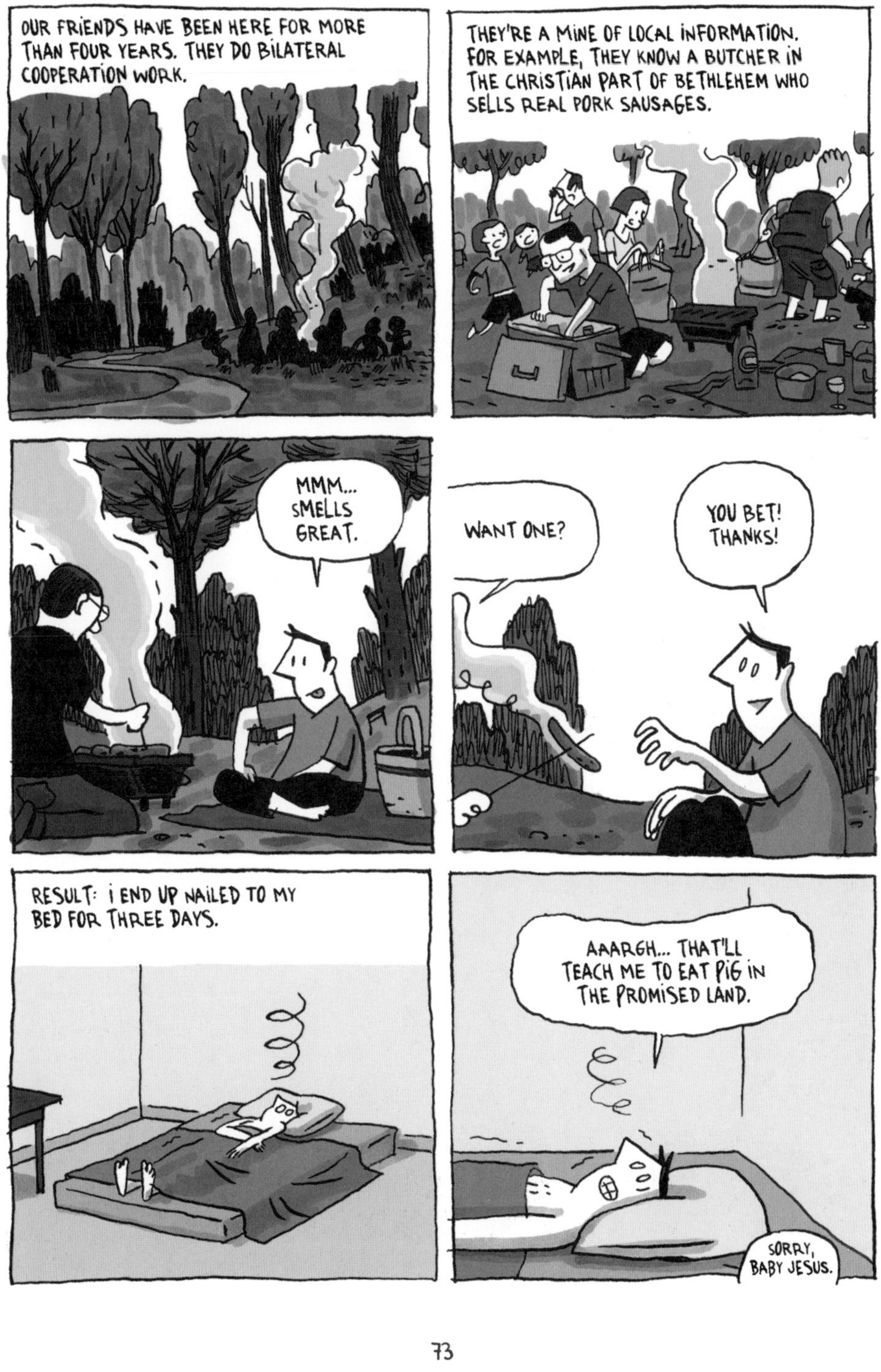
OUR FRIENDS HAVE BEEN HERE FOR MORE THAN FOUR YEARS. THEY DO BILATERAL COOPERATION WORK.
THEY'RE A MINE OF LOCAL INFORMATION. FOR EXAMPLE, THEY KNOW A BUTCHER IN THE CHRISTIAN PART OF BETHLEHEM WHO SELLS REAL PORK SAUSAGES.
MMM... SMELLS GREAT.
WANT ONE?
YOU BET! THANKS!
RESULT: I END UP NAILED TO MY BED FOR THREE DAYS.
AAARGH... THAT'LL TEACH ME TO EAT PIG IN THE PROMISED LAND.
SORRY, BABY JESUS.

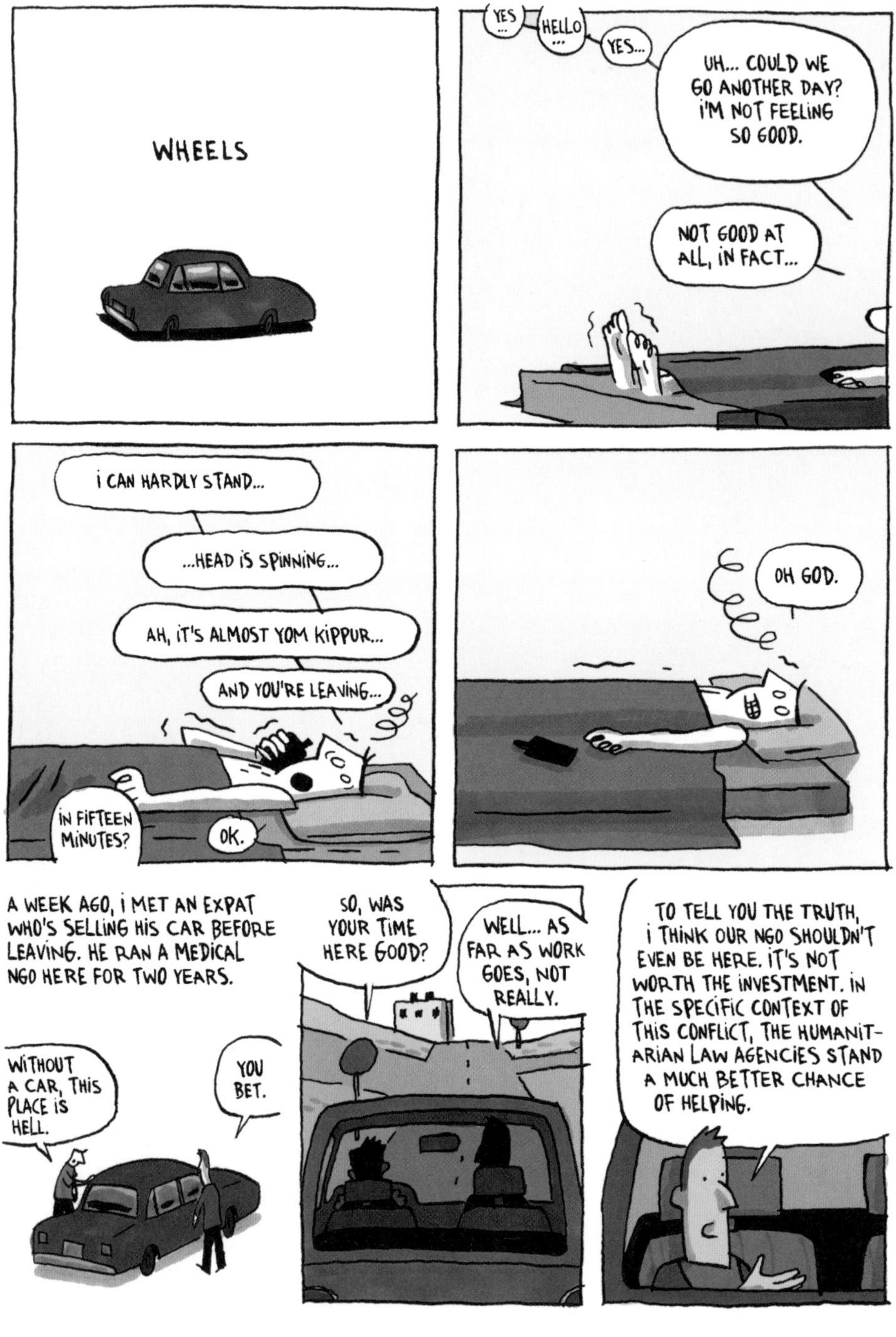
WHEELS
YES...
HELLO...
YES...
UH... COULD WE GO ANOTHER DAY? I'M NOT FEELING SO GOOD.
NOT GOOD AT ALL, IN FACT...
I CAN HARDLY STAND...
...HEAD IS SPINNING...
AH, IT'S ALMOST YOM KIPPUR...
AND YOU'RE LEAVING...
IN FIFTEEN MINUTES?
OK.
OH GOD.
A WEEK AGO, I MET AN EXPAT WHO'S SELLING HIS CAR BEFORE LEAVING. HE RAN A MEDICAL NGO HERE FOR TWO YEARS.
WITHOUT A CAR, THIS PLACE IS HELL.
YOU BET.
SO, WAS YOUR TIME HERE GOOD?
WELL... AS FAR AS WORK GOES, NOT REALLY.
TO TELL YOU THE TRUTH, I THINK OUR NGO SHOULDN'T EVEN BE HERE. IT'S NOT WORTH THE INVESTMENT. IN THE SPECIFIC CONTEXT OF THIS CONFLICT, THE HUMANITARIAN LAW AGENCIES STAND A MUCH BETTER CHANCE OF HELPING.

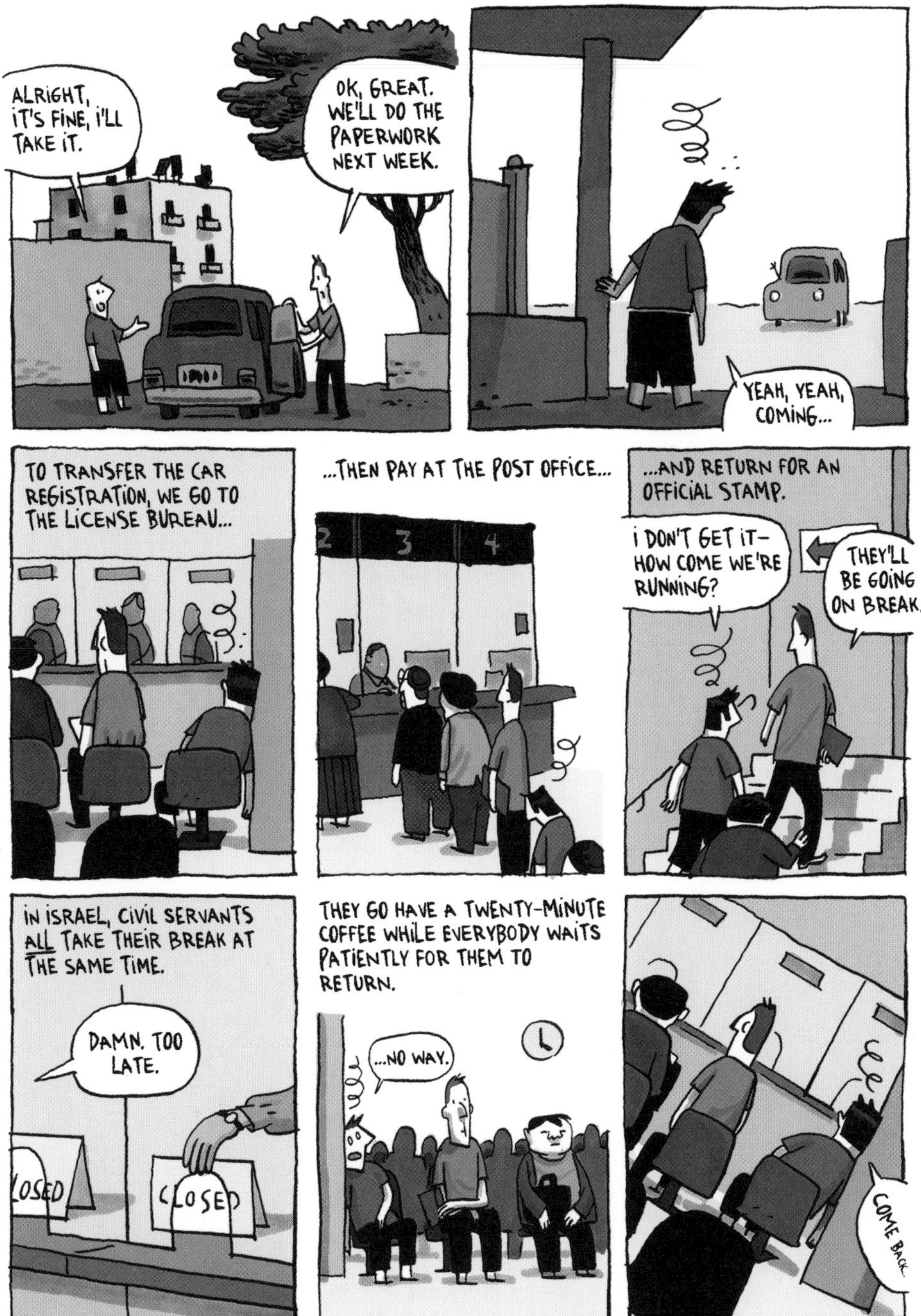
ALRIGHT, IT'S FINE, I'LL TAKE IT.
OK, GREAT. WE'LL DO THE PAPERWORK NEXT WEEK.
YEAH, YEAH, COMING...
TO TRANSFER THE CAR REGISTRATION, WE GO TO THE LICENSE BUREAU...
...THEN PAY AT THE POST OFFICE...
2 3 4
...AND RETURN FOR AN OFFICIAL STAMP.
I DON'T GET IT– HOW COME WE'RE RUNNING?
THEY'LL BE GOING ON BREAK.
IN ISRAEL, CIVIL SERVANTS ALL TAKE THEIR BREAK AT THE SAME TIME.
DAMN. TOO LATE.
LOSED
CLOSED
THEY GO HAVE A TWENTY-MINUTE COFFEE WHILE EVERYBODY WAITS PATIENTLY FOR THEM TO RETURN.
...NO WAY.
COME BACK...

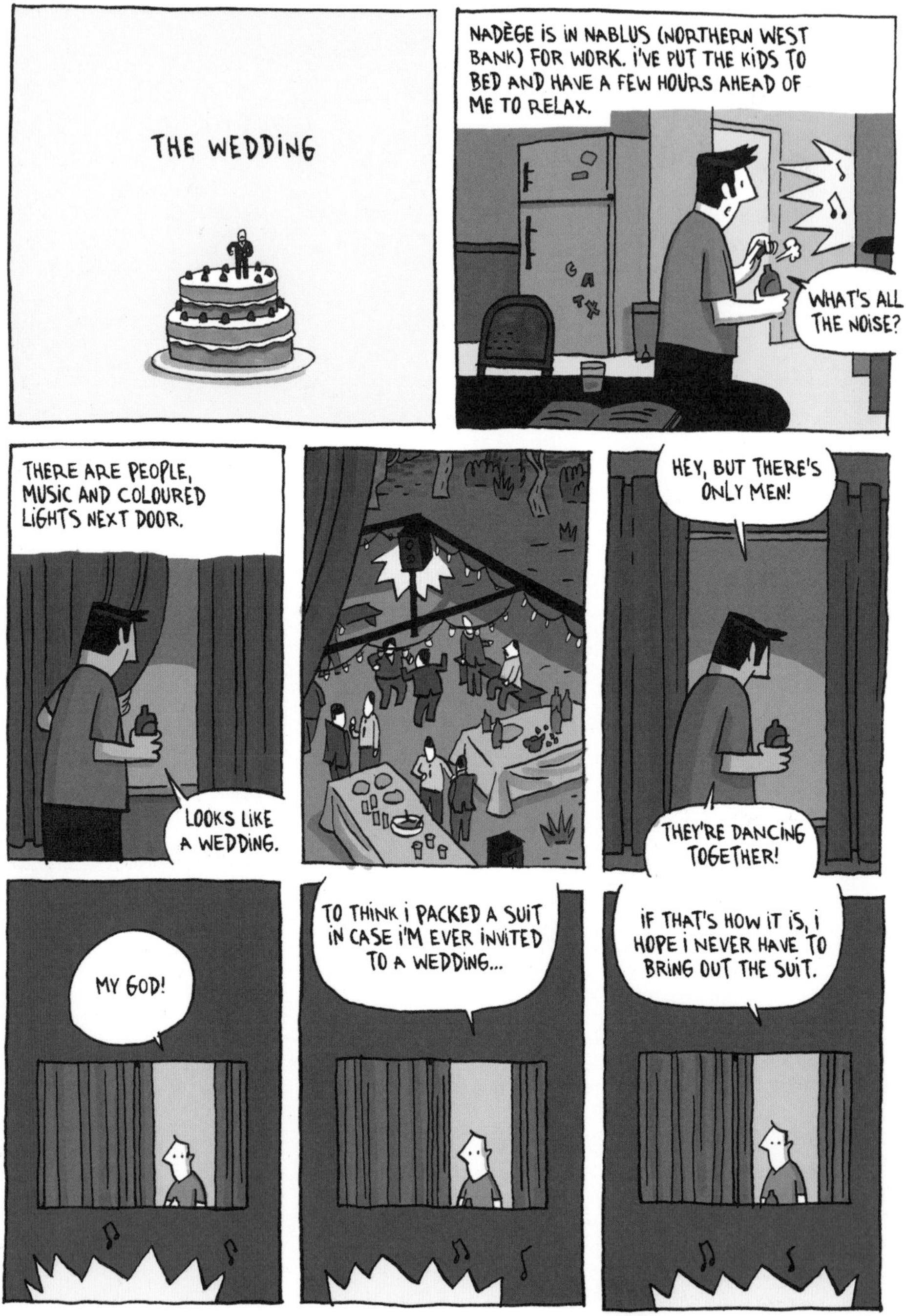
THE WEDDING
NADÈGE IS IN NABLUS (NORTHERN WEST BANK) FOR WORK. I'VE PUT THE KIDS TO BED AND HAVE A FEW HOURS AHEAD OF ME TO RELAX.
WHAT'S ALL THE NOISE?
THERE ARE PEOPLE, MUSIC AND COLOURED LIGHTS NEXT DOOR.
LOOKS LIKE A WEDDING.
HEY, BUT THERE'S ONLY MEN!
THEY'RE DANCING TOGETHER!
MY GOD!
TO THINK I PACKED A SUIT IN CASE I'M EVER INVITED TO A WEDDING...
IF THAT'S HOW IT IS, I HOPE I NEVER HAVE TO BRING OUT THE SUIT.

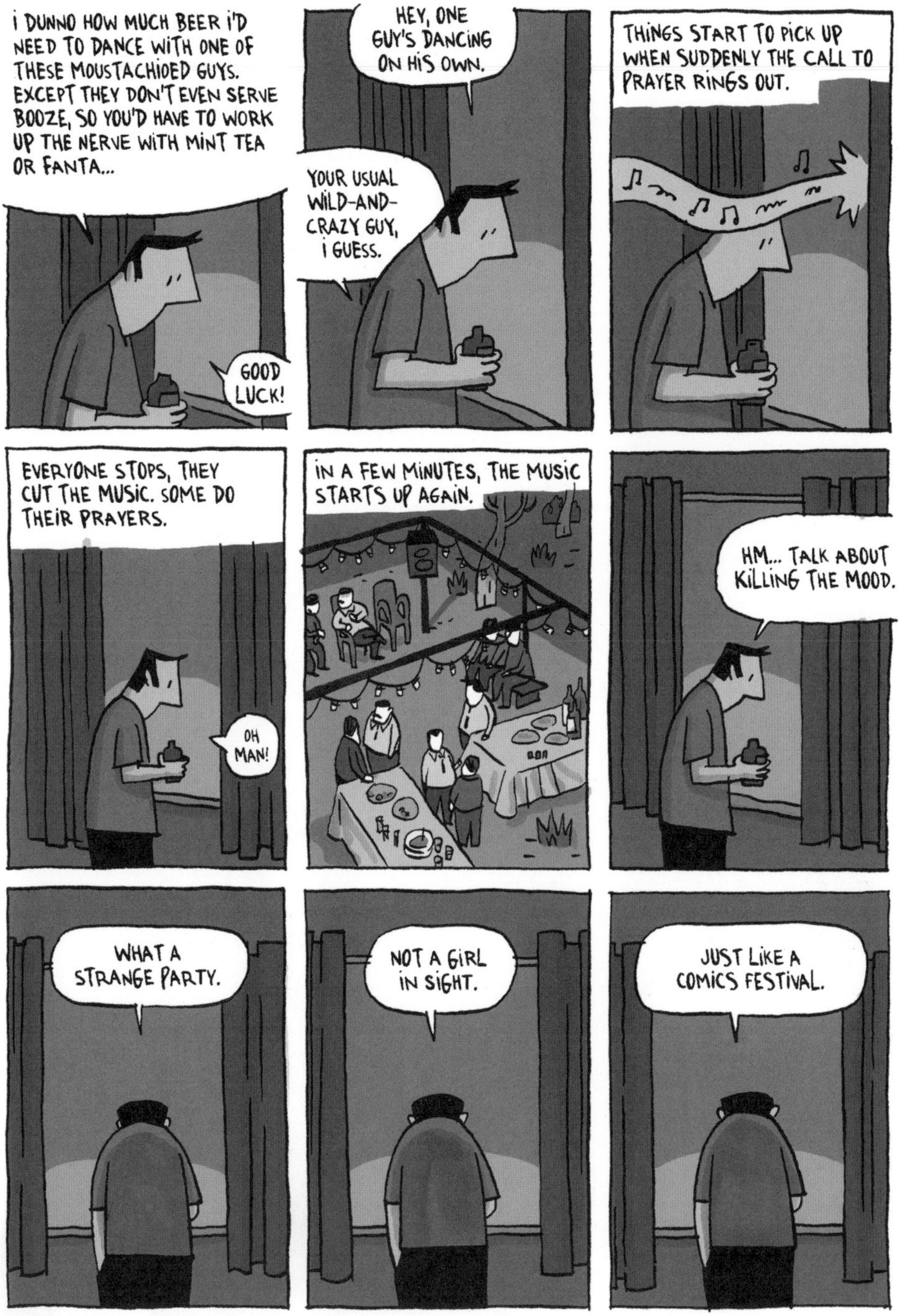
i DUNNO HOW MUCH BEER i'D NEED TO DANCE WITH ONE OF THESE MOUSTACHIOED GUYS. EXCEPT THEY DON'T EVEN SERVE BOOZE, SO YOU'D HAVE TO WORK UP THE NERVE WITH MINT TEA OR FANTA...
GOOD LUCK!
HEY, ONE GUY'S DANCING ON HIS OWN.
YOUR USUAL WILD-AND-CRAZY GUY, i GUESS.
THINGS START TO PICK UP WHEN SUDDENLY THE CALL TO PRAYER RINGS OUT.
EVERYONE STOPS, THEY CUT THE MUSIC. SOME DO THEIR PRAYERS.
OH MAN!
IN A FEW MINUTES, THE MUSIC STARTS UP AGAIN.
HM... TALK ABOUT KILLING THE MOOD.
WHAT A STRANGE PARTY.
NOT A GIRL IN SIGHT.
JUST LIKE A COMICS FESTIVAL.

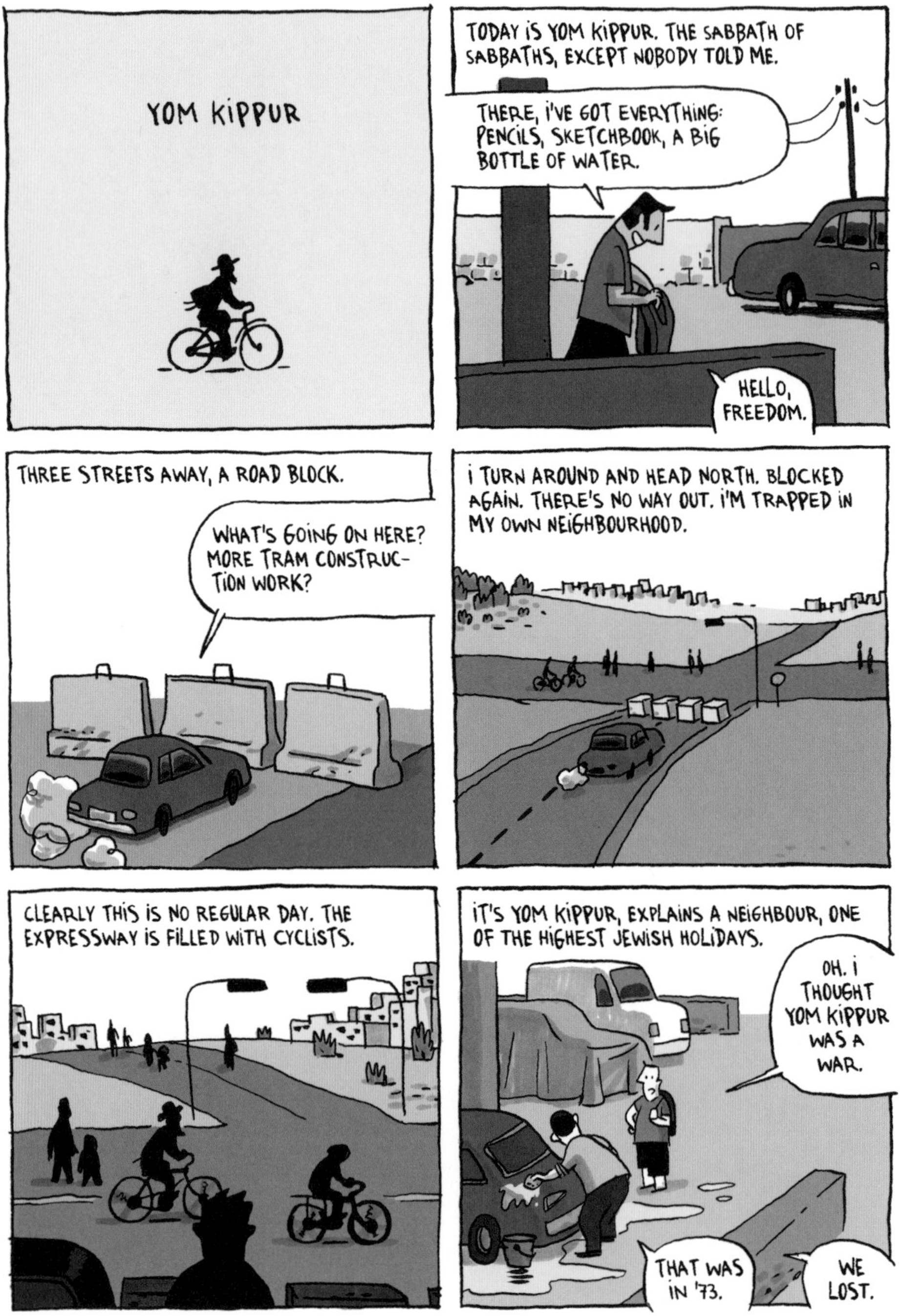
YOM KIPPUR
TODAY IS YOM KIPPUR. THE SABBATH OF SABBATHS, EXCEPT NOBODY TOLD ME.
THERE, I'VE GOT EVERYTHING: PENCILS, SKETCHBOOK, A BIG BOTTLE OF WATER.
HELLO, FREEDOM.
THREE STREETS AWAY, A ROAD BLOCK.
WHAT'S GOING ON HERE? MORE TRAM CONSTRUCTION WORK?
I TURN AROUND AND HEAD NORTH. BLOCKED AGAIN. THERE'S NO WAY OUT. I'M TRAPPED IN MY OWN NEIGHBOURHOOD.
CLEARLY THIS IS NO REGULAR DAY. THE EXPRESSWAY IS FILLED WITH CYCLISTS.
IT'S YOM KIPPUR, EXPLAINS A NEIGHBOUR, ONE OF THE HIGHEST JEWISH HOLIDAYS.
OH. I THOUGHT YOM KIPPUR WAS A WAR.
THAT WAS IN '73.
WE LOST.

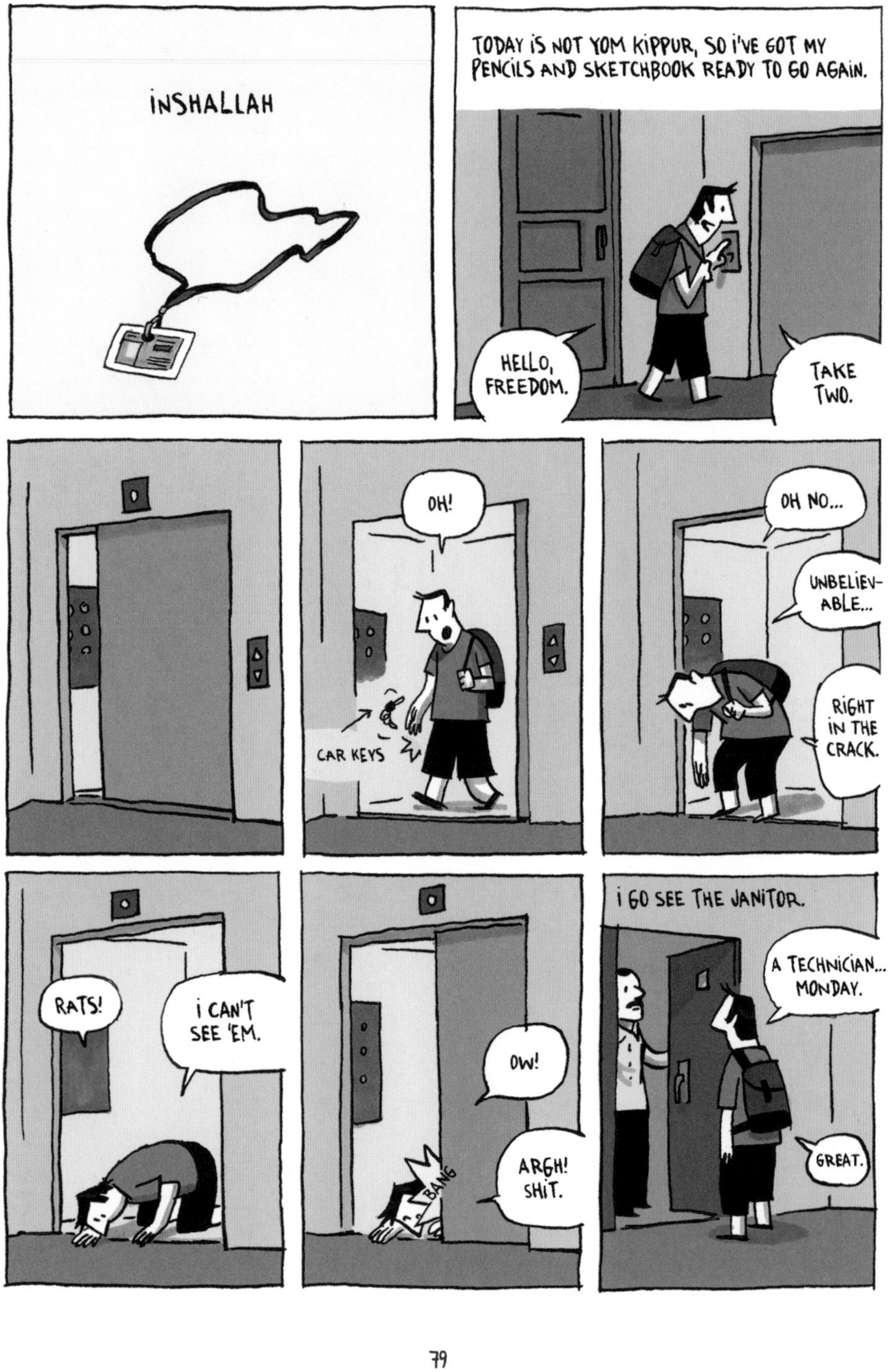
INSHALLAH
TODAY IS NOT YOM KIPPUR, SO I'VE GOT MY PENCILS AND SKETCHBOOK READY TO GO AGAIN.
HELLO, FREEDOM.
TAKE TWO.
OH!
CAR KEYS
OH NO...
UNBELIEVABLE...
RIGHT IN THE CRACK.
RATS!
I CAN'T SEE 'EM.
OW!
BANG
ARGH! SHIT.
I GO SEE THE JANITOR.
A TECHNICIAN... MONDAY.
GREAT.

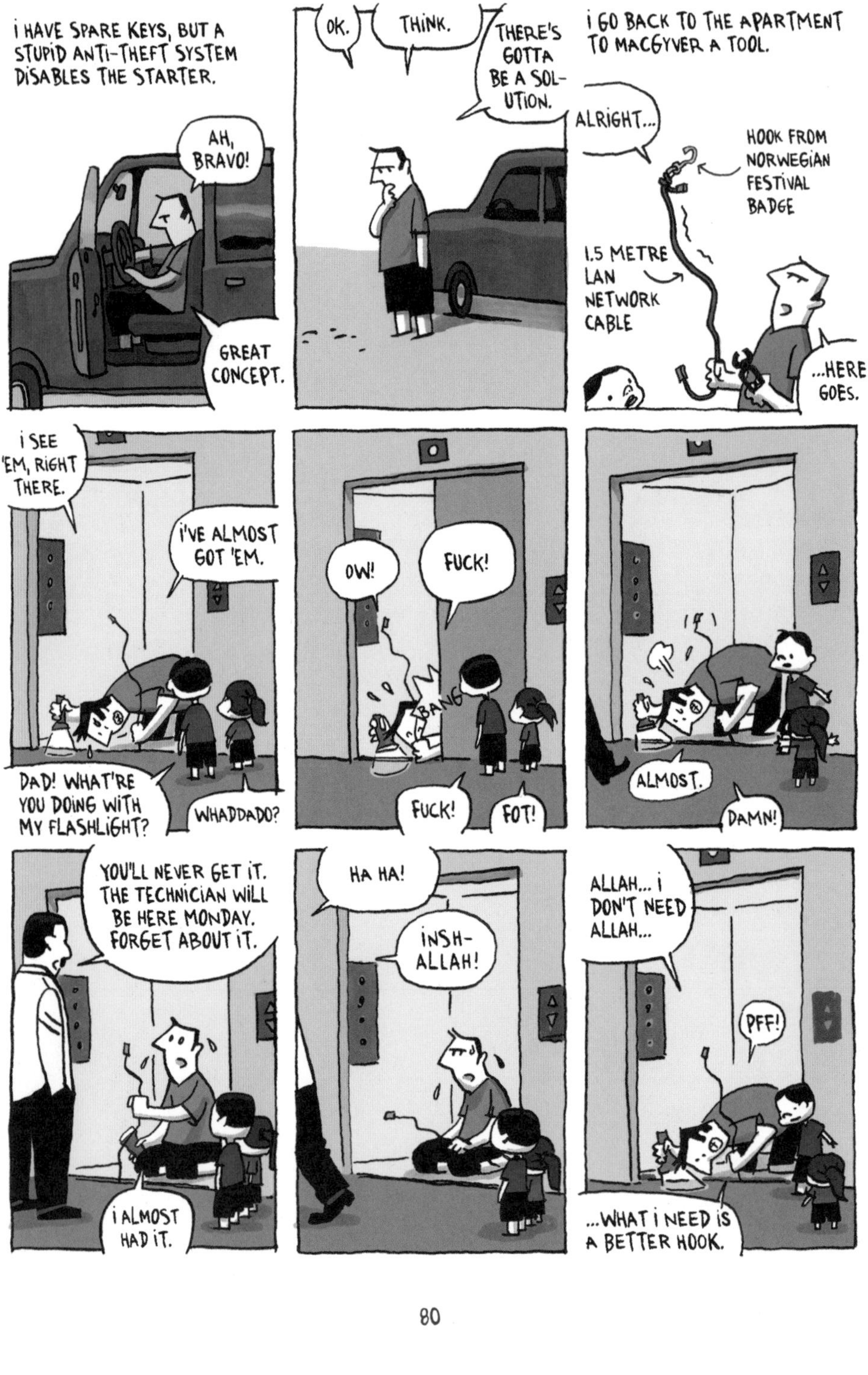
I HAVE SPARE KEYS, BUT A STUPID ANTI-THEFT SYSTEM DISABLES THE STARTER.
AH, BRAVO!
GREAT CONCEPT.
OK.
THINK.
THERE'S GOTTA BE A SOL-UTION.
I GO BACK TO THE APARTMENT TO MACGYVER A TOOL.
ALRIGHT...
HOOK FROM NORWEGIAN FESTIVAL BADGE
1.5 METRE LAN NETWORK CABLE
...HERE GOES.
I SEE 'EM, RIGHT THERE.
I'VE ALMOST GOT 'EM.
DAD! WHAT'RE YOU DOING WITH MY FLASHLIGHT?
WHADDADO?
OW!
FUCK!
BANG
FUCK!
FOT!
ALMOST.
DAMN!
YOU'LL NEVER GET IT. THE TECHNICIAN WILL BE HERE MONDAY. FORGET ABOUT IT.
I ALMOST HAD IT.
HA HA!
INSH-ALLAH!
ALLAH... I DON'T NEED ALLAH...
PFF!
...WHAT I NEED IS A BETTER HOOK.

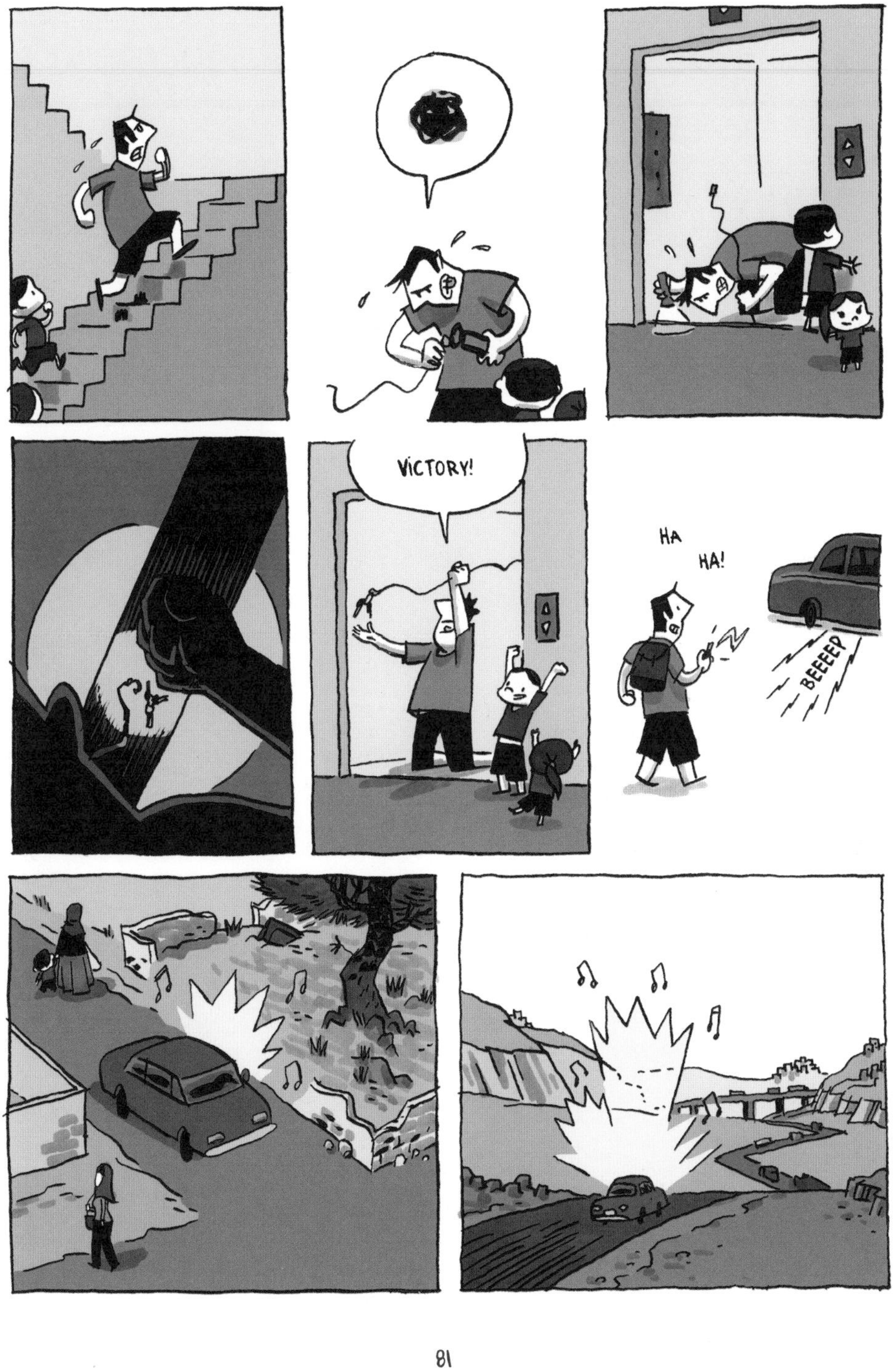
VICTORY!
HA
HA!
BEEEEP

SCRITCH
SCRITCH

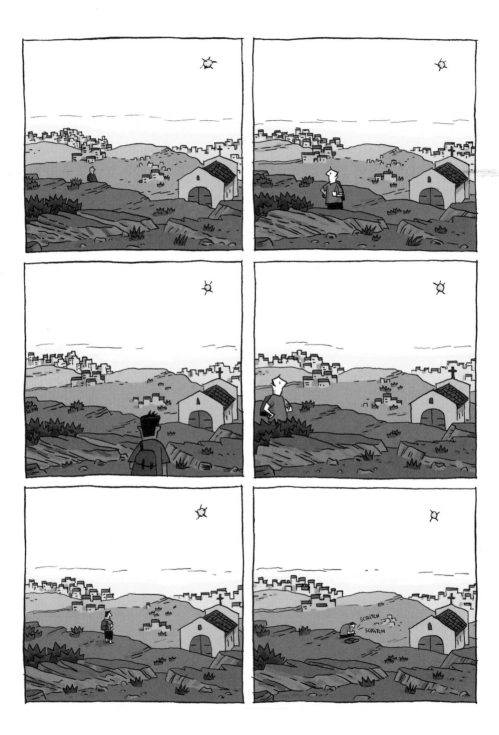

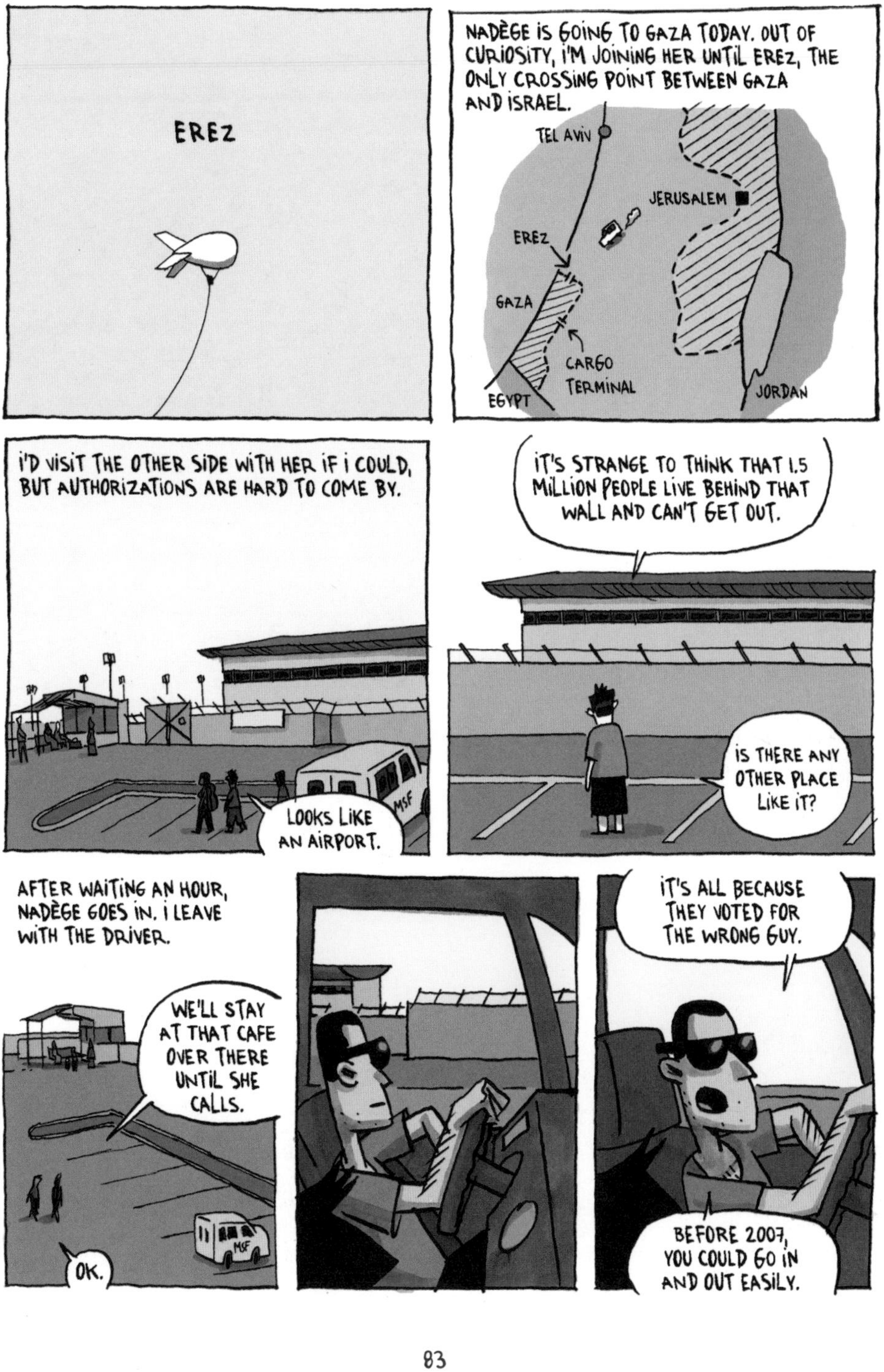
EREZ
NADÈGE IS GOING TO GAZA TODAY. OUT OF CURIOSITY, I'M JOINING HER UNTIL EREZ, THE ONLY CROSSING POINT BETWEEN GAZA AND ISRAEL.
TEL AVIV
JERUSALEM
EREZ
GAZA
CARGO TERMINAL
EGYPT
JORDAN
I'D VISIT THE OTHER SIDE WITH HER IF I COULD, BUT AUTHORIZATIONS ARE HARD TO COME BY.
LOOKS LIKE AN AIRPORT.
MSF
IT'S STRANGE TO THINK THAT 1.5 MILLION PEOPLE LIVE BEHIND THAT WALL AND CAN'T GET OUT.
IS THERE ANY OTHER PLACE LIKE IT?
AFTER WAITING AN HOUR, NADÈGE GOES IN. I LEAVE WITH THE DRIVER.
WE'LL STAY AT THAT CAFE OVER THERE UNTIL SHE CALLS.
OK.
MSF
IT'S ALL BECAUSE THEY VOTED FOR THE WRONG GUY.
BEFORE 2007, YOU COULD GO IN AND OUT EASILY.

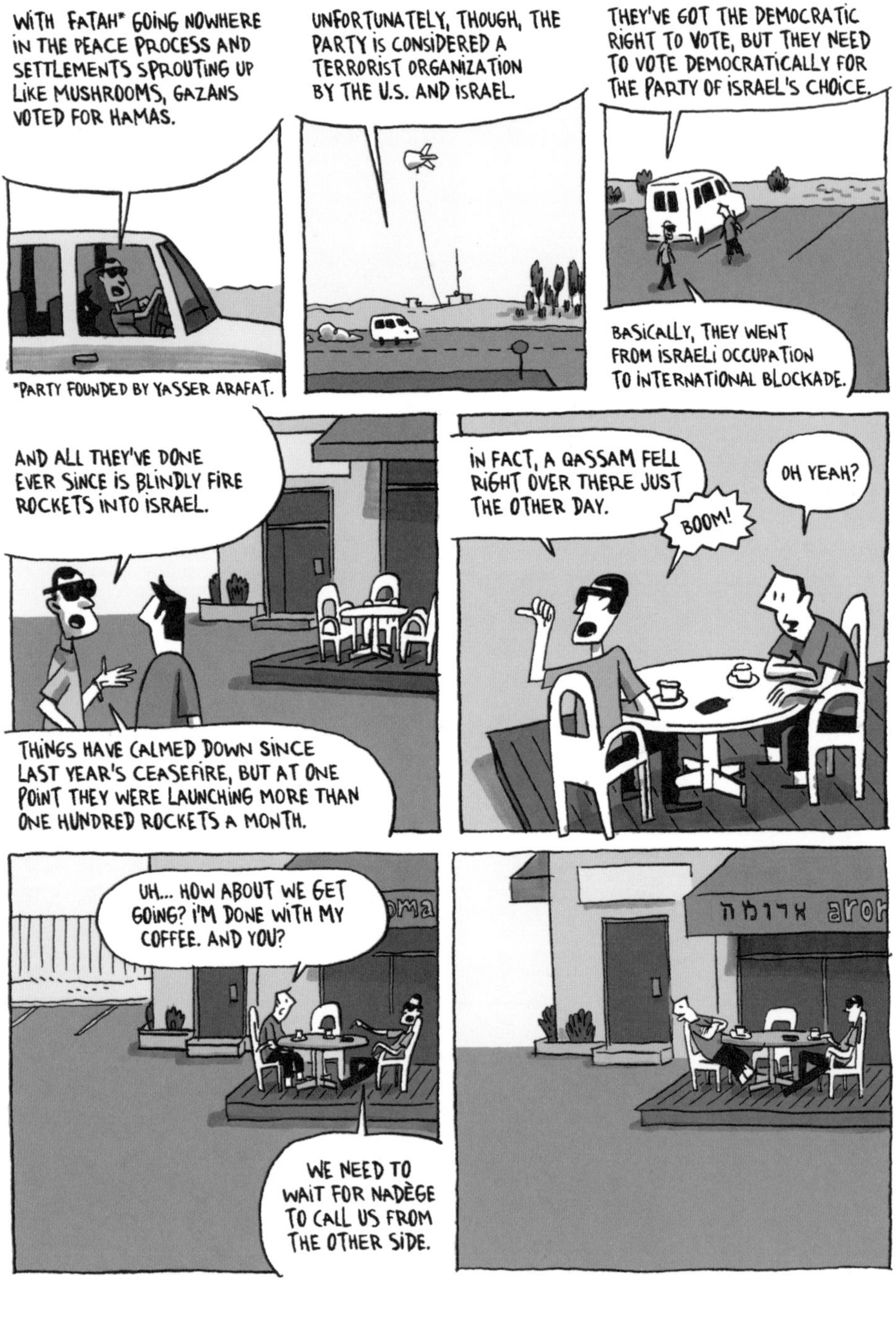
WITH FATAH* GOING NOWHERE IN THE PEACE PROCESS AND SETTLEMENTS SPROUTING UP LIKE MUSHROOMS, GAZANS VOTED FOR HAMAS.
*PARTY FOUNDED BY YASSER ARAFAT.
UNFORTUNATELY, THOUGH, THE PARTY IS CONSIDERED A TERRORIST ORGANIZATION BY THE U.S. AND ISRAEL.
THEY'VE GOT THE DEMOCRATIC RIGHT TO VOTE, BUT THEY NEED TO VOTE DEMOCRATICALLY FOR THE PARTY OF ISRAEL'S CHOICE.
BASICALLY, THEY WENT FROM ISRAELI OCCUPATION TO INTERNATIONAL BLOCKADE.
AND ALL THEY'VE DONE EVER SINCE IS BLINDLY FIRE ROCKETS INTO ISRAEL.
THINGS HAVE CALMED DOWN SINCE LAST YEAR'S CEASEFIRE, BUT AT ONE POINT THEY WERE LAUNCHING MORE THAN ONE HUNDRED ROCKETS A MONTH.
IN FACT, A QASSAM FELL RIGHT OVER THERE JUST THE OTHER DAY.
BOOM!
OH YEAH?
UH... HOW ABOUT WE GET GOING? I'M DONE WITH MY COFFEE. AND YOU?
WE NEED TO WAIT FOR NADÈGE TO CALL US FROM THE OTHER SIDE.
ארומה

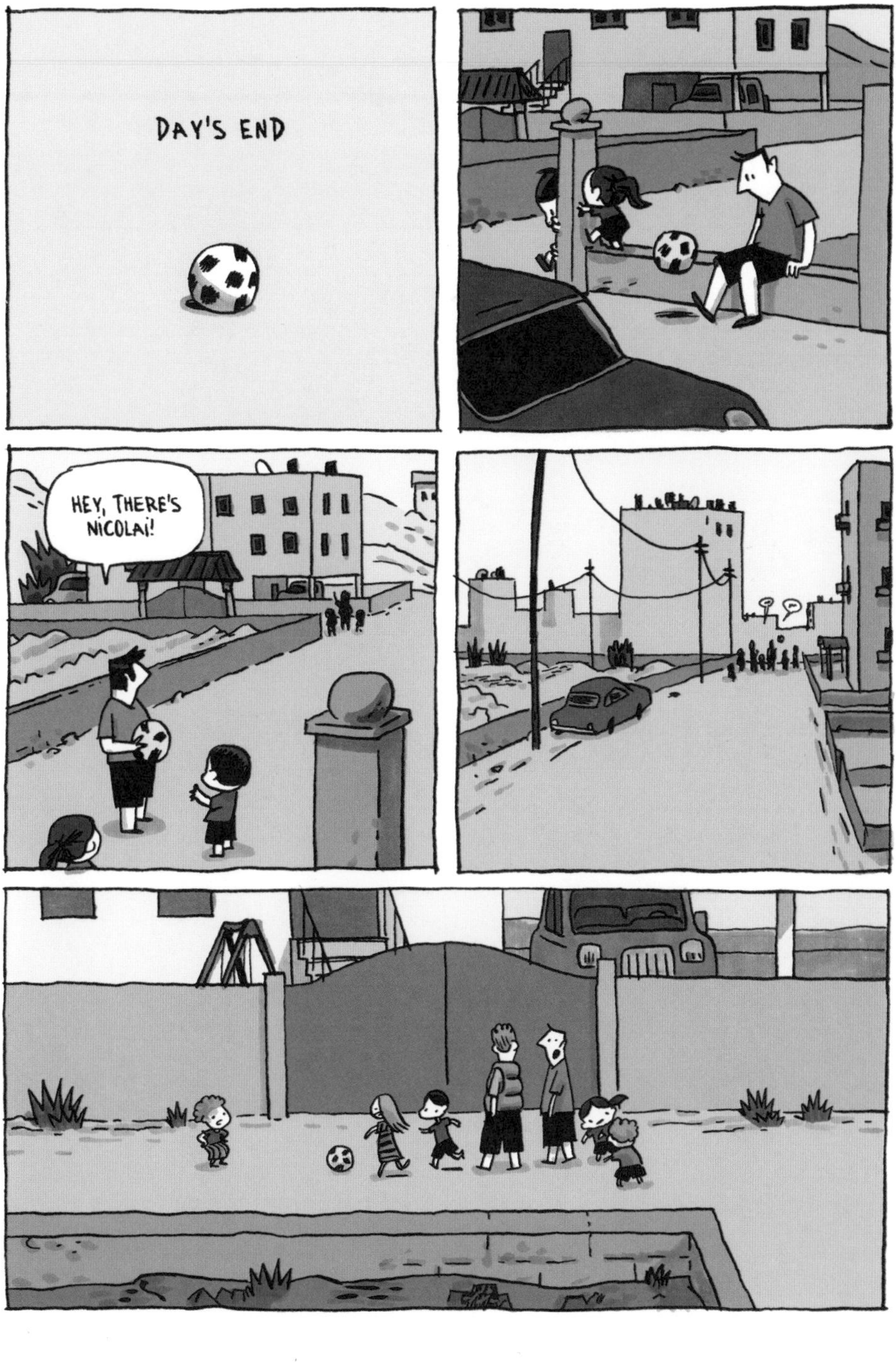
DAY'S END
HEY, THERE'S NICOLAI!

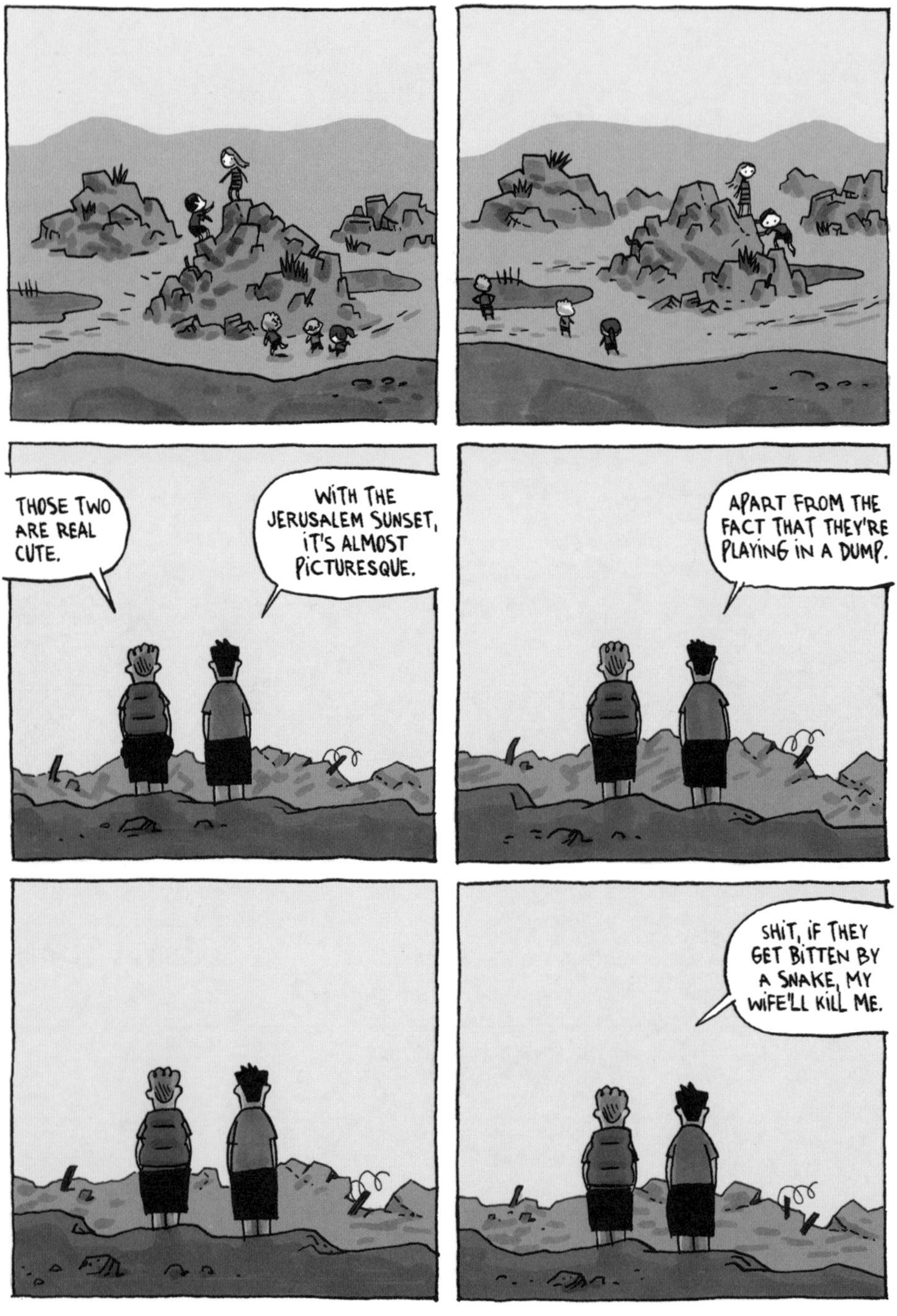
THOSE TWO ARE REAL CUTE.
WITH THE JERUSALEM SUNSET, IT'S ALMOST PICTURESQUE.
APART FROM THE FACT THAT THEY'RE PLAYING IN A DUMP.
SHIT, IF THEY GET BITTEN BY A SNAKE, MY WIFE'LL KILL ME.

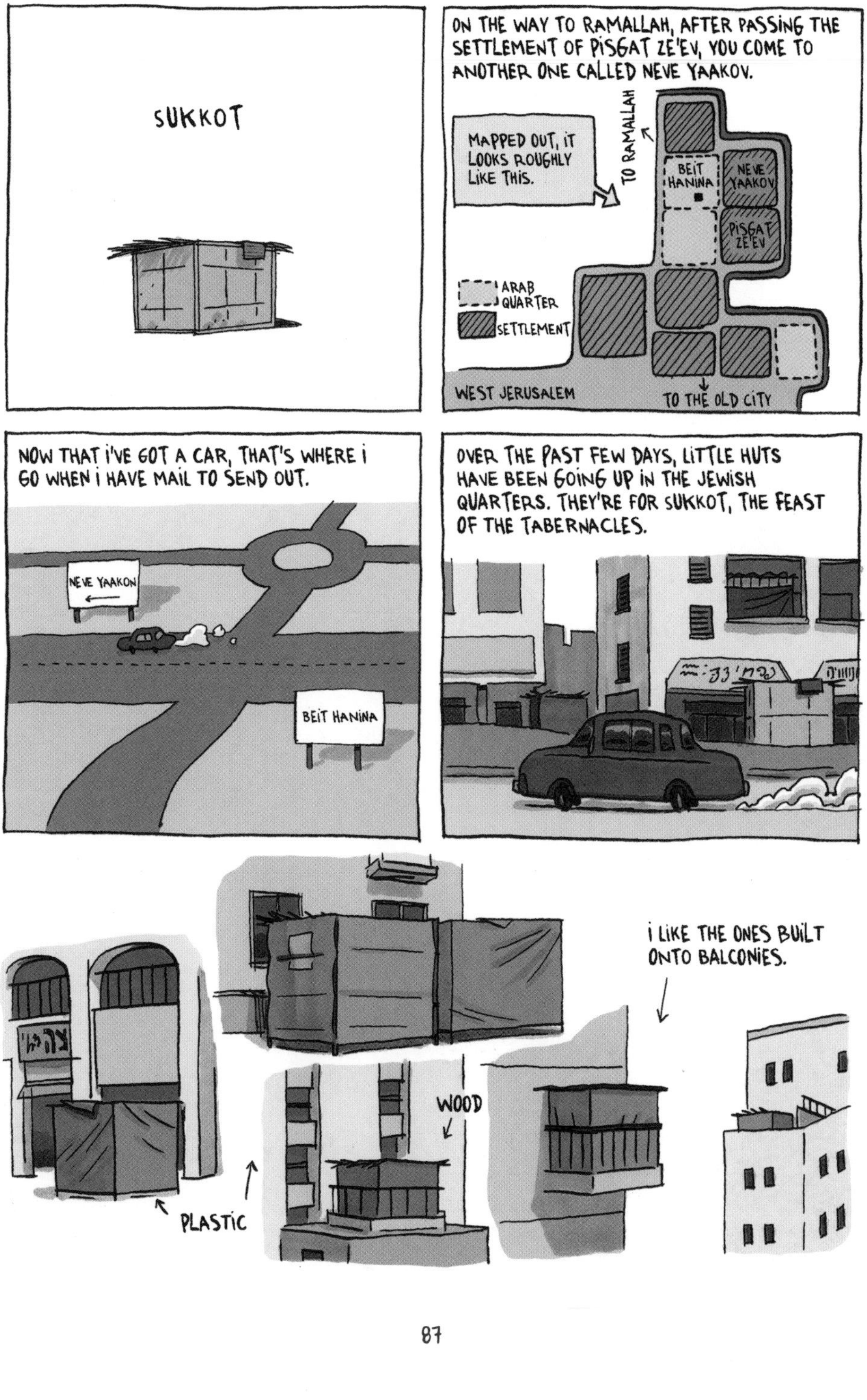
SUKKOT
ON THE WAY TO RAMALLAH, AFTER PASSING THE SETTLEMENT OF PISGAT ZE'EV, YOU COME TO ANOTHER ONE CALLED NEVE YAAKOV.
MAPPED OUT, IT LOOKS ROUGHLY LIKE THIS.
TO RAMALLAH
BEIT HANINA
NEVE YAAKOV
PISGAT ZE'EV
ARAB QUARTER
SETTLEMENT
WEST JERUSALEM
TO THE OLD CITY
NOW THAT I'VE GOT A CAR, THAT'S WHERE I GO WHEN I HAVE MAIL TO SEND OUT.
NEVE YAAKON
BEIT HANINA
OVER THE PAST FEW DAYS, LITTLE HUTS HAVE BEEN GOING UP IN THE JEWISH QUARTERS. THEY'RE FOR SUKKOT, THE FEAST OF THE TABERNACLES.
I LIKE THE ONES BUILT ONTO BALCONIES.
WOOD
PLASTIC

IN THE POST OFFICE, I OFTEN GET SERVED BY A TALL SKINNY GUY WHO'S VERY FRIENDLY, UNLIKE MOST OF HIS COLLEAGUES.

DO YOU HAVE A GUN?

GENERALLY SPEAKING, THE PEOPLE WHO WORK IN JERUSALEM'S SERVICE SECTOR TEND TO BE FAIRLY RUDE.

שלום!

SHALOM!

I SPEAK TO HIM IN ENGLISH. HE ANSWERS FIRST IN ENGLISH, THEN IN HEBREW, TAKING CARE TO ENUNCIATE.

לשלוח מכתב.

HE MUST THINK I'M A NEWCOMER, A RUSSIAN MAYBE, AND THAT I'M GOING TO LEARN HEBREW.

I TRY TO REPEAT PHONETICALLY.

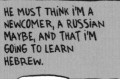

יום טוב ש'יה'ה לך.

שלום

תודה.

TODA.

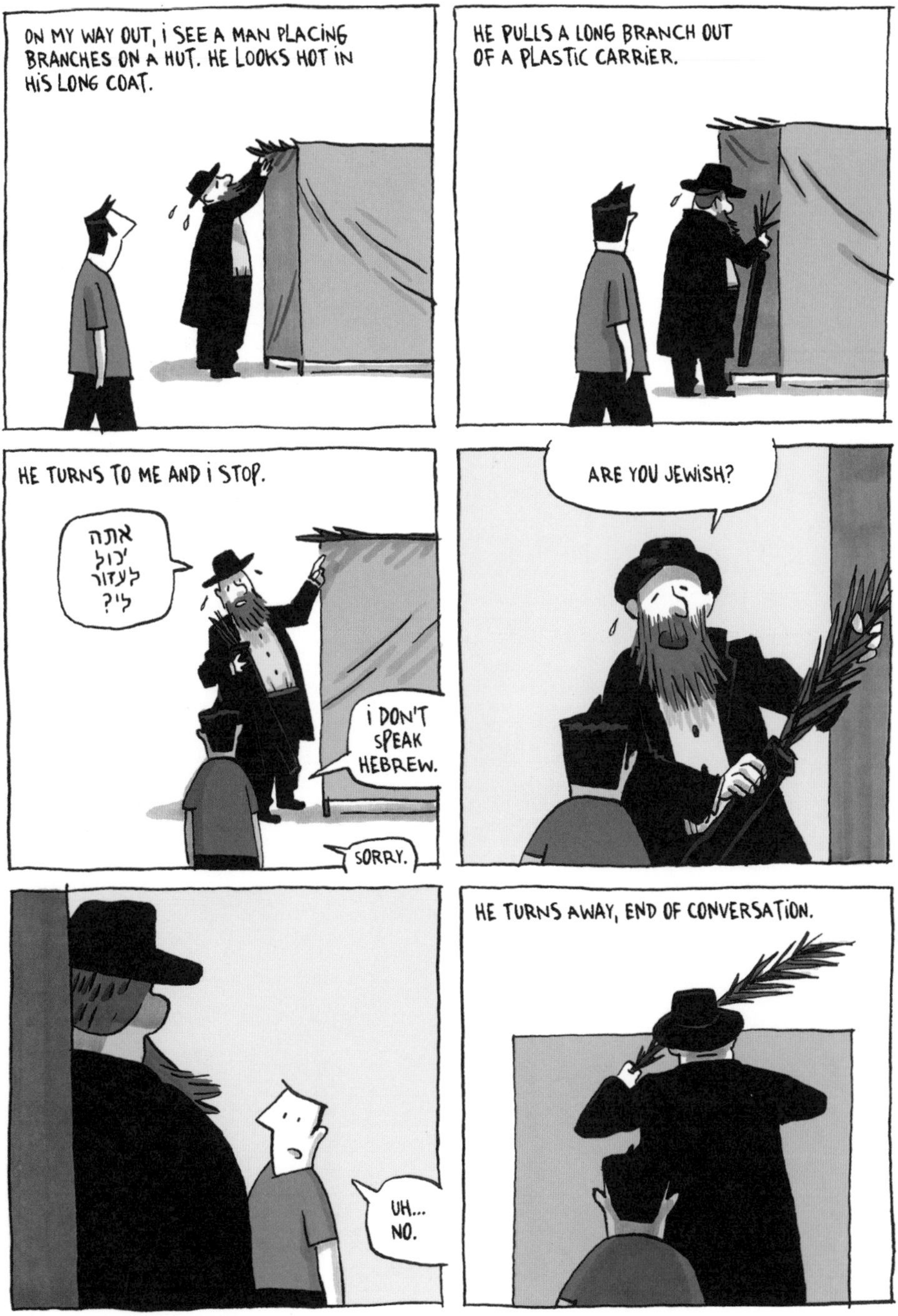
ON MY WAY OUT, I SEE A MAN PLACING BRANCHES ON A HUT. HE LOOKS HOT IN HIS LONG COAT.
HE PULLS A LONG BRANCH OUT OF A PLASTIC CARRIER.
HE TURNS TO ME AND I STOP.
אתה יכול לעזור לי?
I DON'T SPEAK HEBREW.
SORRY.
ARE YOU JEWISH?
UH... NO.
HE TURNS AWAY, END OF CONVERSATION.

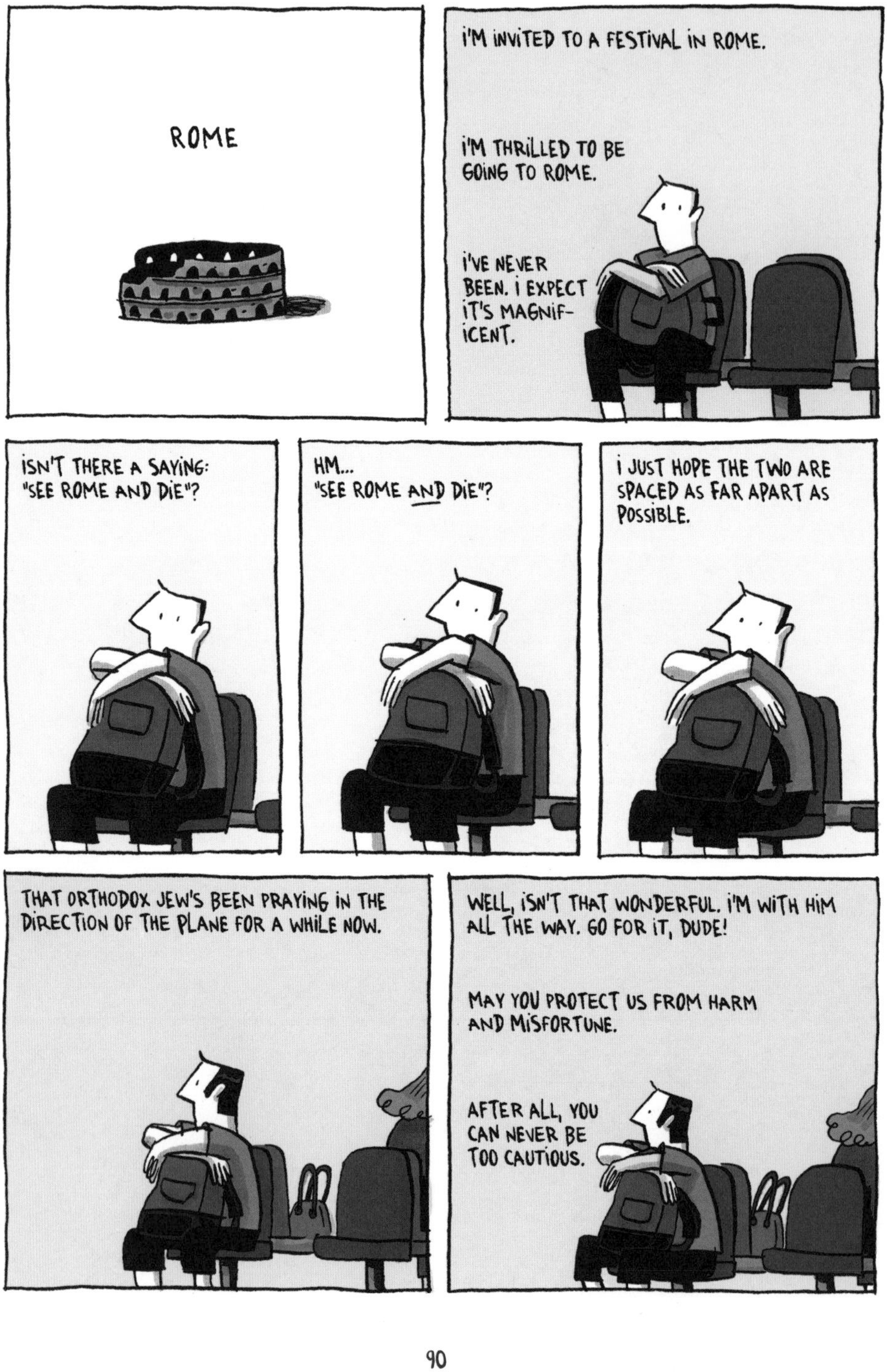
ROME
I'M INVITED TO A FESTIVAL IN ROME.
I'M THRILLED TO BE GOING TO ROME.
I'VE NEVER BEEN. I EXPECT IT'S MAGNIFICENT.
ISN'T THERE A SAYING: "SEE ROME AND DIE"?
HM... "SEE ROME AND DIE"?
I JUST HOPE THE TWO ARE SPACED AS FAR APART AS POSSIBLE.
THAT ORTHODOX JEW'S BEEN PRAYING IN THE DIRECTION OF THE PLANE FOR A WHILE NOW.
WELL, ISN'T THAT WONDERFUL. I'M WITH HIM ALL THE WAY. GO FOR IT, DUDE!
MAY YOU PROTECT US FROM HARM AND MISFORTUNE.
AFTER ALL, YOU CAN NEVER BE TOO CAUTIOUS.

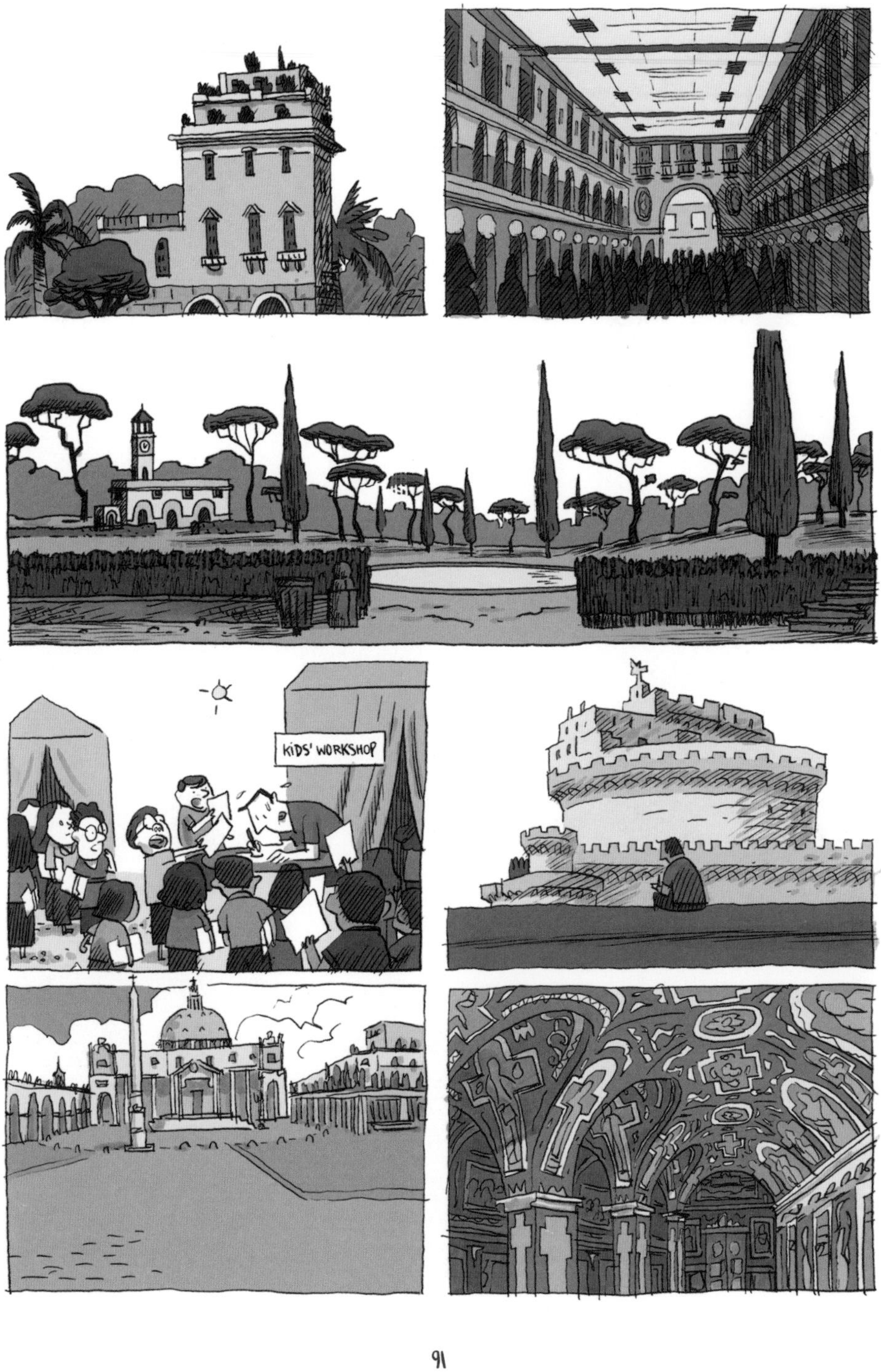
KIDS' WORKSHOP

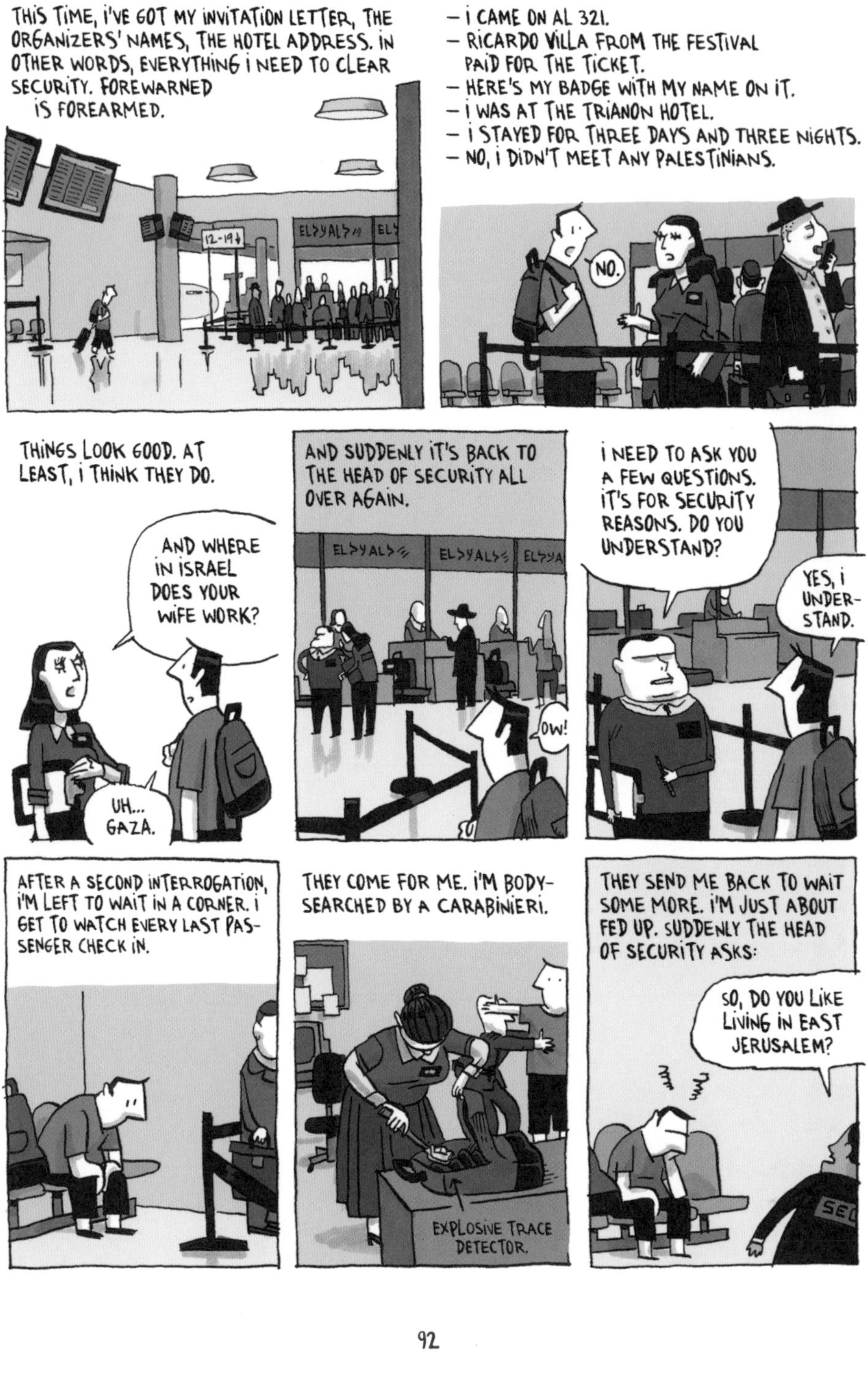
THIS TIME, I'VE GOT MY INVITATION LETTER, THE ORGANIZERS' NAMES, THE HOTEL ADDRESS. IN OTHER WORDS, EVERYTHING I NEED TO CLEAR SECURITY. FOREWARNED IS FOREARMED.
12-19
EL AL
— I CAME ON AL 321.
— RICARDO VILLA FROM THE FESTIVAL PAID FOR THE TICKET.
— HERE'S MY BADGE WITH MY NAME ON IT.
— I WAS AT THE TRIANON HOTEL.
— I STAYED FOR THREE DAYS AND THREE NIGHTS.
— NO, I DIDN'T MEET ANY PALESTINIANS.
NO.
THINGS LOOK GOOD. AT LEAST, I THINK THEY DO.
AND WHERE IN ISRAEL DOES YOUR WIFE WORK?
UH... GAZA.
AND SUDDENLY IT'S BACK TO THE HEAD OF SECURITY ALL OVER AGAIN.
EL AL
OW!
I NEED TO ASK YOU A FEW QUESTIONS. IT'S FOR SECURITY REASONS. DO YOU UNDERSTAND?
YES, I UNDERSTAND.
AFTER A SECOND INTERROGATION, I'M LEFT TO WAIT IN A CORNER. I GET TO WATCH EVERY LAST PASSENGER CHECK IN.
THEY COME FOR ME. I'M BODY-SEARCHED BY A CARABINIERI.
EXPLOSIVE TRACE DETECTOR.
THEY SEND ME BACK TO WAIT SOME MORE. I'M JUST ABOUT FED UP. SUDDENLY THE HEAD OF SECURITY ASKS:
SO, DO YOU LIKE LIVING IN EAST JERUSALEM?

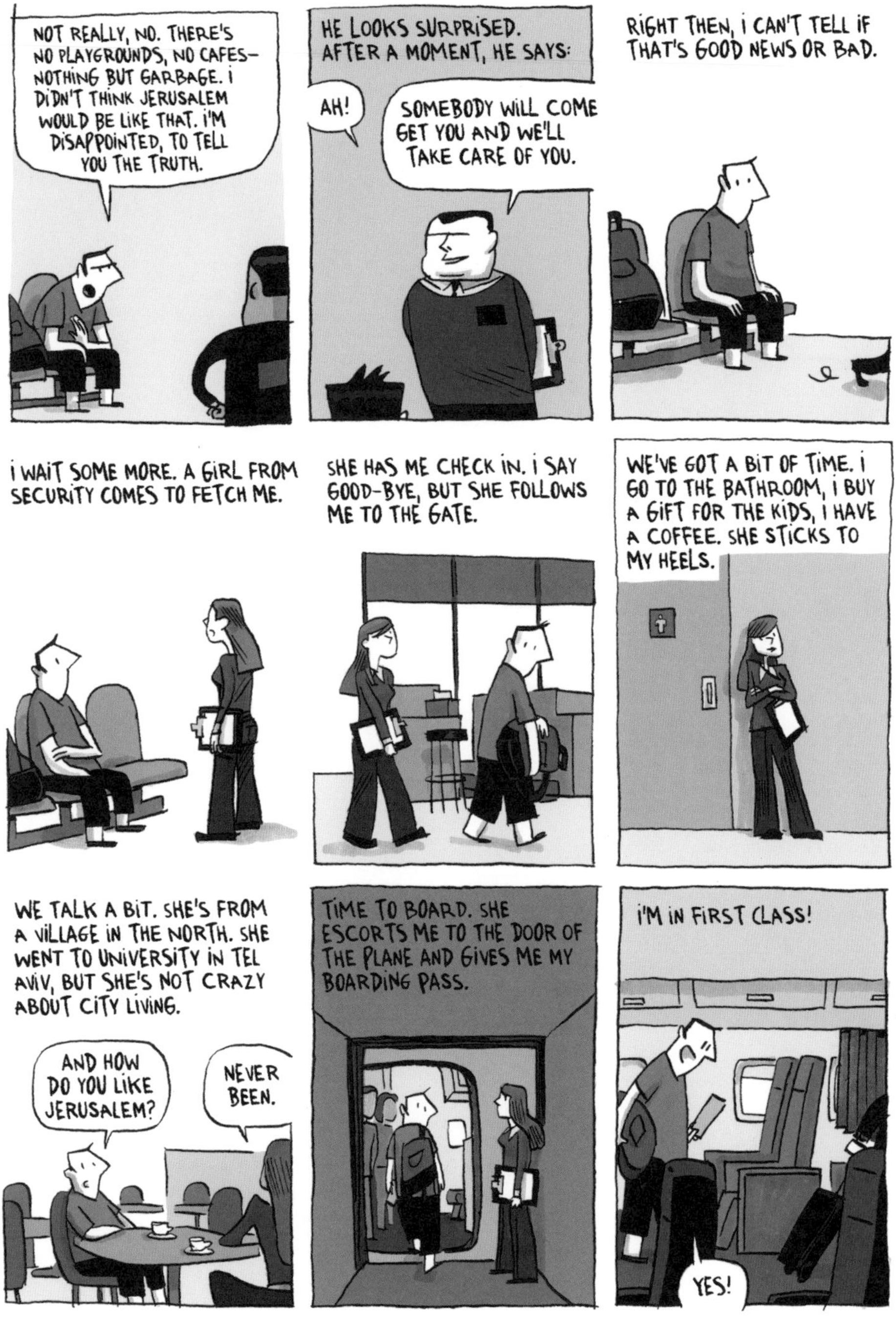

NOT REALLY, NO. THERE'S NO PLAYGROUNDS, NO CAFES— NOTHING BUT GARBAGE. I DIDN'T THINK JERUSALEM WOULD BE LIKE THAT. I'M DISAPPOINTED, TO TELL YOU THE TRUTH.
HE LOOKS SURPRISED. AFTER A MOMENT, HE SAYS:
AH!
SOMEBODY WILL COME GET YOU AND WE'LL TAKE CARE OF YOU.
RIGHT THEN, I CAN'T TELL IF THAT'S GOOD NEWS OR BAD.
I WAIT SOME MORE. A GIRL FROM SECURITY COMES TO FETCH ME.
SHE HAS ME CHECK IN. I SAY GOOD-BYE, BUT SHE FOLLOWS ME TO THE GATE.
WE'VE GOT A BIT OF TIME. I GO TO THE BATHROOM, I BUY A GIFT FOR THE KIDS, I HAVE A COFFEE. SHE STICKS TO MY HEELS.
WE TALK A BIT. SHE'S FROM A VILLAGE IN THE NORTH. SHE WENT TO UNIVERSITY IN TEL AVIV, BUT SHE'S NOT CRAZY ABOUT CITY LIVING.
AND HOW DO YOU LIKE JERUSALEM?
NEVER BEEN.
TIME TO BOARD. SHE ESCORTS ME TO THE DOOR OF THE PLANE AND GIVES ME MY BOARDING PASS.
I'M IN FIRST CLASS!
YES!

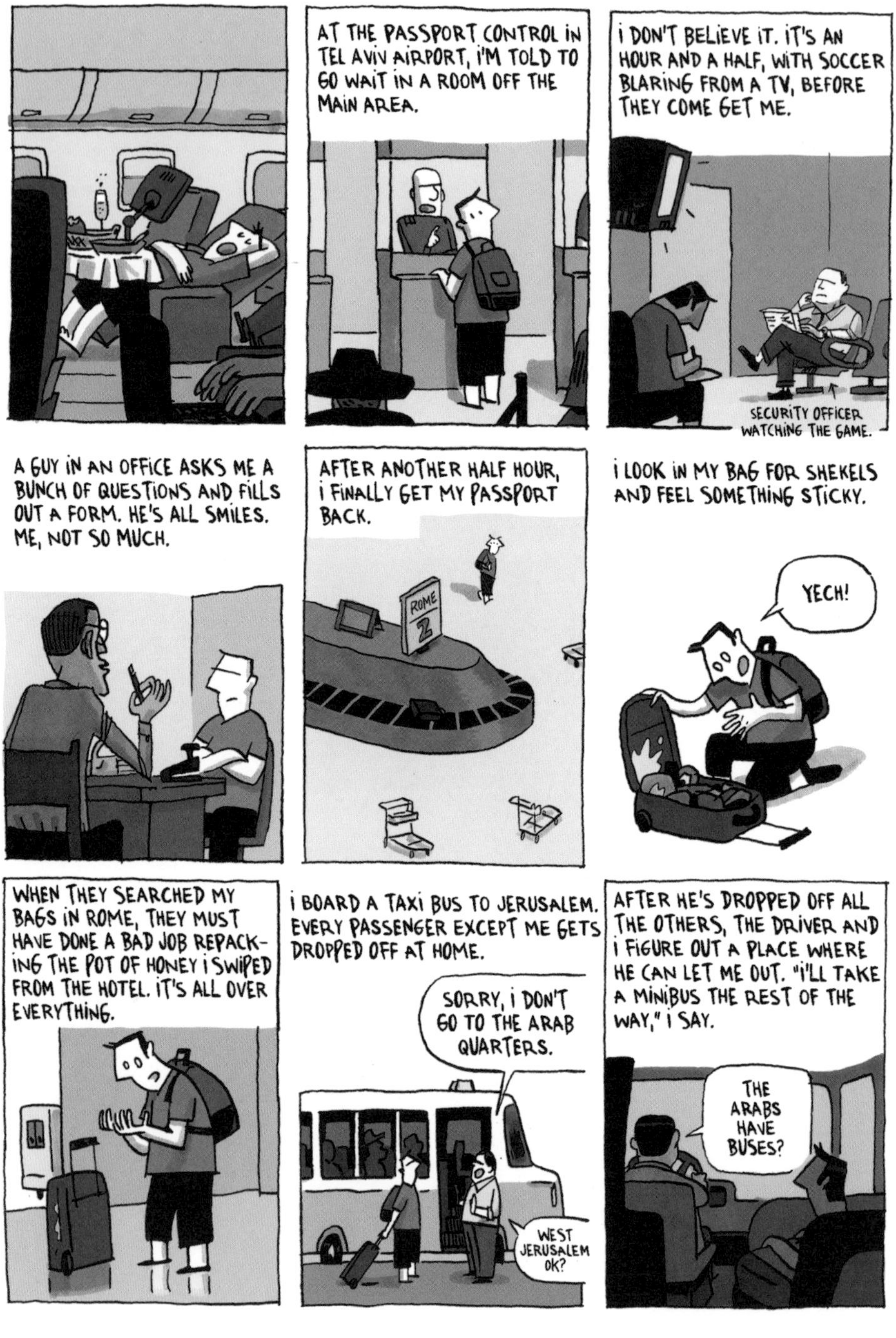
AT THE PASSPORT CONTROL IN TEL AVIV AIRPORT, I'M TOLD TO GO WAIT IN A ROOM OFF THE MAIN AREA.
I DON'T BELIEVE IT. IT'S AN HOUR AND A HALF, WITH SOCCER BLARING FROM A TV, BEFORE THEY COME GET ME.
SECURITY OFFICER WATCHING THE GAME.
A GUY IN AN OFFICE ASKS ME A BUNCH OF QUESTIONS AND FILLS OUT A FORM. HE'S ALL SMILES. ME, NOT SO MUCH.
AFTER ANOTHER HALF HOUR, I FINALLY GET MY PASSPORT BACK.
ROME
2
I LOOK IN MY BAG FOR SHEKELS AND FEEL SOMETHING STICKY.
YECH!
WHEN THEY SEARCHED MY BAGS IN ROME, THEY MUST HAVE DONE A BAD JOB REPACKING THE POT OF HONEY I SWIPED FROM THE HOTEL. IT'S ALL OVER EVERYTHING.
I BOARD A TAXI BUS TO JERUSALEM. EVERY PASSENGER EXCEPT ME GETS DROPPED OFF AT HOME.
SORRY, I DON'T GO TO THE ARAB QUARTERS.
WEST JERUSALEM OK?
AFTER HE'S DROPPED OFF ALL THE OTHERS, THE DRIVER AND I FIGURE OUT A PLACE WHERE HE CAN LET ME OUT. "I'LL TAKE A MINIBUS THE REST OF THE WAY," I SAY.
THE ARABS HAVE BUSES?

NOVEMBER

MONDAY
MORNING

BEFORE WE HAD A CAR I COULD SLEEP IN EVERY MORNING, SINCE I'M NOT AUTHORIZED TO DRIVE MSF VEHICLES.

HOUSEHOLD TRASH

NOW, I'VE GOT THE IMMENSE PRIVILEGE OF TAKING LOUIS TO SCHOOL.

WHICH MEANS PLUNGING FROM OUR NEIGHBOUR-HOOD INTO THE HUGE TRAFFIC JAM CREATED BY SETTLERS COMMUTING TO WORK IN JERUSALEM.

HURRAY.

AND THEN IT'S A GAME OF BUMPER CARS, WITH DRIVERS SWITCHING LANES FOUR TIMES TO MOVE UP A CAR LENGTH OR TWO.

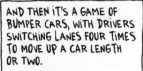

GO AHEAD, PASS. YOU'RE JUST GONNA GET STUCK AGAIN UP AHEAD.

96

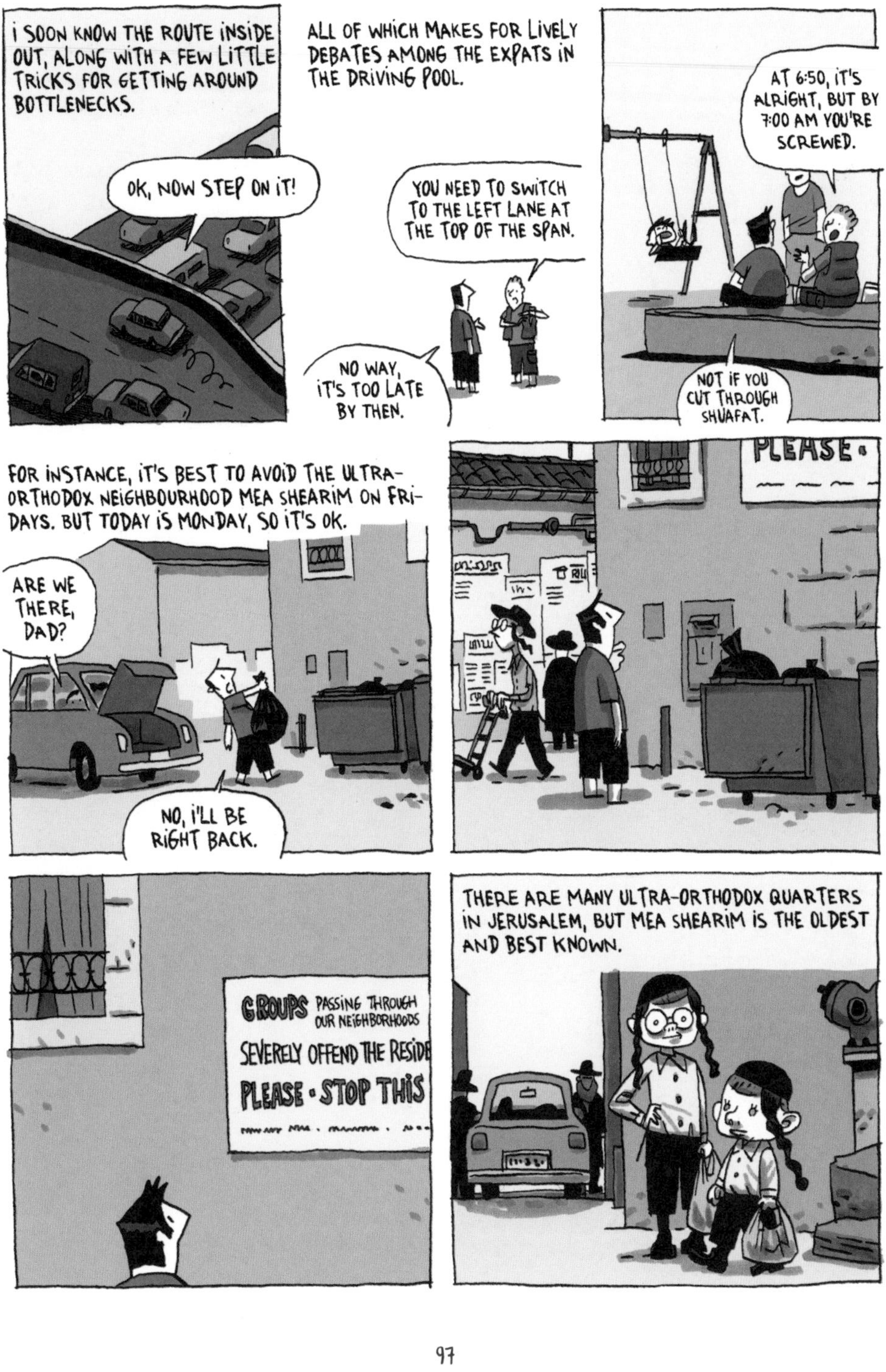
I SOON KNOW THE ROUTE INSIDE OUT, ALONG WITH A FEW LITTLE TRICKS FOR GETTING AROUND BOTTLENECKS.
OK, NOW STEP ON IT!
ALL OF WHICH MAKES FOR LIVELY DEBATES AMONG THE EXPATS IN THE DRIVING POOL.
YOU NEED TO SWITCH TO THE LEFT LANE AT THE TOP OF THE SPAN.
NO WAY, IT'S TOO LATE BY THEN.
AT 6:50, IT'S ALRIGHT, BUT BY 7:00 AM YOU'RE SCREWED.
NOT IF YOU CUT THROUGH SHUAFAT.
FOR INSTANCE, IT'S BEST TO AVOID THE ULTRA-ORTHODOX NEIGHBOURHOOD MEA SHEARIM ON FRIDAYS. BUT TODAY IS MONDAY, SO IT'S OK.
ARE WE THERE, DAD?
NO, I'LL BE RIGHT BACK.
PLEASE
GROUPS PASSING THROUGH OUR NEIGHBORHOODS
SEVERELY OFFEND THE RESIDE
PLEASE • STOP THIS
THERE ARE MANY ULTRA-ORTHODOX QUARTERS IN JERUSALEM, BUT MEA SHEARIM IS THE OLDEST AND BEST KNOWN.

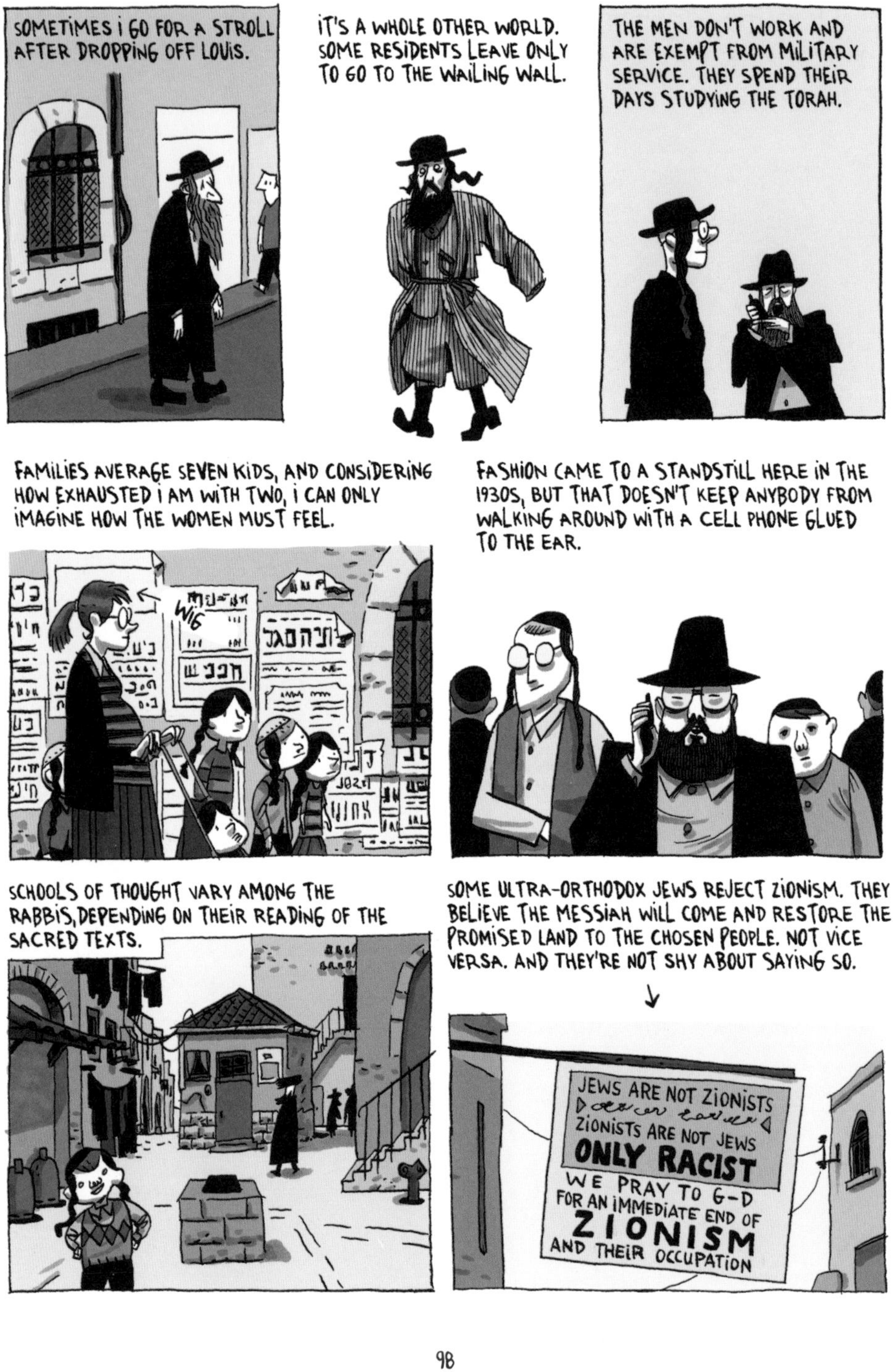
SOMETIMES I GO FOR A STROLL AFTER DROPPING OFF LOUIS.
IT'S A WHOLE OTHER WORLD. SOME RESIDENTS LEAVE ONLY TO GO TO THE WAILING WALL.
THE MEN DON'T WORK AND ARE EXEMPT FROM MILITARY SERVICE. THEY SPEND THEIR DAYS STUDYING THE TORAH.
FAMILIES AVERAGE SEVEN KIDS, AND CONSIDERING HOW EXHAUSTED I AM WITH TWO, I CAN ONLY IMAGINE HOW THE WOMEN MUST FEEL.
WIG
FASHION CAME TO A STANDSTILL HERE IN THE 1930S, BUT THAT DOESN'T KEEP ANYBODY FROM WALKING AROUND WITH A CELL PHONE GLUED TO THE EAR.
SCHOOLS OF THOUGHT VARY AMONG THE RABBIS, DEPENDING ON THEIR READING OF THE SACRED TEXTS.
SOME ULTRA-ORTHODOX JEWS REJECT ZIONISM. THEY BELIEVE THE MESSIAH WILL COME AND RESTORE THE PROMISED LAND TO THE CHOSEN PEOPLE. NOT VICE VERSA. AND THEY'RE NOT SHY ABOUT SAYING SO.
JEWS ARE NOT ZIONISTS
ZIONISTS ARE NOT JEWS
ONLY RACIST
WE PRAY TO G-D
FOR AN IMMEDIATE END OF
ZIONISM
AND THEIR OCCUPATION

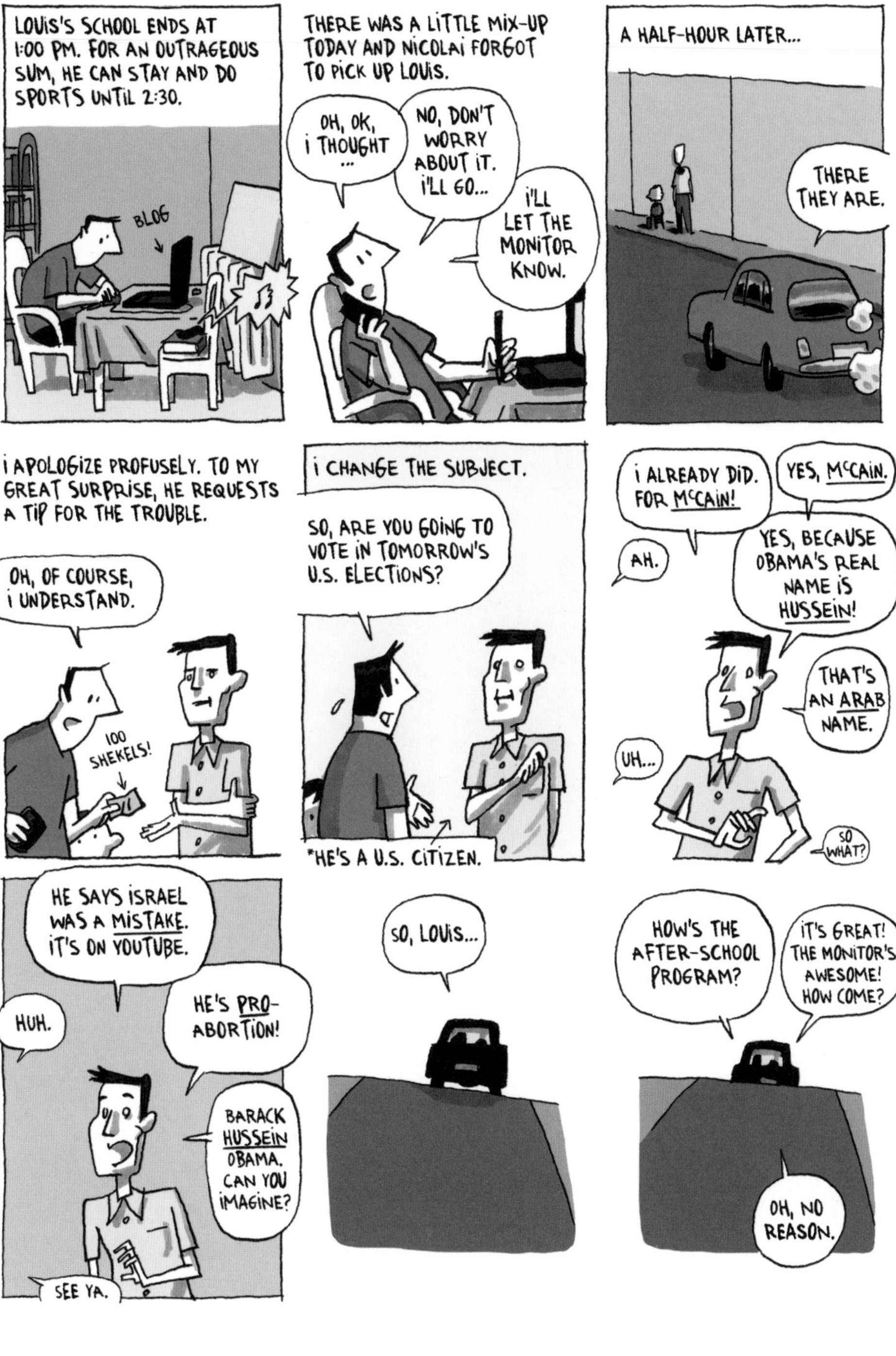
LOUIS'S SCHOOL ENDS AT 1:00 PM. FOR AN OUTRAGEOUS SUM, HE CAN STAY AND DO SPORTS UNTIL 2:30.
BLOG
THERE WAS A LITTLE MIX-UP TODAY AND NICOLAI FORGOT TO PICK UP LOUIS.
OH, OK, I THOUGHT ...
NO, DON'T WORRY ABOUT IT. I'LL GO...
I'LL LET THE MONITOR KNOW.
A HALF-HOUR LATER...
THERE THEY ARE.
I APOLOGIZE PROFUSELY. TO MY GREAT SURPRISE, HE REQUESTS A TIP FOR THE TROUBLE.
OH, OF COURSE, I UNDERSTAND.
100 SHEKELS!
I CHANGE THE SUBJECT.
SO, ARE YOU GOING TO VOTE IN TOMORROW'S U.S. ELECTIONS?
*HE'S A U.S. CITIZEN.
I ALREADY DID. FOR McCAIN!
YES, McCAIN.
AH.
YES, BECAUSE OBAMA'S REAL NAME IS HUSSEIN!
THAT'S AN ARAB NAME.
UH...
SO WHAT?
HE SAYS ISRAEL WAS A MISTAKE. IT'S ON YOUTUBE.
HUH.
HE'S PRO-ABORTION!
BARACK HUSSEIN OBAMA. CAN YOU IMAGINE?
SEE YA.
SO, LOUIS...
HOW'S THE AFTER-SCHOOL PROGRAM?
IT'S GREAT! THE MONITOR'S AWESOME! HOW COME?
OH, NO REASON.

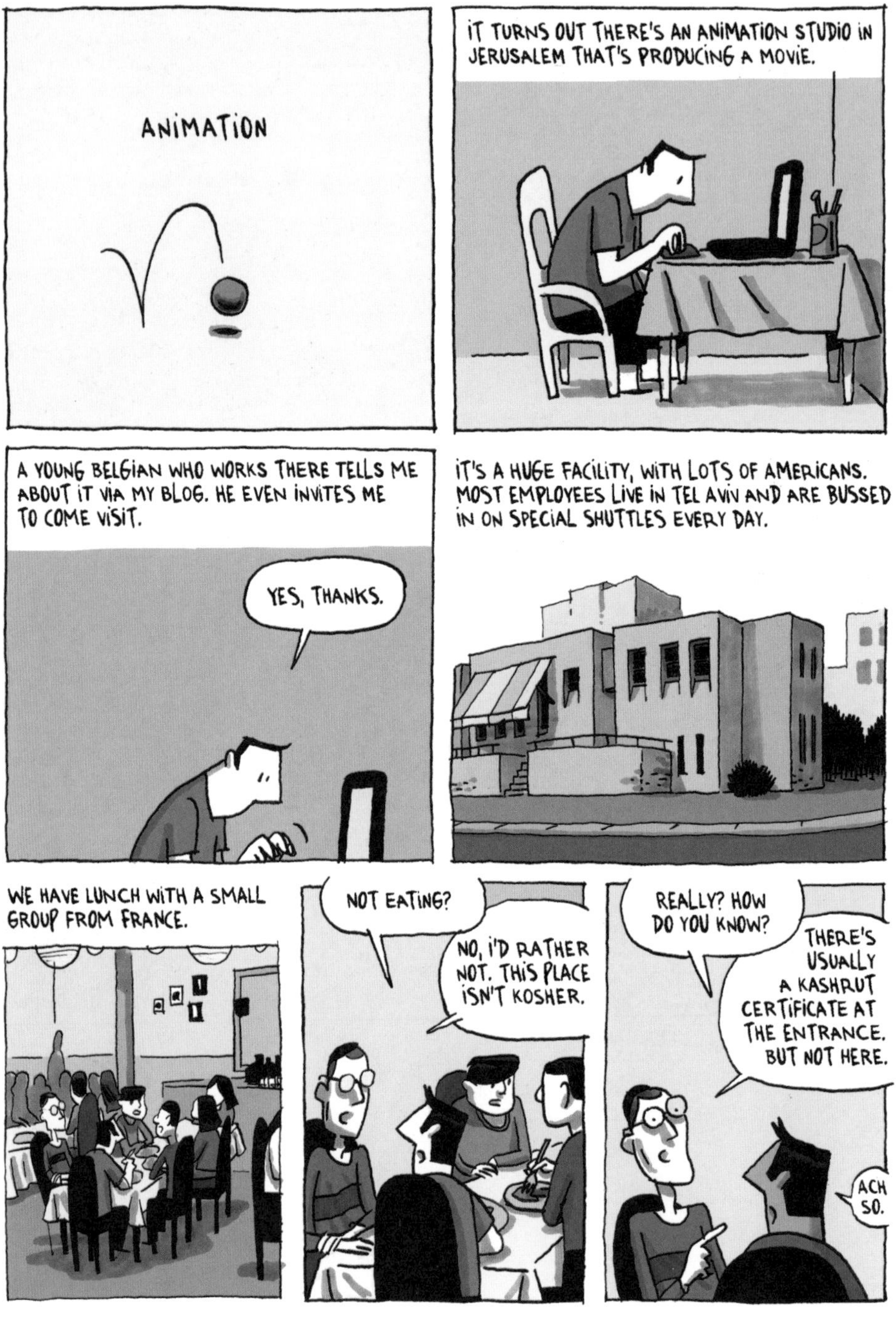
ANIMATION
IT TURNS OUT THERE'S AN ANIMATION STUDIO IN JERUSALEM THAT'S PRODUCING A MOVIE.
A YOUNG BELGIAN WHO WORKS THERE TELLS ME ABOUT IT VIA MY BLOG. HE EVEN INVITES ME TO COME VISIT.
YES, THANKS.
IT'S A HUGE FACILITY, WITH LOTS OF AMERICANS. MOST EMPLOYEES LIVE IN TEL AVIV AND ARE BUSSED IN ON SPECIAL SHUTTLES EVERY DAY.
WE HAVE LUNCH WITH A SMALL GROUP FROM FRANCE.
NOT EATING?
NO, I'D RATHER NOT. THIS PLACE ISN'T KOSHER.
REALLY? HOW DO YOU KNOW?
THERE'S USUALLY A KASHRUT CERTIFICATE AT THE ENTRANCE. BUT NOT HERE.
ACH SO.

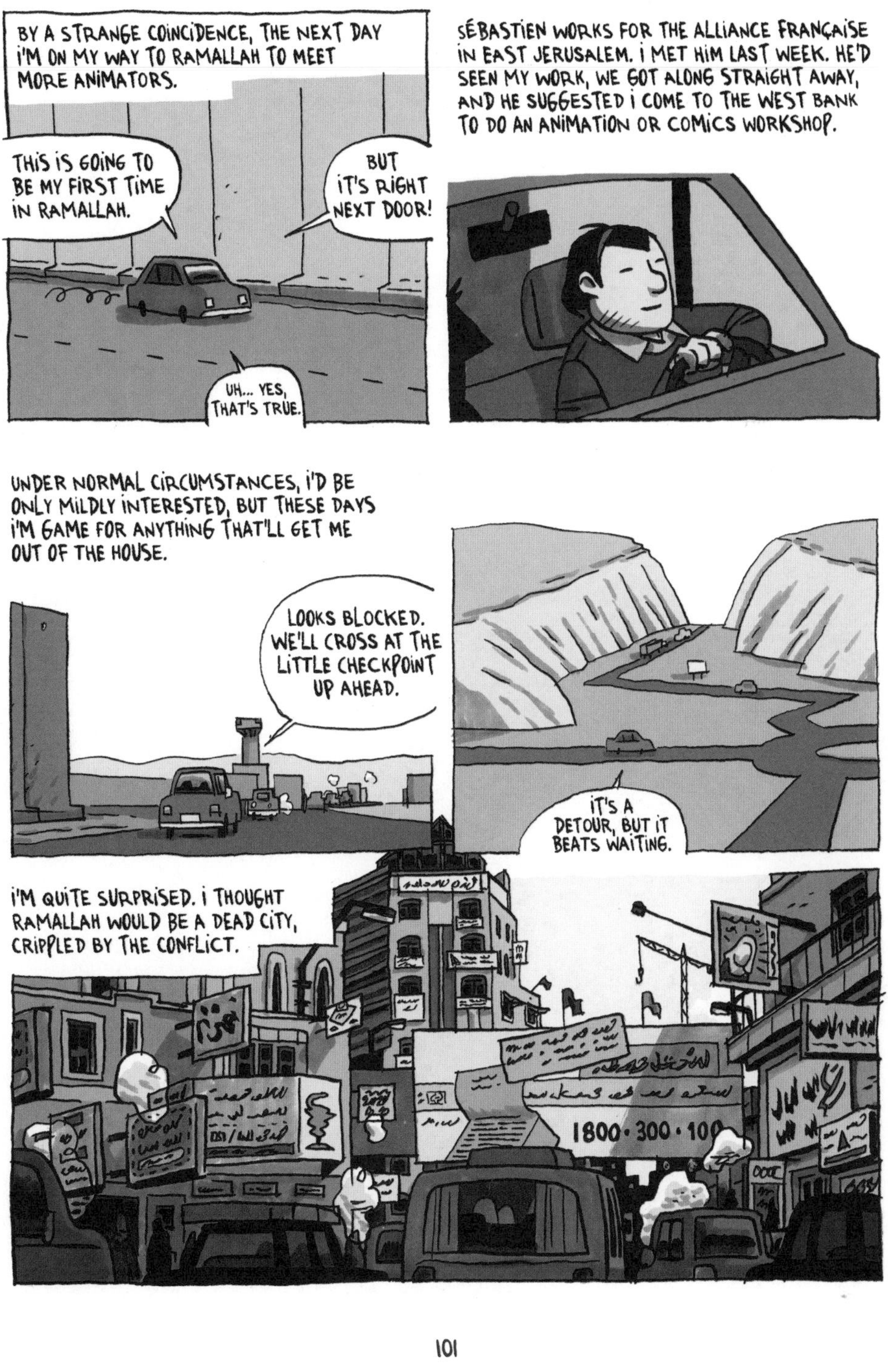
BY A STRANGE COINCIDENCE, THE NEXT DAY I'M ON MY WAY TO RAMALLAH TO MEET MORE ANIMATORS.
THIS IS GOING TO BE MY FIRST TIME IN RAMALLAH.
BUT IT'S RIGHT NEXT DOOR!
UH... YES, THAT'S TRUE.
SÉBASTIEN WORKS FOR THE ALLIANCE FRANÇAISE IN EAST JERUSALEM. I MET HIM LAST WEEK. HE'D SEEN MY WORK, WE GOT ALONG STRAIGHT AWAY, AND HE SUGGESTED I COME TO THE WEST BANK TO DO AN ANIMATION OR COMICS WORKSHOP.
UNDER NORMAL CIRCUMSTANCES, I'D BE ONLY MILDLY INTERESTED, BUT THESE DAYS I'M GAME FOR ANYTHING THAT'LL GET ME OUT OF THE HOUSE.
LOOKS BLOCKED. WE'LL CROSS AT THE LITTLE CHECKPOINT UP AHEAD.
IT'S A DETOUR, BUT IT BEATS WAITING.
I'M QUITE SURPRISED. I THOUGHT RAMALLAH WOULD BE A DEAD CITY, CRIPPLED BY THE CONFLICT.
1800·300·100

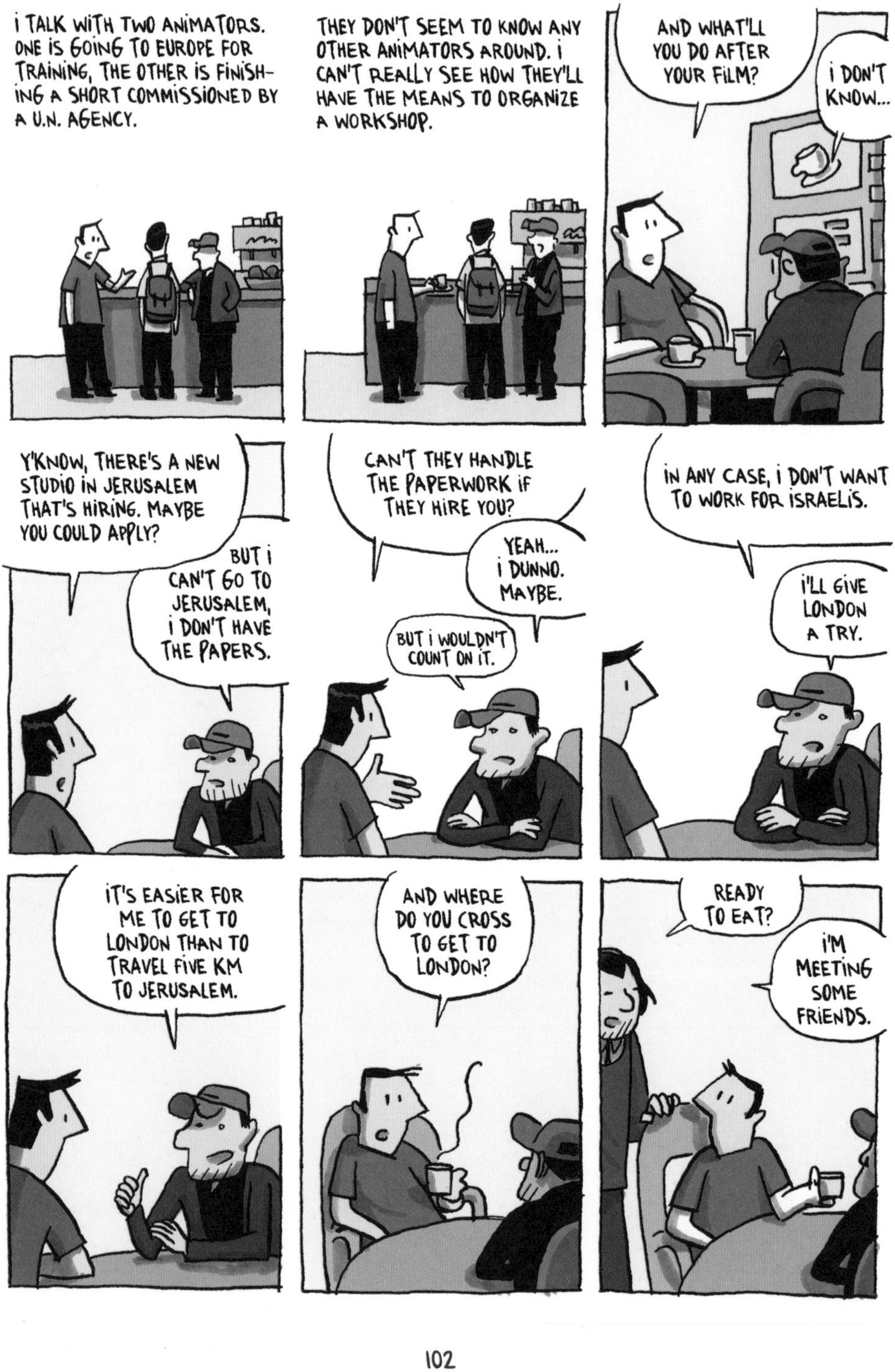
I TALK WITH TWO ANIMATORS. ONE IS GOING TO EUROPE FOR TRAINING, THE OTHER IS FINISHING A SHORT COMMISSIONED BY A U.N. AGENCY.
THEY DON'T SEEM TO KNOW ANY OTHER ANIMATORS AROUND. I CAN'T REALLY SEE HOW THEY'LL HAVE THE MEANS TO ORGANIZE A WORKSHOP.
AND WHAT'LL YOU DO AFTER YOUR FILM?
I DON'T KNOW...
Y'KNOW, THERE'S A NEW STUDIO IN JERUSALEM THAT'S HIRING. MAYBE YOU COULD APPLY?
BUT I CAN'T GO TO JERUSALEM, I DON'T HAVE THE PAPERS.
CAN'T THEY HANDLE THE PAPERWORK IF THEY HIRE YOU?
YEAH... I DUNNO. MAYBE.
BUT I WOULDN'T COUNT ON IT.
IN ANY CASE, I DON'T WANT TO WORK FOR ISRAELIS.
I'LL GIVE LONDON A TRY.
IT'S EASIER FOR ME TO GET TO LONDON THAN TO TRAVEL FIVE KM TO JERUSALEM.
AND WHERE DO YOU CROSS TO GET TO LONDON?
READY TO EAT?
I'M MEETING SOME FRIENDS.

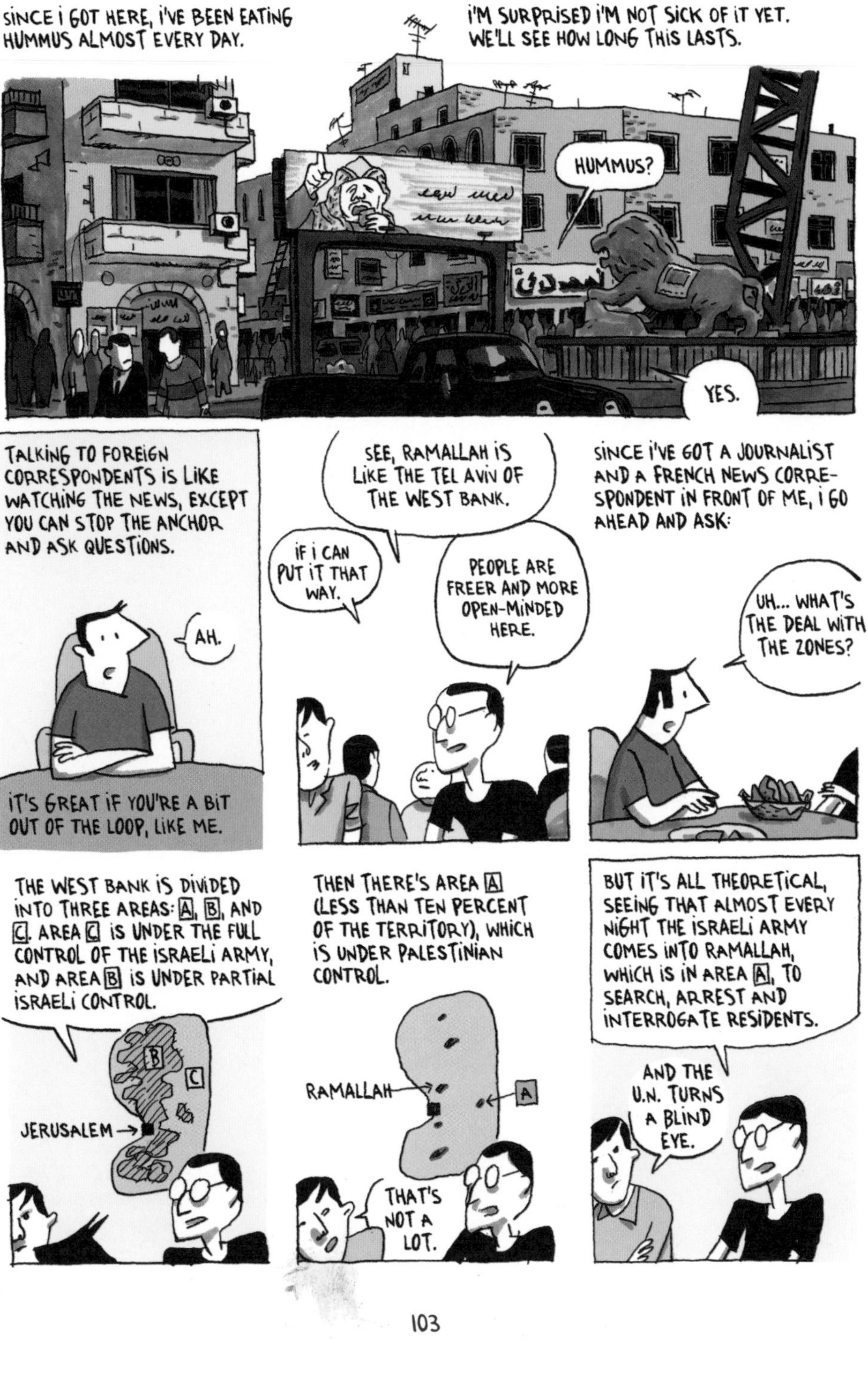

SINCE I GOT HERE, I'VE BEEN EATING HUMMUS ALMOST EVERY DAY.
I'M SURPRISED I'M NOT SICK OF IT YET. WE'LL SEE HOW LONG THIS LASTS.
HUMMUS?
YES.
TALKING TO FOREIGN CORRESPONDENTS IS LIKE WATCHING THE NEWS, EXCEPT YOU CAN STOP THE ANCHOR AND ASK QUESTIONS.
AH.
IT'S GREAT IF YOU'RE A BIT OUT OF THE LOOP, LIKE ME.
SEE, RAMALLAH IS LIKE THE TEL AVIV OF THE WEST BANK.
IF I CAN PUT IT THAT WAY.
PEOPLE ARE FREER AND MORE OPEN-MINDED HERE.
SINCE I'VE GOT A JOURNALIST AND A FRENCH NEWS CORRESPONDENT IN FRONT OF ME, I GO AHEAD AND ASK:
UH... WHAT'S THE DEAL WITH THE ZONES?
THE WEST BANK IS DIVIDED INTO THREE AREAS: A, B, AND C. AREA C IS UNDER THE FULL CONTROL OF THE ISRAELI ARMY, AND AREA B IS UNDER PARTIAL ISRAELI CONTROL.
B
C
JERUSALEM
THEN THERE'S AREA A (LESS THAN TEN PERCENT OF THE TERRITORY), WHICH IS UNDER PALESTINIAN CONTROL.
RAMALLAH
A
THAT'S NOT A LOT.
BUT IT'S ALL THEORETICAL, SEEING THAT ALMOST EVERY NIGHT THE ISRAELI ARMY COMES INTO RAMALLAH, WHICH IS IN AREA A, TO SEARCH, ARREST AND INTERROGATE RESIDENTS.
AND THE U.N. TURNS A BLIND EYE.

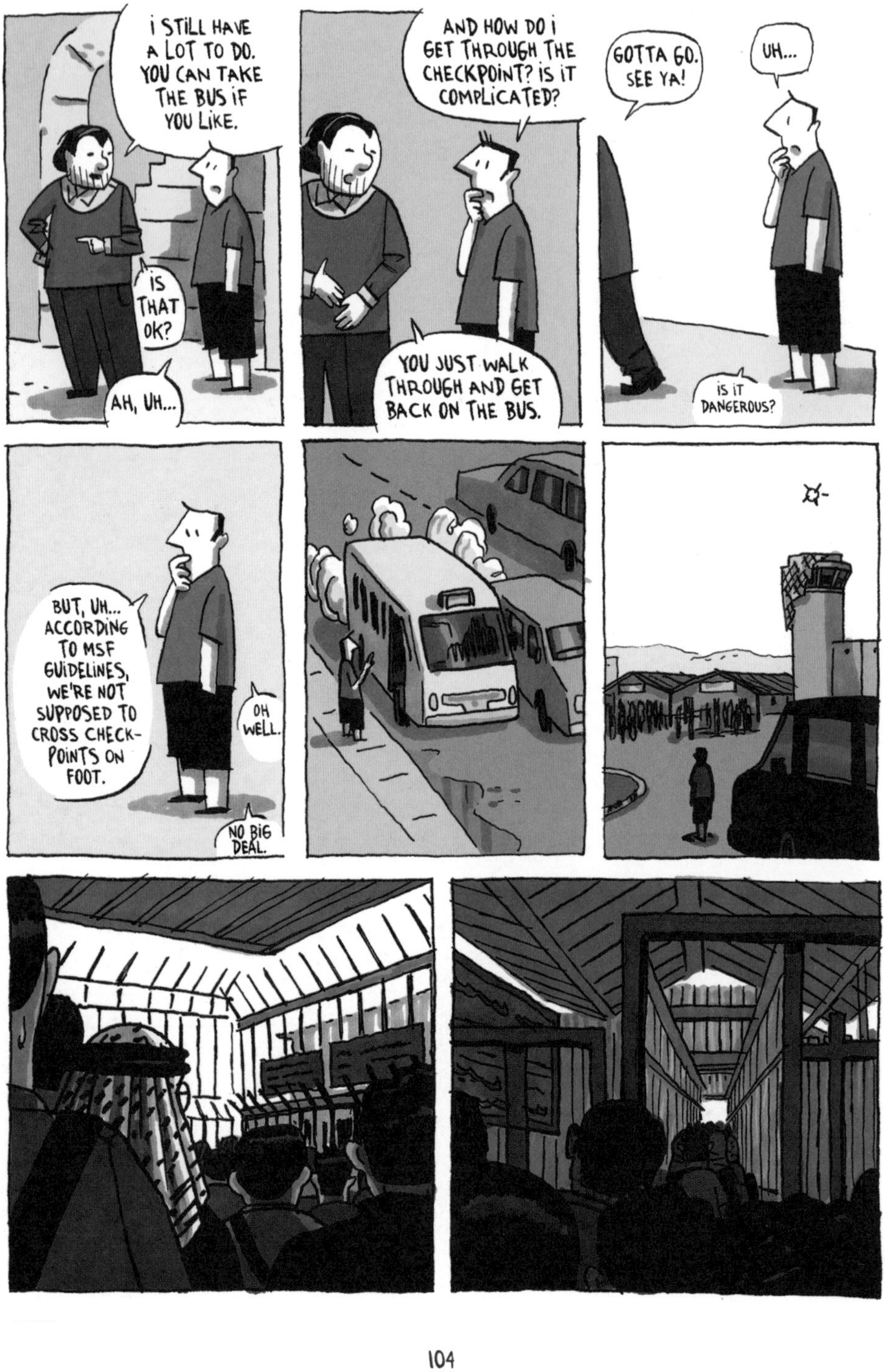
I STILL HAVE A LOT TO DO. YOU CAN TAKE THE BUS IF YOU LIKE.
IS THAT OK?
AH, UH...
AND HOW DO I GET THROUGH THE CHECKPOINT? IS IT COMPLICATED?
YOU JUST WALK THROUGH AND GET BACK ON THE BUS.
GOTTA GO. SEE YA!
UH...
IS IT DANGEROUS?
BUT, UH... ACCORDING TO MSF GUIDELINES, WE'RE NOT SUPPOSED TO CROSS CHECK-POINTS ON FOOT.
OH WELL.
NO BIG DEAL.

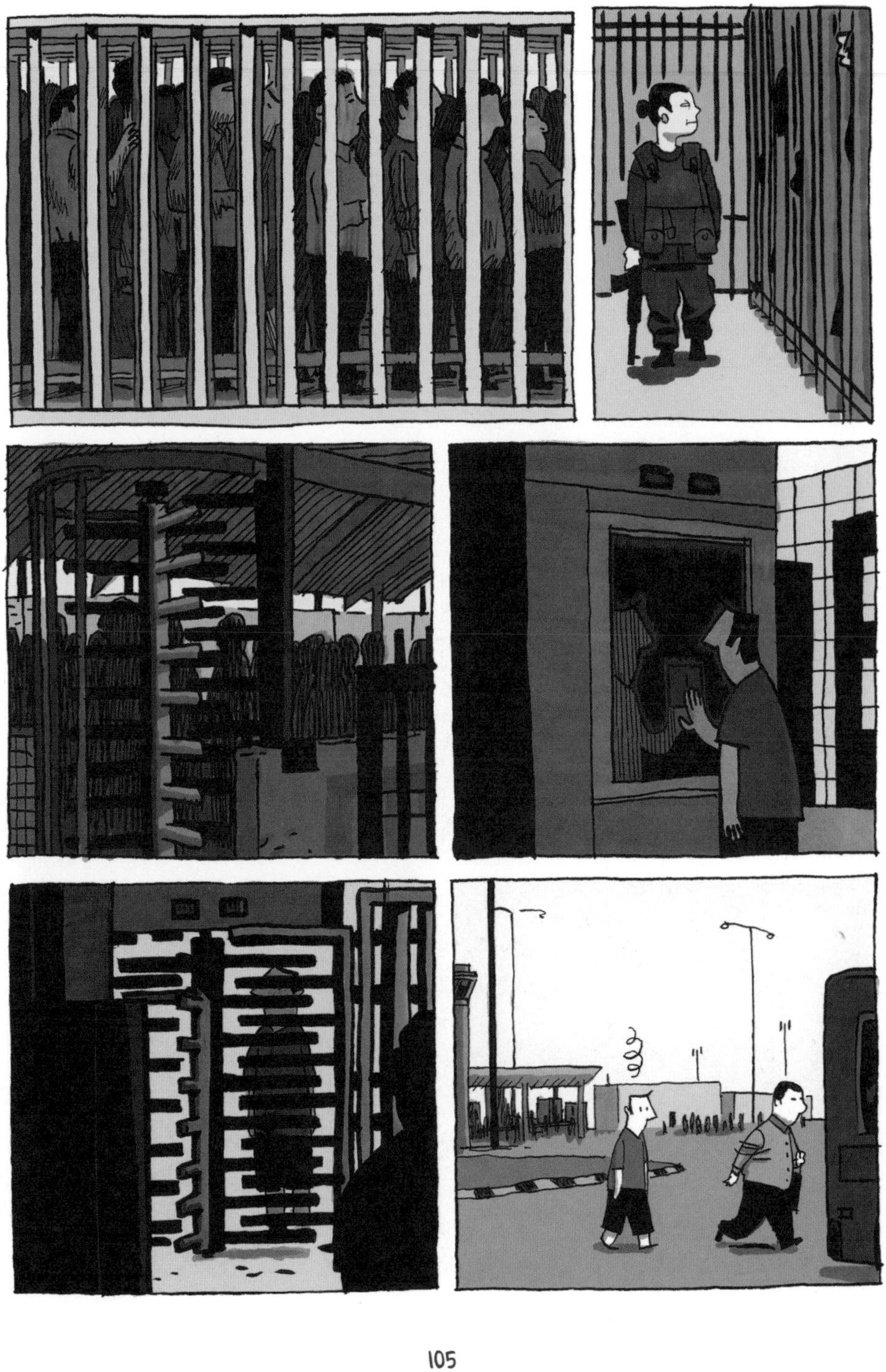

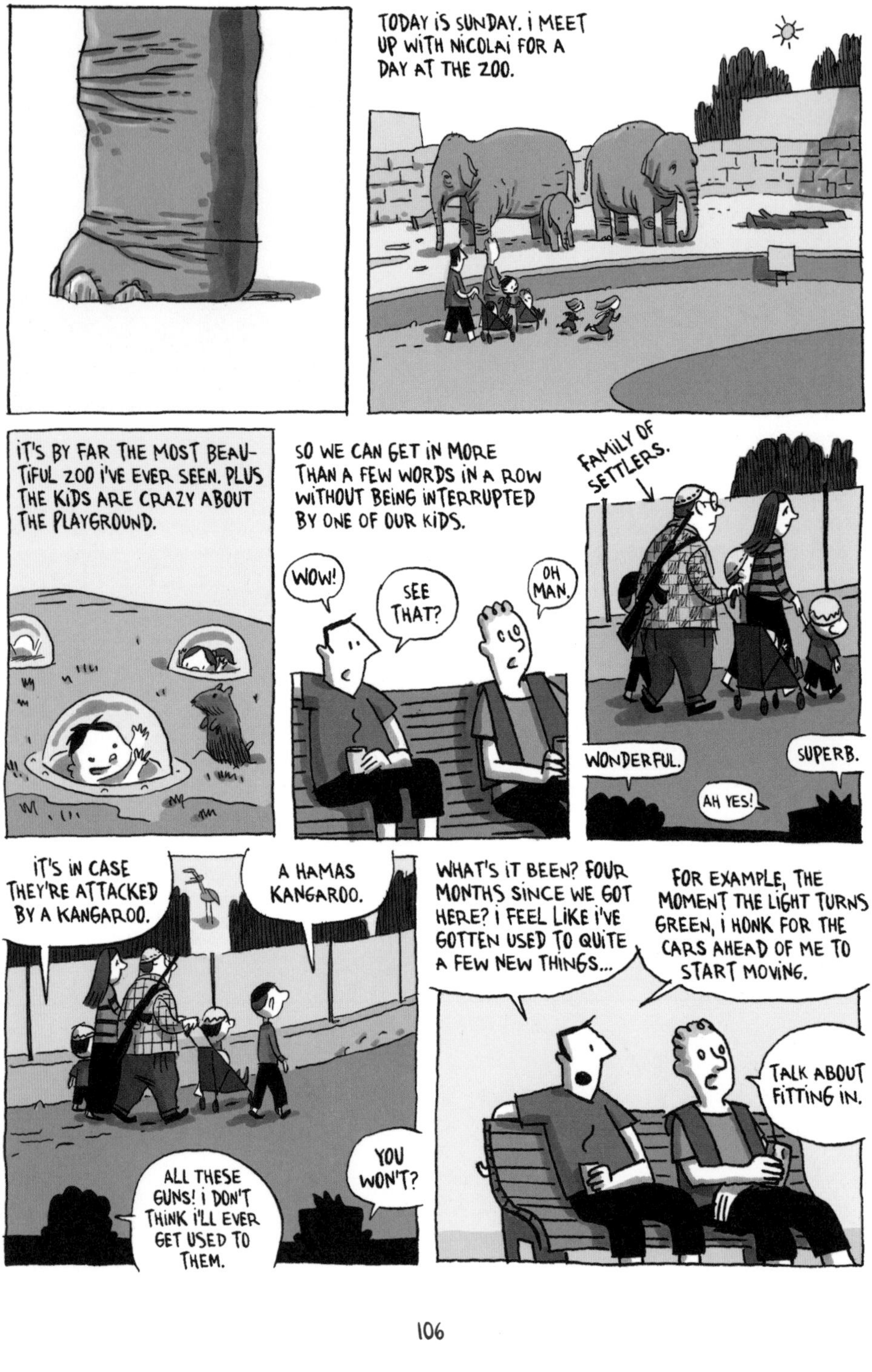
TODAY IS SUNDAY. I MEET UP WITH NICOLAI FOR A DAY AT THE ZOO.
IT'S BY FAR THE MOST BEAUTIFUL ZOO I'VE EVER SEEN. PLUS THE KIDS ARE CRAZY ABOUT THE PLAYGROUND.
SO WE CAN GET IN MORE THAN A FEW WORDS IN A ROW WITHOUT BEING INTERRUPTED BY ONE OF OUR KIDS.
WOW!
SEE THAT?
OH MAN.
FAMILY OF SETTLERS.
WONDERFUL.
AH YES!
SUPERB.
IT'S IN CASE THEY'RE ATTACKED BY A KANGAROO.
A HAMAS KANGAROO.
ALL THESE GUNS! I DON'T THINK I'LL EVER GET USED TO THEM.
YOU WON'T?
WHAT'S IT BEEN? FOUR MONTHS SINCE WE GOT HERE? I FEEL LIKE I'VE GOTTEN USED TO QUITE A FEW NEW THINGS...
FOR EXAMPLE, THE MOMENT THE LIGHT TURNS GREEN, I HONK FOR THE CARS AHEAD OF ME TO START MOVING.
TALK ABOUT FITTING IN.

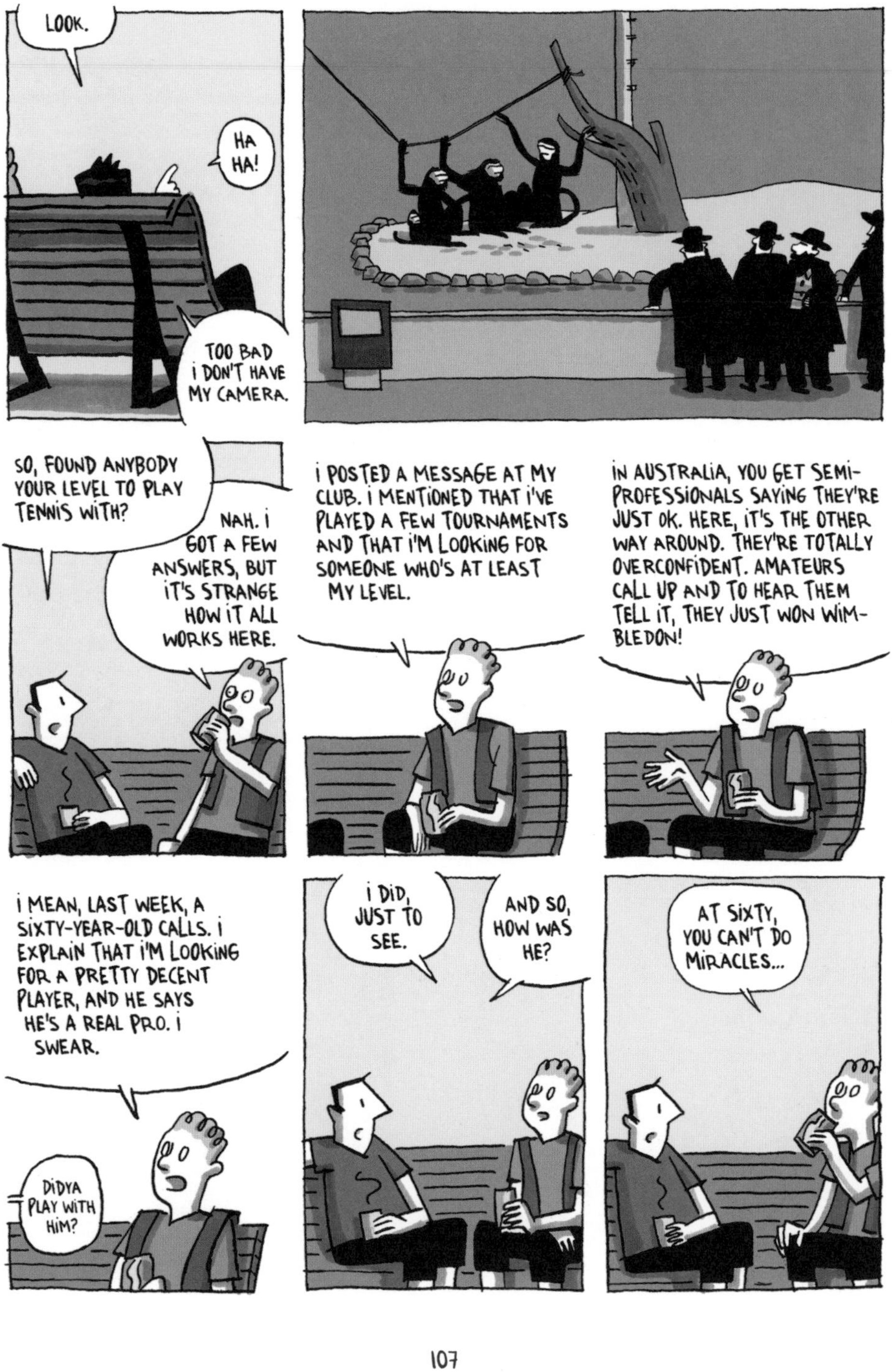
LOOK.
HA HA!
TOO BAD I DON'T HAVE MY CAMERA.
SO, FOUND ANYBODY YOUR LEVEL TO PLAY TENNIS WITH?
NAH. I GOT A FEW ANSWERS, BUT IT'S STRANGE HOW IT ALL WORKS HERE.
I POSTED A MESSAGE AT MY CLUB. I MENTIONED THAT I'VE PLAYED A FEW TOURNAMENTS AND THAT I'M LOOKING FOR SOMEONE WHO'S AT LEAST MY LEVEL.
IN AUSTRALIA, YOU GET SEMI-PROFESSIONALS SAYING THEY'RE JUST OK. HERE, IT'S THE OTHER WAY AROUND. THEY'RE TOTALLY OVERCONFIDENT. AMATEURS CALL UP AND TO HEAR THEM TELL IT, THEY JUST WON WIMBLEDON!
I MEAN, LAST WEEK, A SIXTY-YEAR-OLD CALLS. I EXPLAIN THAT I'M LOOKING FOR A PRETTY DECENT PLAYER, AND HE SAYS HE'S A REAL PRO. I SWEAR.
DIDYA PLAY WITH HIM?
I DID, JUST TO SEE.
AND SO, HOW WAS HE?
AT SIXTY, YOU CAN'T DO MIRACLES...

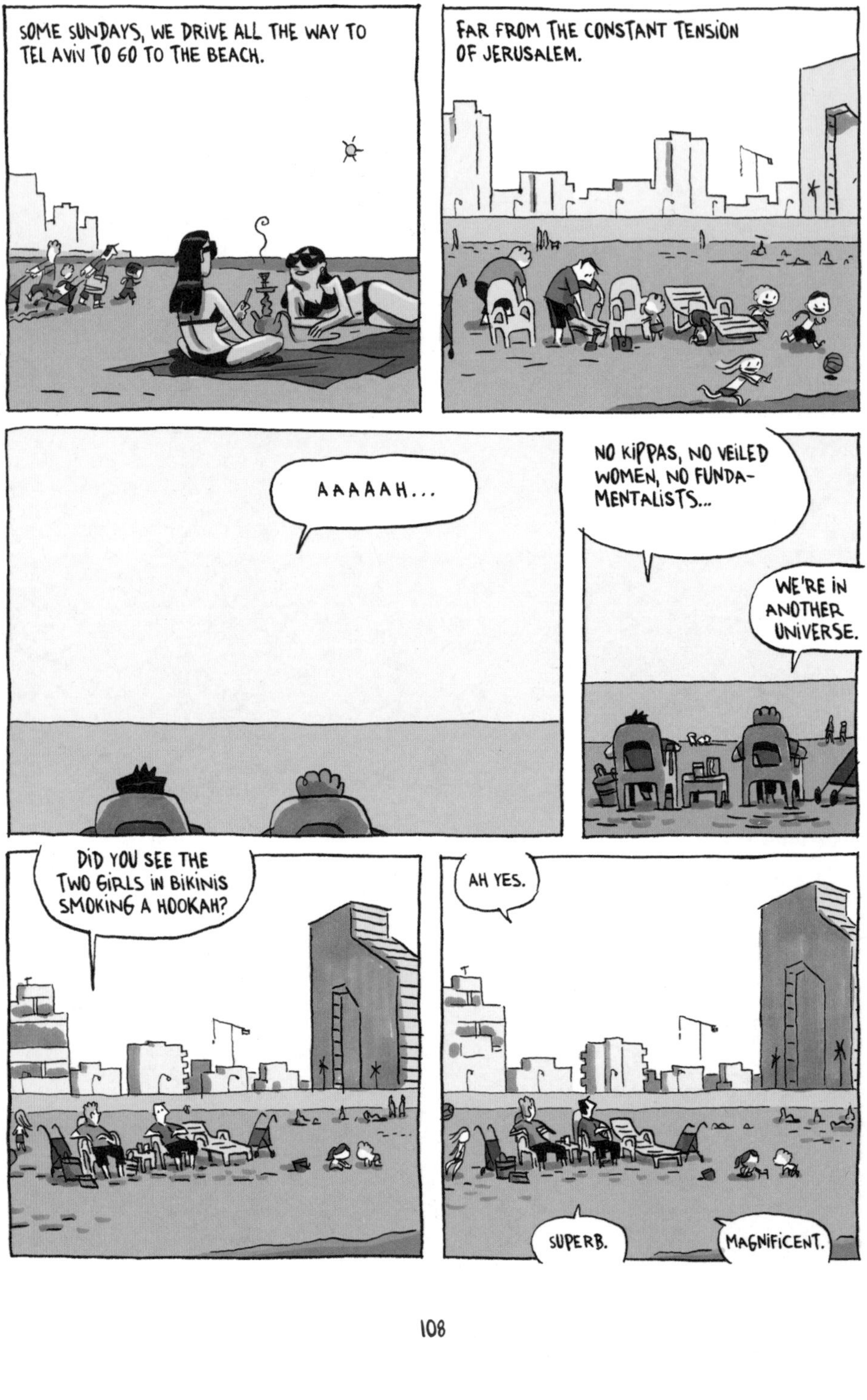
SOME SUNDAYS, WE DRIVE ALL THE WAY TO TEL AVIV TO GO TO THE BEACH.
FAR FROM THE CONSTANT TENSION OF JERUSALEM.
AAAAAH...
NO KIPPAS, NO VEILED WOMEN, NO FUNDA-MENTALISTS...
WE'RE IN ANOTHER UNIVERSE.
DID YOU SEE THE TWO GIRLS IN BIKINIS SMOKING A HOOKAH?
AH YES.
SUPERB.
MAGNIFICENT.

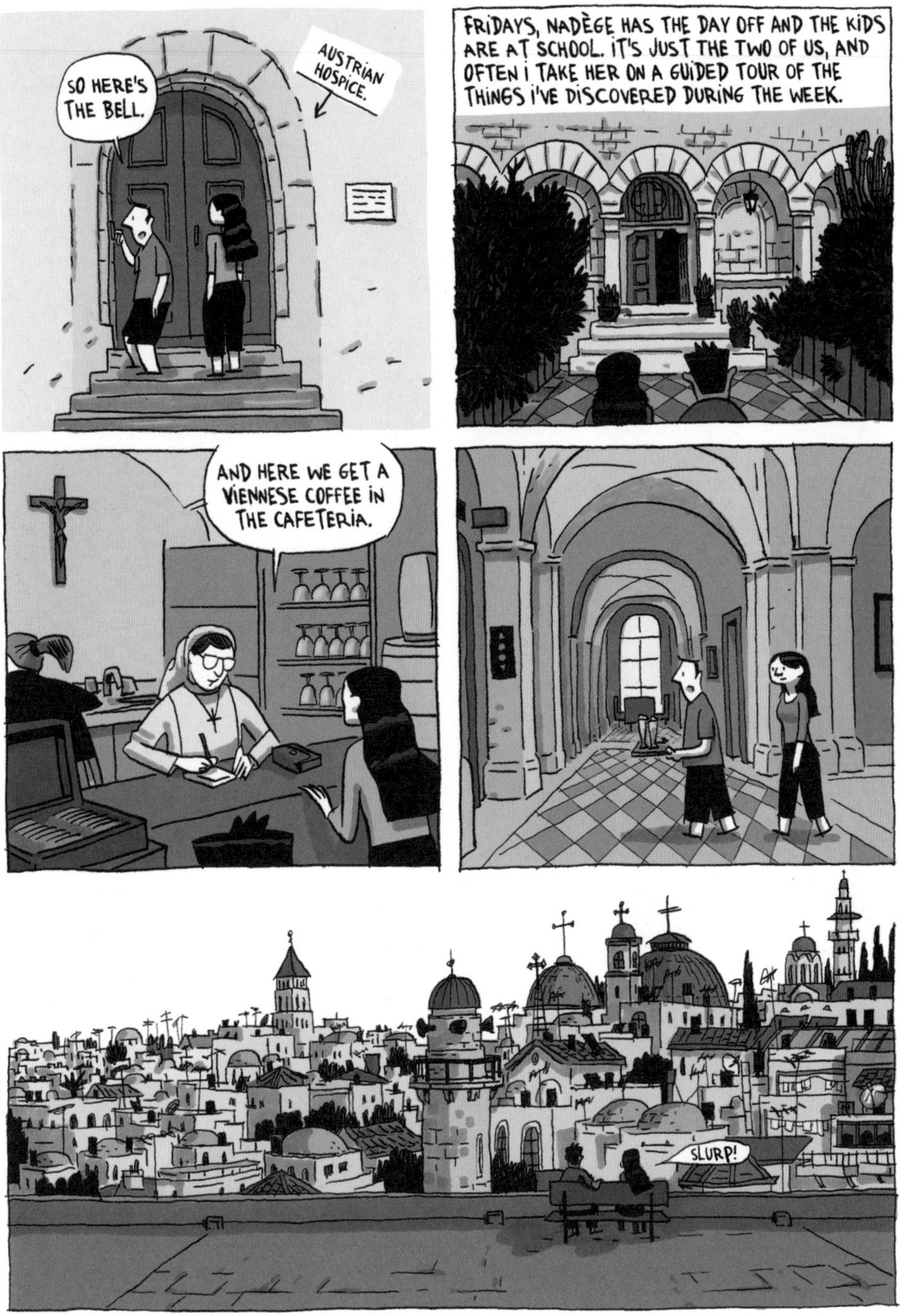
SO HERE'S THE BELL.
AUSTRIAN HOSPICE.
FRIDAYS, NADÈGE HAS THE DAY OFF AND THE KIDS ARE AT SCHOOL. IT'S JUST THE TWO OF US, AND OFTEN I TAKE HER ON A GUIDED TOUR OF THE THINGS I'VE DISCOVERED DURING THE WEEK.
AND HERE WE GET A VIENNESE COFFEE IN THE CAFETERIA.
SLURP!

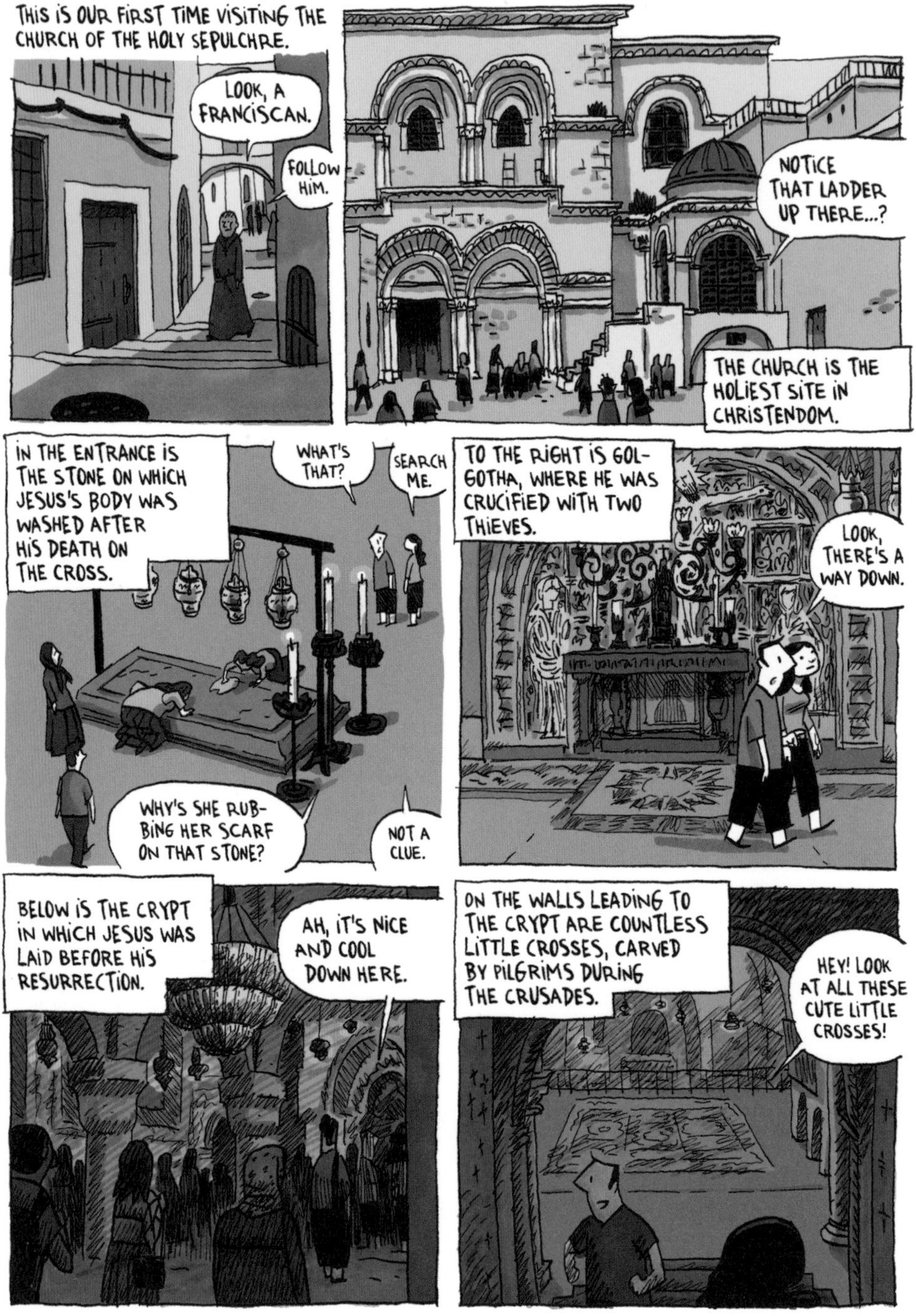
THIS IS OUR FIRST TIME VISITING THE CHURCH OF THE HOLY SEPULCHRE.
LOOK, A FRANCISCAN.
FOLLOW HIM.
NOTICE THAT LADDER UP THERE...?
THE CHURCH IS THE HOLIEST SITE IN CHRISTENDOM.
IN THE ENTRANCE IS THE STONE ON WHICH JESUS'S BODY WAS WASHED AFTER HIS DEATH ON THE CROSS.
WHAT'S THAT?
SEARCH ME.
WHY'S SHE RUBBING HER SCARF ON THAT STONE?
NOT A CLUE.
TO THE RIGHT IS GOLGOTHA, WHERE HE WAS CRUCIFIED WITH TWO THIEVES.
LOOK, THERE'S A WAY DOWN.
BELOW IS THE CRYPT IN WHICH JESUS WAS LAID BEFORE HIS RESURRECTION.
AH, IT'S NICE AND COOL DOWN HERE.
ON THE WALLS LEADING TO THE CRYPT ARE COUNTLESS LITTLE CROSSES, CARVED BY PILGRIMS DURING THE CRUSADES.
HEY! LOOK AT ALL THESE CUTE LITTLE CROSSES!

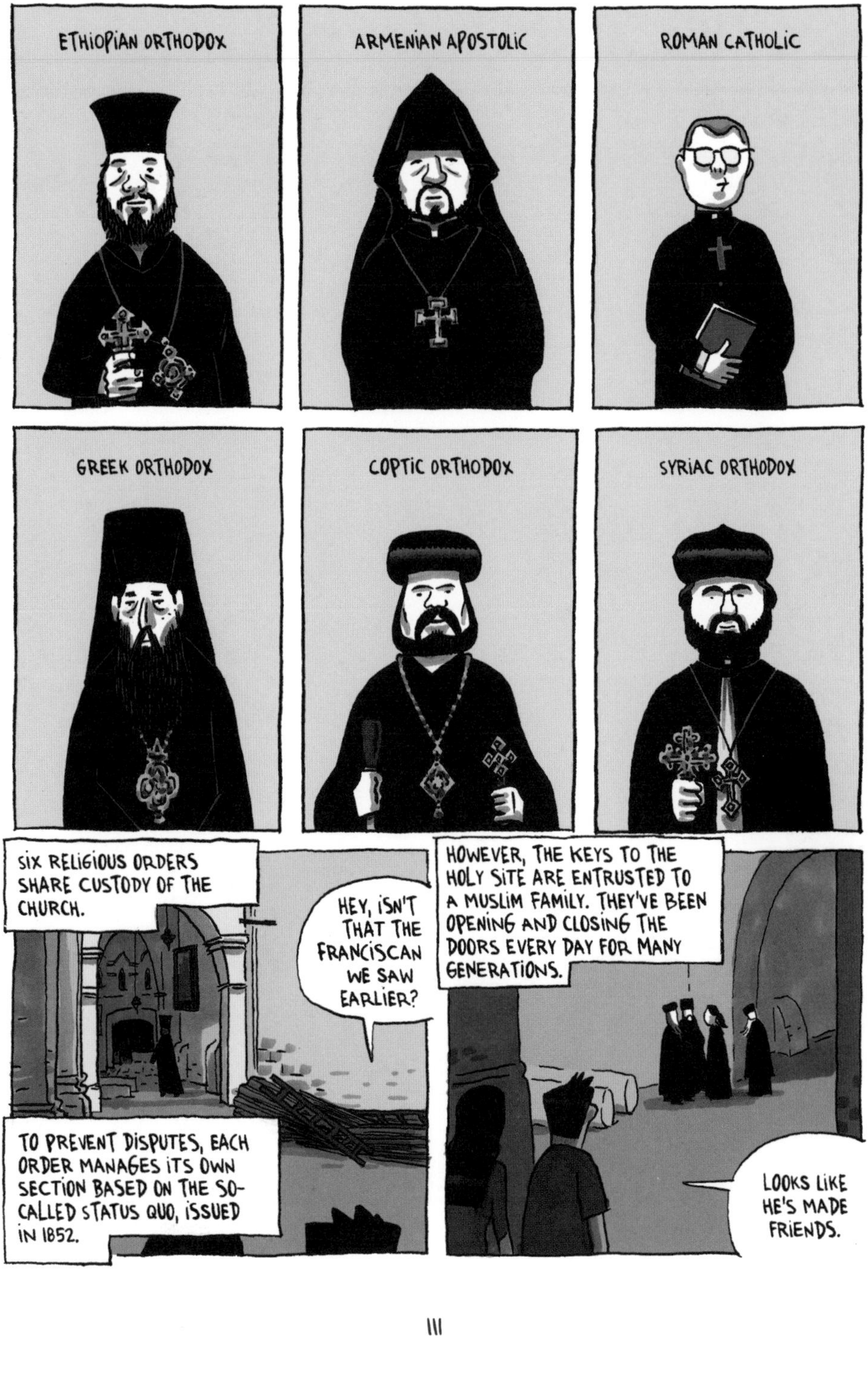

ETHIOPIAN ORTHODOX
ARMENIAN APOSTOLIC
ROMAN CATHOLIC
GREEK ORTHODOX
COPTIC ORTHODOX
SYRIAC ORTHODOX
SIX RELIGIOUS ORDERS SHARE CUSTODY OF THE CHURCH.
TO PREVENT DISPUTES, EACH ORDER MANAGES ITS OWN SECTION BASED ON THE SO-CALLED STATUS QUO, ISSUED IN 1852.
HEY, ISN'T THAT THE FRANCISCAN WE SAW EARLIER?
HOWEVER, THE KEYS TO THE HOLY SITE ARE ENTRUSTED TO A MUSLIM FAMILY. THEY'VE BEEN OPENING AND CLOSING THE DOORS EVERY DAY FOR MANY GENERATIONS.
LOOKS LIKE HE'S MADE FRIENDS.

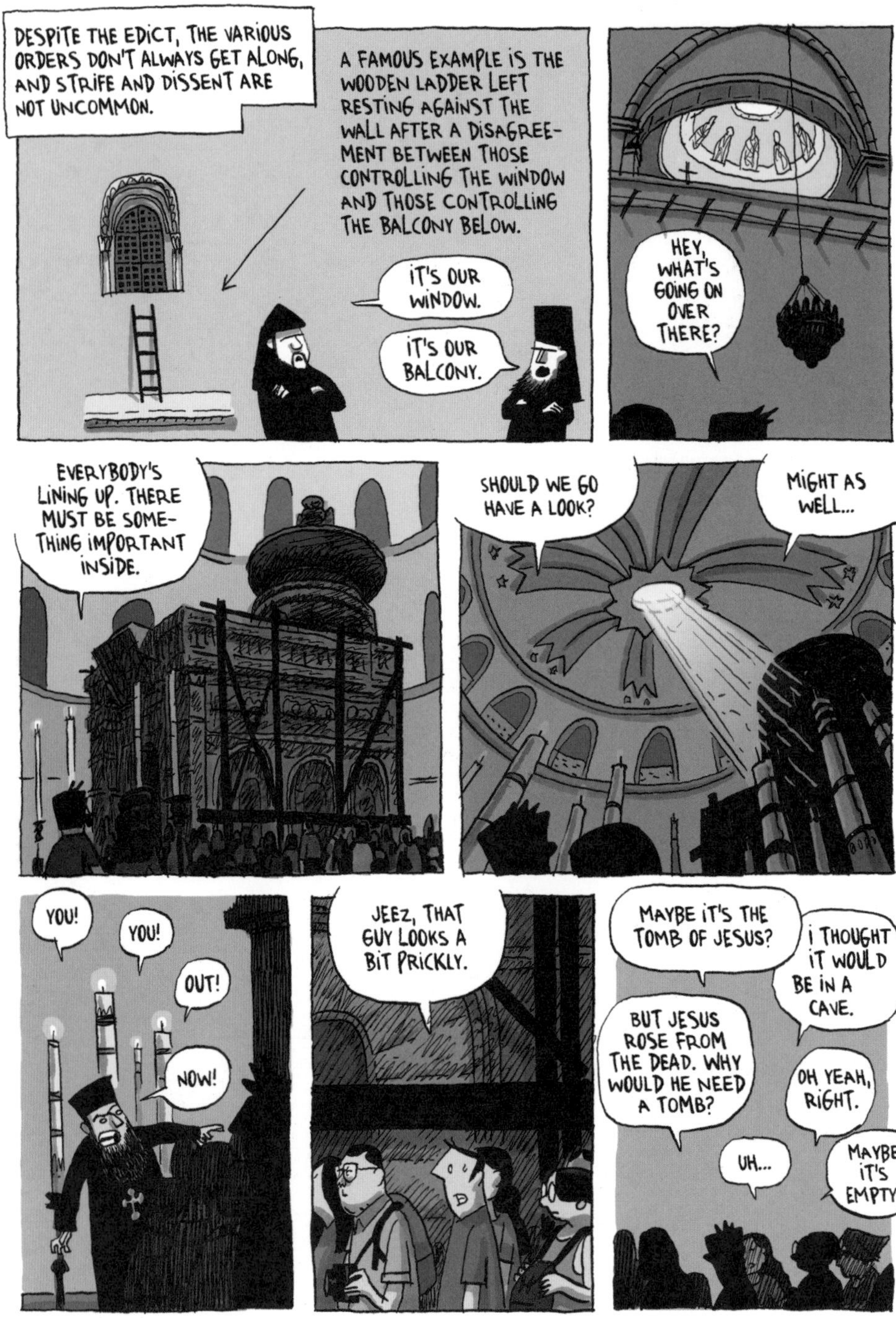
DESPITE THE EDICT, THE VARIOUS ORDERS DON'T ALWAYS GET ALONG, AND STRIFE AND DISSENT ARE NOT UNCOMMON.
A FAMOUS EXAMPLE IS THE WOODEN LADDER LEFT RESTING AGAINST THE WALL AFTER A DISAGREEMENT BETWEEN THOSE CONTROLLING THE WINDOW AND THOSE CONTROLLING THE BALCONY BELOW.
IT'S OUR WINDOW.
IT'S OUR BALCONY.
HEY, WHAT'S GOING ON OVER THERE?
EVERYBODY'S LINING UP. THERE MUST BE SOMETHING IMPORTANT INSIDE.
SHOULD WE GO HAVE A LOOK?
MIGHT AS WELL...
YOU!
YOU!
OUT!
NOW!
JEEZ, THAT GUY LOOKS A BIT PRICKLY.
MAYBE IT'S THE TOMB OF JESUS?
I THOUGHT IT WOULD BE IN A CAVE.
BUT JESUS ROSE FROM THE DEAD. WHY WOULD HE NEED A TOMB?
OH YEAH, RIGHT.
UH...
MAYBE IT'S EMPTY?

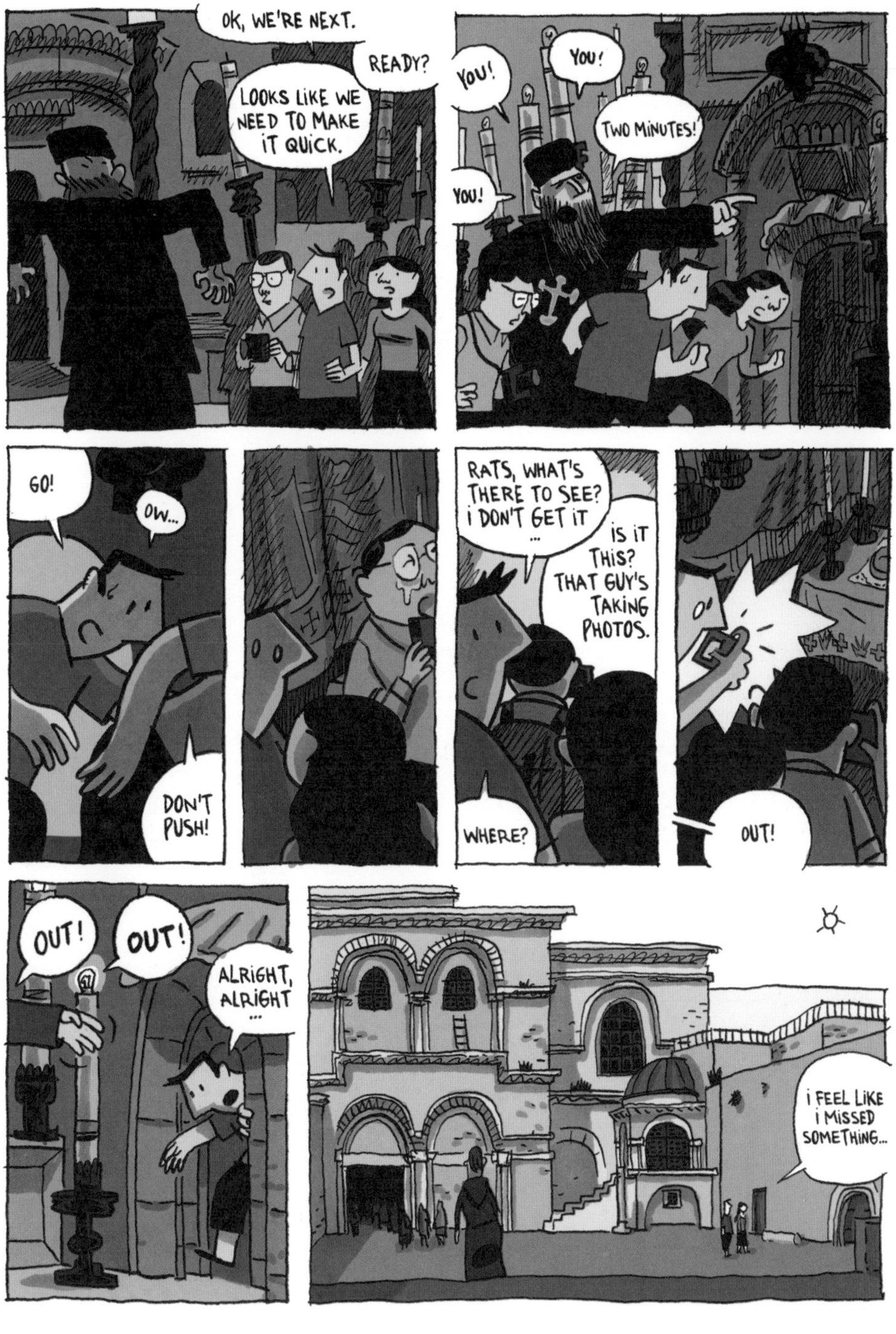
OK, WE'RE NEXT.
READY?
LOOKS LIKE WE NEED TO MAKE IT QUICK.
YOU!
YOU!
TWO MINUTES!
YOU!
GO!
OW...
DON'T PUSH!
RATS, WHAT'S THERE TO SEE? I DON'T GET IT ...
IS IT THIS? THAT GUY'S TAKING PHOTOS.
WHERE?
OUT!
OUT!
OUT!
ALRIGHT, ALRIGHT ...
I FEEL LIKE I MISSED SOMETHING...

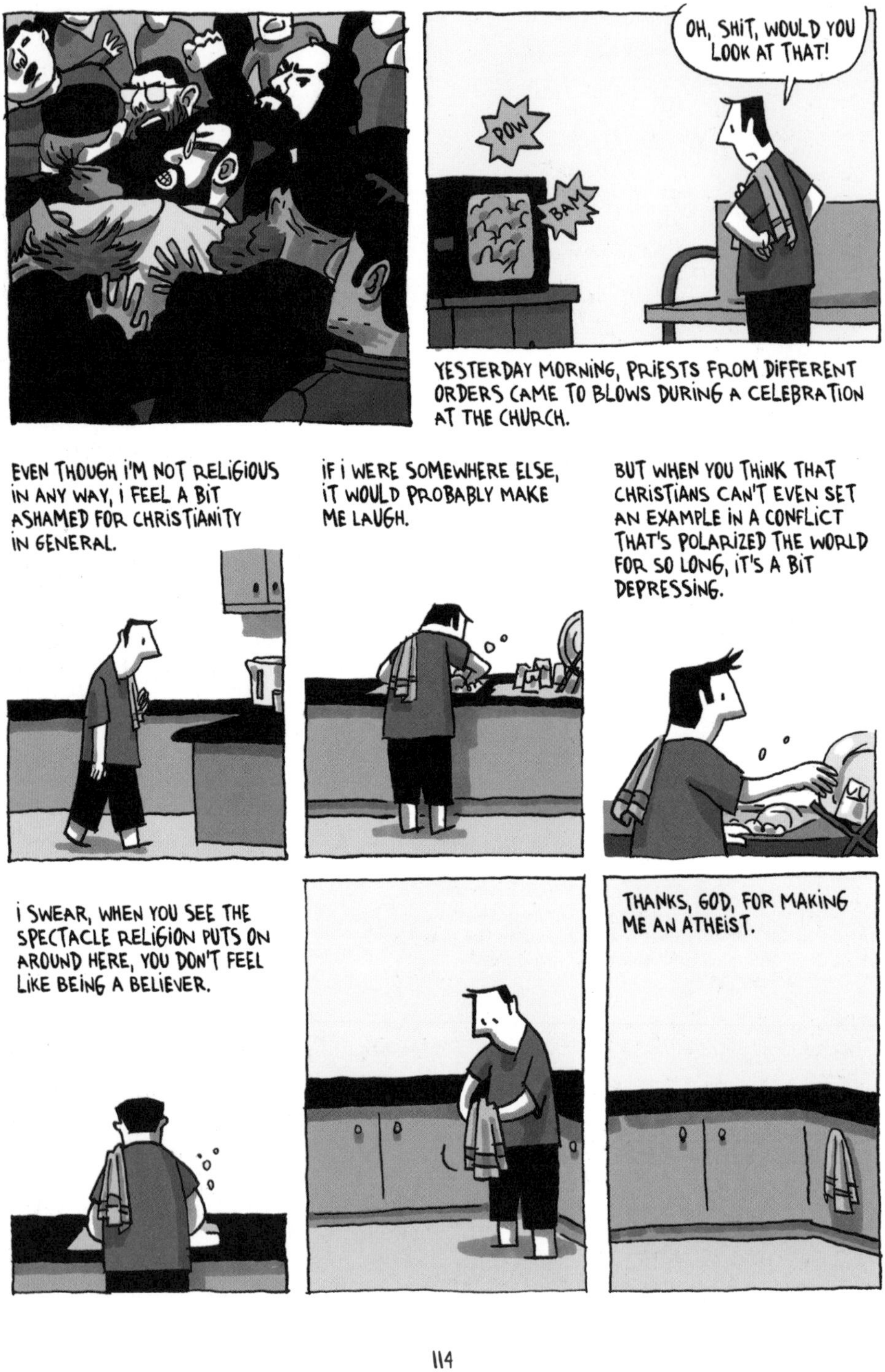
OH, SHIT, WOULD YOU LOOK AT THAT!
POW
BAM
YESTERDAY MORNING, PRIESTS FROM DIFFERENT ORDERS CAME TO BLOWS DURING A CELEBRATION AT THE CHURCH.
EVEN THOUGH I'M NOT RELIGIOUS IN ANY WAY, I FEEL A BIT ASHAMED FOR CHRISTIANITY IN GENERAL.
IF I WERE SOMEWHERE ELSE, IT WOULD PROBABLY MAKE ME LAUGH.
BUT WHEN YOU THINK THAT CHRISTIANS CAN'T EVEN SET AN EXAMPLE IN A CONFLICT THAT'S POLARIZED THE WORLD FOR SO LONG, IT'S A BIT DEPRESSING.
I SWEAR, WHEN YOU SEE THE SPECTACLE RELIGION PUTS ON AROUND HERE, YOU DON'T FEEL LIKE BEING A BELIEVER.
THANKS, GOD, FOR MAKING ME AN ATHEIST.

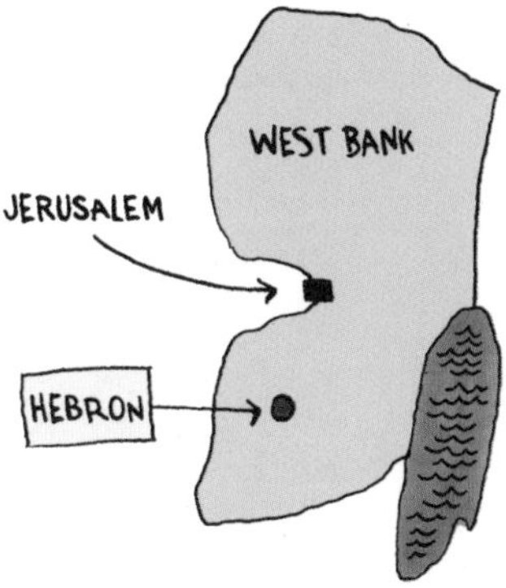
WEST BANK
JERUSALEM
HEBRON

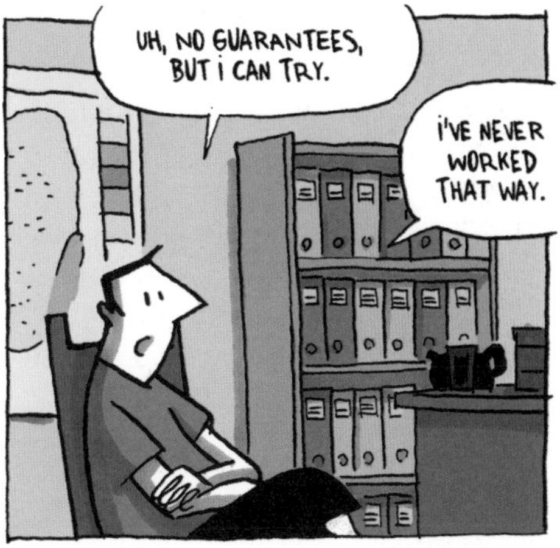
UH, NO GUARANTEES, BUT I CAN TRY.
I'VE NEVER WORKED THAT WAY.

THE HEAD OF MSF SPAIN (WHO KNOWS MY WORK) ASKED IF I COULD DO A GRAPHIC REPORTAGE FOR THE AGENCY. THE IDEA IS FOR ME, IN MY OWN WAY, TO TALK ABOUT WHAT THEY'RE DOING IN HEBRON, A WEST BANK CITY WHERE THE SETTLERS ARE KNOWN TO BE ESPECIALLY MILITANT.

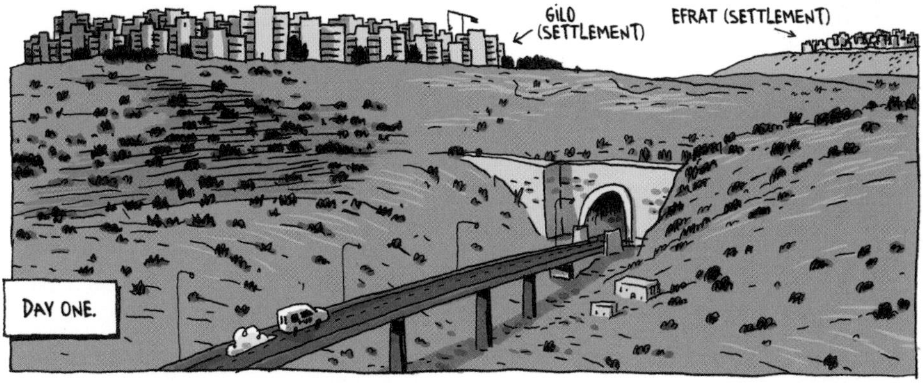
GILO (SETTLEMENT)
EFRAT (SETTLEMENT)
DAY ONE.

HEBRON IS A BIG CITY OF ABOUT 130,000 INHABITANTS. AMONG THE PALESTINIANS LIVE SOME 400 SETTLERS, WHO ARE GUARDED BY A SURPRISING NUMBER OF SOLDIERS.

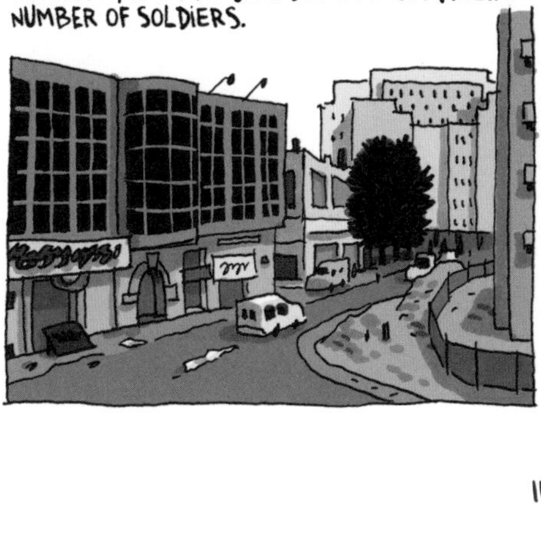

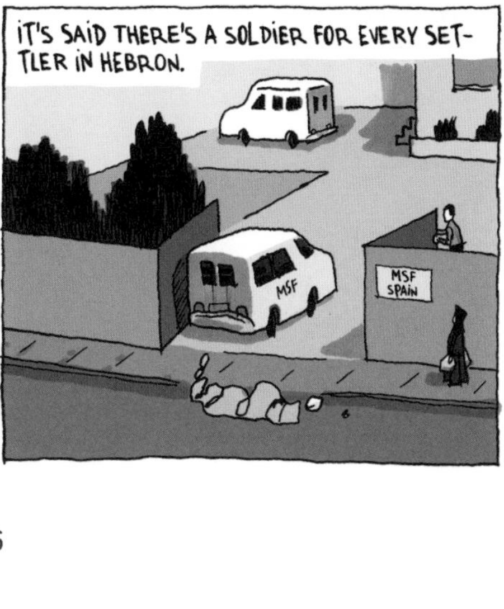
IT'S SAID THERE'S A SOLDIER FOR EVERY SETTLER IN HEBRON.
MSF
MSF SPAIN

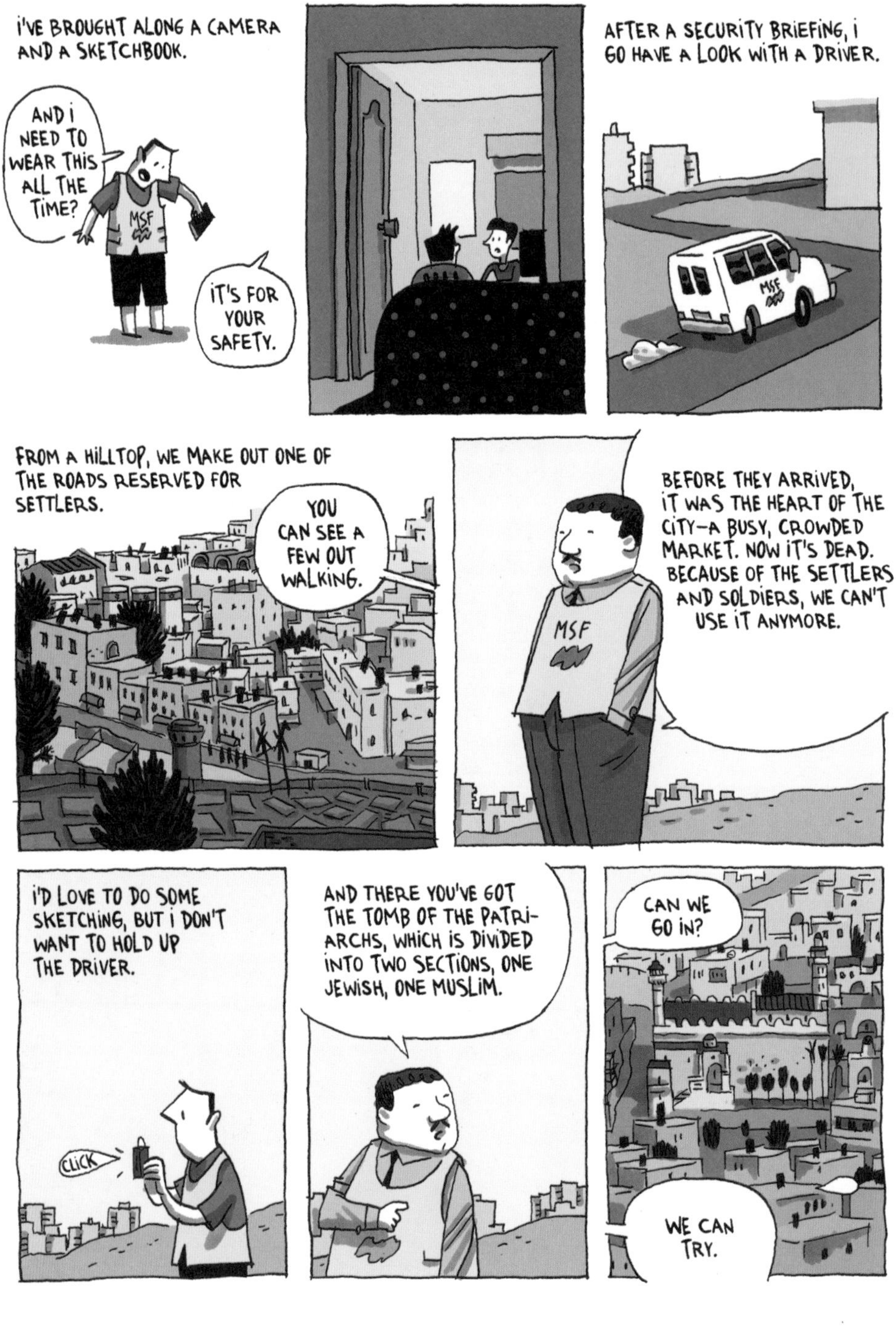
I'VE BROUGHT ALONG A CAMERA AND A SKETCHBOOK.
AND I NEED TO WEAR THIS ALL THE TIME?
MSF
IT'S FOR YOUR SAFETY.
AFTER A SECURITY BRIEFING, I GO HAVE A LOOK WITH A DRIVER.
MSF
FROM A HILLTOP, WE MAKE OUT ONE OF THE ROADS RESERVED FOR SETTLERS.
YOU CAN SEE A FEW OUT WALKING.
BEFORE THEY ARRIVED, IT WAS THE HEART OF THE CITY—A BUSY, CROWDED MARKET. NOW IT'S DEAD. BECAUSE OF THE SETTLERS AND SOLDIERS, WE CAN'T USE IT ANYMORE.
MSF
I'D LOVE TO DO SOME SKETCHING, BUT I DON'T WANT TO HOLD UP THE DRIVER.
CLICK
AND THERE YOU'VE GOT THE TOMB OF THE PATRIARCHS, WHICH IS DIVIDED INTO TWO SECTIONS, ONE JEWISH, ONE MUSLIM.
CAN WE GO IN?
WE CAN TRY.

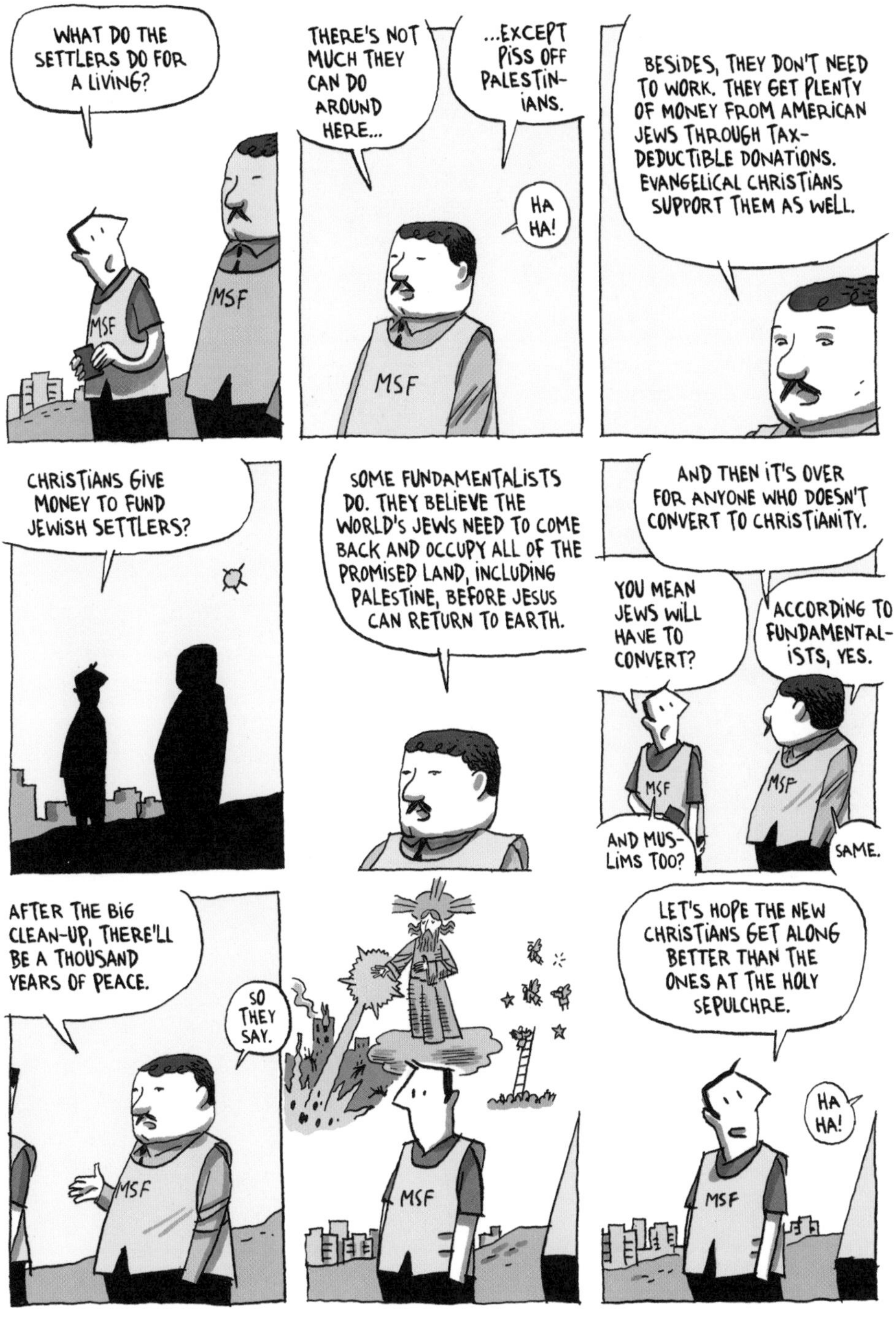
WHAT DO THE SETTLERS DO FOR A LIVING?
MSF
MSF
THERE'S NOT MUCH THEY CAN DO AROUND HERE...
...EXCEPT PISS OFF PALESTIN-IANS.
HA HA!
MSF
BESIDES, THEY DON'T NEED TO WORK. THEY GET PLENTY OF MONEY FROM AMERICAN JEWS THROUGH TAX-DEDUCTIBLE DONATIONS. EVANGELICAL CHRISTIANS SUPPORT THEM AS WELL.
CHRISTIANS GIVE MONEY TO FUND JEWISH SETTLERS?
SOME FUNDAMENTALISTS DO. THEY BELIEVE THE WORLD'S JEWS NEED TO COME BACK AND OCCUPY ALL OF THE PROMISED LAND, INCLUDING PALESTINE, BEFORE JESUS CAN RETURN TO EARTH.
AND THEN IT'S OVER FOR ANYONE WHO DOESN'T CONVERT TO CHRISTIANITY.
YOU MEAN JEWS WILL HAVE TO CONVERT?
ACCORDING TO FUNDAMENTAL-ISTS, YES.
MSF
MSF
AND MUS-LIMS TOO?
SAME.
AFTER THE BIG CLEAN-UP, THERE'LL BE A THOUSAND YEARS OF PEACE.
SO THEY SAY.
MSF
MSF
LET'S HOPE THE NEW CHRISTIANS GET ALONG BETTER THAN THE ONES AT THE HOLY SEPULCHRE.
HA HA!
MSF

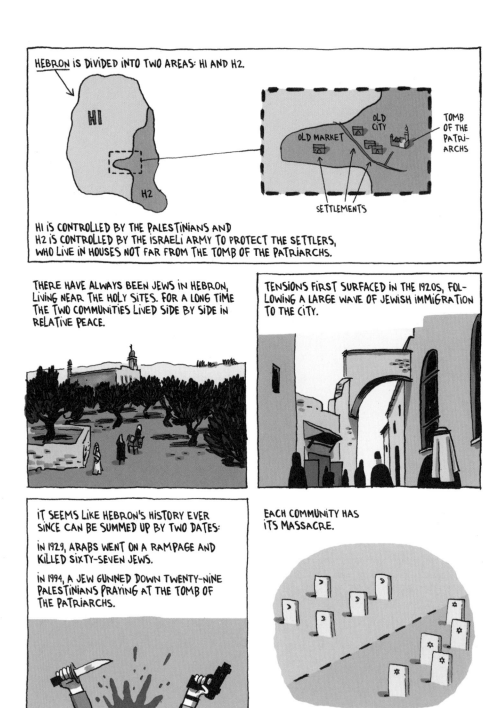

HEBRON IS DIVIDED INTO TWO AREAS: H1 AND H2.

H1

H2

OLD MARKET

OLD CITY

TOMB OF THE PATRI-ARCHS

SETTLEMENTS

H1 IS CONTROLLED BY THE PALESTINIANS AND H2 IS CONTROLLED BY THE ISRAELI ARMY TO PROTECT THE SETTLERS, WHO LIVE IN HOUSES NOT FAR FROM THE TOMB OF THE PATRIARCHS.

THERE HAVE ALWAYS BEEN JEWS IN HEBRON, LIVING NEAR THE HOLY SITES. FOR A LONG TIME THE TWO COMMUNITIES LIVED SIDE BY SIDE IN RELATIVE PEACE.

TENSIONS FIRST SURFACED IN THE 1920S, FOLLOWING A LARGE WAVE OF JEWISH IMMIGRATION TO THE CITY.

IT SEEMS LIKE HEBRON'S HISTORY EVER SINCE CAN BE SUMMED UP BY TWO DATES:

IN 1929, ARABS WENT ON A RAMPAGE AND KILLED SIXTY-SEVEN JEWS.

IN 1994, A JEW GUNNED DOWN TWENTY-NINE PALESTINIANS PRAYING AT THE TOMB OF THE PATRIARCHS.

EACH COMMUNITY HAS ITS MASSACRE.

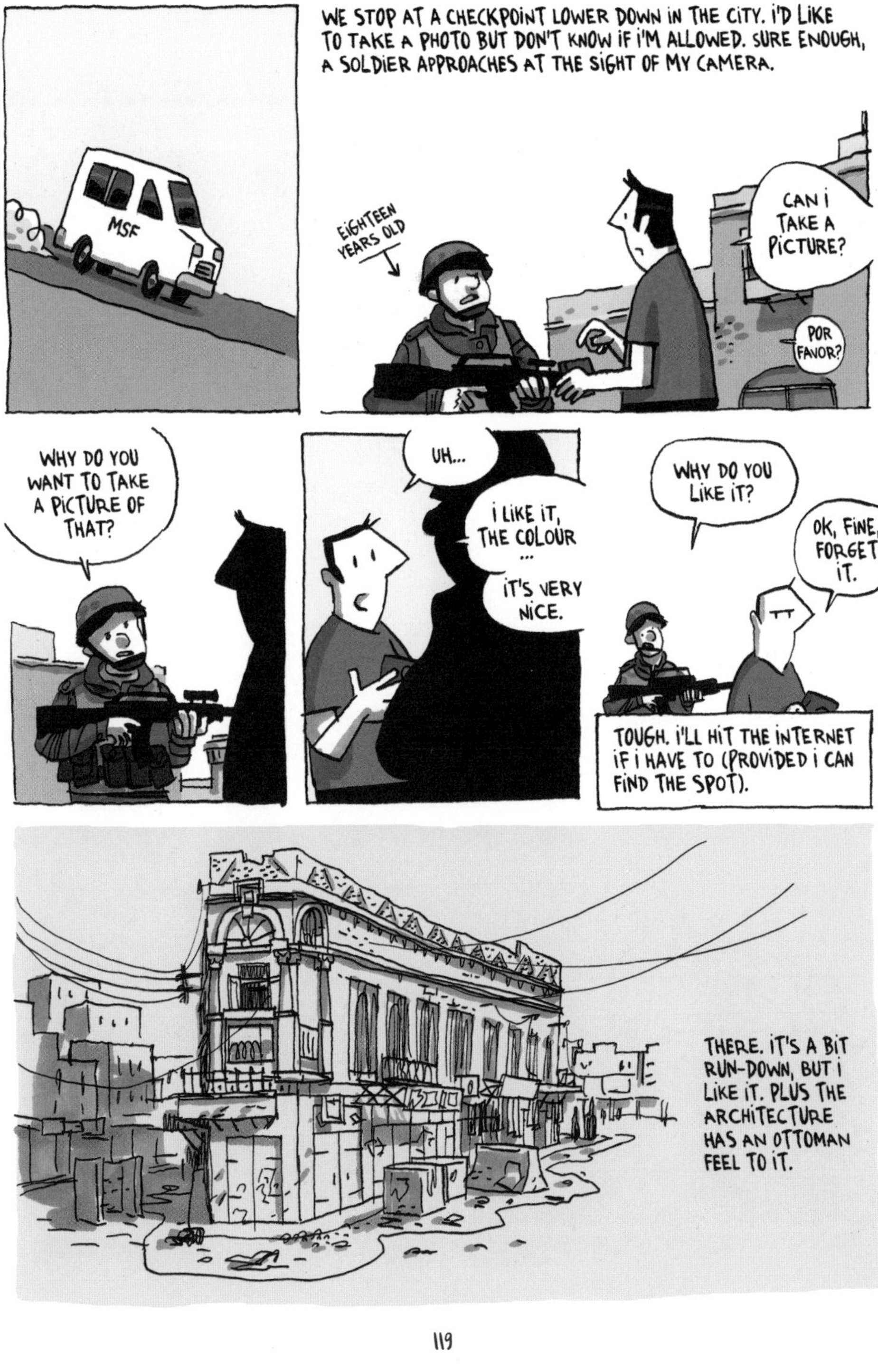

WE STOP AT A CHECKPOINT LOWER DOWN IN THE CITY. I'D LIKE TO TAKE A PHOTO BUT DON'T KNOW IF I'M ALLOWED. SURE ENOUGH, A SOLDIER APPROACHES AT THE SIGHT OF MY CAMERA.
MSF
EIGHTEEN YEARS OLD
CAN I TAKE A PICTURE?
POR FAVOR?
WHY DO YOU WANT TO TAKE A PICTURE OF THAT?
UH...
I LIKE IT, THE COLOUR ...
IT'S VERY NICE.
WHY DO YOU LIKE IT?
OK, FINE, FORGET IT.
TOUGH. I'LL HIT THE INTERNET IF I HAVE TO (PROVIDED I CAN FIND THE SPOT).
THERE. IT'S A BIT RUN-DOWN, BUT I LIKE IT. PLUS THE ARCHITECTURE HAS AN OTTOMAN FEEL TO IT.

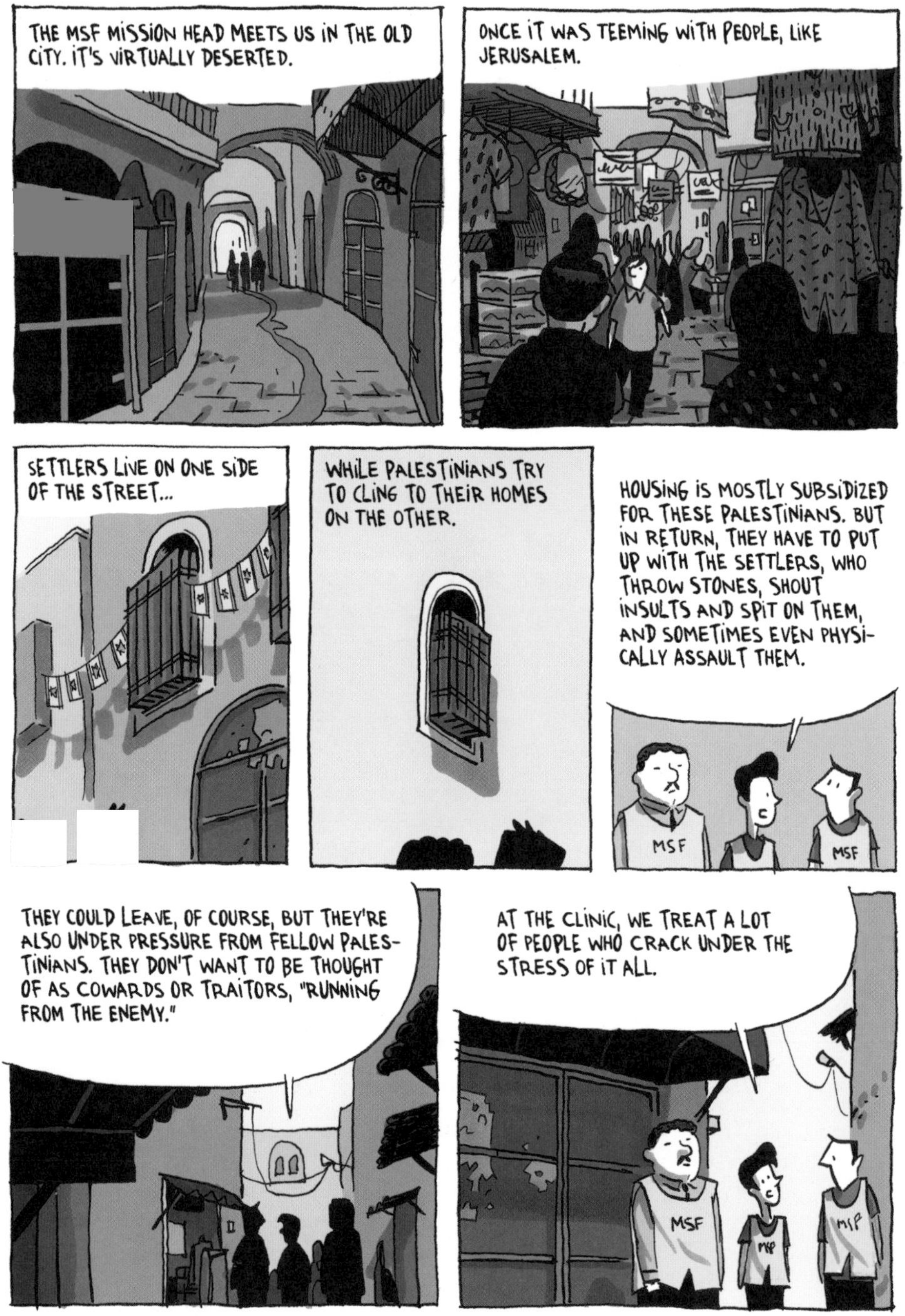
THE MSF MISSION HEAD MEETS US IN THE OLD CITY. IT'S VIRTUALLY DESERTED.
ONCE IT WAS TEEMING WITH PEOPLE, LIKE JERUSALEM.
SETTLERS LIVE ON ONE SIDE OF THE STREET...
WHILE PALESTINIANS TRY TO CLING TO THEIR HOMES ON THE OTHER.
HOUSING IS MOSTLY SUBSIDIZED FOR THESE PALESTINIANS. BUT IN RETURN, THEY HAVE TO PUT UP WITH THE SETTLERS, WHO THROW STONES, SHOUT INSULTS AND SPIT ON THEM, AND SOMETIMES EVEN PHYSICALLY ASSAULT THEM.
MSF
MSF
THEY COULD LEAVE, OF COURSE, BUT THEY'RE ALSO UNDER PRESSURE FROM FELLOW PALESTINIANS. THEY DON'T WANT TO BE THOUGHT OF AS COWARDS OR TRAITORS, "RUNNING FROM THE ENEMY."
AT THE CLINIC, WE TREAT A LOT OF PEOPLE WHO CRACK UNDER THE STRESS OF IT ALL.
MSF
MSF

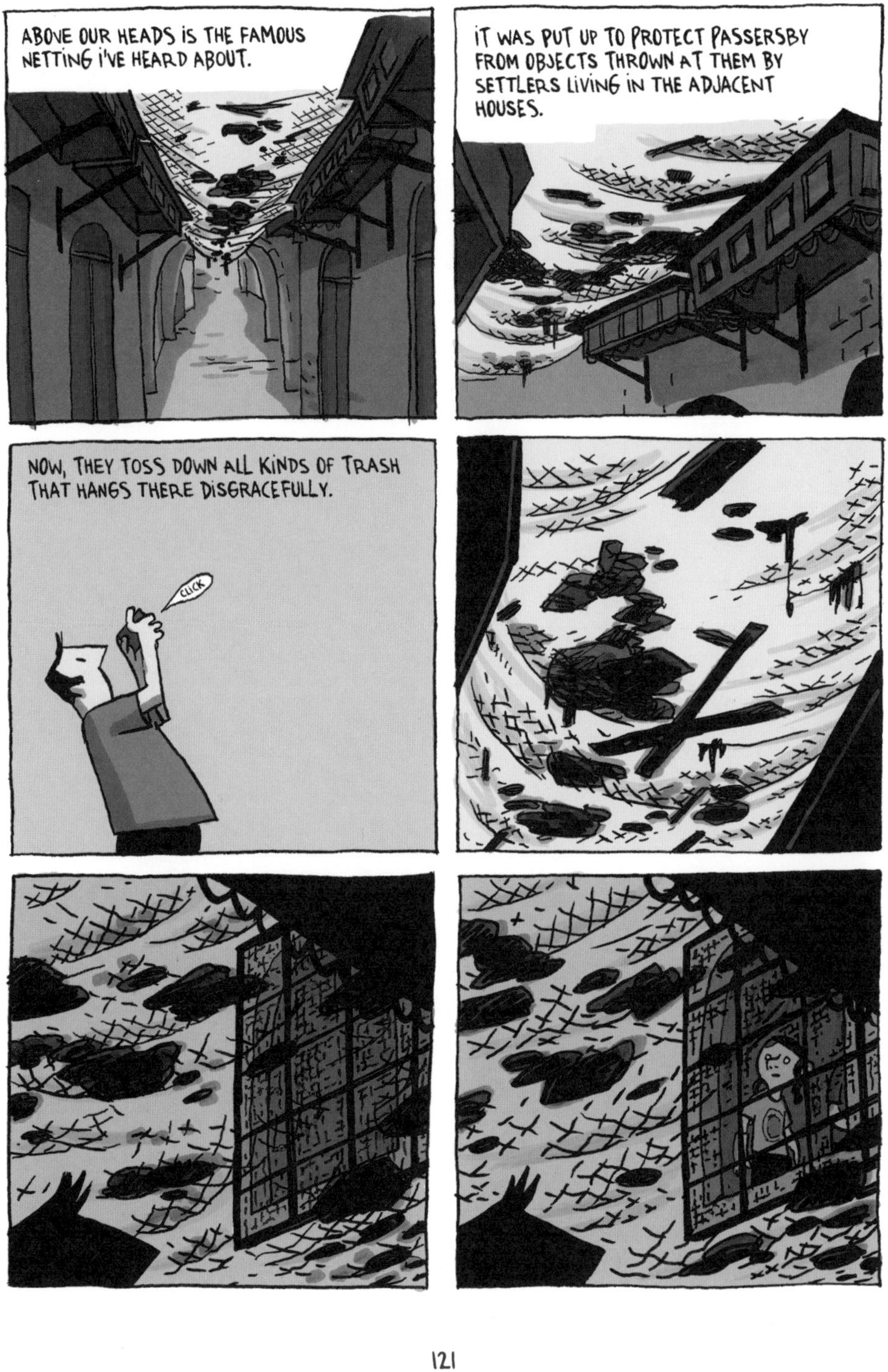
ABOVE OUR HEADS IS THE FAMOUS NETTING I'VE HEARD ABOUT.
IT WAS PUT UP TO PROTECT PASSERSBY FROM OBJECTS THROWN AT THEM BY SETTLERS LIVING IN THE ADJACENT HOUSES.
NOW, THEY TOSS DOWN ALL KINDS OF TRASH THAT HANGS THERE DISGRACEFULLY.
CLICK

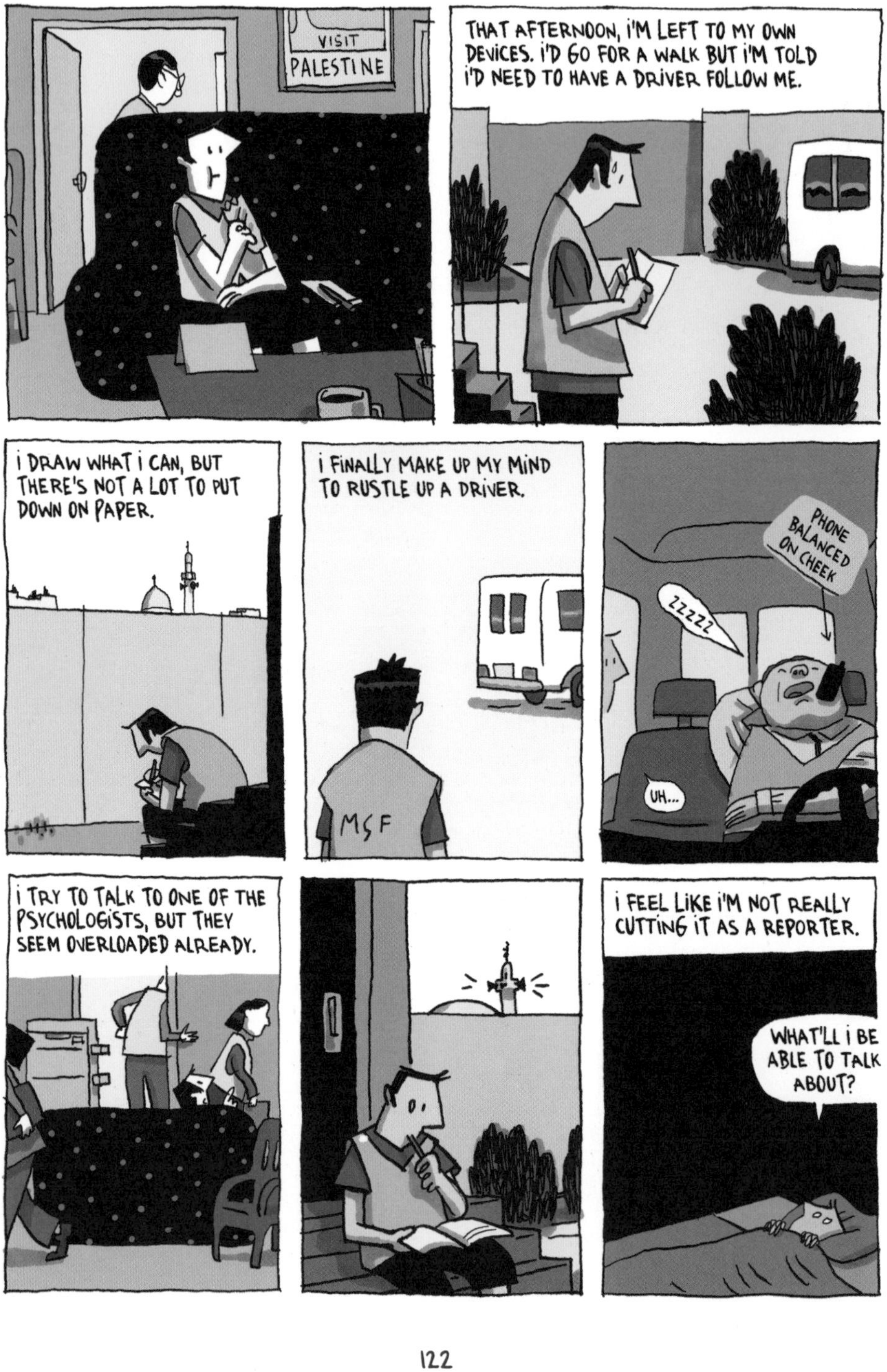
VISIT PALESTINE
THAT AFTERNOON, I'M LEFT TO MY OWN DEVICES. I'D GO FOR A WALK BUT I'M TOLD I'D NEED TO HAVE A DRIVER FOLLOW ME.
I DRAW WHAT I CAN, BUT THERE'S NOT A LOT TO PUT DOWN ON PAPER.
I FINALLY MAKE UP MY MIND TO RUSTLE UP A DRIVER.
MSF
PHONE BALANCED ON CHEEK
ZZZZZ
UH...
I TRY TO TALK TO ONE OF THE PSYCHOLOGISTS, BUT THEY SEEM OVERLOADED ALREADY.
I FEEL LIKE I'M NOT REALLY CUTTING IT AS A REPORTER.
WHAT'LL I BE ABLE TO TALK ABOUT?

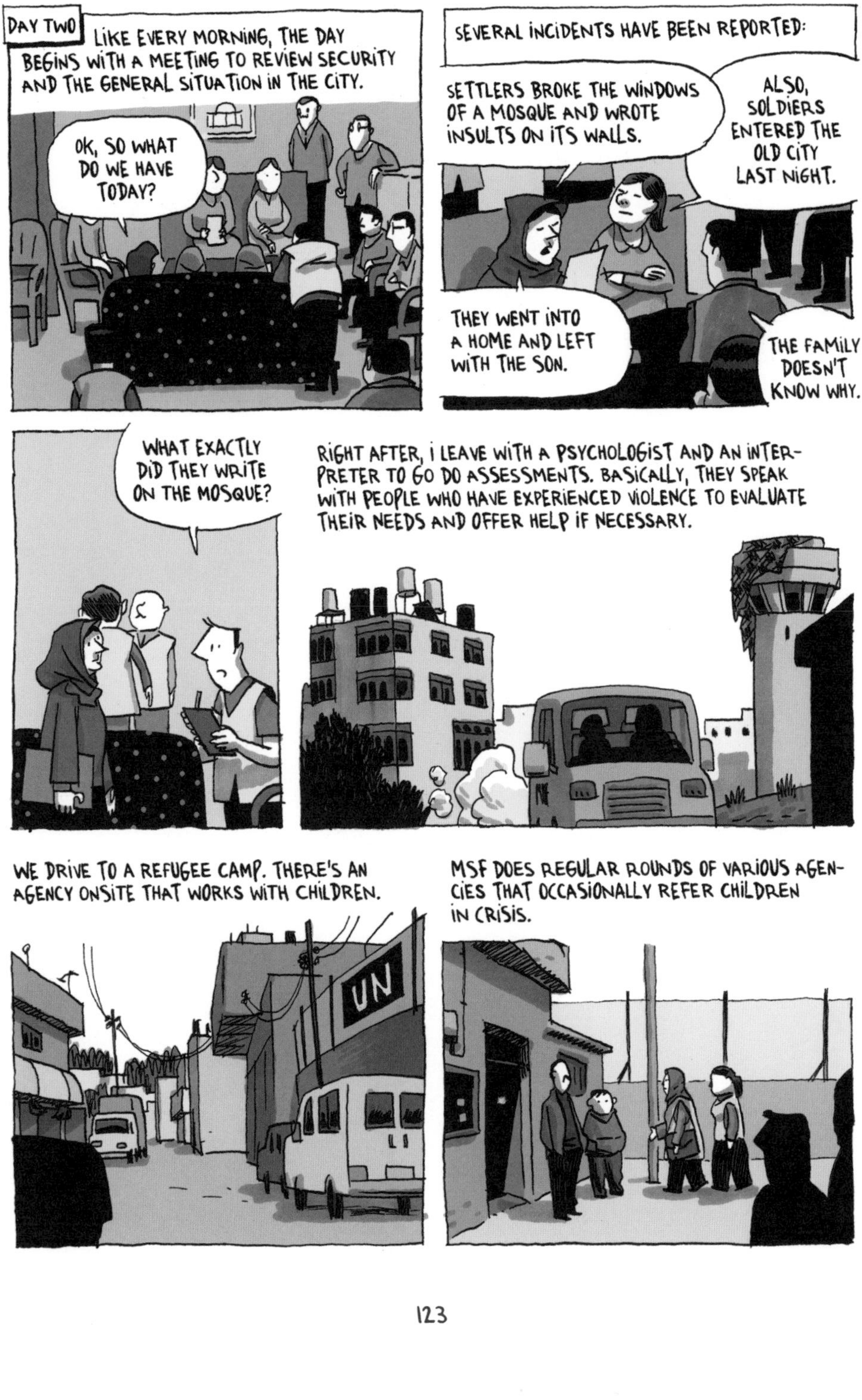
DAY TWO
LIKE EVERY MORNING, THE DAY BEGINS WITH A MEETING TO REVIEW SECURITY AND THE GENERAL SITUATION IN THE CITY.
OK, SO WHAT DO WE HAVE TODAY?
SEVERAL INCIDENTS HAVE BEEN REPORTED:
SETTLERS BROKE THE WINDOWS OF A MOSQUE AND WROTE INSULTS ON ITS WALLS.
ALSO, SOLDIERS ENTERED THE OLD CITY LAST NIGHT.
THEY WENT INTO A HOME AND LEFT WITH THE SON.
THE FAMILY DOESN'T KNOW WHY.
WHAT EXACTLY DID THEY WRITE ON THE MOSQUE?
RIGHT AFTER, I LEAVE WITH A PSYCHOLOGIST AND AN INTERPRETER TO GO DO ASSESSMENTS. BASICALLY, THEY SPEAK WITH PEOPLE WHO HAVE EXPERIENCED VIOLENCE TO EVALUATE THEIR NEEDS AND OFFER HELP IF NECESSARY.
WE DRIVE TO A REFUGEE CAMP. THERE'S AN AGENCY ONSITE THAT WORKS WITH CHILDREN.
UN
MSF DOES REGULAR ROUNDS OF VARIOUS AGENCIES THAT OCCASIONALLY REFER CHILDREN IN CRISIS.

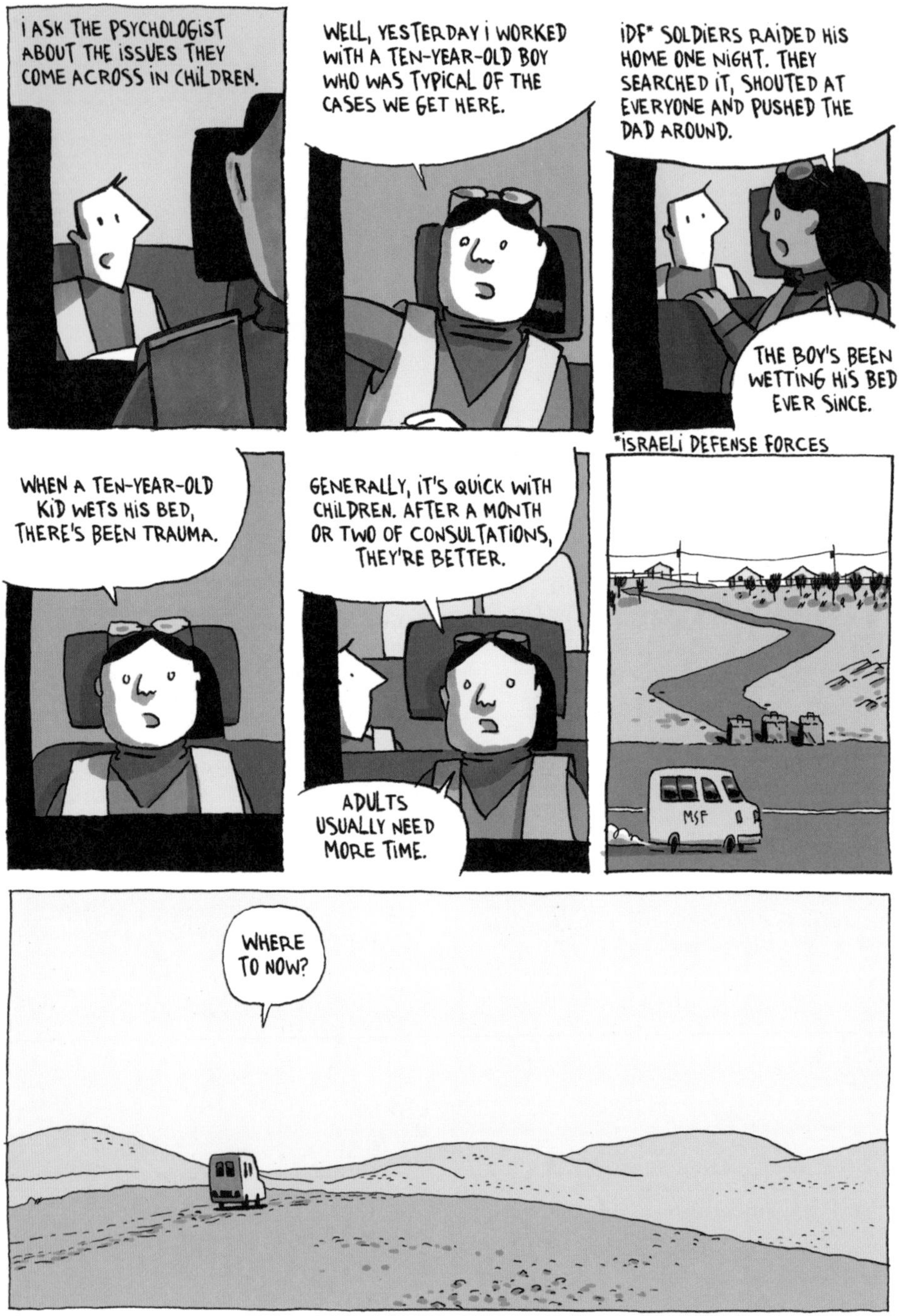
I ASK THE PSYCHOLOGIST ABOUT THE ISSUES THEY COME ACROSS IN CHILDREN.
WELL, YESTERDAY I WORKED WITH A TEN-YEAR-OLD BOY WHO WAS TYPICAL OF THE CASES WE GET HERE.
IDF* SOLDIERS RAIDED HIS HOME ONE NIGHT. THEY SEARCHED IT, SHOUTED AT EVERYONE AND PUSHED THE DAD AROUND.
THE BOY'S BEEN WETTING HIS BED EVER SINCE.
*ISRAELI DEFENSE FORCES
WHEN A TEN-YEAR-OLD KID WETS HIS BED, THERE'S BEEN TRAUMA.
GENERALLY, IT'S QUICK WITH CHILDREN. AFTER A MONTH OR TWO OF CONSULTATIONS, THEY'RE BETTER.
ADULTS USUALLY NEED MORE TIME.
MSF
WHERE TO NOW?

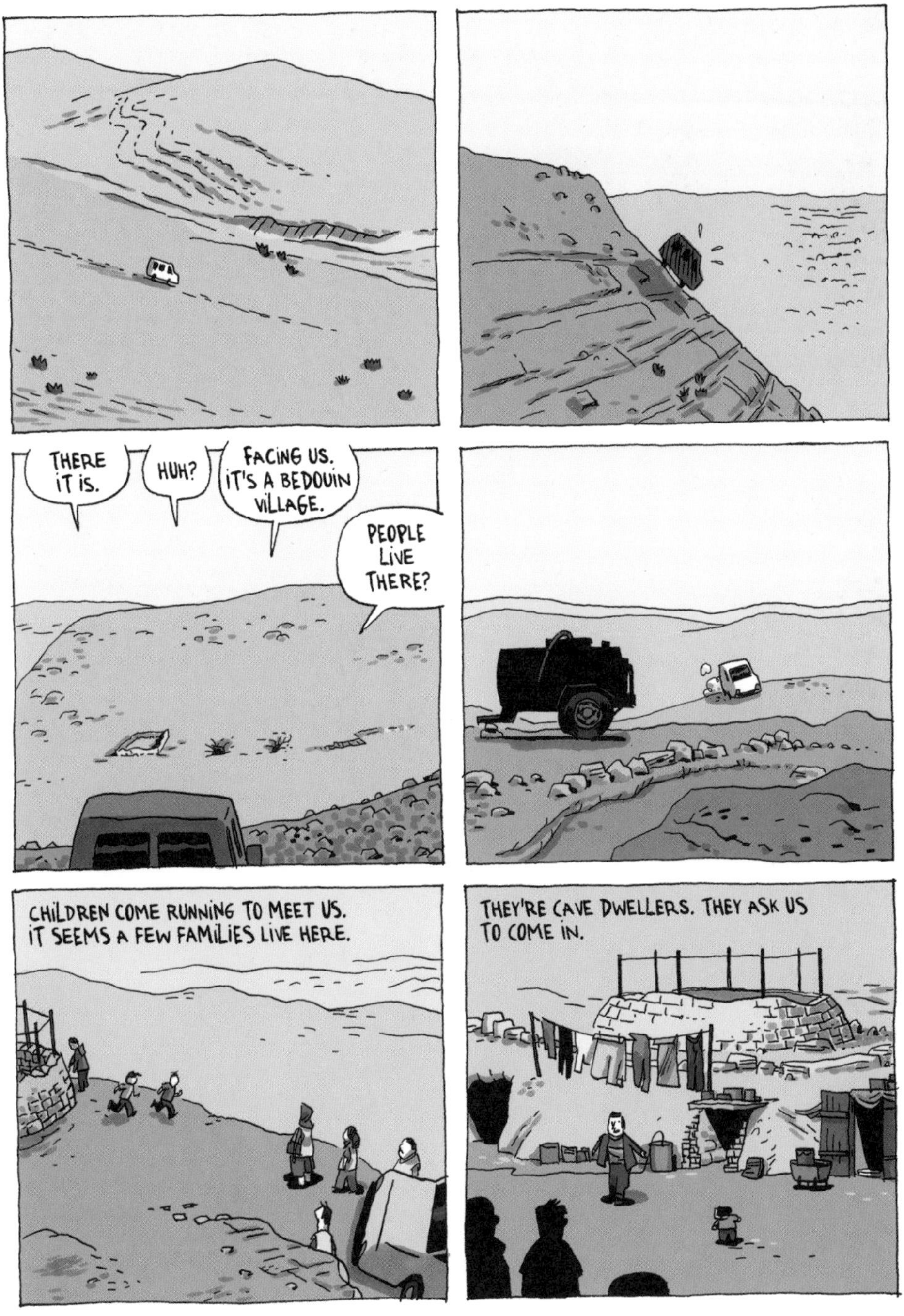
THERE IT IS.
HUH?
FACING US. IT'S A BEDOUIN VILLAGE.
PEOPLE LIVE THERE?
CHILDREN COME RUNNING TO MEET US. IT SEEMS A FEW FAMILIES LIVE HERE.
THEY'RE CAVE DWELLERS. THEY ASK US TO COME IN.

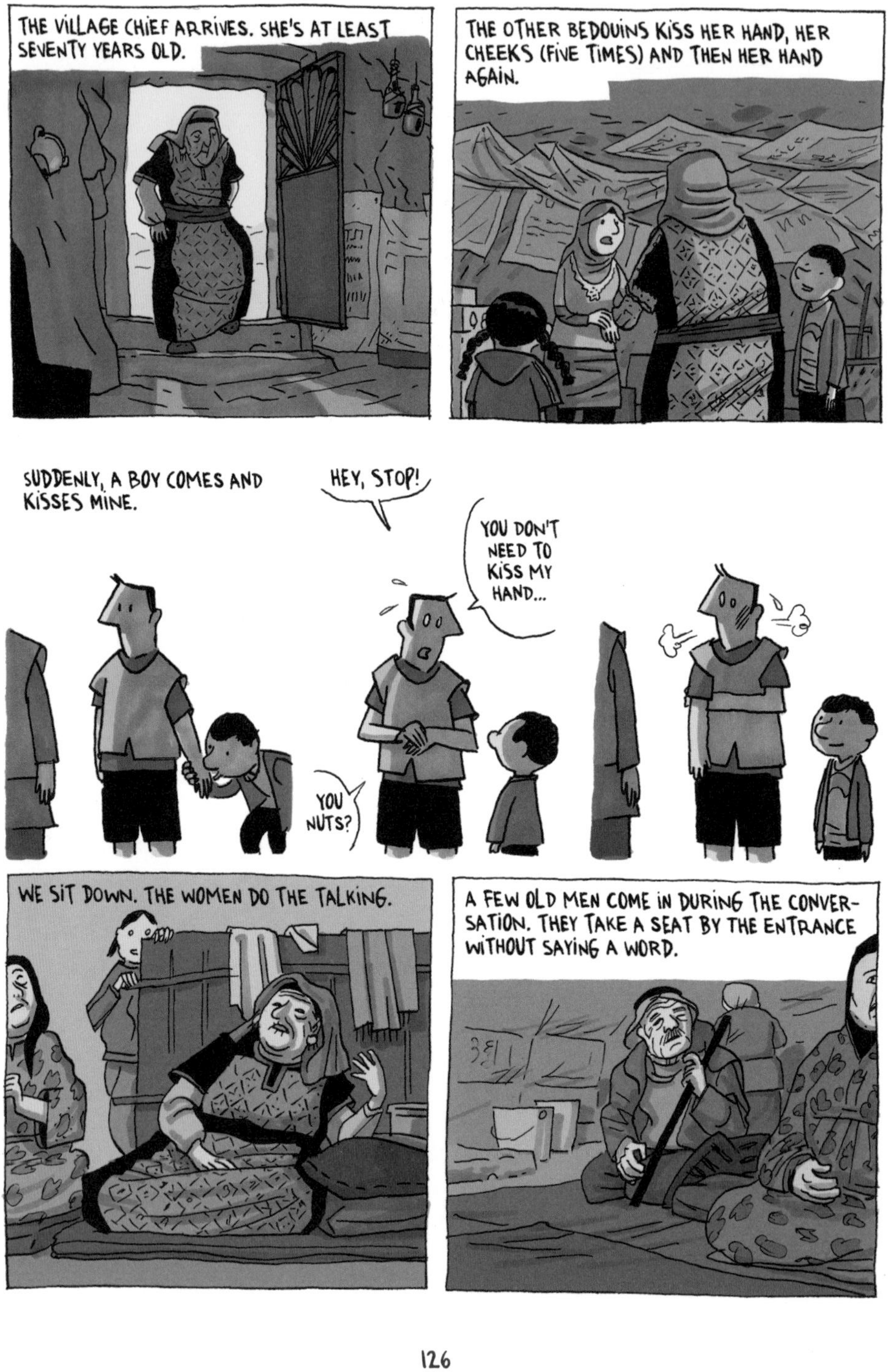

THE VILLAGE CHIEF ARRIVES. SHE'S AT LEAST SEVENTY YEARS OLD.
THE OTHER BEDOUINS KISS HER HAND, HER CHEEKS (FIVE TIMES) AND THEN HER HAND AGAIN.
SUDDENLY, A BOY COMES AND KISSES MINE.
HEY, STOP!
YOU NUTS?
YOU DON'T NEED TO KISS MY HAND...
WE SIT DOWN. THE WOMEN DO THE TALKING.
A FEW OLD MEN COME IN DURING THE CONVERSATION. THEY TAKE A SEAT BY THE ENTRANCE WITHOUT SAYING A WORD.

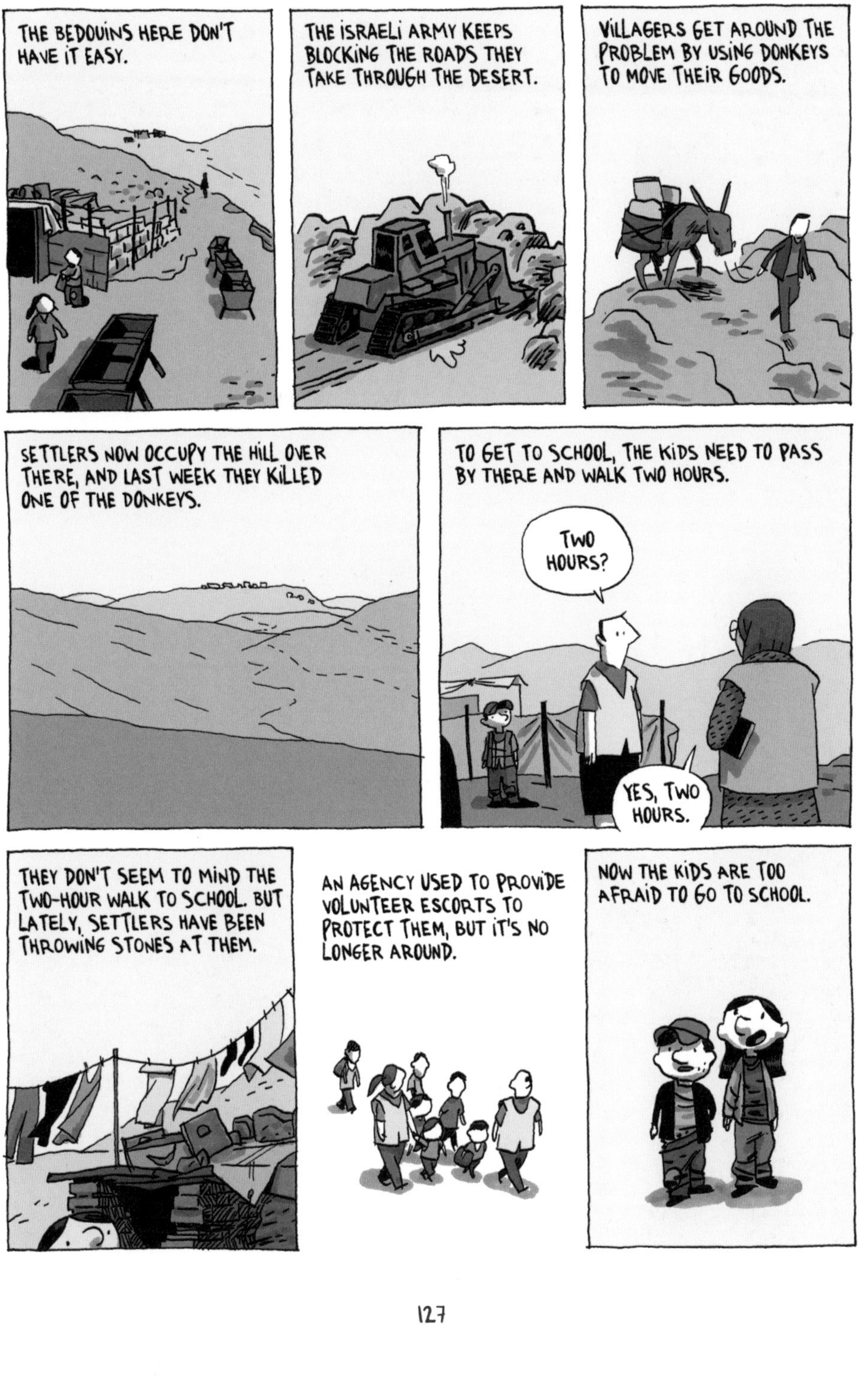
THE BEDOUINS HERE DON'T HAVE IT EASY.
THE ISRAELI ARMY KEEPS BLOCKING THE ROADS THEY TAKE THROUGH THE DESERT.
VILLAGERS GET AROUND THE PROBLEM BY USING DONKEYS TO MOVE THEIR GOODS.
SETTLERS NOW OCCUPY THE HILL OVER THERE, AND LAST WEEK THEY KILLED ONE OF THE DONKEYS.
TO GET TO SCHOOL, THE KIDS NEED TO PASS BY THERE AND WALK TWO HOURS.
TWO HOURS?
YES, TWO HOURS.
THEY DON'T SEEM TO MIND THE TWO-HOUR WALK TO SCHOOL. BUT LATELY, SETTLERS HAVE BEEN THROWING STONES AT THEM.
AN AGENCY USED TO PROVIDE VOLUNTEER ESCORTS TO PROTECT THEM, BUT IT'S NO LONGER AROUND.
NOW THE KIDS ARE TOO AFRAID TO GO TO SCHOOL.

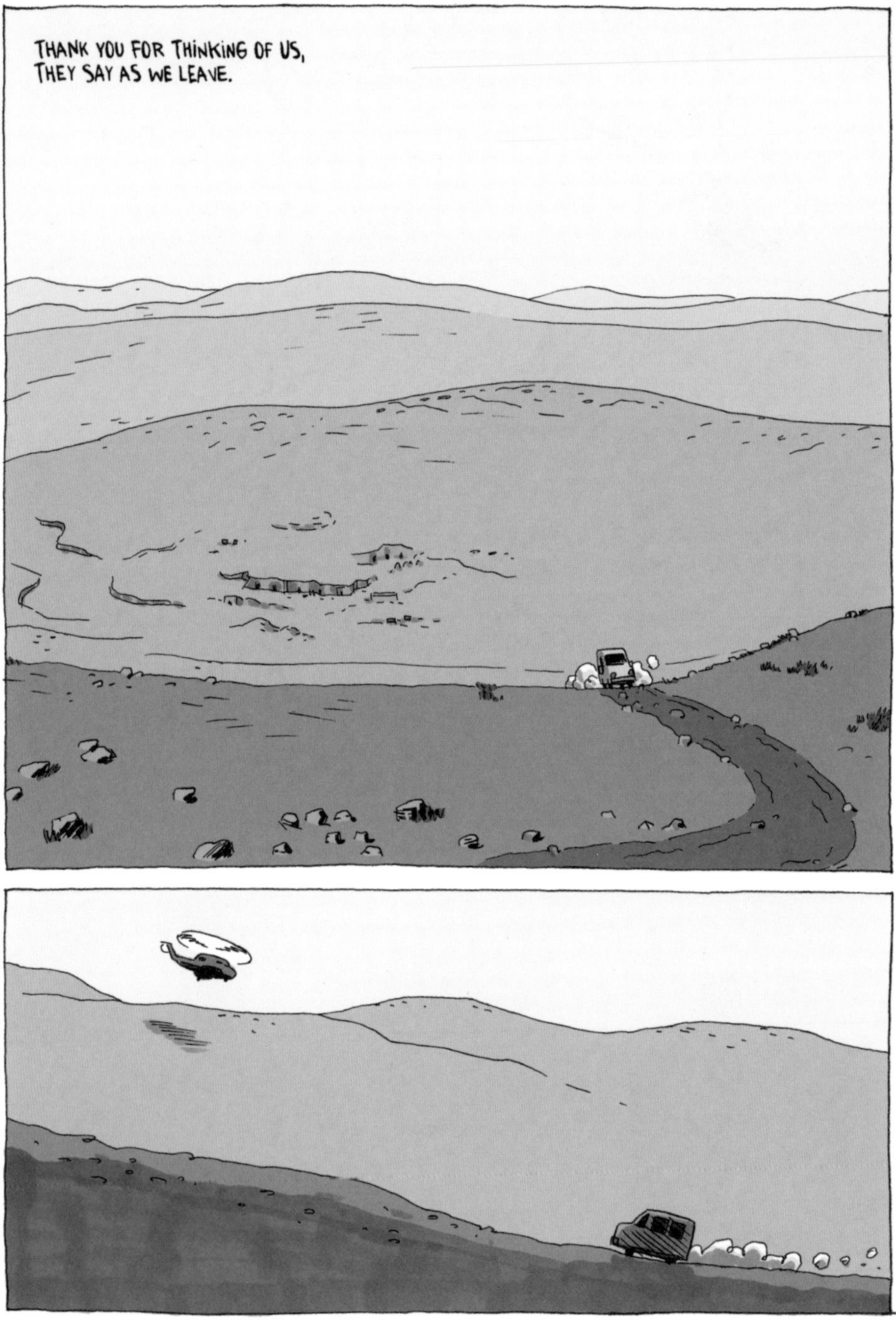
THANK YOU FOR THINKING OF US, THEY SAY AS WE LEAVE.

DECEMBER

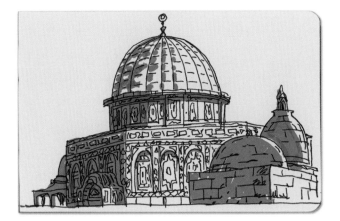

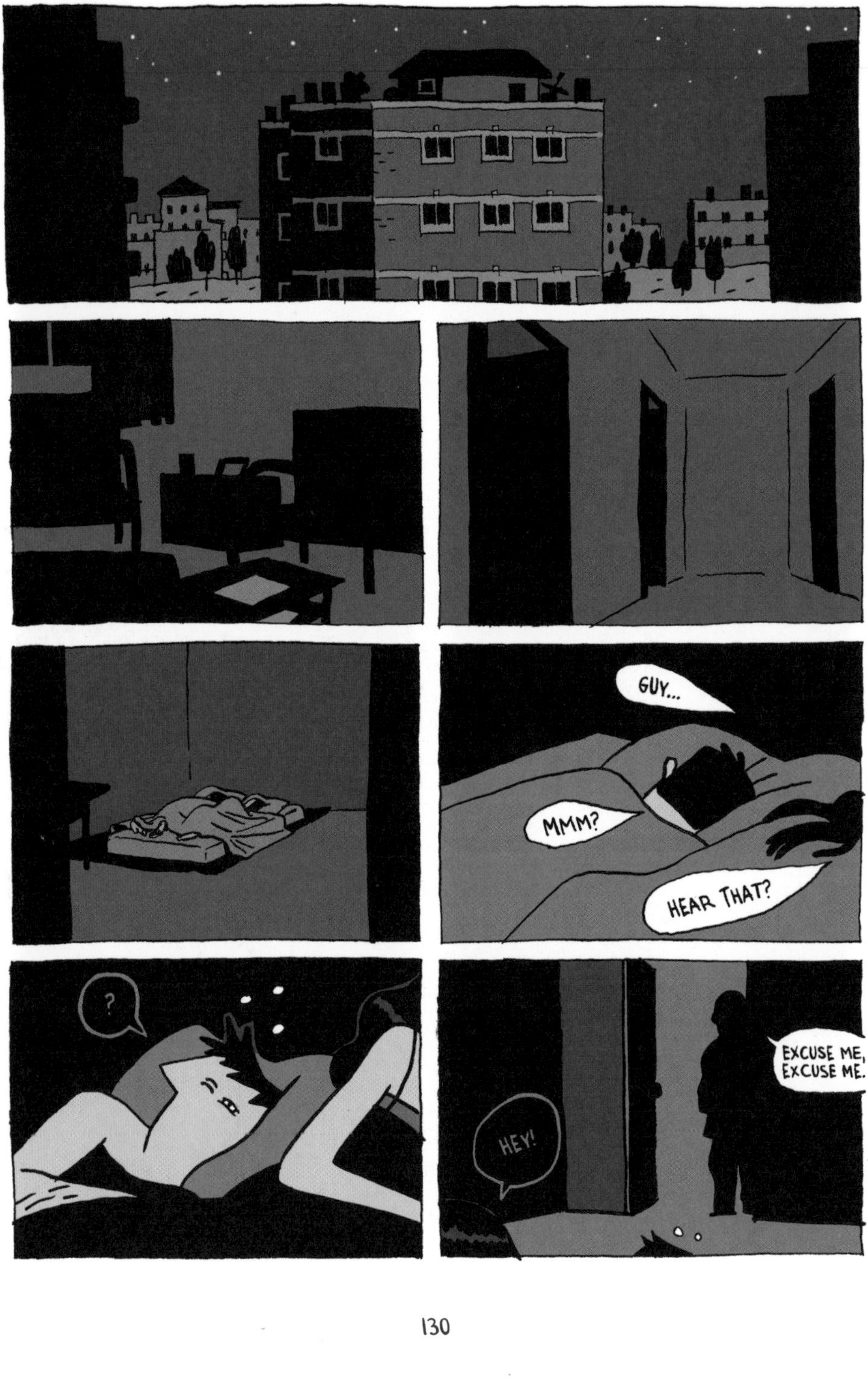
GUY...
MMM?
HEAR THAT?
?
EXCUSE ME, EXCUSE ME.
HEY!

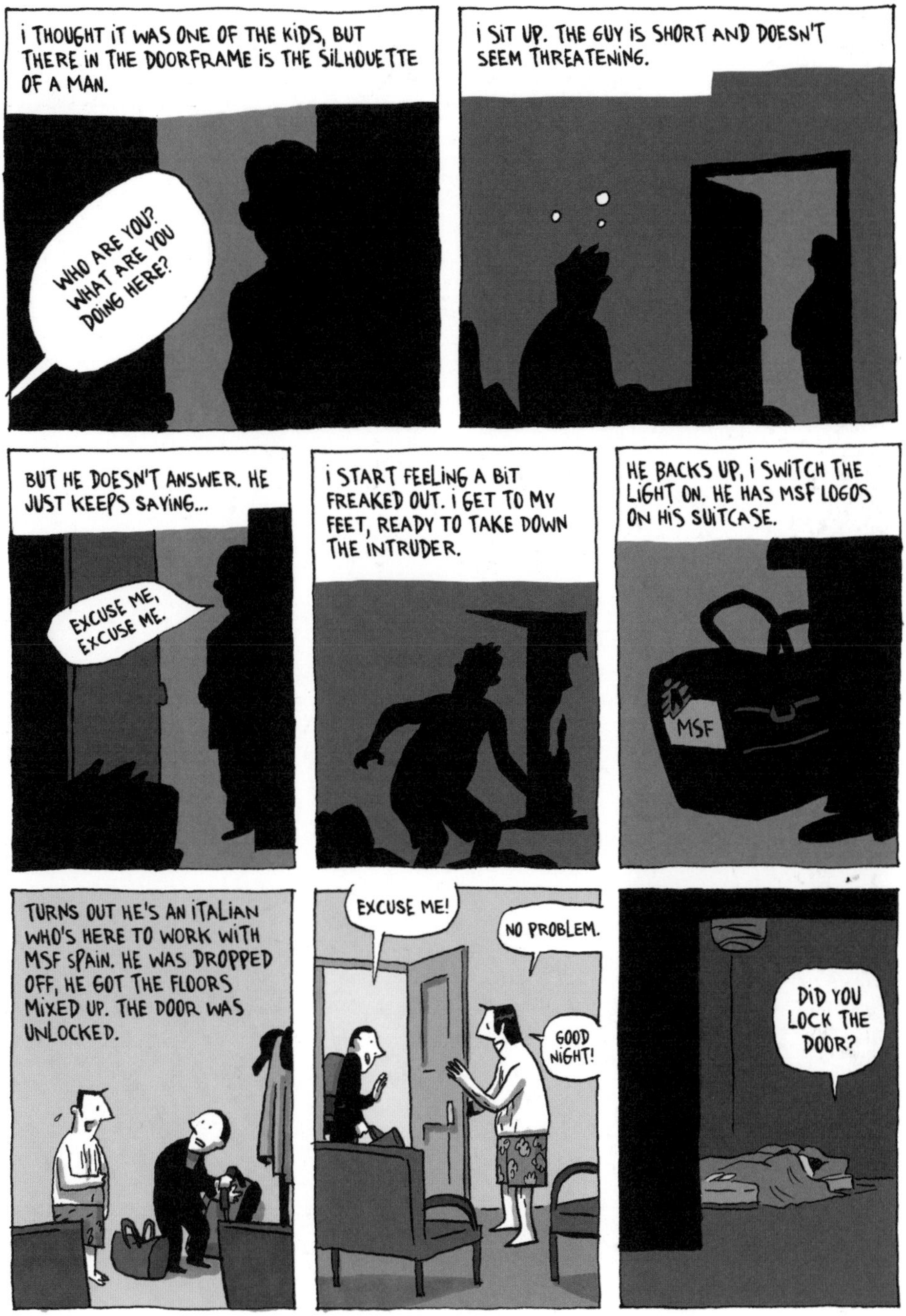
I THOUGHT IT WAS ONE OF THE KIDS, BUT THERE IN THE DOORFRAME IS THE SILHOUETTE OF A MAN.
WHO ARE YOU? WHAT ARE YOU DOING HERE?
I SIT UP. THE GUY IS SHORT AND DOESN'T SEEM THREATENING.
BUT HE DOESN'T ANSWER. HE JUST KEEPS SAYING...
EXCUSE ME, EXCUSE ME.
I START FEELING A BIT FREAKED OUT. I GET TO MY FEET, READY TO TAKE DOWN THE INTRUDER.
HE BACKS UP, I SWITCH THE LIGHT ON. HE HAS MSF LOGOS ON HIS SUITCASE.
MSF
TURNS OUT HE'S AN ITALIAN WHO'S HERE TO WORK WITH MSF SPAIN. HE WAS DROPPED OFF, HE GOT THE FLOORS MIXED UP. THE DOOR WAS UNLOCKED.
EXCUSE ME!
NO PROBLEM.
GOOD NIGHT!
DID YOU LOCK THE DOOR?

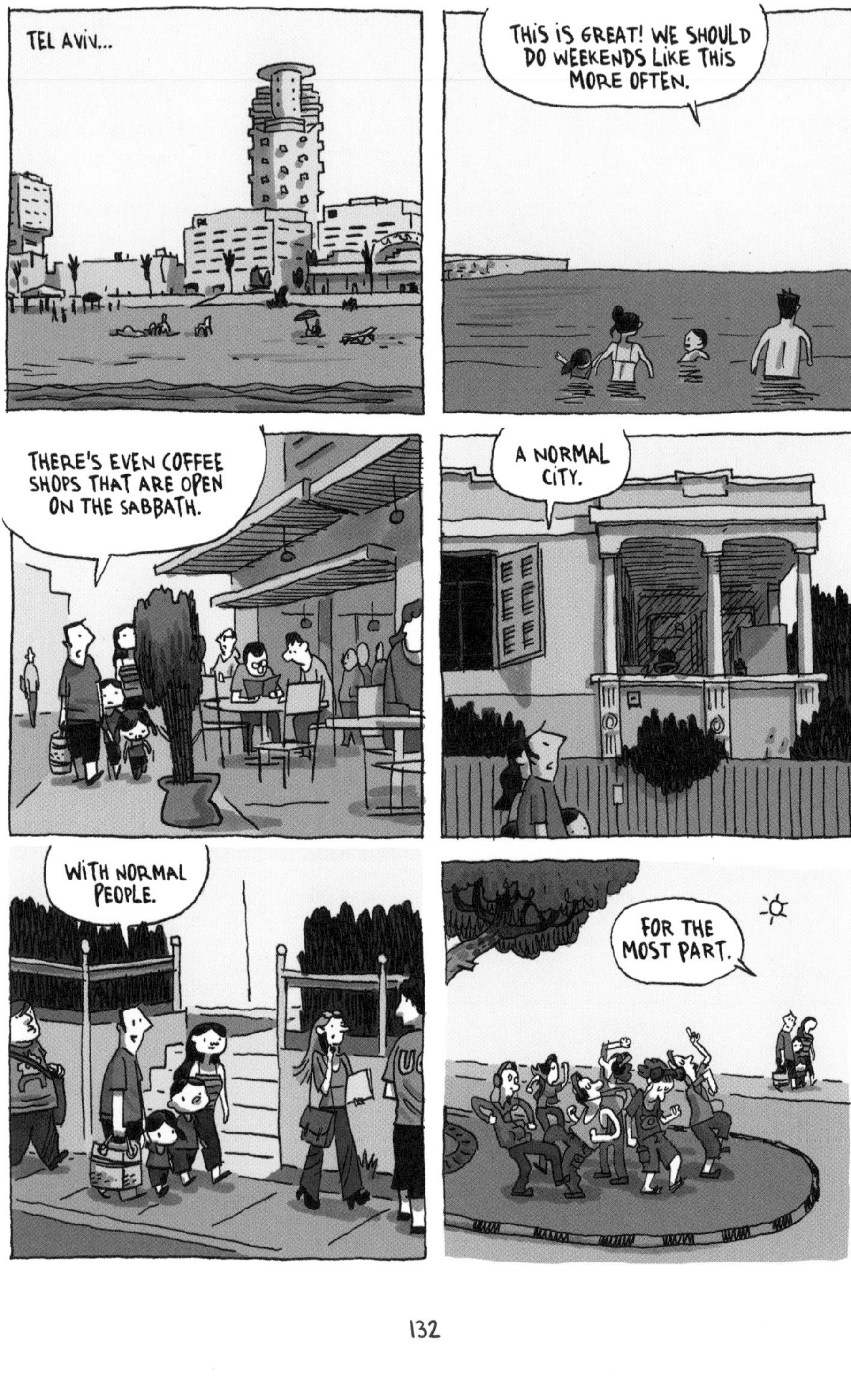
TEL AVIV...
THIS IS GREAT! WE SHOULD DO WEEKENDS LIKE THIS MORE OFTEN.
THERE'S EVEN COFFEE SHOPS THAT ARE OPEN ON THE SABBATH.
A NORMAL CITY.
WITH NORMAL PEOPLE.
FOR THE MOST PART.

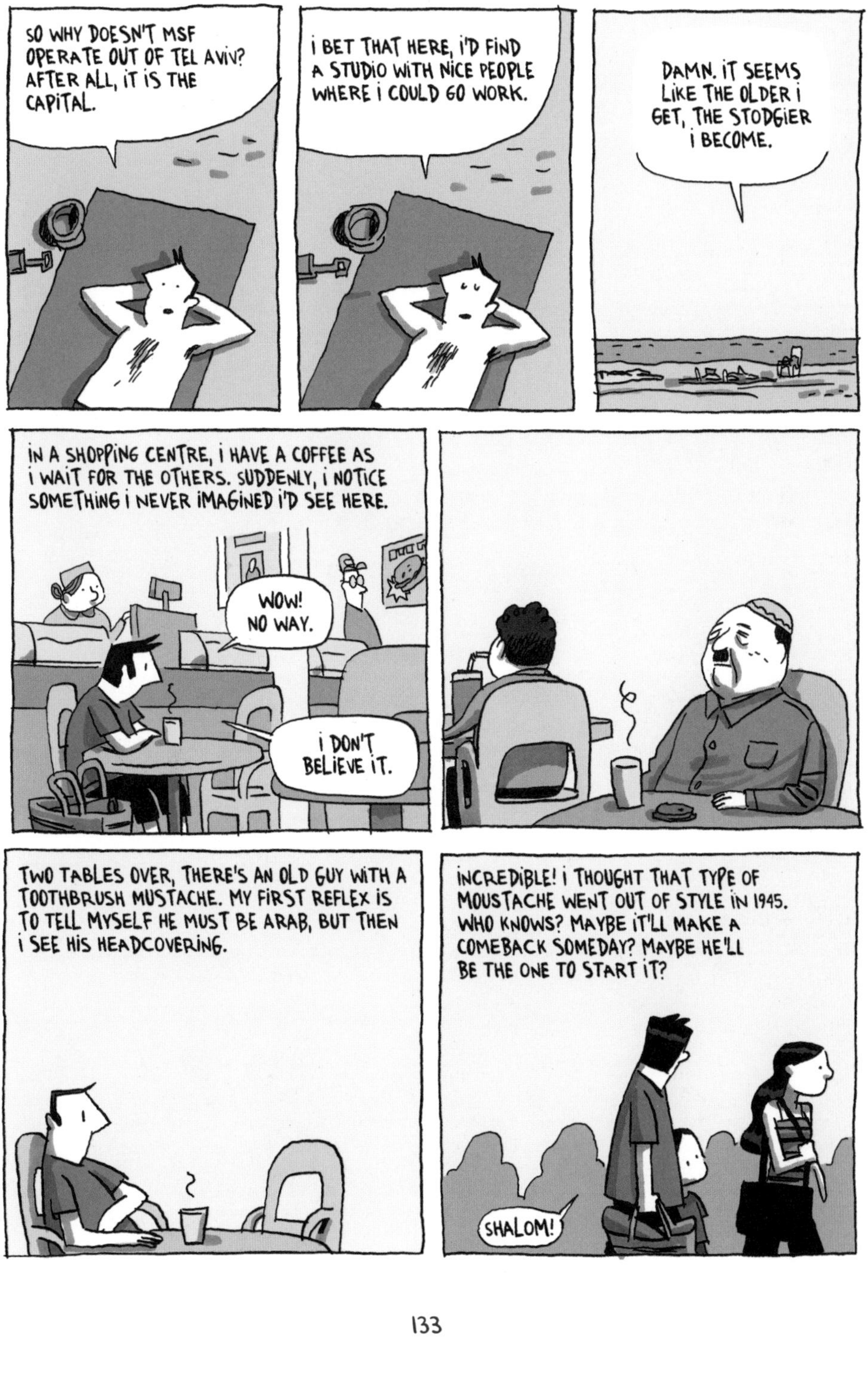
SO WHY DOESN'T MSF OPERATE OUT OF TEL AVIV? AFTER ALL, IT IS THE CAPITAL.
I BET THAT HERE, I'D FIND A STUDIO WITH NICE PEOPLE WHERE I COULD GO WORK.
DAMN. IT SEEMS LIKE THE OLDER I GET, THE STODGIER I BECOME.
IN A SHOPPING CENTRE, I HAVE A COFFEE AS I WAIT FOR THE OTHERS. SUDDENLY, I NOTICE SOMETHING I NEVER IMAGINED I'D SEE HERE.
WOW! NO WAY.
I DON'T BELIEVE IT.
TWO TABLES OVER, THERE'S AN OLD GUY WITH A TOOTHBRUSH MUSTACHE. MY FIRST REFLEX IS TO TELL MYSELF HE MUST BE ARAB, BUT THEN I SEE HIS HEADCOVERING.
INCREDIBLE! I THOUGHT THAT TYPE OF MOUSTACHE WENT OUT OF STYLE IN 1945. WHO KNOWS? MAYBE IT'LL MAKE A COMEBACK SOMEDAY? MAYBE HE'LL BE THE ONE TO START IT?
SHALOM!

POGROMS AND TERRORISTS

ON DECEMBER 4, SETTLERS OCCUPYING A BUILDING IN CENTRAL HEBRON WERE EVACUATED BY THE ISRAELI ARMY.

THE SETTLERS PUT UP A FIERCE FIGHT, AND SIX SOLDIERS WERE INJURED DURING THE OPERATION.

OTHER SETTLERS RESPONDED WITH VIOLENT ATTACKS ON ARAB FAMILIES, ALL UNDER THE EYES OF JOURNALISTS.

THE STORY MADE THE FRONT PAGE OF THE PAPERS.

THE VAST MAJORITY OF ISRAELIS VIGOROUSLY DISAPPROVE OF THE EXTREME BEHAVIOUR OF THE HEBRON SETTLERS.

IN A STATEMENT FOLLOWING THESE INCIDENTS, EHUD OLMERT SPOKE OF "POGROMS" PERPETRATED BY JEWS AGAINST ARABS.

HARSH WORDS, DELIBERATELY USED BY THE PRIME MINISTER TO MAKE AN IMPRESSION.

For foreigners living in Israel, the tone employed by local journalists can be very surprising.

If you're used to more restrained criticism of Israel and its government, it's almost shocking.

On September 24, Zeev Sternhell, a founding member of Peace Now, escaped an assassination attempt by Jewish right-wing extremists.

The newspapers called it Zionist terrorism.

Elsewhere, you might think twice before accusing Jews of carrying out pogroms or terrorist activities.

In Israel, it's not an issue. The country is a democracy with a free press. That's not something you can say of its neighbours (for now).

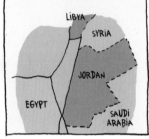

LIBYA
SYRIA
JORDAN
EGYPT
SAUDI ARABIA

But here journalists are openly critical and you'll often come across comments like this one: "Israel is a democracy for Jews, but not for the Arabs who live within its borders."

Spare the rod, spoil the child.

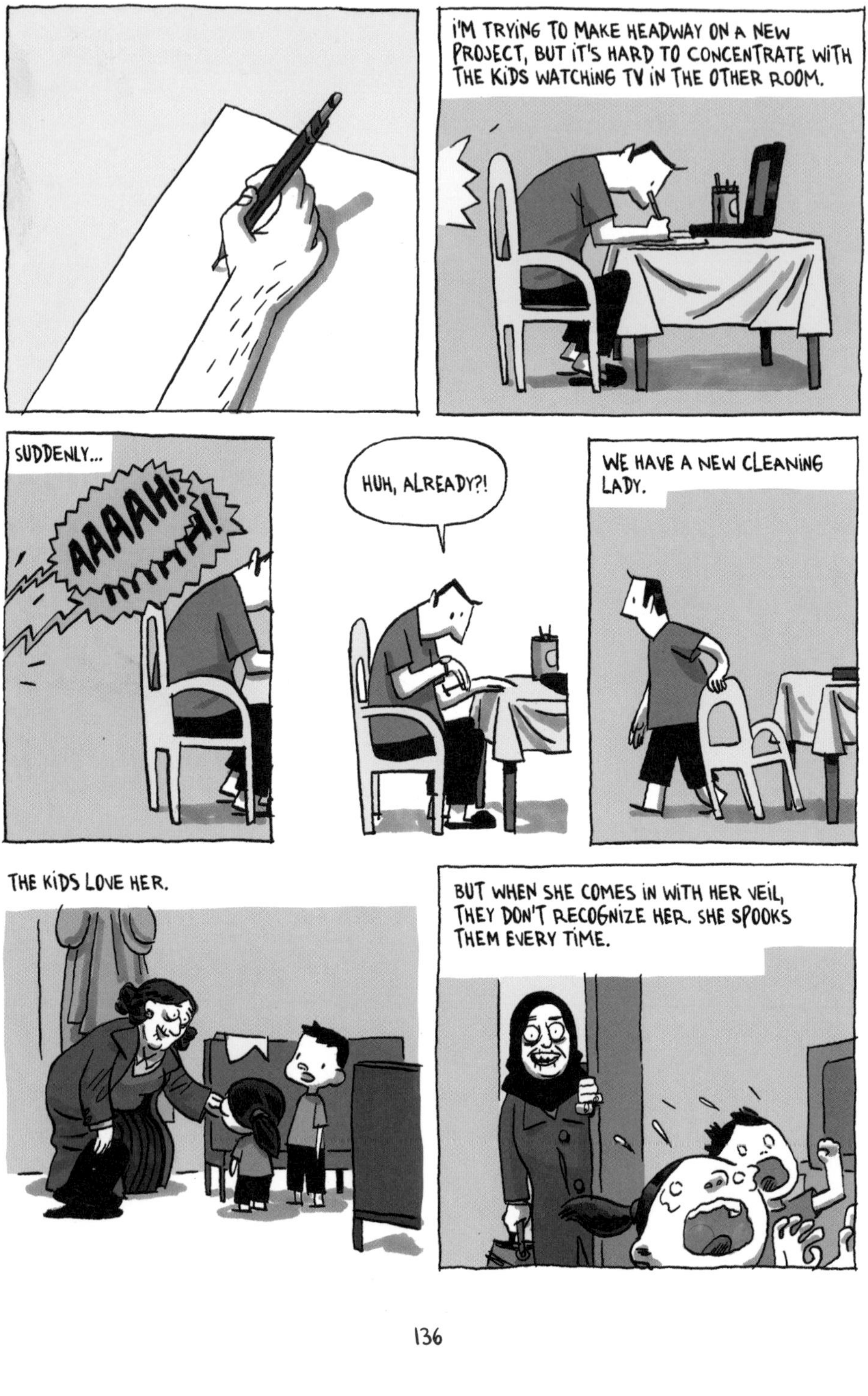
I'M TRYING TO MAKE HEADWAY ON A NEW PROJECT, BUT IT'S HARD TO CONCENTRATE WITH THE KIDS WATCHING TV IN THE OTHER ROOM.
SUDDENLY...
AAAAH!
HUH, ALREADY?!
WE HAVE A NEW CLEANING LADY.
THE KIDS LOVE HER.
BUT WHEN SHE COMES IN WITH HER VEIL, THEY DON'T RECOGNIZE HER. SHE SPOOKS THEM EVERY TIME.

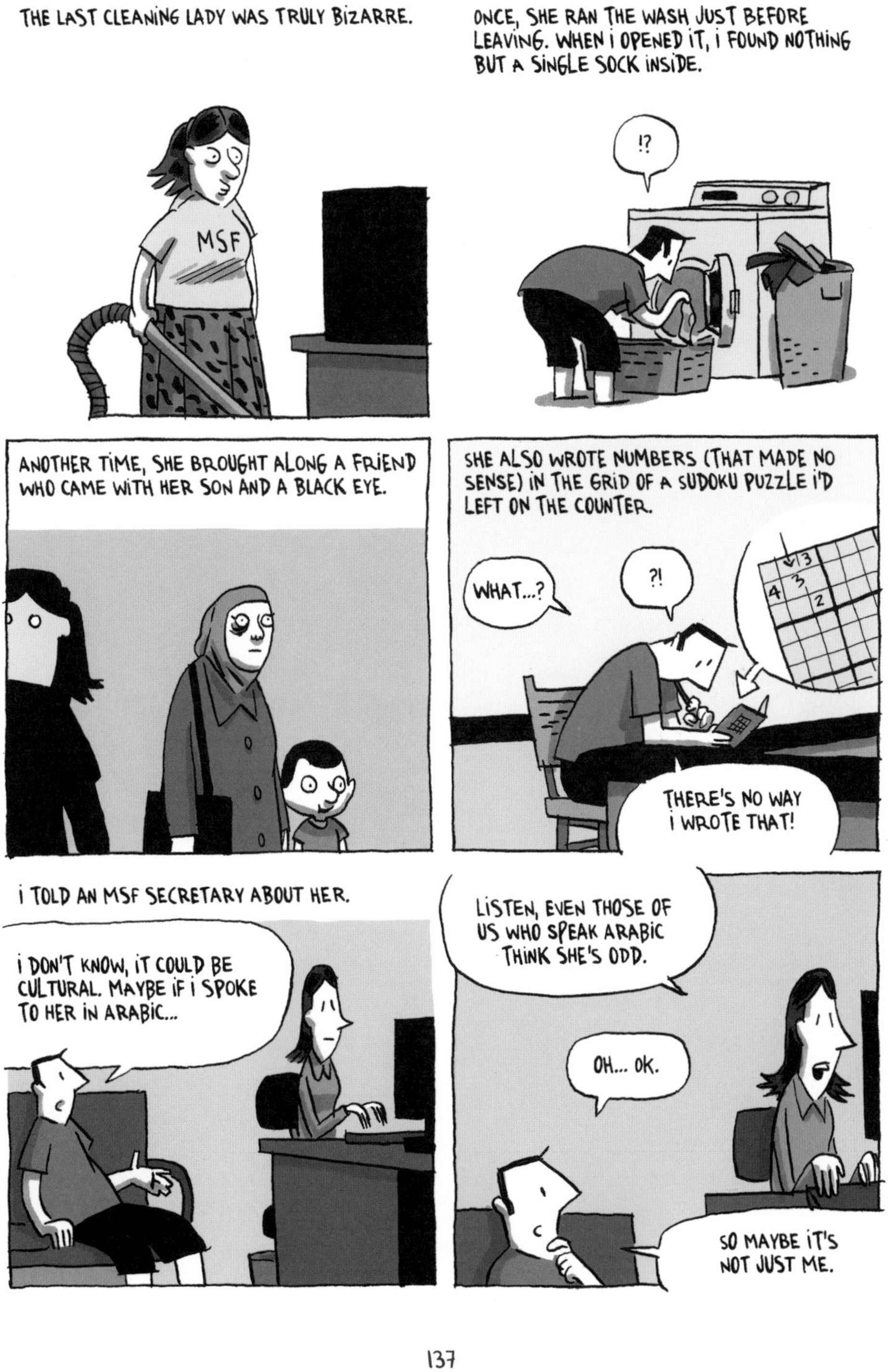
THE LAST CLEANING LADY WAS TRULY BIZARRE.
ONCE, SHE RAN THE WASH JUST BEFORE LEAVING. WHEN I OPENED IT, I FOUND NOTHING BUT A SINGLE SOCK INSIDE.
!?
MSF
ANOTHER TIME, SHE BROUGHT ALONG A FRIEND WHO CAME WITH HER SON AND A BLACK EYE.
SHE ALSO WROTE NUMBERS (THAT MADE NO SENSE) IN THE GRID OF A SUDOKU PUZZLE I'D LEFT ON THE COUNTER.
WHAT...?
?!
THERE'S NO WAY I WROTE THAT!
I TOLD AN MSF SECRETARY ABOUT HER.
I DON'T KNOW, IT COULD BE CULTURAL. MAYBE IF I SPOKE TO HER IN ARABIC...
LISTEN, EVEN THOSE OF US WHO SPEAK ARABIC THINK SHE'S ODD.
OH... OK.
SO MAYBE IT'S NOT JUST ME.

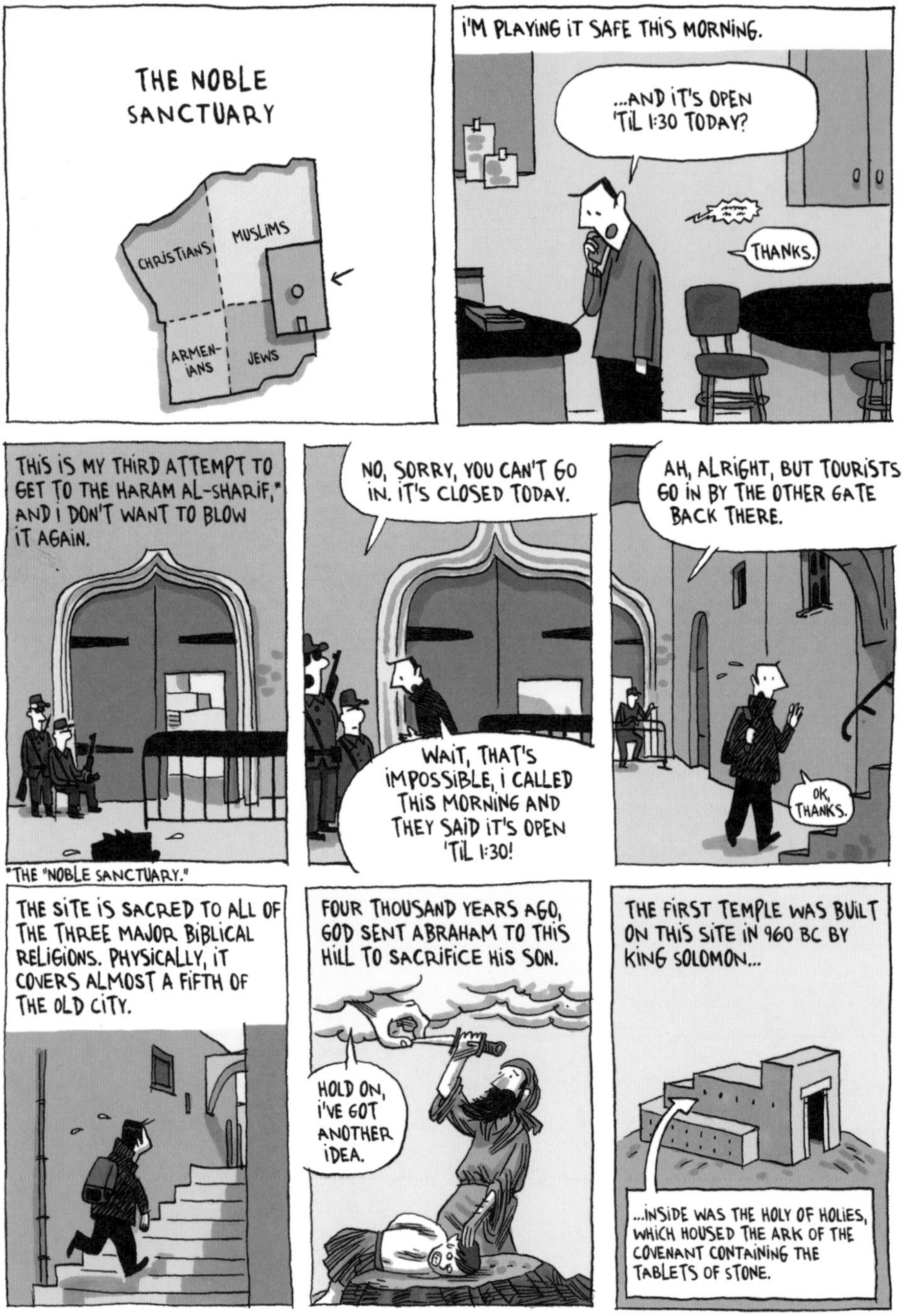
THE NOBLE SANCTUARY
CHRISTIANS
MUSLIMS
ARMEN-IANS
JEWS
I'M PLAYING IT SAFE THIS MORNING.
...AND IT'S OPEN 'TIL 1:30 TODAY?
THANKS.
THIS IS MY THIRD ATTEMPT TO GET TO THE HARAM AL-SHARIF,* AND I DON'T WANT TO BLOW IT AGAIN.
NO, SORRY, YOU CAN'T GO IN. IT'S CLOSED TODAY.
WAIT, THAT'S IMPOSSIBLE, I CALLED THIS MORNING AND THEY SAID IT'S OPEN 'TIL 1:30!
AH, ALRIGHT, BUT TOURISTS GO IN BY THE OTHER GATE BACK THERE.
OK, THANKS.
*THE "NOBLE SANCTUARY."
THE SITE IS SACRED TO ALL OF THE THREE MAJOR BIBLICAL RELIGIONS. PHYSICALLY, IT COVERS ALMOST A FIFTH OF THE OLD CITY.
FOUR THOUSAND YEARS AGO, GOD SENT ABRAHAM TO THIS HILL TO SACRIFICE HIS SON.
HOLD ON, I'VE GOT ANOTHER IDEA.
THE FIRST TEMPLE WAS BUILT ON THIS SITE IN 960 BC BY KING SOLOMON...
...INSIDE WAS THE HOLY OF HOLIES, WHICH HOUSED THE ARK OF THE COVENANT CONTAINING THE TABLETS OF STONE.

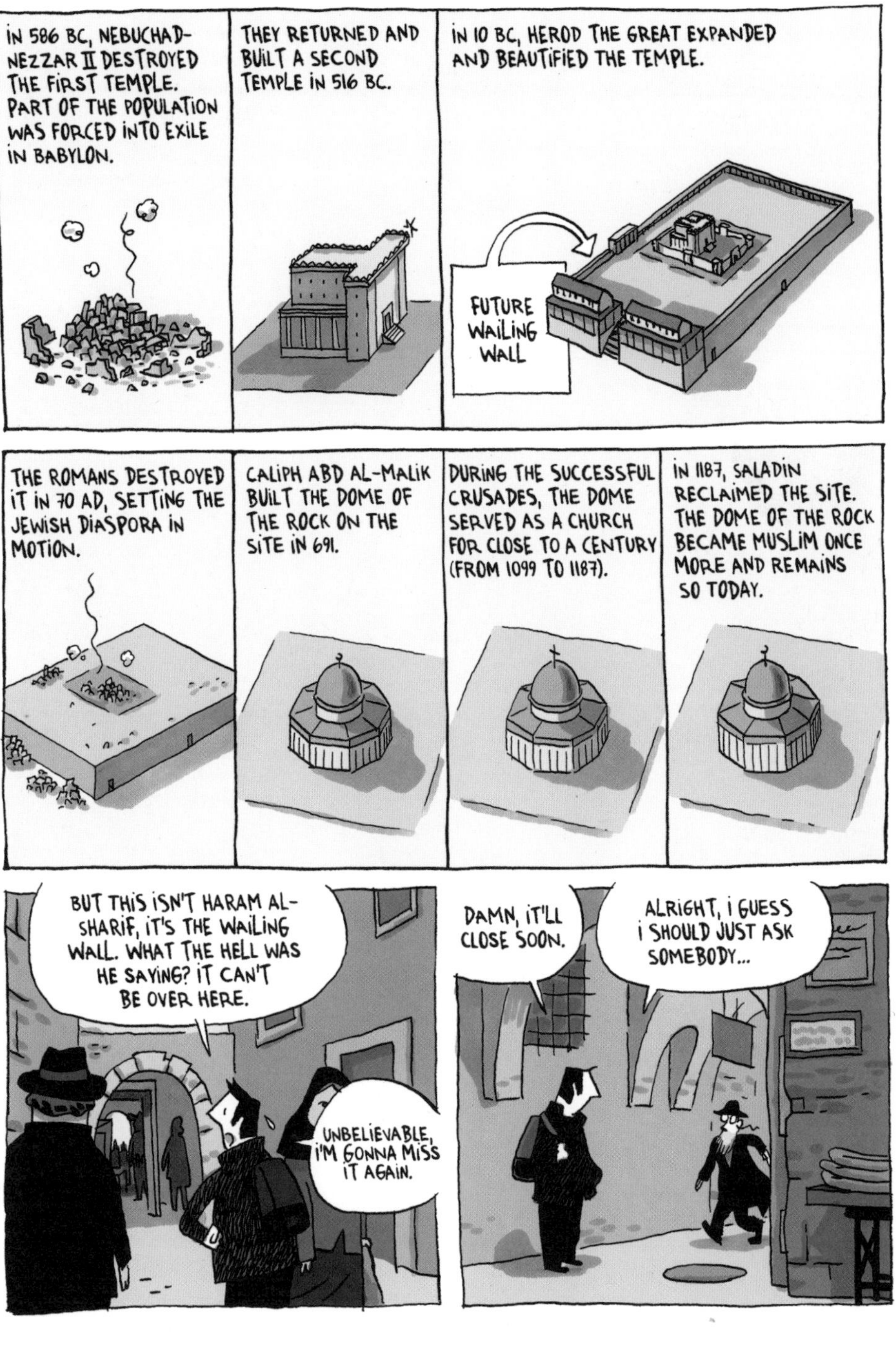

IN 586 BC, NEBUCHADNEZZAR II DESTROYED THE FIRST TEMPLE. PART OF THE POPULATION WAS FORCED INTO EXILE IN BABYLON.
THEY RETURNED AND BUILT A SECOND TEMPLE IN 516 BC.
IN 10 BC, HEROD THE GREAT EXPANDED AND BEAUTIFIED THE TEMPLE.
FUTURE WAILING WALL
THE ROMANS DESTROYED IT IN 70 AD, SETTING THE JEWISH DIASPORA IN MOTION.
CALIPH ABD AL-MALIK BUILT THE DOME OF THE ROCK ON THE SITE IN 691.
DURING THE SUCCESSFUL CRUSADES, THE DOME SERVED AS A CHURCH FOR CLOSE TO A CENTURY (FROM 1099 TO 1187).
IN 1187, SALADIN RECLAIMED THE SITE. THE DOME OF THE ROCK BECAME MUSLIM ONCE MORE AND REMAINS SO TODAY.
BUT THIS ISN'T HARAM AL-SHARIF, IT'S THE WAILING WALL. WHAT THE HELL WAS HE SAYING? IT CAN'T BE OVER HERE.
UNBELIEVABLE, I'M GONNA MISS IT AGAIN.
DAMN, IT'LL CLOSE SOON.
ALRIGHT, I GUESS I SHOULD JUST ASK SOMEBODY...

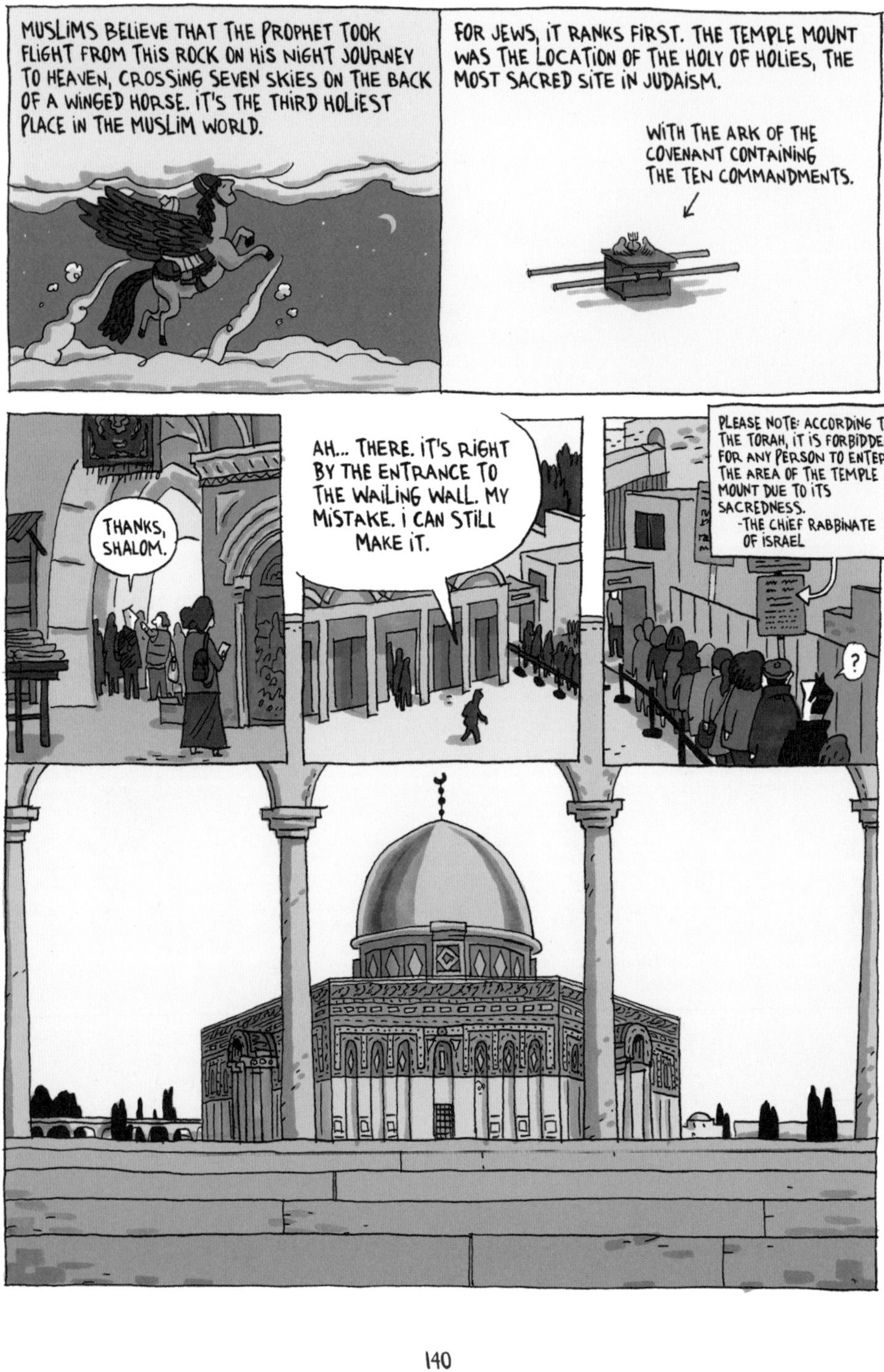
MUSLIMS BELIEVE THAT THE PROPHET TOOK FLIGHT FROM THIS ROCK ON HIS NIGHT JOURNEY TO HEAVEN, CROSSING SEVEN SKIES ON THE BACK OF A WINGED HORSE. IT'S THE THIRD HOLIEST PLACE IN THE MUSLIM WORLD.
FOR JEWS, IT RANKS FIRST. THE TEMPLE MOUNT WAS THE LOCATION OF THE HOLY OF HOLIES, THE MOST SACRED SITE IN JUDAISM.
WITH THE ARK OF THE COVENANT CONTAINING THE TEN COMMANDMENTS.
THANKS, SHALOM.
AH... THERE. IT'S RIGHT BY THE ENTRANCE TO THE WAILING WALL. MY MISTAKE. I CAN STILL MAKE IT.
PLEASE NOTE: ACCORDING TO THE TORAH, IT IS FORBIDDEN FOR ANY PERSON TO ENTER THE AREA OF THE TEMPLE MOUNT DUE TO ITS SACREDNESS.
-THE CHIEF RABBINATE OF ISRAEL
?

I'M FINALLY ON THE ESPLANADE. I DON'T KNOW IF IT'S THE FACT THAT IT TOOK ME A FEW TRIES TO FIND IT, OR THE CONTRAST BETWEEN THIS VAST SPACE AND THE BUSTLE OF THE NARROW STREETS BEYOND, BUT I FEEL QUITE MOVED TO BE HERE, JUST TO BE ABLE TO TAKE IT ALL IN.

SHADED BY GREENERY, THE COMPLEX IS THE SIZE OF A NEIGHBOURHOOD.

I PASS A GROUP OF JEWS. I GUESS THEY WEREN'T PUT OFF BY THE POSTER AT THE ENTRANCE.

THE RABBIS HAVE FORBIDDEN JEWS FROM ENTERING THE TEMPLE MOUNT SINCE THEY MIGHT INADVERTENTLY SET FOOT ON THE HOLY OF HOLIES.

ONE RABBI EVEN CALLED FOR A NO-FLY ZONE OVER THE SITE...

ONLY THE HIGH PRIEST IS ALLOWED TO ENTER THE HOLY OF HOLIES.

141

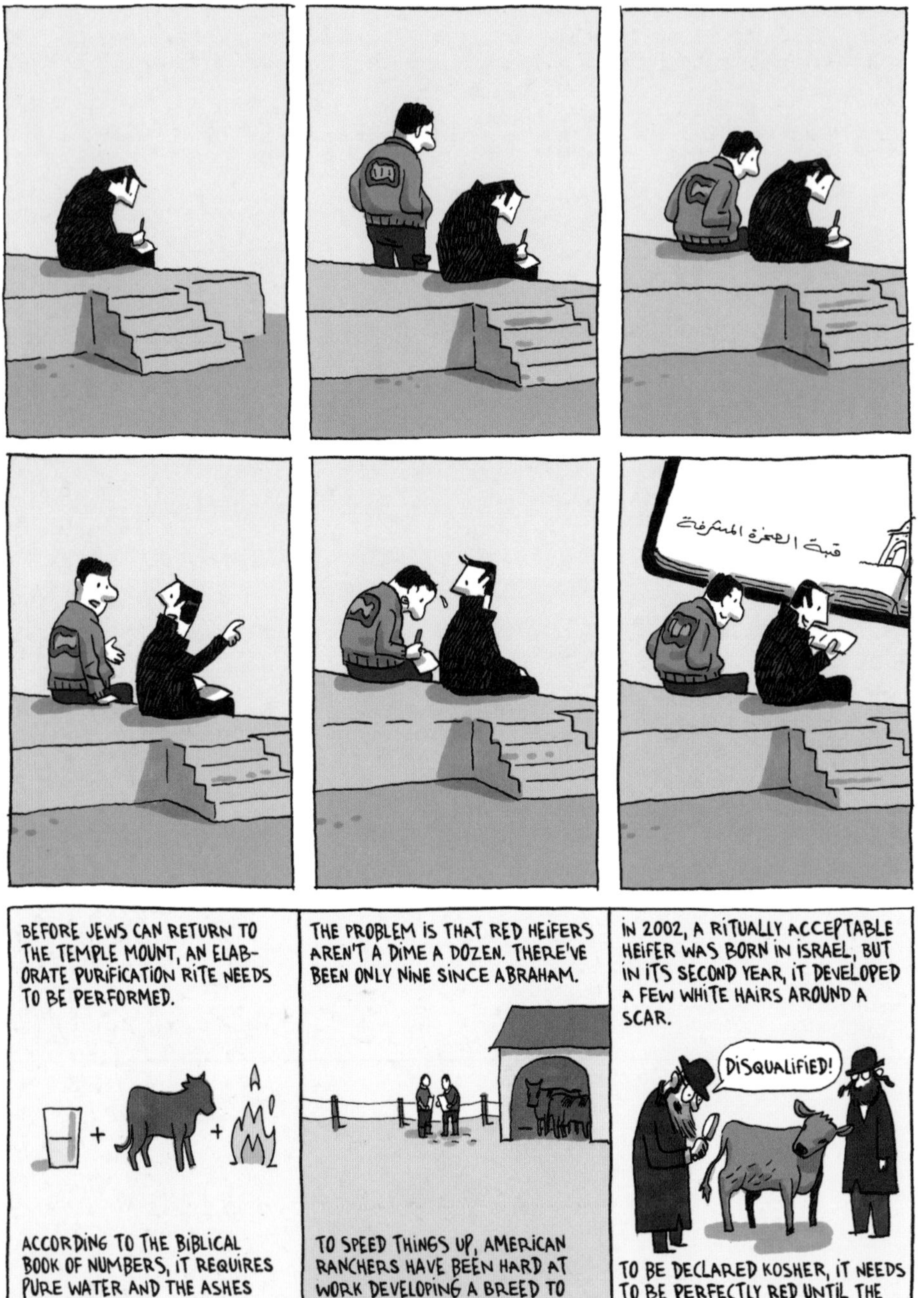

قبة الصخرة المشرفة
BEFORE JEWS CAN RETURN TO THE TEMPLE MOUNT, AN ELABORATE PURIFICATION RITE NEEDS TO BE PERFORMED.
ACCORDING TO THE BIBLICAL BOOK OF NUMBERS, IT REQUIRES PURE WATER AND THE ASHES OF A RED HEIFER.
THE PROBLEM IS THAT RED HEIFERS AREN'T A DIME A DOZEN. THERE'VE BEEN ONLY NINE SINCE ABRAHAM.
TO SPEED THINGS UP, AMERICAN RANCHERS HAVE BEEN HARD AT WORK DEVELOPING A BREED TO CREATE THE TENTH HEIFER.
IN 2002, A RITUALLY ACCEPTABLE HEIFER WAS BORN IN ISRAEL, BUT IN ITS SECOND YEAR, IT DEVELOPED A FEW WHITE HAIRS AROUND A SCAR.
DISQUALIFIED!
TO BE DECLARED KOSHER, IT NEEDS TO BE PERFECTLY RED UNTIL THE AGE OF THREE, HOOVES AND ALL.

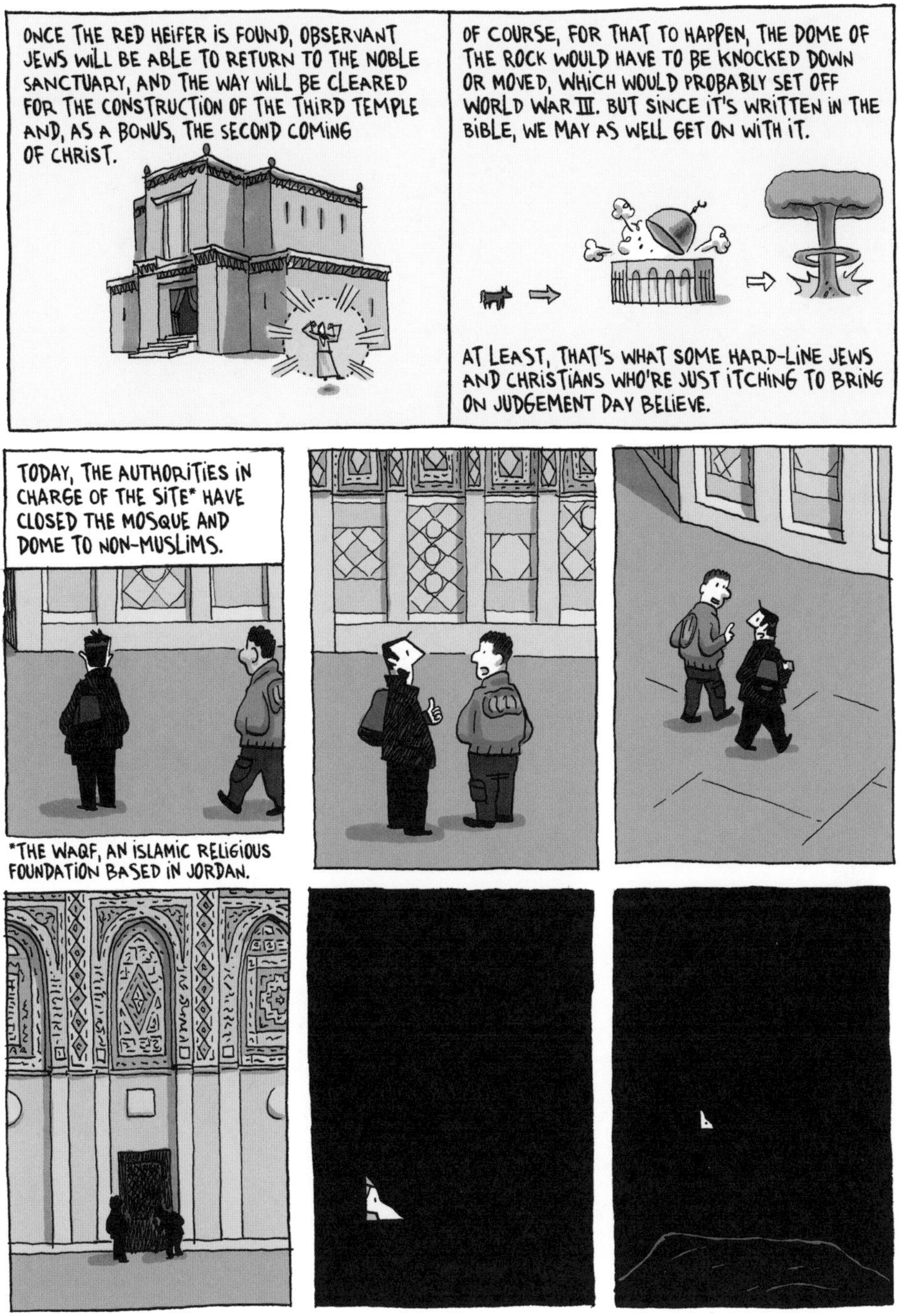
ONCE THE RED HEIFER IS FOUND, OBSERVANT JEWS WILL BE ABLE TO RETURN TO THE NOBLE SANCTUARY, AND THE WAY WILL BE CLEARED FOR THE CONSTRUCTION OF THE THIRD TEMPLE AND, AS A BONUS, THE SECOND COMING OF CHRIST.
OF COURSE, FOR THAT TO HAPPEN, THE DOME OF THE ROCK WOULD HAVE TO BE KNOCKED DOWN OR MOVED, WHICH WOULD PROBABLY SET OFF WORLD WAR III. BUT SINCE IT'S WRITTEN IN THE BIBLE, WE MAY AS WELL GET ON WITH IT.
AT LEAST, THAT'S WHAT SOME HARD-LINE JEWS AND CHRISTIANS WHO'RE JUST ITCHING TO BRING ON JUDGEMENT DAY BELIEVE.
TODAY, THE AUTHORITIES IN CHARGE OF THE SITE* HAVE CLOSED THE MOSQUE AND DOME TO NON-MUSLIMS.
*THE WAQF, AN ISLAMIC RELIGIOUS FOUNDATION BASED IN JORDAN.

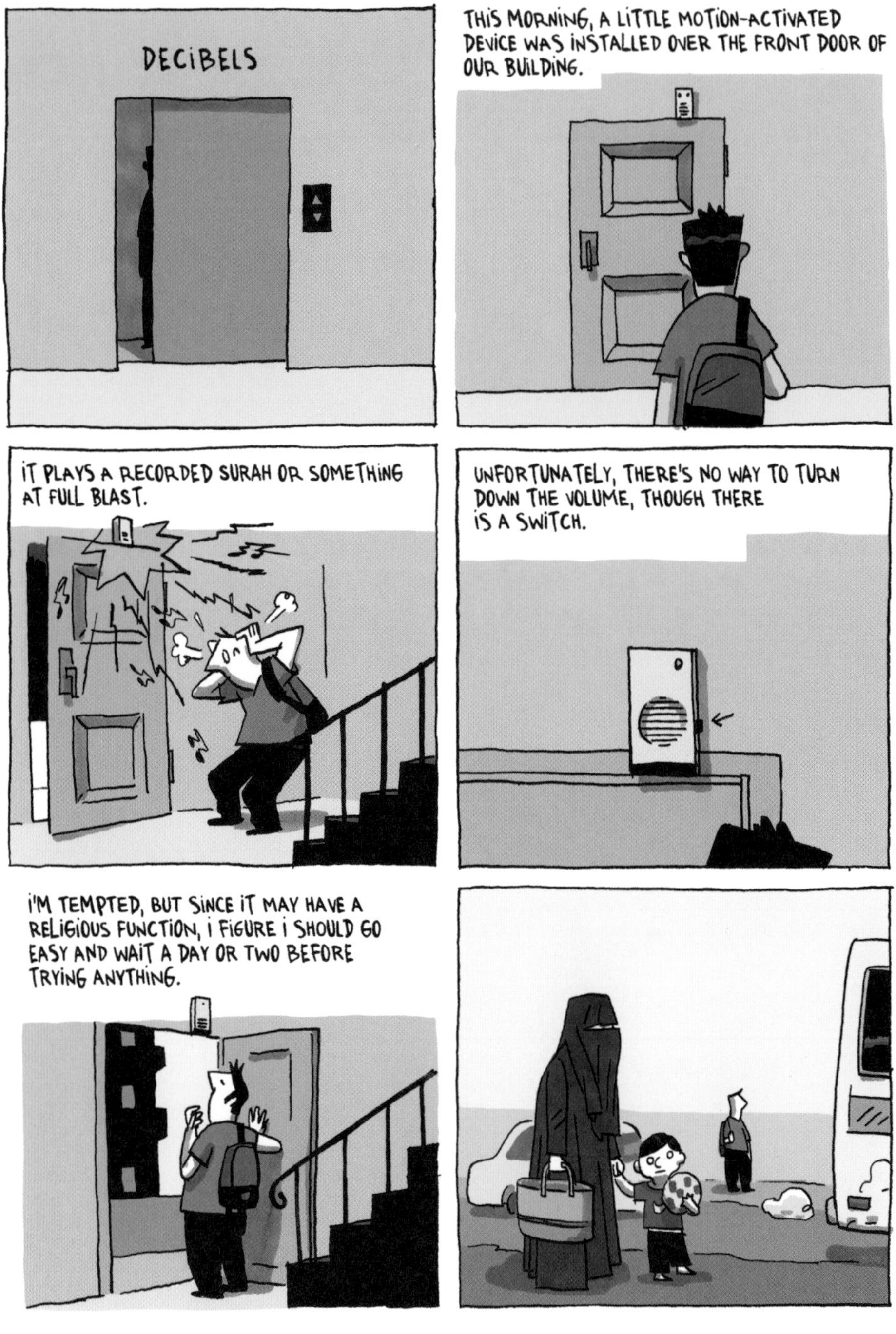
DECIBELS
THIS MORNING, A LITTLE MOTION-ACTIVATED DEVICE WAS INSTALLED OVER THE FRONT DOOR OF OUR BUILDING.
IT PLAYS A RECORDED SURAH OR SOMETHING AT FULL BLAST.
UNFORTUNATELY, THERE'S NO WAY TO TURN DOWN THE VOLUME, THOUGH THERE IS A SWITCH.
I'M TEMPTED, BUT SINCE IT MAY HAVE A RELIGIOUS FUNCTION, I FIGURE I SHOULD GO EASY AND WAIT A DAY OR TWO BEFORE TRYING ANYTHING.

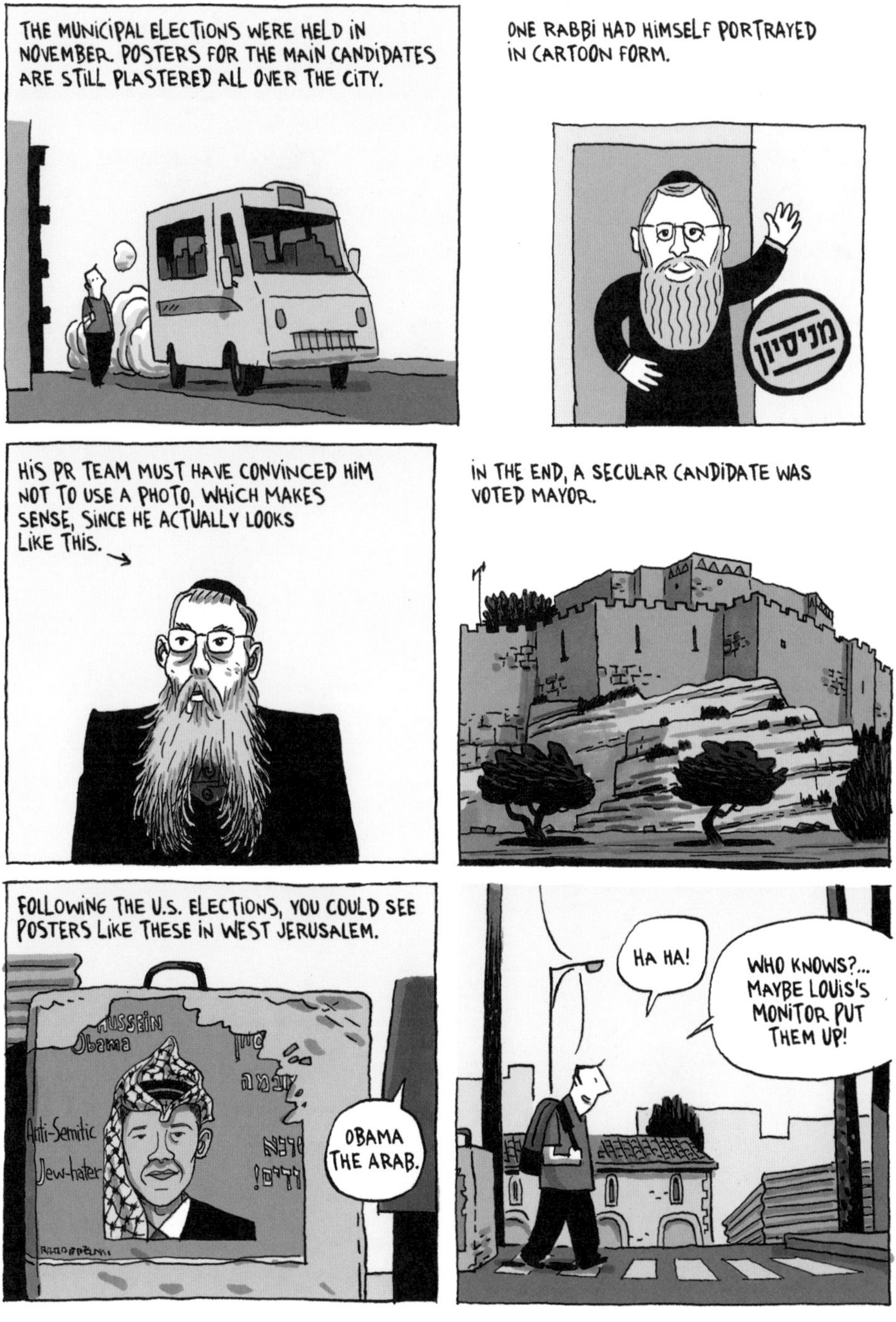
THE MUNICIPAL ELECTIONS WERE HELD IN NOVEMBER. POSTERS FOR THE MAIN CANDIDATES ARE STILL PLASTERED ALL OVER THE CITY.
ONE RABBI HAD HIMSELF PORTRAYED IN CARTOON FORM.
HIS PR TEAM MUST HAVE CONVINCED HIM NOT TO USE A PHOTO, WHICH MAKES SENSE, SINCE HE ACTUALLY LOOKS LIKE THIS.
IN THE END, A SECULAR CANDIDATE WAS VOTED MAYOR.
FOLLOWING THE U.S. ELECTIONS, YOU COULD SEE POSTERS LIKE THESE IN WEST JERUSALEM.
HUSSEIN
Obama
Anti-Semitic
Jew-hater
OBAMA THE ARAB.
HA HA!
WHO KNOWS?... MAYBE LOUIS'S MONITOR PUT THEM UP!

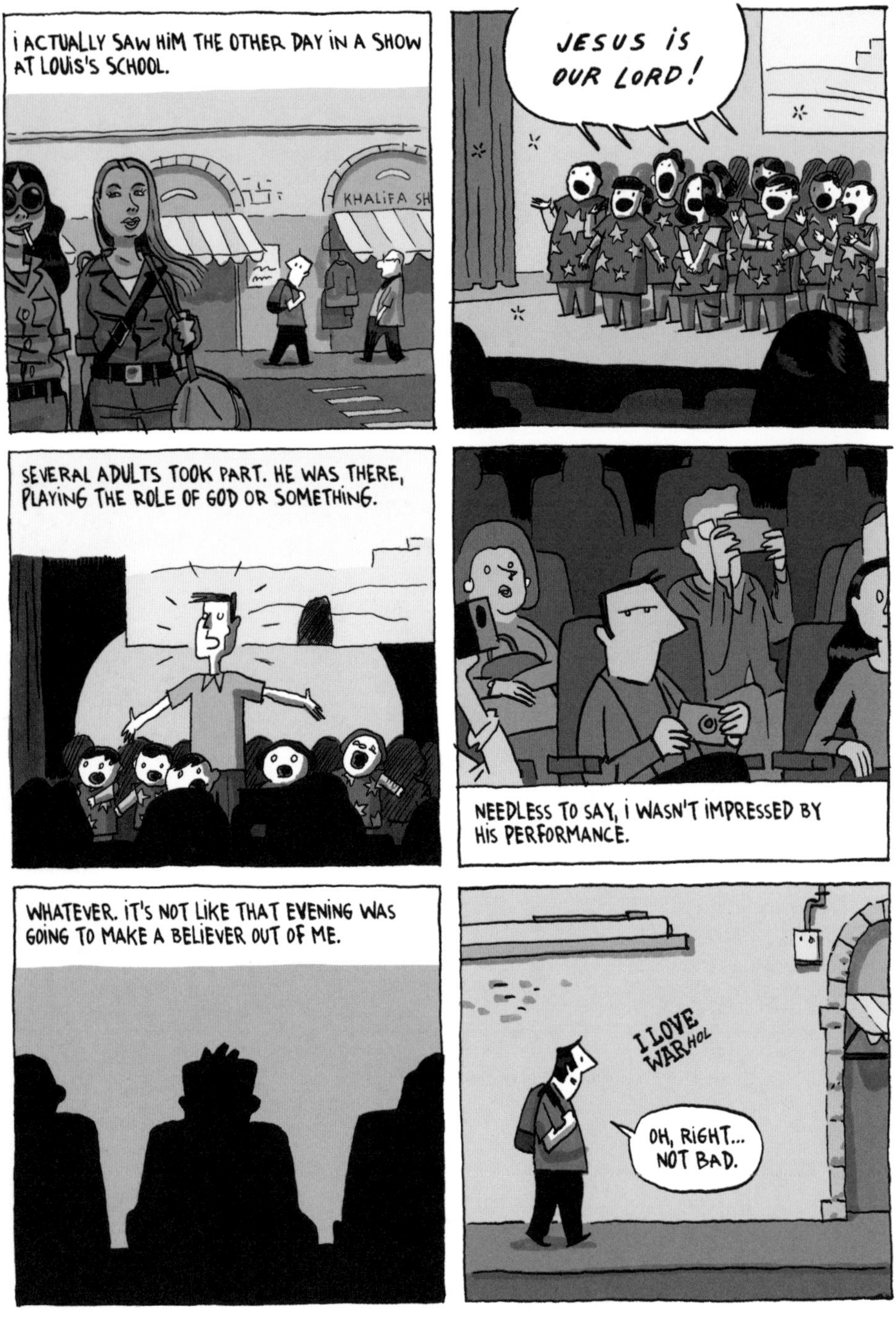
i ACTUALLY SAW HIM THE OTHER DAY iN A SHOW AT LOUiS'S SCHOOL.
KHALiFA SH
JESUS iS OUR LORD!
SEVERAL ADULTS TOOK PART. HE WAS THERE, PLAYiNG THE ROLE OF GOD OR SOMETHiNG.
NEEDLESS TO SAY, i WASN'T iMPRESSED BY HiS PERFORMANCE.
WHATEVER. iT'S NOT LIKE THAT EVENiNG WAS GOiNG TO MAKE A BELiEVER OUT OF ME.
I LOVE WARHOL
OH, RiGHT... NOT BAD.

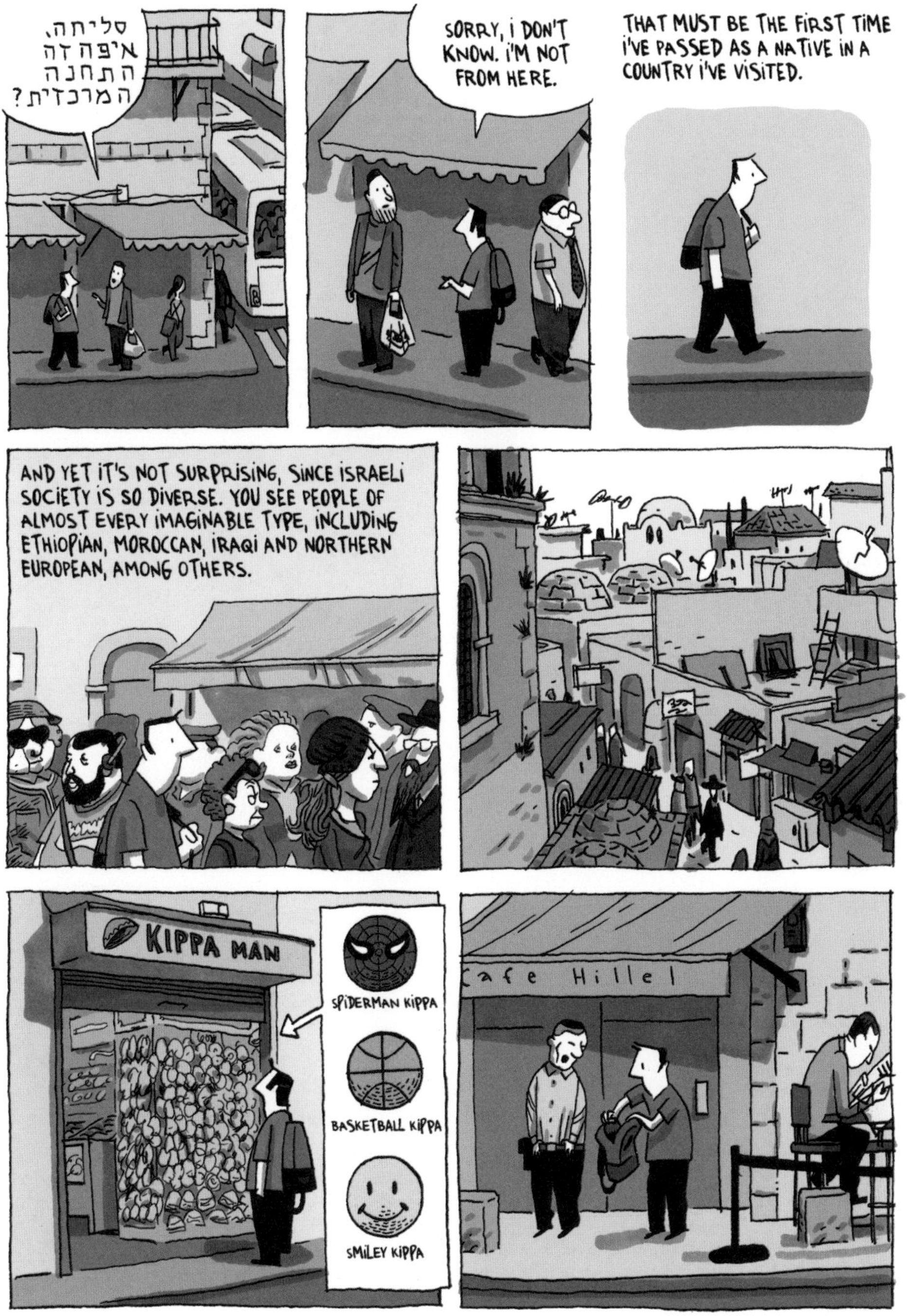
סליחה, איפה זה התחנה המרכזית?
SORRY, I DON'T KNOW. I'M NOT FROM HERE.
THAT MUST BE THE FIRST TIME I'VE PASSED AS A NATIVE IN A COUNTRY I'VE VISITED.
AND YET IT'S NOT SURPRISING, SINCE ISRAELI SOCIETY IS SO DIVERSE. YOU SEE PEOPLE OF ALMOST EVERY IMAGINABLE TYPE, INCLUDING ETHIOPIAN, MOROCCAN, IRAQI AND NORTHERN EUROPEAN, AMONG OTHERS.
KIPPA MAN
SPIDERMAN KIPPA
BASKETBALL KIPPA
SMILEY KIPPA
Cafe Hillel

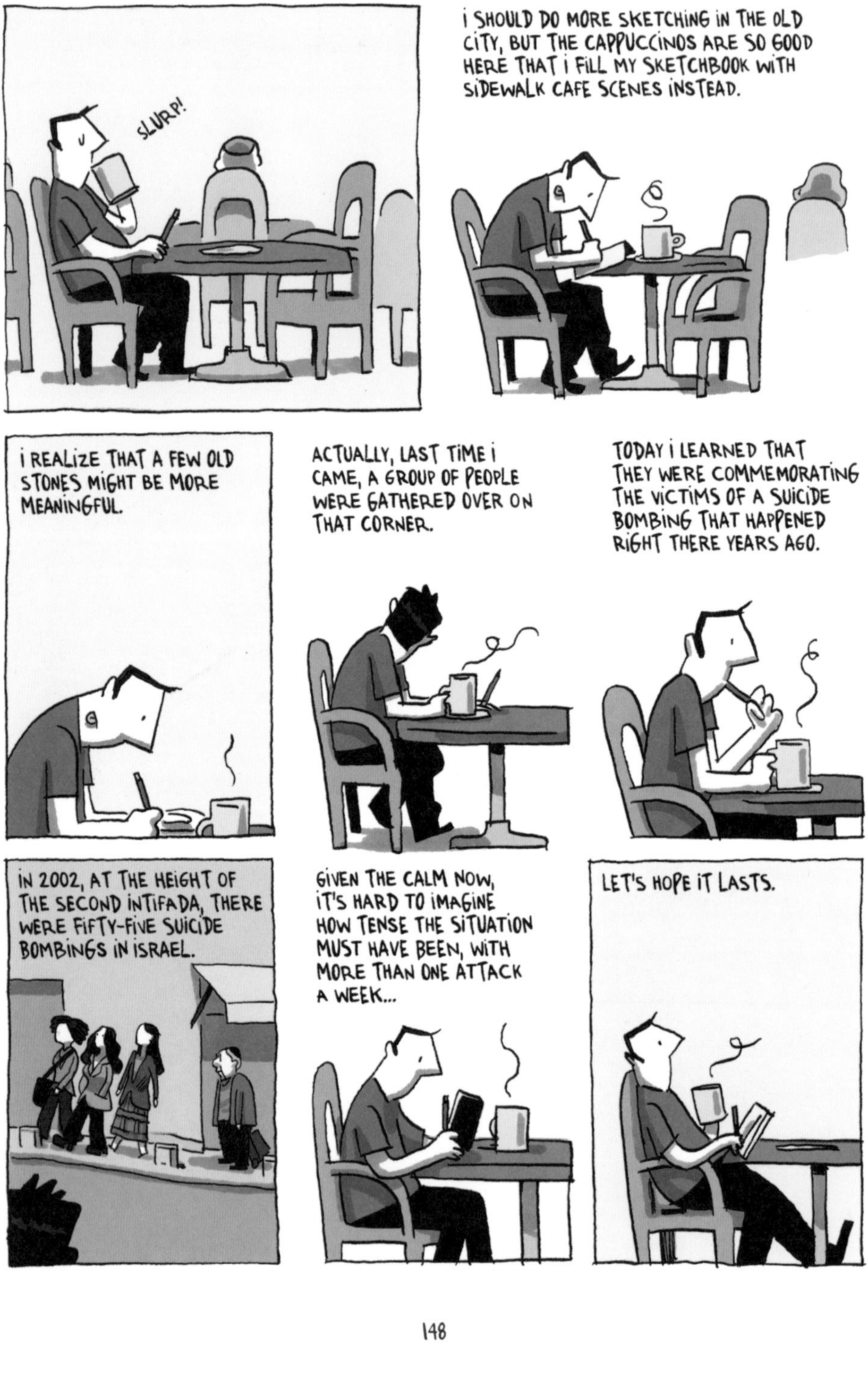
SLURP!
I SHOULD DO MORE SKETCHING IN THE OLD CITY, BUT THE CAPPUCCINOS ARE SO GOOD HERE THAT I FILL MY SKETCHBOOK WITH SIDEWALK CAFE SCENES INSTEAD.
I REALIZE THAT A FEW OLD STONES MIGHT BE MORE MEANINGFUL.
ACTUALLY, LAST TIME I CAME, A GROUP OF PEOPLE WERE GATHERED OVER ON THAT CORNER.
TODAY I LEARNED THAT THEY WERE COMMEMORATING THE VICTIMS OF A SUICIDE BOMBING THAT HAPPENED RIGHT THERE YEARS AGO.
IN 2002, AT THE HEIGHT OF THE SECOND INTIFADA, THERE WERE FIFTY-FIVE SUICIDE BOMBINGS IN ISRAEL.
GIVEN THE CALM NOW, IT'S HARD TO IMAGINE HOW TENSE THE SITUATION MUST HAVE BEEN, WITH MORE THAN ONE ATTACK A WEEK...
LET'S HOPE IT LASTS.

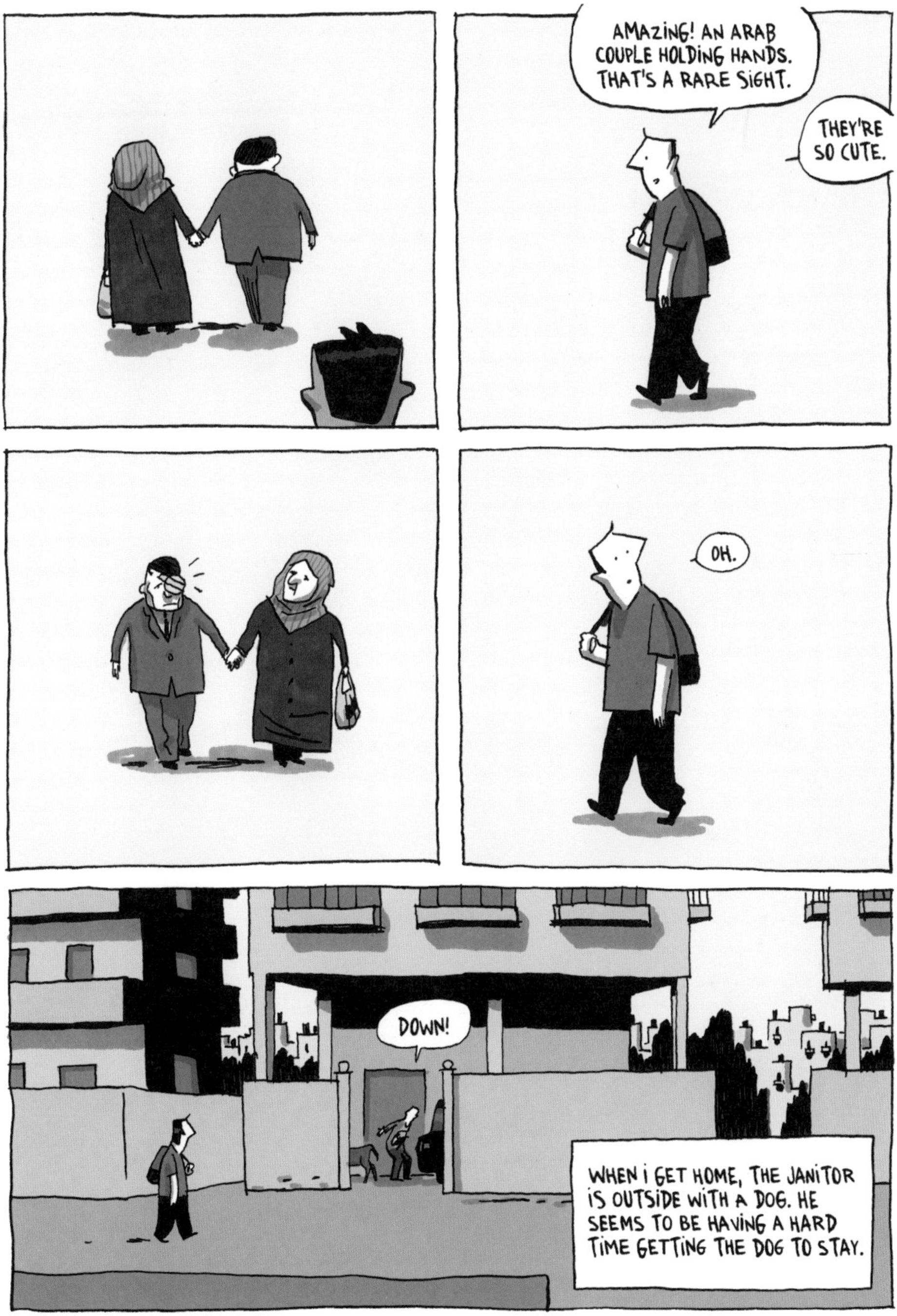
AMAZING! AN ARAB COUPLE HOLDING HANDS. THAT'S A RARE SIGHT.
THEY'RE SO CUTE.
OH.
DOWN!
WHEN I GET HOME, THE JANITOR IS OUTSIDE WITH A DOG. HE SEEMS TO BE HAVING A HARD TIME GETTING THE DOG TO STAY.

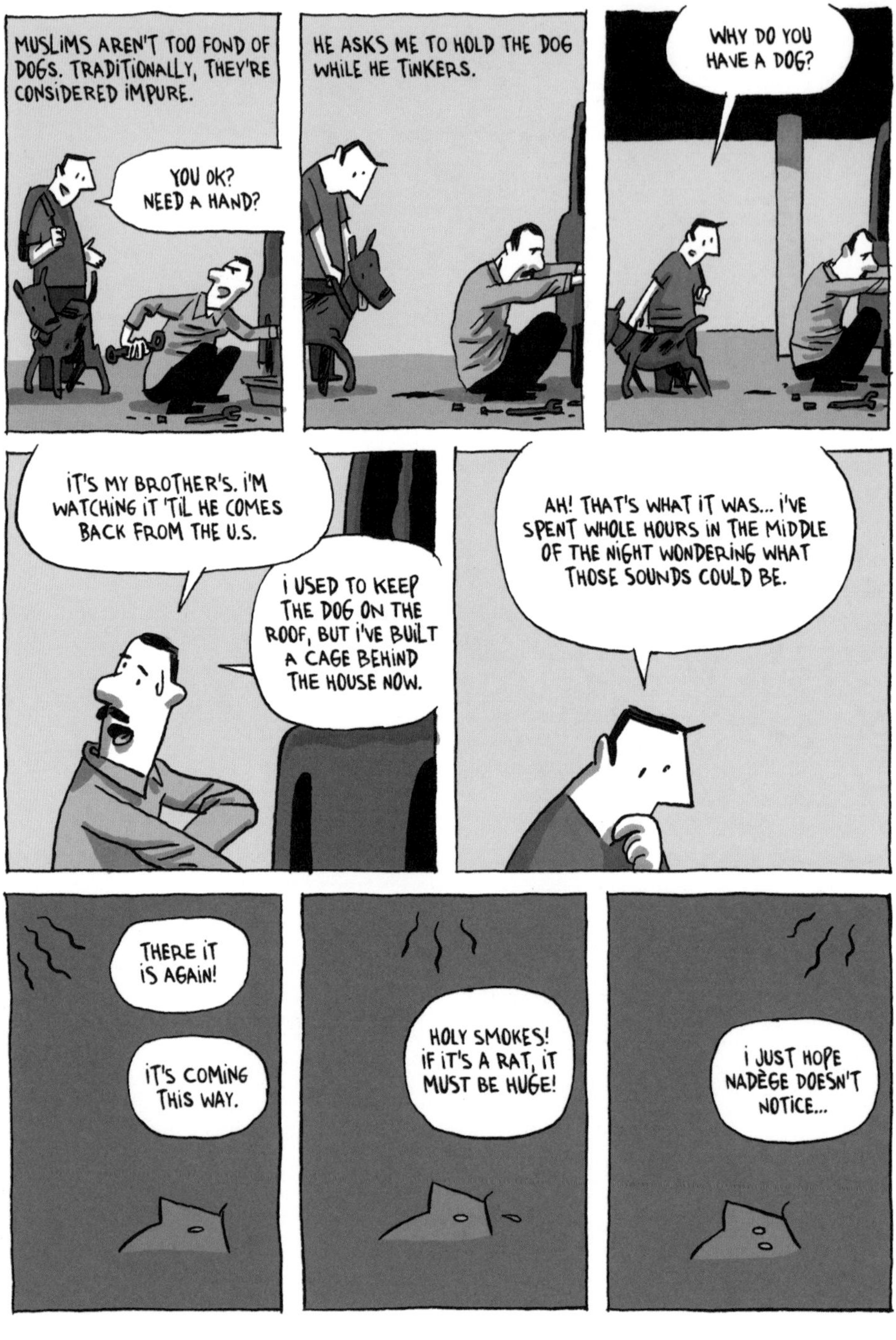
MUSLIMS AREN'T TOO FOND OF DOGS. TRADITIONALLY, THEY'RE CONSIDERED IMPURE.
YOU OK? NEED A HAND?
HE ASKS ME TO HOLD THE DOG WHILE HE TINKERS.
WHY DO YOU HAVE A DOG?
IT'S MY BROTHER'S. I'M WATCHING IT 'TIL HE COMES BACK FROM THE U.S.
I USED TO KEEP THE DOG ON THE ROOF, BUT I'VE BUILT A CAGE BEHIND THE HOUSE NOW.
AH! THAT'S WHAT IT WAS... I'VE SPENT WHOLE HOURS IN THE MIDDLE OF THE NIGHT WONDERING WHAT THOSE SOUNDS COULD BE.
THERE IT IS AGAIN!
IT'S COMING THIS WAY.
HOLY SMOKES! IF IT'S A RAT, IT MUST BE HUGE!
I JUST HOPE NADÈGE DOESN'T NOTICE...

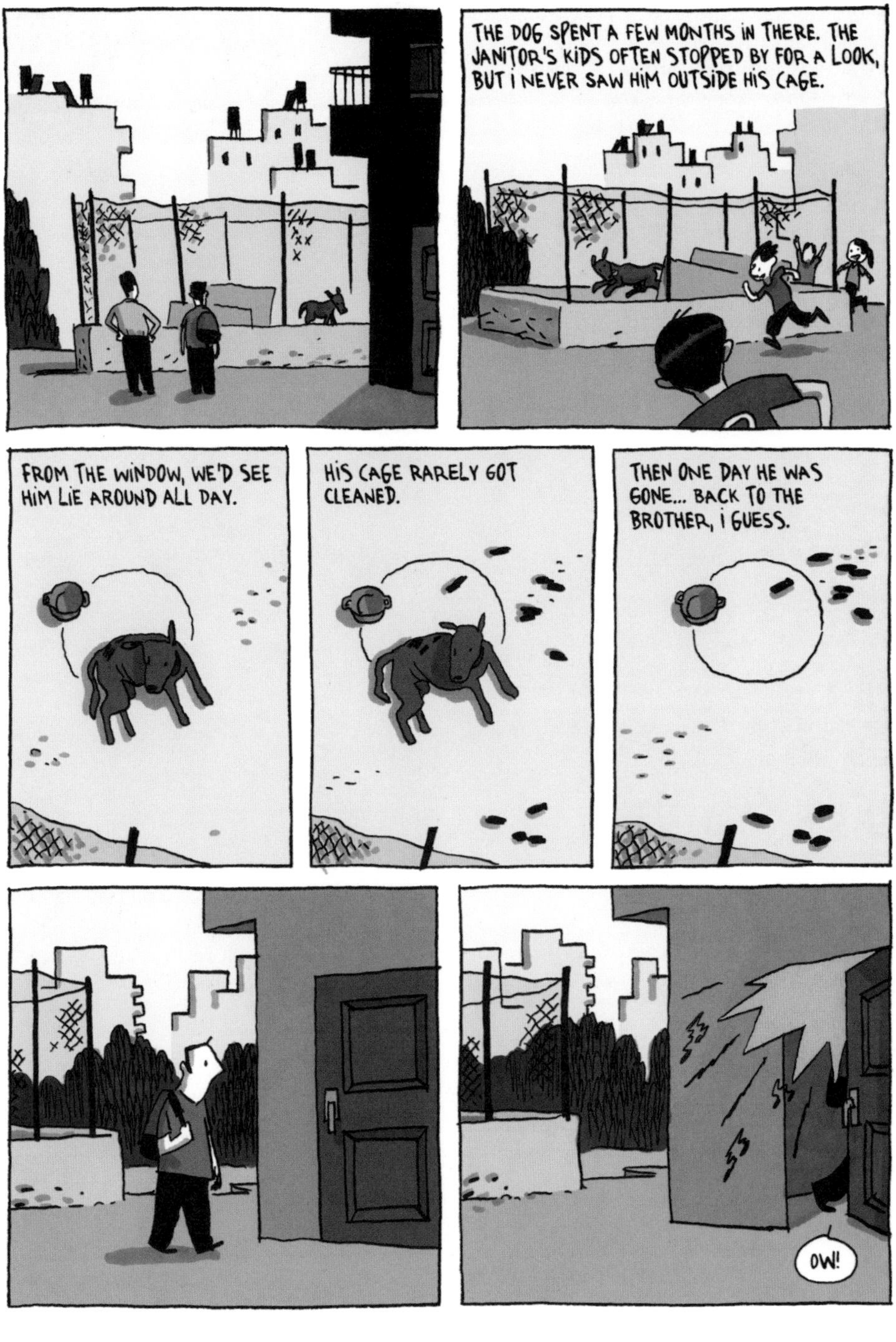
THE DOG SPENT A FEW MONTHS IN THERE. THE JANITOR'S KIDS OFTEN STOPPED BY FOR A LOOK, BUT I NEVER SAW HIM OUTSIDE HIS CAGE.
FROM THE WINDOW, WE'D SEE HIM LIE AROUND ALL DAY.
HIS CAGE RARELY GOT CLEANED.
THEN ONE DAY HE WAS GONE... BACK TO THE BROTHER, I GUESS.
OW!

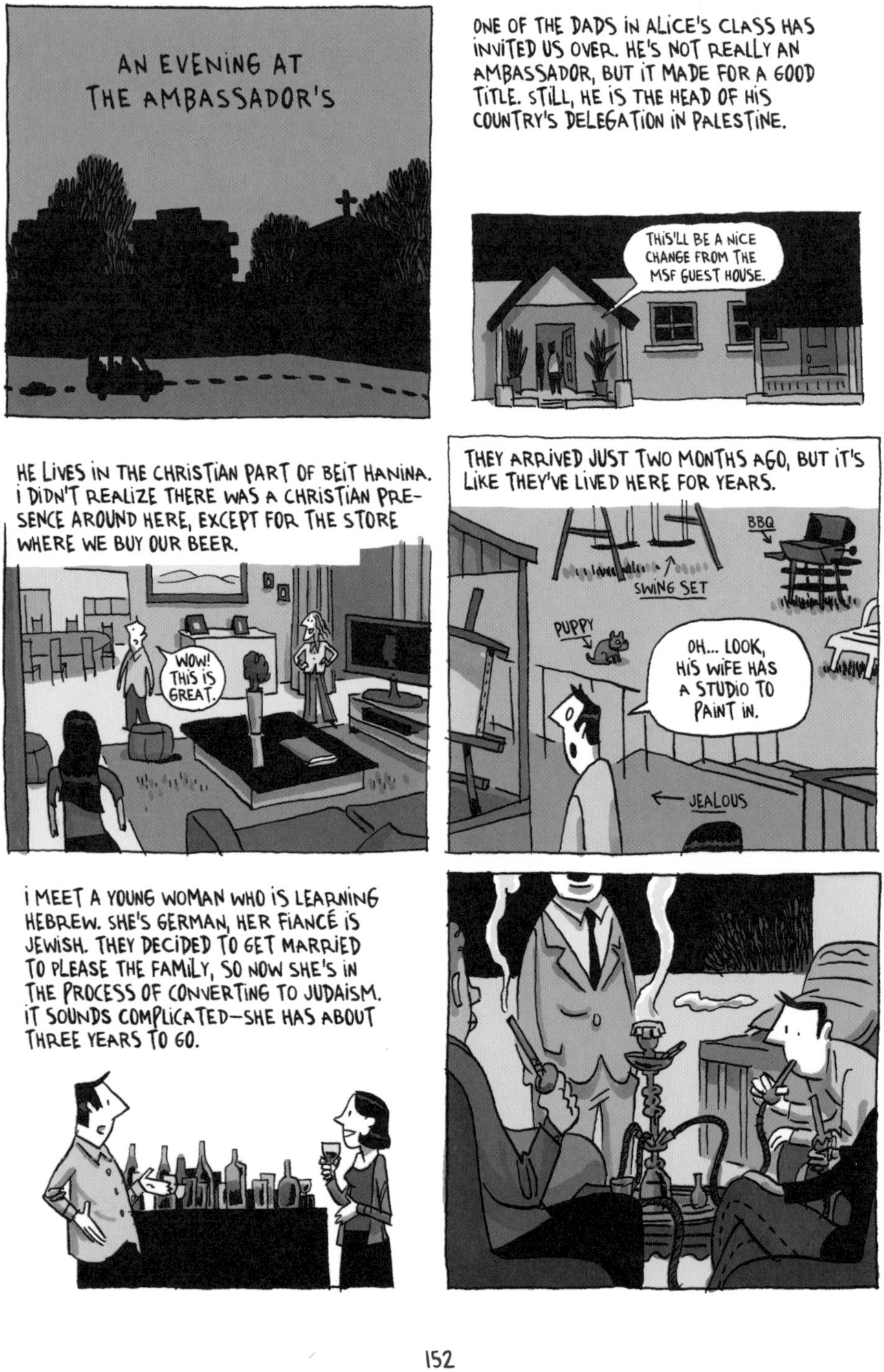
AN EVENING AT THE AMBASSADOR'S
ONE OF THE DADS IN ALICE'S CLASS HAS INVITED US OVER. HE'S NOT REALLY AN AMBASSADOR, BUT IT MADE FOR A GOOD TITLE. STILL, HE IS THE HEAD OF HIS COUNTRY'S DELEGATION IN PALESTINE.
THIS'LL BE A NICE CHANGE FROM THE MSF GUEST HOUSE.
HE LIVES IN THE CHRISTIAN PART OF BEIT HANINA. I DIDN'T REALIZE THERE WAS A CHRISTIAN PRESENCE AROUND HERE, EXCEPT FOR THE STORE WHERE WE BUY OUR BEER.
WOW! THIS IS GREAT.
THEY ARRIVED JUST TWO MONTHS AGO, BUT IT'S LIKE THEY'VE LIVED HERE FOR YEARS.
BBQ
SWING SET
PUPPY
OH... LOOK, HIS WIFE HAS A STUDIO TO PAINT IN.
JEALOUS
I MEET A YOUNG WOMAN WHO IS LEARNING HEBREW. SHE'S GERMAN, HER FIANCÉ IS JEWISH. THEY DECIDED TO GET MARRIED TO PLEASE THE FAMILY, SO NOW SHE'S IN THE PROCESS OF CONVERTING TO JUDAISM. IT SOUNDS COMPLICATED—SHE HAS ABOUT THREE YEARS TO GO.

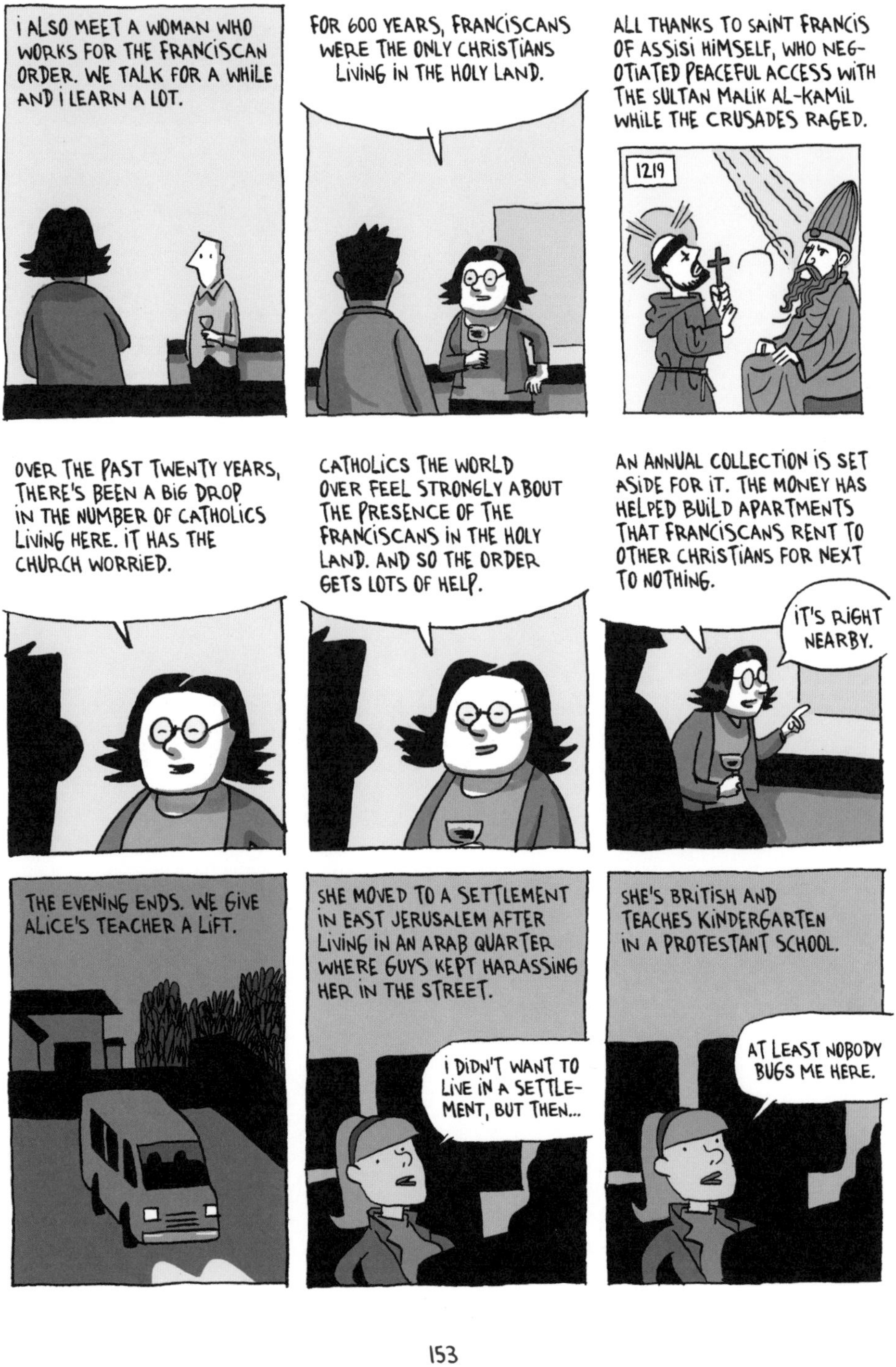
I ALSO MEET A WOMAN WHO WORKS FOR THE FRANCISCAN ORDER. WE TALK FOR A WHILE AND I LEARN A LOT.
FOR 600 YEARS, FRANCISCANS WERE THE ONLY CHRISTIANS LIVING IN THE HOLY LAND.
ALL THANKS TO SAINT FRANCIS OF ASSISI HIMSELF, WHO NEGOTIATED PEACEFUL ACCESS WITH THE SULTAN MALIK AL-KAMIL WHILE THE CRUSADES RAGED.
1219
OVER THE PAST TWENTY YEARS, THERE'S BEEN A BIG DROP IN THE NUMBER OF CATHOLICS LIVING HERE. IT HAS THE CHURCH WORRIED.
CATHOLICS THE WORLD OVER FEEL STRONGLY ABOUT THE PRESENCE OF THE FRANCISCANS IN THE HOLY LAND. AND SO THE ORDER GETS LOTS OF HELP.
AN ANNUAL COLLECTION IS SET ASIDE FOR IT. THE MONEY HAS HELPED BUILD APARTMENTS THAT FRANCISCANS RENT TO OTHER CHRISTIANS FOR NEXT TO NOTHING.
IT'S RIGHT NEARBY.
THE EVENING ENDS. WE GIVE ALICE'S TEACHER A LIFT.
SHE MOVED TO A SETTLEMENT IN EAST JERUSALEM AFTER LIVING IN AN ARAB QUARTER WHERE GUYS KEPT HARASSING HER IN THE STREET.
I DIDN'T WANT TO LIVE IN A SETTLEMENT, BUT THEN...
SHE'S BRITISH AND TEACHES KINDERGARTEN IN A PROTESTANT SCHOOL.
AT LEAST NOBODY BUGS ME HERE.

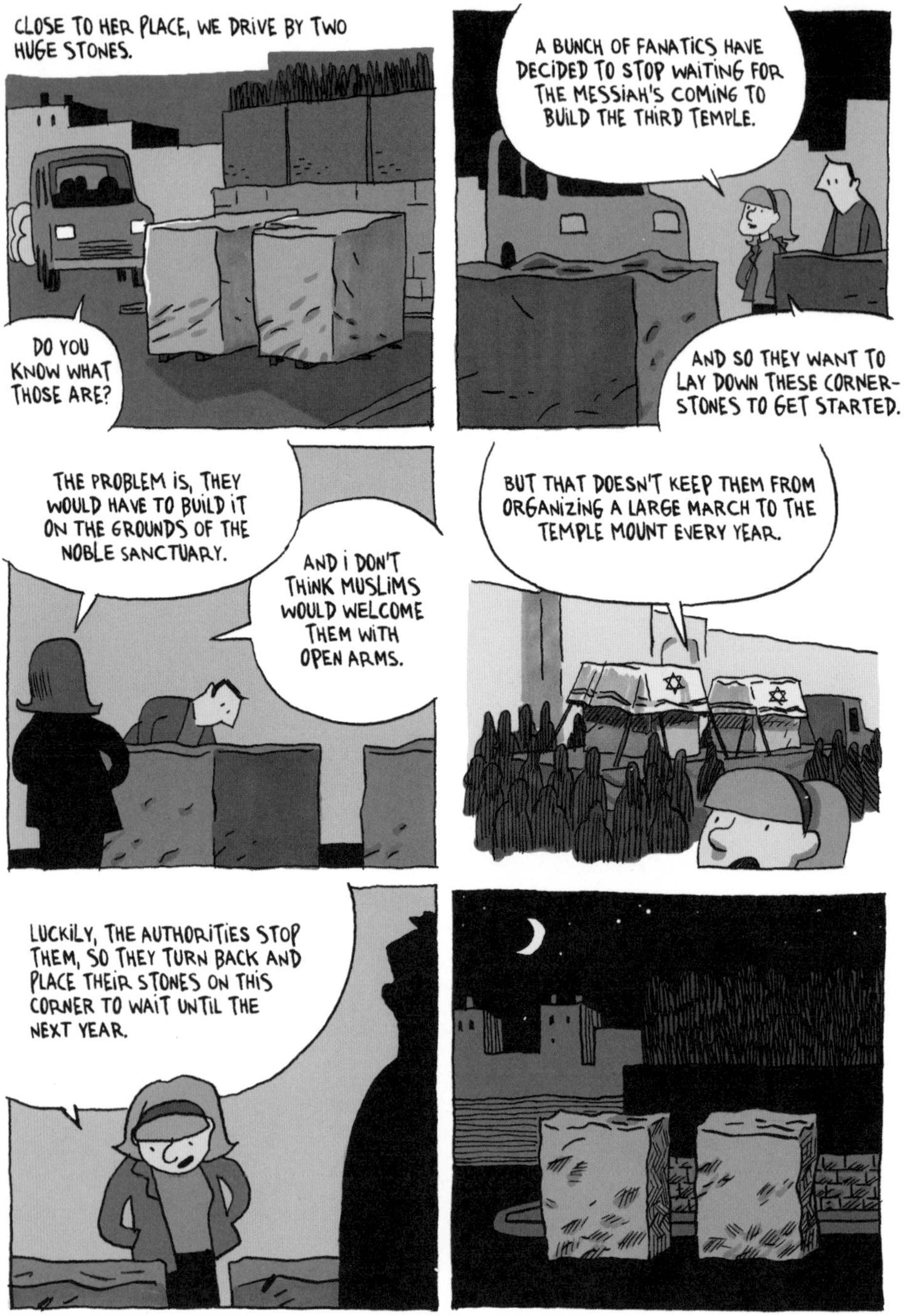

CLOSE TO HER PLACE, WE DRIVE BY TWO HUGE STONES.
DO YOU KNOW WHAT THOSE ARE?
A BUNCH OF FANATICS HAVE DECIDED TO STOP WAITING FOR THE MESSIAH'S COMING TO BUILD THE THIRD TEMPLE.
AND SO THEY WANT TO LAY DOWN THESE CORNER-STONES TO GET STARTED.
THE PROBLEM IS, THEY WOULD HAVE TO BUILD IT ON THE GROUNDS OF THE NOBLE SANCTUARY.
AND I DON'T THINK MUSLIMS WOULD WELCOME THEM WITH OPEN ARMS.
BUT THAT DOESN'T KEEP THEM FROM ORGANIZING A LARGE MARCH TO THE TEMPLE MOUNT EVERY YEAR.
LUCKILY, THE AUTHORITIES STOP THEM, SO THEY TURN BACK AND PLACE THEIR STONES ON THIS CORNER TO WAIT UNTIL THE NEXT YEAR.

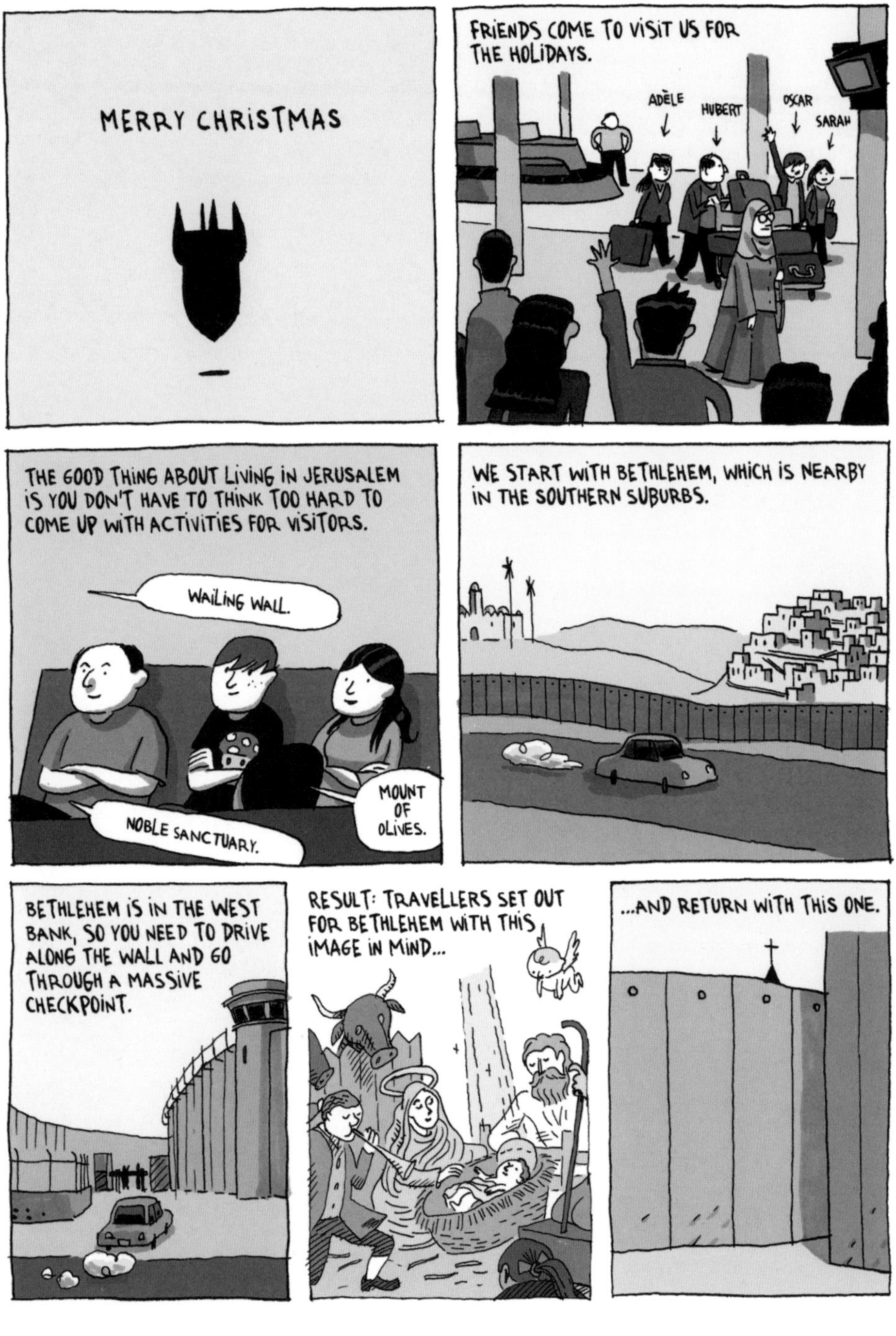
MERRY CHRISTMAS
FRIENDS COME TO VISIT US FOR THE HOLIDAYS.
ADÈLE
HUBERT
OSCAR
SARAH
THE GOOD THING ABOUT LIVING IN JERUSALEM IS YOU DON'T HAVE TO THINK TOO HARD TO COME UP WITH ACTIVITIES FOR VISITORS.
WAILING WALL.
MOUNT OF OLIVES.
NOBLE SANCTUARY.
WE START WITH BETHLEHEM, WHICH IS NEARBY IN THE SOUTHERN SUBURBS.
BETHLEHEM IS IN THE WEST BANK, SO YOU NEED TO DRIVE ALONG THE WALL AND GO THROUGH A MASSIVE CHECKPOINT.
RESULT: TRAVELLERS SET OUT FOR BETHLEHEM WITH THIS IMAGE IN MIND...
...AND RETURN WITH THIS ONE.

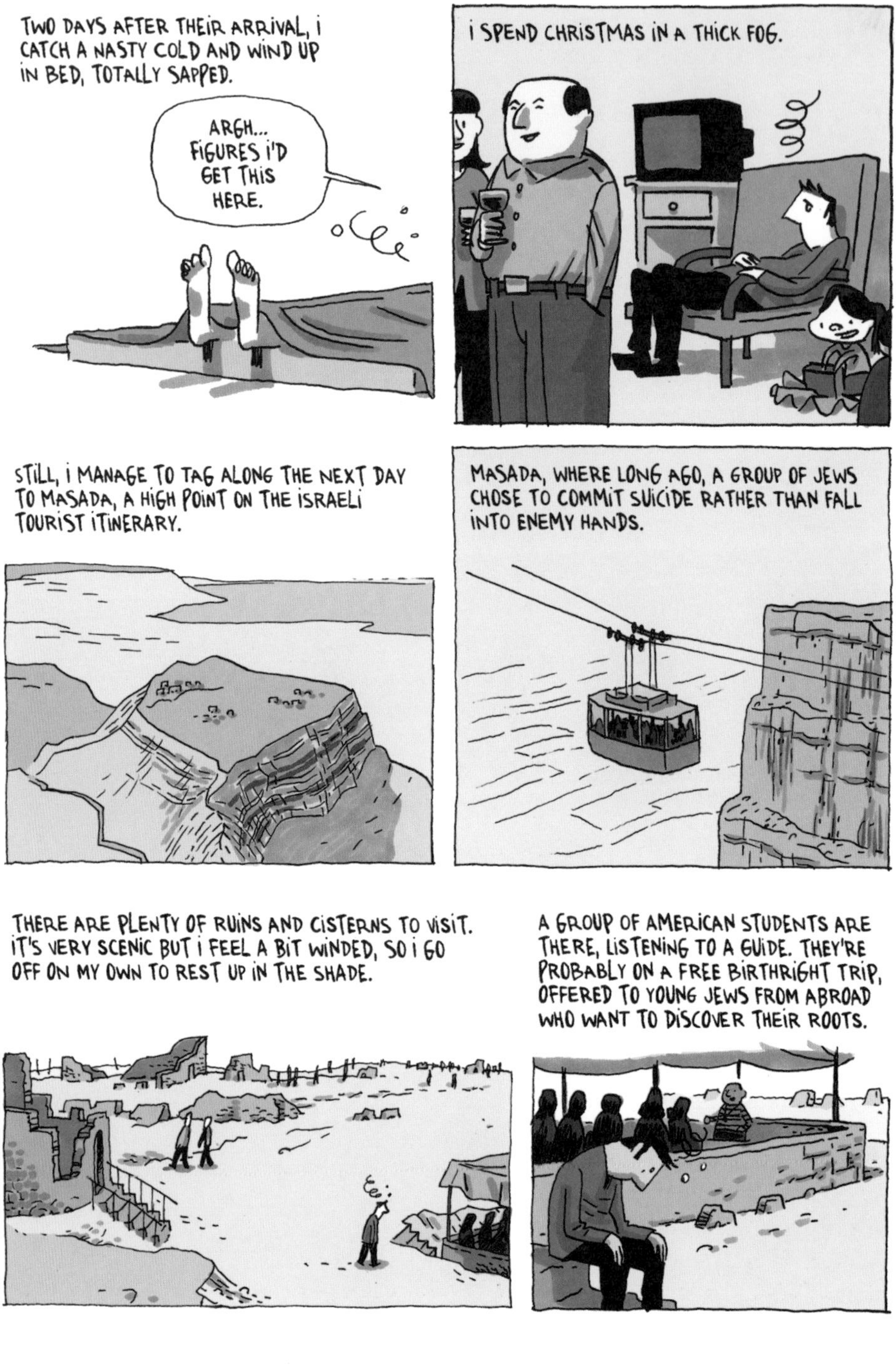
TWO DAYS AFTER THEIR ARRIVAL, I CATCH A NASTY COLD AND WIND UP IN BED, TOTALLY SAPPED.
ARGH... FIGURES I'D GET THIS HERE.
I SPEND CHRISTMAS IN A THICK FOG.
STILL, I MANAGE TO TAG ALONG THE NEXT DAY TO MASADA, A HIGH POINT ON THE ISRAELI TOURIST ITINERARY.
MASADA, WHERE LONG AGO, A GROUP OF JEWS CHOSE TO COMMIT SUICIDE RATHER THAN FALL INTO ENEMY HANDS.
THERE ARE PLENTY OF RUINS AND CISTERNS TO VISIT. IT'S VERY SCENIC BUT I FEEL A BIT WINDED, SO I GO OFF ON MY OWN TO REST UP IN THE SHADE.
A GROUP OF AMERICAN STUDENTS ARE THERE, LISTENING TO A GUIDE. THEY'RE PROBABLY ON A FREE BIRTHRIGHT TRIP, OFFERED TO YOUNG JEWS FROM ABROAD WHO WANT TO DISCOVER THEIR ROOTS.

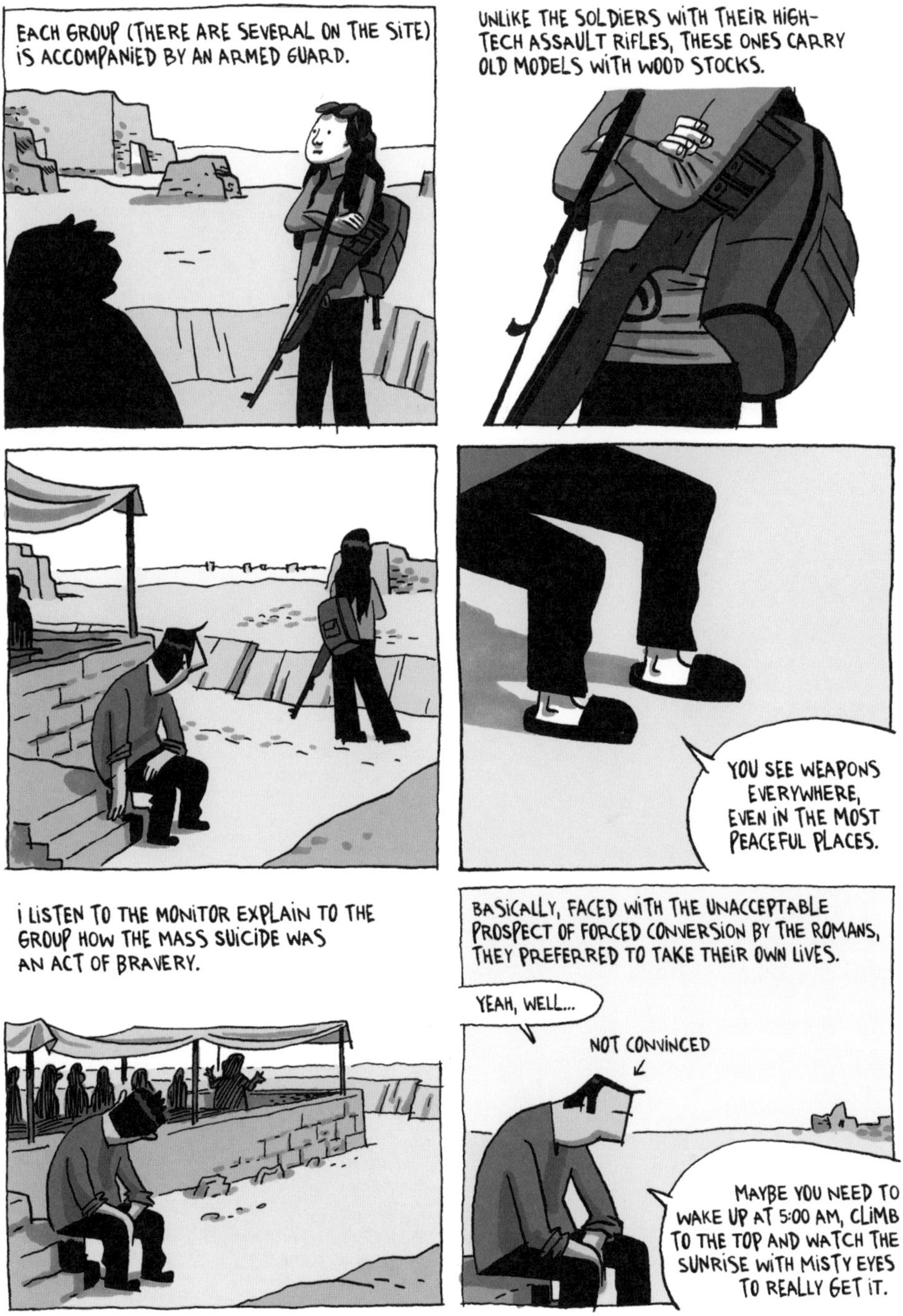
EACH GROUP (THERE ARE SEVERAL ON THE SITE) IS ACCOMPANIED BY AN ARMED GUARD.
UNLIKE THE SOLDIERS WITH THEIR HIGH-TECH ASSAULT RIFLES, THESE ONES CARRY OLD MODELS WITH WOOD STOCKS.
YOU SEE WEAPONS EVERYWHERE, EVEN IN THE MOST PEACEFUL PLACES.
I LISTEN TO THE MONITOR EXPLAIN TO THE GROUP HOW THE MASS SUICIDE WAS AN ACT OF BRAVERY.
BASICALLY, FACED WITH THE UNACCEPTABLE PROSPECT OF FORCED CONVERSION BY THE ROMANS, THEY PREFERRED TO TAKE THEIR OWN LIVES.
YEAH, WELL...
NOT CONVINCED
MAYBE YOU NEED TO WAKE UP AT 5:00 AM, CLIMB TO THE TOP AND WATCH THE SUNRISE WITH MISTY EYES TO REALLY GET IT.

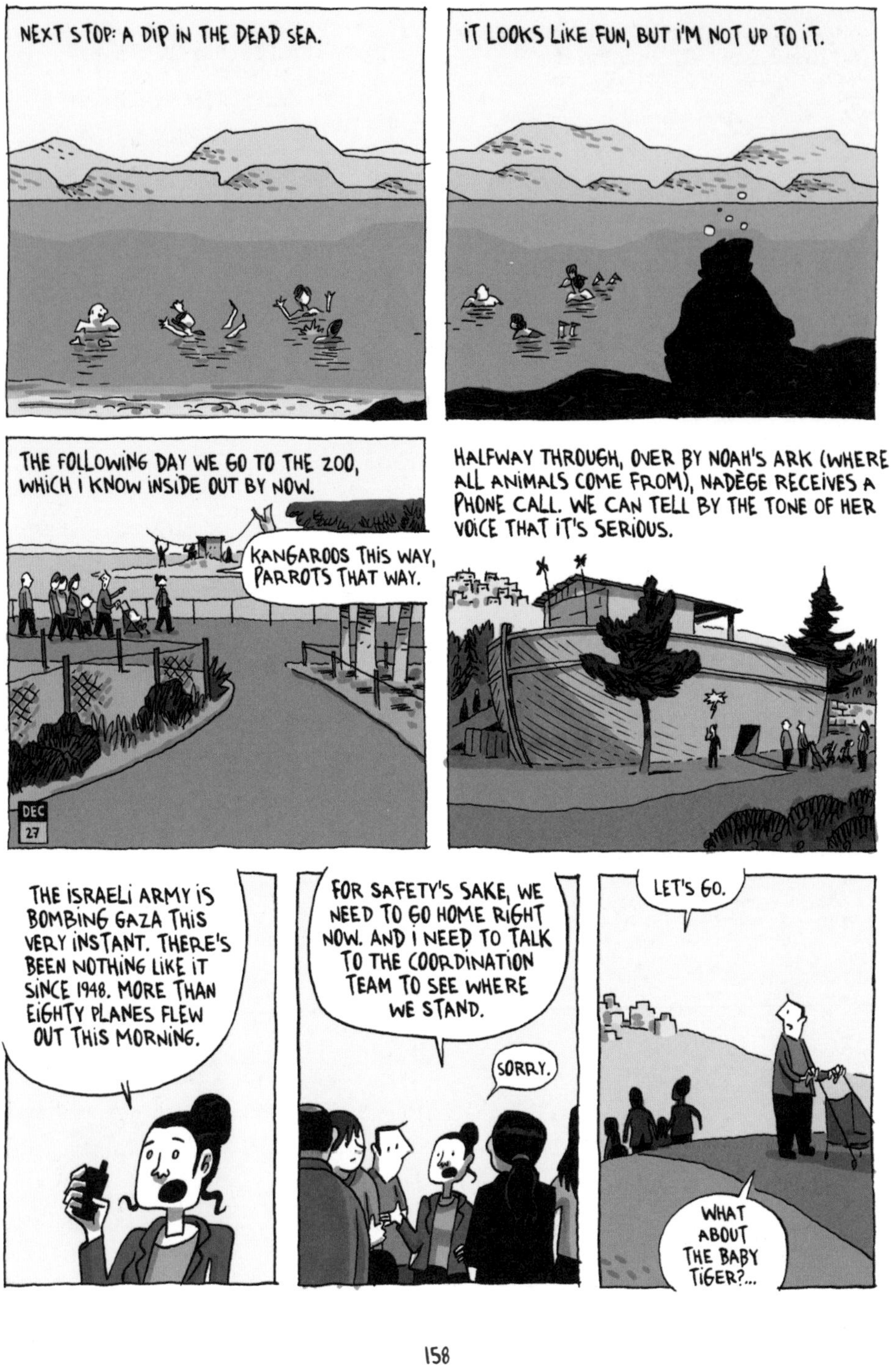
NEXT STOP: A DIP IN THE DEAD SEA.
IT LOOKS LIKE FUN, BUT I'M NOT UP TO IT.
THE FOLLOWING DAY WE GO TO THE ZOO, WHICH I KNOW INSIDE OUT BY NOW.
KANGAROOS THIS WAY, PARROTS THAT WAY.
DEC 27
HALFWAY THROUGH, OVER BY NOAH'S ARK (WHERE ALL ANIMALS COME FROM), NADÈGE RECEIVES A PHONE CALL. WE CAN TELL BY THE TONE OF HER VOICE THAT IT'S SERIOUS.
THE ISRAELI ARMY IS BOMBING GAZA THIS VERY INSTANT. THERE'S BEEN NOTHING LIKE IT SINCE 1948. MORE THAN EIGHTY PLANES FLEW OUT THIS MORNING.
FOR SAFETY'S SAKE, WE NEED TO GO HOME RIGHT NOW. AND I NEED TO TALK TO THE COORDINATION TEAM TO SEE WHERE WE STAND.
SORRY.
LET'S GO.
WHAT ABOUT THE BABY TIGER?...

NADÈGE CHECKS IN WITH THE TEAM IN GAZA. THERE ARE NO EXPATS ON SITE BECAUSE THEY'VE ALL LEFT THE STRIP FOR THE HOLIDAYS.

IN GAZA, THE OFFICES HAVE BEEN TURNED INTO DORMITORIES FOR EMPLOYEES WHO'D RATHER SLEEP THERE. IT'S IN A QUARTER THAT'S LESS LIKELY TO GET BOMBED THAN THEIR OWN.

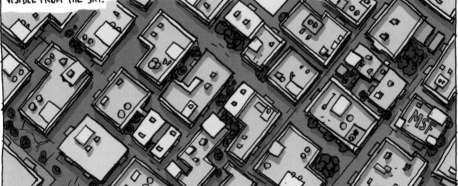

THEY'VE PAINTED THE THREE-LETTER LOGO IN HUGE LETTERS ON THE ROOF TO BE CLEARLY VISIBLE FROM THE SKY.

DEC 28

THE AIR STRIKES INTENSIFY, TEMPERS FLARE. HAMAS CALLS FOR A THIRD INTIFADA.

THE STREETS ARE CALM, THE ATMOSPHERE STRANGE. WHEN YOU THINK THAT NEARBY, THEY'RE BOMBING PEOPLE WITH FIGHTER JETS...

159

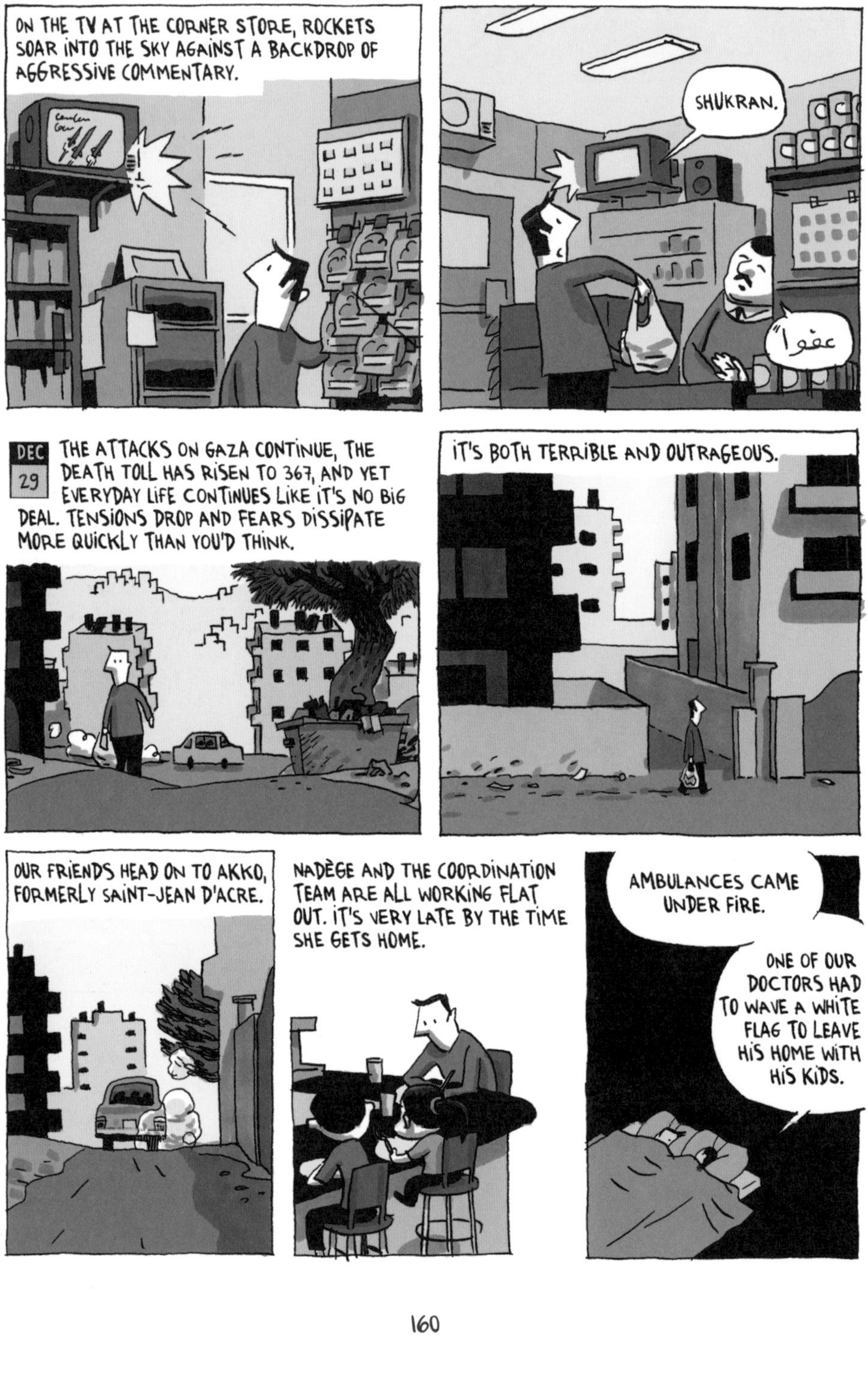
ON THE TV AT THE CORNER STORE, ROCKETS SOAR INTO THE SKY AGAINST A BACKDROP OF AGGRESSIVE COMMENTARY.
SHUKRAN.
"عفوا"
DEC 29
THE ATTACKS ON GAZA CONTINUE, THE DEATH TOLL HAS RISEN TO 367, AND YET EVERYDAY LIFE CONTINUES LIKE IT'S NO BIG DEAL. TENSIONS DROP AND FEARS DISSIPATE MORE QUICKLY THAN YOU'D THINK.
IT'S BOTH TERRIBLE AND OUTRAGEOUS.
OUR FRIENDS HEAD ON TO AKKO, FORMERLY SAINT-JEAN D'ACRE.
NADÈGE AND THE COORDINATION TEAM ARE ALL WORKING FLAT OUT. IT'S VERY LATE BY THE TIME SHE GETS HOME.
AMBULANCES CAME UNDER FIRE.
ONE OF OUR DOCTORS HAD TO WAVE A WHITE FLAG TO LEAVE HIS HOME WITH HIS KIDS.

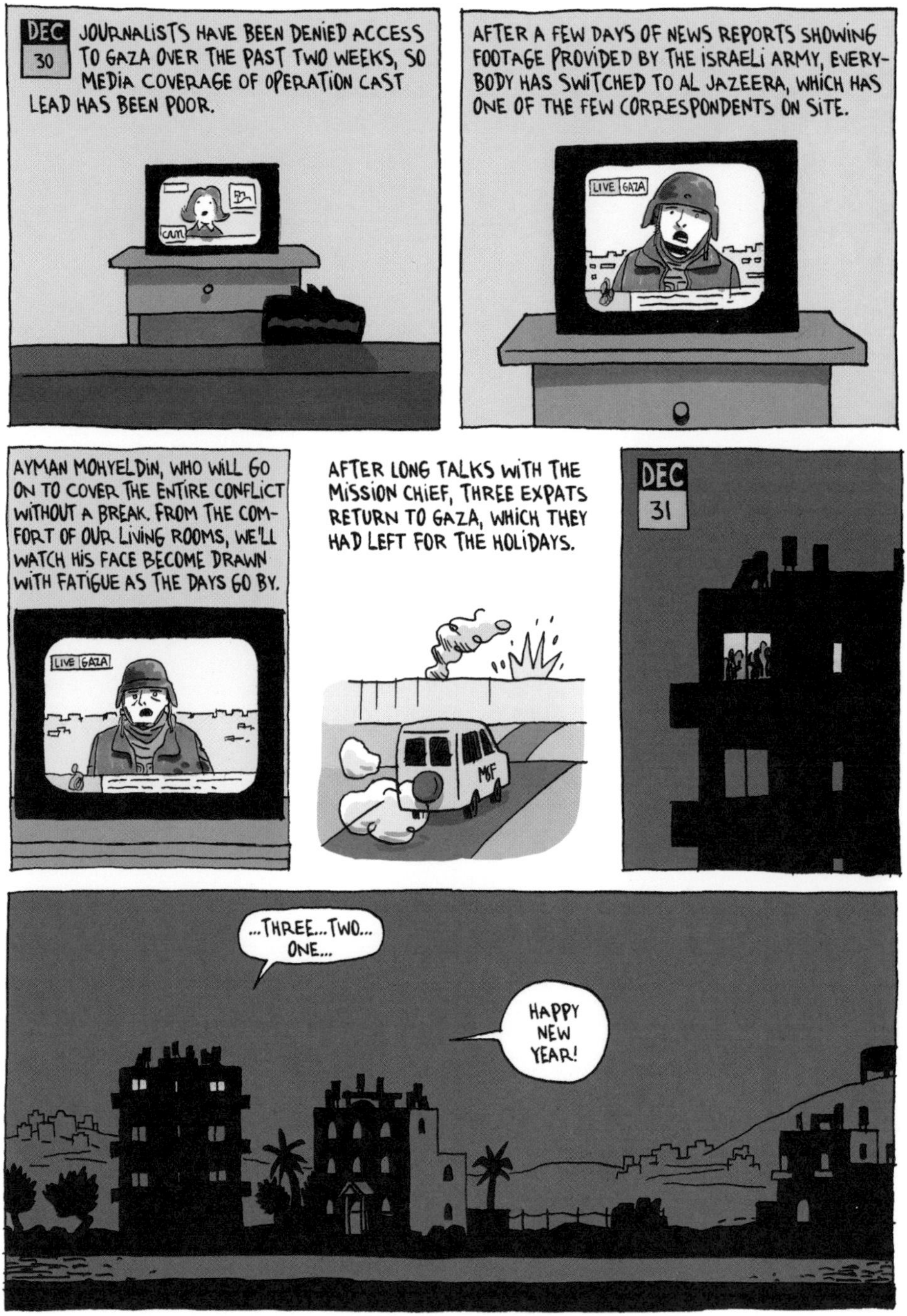
DEC 30
JOURNALISTS HAVE BEEN DENIED ACCESS TO GAZA OVER THE PAST TWO WEEKS, SO MEDIA COVERAGE OF OPERATION CAST LEAD HAS BEEN POOR.
AFTER A FEW DAYS OF NEWS REPORTS SHOWING FOOTAGE PROVIDED BY THE ISRAELI ARMY, EVERYBODY HAS SWITCHED TO AL JAZEERA, WHICH HAS ONE OF THE FEW CORRESPONDENTS ON SITE.
LIVE GAZA
AYMAN MOHYELDIN, WHO WILL GO ON TO COVER THE ENTIRE CONFLICT WITHOUT A BREAK. FROM THE COMFORT OF OUR LIVING ROOMS, WE'LL WATCH HIS FACE BECOME DRAWN WITH FATIGUE AS THE DAYS GO BY.
LIVE GAZA
AFTER LONG TALKS WITH THE MISSION CHIEF, THREE EXPATS RETURN TO GAZA, WHICH THEY HAD LEFT FOR THE HOLIDAYS.
MSF
DEC 31
...THREE...TWO... ONE...
HAPPY NEW YEAR!

JANUARY

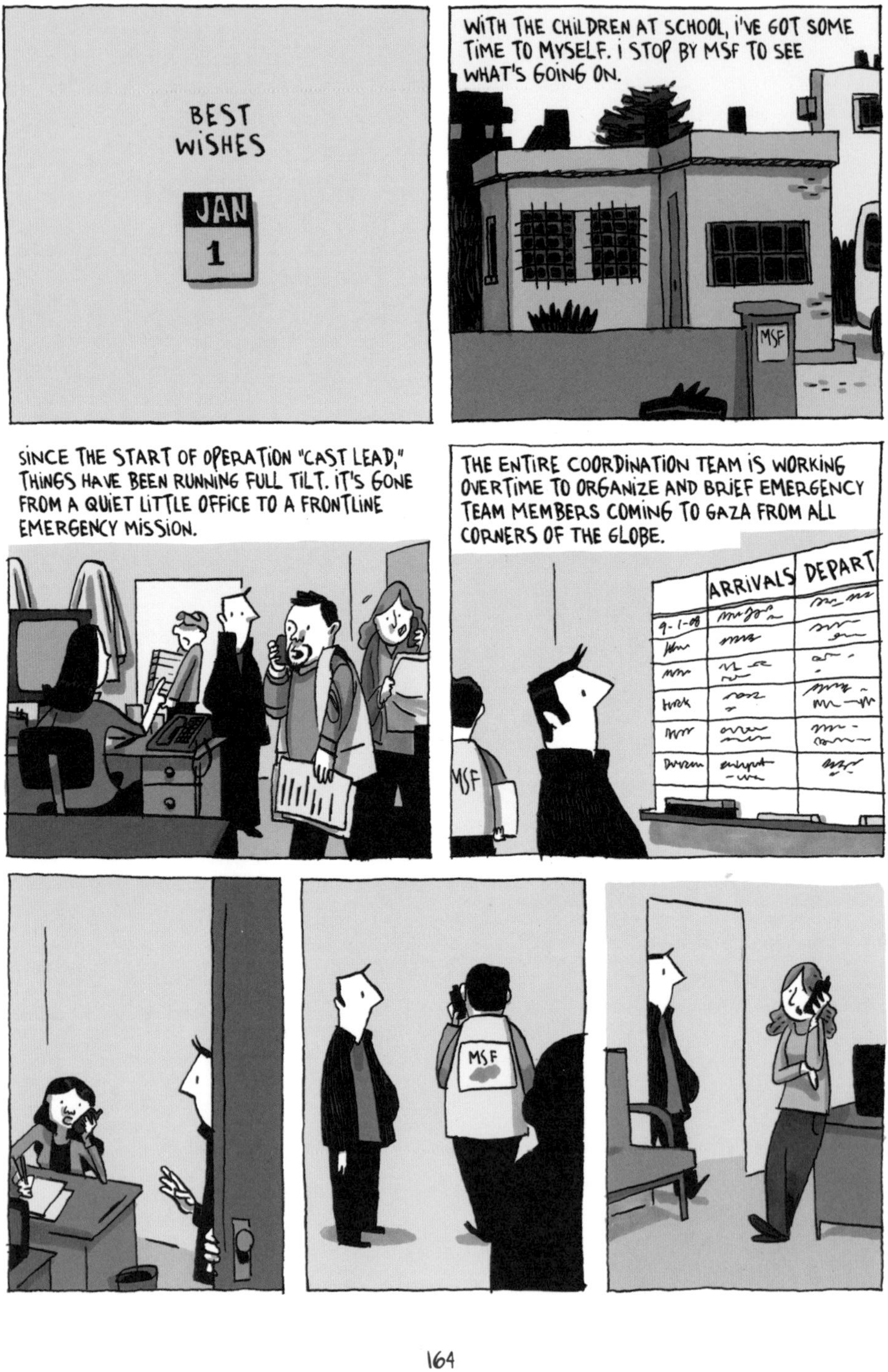
BEST WISHES
JAN
1
WITH THE CHILDREN AT SCHOOL, I'VE GOT SOME TIME TO MYSELF. I STOP BY MSF TO SEE WHAT'S GOING ON.
MSF
SINCE THE START OF OPERATION "CAST LEAD," THINGS HAVE BEEN RUNNING FULL TILT. IT'S GONE FROM A QUIET LITTLE OFFICE TO A FRONTLINE EMERGENCY MISSION.
THE ENTIRE COORDINATION TEAM IS WORKING OVERTIME TO ORGANIZE AND BRIEF EMERGENCY TEAM MEMBERS COMING TO GAZA FROM ALL CORNERS OF THE GLOBE.
ARRIVALS
DEPART
MSF
MSF

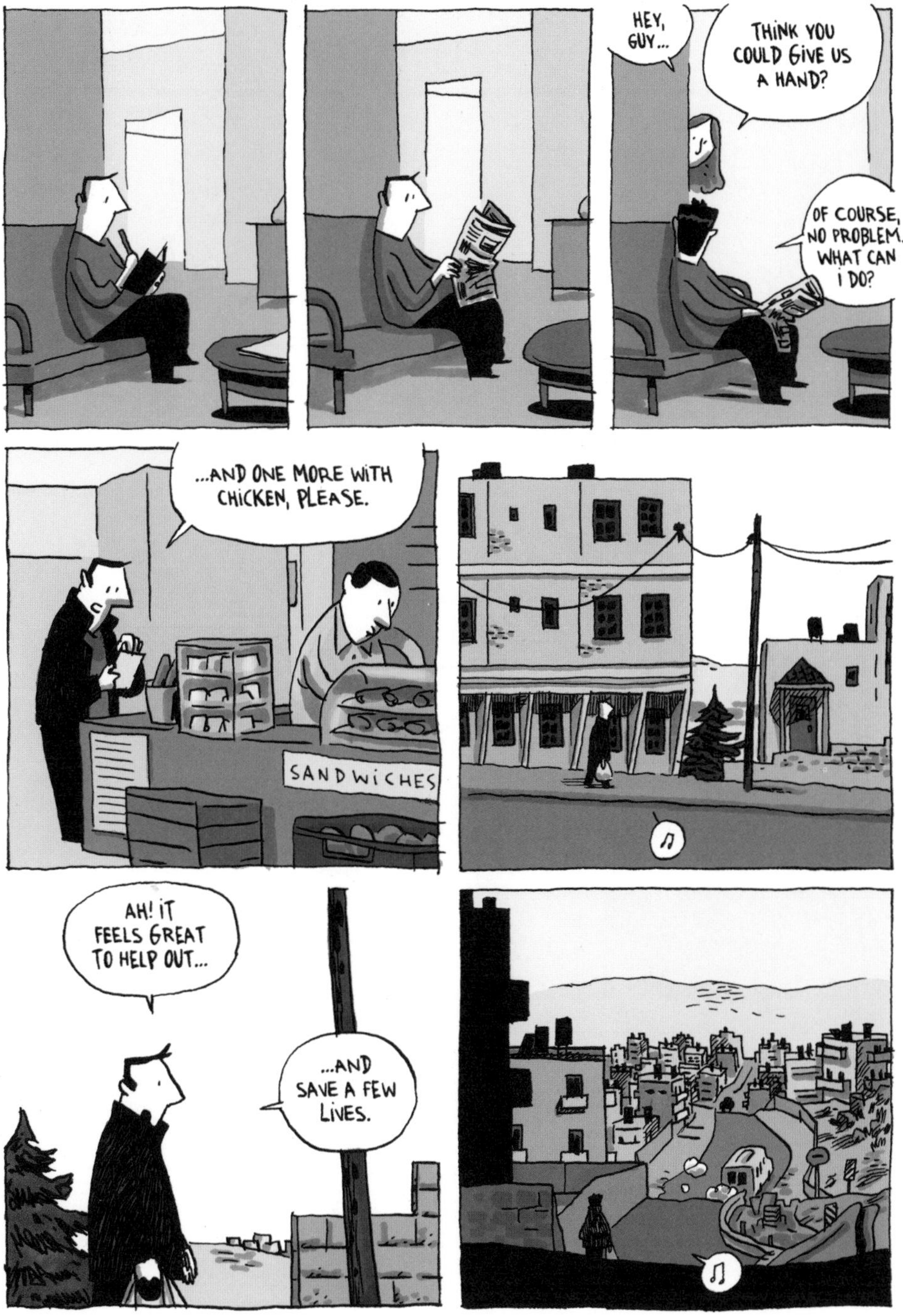
HEY, GUY...
THINK YOU COULD GIVE US A HAND?
OF COURSE, NO PROBLEM. WHAT CAN I DO?
...AND ONE MORE WITH CHICKEN, PLEASE.
SANDWICHES
AH! IT FEELS GREAT TO HELP OUT...
...AND SAVE A FEW LIVES.

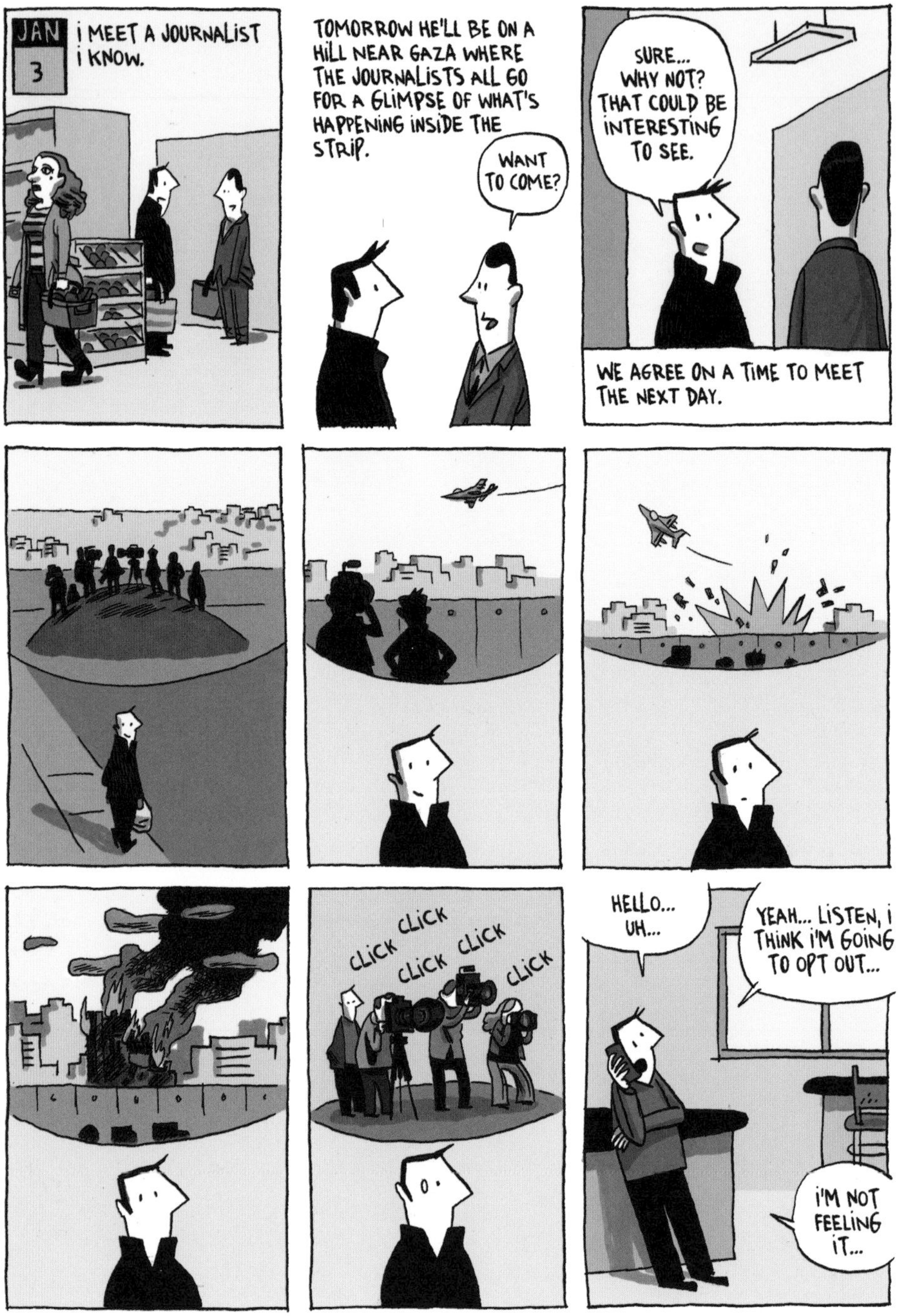

JAN 3
i MEET A JOURNALIST i KNOW.
TOMORROW HE'LL BE ON A HiLL NEAR GAZA WHERE THE JOURNALISTS ALL GO FOR A GLiMPSE OF WHAT'S HAPPENiNG iNSiDE THE STRiP.
WANT TO COME?
SURE... WHY NOT? THAT COULD BE INTERESTING TO SEE.
WE AGREE ON A TiME TO MEET THE NEXT DAY.
CLiCK CLiCK CLiCK CLiCK CLiCK
HELLO... UH...
YEAH... LiSTEN, i THiNK i'M GOiNG TO OPT OUT...
i'M NOT FEELiNG iT...

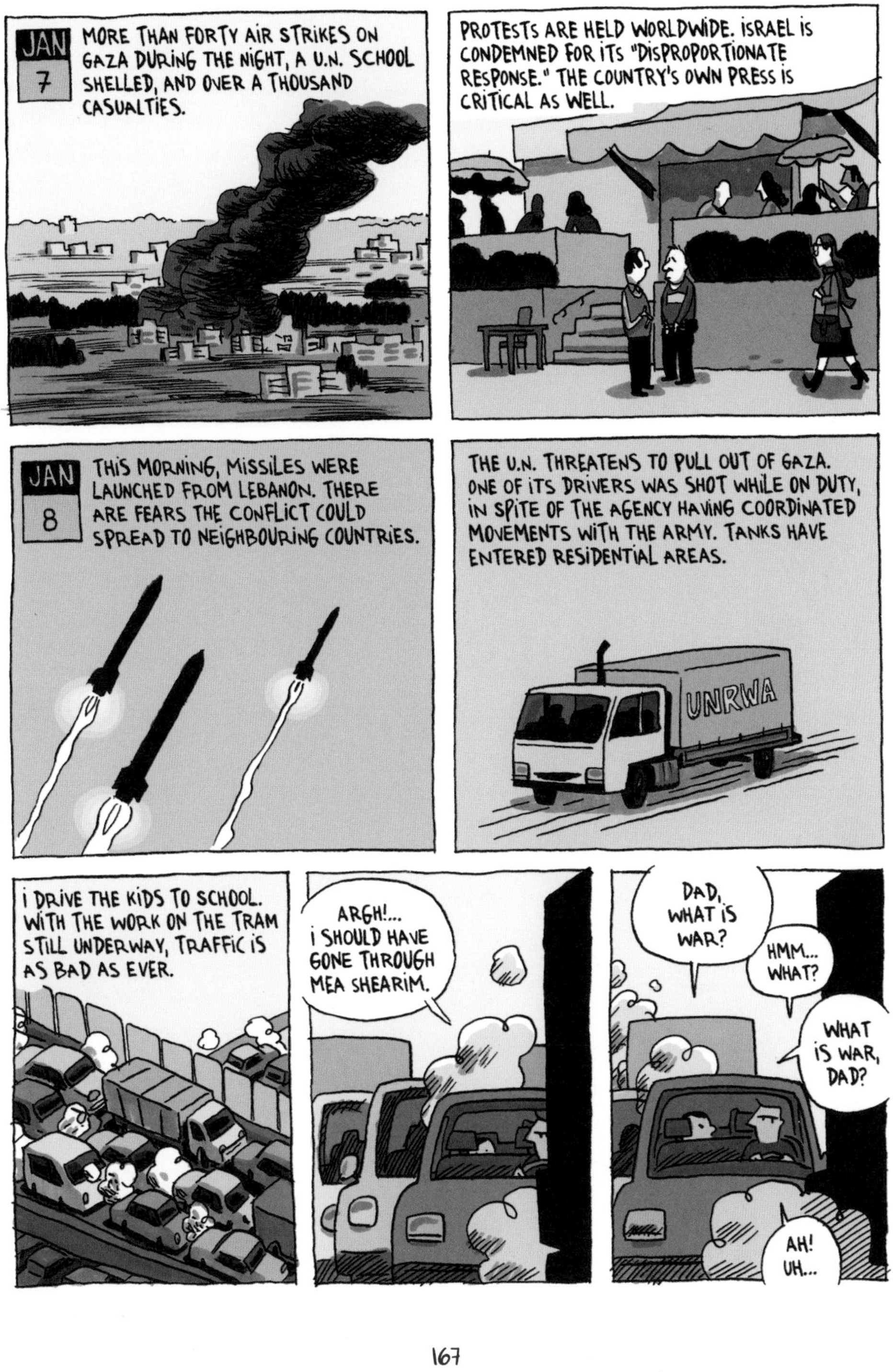
JAN 7
MORE THAN FORTY AIR STRIKES ON GAZA DURING THE NIGHT, A U.N. SCHOOL SHELLED, AND OVER A THOUSAND CASUALTIES.
PROTESTS ARE HELD WORLDWIDE. ISRAEL IS CONDEMNED FOR ITS "DISPROPORTIONATE RESPONSE." THE COUNTRY'S OWN PRESS IS CRITICAL AS WELL.
JAN 8
THIS MORNING, MISSILES WERE LAUNCHED FROM LEBANON. THERE ARE FEARS THE CONFLICT COULD SPREAD TO NEIGHBOURING COUNTRIES.
THE U.N. THREATENS TO PULL OUT OF GAZA. ONE OF ITS DRIVERS WAS SHOT WHILE ON DUTY, IN SPITE OF THE AGENCY HAVING COORDINATED MOVEMENTS WITH THE ARMY. TANKS HAVE ENTERED RESIDENTIAL AREAS.
UNRWA
I DRIVE THE KIDS TO SCHOOL. WITH THE WORK ON THE TRAM STILL UNDERWAY, TRAFFIC IS AS BAD AS EVER.
ARGH!... I SHOULD HAVE GONE THROUGH MEA SHEARIM.
DAD, WHAT IS WAR?
HMM... WHAT?
WHAT IS WAR, DAD?
AH! UH...

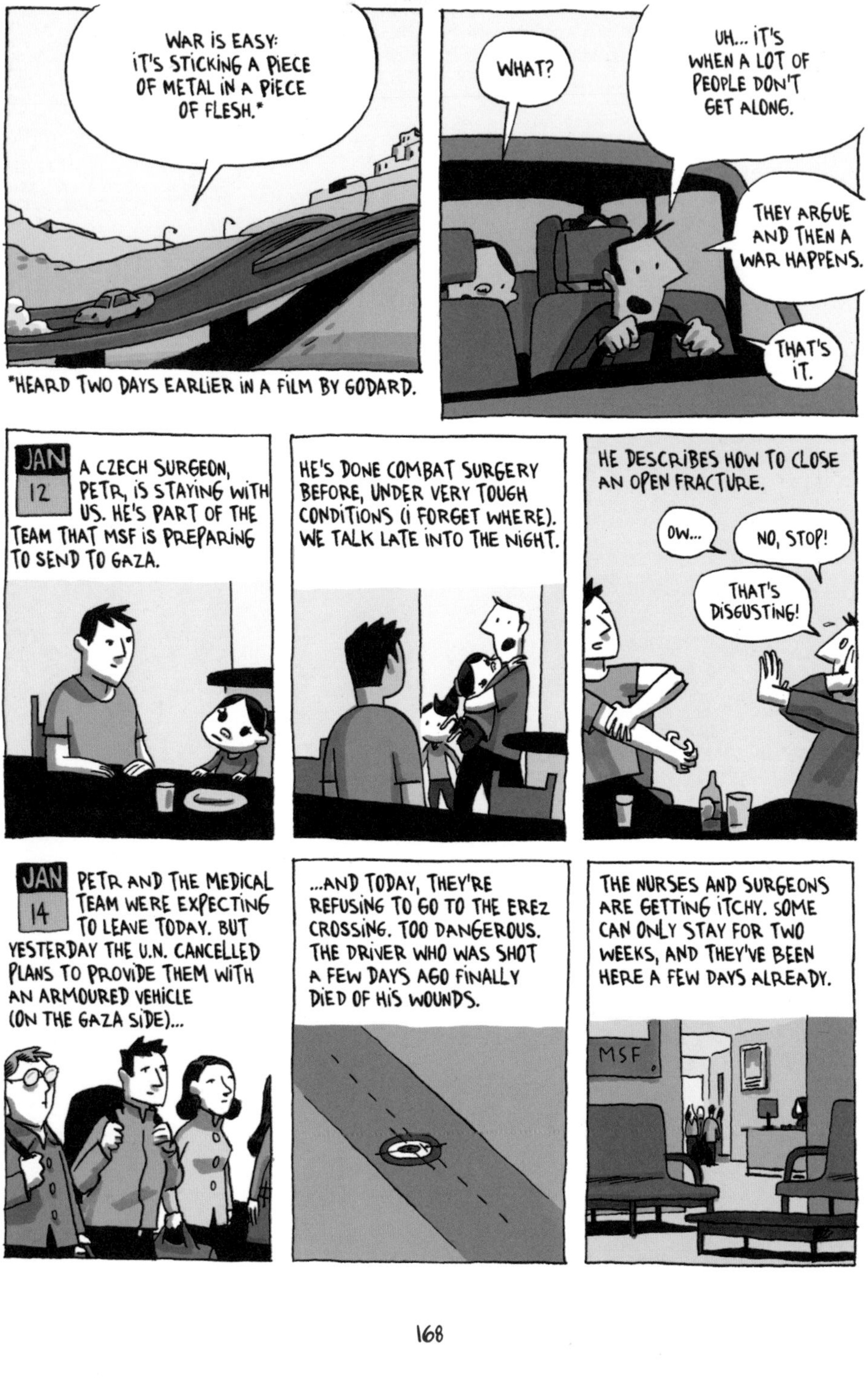
WAR IS EASY: IT'S STICKING A PIECE OF METAL IN A PIECE OF FLESH.*
*HEARD TWO DAYS EARLIER IN A FILM BY GODARD.
WHAT?
UH... IT'S WHEN A LOT OF PEOPLE DON'T GET ALONG.
THEY ARGUE AND THEN A WAR HAPPENS.
THAT'S IT.
JAN 12
A CZECH SURGEON, PETR, IS STAYING WITH US. HE'S PART OF THE TEAM THAT MSF IS PREPARING TO SEND TO GAZA.
HE'S DONE COMBAT SURGERY BEFORE, UNDER VERY TOUGH CONDITIONS (I FORGET WHERE). WE TALK LATE INTO THE NIGHT.
HE DESCRIBES HOW TO CLOSE AN OPEN FRACTURE.
OW...
NO, STOP!
THAT'S DISGUSTING!
JAN 14
PETR AND THE MEDICAL TEAM WERE EXPECTING TO LEAVE TODAY. BUT YESTERDAY THE U.N. CANCELLED PLANS TO PROVIDE THEM WITH AN ARMOURED VEHICLE (ON THE GAZA SIDE)...
...AND TODAY, THEY'RE REFUSING TO GO TO THE EREZ CROSSING. TOO DANGEROUS. THE DRIVER WHO WAS SHOT A FEW DAYS AGO FINALLY DIED OF HIS WOUNDS.
THE NURSES AND SURGEONS ARE GETTING ITCHY. SOME CAN ONLY STAY FOR TWO WEEKS, AND THEY'VE BEEN HERE A FEW DAYS ALREADY.
MSF

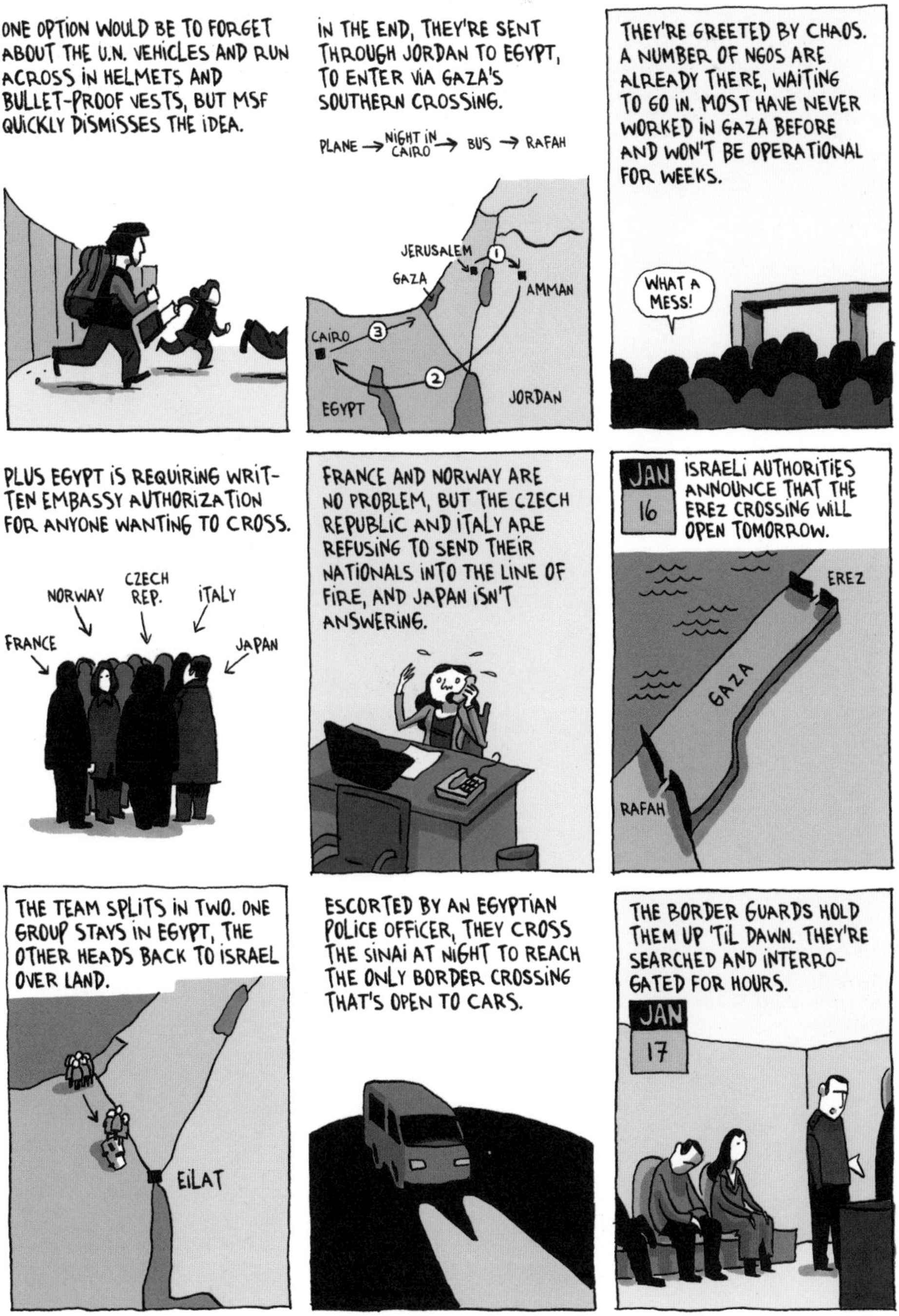
ONE OPTION WOULD BE TO FORGET ABOUT THE U.N. VEHICLES AND RUN ACROSS IN HELMETS AND BULLET-PROOF VESTS, BUT MSF QUICKLY DISMISSES THE IDEA.
IN THE END, THEY'RE SENT THROUGH JORDAN TO EGYPT, TO ENTER VIA GAZA'S SOUTHERN CROSSING.
PLANE → NIGHT IN CAIRO → BUS → RAFAH
JERUSALEM
GAZA
AMMAN
CAIRO
EGYPT
JORDAN
THEY'RE GREETED BY CHAOS. A NUMBER OF NGOS ARE ALREADY THERE, WAITING TO GO IN. MOST HAVE NEVER WORKED IN GAZA BEFORE AND WON'T BE OPERATIONAL FOR WEEKS.
WHAT A MESS!
PLUS EGYPT IS REQUIRING WRIT-TEN EMBASSY AUTHORIZATION FOR ANYONE WANTING TO CROSS.
NORWAY
CZECH REP.
ITALY
FRANCE
JAPAN
FRANCE AND NORWAY ARE NO PROBLEM, BUT THE CZECH REPUBLIC AND ITALY ARE REFUSING TO SEND THEIR NATIONALS INTO THE LINE OF FIRE, AND JAPAN ISN'T ANSWERING.
JAN 16
ISRAELI AUTHORITIES ANNOUNCE THAT THE EREZ CROSSING WILL OPEN TOMORROW.
EREZ
GAZA
RAFAH
THE TEAM SPLITS IN TWO. ONE GROUP STAYS IN EGYPT, THE OTHER HEADS BACK TO ISRAEL OVER LAND.
EILAT
ESCORTED BY AN EGYPTIAN POLICE OFFICER, THEY CROSS THE SINAI AT NIGHT TO REACH THE ONLY BORDER CROSSING THAT'S OPEN TO CARS.
THE BORDER GUARDS HOLD THEM UP 'TIL DAWN. THEY'RE SEARCHED AND INTERRO-GATED FOR HOURS.
JAN 17

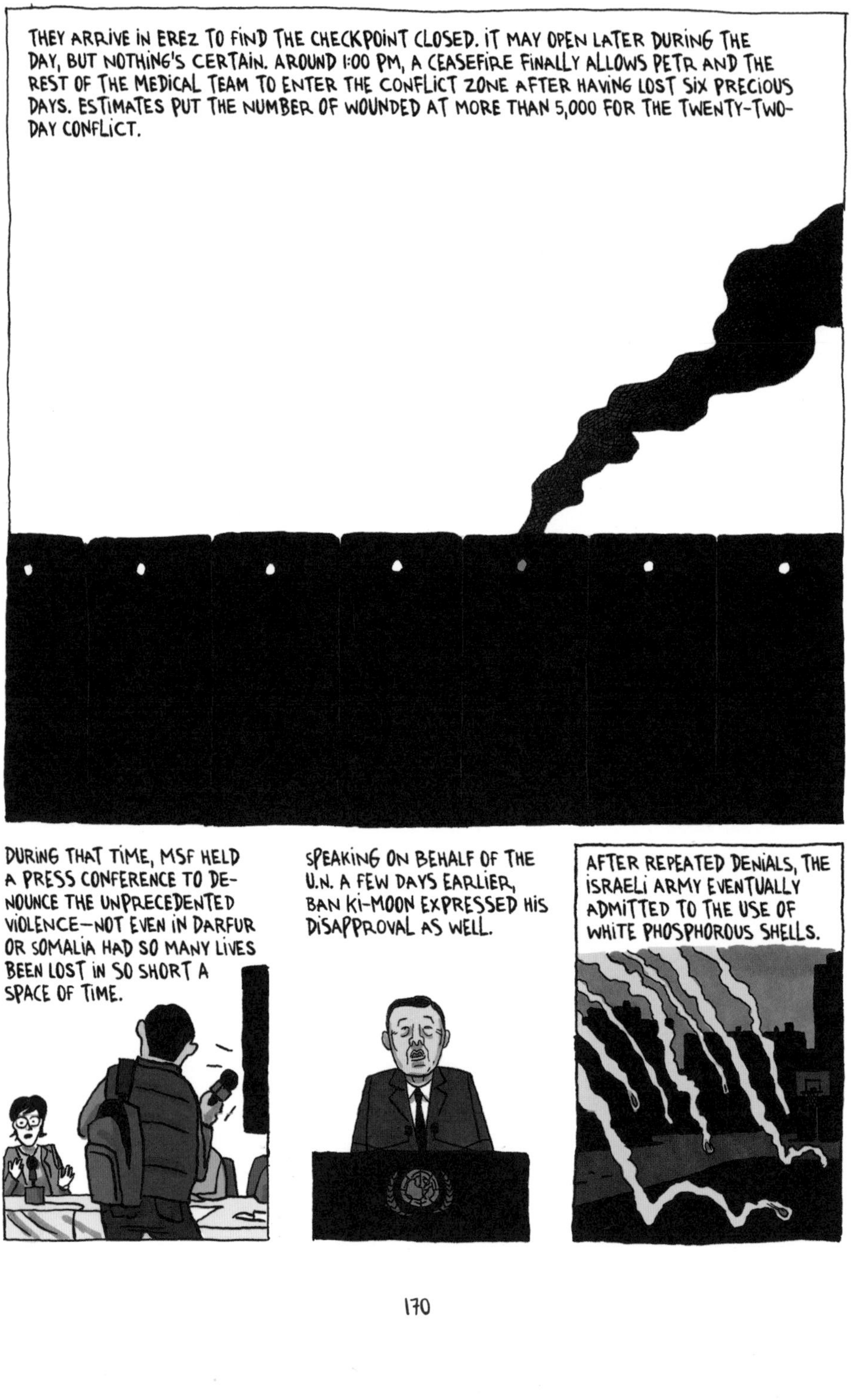
THEY ARRIVE IN EREZ TO FIND THE CHECKPOINT CLOSED. IT MAY OPEN LATER DURING THE DAY, BUT NOTHING'S CERTAIN. AROUND 1:00 PM, A CEASEFIRE FINALLY ALLOWS PETR AND THE REST OF THE MEDICAL TEAM TO ENTER THE CONFLICT ZONE AFTER HAVING LOST SIX PRECIOUS DAYS. ESTIMATES PUT THE NUMBER OF WOUNDED AT MORE THAN 5,000 FOR THE TWENTY-TWO-DAY CONFLICT.
DURING THAT TIME, MSF HELD A PRESS CONFERENCE TO DENOUNCE THE UNPRECEDENTED VIOLENCE—NOT EVEN IN DARFUR OR SOMALIA HAD SO MANY LIVES BEEN LOST IN SO SHORT A SPACE OF TIME.
SPEAKING ON BEHALF OF THE U.N. A FEW DAYS EARLIER, BAN KI-MOON EXPRESSED HIS DISAPPROVAL AS WELL.
AFTER REPEATED DENIALS, THE ISRAELI ARMY EVENTUALLY ADMITTED TO THE USE OF WHITE PHOSPHOROUS SHELLS.

ON THE EVENING OF THE 16TH, A REAL-LIFE DRAMA PLAYS OUT ON NATIONAL TV. THE INCIDENT HAS A PROFOUND IMPACT ON PUBLIC OPINION IN ISRAEL.

DR. EZZEDINE ABU AL-AISH IS ON THE LINE FROM GAZA WITH A CHANNEL 10 REPORTER WHEN A SHELL HITS HIS HOME AND KILLS THREE OF HIS DAUGHTERS.

SHLOMI ELDAR →

SHLOMI, COME QUICK, COME!

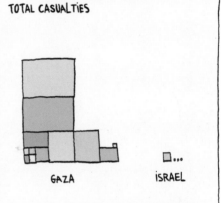

A FEW DAYS LATER, ISRAELI TANKS PULL OUT OF GAZA. OPERATION CAST LEAD IS OVER.

TOTAL CASUALTIES

GAZA   ISRAEL
                     ☐...

AT THE END OF THE MONTH, I GET TOGETHER WITH SOME OF THE DOCTORS, NOW ON THEIR WAY HOME. I TAKE THEM OUT THREE EVENINGS IN A ROW TO HELP THEM WIND DOWN. I MEET A SURGEON FROM HONG KONG.

PETR IS BACK, TOO. FROM OUR CONVERSATION, I CAN GUESS HE'S SEEN SOME TERRIBLE THINGS (YOUNG BURN VICTIMS, I'M TOLD LATER), BUT NOW'S NOT THE TIME OR PLACE TO TALK ABOUT IT. WE'RE HERE TO HAVE A NICE EVENING.

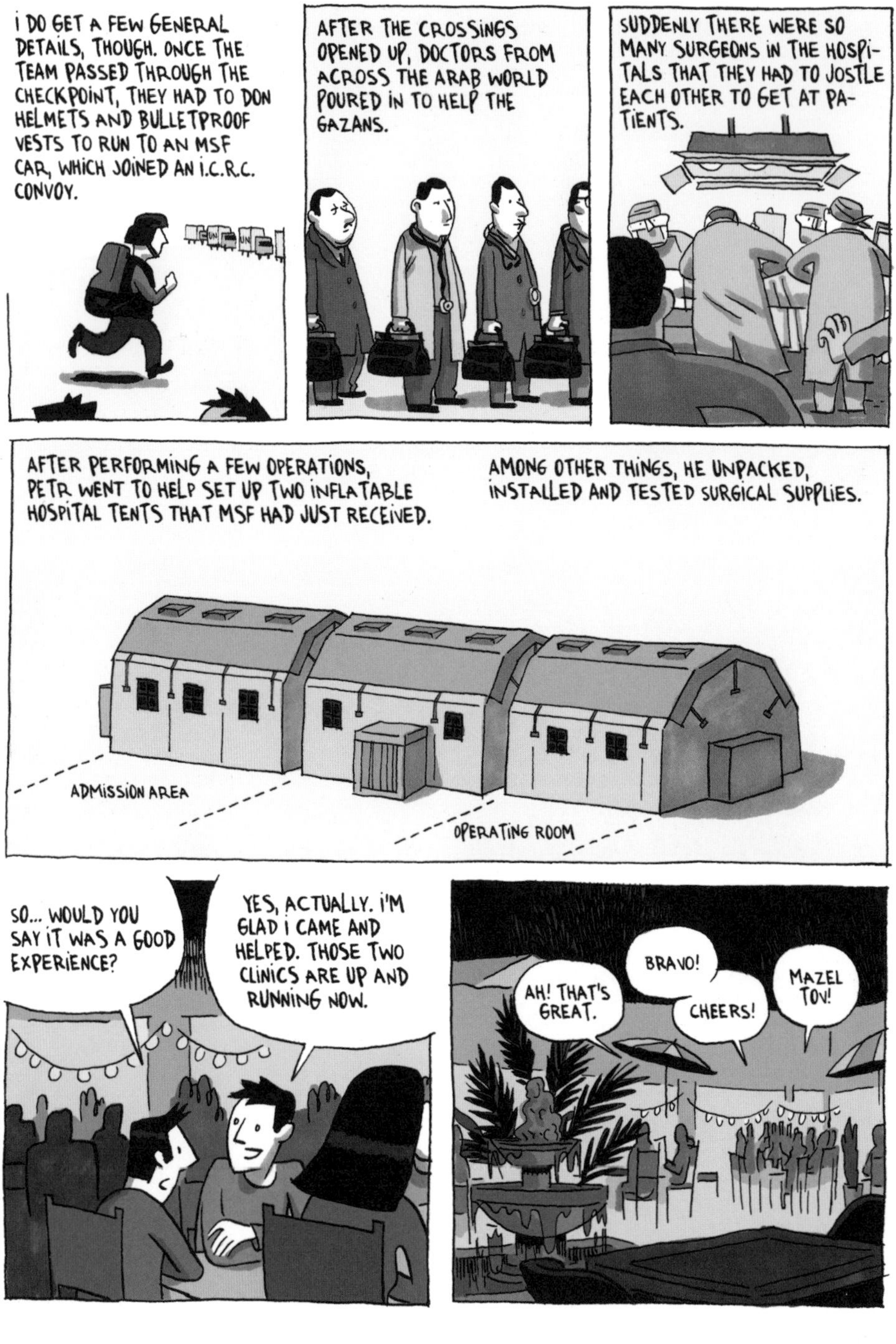
I DO GET A FEW GENERAL DETAILS, THOUGH. ONCE THE TEAM PASSED THROUGH THE CHECKPOINT, THEY HAD TO DON HELMETS AND BULLETPROOF VESTS TO RUN TO AN MSF CAR, WHICH JOINED AN I.C.R.C. CONVOY.
AFTER THE CROSSINGS OPENED UP, DOCTORS FROM ACROSS THE ARAB WORLD POURED IN TO HELP THE GAZANS.
SUDDENLY THERE WERE SO MANY SURGEONS IN THE HOSPITALS THAT THEY HAD TO JOSTLE EACH OTHER TO GET AT PATIENTS.
AFTER PERFORMING A FEW OPERATIONS, PETR WENT TO HELP SET UP TWO INFLATABLE HOSPITAL TENTS THAT MSF HAD JUST RECEIVED.
AMONG OTHER THINGS, HE UNPACKED, INSTALLED AND TESTED SURGICAL SUPPLIES.
ADMISSION AREA
OPERATING ROOM
SO... WOULD YOU SAY IT WAS A GOOD EXPERIENCE?
YES, ACTUALLY. I'M GLAD I CAME AND HELPED. THOSE TWO CLINICS ARE UP AND RUNNING NOW.
AH! THAT'S GREAT.
BRAVO!
CHEERS!
MAZEL TOV!

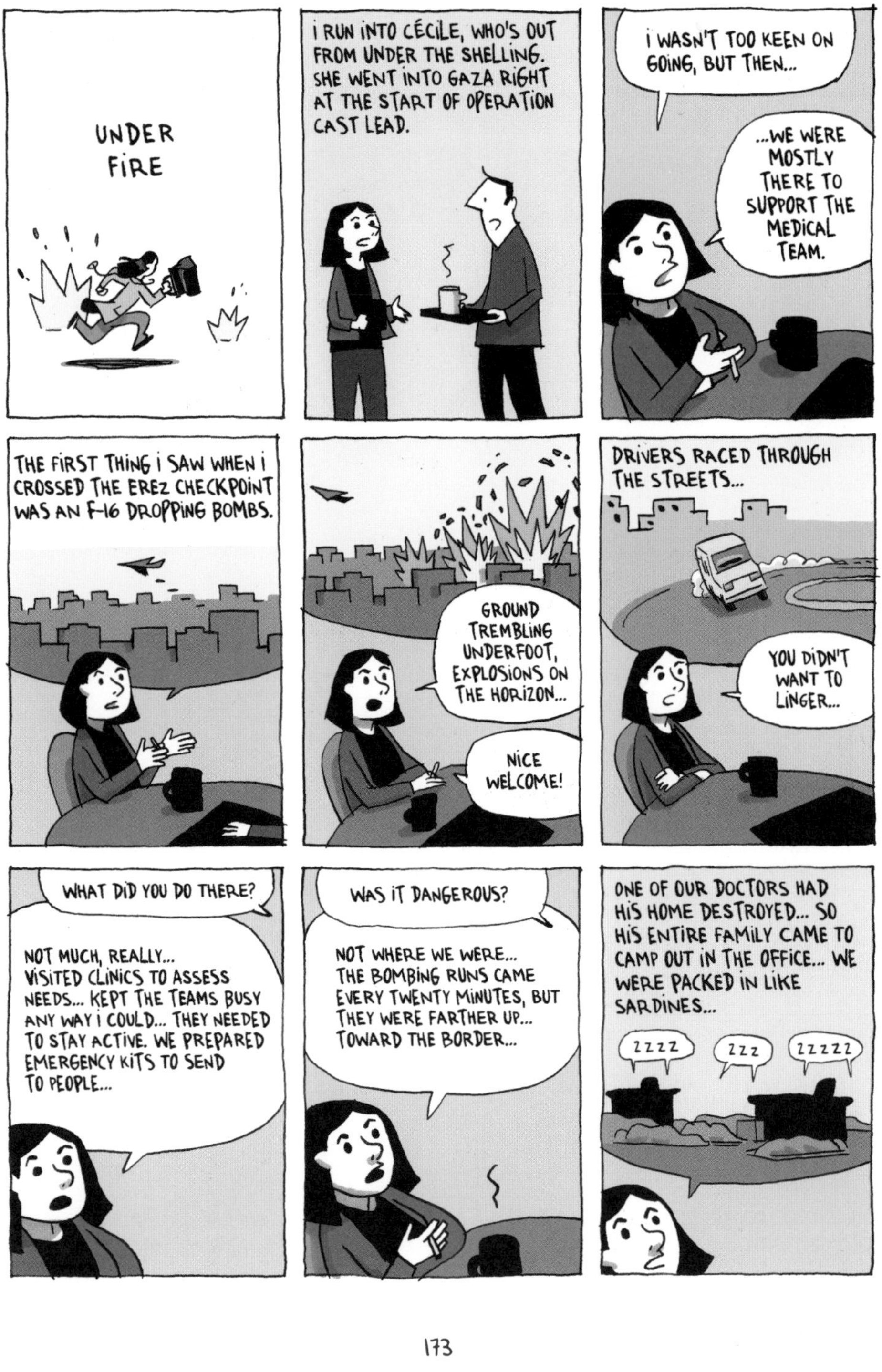
UNDER FIRE
i RUN INTO CÉCILE, WHO'S OUT FROM UNDER THE SHELLING. SHE WENT INTO GAZA RIGHT AT THE START OF OPERATION CAST LEAD.
i WASN'T TOO KEEN ON GOING, BUT THEN...
...WE WERE MOSTLY THERE TO SUPPORT THE MEDICAL TEAM.
THE FIRST THING i SAW WHEN i CROSSED THE EREZ CHECKPOINT WAS AN F-16 DROPPING BOMBS.
GROUND TREMBLING UNDERFOOT, EXPLOSIONS ON THE HORIZON...
NICE WELCOME!
DRIVERS RACED THROUGH THE STREETS...
YOU DIDN'T WANT TO LINGER...
WHAT DID YOU DO THERE?
NOT MUCH, REALLY... VISITED CLINICS TO ASSESS NEEDS... KEPT THE TEAMS BUSY ANY WAY i COULD... THEY NEEDED TO STAY ACTIVE. WE PREPARED EMERGENCY KITS TO SEND TO PEOPLE...
WAS iT DANGEROUS?
NOT WHERE WE WERE... THE BOMBING RUNS CAME EVERY TWENTY MINUTES, BUT THEY WERE FARTHER UP... TOWARD THE BORDER...
ONE OF OUR DOCTORS HAD HIS HOME DESTROYED... SO HIS ENTIRE FAMILY CAME TO CAMP OUT IN THE OFFICE... WE WERE PACKED IN LIKE SARDINES...
ZZZZ
ZZZ
ZZZZZ

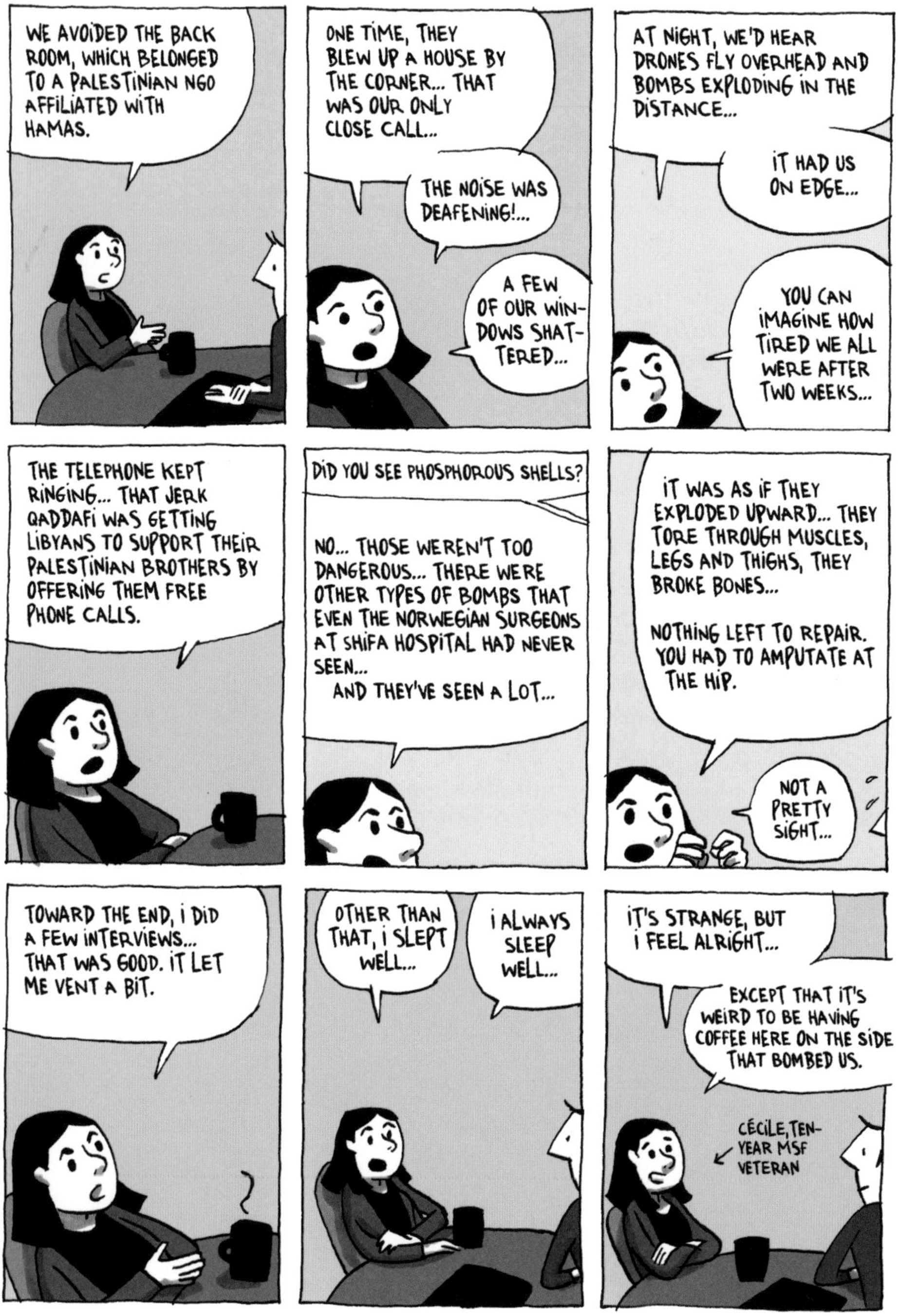
WE AVOIDED THE BACK ROOM, WHICH BELONGED TO A PALESTINIAN NGO AFFILIATED WITH HAMAS.
ONE TIME, THEY BLEW UP A HOUSE BY THE CORNER... THAT WAS OUR ONLY CLOSE CALL...
THE NOISE WAS DEAFENING!...
A FEW OF OUR WINDOWS SHATTERED...
AT NIGHT, WE'D HEAR DRONES FLY OVERHEAD AND BOMBS EXPLODING IN THE DISTANCE...
IT HAD US ON EDGE...
YOU CAN IMAGINE HOW TIRED WE ALL WERE AFTER TWO WEEKS...
THE TELEPHONE KEPT RINGING... THAT JERK QADDAFI WAS GETTING LIBYANS TO SUPPORT THEIR PALESTINIAN BROTHERS BY OFFERING THEM FREE PHONE CALLS.
DID YOU SEE PHOSPHOROUS SHELLS?
NO... THOSE WEREN'T TOO DANGEROUS... THERE WERE OTHER TYPES OF BOMBS THAT EVEN THE NORWEGIAN SURGEONS AT SHIFA HOSPITAL HAD NEVER SEEN...
AND THEY'VE SEEN A LOT...
IT WAS AS IF THEY EXPLODED UPWARD... THEY TORE THROUGH MUSCLES, LEGS AND THIGHS, THEY BROKE BONES...
NOTHING LEFT TO REPAIR. YOU HAD TO AMPUTATE AT THE HIP.
NOT A PRETTY SIGHT...
TOWARD THE END, I DID A FEW INTERVIEWS... THAT WAS GOOD. IT LET ME VENT A BIT.
OTHER THAN THAT, I SLEPT WELL...
I ALWAYS SLEEP WELL...
IT'S STRANGE, BUT I FEEL ALRIGHT...
EXCEPT THAT IT'S WEIRD TO BE HAVING COFFEE HERE ON THE SIDE THAT BOMBED US.
CÉCILE, TEN-YEAR MSF VETERAN

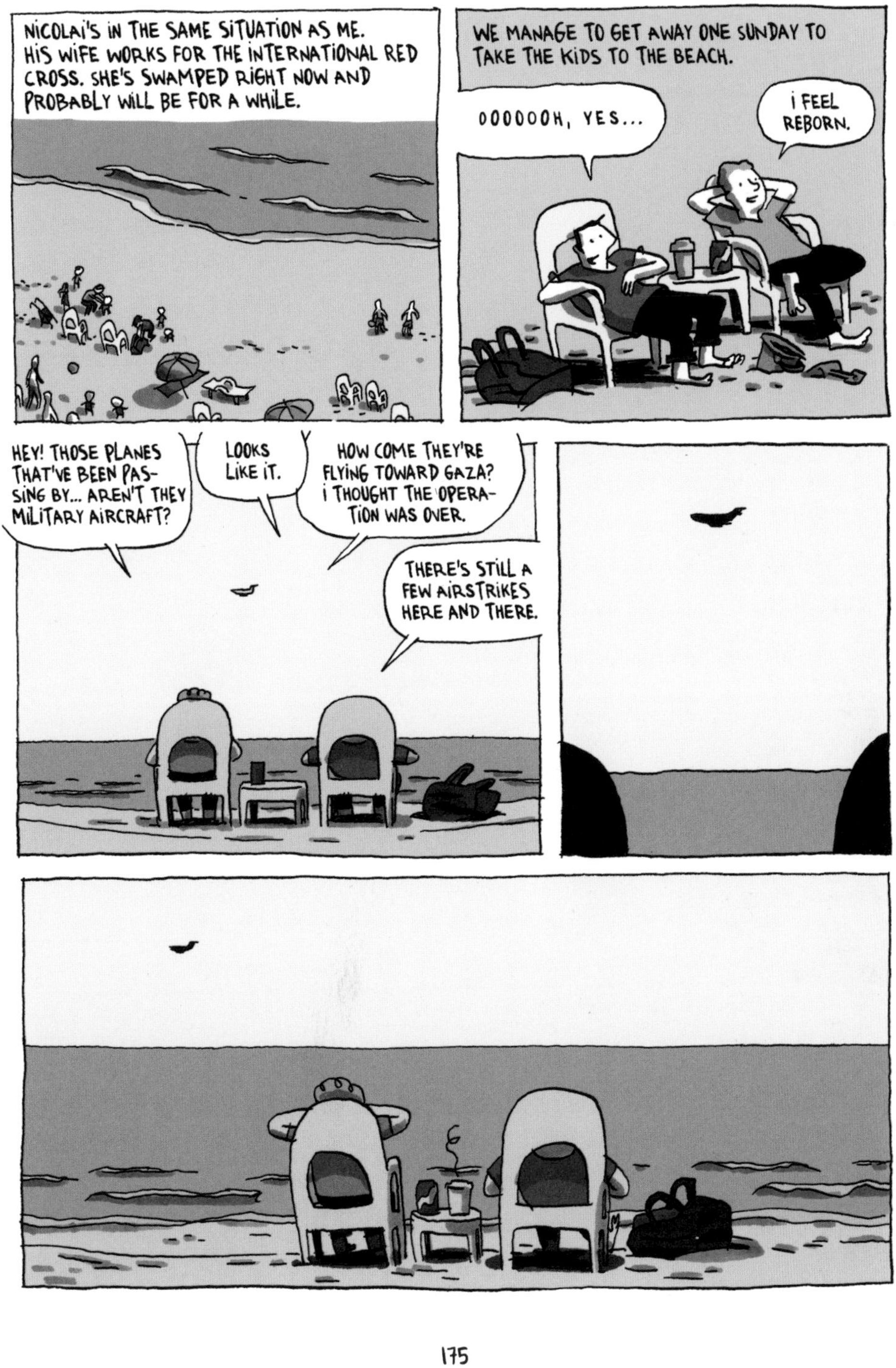
NICOLAI'S IN THE SAME SITUATION AS ME. HIS WIFE WORKS FOR THE INTERNATIONAL RED CROSS. SHE'S SWAMPED RIGHT NOW AND PROBABLY WILL BE FOR A WHILE.
WE MANAGE TO GET AWAY ONE SUNDAY TO TAKE THE KIDS TO THE BEACH.
OOOOOOH, YES...
I FEEL REBORN.
HEY! THOSE PLANES THAT'VE BEEN PASSING BY... AREN'T THEY MILITARY AIRCRAFT?
LOOKS LIKE IT.
HOW COME THEY'RE FLYING TOWARD GAZA? I THOUGHT THE OPERATION WAS OVER.
THERE'S STILL A FEW AIRSTRIKES HERE AND THERE.

FEBRUARY

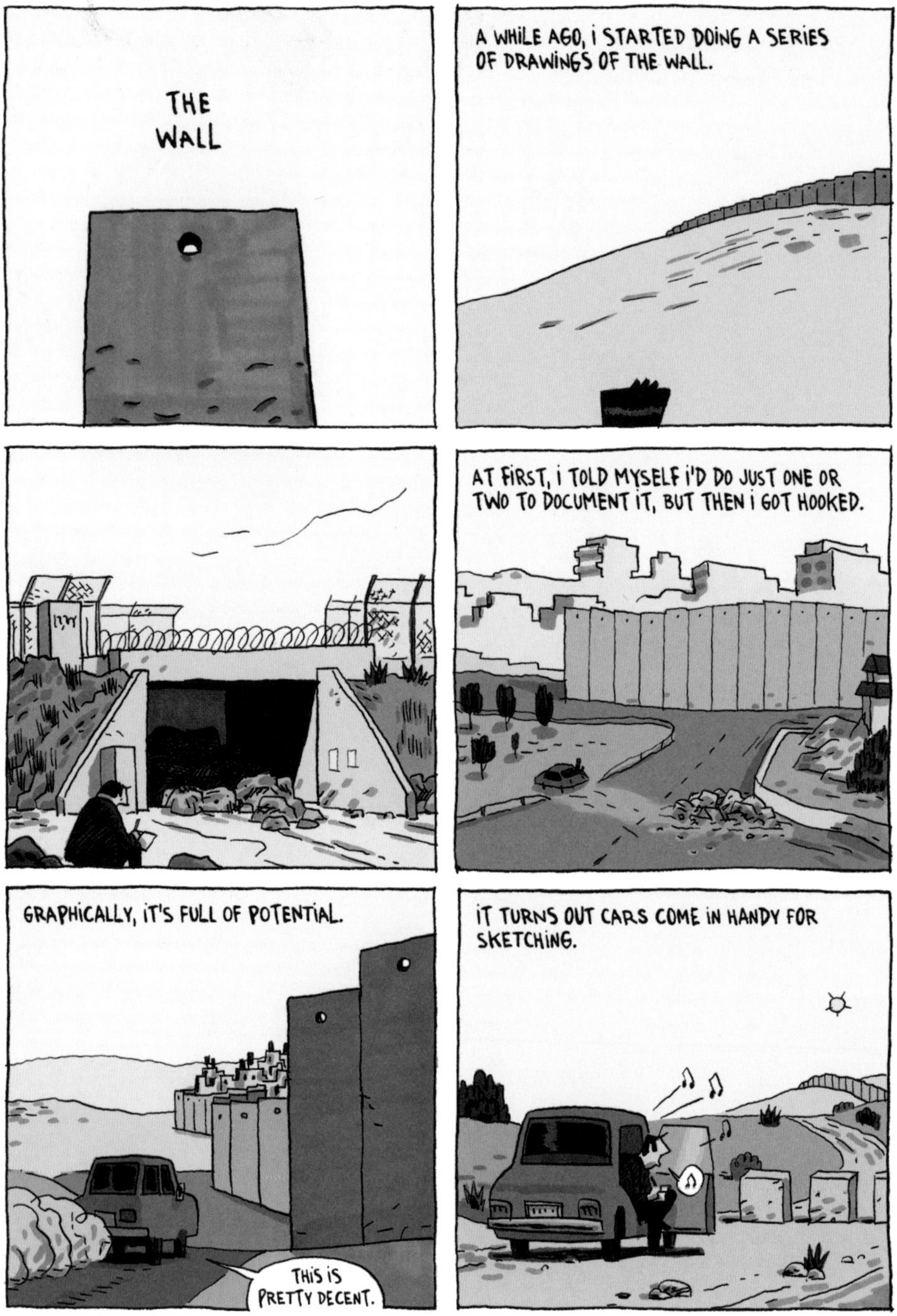
THE WALL
A WHILE AGO, I STARTED DOING A SERIES OF DRAWINGS OF THE WALL.
AT FIRST, I TOLD MYSELF I'D DO JUST ONE OR TWO TO DOCUMENT IT, BUT THEN I GOT HOOKED.
GRAPHICALLY, IT'S FULL OF POTENTIAL.
THIS IS PRETTY DECENT.
IT TURNS OUT CARS COME IN HANDY FOR SKETCHING.

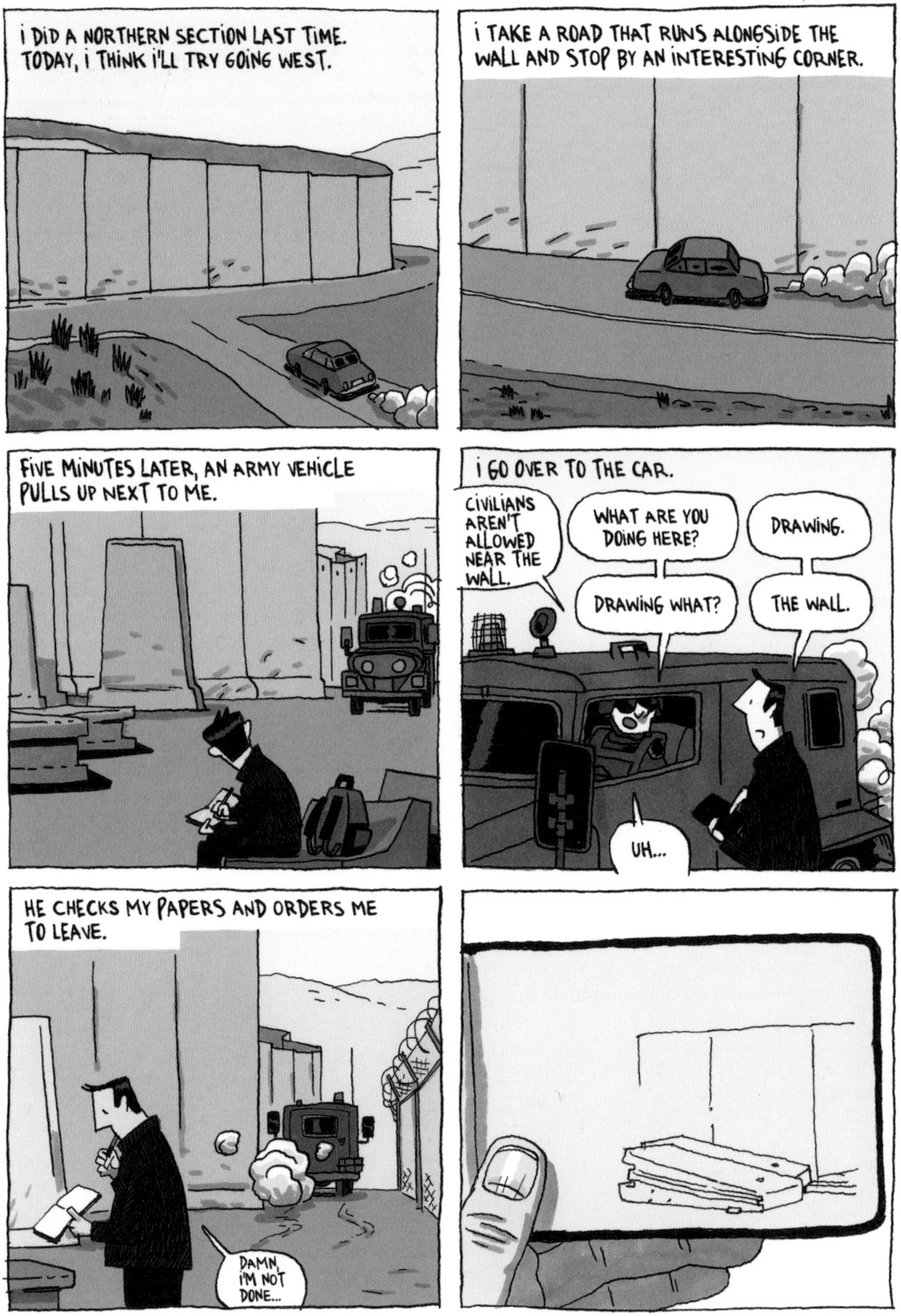
I DID A NORTHERN SECTION LAST TIME. TODAY, I THINK I'LL TRY GOING WEST.
I TAKE A ROAD THAT RUNS ALONGSIDE THE WALL AND STOP BY AN INTERESTING CORNER.
FIVE MINUTES LATER, AN ARMY VEHICLE PULLS UP NEXT TO ME.
I GO OVER TO THE CAR.
WHAT ARE YOU DOING HERE?
DRAWING.
DRAWING WHAT?
THE WALL.
CIVILIANS AREN'T ALLOWED NEAR THE WALL.
UH...
HE CHECKS MY PAPERS AND ORDERS ME TO LEAVE.
DAMN, I'M NOT DONE...

MOUNT OF OLIVES

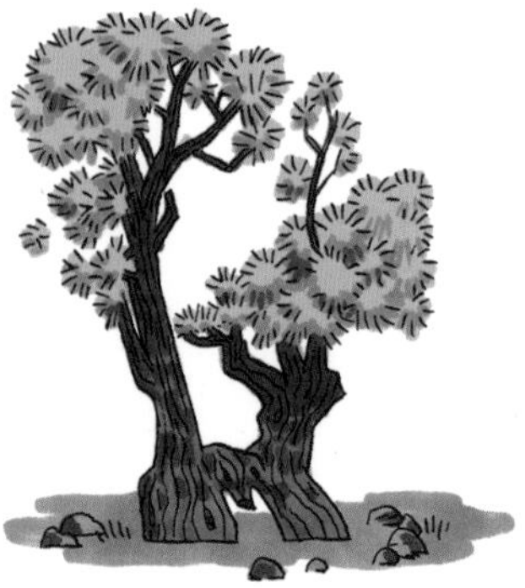

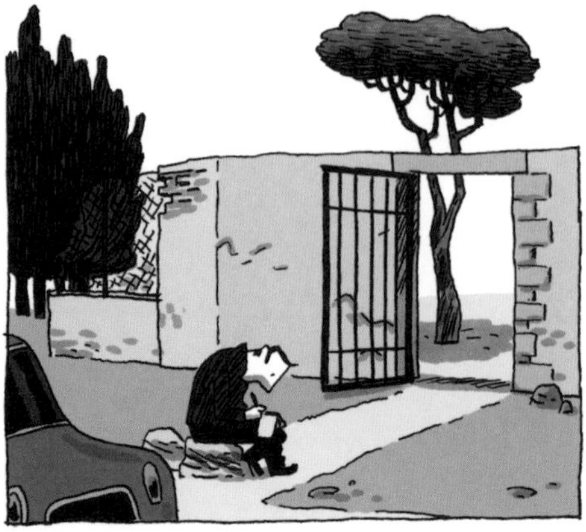

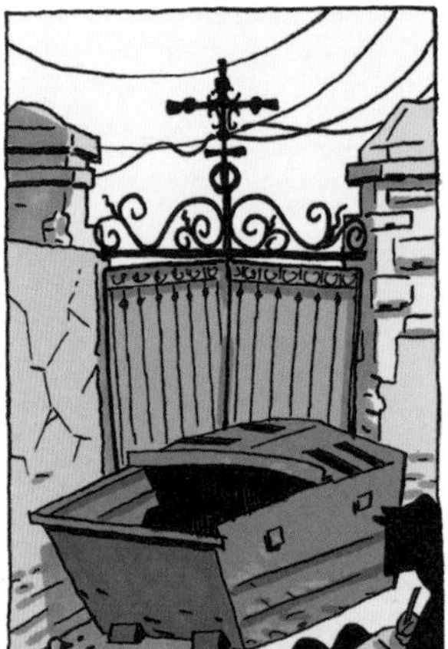

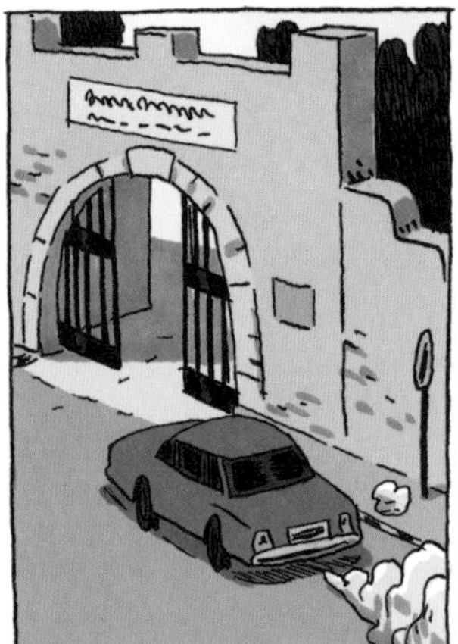

EXPLORING THE MOUNT OF OLIVES ONE DAY, I FIND A GREAT KIDS' PARK ON THE GROUNDS OF A HOSPITAL.

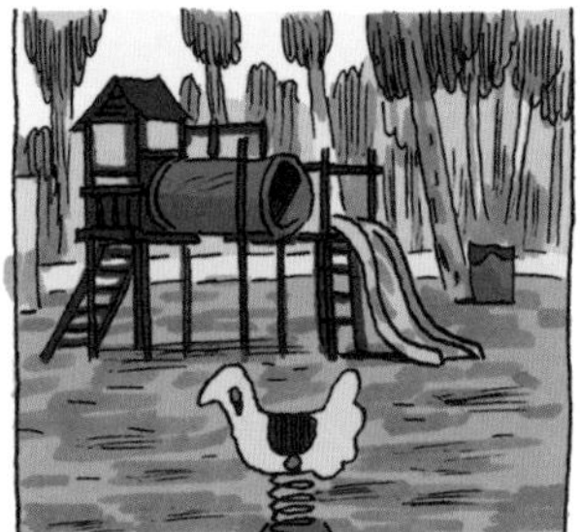

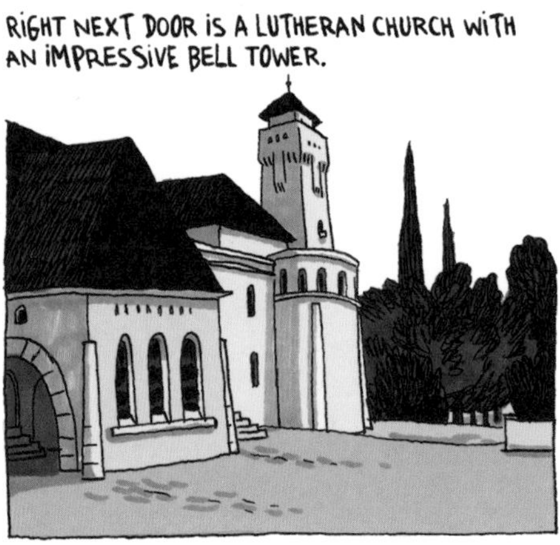
RIGHT NEXT DOOR IS A LUTHERAN CHURCH WITH AN IMPRESSIVE BELL TOWER.

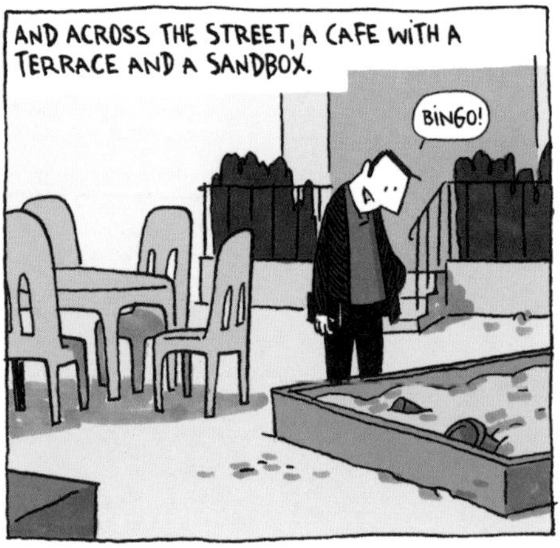
AND ACROSS THE STREET, A CAFE WITH A TERRACE AND A SANDBOX.
BINGO!

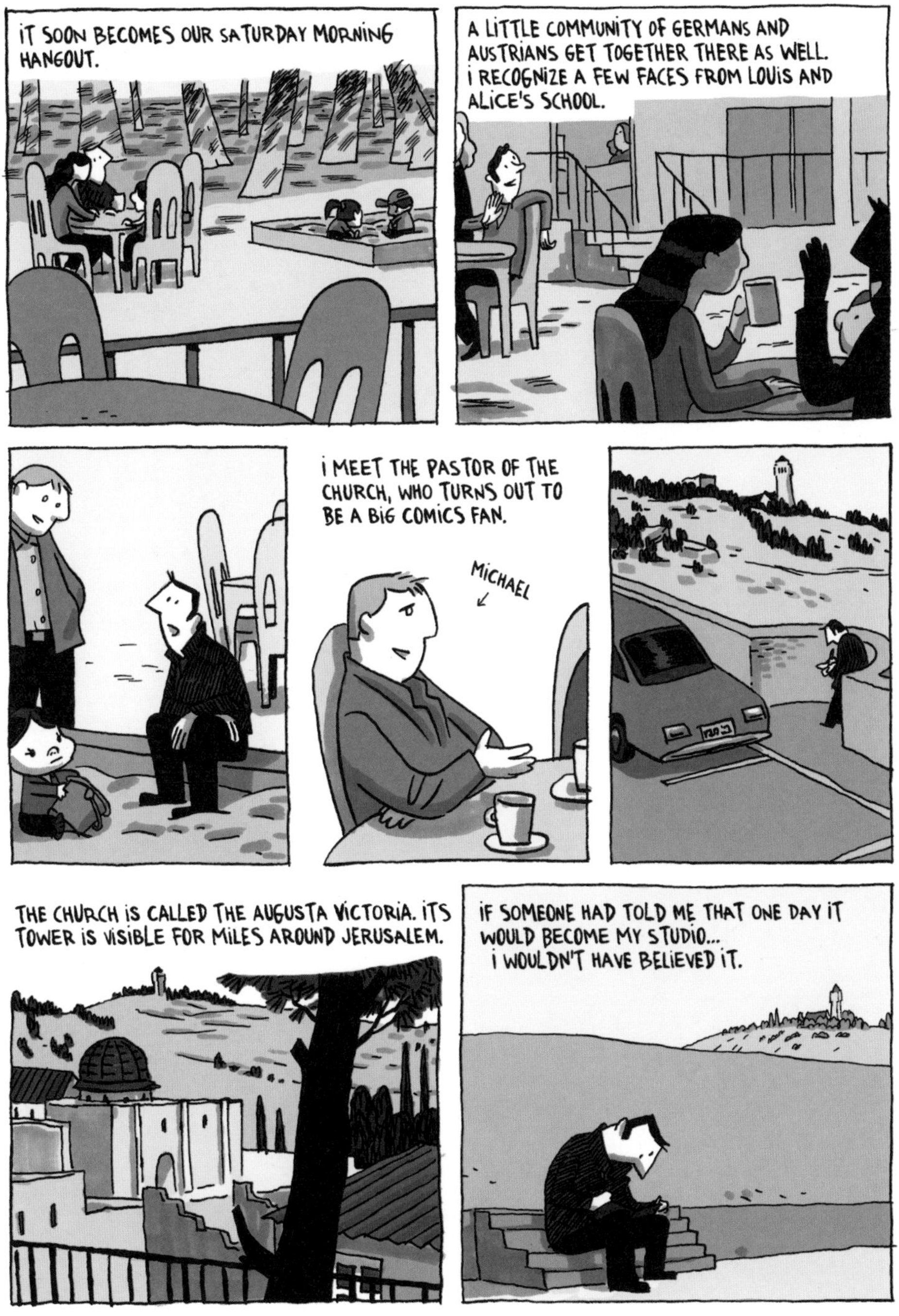
IT SOON BECOMES OUR SATURDAY MORNING HANGOUT.
A LITTLE COMMUNITY OF GERMANS AND AUSTRIANS GET TOGETHER THERE AS WELL. I RECOGNIZE A FEW FACES FROM LOUIS AND ALICE'S SCHOOL.
I MEET THE PASTOR OF THE CHURCH, WHO TURNS OUT TO BE A BIG COMICS FAN.
MICHAEL
THE CHURCH IS CALLED THE AUGUSTA VICTORIA. ITS TOWER IS VISIBLE FOR MILES AROUND JERUSALEM.
IF SOMEONE HAD TOLD ME THAT ONE DAY IT WOULD BECOME MY STUDIO...
I WOULDN'T HAVE BELIEVED IT.

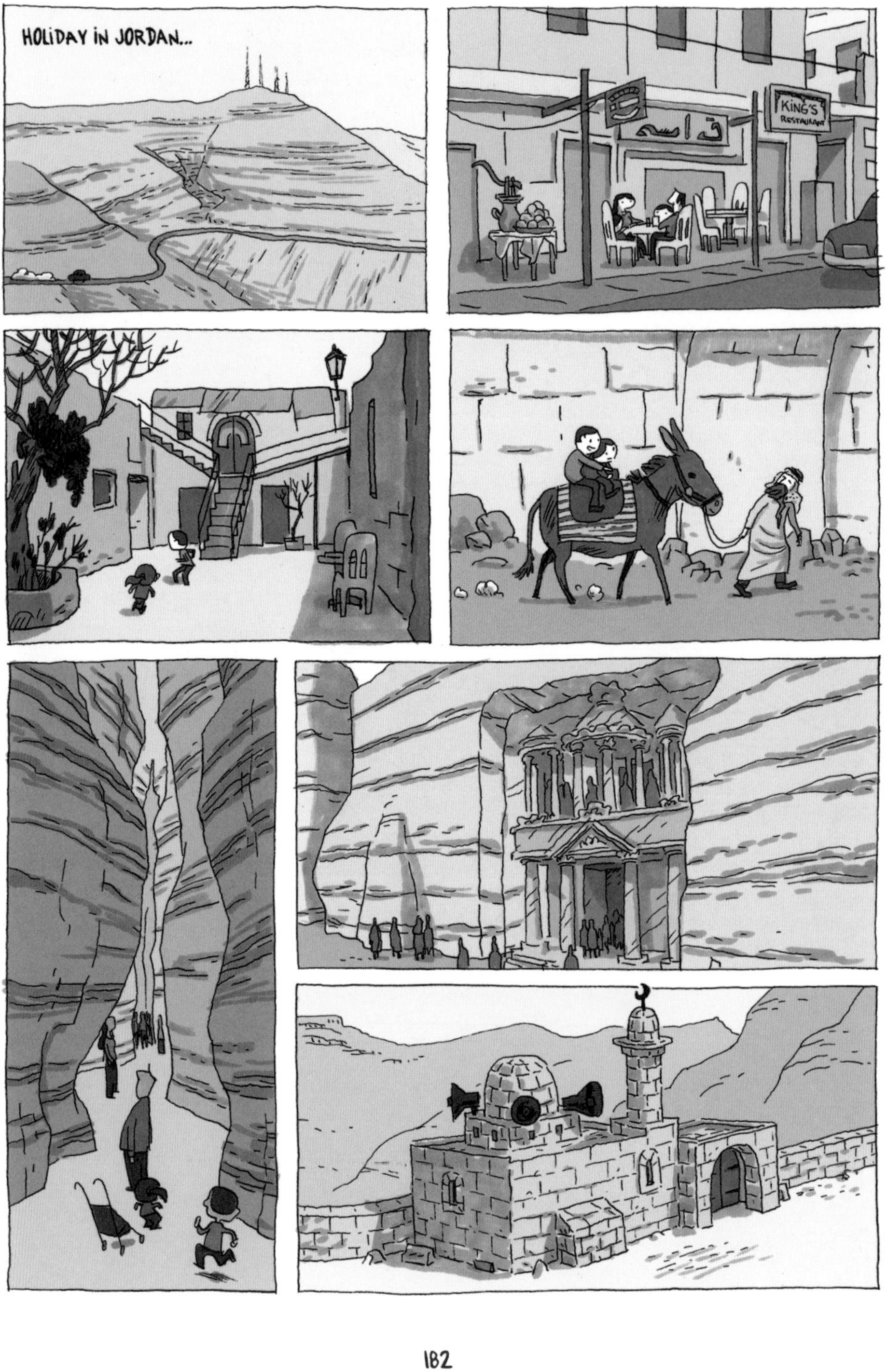
HOLIDAY IN JORDAN...
KING'S RESTAURANT

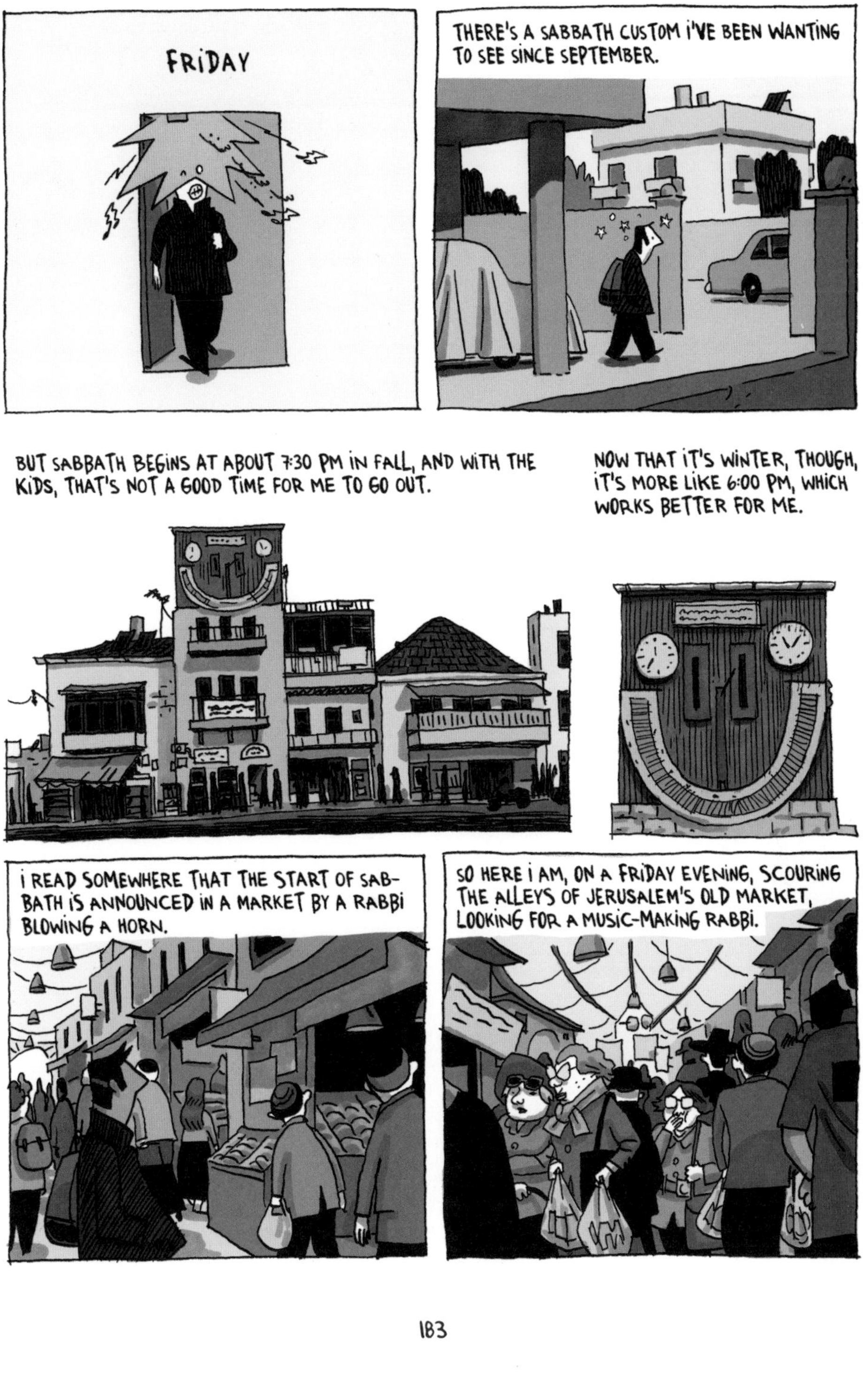
FRIDAY
THERE'S A SABBATH CUSTOM I'VE BEEN WANTING TO SEE SINCE SEPTEMBER.
BUT SABBATH BEGINS AT ABOUT 7:30 PM IN FALL, AND WITH THE KIDS, THAT'S NOT A GOOD TIME FOR ME TO GO OUT.
NOW THAT IT'S WINTER, THOUGH, IT'S MORE LIKE 6:00 PM, WHICH WORKS BETTER FOR ME.
I READ SOMEWHERE THAT THE START OF SAB-BATH IS ANNOUNCED IN A MARKET BY A RABBI BLOWING A HORN.
SO HERE I AM, ON A FRIDAY EVENING, SCOURING THE ALLEYS OF JERUSALEM'S OLD MARKET, LOOKING FOR A MUSIC-MAKING RABBI.

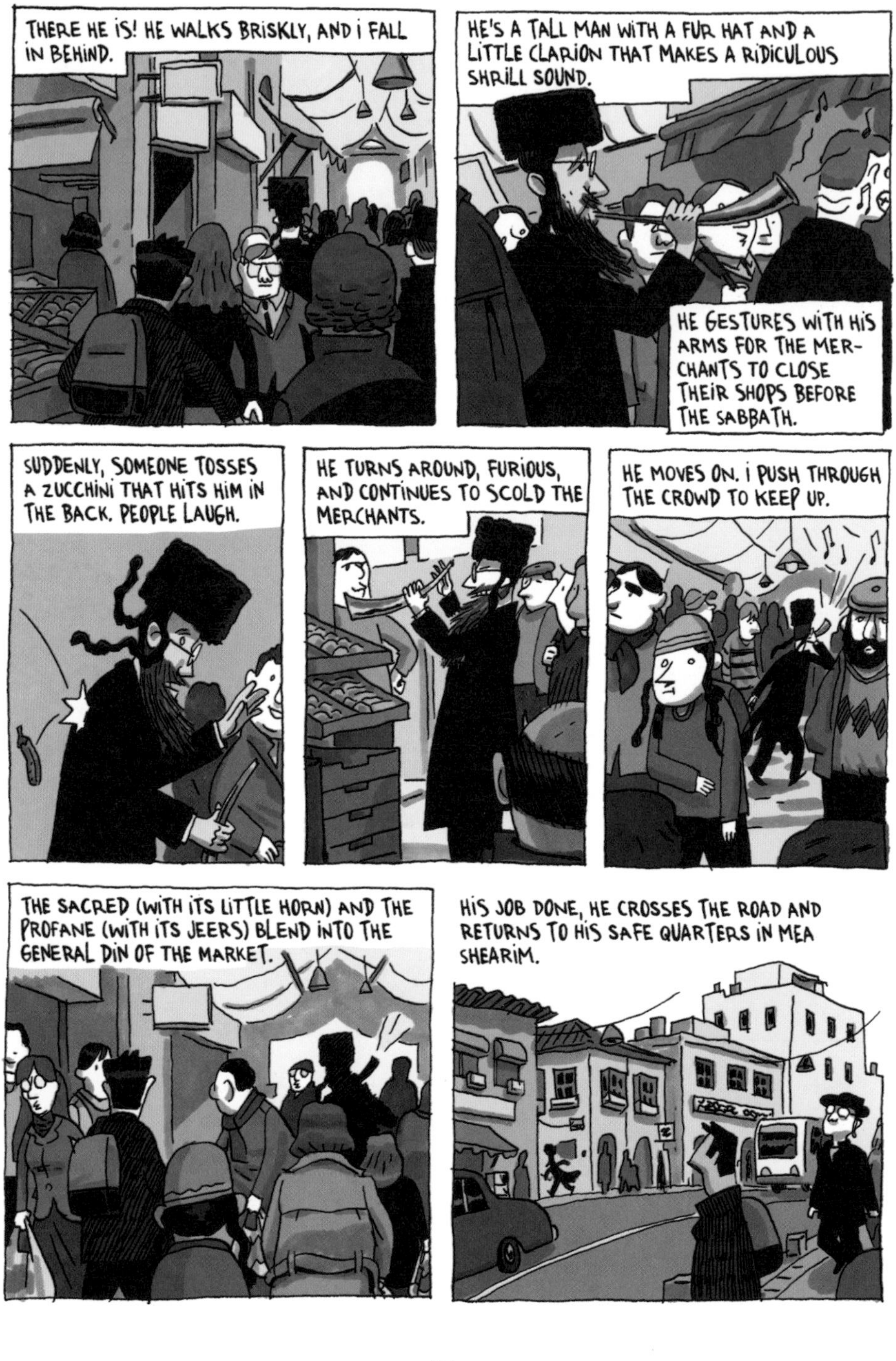
THERE HE IS! HE WALKS BRISKLY, AND I FALL IN BEHIND.
HE'S A TALL MAN WITH A FUR HAT AND A LITTLE CLARION THAT MAKES A RIDICULOUS SHRILL SOUND.
HE GESTURES WITH HIS ARMS FOR THE MERCHANTS TO CLOSE THEIR SHOPS BEFORE THE SABBATH.
SUDDENLY, SOMEONE TOSSES A ZUCCHINI THAT HITS HIM IN THE BACK. PEOPLE LAUGH.
HE TURNS AROUND, FURIOUS, AND CONTINUES TO SCOLD THE MERCHANTS.
HE MOVES ON. I PUSH THROUGH THE CROWD TO KEEP UP.
THE SACRED (WITH ITS LITTLE HORN) AND THE PROFANE (WITH ITS JEERS) BLEND INTO THE GENERAL DIN OF THE MARKET.
HIS JOB DONE, HE CROSSES THE ROAD AND RETURNS TO HIS SAFE QUARTERS IN MEA SHEARIM.

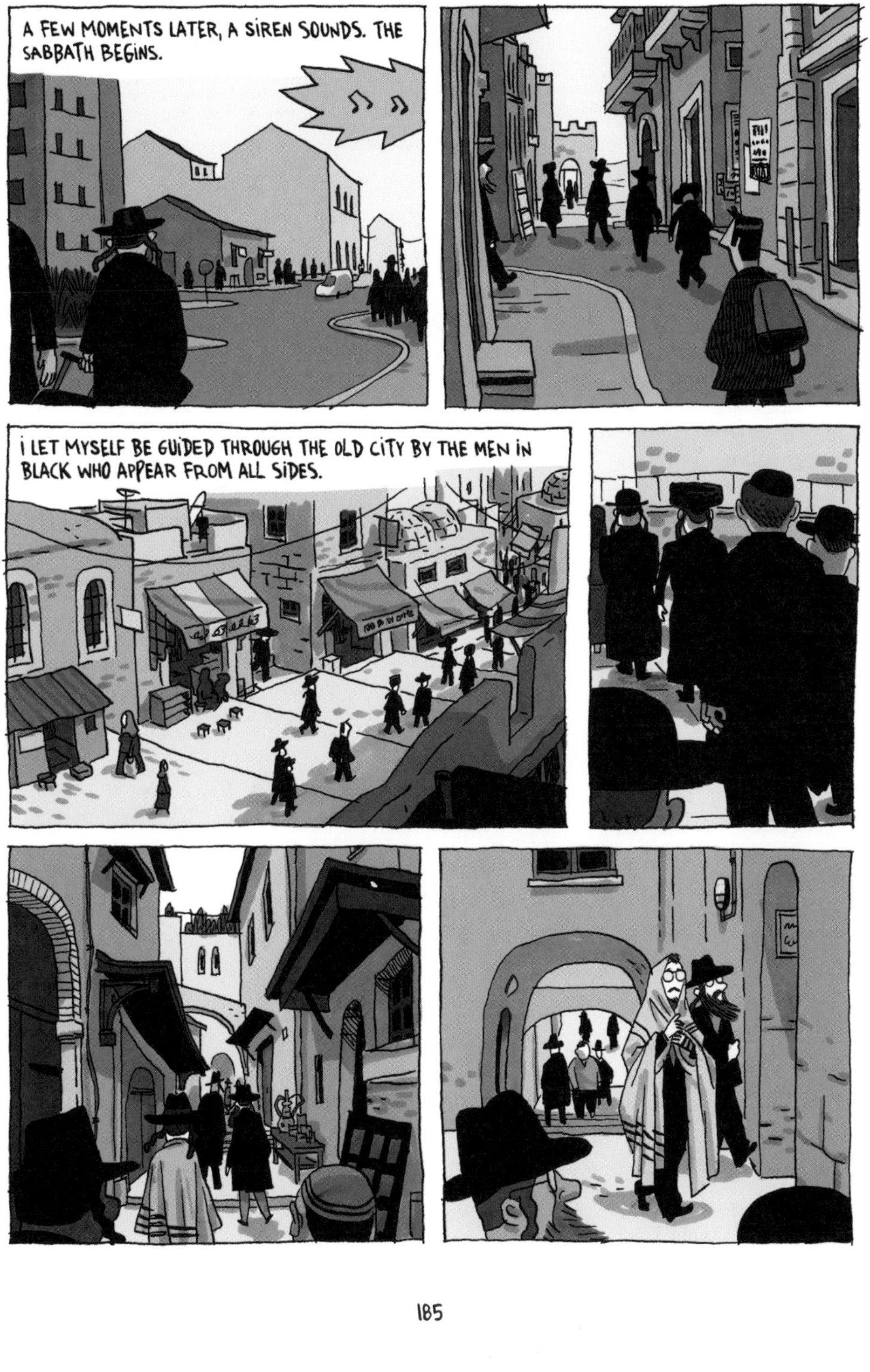
A FEW MOMENTS LATER, A SIREN SOUNDS. THE SABBATH BEGINS.
I LET MYSELF BE GUIDED THROUGH THE OLD CITY BY THE MEN IN BLACK WHO APPEAR FROM ALL SIDES.

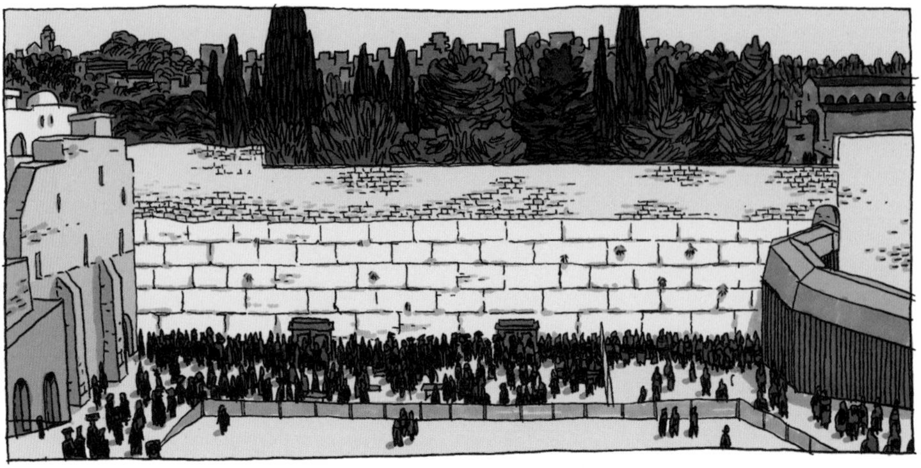

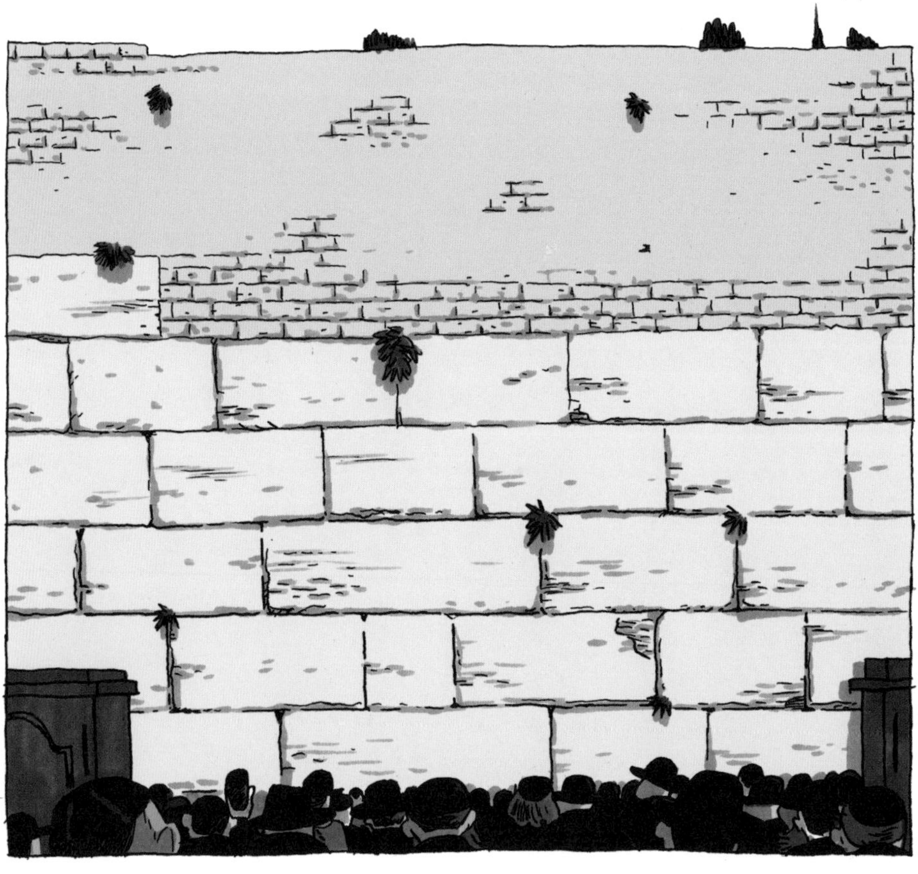

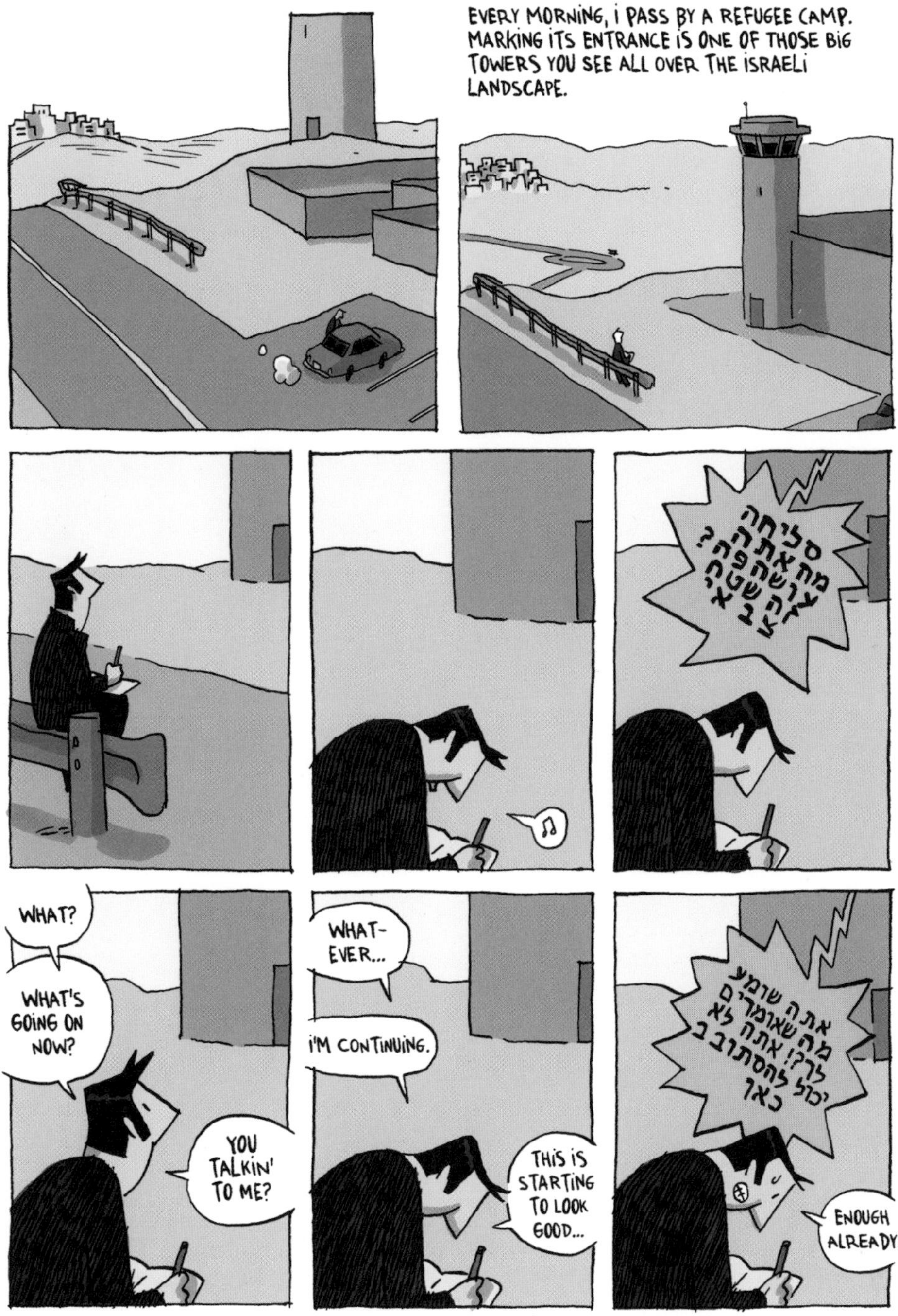
EVERY MORNING, I PASS BY A REFUGEE CAMP. MARKING ITS ENTRANCE IS ONE OF THOSE BIG TOWERS YOU SEE ALL OVER THE ISRAELI LANDSCAPE.
סליחה מה אתה פה? ערשה זה שטח צבא
WHAT?
WHAT'S GOING ON NOW?
YOU TALKIN' TO ME?
WHAT-EVER...
I'M CONTINUING.
THIS IS STARTING TO LOOK GOOD...
אתה שרמע מה שאומרים לא לך?! אתה יכול להסתובב כאן
ENOUGH ALREADY.

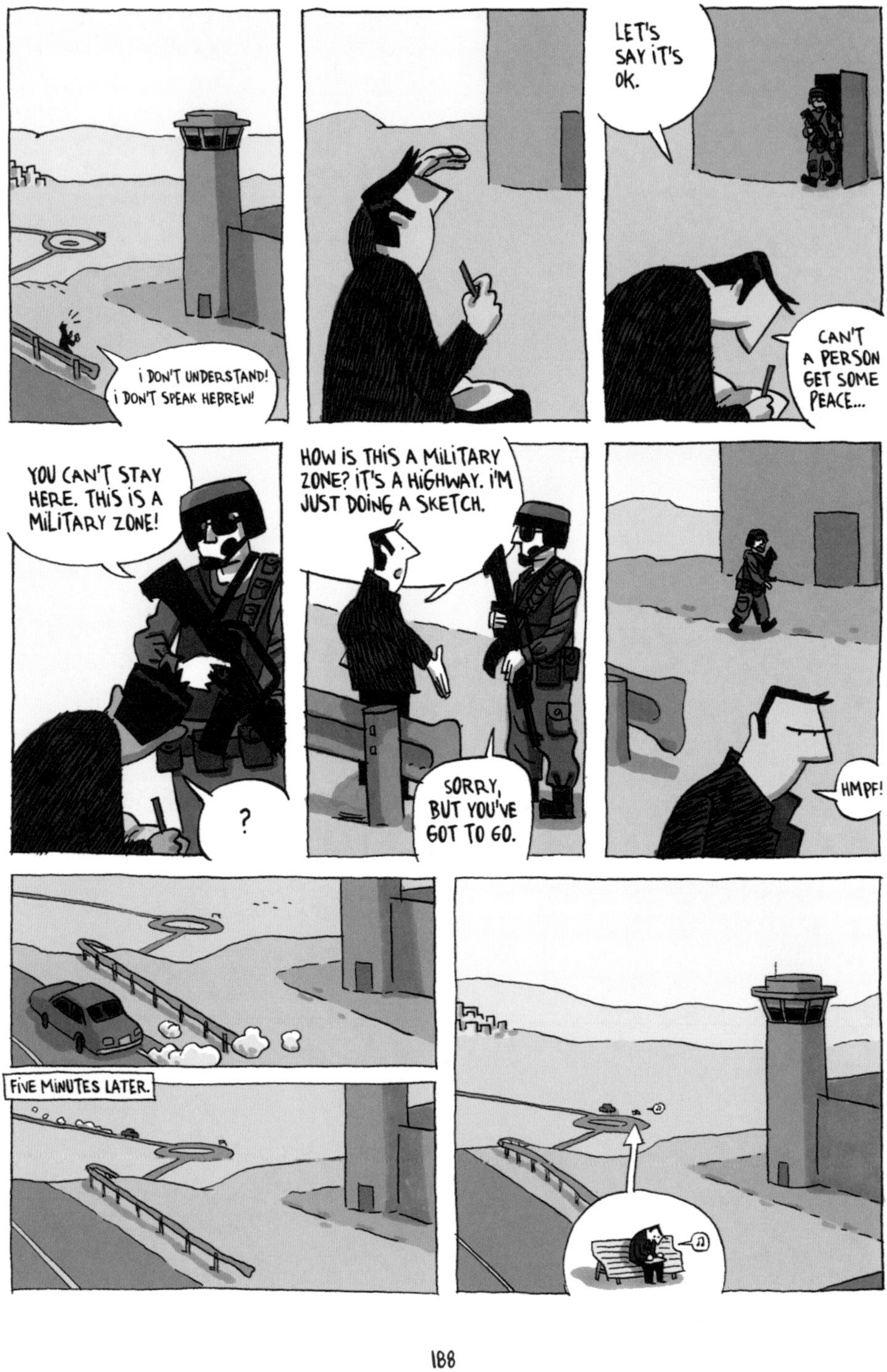
I DON'T UNDERSTAND!
I DON'T SPEAK HEBREW!
LET'S SAY IT'S OK.
CAN'T A PERSON GET SOME PEACE...
YOU CAN'T STAY HERE. THIS IS A MILITARY ZONE!
?
HOW IS THIS A MILITARY ZONE? IT'S A HIGHWAY. I'M JUST DOING A SKETCH.
SORRY, BUT YOU'VE GOT TO GO.
HMPF!
FIVE MINUTES LATER.

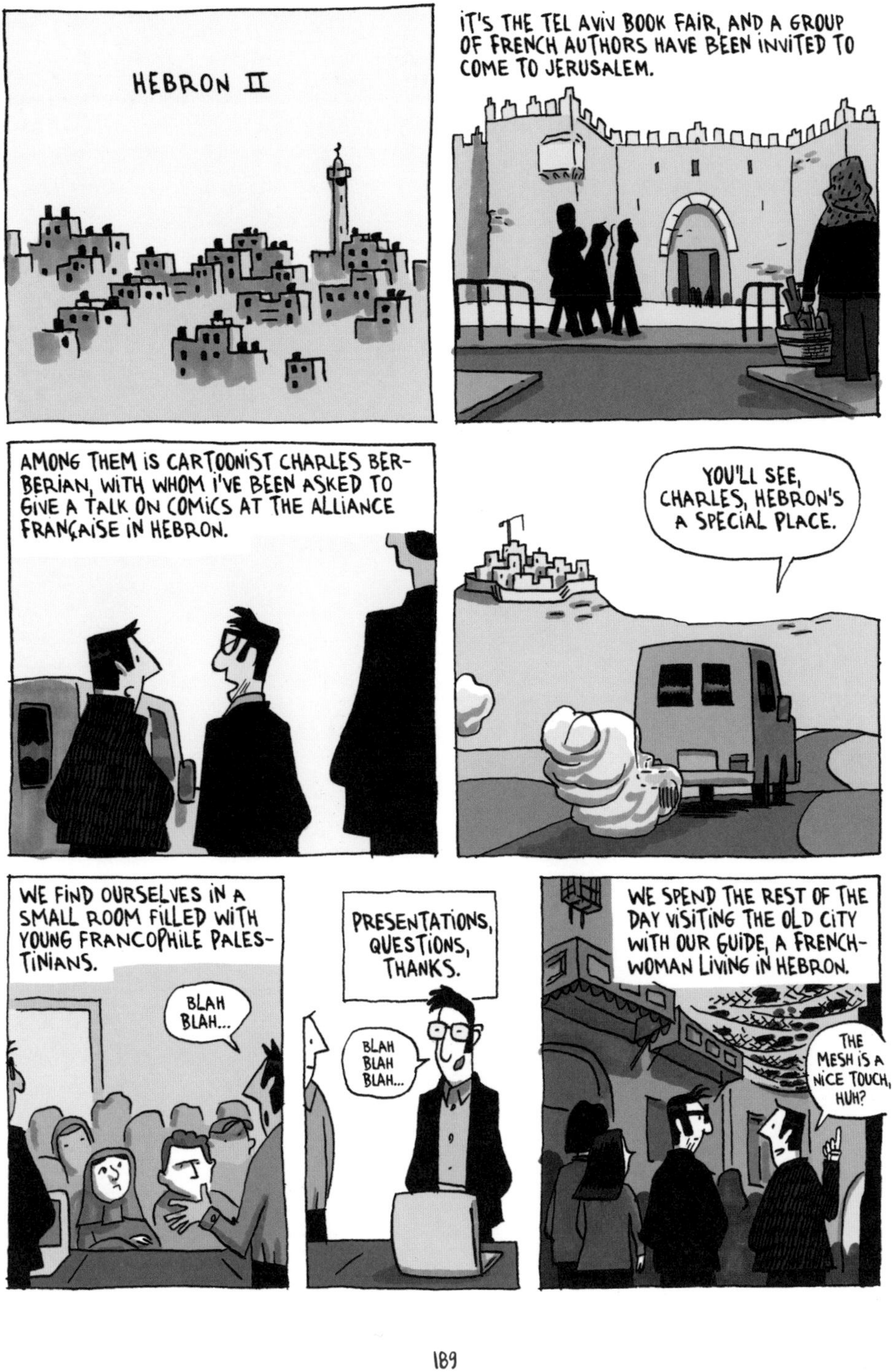
HEBRON II
IT'S THE TEL AVIV BOOK FAIR, AND A GROUP OF FRENCH AUTHORS HAVE BEEN INVITED TO COME TO JERUSALEM.
AMONG THEM IS CARTOONIST CHARLES BERBERIAN, WITH WHOM I'VE BEEN ASKED TO GIVE A TALK ON COMICS AT THE ALLIANCE FRANÇAISE IN HEBRON.
YOU'LL SEE, CHARLES, HEBRON'S A SPECIAL PLACE.
WE FIND OURSELVES IN A SMALL ROOM FILLED WITH YOUNG FRANCOPHILE PALESTINIANS.
BLAH BLAH...
PRESENTATIONS, QUESTIONS, THANKS.
BLAH BLAH BLAH...
WE SPEND THE REST OF THE DAY VISITING THE OLD CITY WITH OUR GUIDE, A FRENCHWOMAN LIVING IN HEBRON.
THE MESH IS A NICE TOUCH, HUH?

THE TOMB OF THE PATRIARCHS IS CLOSED.

DAMN.

TOUGH LUCK!

SECOND TIME FOR ME.

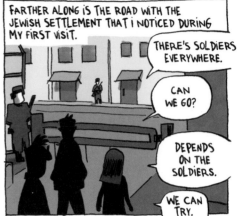

FARTHER ALONG IS THE ROAD WITH THE JEWISH SETTLEMENT THAT I NOTICED DURING MY FIRST VISIT.

THERE'S SOLDIERS EVERYWHERE.

CAN WE GO?

DEPENDS ON THE SOLDIERS.

WE CAN TRY.

THIS ROAD IS UNUSUAL BECAUSE PALESTINIANS CAN USE IT TO GET TO AN ADMINISTRATIVE OFFICE UP AHEAD.

BUT SINCE PALESTINIANS AND SETTLERS PASS BY EACH OTHER HERE, THEY'VE DRAWN A YELLOW LINE DOWN THE MIDDLE TO KEEP THEM APART.

ARABS ON ONE SIDE, JEWS ON THE OTHER.

AND WHAT ABOUT US?

A YOUNG WOMAN WALKS BY. SHE MUST LIVE AROUND HERE. NO OBVIOUS SIGN OF RELIGIOUS AFFILIATION.

UNLIKE THE FOUR GUYS WHO ARE OUT FOR A JOG. THEY'RE NOT FLASHING CONSPICUOUS RELIGIOUS SYMBOLS EITHER, BUT...

...ONE HAS AN ASSAULT RIFLE SLUNG OVER HIS SHOULDER.

IT SAYS SOMETHING ABOUT THE GENERAL FEEL OF THE NEIGHBOURHOOD.

I TOLD YOU IT WAS SPECIAL.

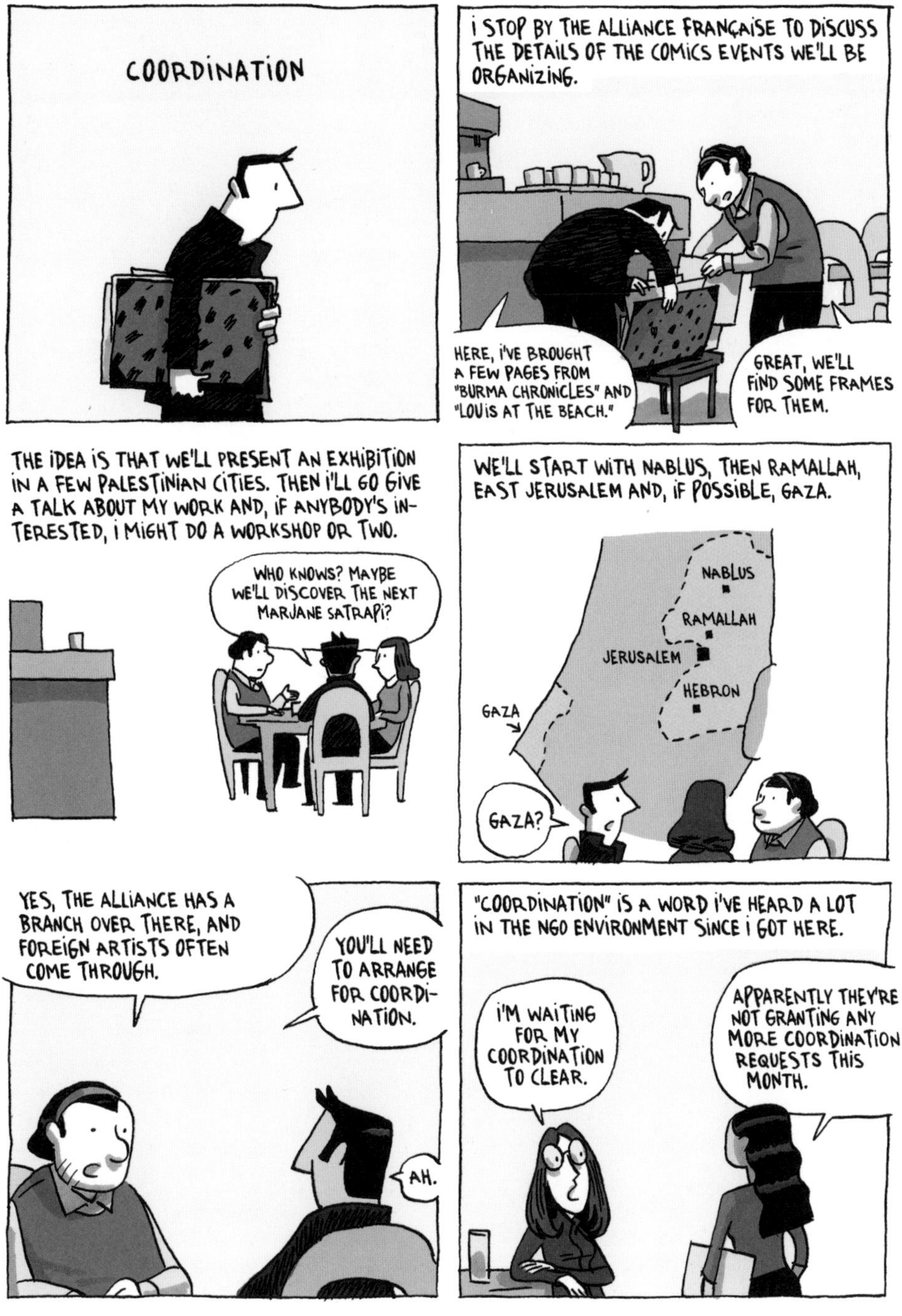
COORDINATION
I STOP BY THE ALLIANCE FRANÇAISE TO DISCUSS THE DETAILS OF THE COMICS EVENTS WE'LL BE ORGANIZING.
HERE, I'VE BROUGHT A FEW PAGES FROM "BURMA CHRONICLES" AND "LOUIS AT THE BEACH."
GREAT, WE'LL FIND SOME FRAMES FOR THEM.
THE IDEA IS THAT WE'LL PRESENT AN EXHIBITION IN A FEW PALESTINIAN CITIES. THEN I'LL GO GIVE A TALK ABOUT MY WORK AND, IF ANYBODY'S INTERESTED, I MIGHT DO A WORKSHOP OR TWO.
WHO KNOWS? MAYBE WE'LL DISCOVER THE NEXT MARJANE SATRAPI?
WE'LL START WITH NABLUS, THEN RAMALLAH, EAST JERUSALEM AND, IF POSSIBLE, GAZA.
NABLUS
RAMALLAH
JERUSALEM
HEBRON
GAZA
GAZA?
YES, THE ALLIANCE HAS A BRANCH OVER THERE, AND FOREIGN ARTISTS OFTEN COME THROUGH.
YOU'LL NEED TO ARRANGE FOR COORDINATION.
AH.
"COORDINATION" IS A WORD I'VE HEARD A LOT IN THE NGO ENVIRONMENT SINCE I GOT HERE.
I'M WAITING FOR MY COORDINATION TO CLEAR.
APPARENTLY THEY'RE NOT GRANTING ANY MORE COORDINATION REQUESTS THIS MONTH.

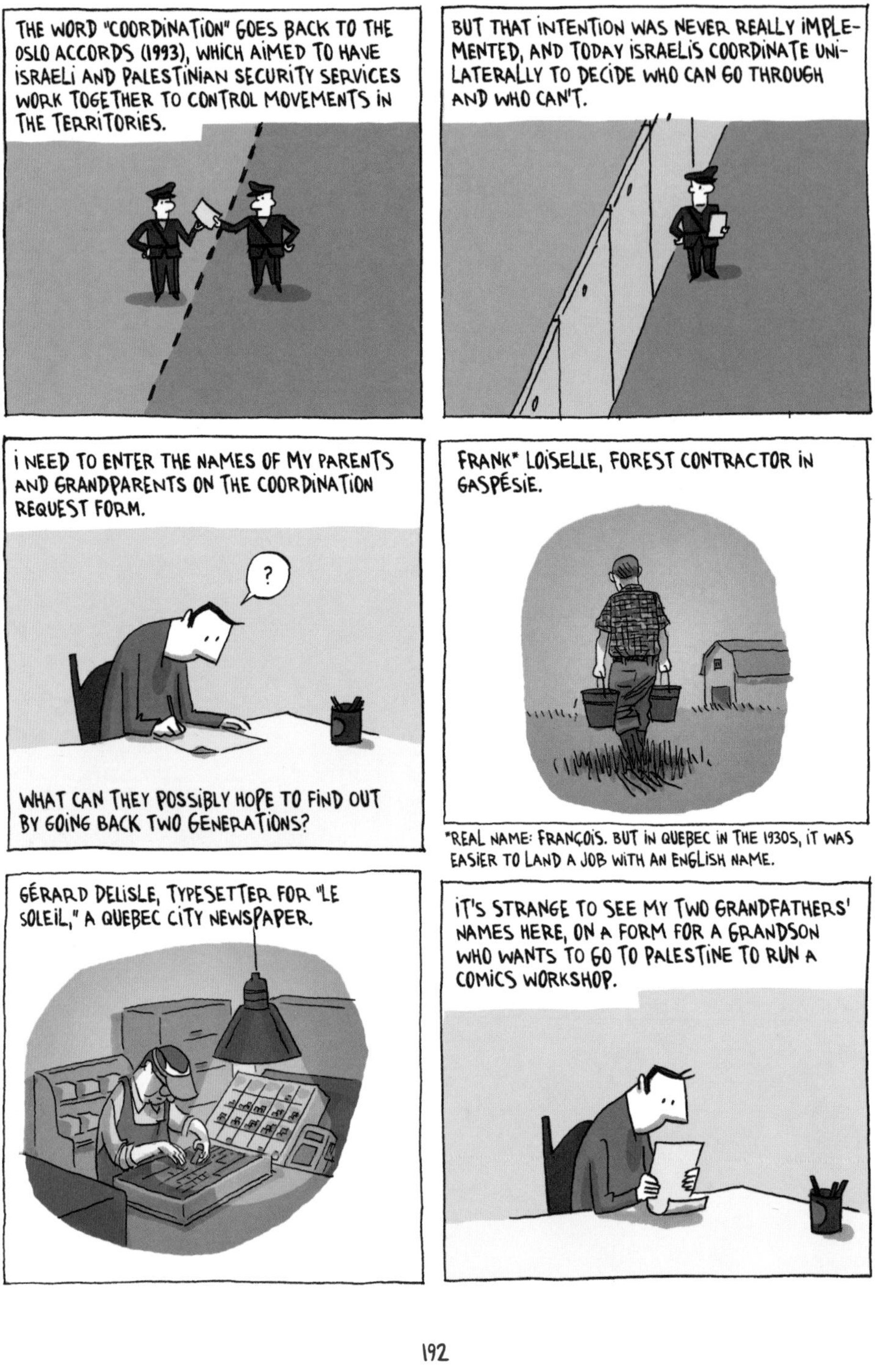
THE WORD "COORDINATION" GOES BACK TO THE OSLO ACCORDS (1993), WHICH AIMED TO HAVE ISRAELI AND PALESTINIAN SECURITY SERVICES WORK TOGETHER TO CONTROL MOVEMENTS IN THE TERRITORIES.
BUT THAT INTENTION WAS NEVER REALLY IMPLEMENTED, AND TODAY ISRAELIS COORDINATE UNILATERALLY TO DECIDE WHO CAN GO THROUGH AND WHO CAN'T.
I NEED TO ENTER THE NAMES OF MY PARENTS AND GRANDPARENTS ON THE COORDINATION REQUEST FORM.
?
WHAT CAN THEY POSSIBLY HOPE TO FIND OUT BY GOING BACK TWO GENERATIONS?
FRANK* LOISELLE, FOREST CONTRACTOR IN GASPÉSIE.
*REAL NAME: FRANÇOIS. BUT IN QUEBEC IN THE 1930S, IT WAS EASIER TO LAND A JOB WITH AN ENGLISH NAME.
GÉRARD DELISLE, TYPESETTER FOR "LE SOLEIL," A QUEBEC CITY NEWSPAPER.
IT'S STRANGE TO SEE MY TWO GRANDFATHERS' NAMES HERE, ON A FORM FOR A GRANDSON WHO WANTS TO GO TO PALESTINE TO RUN A COMICS WORKSHOP.

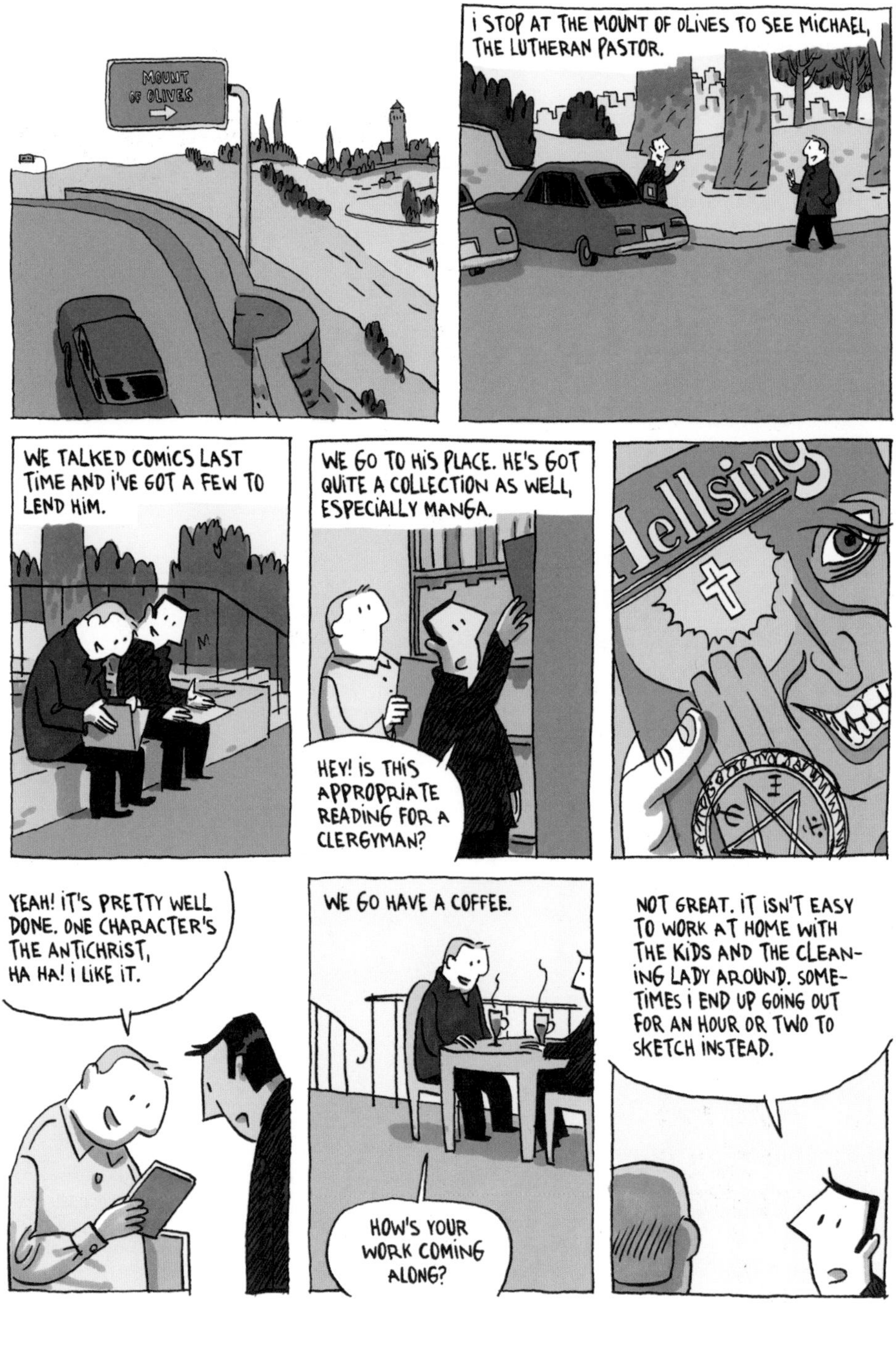
MOUNT OF OLIVES
I STOP AT THE MOUNT OF OLIVES TO SEE MICHAEL, THE LUTHERAN PASTOR.
WE TALKED COMICS LAST TIME AND I'VE GOT A FEW TO LEND HIM.
WE GO TO HIS PLACE. HE'S GOT QUITE A COLLECTION AS WELL, ESPECIALLY MANGA.
HEY! IS THIS APPROPRIATE READING FOR A CLERGYMAN?
Hellsing
YEAH! IT'S PRETTY WELL DONE. ONE CHARACTER'S THE ANTICHRIST, HA HA! I LIKE IT.
WE GO HAVE A COFFEE.
HOW'S YOUR WORK COMING ALONG?
NOT GREAT. IT ISN'T EASY TO WORK AT HOME WITH THE KIDS AND THE CLEANING LADY AROUND. SOMETIMES I END UP GOING OUT FOR AN HOUR OR TWO TO SKETCH INSTEAD.

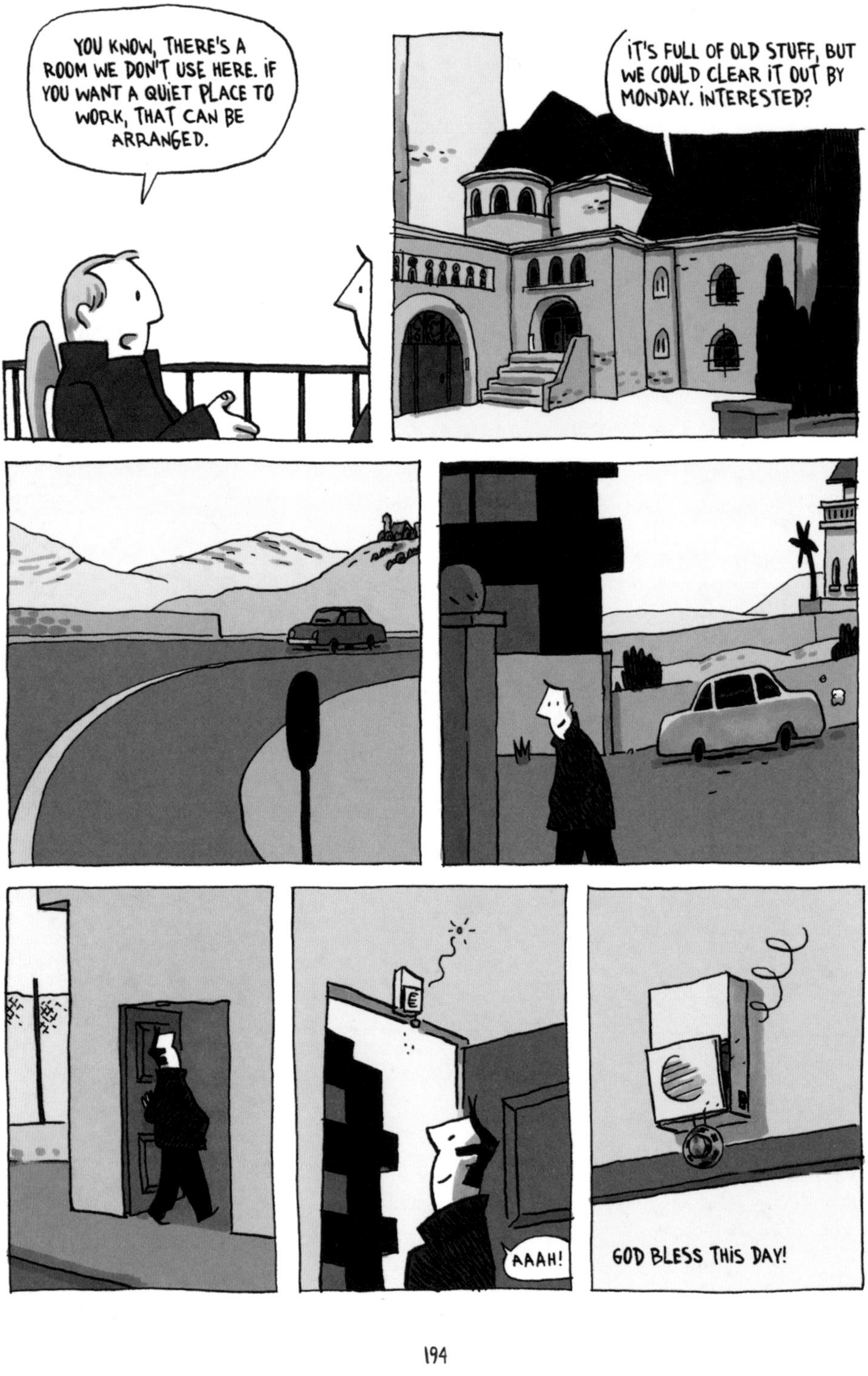
YOU KNOW, THERE'S A ROOM WE DON'T USE HERE. IF YOU WANT A QUIET PLACE TO WORK, THAT CAN BE ARRANGED.
IT'S FULL OF OLD STUFF, BUT WE COULD CLEAR IT OUT BY MONDAY. INTERESTED?
AAAH!
GOD BLESS THIS DAY!

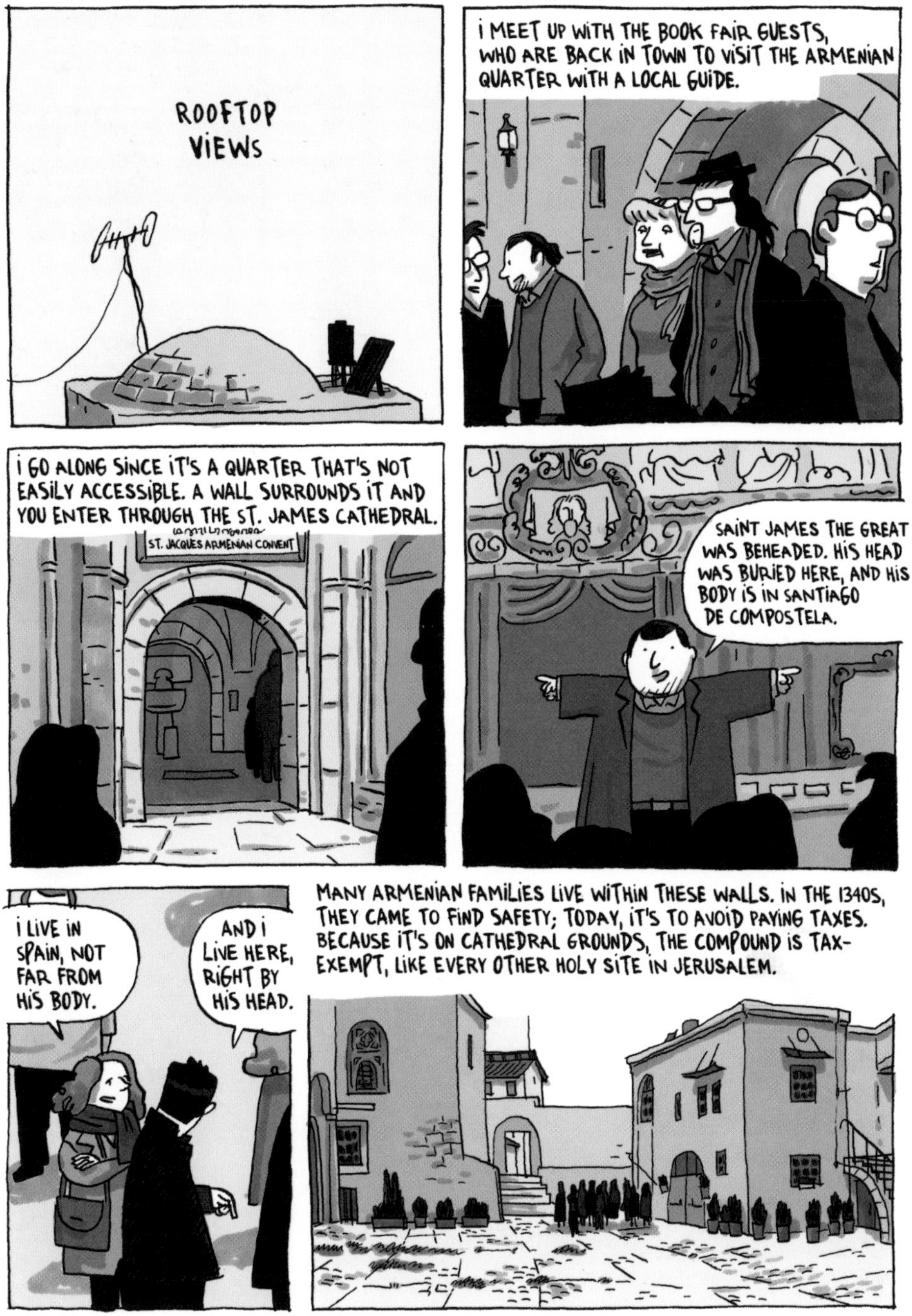
ROOFTOP VIEWS
I MEET UP WITH THE BOOK FAIR GUESTS, WHO ARE BACK IN TOWN TO VISIT THE ARMENIAN QUARTER WITH A LOCAL GUIDE.
I GO ALONG SINCE IT'S A QUARTER THAT'S NOT EASILY ACCESSIBLE. A WALL SURROUNDS IT AND YOU ENTER THROUGH THE ST. JAMES CATHEDRAL.
ST. JACQUES ARMENIAN CONVENT
SAINT JAMES THE GREAT WAS BEHEADED. HIS HEAD WAS BURIED HERE, AND HIS BODY IS IN SANTIAGO DE COMPOSTELA.
I LIVE IN SPAIN, NOT FAR FROM HIS BODY.
AND I LIVE HERE, RIGHT BY HIS HEAD.
MANY ARMENIAN FAMILIES LIVE WITHIN THESE WALLS. IN THE 1340S, THEY CAME TO FIND SAFETY; TODAY, IT'S TO AVOID PAYING TAXES. BECAUSE IT'S ON CATHEDRAL GROUNDS, THE COMPOUND IS TAX-EXEMPT, LIKE EVERY OTHER HOLY SITE IN JERUSALEM.

IT'S EVEN CARVED IN STONE BY THE ENTRANCE.

ANYONE WHO COLLECTS TAXES ON THESE GROUNDS SHALL BE DAMNED, AND THEIR SONS TOO, AND THE CURSE OF ALLAH SHALL BE UPON THEM.

SULTAN CHAQMAQ 1451

SO IT'S NOT SURPRISING THAT THE COMPOUND HAS GROWN SOME OVER THE CENTURIES.

ENTRANCE

TODAY, IT COVERS ONE SIXTH OF JERUSALEM'S OLD CITY.

MUSLIMS

CHRISTIANS

JEWS

ARMENIANS

IT HAS EVERYTHING: A MUSEUM, CHURCHES, A SCHOOL WITH A SOCCER FIELD....

...THE ONLY SOCCER FIELD IN THE WORLD BUILT ON THE GROUNDS OF A CATHEDRAL.

AFTER THE VISIT, THE GROUP SPLITS UP AND I FIND MYSELF HAVING LUNCH WITH AN IMPROBABLE MIX OF AUTHORS.

THERE'S THE AUTHOR OF THE COMIC BOOK VERSION OF "REMEMBRANCE OF THINGS PAST,"* THE STAND-UP COMEDIAN CHARLOTTE DE TURCKHEIM...

WE KNOW PROUST OFTEN WENT TO BROTHELS...

*STÉPHANE HEUET

ATIQ RAHIMI, THE FRENCH-AFGHAN WRITER WHO WON THE PRIX GONCOURT THIS YEAR, AND CHARLES BERBERIAN.

MY MOTHER WAS BORN IN JERUSALEM...

AT THE END OF THE MEAL, SEVERAL OF THEM WANT TO VISIT THE DOME OF THE ROCK.

YOU'LL NEED TO HURRY. IT CLOSES AT 1:30 TODAY.

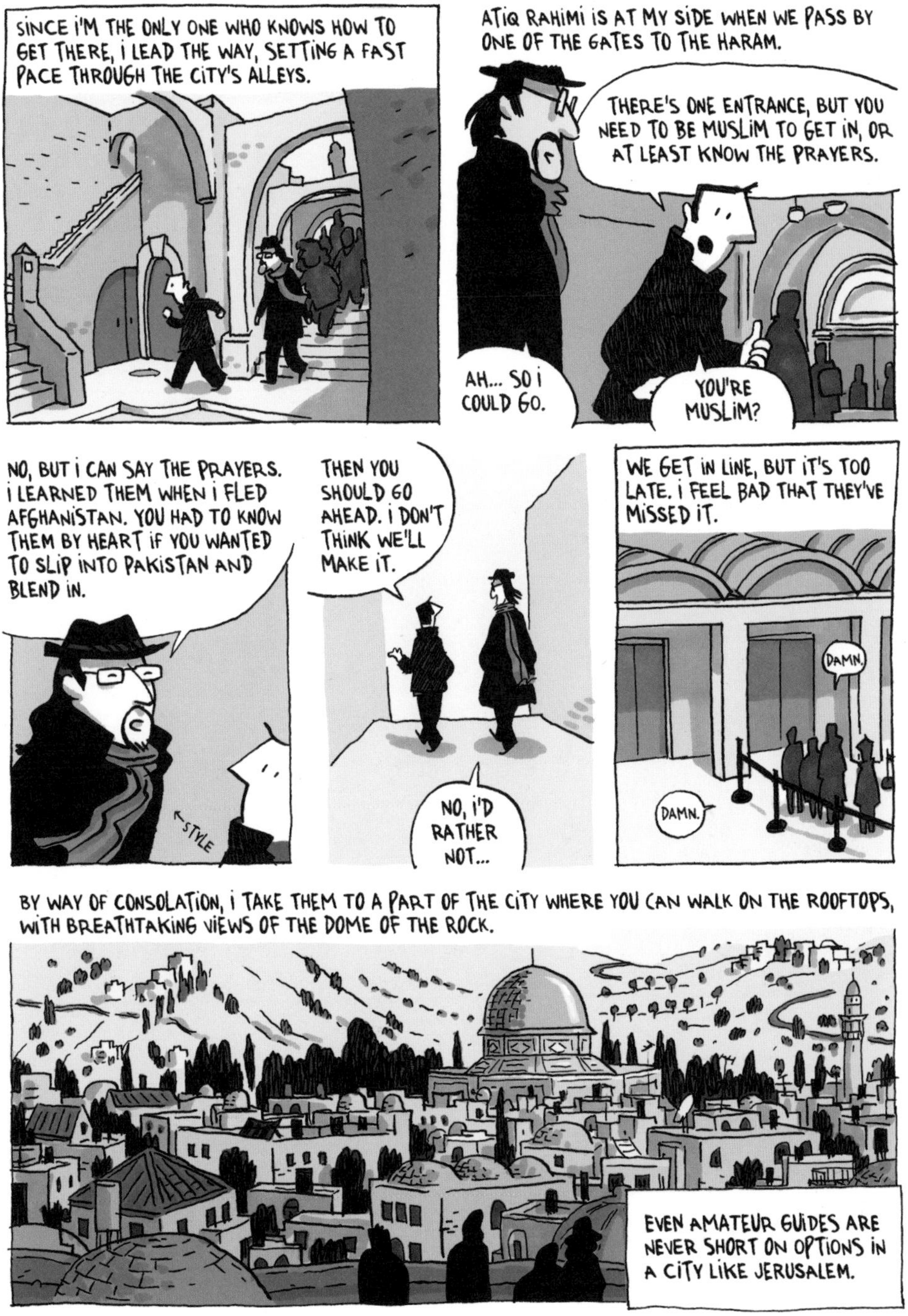
SINCE I'M THE ONLY ONE WHO KNOWS HOW TO GET THERE, I LEAD THE WAY, SETTING A FAST PACE THROUGH THE CITY'S ALLEYS.
ATIQ RAHIMI IS AT MY SIDE WHEN WE PASS BY ONE OF THE GATES TO THE HARAM.
THERE'S ONE ENTRANCE, BUT YOU NEED TO BE MUSLIM TO GET IN, OR AT LEAST KNOW THE PRAYERS.
AH... SO I COULD GO.
YOU'RE MUSLIM?
NO, BUT I CAN SAY THE PRAYERS. I LEARNED THEM WHEN I FLED AFGHANISTAN. YOU HAD TO KNOW THEM BY HEART IF YOU WANTED TO SLIP INTO PAKISTAN AND BLEND IN.
←STYLE
THEN YOU SHOULD GO AHEAD. I DON'T THINK WE'LL MAKE IT.
NO, I'D RATHER NOT...
WE GET IN LINE, BUT IT'S TOO LATE. I FEEL BAD THAT THEY'VE MISSED IT.
DAMN.
DAMN.
BY WAY OF CONSOLATION, I TAKE THEM TO A PART OF THE CITY WHERE YOU CAN WALK ON THE ROOFTOPS, WITH BREATHTAKING VIEWS OF THE DOME OF THE ROCK.
EVEN AMATEUR GUIDES ARE NEVER SHORT ON OPTIONS IN A CITY LIKE JERUSALEM.

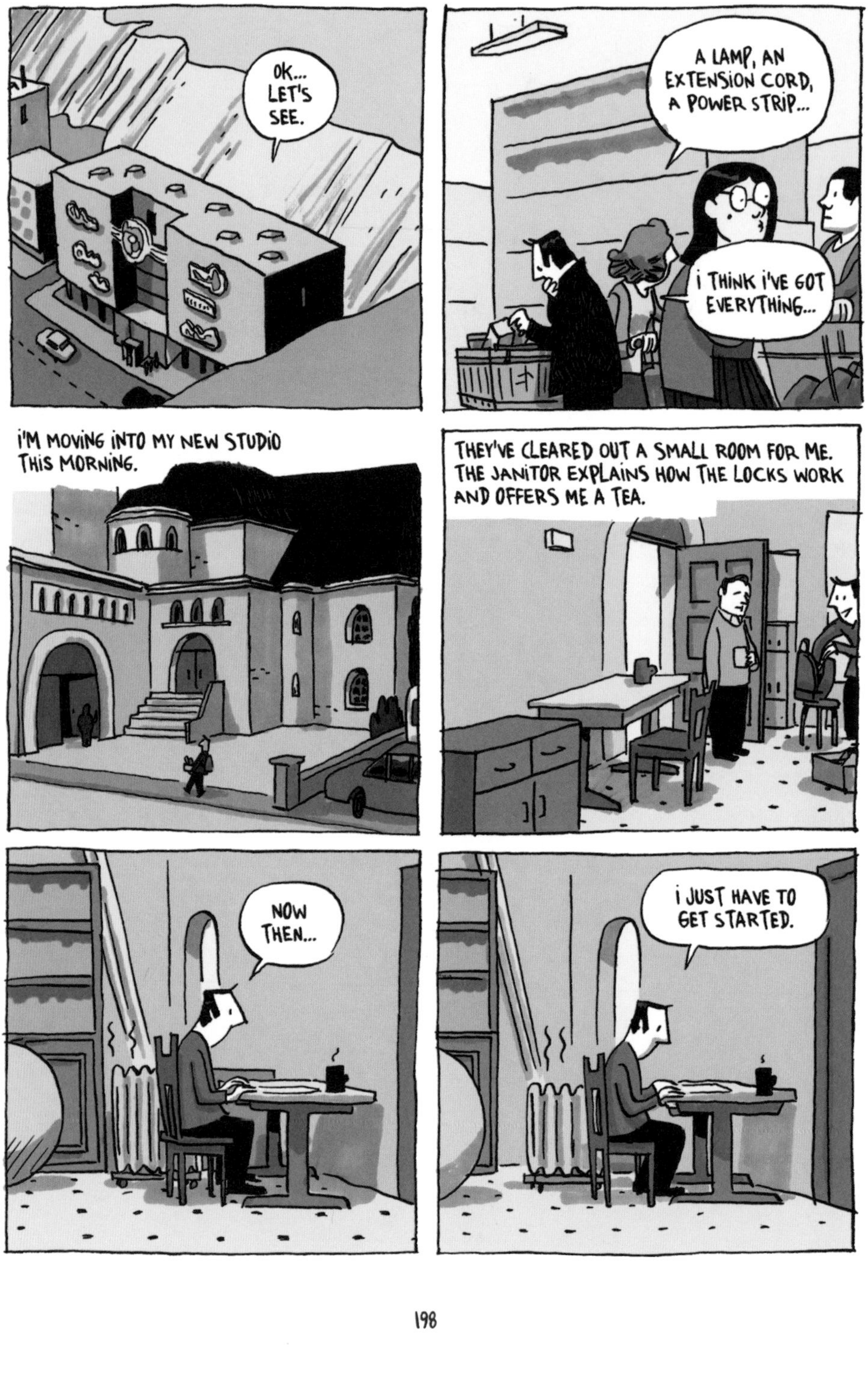
OK... LET'S SEE.
A LAMP, AN EXTENSION CORD, A POWER STRIP...
I THINK I'VE GOT EVERYTHING...
I'M MOVING INTO MY NEW STUDIO THIS MORNING.
THEY'VE CLEARED OUT A SMALL ROOM FOR ME. THE JANITOR EXPLAINS HOW THE LOCKS WORK AND OFFERS ME A TEA.
NOW THEN...
I JUST HAVE TO GET STARTED.

THERE ARE CURIOUS OBJECTS IN THE ROOM.

A BUST OF SOME BIGWIG.

MAYBE BISMARCK?

FIVE LARGE BALLS THAT ARE USED BY A REHA-BILITATION PROGRAM FOR KIDS AT THE HOSPITAL NEXT DOOR.

AN OLD DUST-COVERED STRETCHER, A LITTLE SIGN IN FOUR LANGUAGES.

WORSHIP-DO NOT DISTURB
خدمة دينية - الرجاء وعدم الازعاج
בבקשה - לא להפריע
GOTTESDIENST-BITTE NICHT STOREN

RIGHT BEHIND ME, A REPLICA OF THE ARK OF THE COVENANT, PAINTED GOLD. INSIDE IT, THE STONE TABLETS. THE THING MUST WEIGH 300 POUNDS.

HOLY COW, IT'S HEAVY!

MICHAEL ONCE TOLD ME ABOUT IT. A GERMAN NAMED MANFRED MISS-FELDER BUILT IT AND BROUGHT IT HERE ON FOOT IN 1995. HIS JOURNEY TOOK MORE THAN A YEAR.

WHEN HE ARRIVED, SOME CON-SERVATIVE JEWS TOOK OFFENSE AT HIS TREATMENT OF THE SAC-RED SYMBOL. HE GOT BEAT UP AND LEFT HIS ARK WITH ANYONE WILLING TO STORE IT.

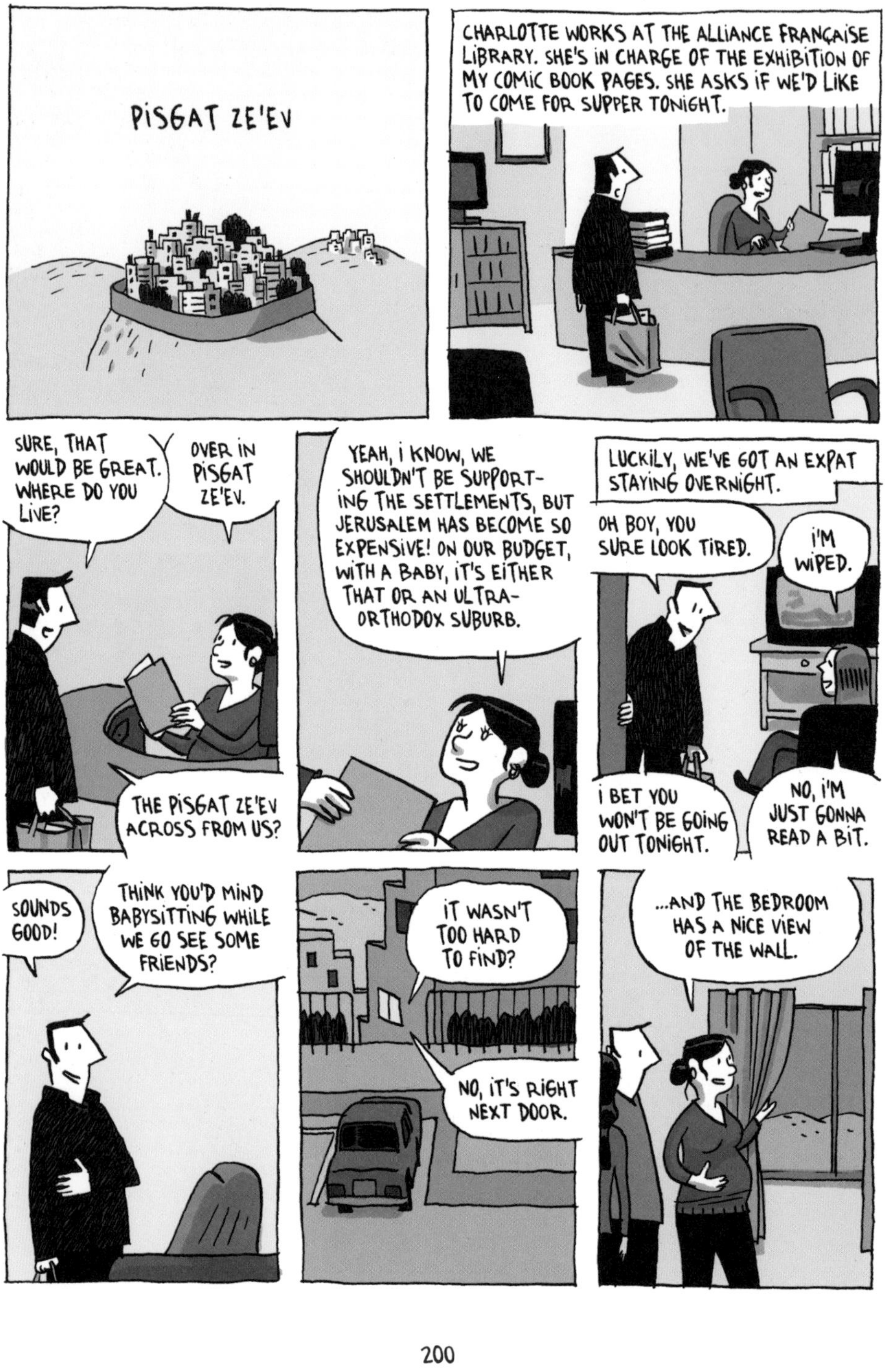
PISGAT ZE'EV
CHARLOTTE WORKS AT THE ALLIANCE FRANÇAISE LIBRARY. SHE'S IN CHARGE OF THE EXHIBITION OF MY COMIC BOOK PAGES. SHE ASKS IF WE'D LIKE TO COME FOR SUPPER TONIGHT.
SURE, THAT WOULD BE GREAT. WHERE DO YOU LIVE?
OVER IN PISGAT ZE'EV.
THE PISGAT ZE'EV ACROSS FROM US?
YEAH, I KNOW, WE SHOULDN'T BE SUPPORT-ING THE SETTLEMENTS, BUT JERUSALEM HAS BECOME SO EXPENSIVE! ON OUR BUDGET, WITH A BABY, IT'S EITHER THAT OR AN ULTRA-ORTHODOX SUBURB.
LUCKILY, WE'VE GOT AN EXPAT STAYING OVERNIGHT.
OH BOY, YOU SURE LOOK TIRED.
I'M WIPED.
I BET YOU WON'T BE GOING OUT TONIGHT.
NO, I'M JUST GONNA READ A BIT.
SOUNDS GOOD!
THINK YOU'D MIND BABYSITTING WHILE WE GO SEE SOME FRIENDS?
IT WASN'T TOO HARD TO FIND?
NO, IT'S RIGHT NEXT DOOR.
...AND THE BEDROOM HAS A NICE VIEW OF THE WALL.

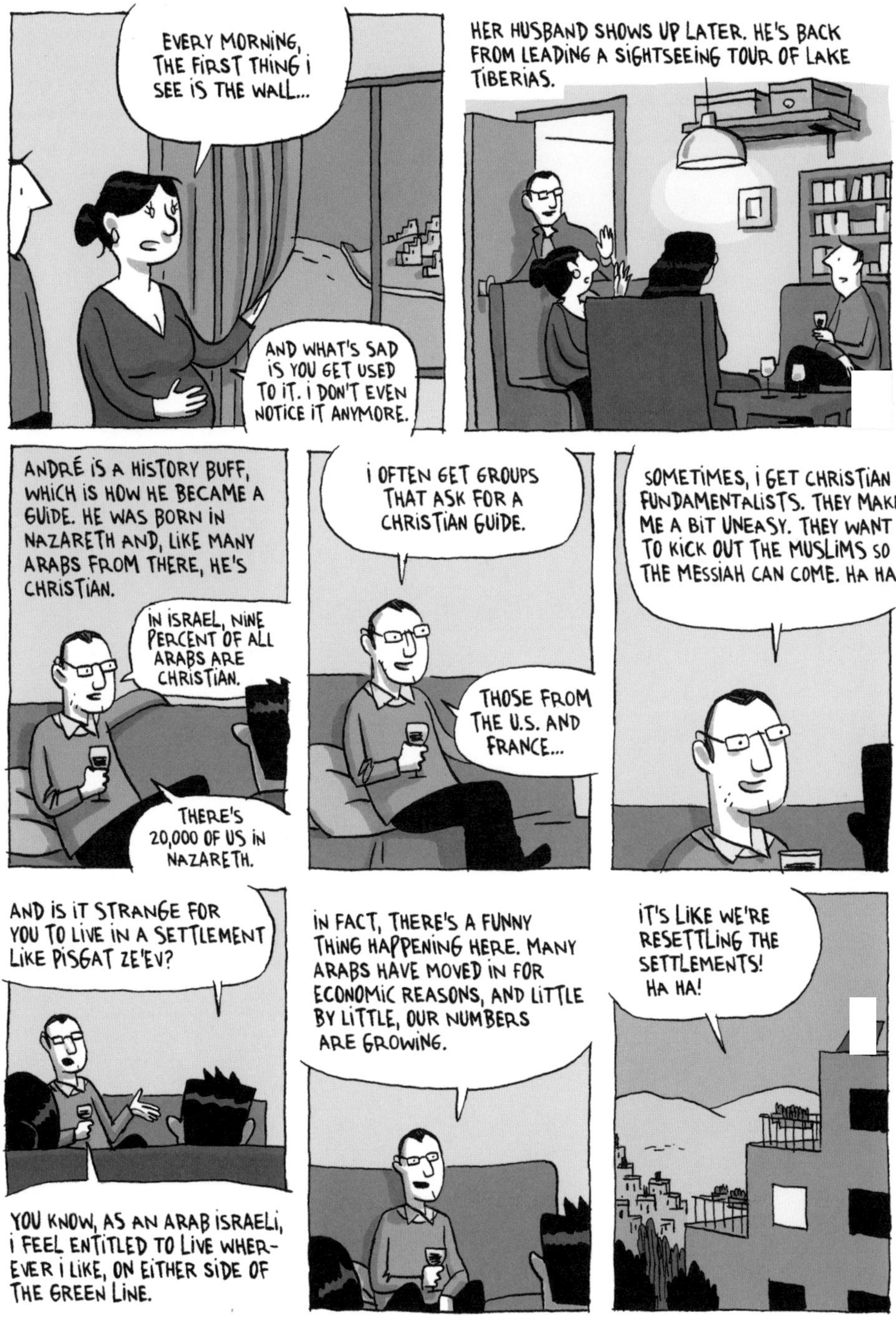
EVERY MORNING, THE FIRST THING I SEE IS THE WALL...
AND WHAT'S SAD IS YOU GET USED TO IT. I DON'T EVEN NOTICE IT ANYMORE.
HER HUSBAND SHOWS UP LATER. HE'S BACK FROM LEADING A SIGHTSEEING TOUR OF LAKE TIBERIAS.
ANDRÉ IS A HISTORY BUFF, WHICH IS HOW HE BECAME A GUIDE. HE WAS BORN IN NAZARETH AND, LIKE MANY ARABS FROM THERE, HE'S CHRISTIAN.
IN ISRAEL, NINE PERCENT OF ALL ARABS ARE CHRISTIAN.
THERE'S 20,000 OF US IN NAZARETH.
I OFTEN GET GROUPS THAT ASK FOR A CHRISTIAN GUIDE.
THOSE FROM THE U.S. AND FRANCE...
SOMETIMES, I GET CHRISTIAN FUNDAMENTALISTS. THEY MAKE ME A BIT UNEASY. THEY WANT TO KICK OUT THE MUSLIMS SO THE MESSIAH CAN COME. HA HA!
AND IS IT STRANGE FOR YOU TO LIVE IN A SETTLEMENT LIKE PISGAT ZE'EV?
YOU KNOW, AS AN ARAB ISRAELI, I FEEL ENTITLED TO LIVE WHEREVER I LIKE, ON EITHER SIDE OF THE GREEN LINE.
IN FACT, THERE'S A FUNNY THING HAPPENING HERE. MANY ARABS HAVE MOVED IN FOR ECONOMIC REASONS, AND LITTLE BY LITTLE, OUR NUMBERS ARE GROWING.
IT'S LIKE WE'RE RESETTLING THE SETTLEMENTS! HA HA!

MARCH

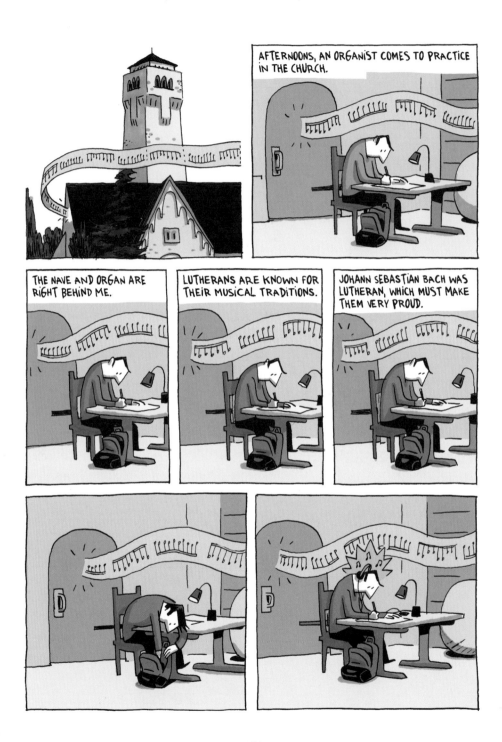

AFTERNOONS, AN ORGANIST COMES TO PRACTICE IN THE CHURCH.

THE NAVE AND ORGAN ARE RIGHT BEHIND ME.

LUTHERANS ARE KNOWN FOR THEIR MUSICAL TRADITIONS.

JOHANN SEBASTIAN BACH WAS LUTHERAN, WHICH MUST MAKE THEM VERY PROUD.

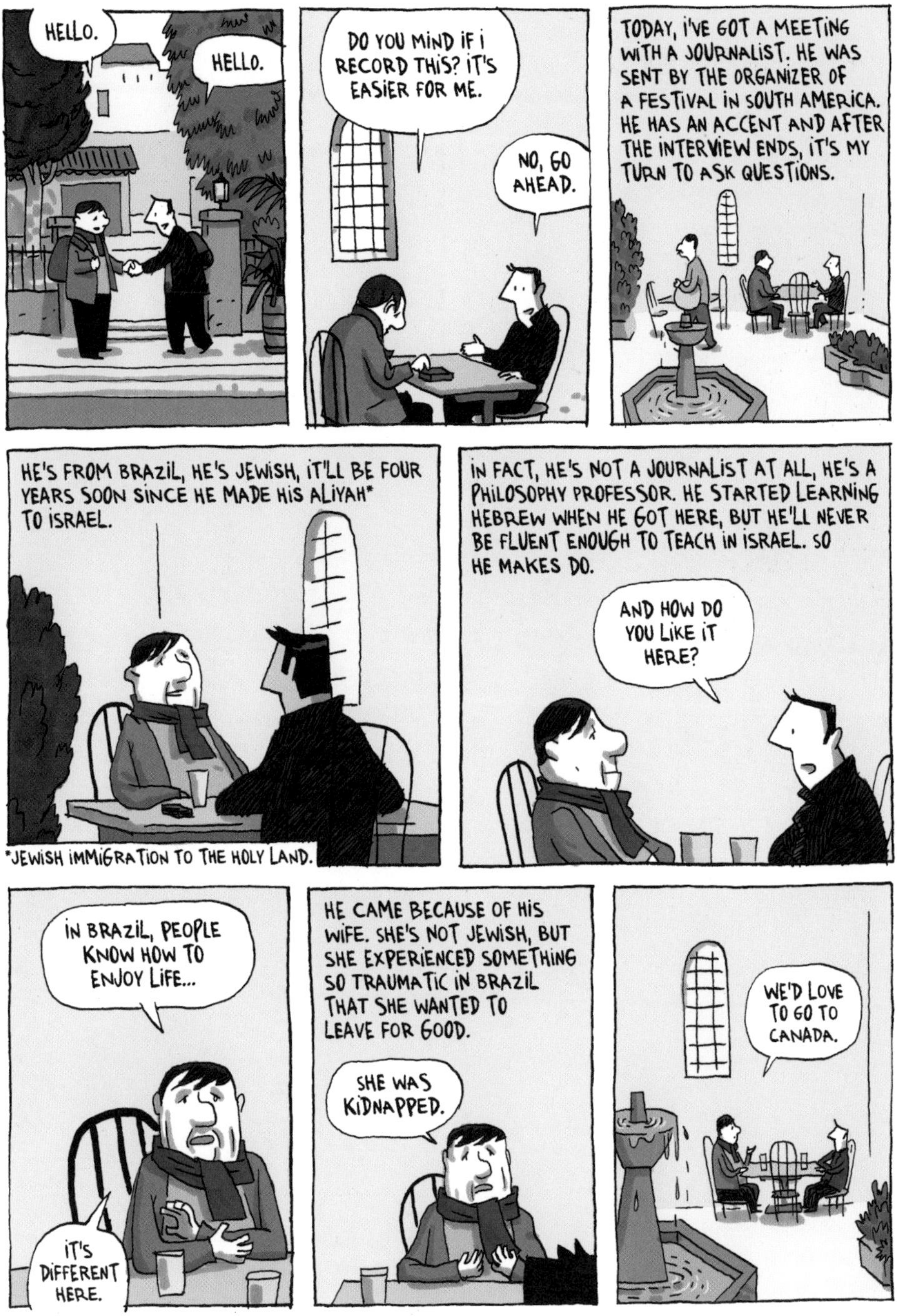
HELLO.
HELLO.
DO YOU MIND IF I RECORD THIS? IT'S EASIER FOR ME.
NO, GO AHEAD.
TODAY, I'VE GOT A MEETING WITH A JOURNALIST. HE WAS SENT BY THE ORGANIZER OF A FESTIVAL IN SOUTH AMERICA. HE HAS AN ACCENT AND AFTER THE INTERVIEW ENDS, IT'S MY TURN TO ASK QUESTIONS.
HE'S FROM BRAZIL, HE'S JEWISH, IT'LL BE FOUR YEARS SOON SINCE HE MADE HIS ALIYAH* TO ISRAEL.
*JEWISH IMMIGRATION TO THE HOLY LAND.
IN FACT, HE'S NOT A JOURNALIST AT ALL, HE'S A PHILOSOPHY PROFESSOR. HE STARTED LEARNING HEBREW WHEN HE GOT HERE, BUT HE'LL NEVER BE FLUENT ENOUGH TO TEACH IN ISRAEL. SO HE MAKES DO.
AND HOW DO YOU LIKE IT HERE?
IN BRAZIL, PEOPLE KNOW HOW TO ENJOY LIFE...
IT'S DIFFERENT HERE.
HE CAME BECAUSE OF HIS WIFE. SHE'S NOT JEWISH, BUT SHE EXPERIENCED SOMETHING SO TRAUMATIC IN BRAZIL THAT SHE WANTED TO LEAVE FOR GOOD.
SHE WAS KIDNAPPED.
WE'D LOVE TO GO TO CANADA.

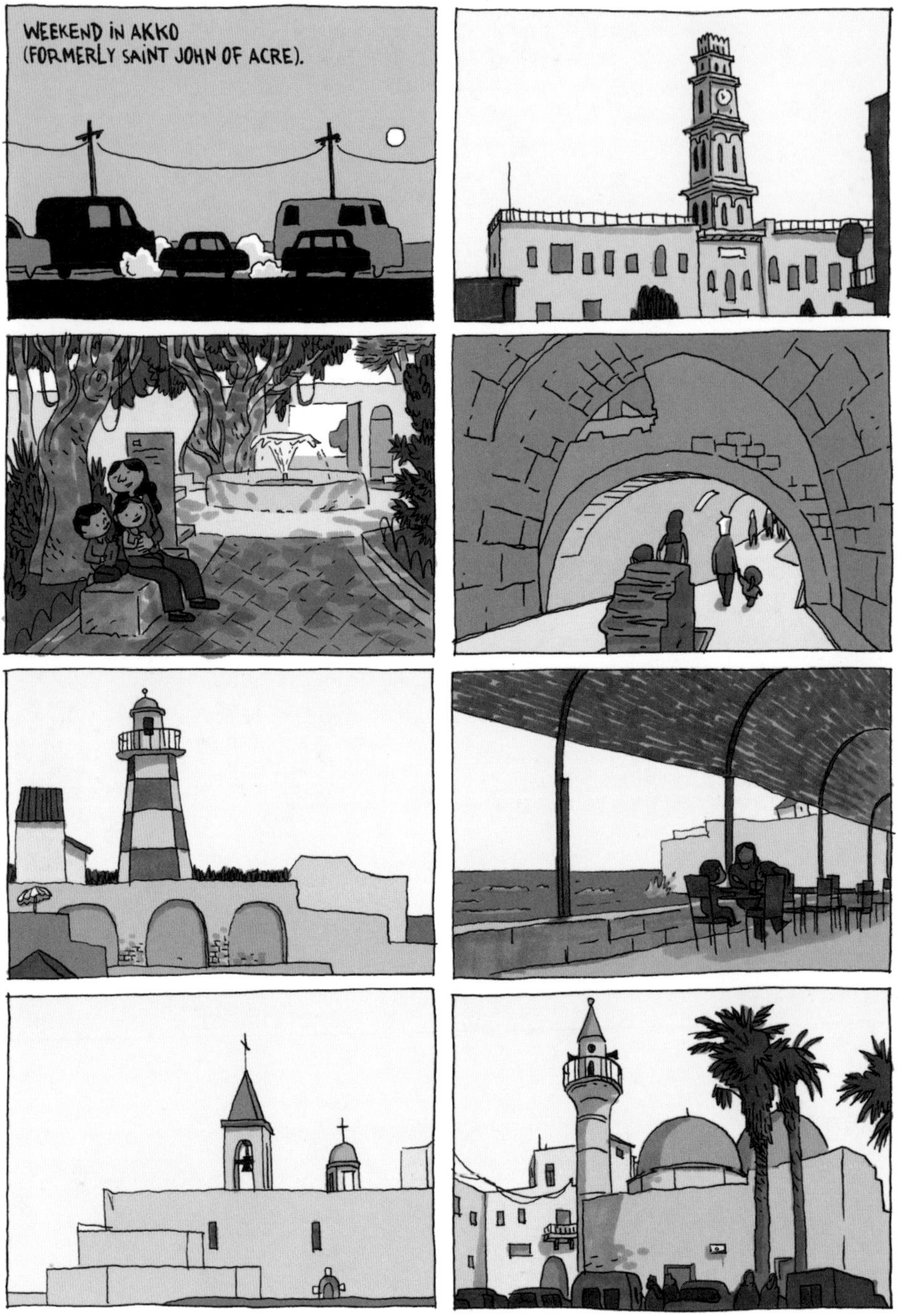
WEEKEND IN AKKO
(FORMERLY SAINT JOHN OF ACRE).

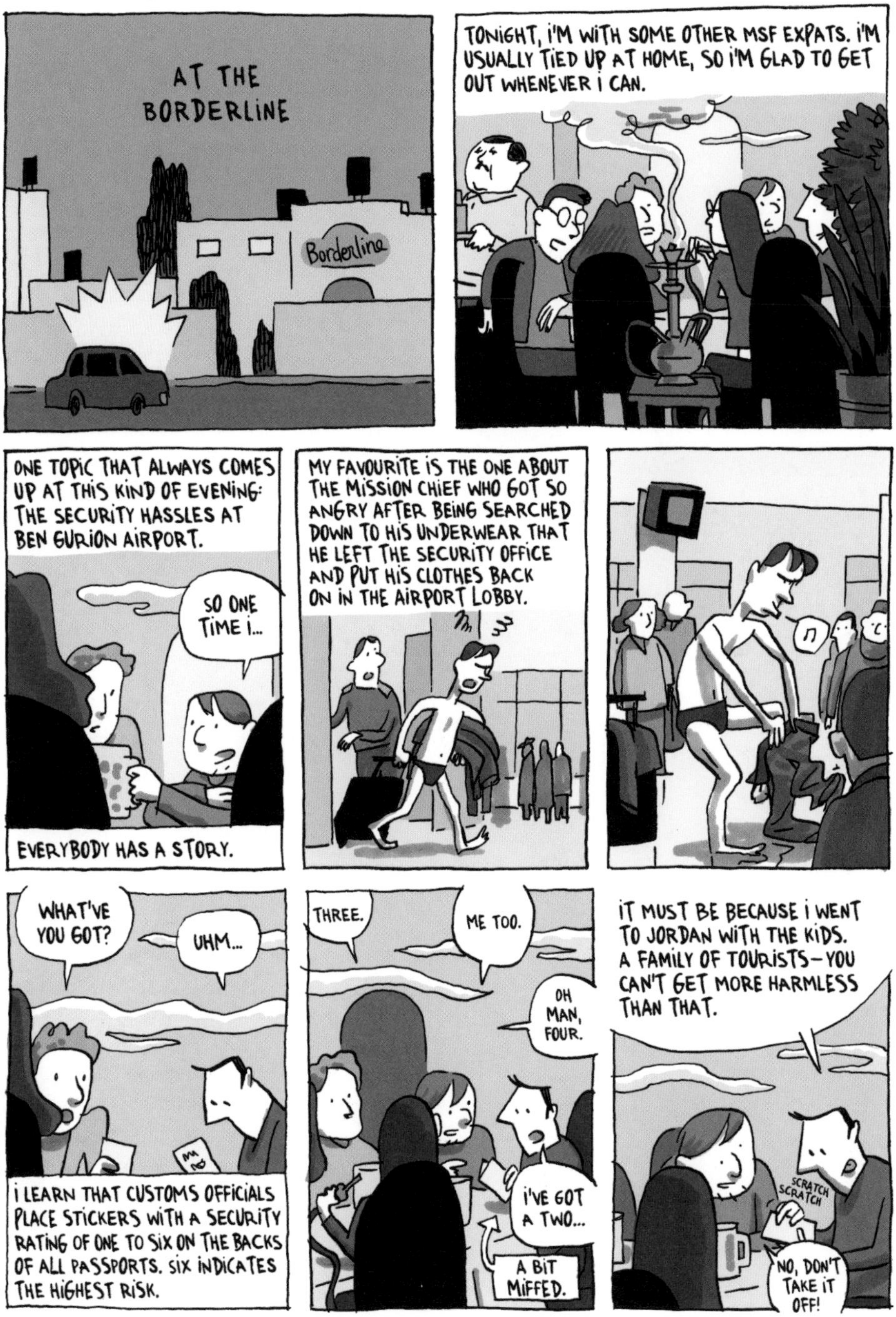
AT THE BORDERLINE
Borderline
TONIGHT, I'M WITH SOME OTHER MSF EXPATS. I'M USUALLY TIED UP AT HOME, SO I'M GLAD TO GET OUT WHENEVER I CAN.
ONE TOPIC THAT ALWAYS COMES UP AT THIS KIND OF EVENING: THE SECURITY HASSLES AT BEN GURION AIRPORT.
SO ONE TIME I...
EVERYBODY HAS A STORY.
MY FAVOURITE IS THE ONE ABOUT THE MISSION CHIEF WHO GOT SO ANGRY AFTER BEING SEARCHED DOWN TO HIS UNDERWEAR THAT HE LEFT THE SECURITY OFFICE AND PUT HIS CLOTHES BACK ON IN THE AIRPORT LOBBY.
WHAT'VE YOU GOT?
UHM...
I LEARN THAT CUSTOMS OFFICIALS PLACE STICKERS WITH A SECURITY RATING OF ONE TO SIX ON THE BACKS OF ALL PASSPORTS. SIX INDICATES THE HIGHEST RISK.
THREE.
ME TOO.
OH MAN, FOUR.
I'VE GOT A TWO...
A BIT MIFFED.
IT MUST BE BECAUSE I WENT TO JORDAN WITH THE KIDS. A FAMILY OF TOURISTS—YOU CAN'T GET MORE HARMLESS THAN THAT.
SCRATCH SCRATCH
NO, DON'T TAKE IT OFF!

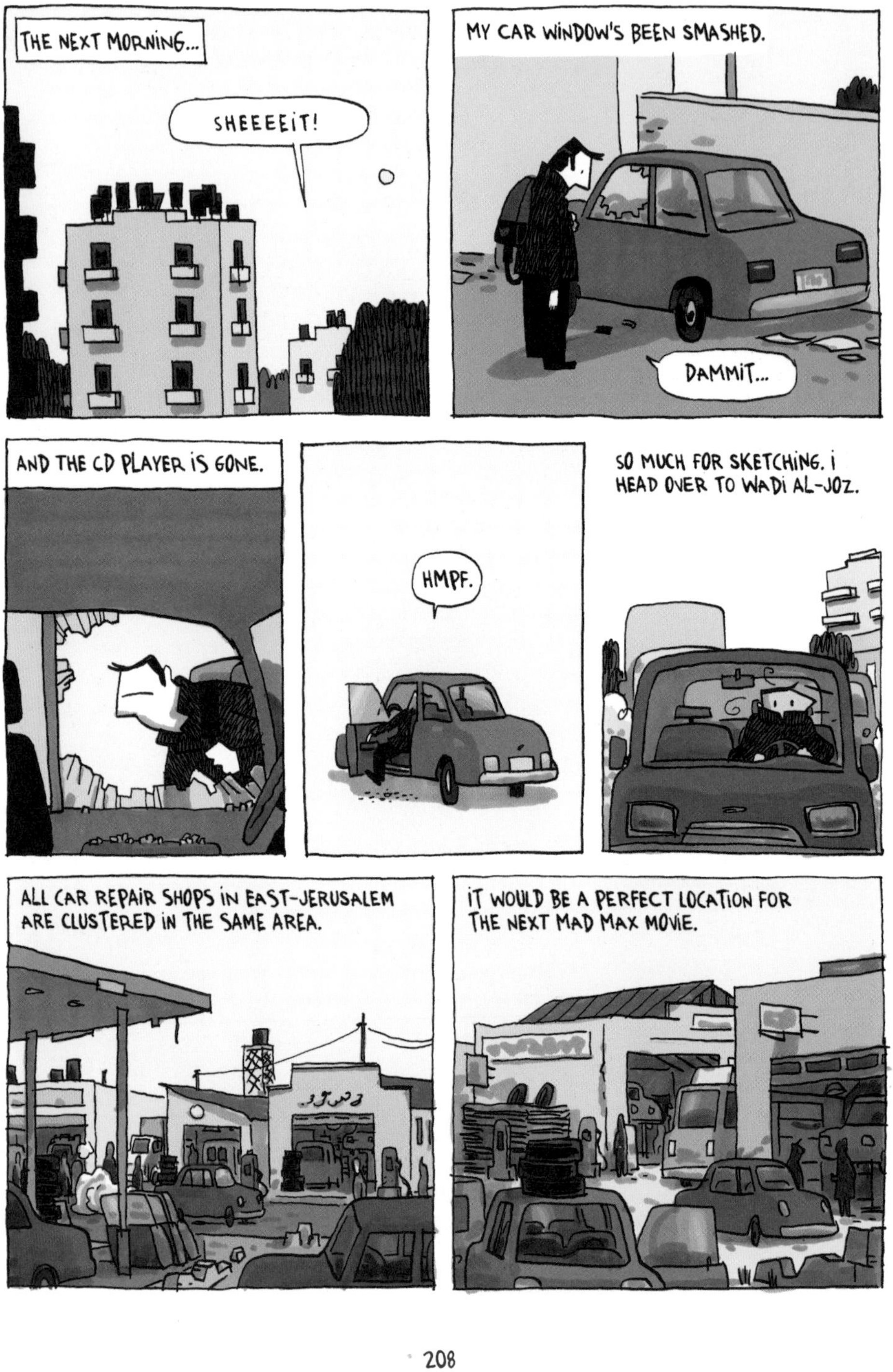
THE NEXT MORNING...
SHEEEEIT!
MY CAR WINDOW'S BEEN SMASHED.
DAMMIT...
AND THE CD PLAYER IS GONE.
HMPF.
SO MUCH FOR SKETCHING. I HEAD OVER TO WADI AL-JOZ.
ALL CAR REPAIR SHOPS IN EAST-JERUSALEM ARE CLUSTERED IN THE SAME AREA.
IT WOULD BE A PERFECT LOCATION FOR THE NEXT MAD MAX MOVIE.

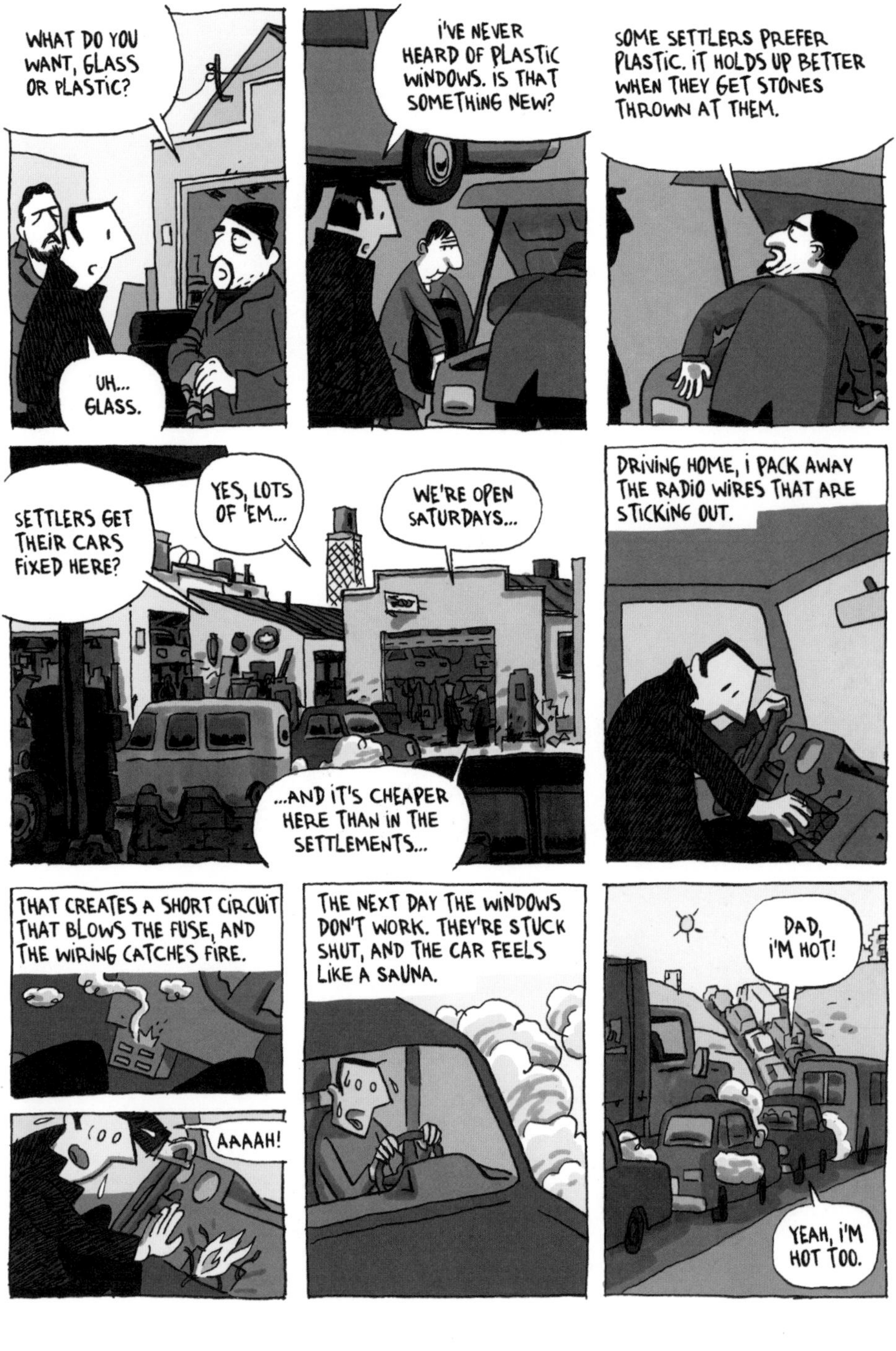
WHAT DO YOU WANT, GLASS OR PLASTIC?
UH... GLASS.
I'VE NEVER HEARD OF PLASTIC WINDOWS. IS THAT SOMETHING NEW?
SOME SETTLERS PREFER PLASTIC. IT HOLDS UP BETTER WHEN THEY GET STONES THROWN AT THEM.
SETTLERS GET THEIR CARS FIXED HERE?
YES, LOTS OF 'EM...
WE'RE OPEN SATURDAYS...
...AND IT'S CHEAPER HERE THAN IN THE SETTLEMENTS...
DRIVING HOME, I PACK AWAY THE RADIO WIRES THAT ARE STICKING OUT.
THAT CREATES A SHORT CIRCUIT THAT BLOWS THE FUSE, AND THE WIRING CATCHES FIRE.
AAAAH!
THE NEXT DAY THE WINDOWS DON'T WORK. THEY'RE STUCK SHUT, AND THE CAR FEELS LIKE A SAUNA.
DAD, I'M HOT!
YEAH, I'M HOT TOO.

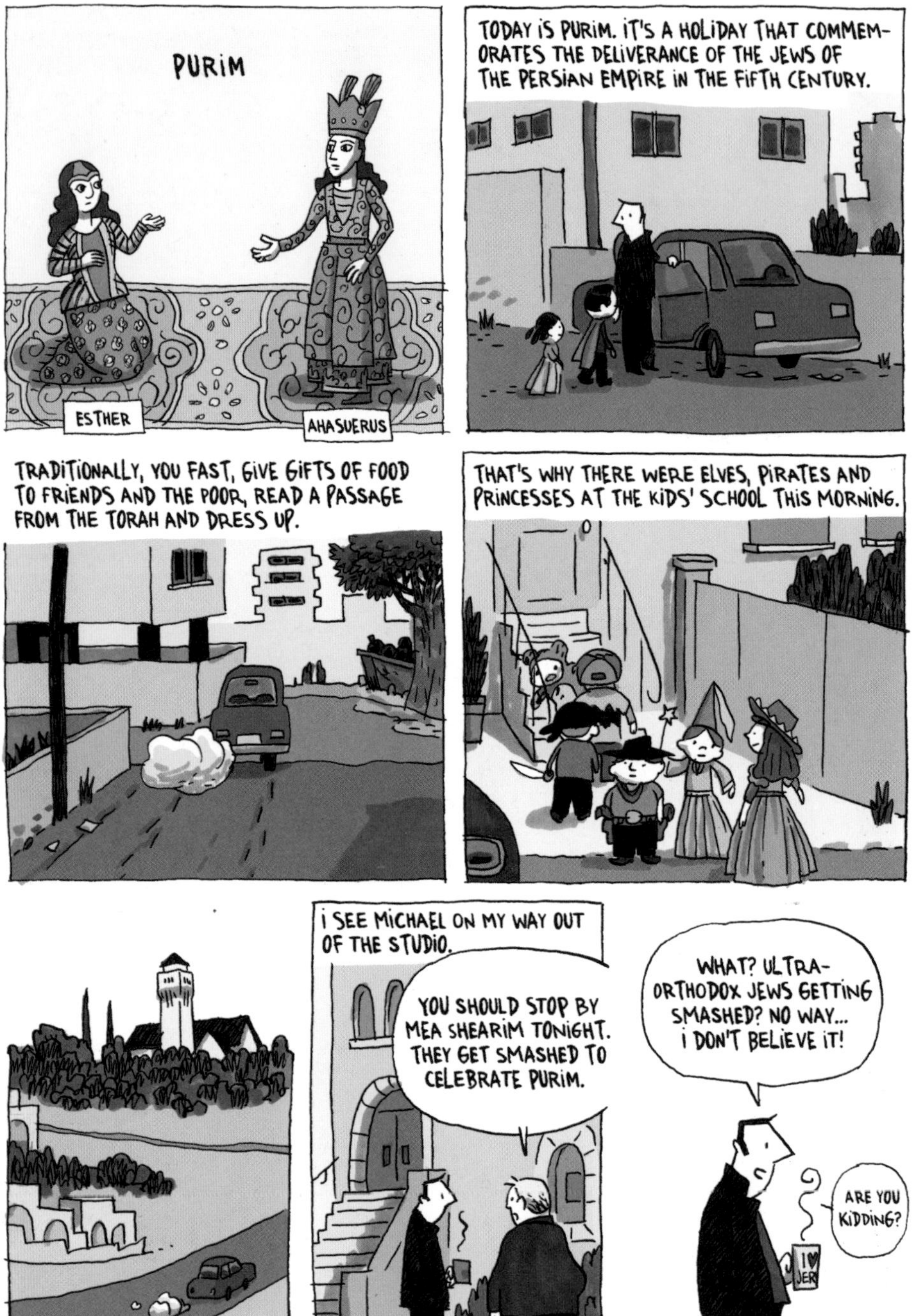
PURIM
ESTHER
AHASUERUS
TODAY IS PURIM. IT'S A HOLIDAY THAT COMMEMORATES THE DELIVERANCE OF THE JEWS OF THE PERSIAN EMPIRE IN THE FIFTH CENTURY.
TRADITIONALLY, YOU FAST, GIVE GIFTS OF FOOD TO FRIENDS AND THE POOR, READ A PASSAGE FROM THE TORAH AND DRESS UP.
THAT'S WHY THERE WERE ELVES, PIRATES AND PRINCESSES AT THE KIDS' SCHOOL THIS MORNING.
I SEE MICHAEL ON MY WAY OUT OF THE STUDIO.
YOU SHOULD STOP BY MEA SHEARIM TONIGHT. THEY GET SMASHED TO CELEBRATE PURIM.
WHAT? ULTRA-ORTHODOX JEWS GETTING SMASHED? NO WAY... I DON'T BELIEVE IT!
ARE YOU KIDDING?

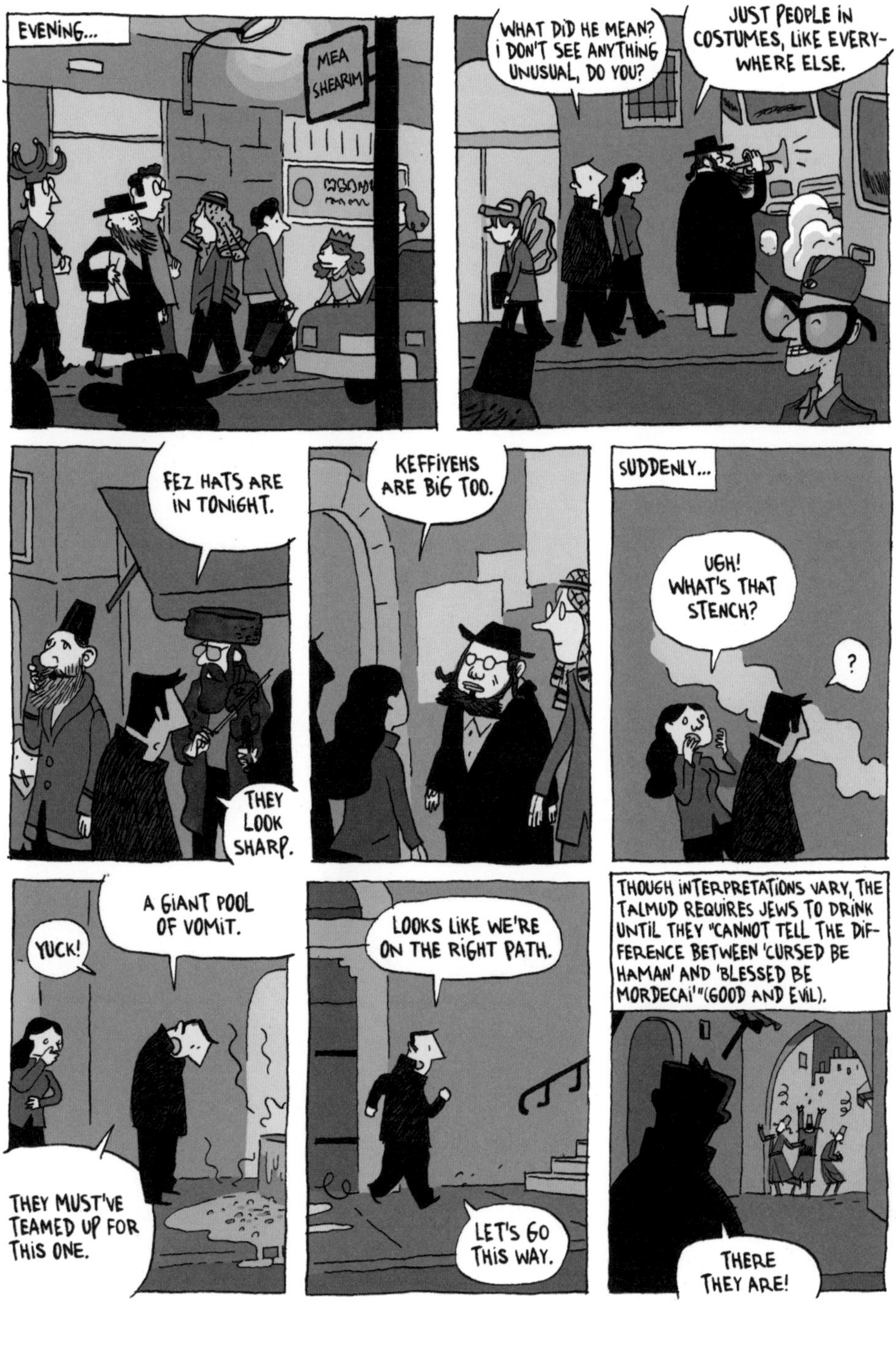

EVENING...
MEA SHEARIM
WHAT DID HE MEAN? I DON'T SEE ANYTHING UNUSUAL, DO YOU?
JUST PEOPLE IN COSTUMES, LIKE EVERYWHERE ELSE.
FEZ HATS ARE IN TONIGHT.
THEY LOOK SHARP.
KEFFIYEHS ARE BIG TOO.
SUDDENLY...
UGH! WHAT'S THAT STENCH?
?
A GIANT POOL OF VOMIT.
YUCK!
THEY MUST'VE TEAMED UP FOR THIS ONE.
LOOKS LIKE WE'RE ON THE RIGHT PATH.
LET'S GO THIS WAY.
THOUGH INTERPRETATIONS VARY, THE TALMUD REQUIRES JEWS TO DRINK UNTIL THEY "CANNOT TELL THE DIFFERENCE BETWEEN 'CURSED BE HAMAN' AND 'BLESSED BE MORDECAI'" (GOOD AND EVIL).
THERE THEY ARE!

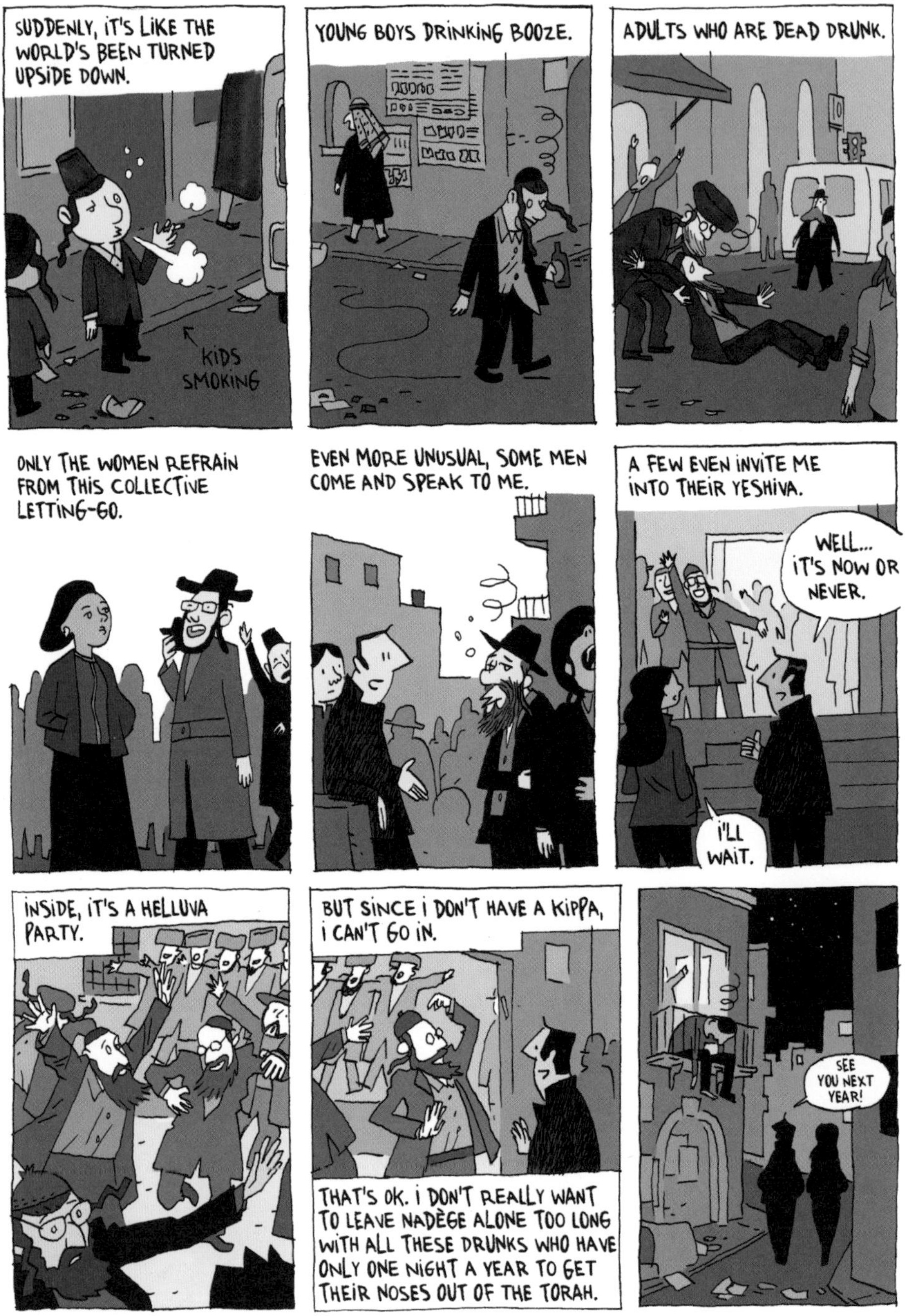
SUDDENLY, IT'S LIKE THE WORLD'S BEEN TURNED UPSIDE DOWN.
KIDS SMOKING
YOUNG BOYS DRINKING BOOZE.
ADULTS WHO ARE DEAD DRUNK.
ONLY THE WOMEN REFRAIN FROM THIS COLLECTIVE LETTING-GO.
EVEN MORE UNUSUAL, SOME MEN COME AND SPEAK TO ME.
A FEW EVEN INVITE ME INTO THEIR YESHIVA.
WELL... IT'S NOW OR NEVER.
I'LL WAIT.
INSIDE, IT'S A HELLUVA PARTY.
BUT SINCE I DON'T HAVE A KIPPA, I CAN'T GO IN.
THAT'S OK. I DON'T REALLY WANT TO LEAVE NADÈGE ALONE TOO LONG WITH ALL THESE DRUNKS WHO HAVE ONLY ONE NIGHT A YEAR TO GET THEIR NOSES OUT OF THE TORAH.
SEE YOU NEXT YEAR!

NABLUS

I ATTEND THE OPENING OF AN EXHIBITION DEDICATED TO MY WORK. IN ALL, SOME TWENTY PAGES ARE ON DISPLAY IN THE ENTRANCE HALL OF NABLUS UNIVERSITY.

I'VE NEVER SHOWN MY WORK IN A MORE BEAUTIFUL SPACE. IT'S HUGE AND ALMOST BRAND NEW.

I WALK THROUGH THE EXHIBIT WITH A REPRESENTATIVE OF THE CITY (OR THE UNIVERSITY, I DIDN'T UNDERSTAND WHICH).

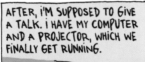

NO, ACTUALLY... PYONGYANG IS IN NORTH KOREA.

COFFEE, CAKE. I MEET A FEW YOUNG PEOPLE WHO SEEM INTERESTED IN COMICS.

AFTER, I'M SUPPOSED TO GIVE A TALK. I HAVE MY COMPUTER AND A PROJECTOR, WHICH WE FINALLY GET RUNNING.

THE CLASS IS FULL OF FINE ARTS STUDENTS. HALF GIRLS, HALF GUYS.

SALAMALEKUM.

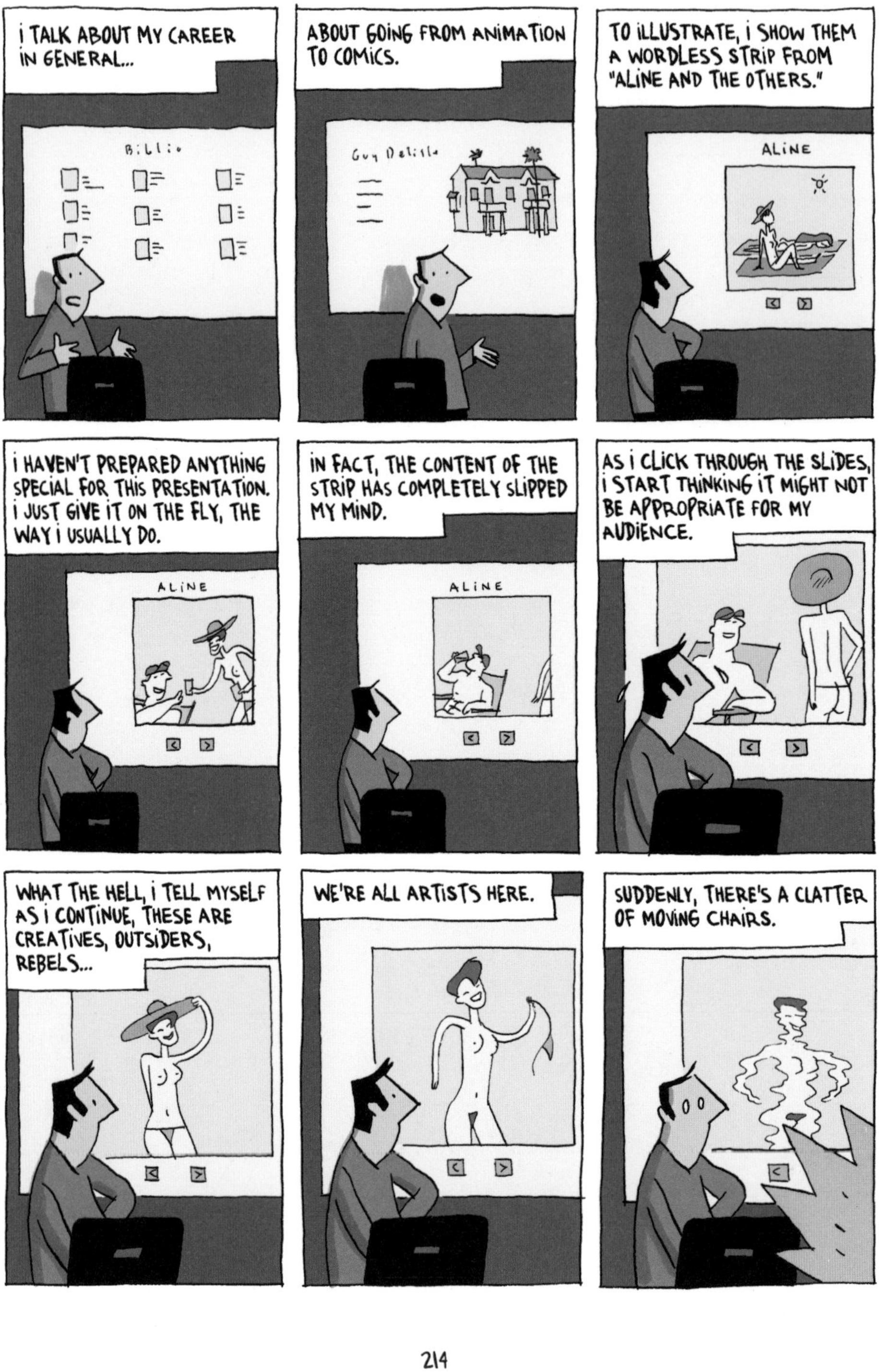
I TALK ABOUT MY CAREER IN GENERAL...
Biblio
ABOUT GOING FROM ANIMATION TO COMICS.
Guy Delisle
TO ILLUSTRATE, I SHOW THEM A WORDLESS STRIP FROM "ALINE AND THE OTHERS."
ALINE
I HAVEN'T PREPARED ANYTHING SPECIAL FOR THIS PRESENTATION. I JUST GIVE IT ON THE FLY, THE WAY I USUALLY DO.
ALINE
IN FACT, THE CONTENT OF THE STRIP HAS COMPLETELY SLIPPED MY MIND.
ALINE
AS I CLICK THROUGH THE SLIDES, I START THINKING IT MIGHT NOT BE APPROPRIATE FOR MY AUDIENCE.
WHAT THE HELL, I TELL MYSELF AS I CONTINUE, THESE ARE CREATIVES, OUTSIDERS, REBELS...
WE'RE ALL ARTISTS HERE.
SUDDENLY, THERE'S A CLATTER OF MOVING CHAIRS.

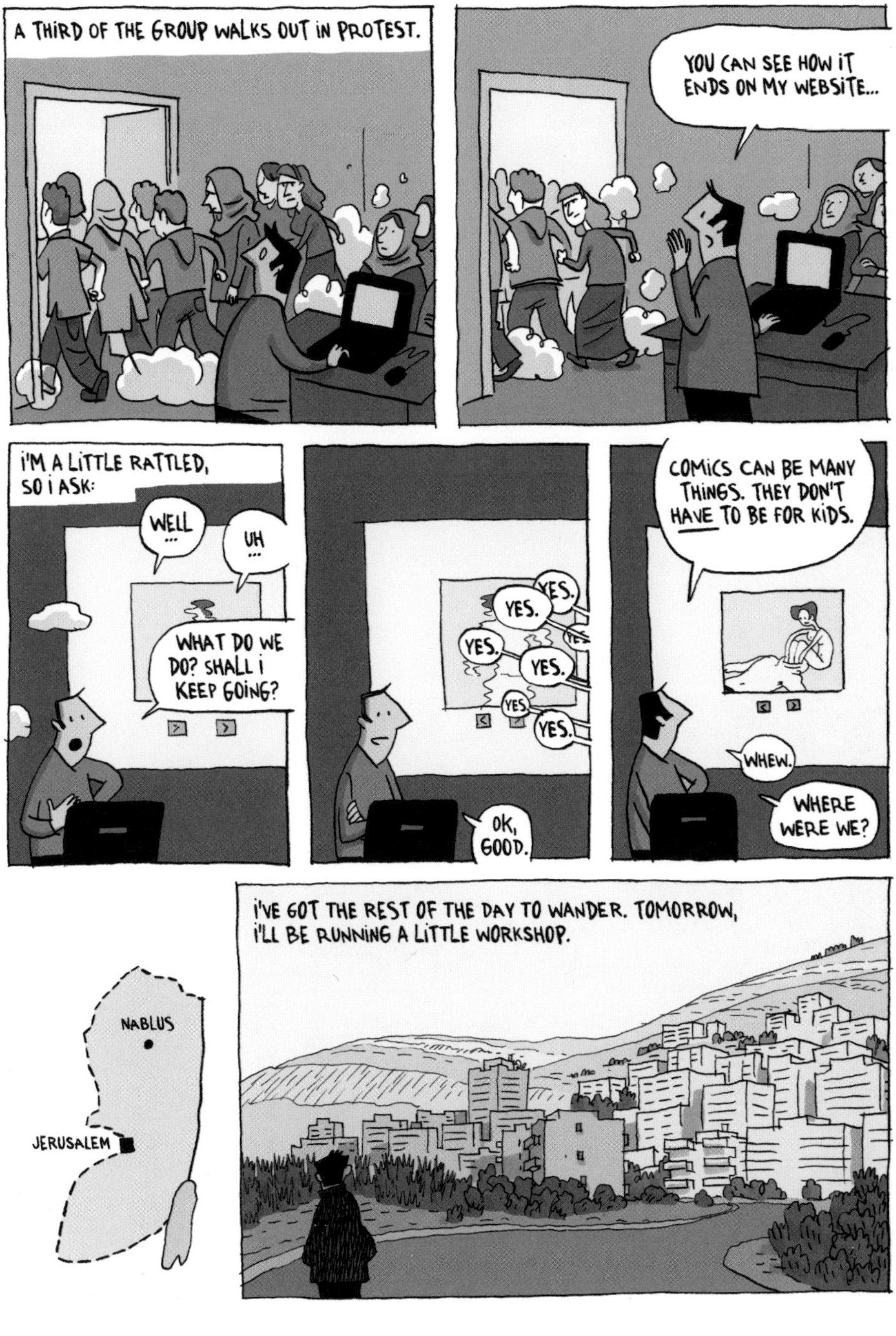
A THIRD OF THE GROUP WALKS OUT IN PROTEST.
YOU CAN SEE HOW IT ENDS ON MY WEBSITE...
I'M A LITTLE RATTLED, SO I ASK:
WELL ...
UH ...
WHAT DO WE DO? SHALL I KEEP GOING?
YES.
YES.
YES.
YES.
YES.
YES.
OK, GOOD.
COMICS CAN BE MANY THINGS. THEY DON'T HAVE TO BE FOR KIDS.
WHEW.
WHERE WERE WE?
I'VE GOT THE REST OF THE DAY TO WANDER. TOMORROW, I'LL BE RUNNING A LITTLE WORKSHOP.
NABLUS
JERUSALEM

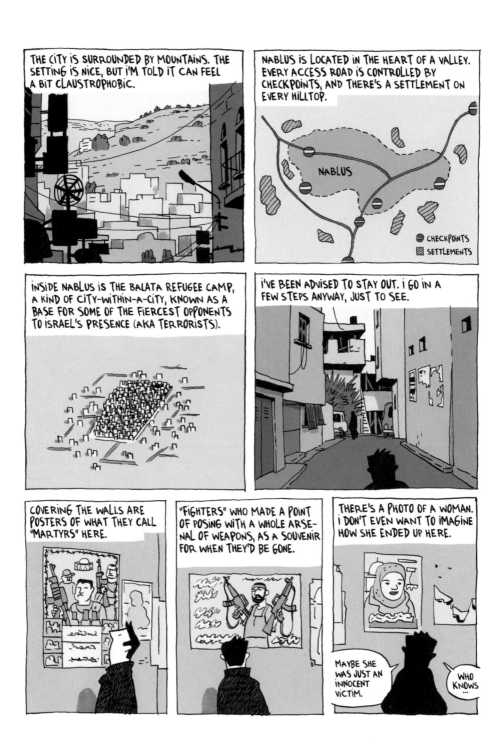

THE CITY IS SURROUNDED BY MOUNTAINS. THE SETTING IS NICE, BUT I'M TOLD IT CAN FEEL A BIT CLAUSTROPHOBIC.

NABLUS IS LOCATED IN THE HEART OF A VALLEY. EVERY ACCESS ROAD IS CONTROLLED BY CHECKPOINTS, AND THERE'S A SETTLEMENT ON EVERY HILLTOP.

NABLUS

● CHECKPOINTS
▨ SETTLEMENTS

INSIDE NABLUS IS THE BALATA REFUGEE CAMP, A KIND OF CITY-WITHIN-A-CITY, KNOWN AS A BASE FOR SOME OF THE FIERCEST OPPONENTS TO ISRAEL'S PRESENCE (AKA TERRORISTS).

I'VE BEEN ADVISED TO STAY OUT. I GO IN A FEW STEPS ANYWAY, JUST TO SEE.

COVERING THE WALLS ARE POSTERS OF WHAT THEY CALL "MARTYRS" HERE.

"FIGHTERS" WHO MADE A POINT OF POSING WITH A WHOLE ARSENAL OF WEAPONS, AS A SOUVENIR FOR WHEN THEY'D BE GONE.

THERE'S A PHOTO OF A WOMAN. I DON'T EVEN WANT TO IMAGINE HOW SHE ENDED UP HERE.

MAYBE SHE WAS JUST AN INNOCENT VICTIM.

WHO KNOWS...

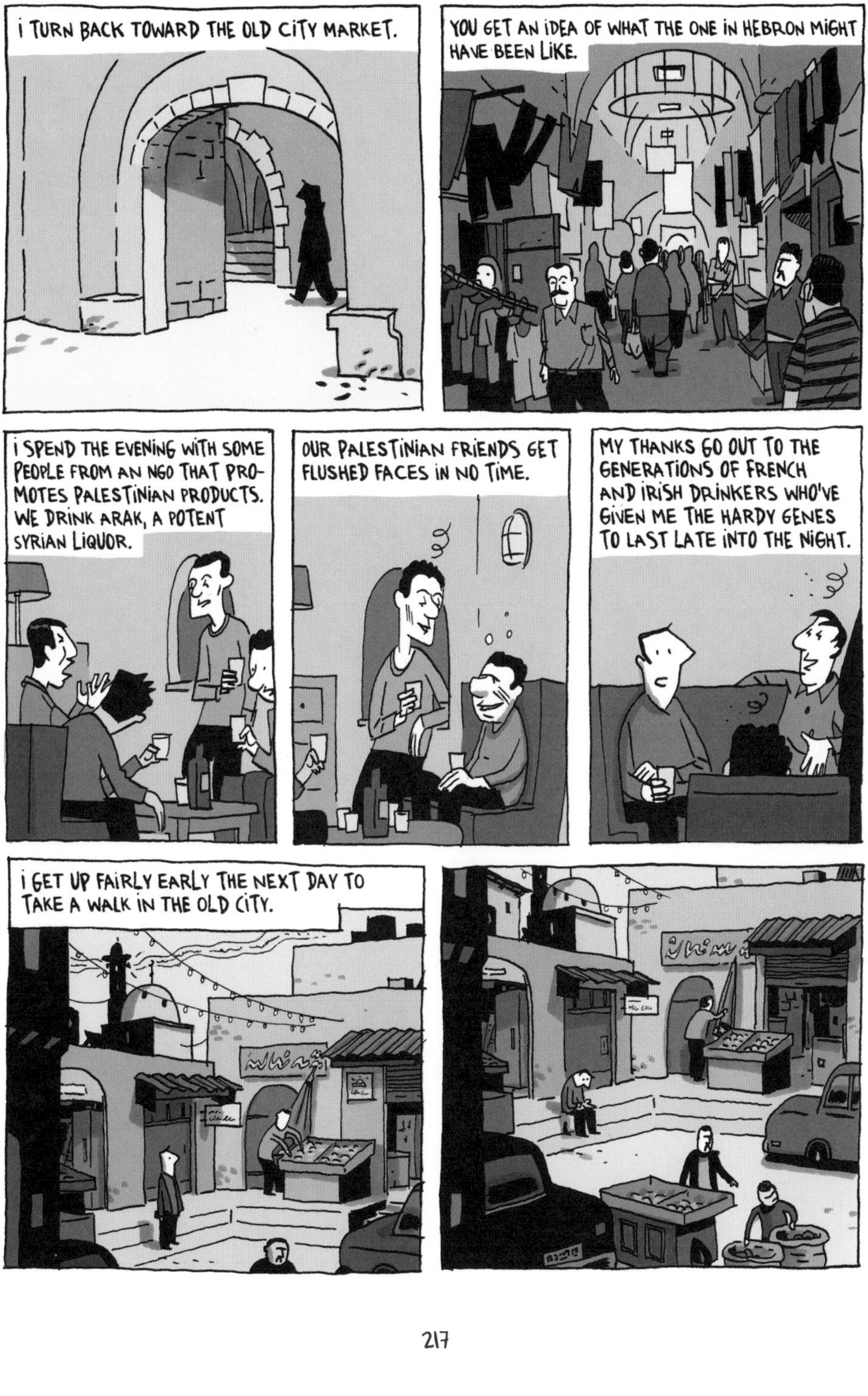
I TURN BACK TOWARD THE OLD CITY MARKET.
YOU GET AN IDEA OF WHAT THE ONE IN HEBRON MIGHT HAVE BEEN LIKE.
I SPEND THE EVENING WITH SOME PEOPLE FROM AN NGO THAT PROMOTES PALESTINIAN PRODUCTS. WE DRINK ARAK, A POTENT SYRIAN LIQUOR.
OUR PALESTINIAN FRIENDS GET FLUSHED FACES IN NO TIME.
MY THANKS GO OUT TO THE GENERATIONS OF FRENCH AND IRISH DRINKERS WHO'VE GIVEN ME THE HARDY GENES TO LAST LATE INTO THE NIGHT.
I GET UP FAIRLY EARLY THE NEXT DAY TO TAKE A WALK IN THE OLD CITY.

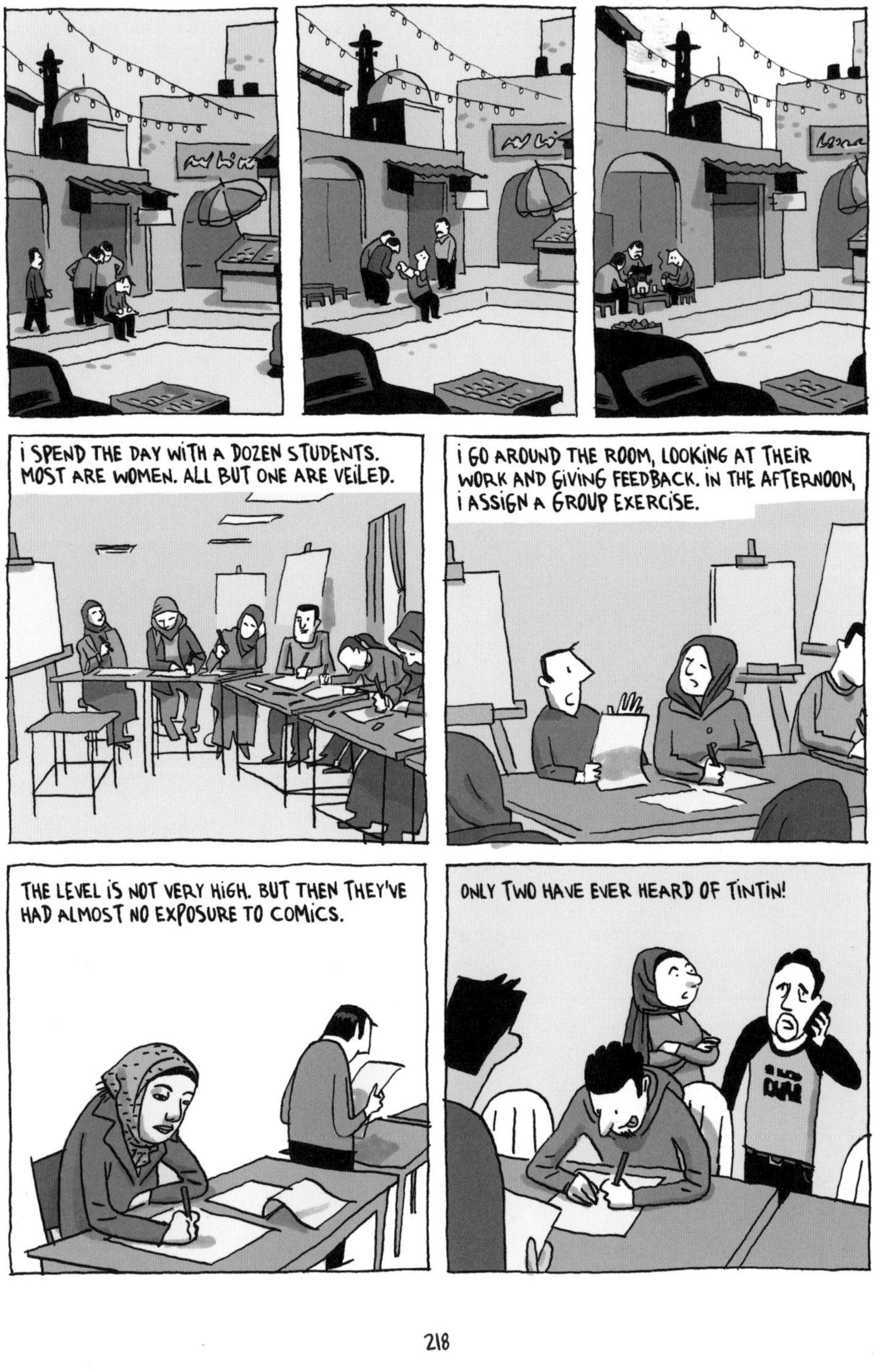
I SPEND THE DAY WITH A DOZEN STUDENTS. MOST ARE WOMEN. ALL BUT ONE ARE VEILED.
I GO AROUND THE ROOM, LOOKING AT THEIR WORK AND GIVING FEEDBACK. IN THE AFTERNOON, I ASSIGN A GROUP EXERCISE.
THE LEVEL IS NOT VERY HIGH. BUT THEN THEY'VE HAD ALMOST NO EXPOSURE TO COMICS.
ONLY TWO HAVE EVER HEARD OF TINTIN!

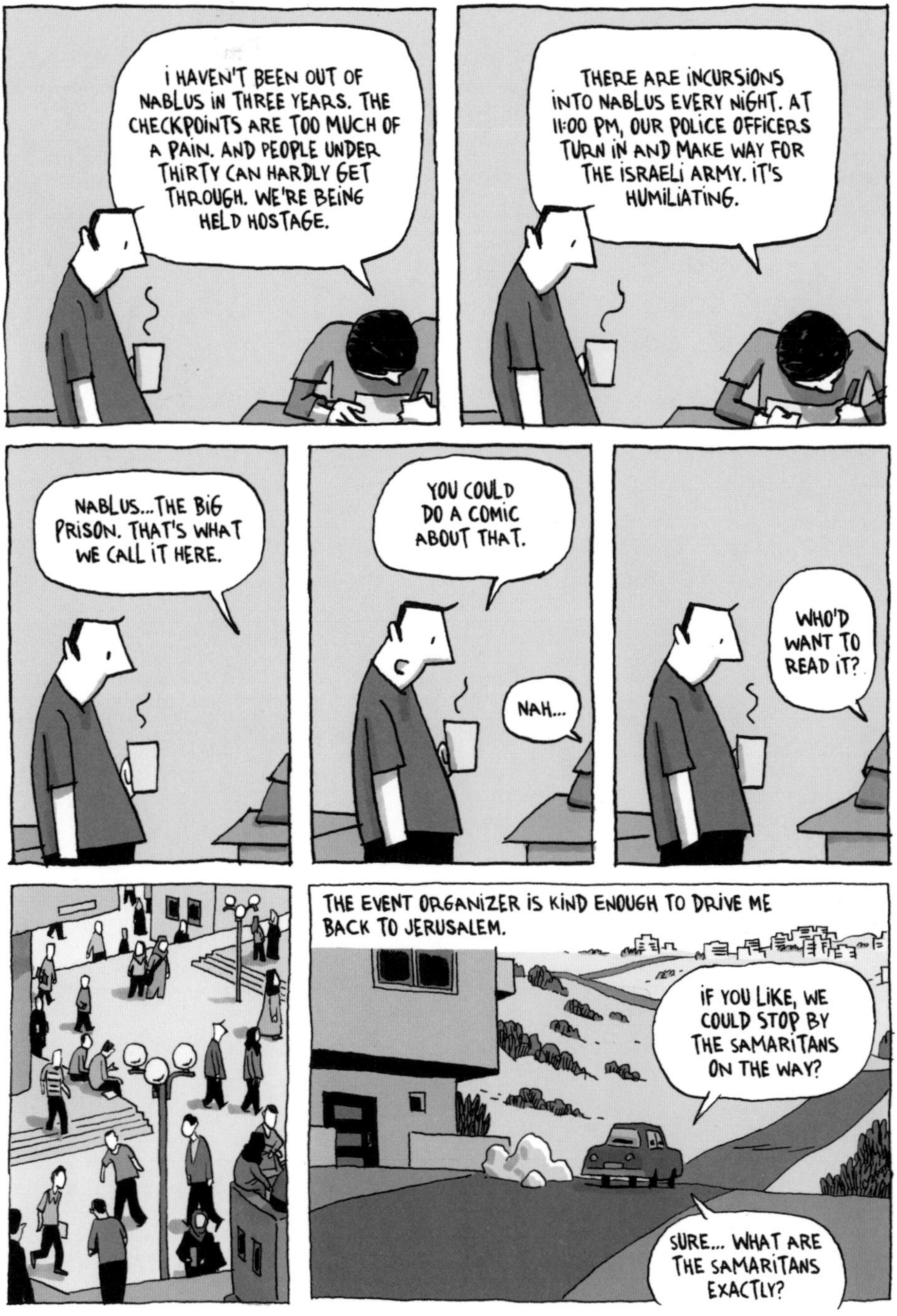

I HAVEN'T BEEN OUT OF NABLUS IN THREE YEARS. THE CHECKPOINTS ARE TOO MUCH OF A PAIN. AND PEOPLE UNDER THIRTY CAN HARDLY GET THROUGH. WE'RE BEING HELD HOSTAGE.
THERE ARE INCURSIONS INTO NABLUS EVERY NIGHT. AT 11:00 PM, OUR POLICE OFFICERS TURN IN AND MAKE WAY FOR THE ISRAELI ARMY. IT'S HUMILIATING.
NABLUS... THE BIG PRISON. THAT'S WHAT WE CALL IT HERE.
YOU COULD DO A COMIC ABOUT THAT.
NAH...
WHO'D WANT TO READ IT?
THE EVENT ORGANIZER IS KIND ENOUGH TO DRIVE ME BACK TO JERUSALEM.
IF YOU LIKE, WE COULD STOP BY THE SAMARITANS ON THE WAY?
SURE... WHAT ARE THE SAMARITANS EXACTLY?

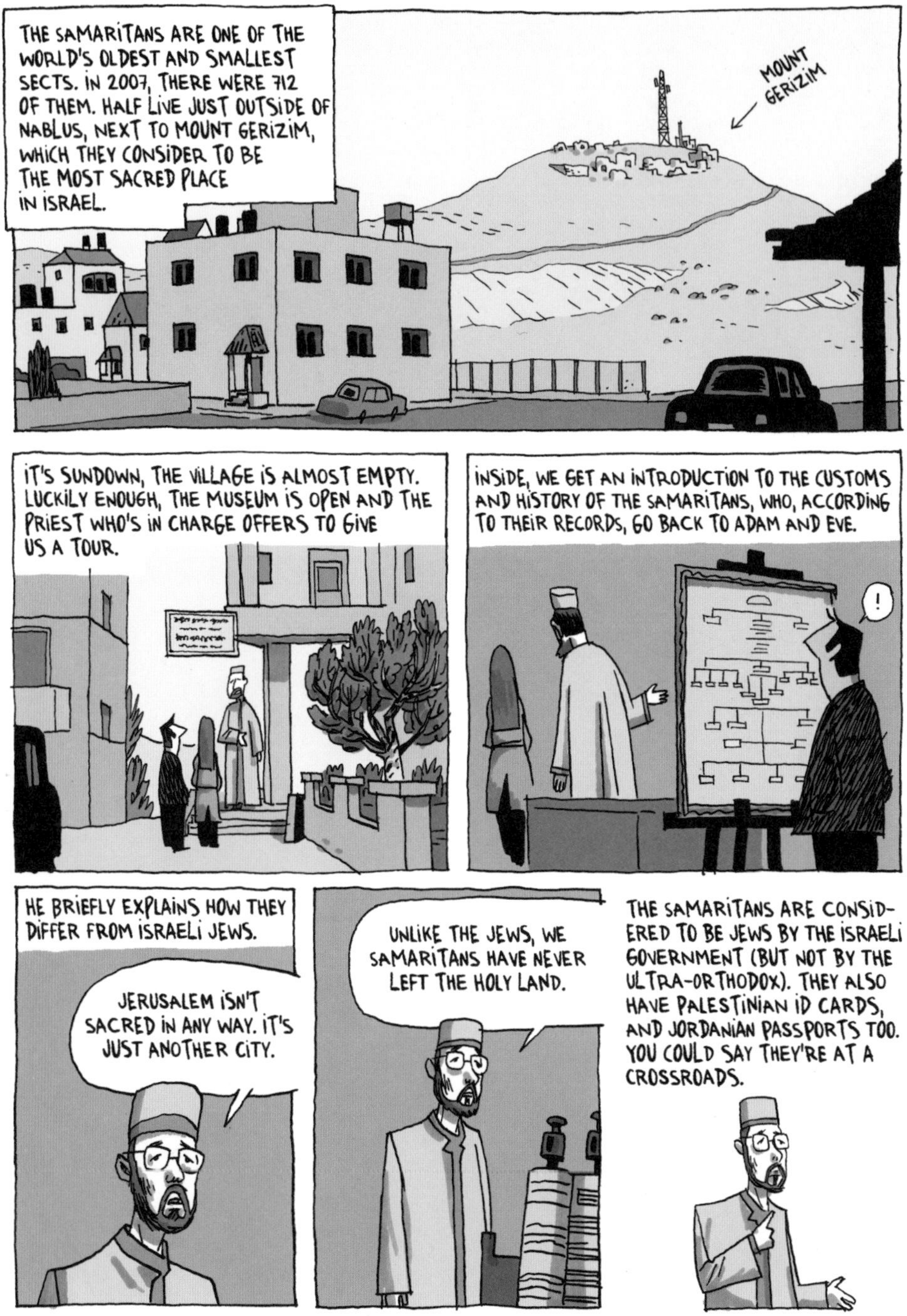
THE SAMARITANS ARE ONE OF THE WORLD'S OLDEST AND SMALLEST SECTS. IN 2007, THERE WERE 712 OF THEM. HALF LIVE JUST OUTSIDE OF NABLUS, NEXT TO MOUNT GERIZIM, WHICH THEY CONSIDER TO BE THE MOST SACRED PLACE IN ISRAEL.
MOUNT GERIZIM
IT'S SUNDOWN, THE VILLAGE IS ALMOST EMPTY. LUCKILY ENOUGH, THE MUSEUM IS OPEN AND THE PRIEST WHO'S IN CHARGE OFFERS TO GIVE US A TOUR.
INSIDE, WE GET AN INTRODUCTION TO THE CUSTOMS AND HISTORY OF THE SAMARITANS, WHO, ACCORDING TO THEIR RECORDS, GO BACK TO ADAM AND EVE.
!
HE BRIEFLY EXPLAINS HOW THEY DIFFER FROM ISRAELI JEWS.
JERUSALEM ISN'T SACRED IN ANY WAY. IT'S JUST ANOTHER CITY.
UNLIKE THE JEWS, WE SAMARITANS HAVE NEVER LEFT THE HOLY LAND.
THE SAMARITANS ARE CONSIDERED TO BE JEWS BY THE ISRAELI GOVERNMENT (BUT NOT BY THE ULTRA-ORTHODOX). THEY ALSO HAVE PALESTINIAN ID CARDS, AND JORDANIAN PASSPORTS TOO. YOU COULD SAY THEY'RE AT A CROSSROADS.

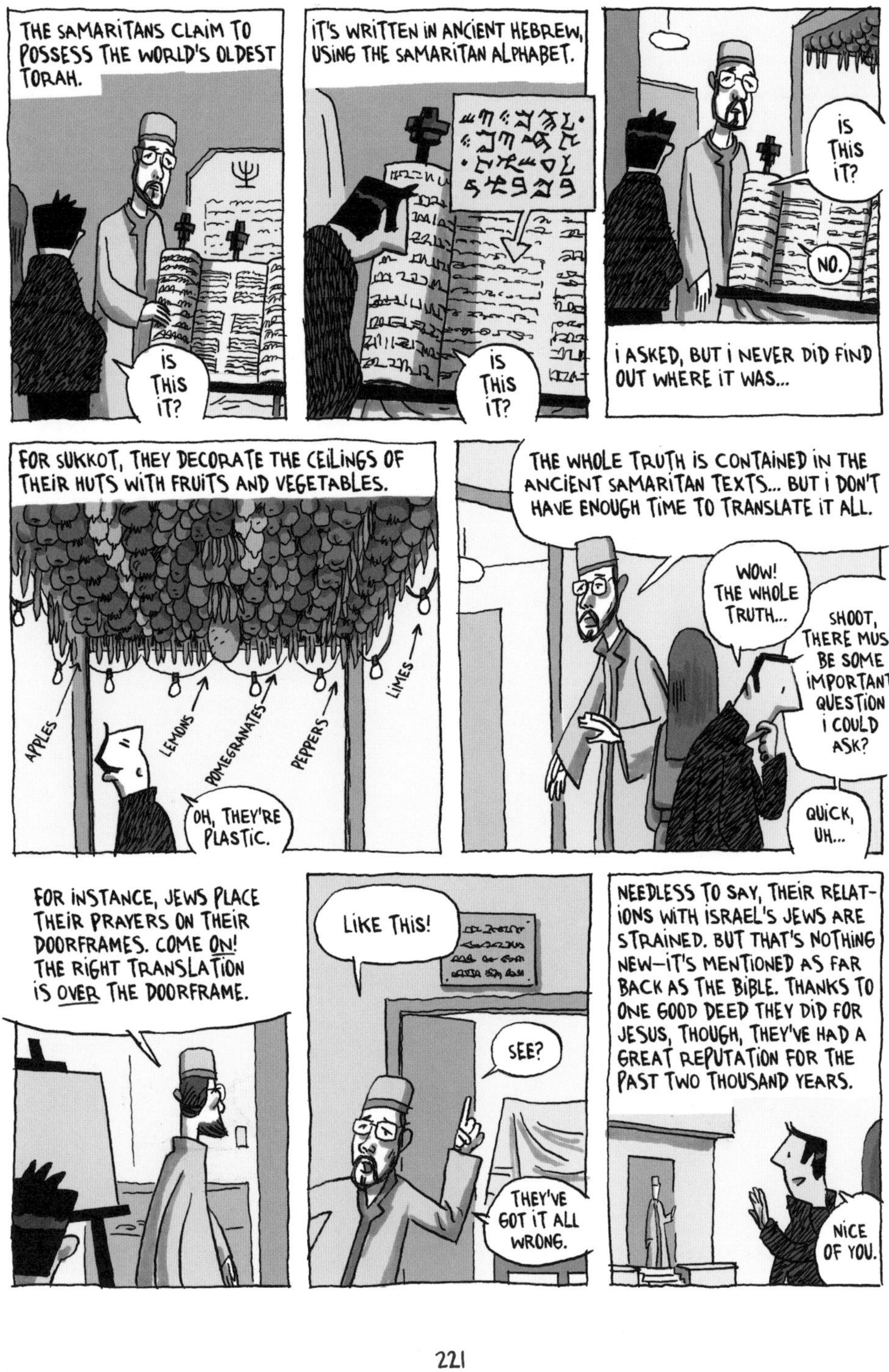
THE SAMARITANS CLAIM TO POSSESS THE WORLD'S OLDEST TORAH.
IS THIS IT?
IT'S WRITTEN IN ANCIENT HEBREW, USING THE SAMARITAN ALPHABET.
IS THIS IT?
IS THIS IT?
NO.
I ASKED, BUT I NEVER DID FIND OUT WHERE IT WAS...
FOR SUKKOT, THEY DECORATE THE CEILINGS OF THEIR HUTS WITH FRUITS AND VEGETABLES.
APPLES
LEMONS
POMEGRANATES
PEPPERS
LIMES
OH, THEY'RE PLASTIC.
THE WHOLE TRUTH IS CONTAINED IN THE ANCIENT SAMARITAN TEXTS... BUT I DON'T HAVE ENOUGH TIME TO TRANSLATE IT ALL.
WOW! THE WHOLE TRUTH...
SHOOT, THERE MUST BE SOME IMPORTANT QUESTION I COULD ASK?
QUICK, UH...
FOR INSTANCE, JEWS PLACE THEIR PRAYERS ON THEIR DOORFRAMES. COME ON! THE RIGHT TRANSLATION IS OVER THE DOORFRAME.
LIKE THIS!
SEE?
THEY'VE GOT IT ALL WRONG.
NEEDLESS TO SAY, THEIR RELATIONS WITH ISRAEL'S JEWS ARE STRAINED. BUT THAT'S NOTHING NEW—IT'S MENTIONED AS FAR BACK AS THE BIBLE. THANKS TO ONE GOOD DEED THEY DID FOR JESUS, THOUGH, THEY'VE HAD A GREAT REPUTATION FOR THE PAST TWO THOUSAND YEARS.
NICE OF YOU.

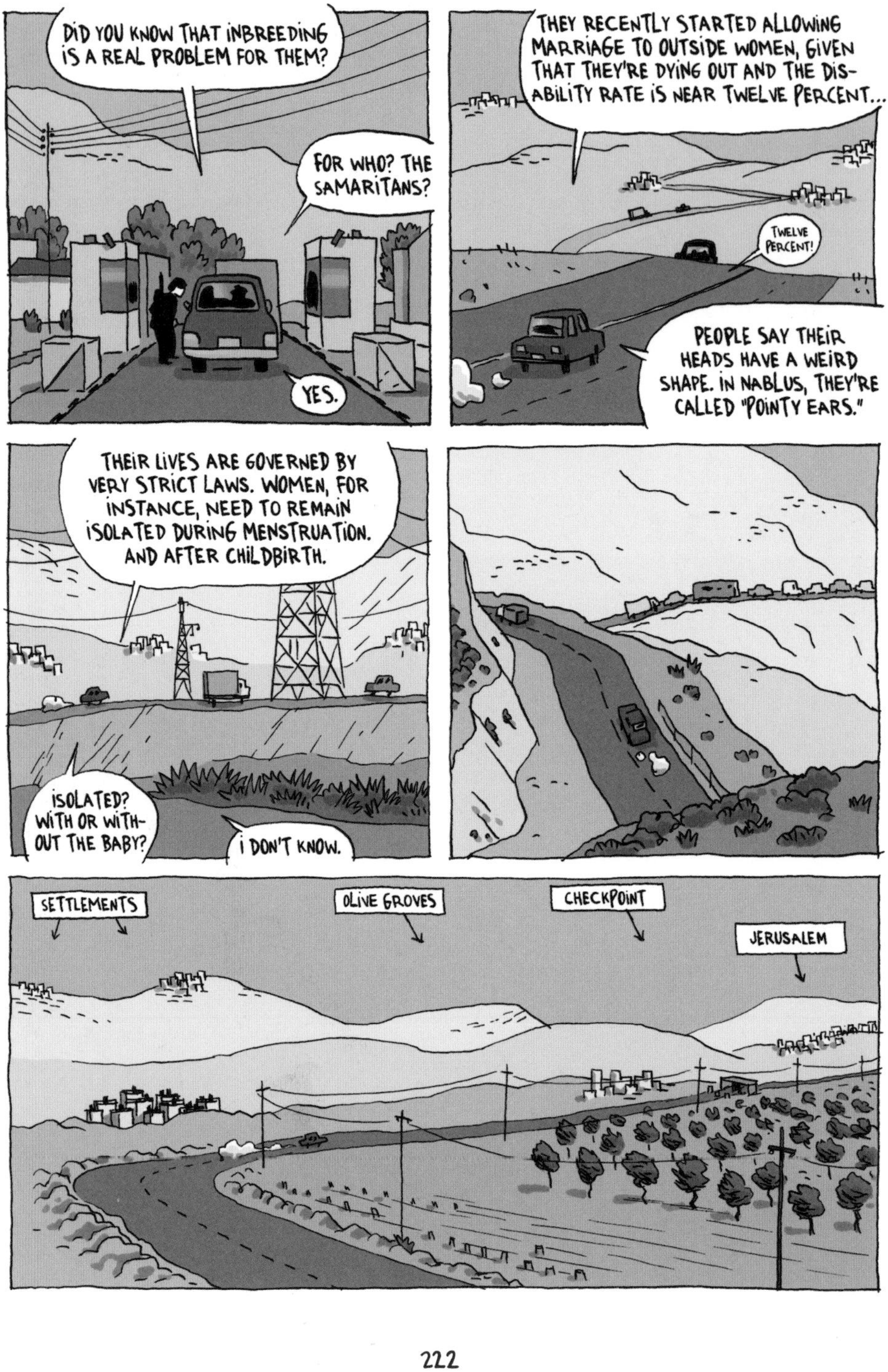
DID YOU KNOW THAT INBREEDING IS A REAL PROBLEM FOR THEM?
FOR WHO? THE SAMARITANS?
YES.
THEY RECENTLY STARTED ALLOWING MARRIAGE TO OUTSIDE WOMEN, GIVEN THAT THEY'RE DYING OUT AND THE DISABILITY RATE IS NEAR TWELVE PERCENT...
TWELVE PERCENT!
PEOPLE SAY THEIR HEADS HAVE A WEIRD SHAPE. IN NABLUS, THEY'RE CALLED "POINTY EARS."
THEIR LIVES ARE GOVERNED BY VERY STRICT LAWS. WOMEN, FOR INSTANCE, NEED TO REMAIN ISOLATED DURING MENSTRUATION. AND AFTER CHILDBIRTH.
ISOLATED? WITH OR WITHOUT THE BABY?
I DON'T KNOW.
SETTLEMENTS
OLIVE GROVES
CHECKPOINT
JERUSALEM

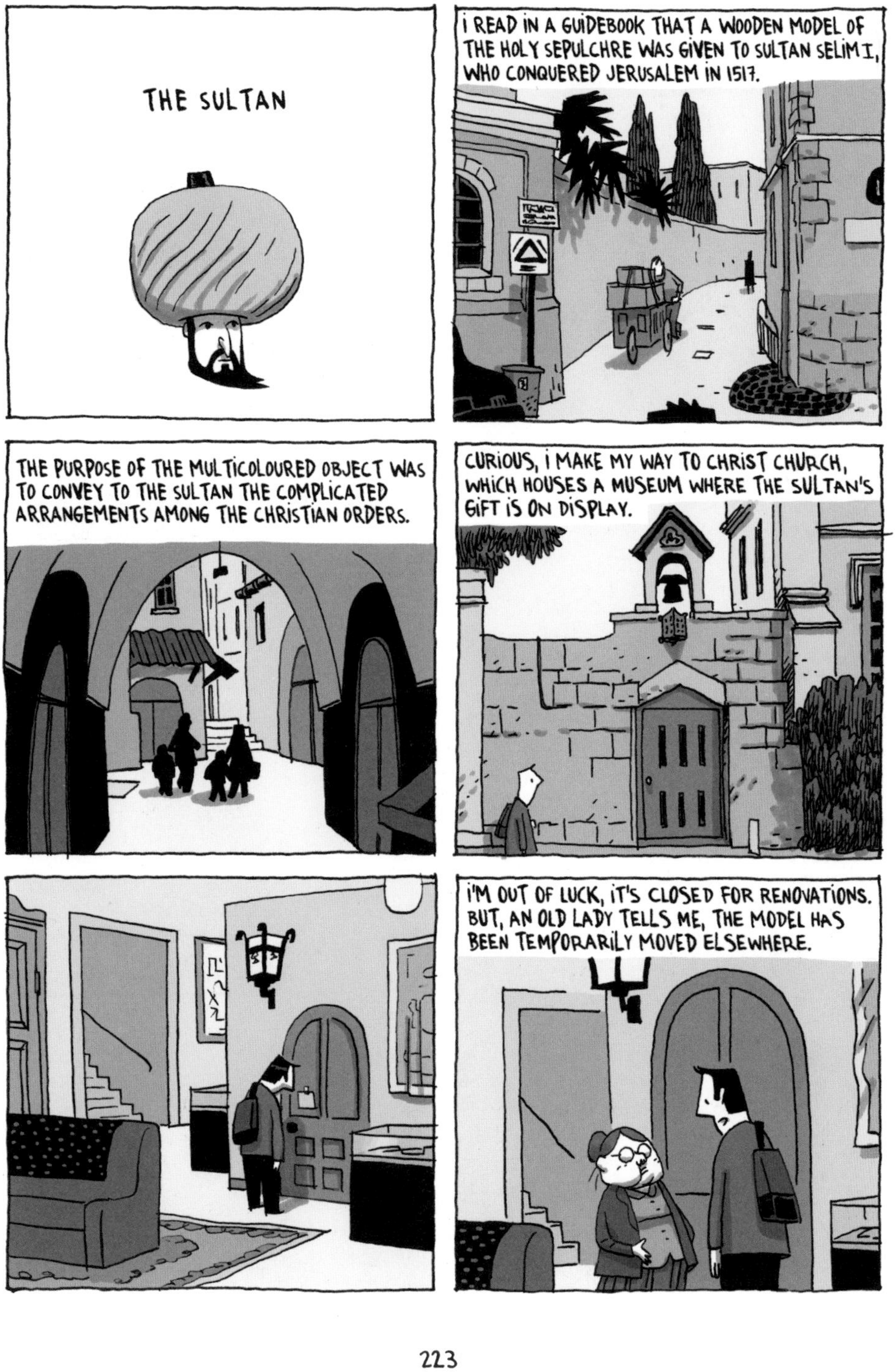
THE SULTAN
I READ IN A GUIDEBOOK THAT A WOODEN MODEL OF THE HOLY SEPULCHRE WAS GIVEN TO SULTAN SELIM I, WHO CONQUERED JERUSALEM IN 1517.
THE PURPOSE OF THE MULTICOLOURED OBJECT WAS TO CONVEY TO THE SULTAN THE COMPLICATED ARRANGEMENTS AMONG THE CHRISTIAN ORDERS.
CURIOUS, I MAKE MY WAY TO CHRIST CHURCH, WHICH HOUSES A MUSEUM WHERE THE SULTAN'S GIFT IS ON DISPLAY.
I'M OUT OF LUCK, IT'S CLOSED FOR RENOVATIONS. BUT, AN OLD LADY TELLS ME, THE MODEL HAS BEEN TEMPORARILY MOVED ELSEWHERE.

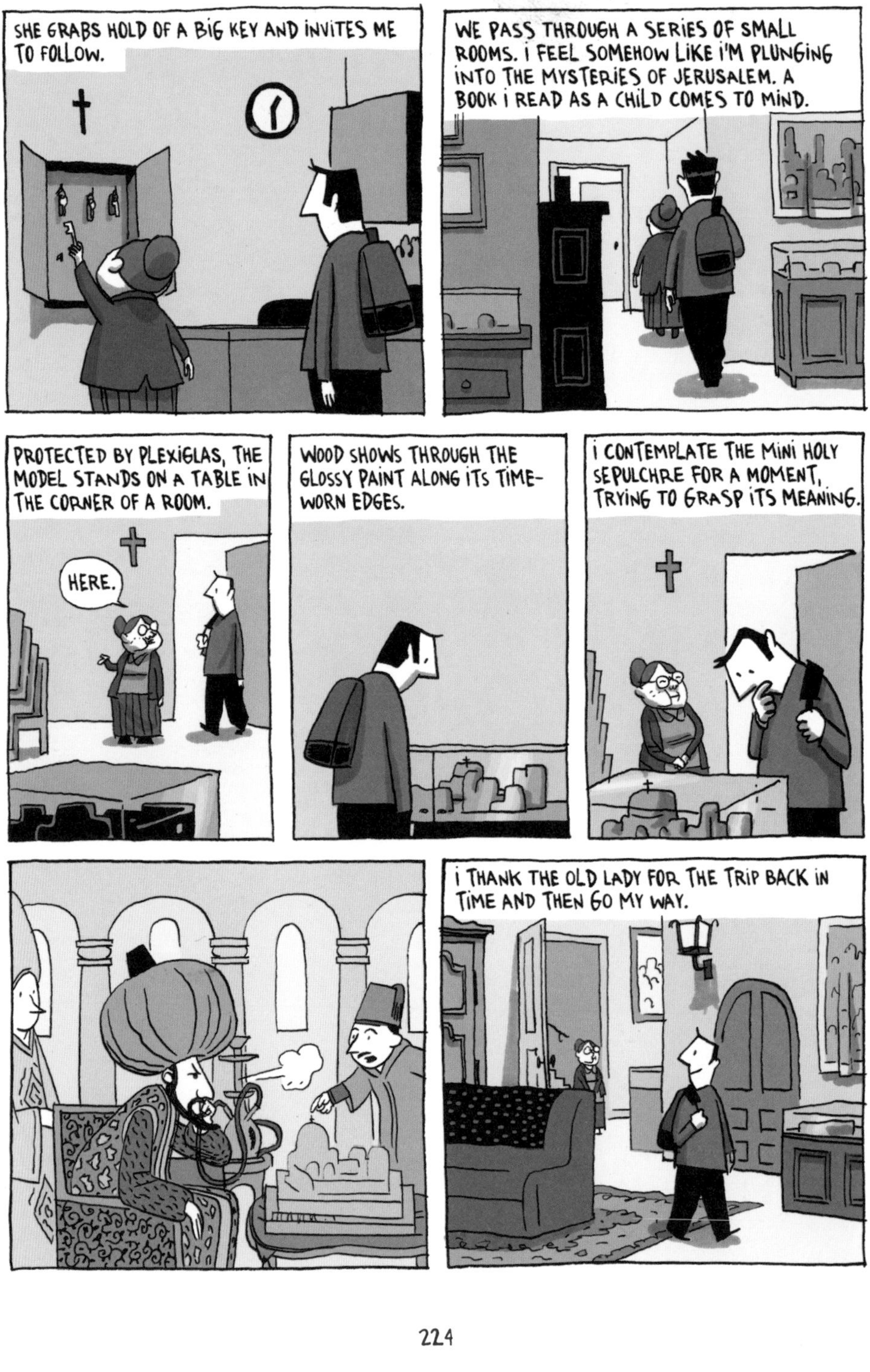
SHE GRABS HOLD OF A BIG KEY AND INVITES ME TO FOLLOW.
WE PASS THROUGH A SERIES OF SMALL ROOMS. I FEEL SOMEHOW LIKE I'M PLUNGING INTO THE MYSTERIES OF JERUSALEM. A BOOK I READ AS A CHILD COMES TO MIND.
PROTECTED BY PLEXIGLAS, THE MODEL STANDS ON A TABLE IN THE CORNER OF A ROOM.
HERE.
WOOD SHOWS THROUGH THE GLOSSY PAINT ALONG ITS TIME-WORN EDGES.
I CONTEMPLATE THE MINI HOLY SEPULCHRE FOR A MOMENT, TRYING TO GRASP ITS MEANING.
I THANK THE OLD LADY FOR THE TRIP BACK IN TIME AND THEN GO MY WAY.

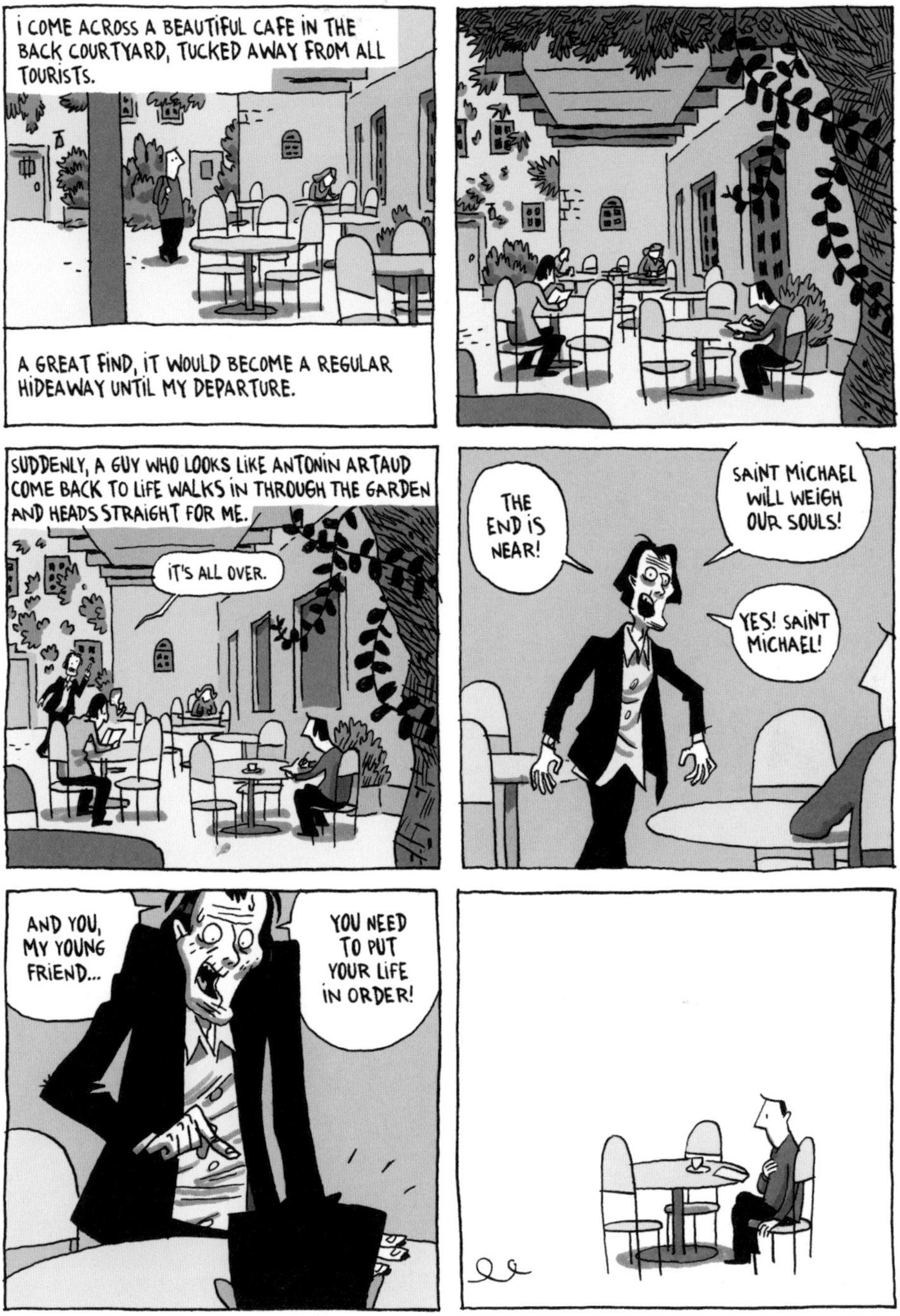
I COME ACROSS A BEAUTIFUL CAFE IN THE BACK COURTYARD, TUCKED AWAY FROM ALL TOURISTS.
A GREAT FIND, IT WOULD BECOME A REGULAR HIDEAWAY UNTIL MY DEPARTURE.
SUDDENLY, A GUY WHO LOOKS LIKE ANTONIN ARTAUD COME BACK TO LIFE WALKS IN THROUGH THE GARDEN AND HEADS STRAIGHT FOR ME.
IT'S ALL OVER.
THE END IS NEAR!
SAINT MICHAEL WILL WEIGH OUR SOULS!
YES! SAINT MICHAEL!
AND YOU, MY YOUNG FRIEND...
YOU NEED TO PUT YOUR LIFE IN ORDER!

APRIL

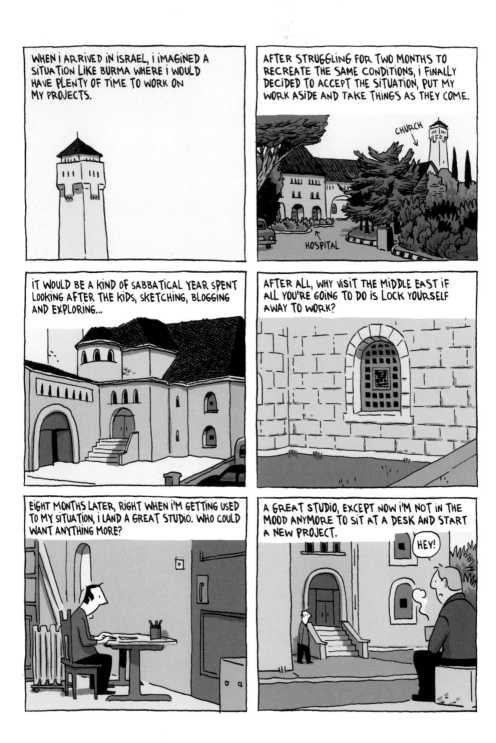

WHEN I ARRIVED IN ISRAEL, I IMAGINED A SITUATION LIKE BURMA WHERE I WOULD HAVE PLENTY OF TIME TO WORK ON MY PROJECTS.

AFTER STRUGGLING FOR TWO MONTHS TO RECREATE THE SAME CONDITIONS, I FINALLY DECIDED TO ACCEPT THE SITUATION, PUT MY WORK ASIDE AND TAKE THINGS AS THEY COME.

CHURCH

HOSPITAL

IT WOULD BE A KIND OF SABBATICAL YEAR SPENT LOOKING AFTER THE KIDS, SKETCHING, BLOGGING AND EXPLORING...

AFTER ALL, WHY VISIT THE MIDDLE EAST IF ALL YOU'RE GOING TO DO IS LOCK YOURSELF AWAY TO WORK?

EIGHT MONTHS LATER, RIGHT WHEN I'M GETTING USED TO MY SITUATION, I LAND A GREAT STUDIO. WHO COULD WANT ANYTHING MORE?

A GREAT STUDIO, EXCEPT NOW I'M NOT IN THE MOOD ANYMORE TO SIT AT A DESK AND START A NEW PROJECT.

HEY!

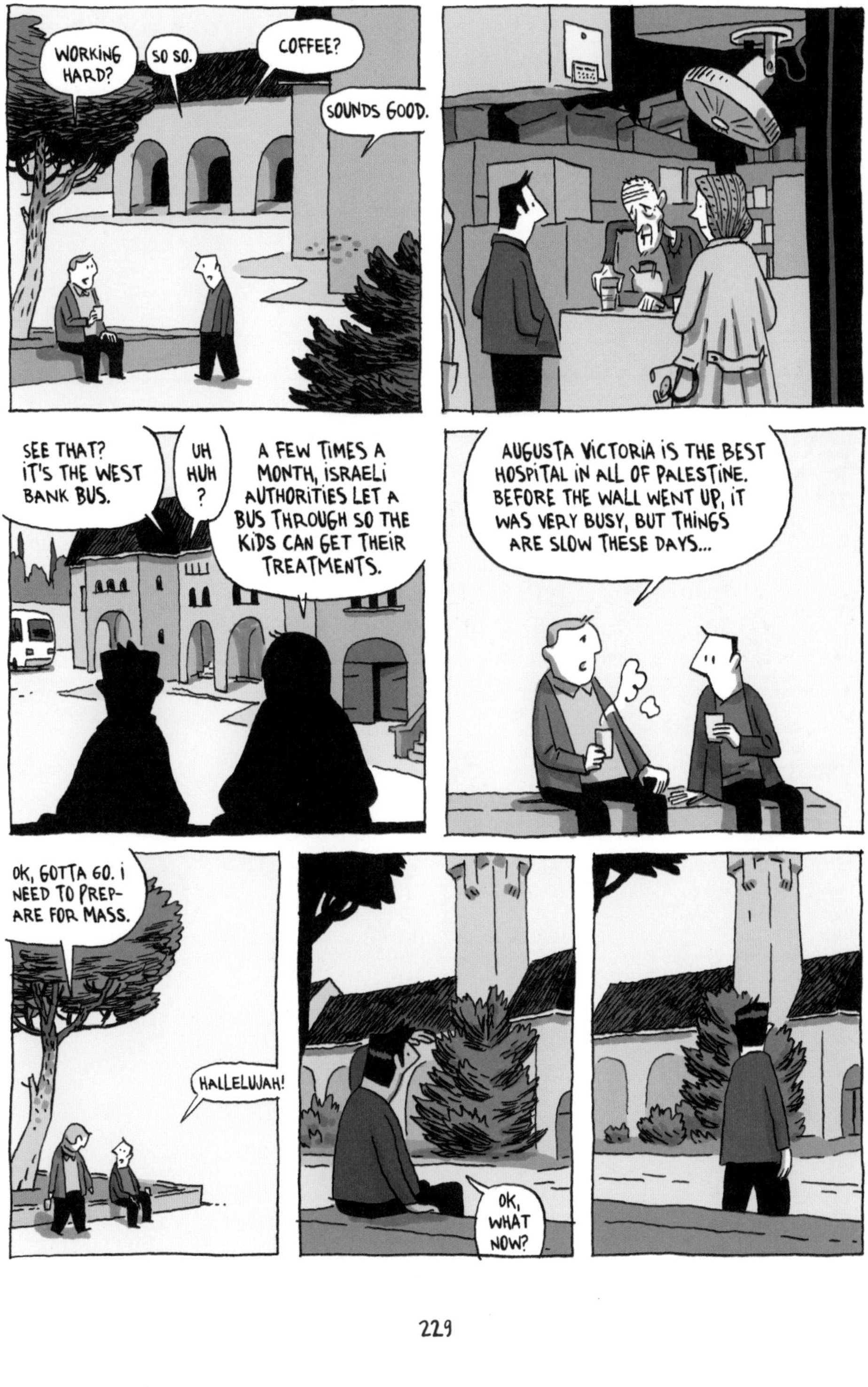

WORKING HARD?
SO SO.
COFFEE?
SOUNDS GOOD.
SEE THAT? IT'S THE WEST BANK BUS.
UH HUH ?
A FEW TIMES A MONTH, ISRAELI AUTHORITIES LET A BUS THROUGH SO THE KIDS CAN GET THEIR TREATMENTS.
AUGUSTA VICTORIA IS THE BEST HOSPITAL IN ALL OF PALESTINE. BEFORE THE WALL WENT UP, IT WAS VERY BUSY, BUT THINGS ARE SLOW THESE DAYS...
OK, GOTTA GO. I NEED TO PREPARE FOR MASS.
HALLELUJAH!
OK, WHAT NOW?

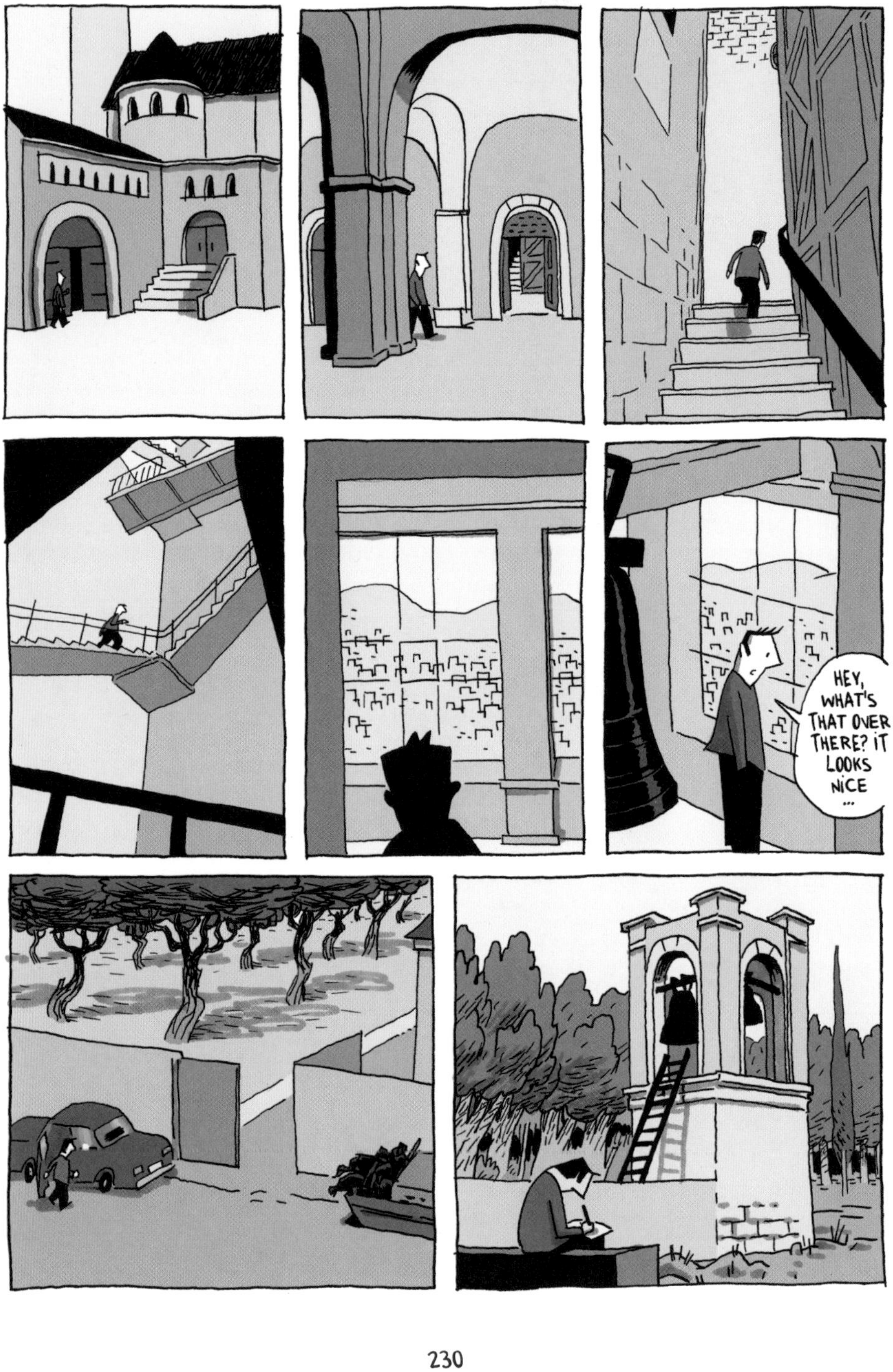
HEY, WHAT'S THAT OVER THERE? IT LOOKS NICE ...

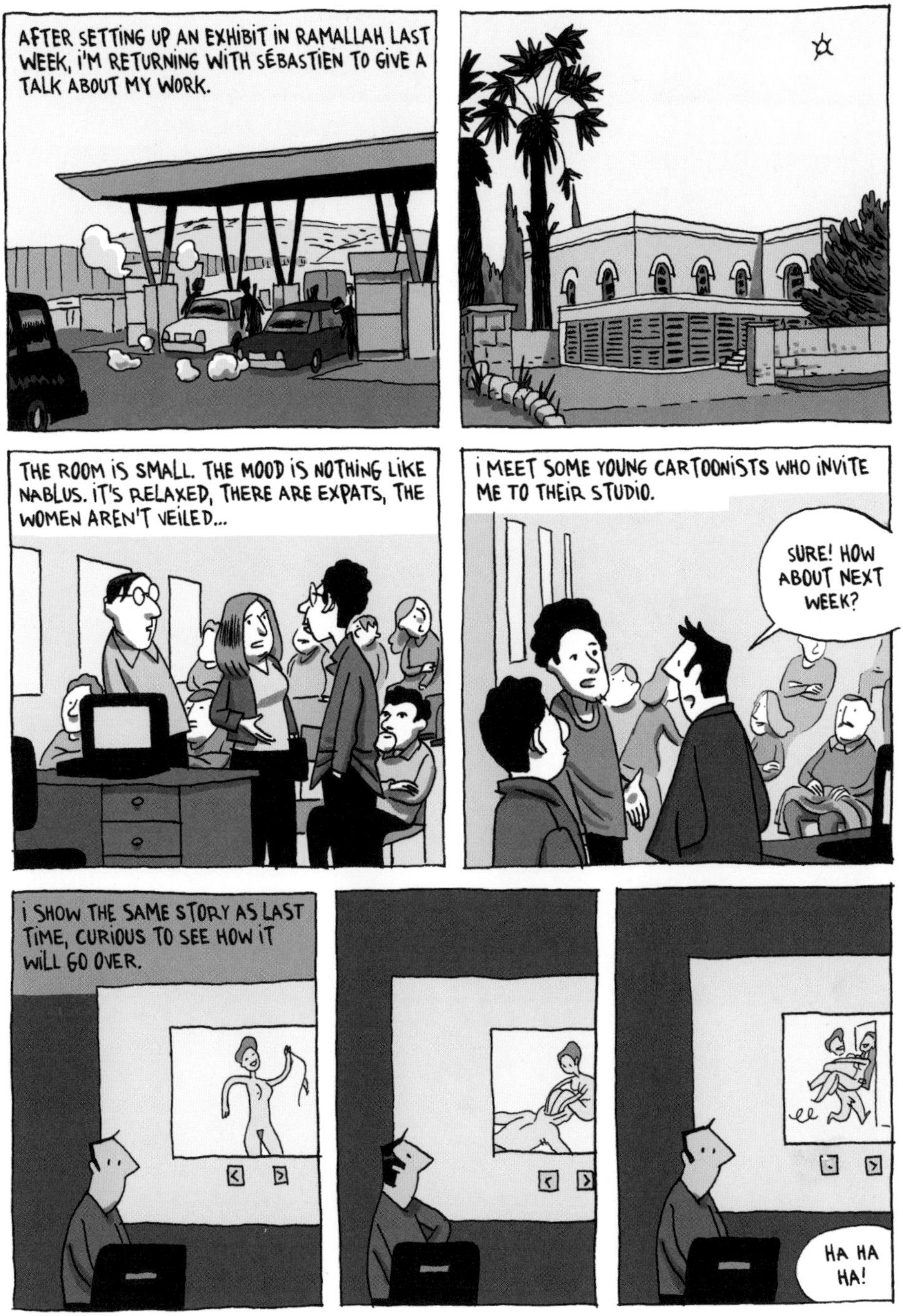
AFTER SETTING UP AN EXHIBIT IN RAMALLAH LAST WEEK, I'M RETURNING WITH SÉBASTIEN TO GIVE A TALK ABOUT MY WORK.
THE ROOM IS SMALL. THE MOOD IS NOTHING LIKE NABLUS. IT'S RELAXED, THERE ARE EXPATS, THE WOMEN AREN'T VEILED...
I MEET SOME YOUNG CARTOONISTS WHO INVITE ME TO THEIR STUDIO.
SURE! HOW ABOUT NEXT WEEK?
I SHOW THE SAME STORY AS LAST TIME, CURIOUS TO SEE HOW IT WILL GO OVER.
HA HA HA!

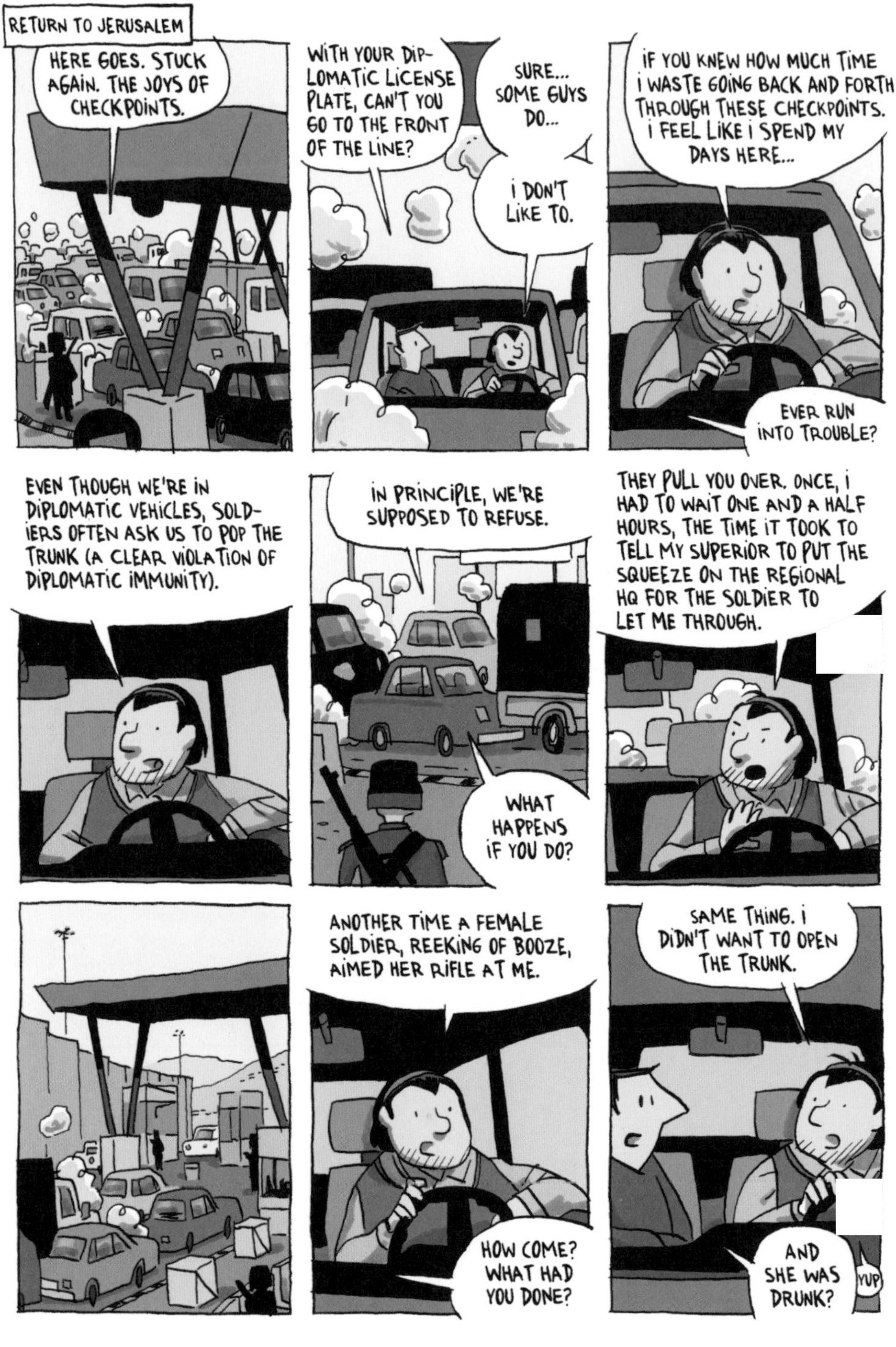
RETURN TO JERUSALEM
HERE GOES. STUCK AGAIN. THE JOYS OF CHECKPOINTS.
WITH YOUR DIPLOMATIC LICENSE PLATE, CAN'T YOU GO TO THE FRONT OF THE LINE?
SURE... SOME GUYS DO...
I DON'T LIKE TO.
IF YOU KNEW HOW MUCH TIME I WASTE GOING BACK AND FORTH THROUGH THESE CHECKPOINTS. I FEEL LIKE I SPEND MY DAYS HERE...
EVER RUN INTO TROUBLE?
EVEN THOUGH WE'RE IN DIPLOMATIC VEHICLES, SOLDIERS OFTEN ASK US TO POP THE TRUNK (A CLEAR VIOLATION OF DIPLOMATIC IMMUNITY).
IN PRINCIPLE, WE'RE SUPPOSED TO REFUSE.
WHAT HAPPENS IF YOU DO?
THEY PULL YOU OVER. ONCE, I HAD TO WAIT ONE AND A HALF HOURS, THE TIME IT TOOK TO TELL MY SUPERIOR TO PUT THE SQUEEZE ON THE REGIONAL HQ FOR THE SOLDIER TO LET ME THROUGH.
ANOTHER TIME A FEMALE SOLDIER, REEKING OF BOOZE, AIMED HER RIFLE AT ME.
HOW COME? WHAT HAD YOU DONE?
SAME THING. I DIDN'T WANT TO OPEN THE TRUNK.
AND SHE WAS DRUNK?
YUP

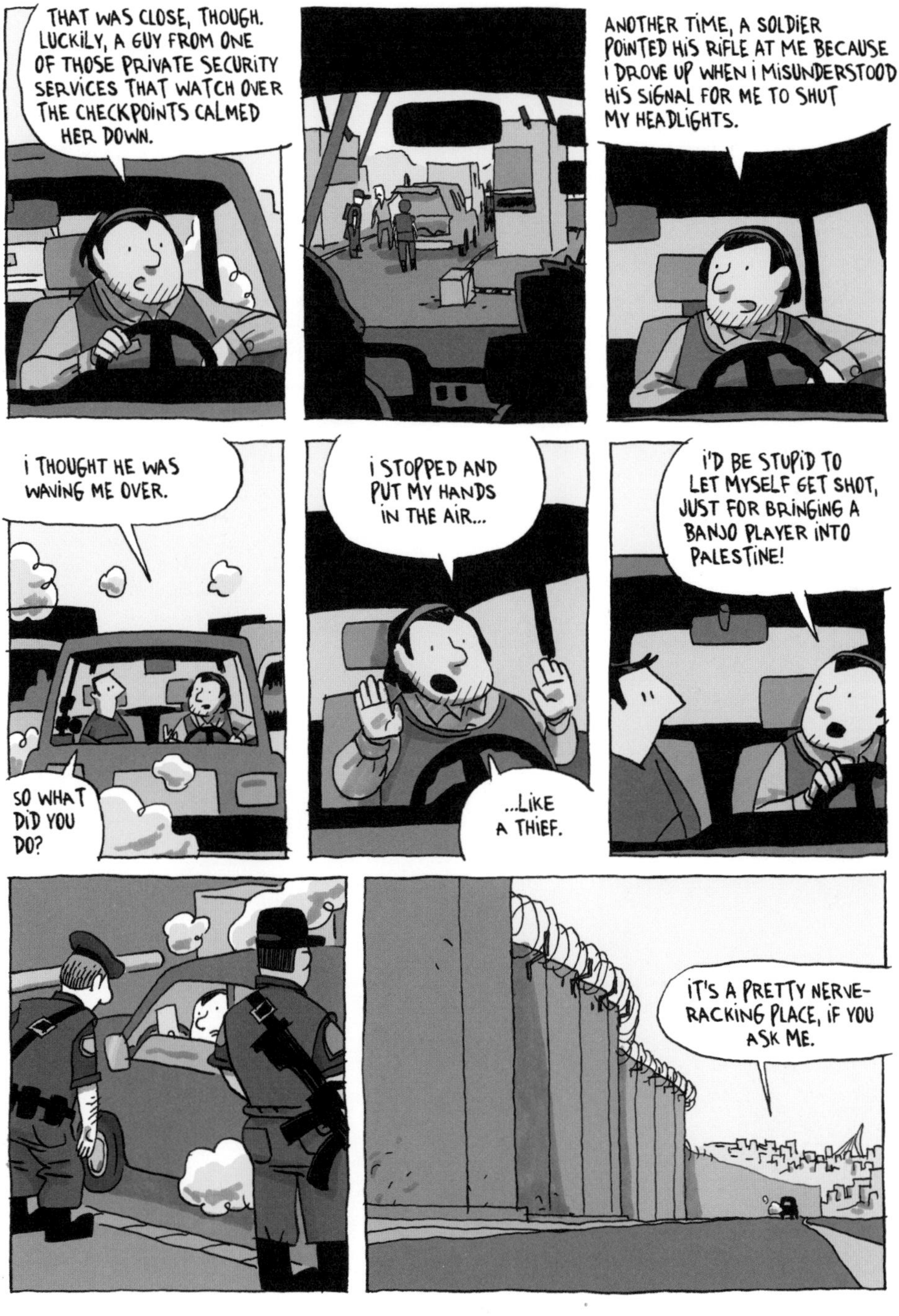
THAT WAS CLOSE, THOUGH. LUCKILY, A GUY FROM ONE OF THOSE PRIVATE SECURITY SERVICES THAT WATCH OVER THE CHECKPOINTS CALMED HER DOWN.
ANOTHER TIME, A SOLDIER POINTED HIS RIFLE AT ME BECAUSE I DROVE UP WHEN I MISUNDERSTOOD HIS SIGNAL FOR ME TO SHUT MY HEADLIGHTS.
I THOUGHT HE WAS WAVING ME OVER.
SO WHAT DID YOU DO?
I STOPPED AND PUT MY HANDS IN THE AIR...
...LIKE A THIEF.
I'D BE STUPID TO LET MYSELF GET SHOT, JUST FOR BRINGING A BANJO PLAYER INTO PALESTINE!
IT'S A PRETTY NERVE-RACKING PLACE, IF YOU ASK ME.

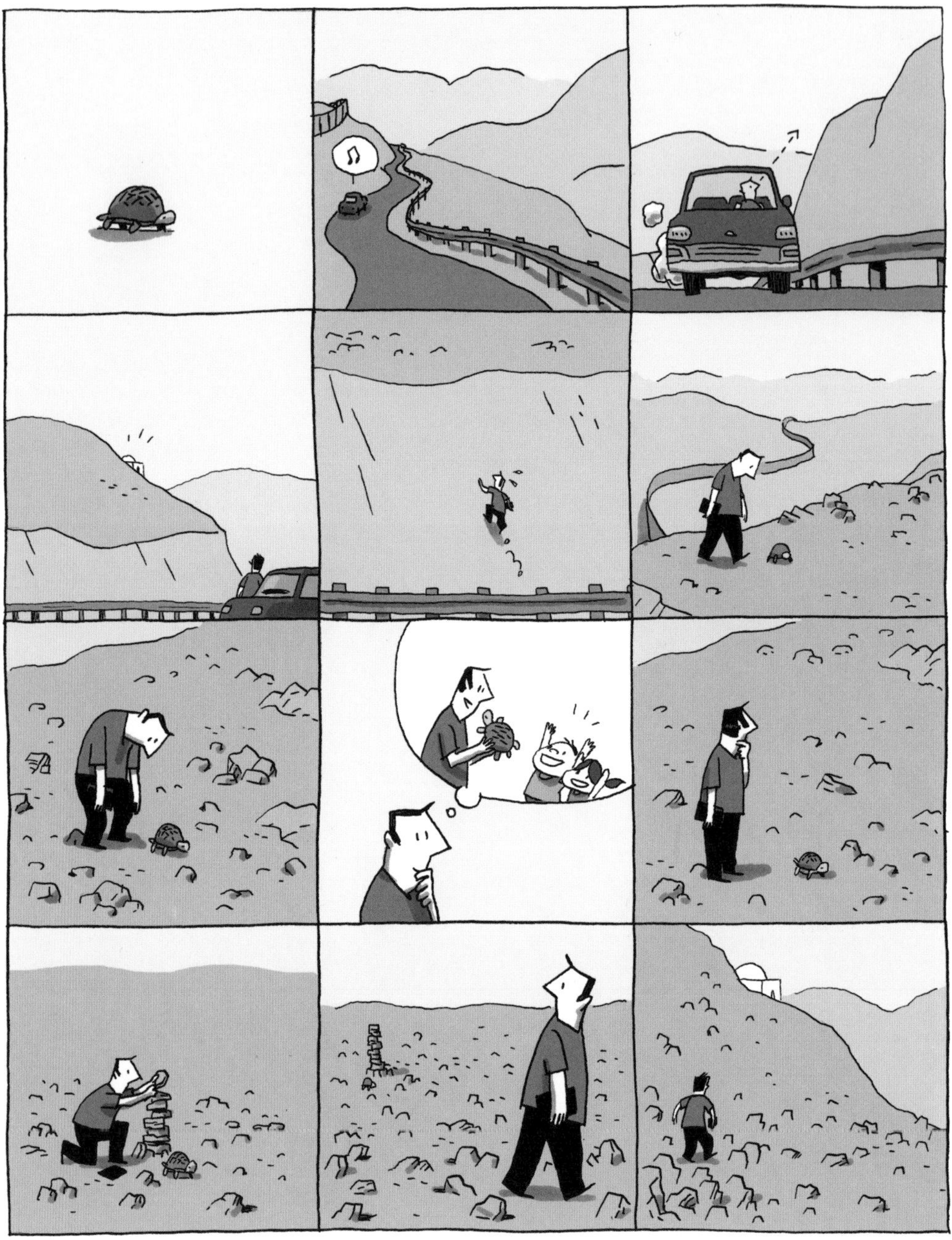

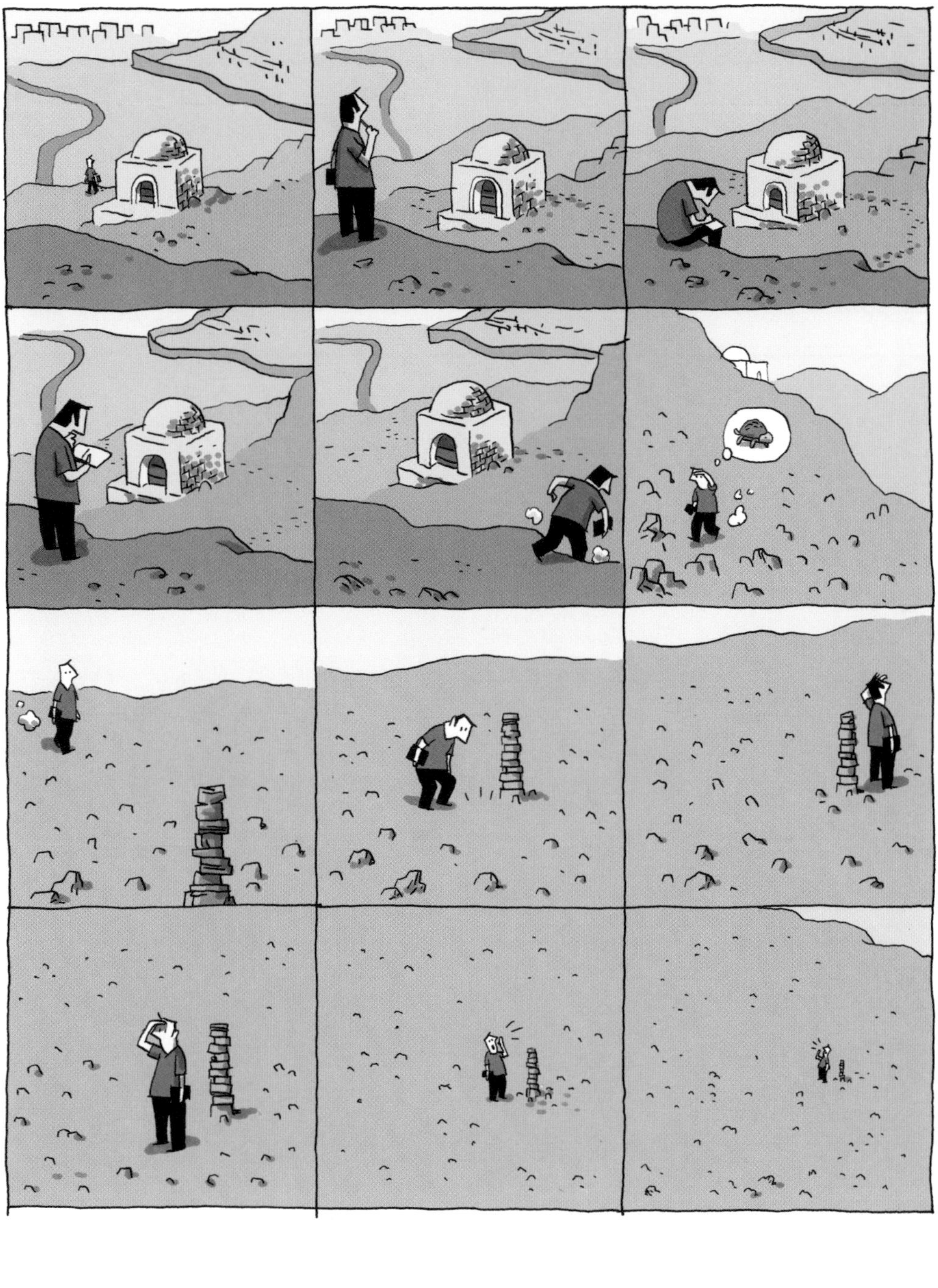

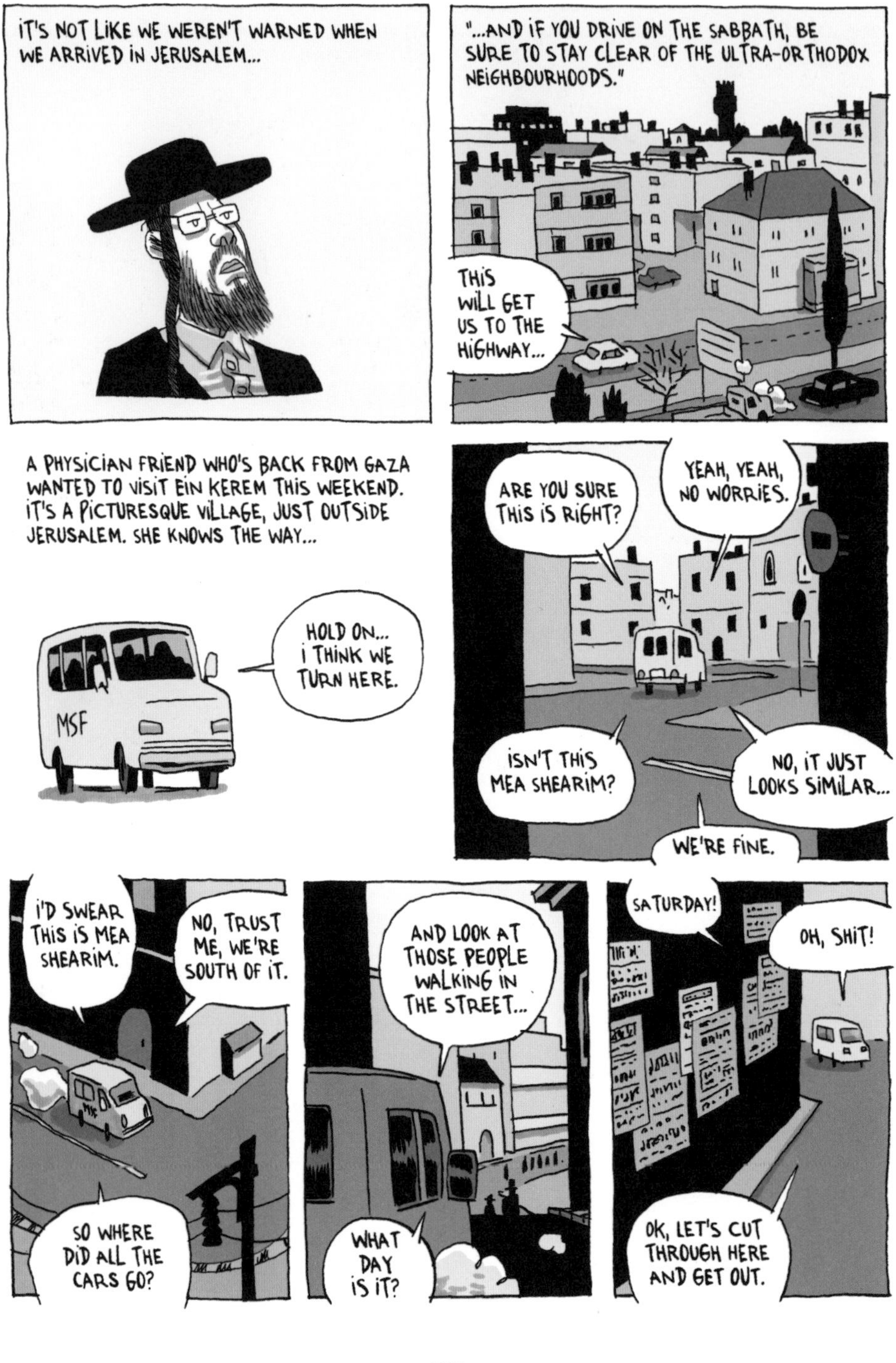
IT'S NOT LIKE WE WEREN'T WARNED WHEN WE ARRIVED IN JERUSALEM...
"...AND IF YOU DRIVE ON THE SABBATH, BE SURE TO STAY CLEAR OF THE ULTRA-ORTHODOX NEIGHBOURHOODS."
THIS WILL GET US TO THE HIGHWAY...
A PHYSICIAN FRIEND WHO'S BACK FROM GAZA WANTED TO VISIT EIN KEREM THIS WEEKEND. IT'S A PICTURESQUE VILLAGE, JUST OUTSIDE JERUSALEM. SHE KNOWS THE WAY...
MSF
HOLD ON... I THINK WE TURN HERE.
ARE YOU SURE THIS IS RIGHT?
YEAH, YEAH, NO WORRIES.
ISN'T THIS MEA SHEARIM?
NO, IT JUST LOOKS SIMILAR...
WE'RE FINE.
I'D SWEAR THIS IS MEA SHEARIM.
NO, TRUST ME, WE'RE SOUTH OF IT.
SO WHERE DID ALL THE CARS GO?
AND LOOK AT THOSE PEOPLE WALKING IN THE STREET...
WHAT DAY IS IT?
SATURDAY!
OH, SHIT!
OK, LET'S CUT THROUGH HERE AND GET OUT.

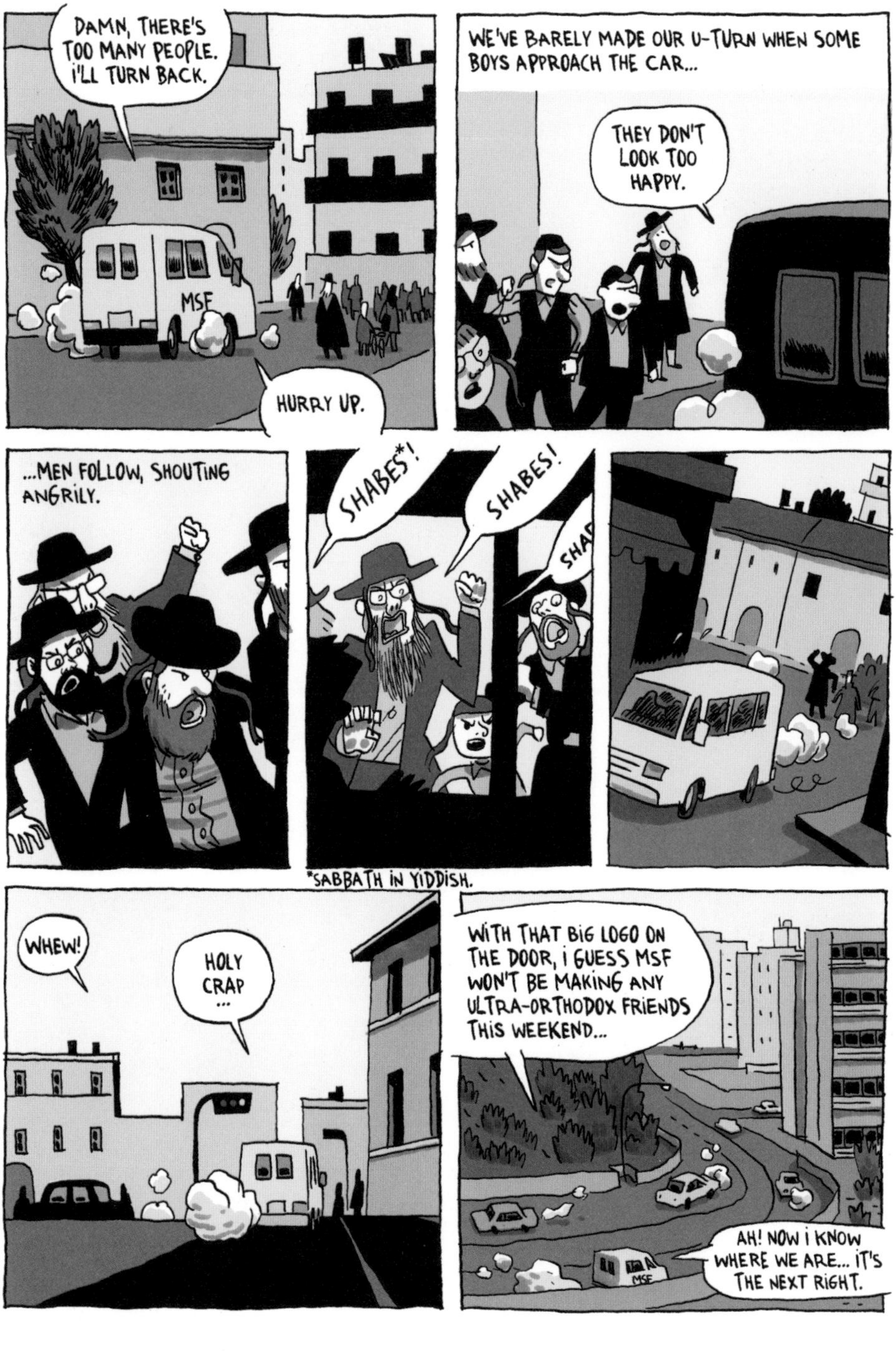
DAMN, THERE'S TOO MANY PEOPLE. I'LL TURN BACK.
MSF
HURRY UP.
WE'VE BARELY MADE OUR U-TURN WHEN SOME BOYS APPROACH THE CAR...
THEY DON'T LOOK TOO HAPPY.
...MEN FOLLOW, SHOUTING ANGRILY.
SHABES*!
SHABES!
*SABBATH IN YIDDISH.
WHEW!
HOLY CRAP ...
WITH THAT BIG LOGO ON THE DOOR, I GUESS MSF WON'T BE MAKING ANY ULTRA-ORTHODOX FRIENDS THIS WEEKEND...
MSF
AH! NOW I KNOW WHERE WE ARE... IT'S THE NEXT RIGHT.

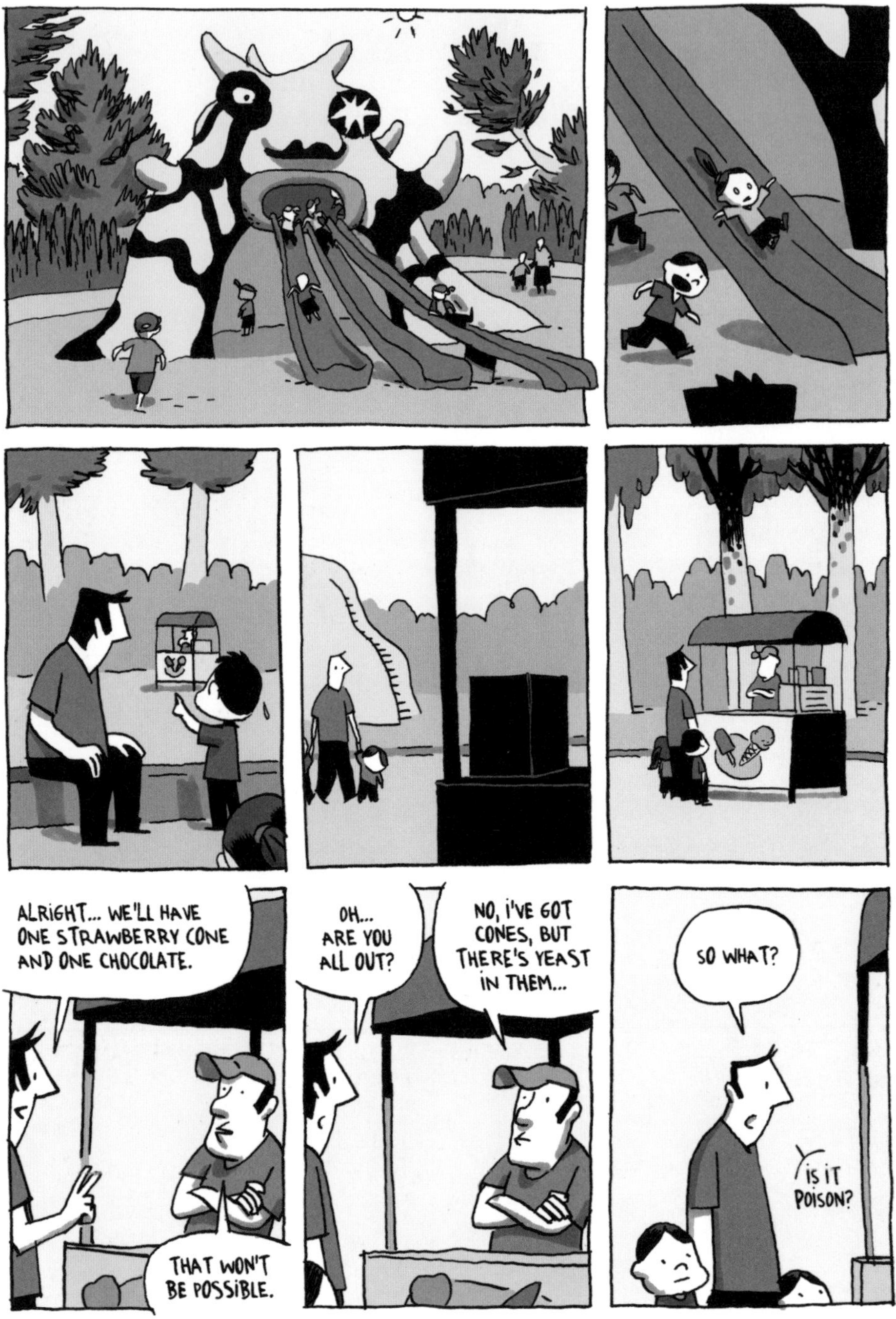
ALRIGHT... WE'LL HAVE ONE STRAWBERRY CONE AND ONE CHOCOLATE.
THAT WON'T BE POSSIBLE.
OH... ARE YOU ALL OUT?
NO, I'VE GOT CONES, BUT THERE'S YEAST IN THEM...
SO WHAT?
IS IT POISON?

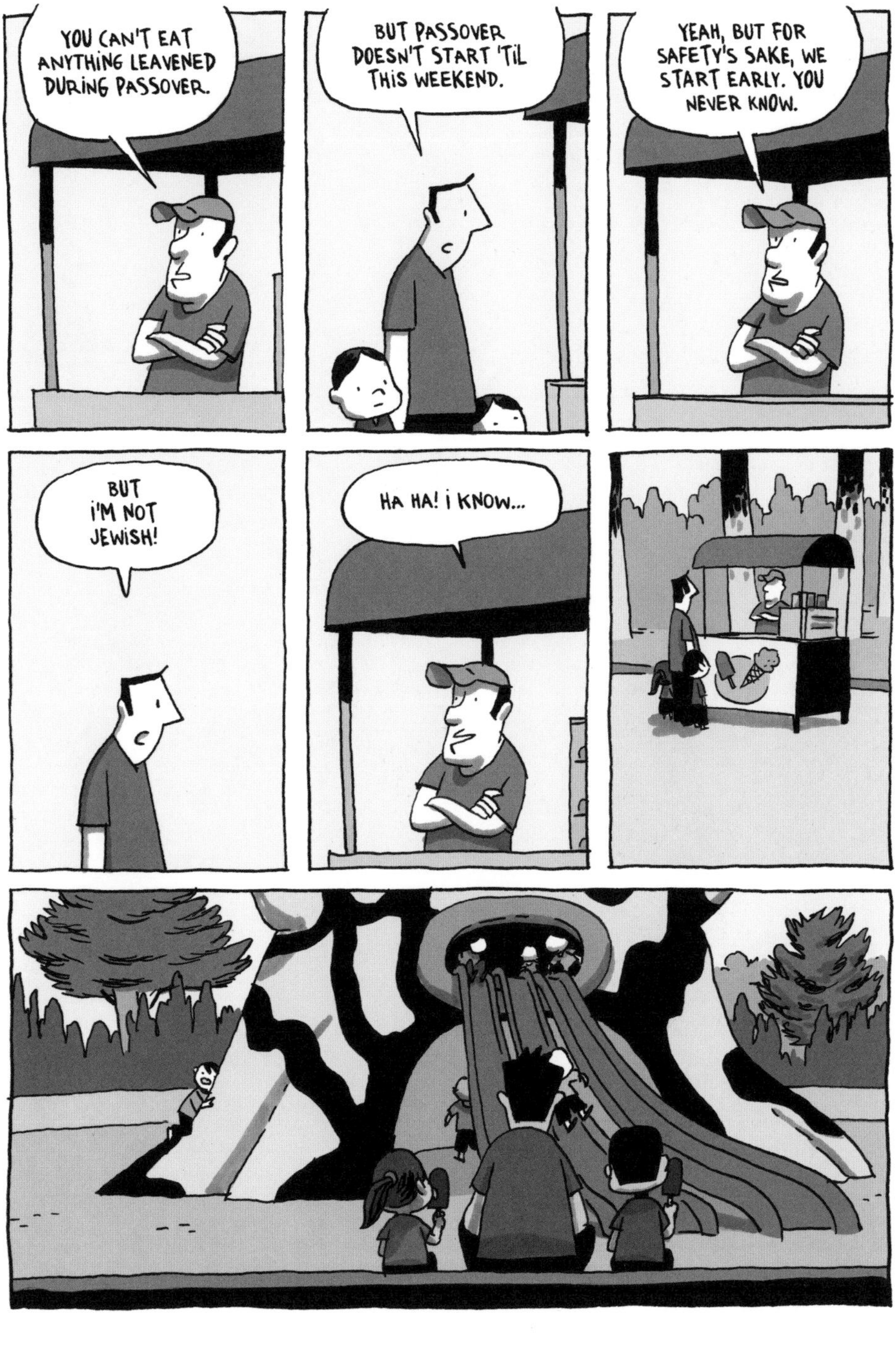
YOU CAN'T EAT ANYTHING LEAVENED DURING PASSOVER.
BUT PASSOVER DOESN'T START 'TIL THIS WEEKEND.
YEAH, BUT FOR SAFETY'S SAKE, WE START EARLY. YOU NEVER KNOW.
BUT I'M NOT JEWISH!
HA HA! I KNOW...

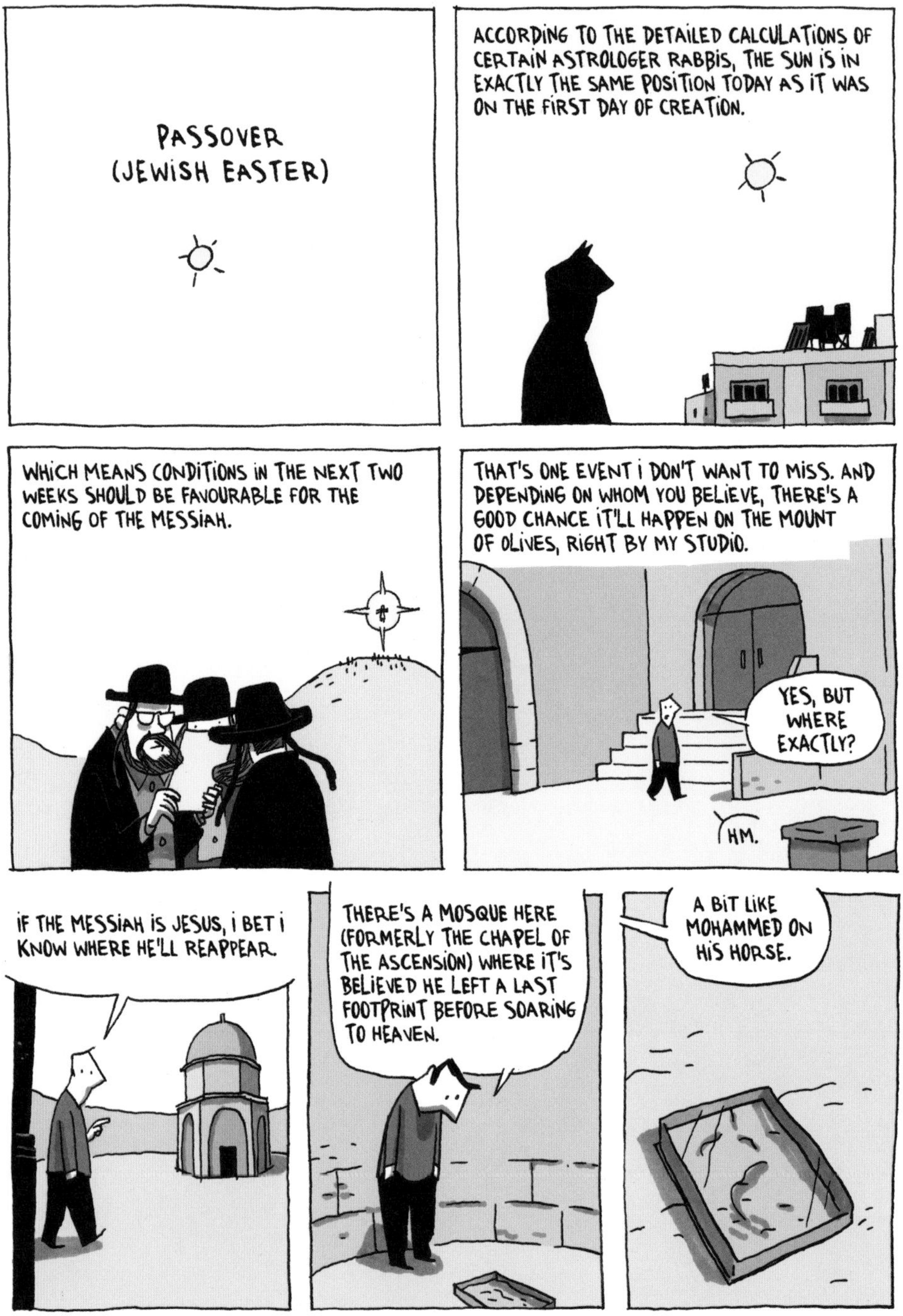
PASSOVER (JEWISH EASTER)
ACCORDING TO THE DETAILED CALCULATIONS OF CERTAIN ASTROLOGER RABBIS, THE SUN IS IN EXACTLY THE SAME POSITION TODAY AS IT WAS ON THE FIRST DAY OF CREATION.
WHICH MEANS CONDITIONS IN THE NEXT TWO WEEKS SHOULD BE FAVOURABLE FOR THE COMING OF THE MESSIAH.
THAT'S ONE EVENT I DON'T WANT TO MISS. AND DEPENDING ON WHOM YOU BELIEVE, THERE'S A GOOD CHANCE IT'LL HAPPEN ON THE MOUNT OF OLIVES, RIGHT BY MY STUDIO.
YES, BUT WHERE EXACTLY?
HM.
IF THE MESSIAH IS JESUS, I BET I KNOW WHERE HE'LL REAPPEAR.
THERE'S A MOSQUE HERE (FORMERLY THE CHAPEL OF THE ASCENSION) WHERE IT'S BELIEVED HE LEFT A LAST FOOTPRINT BEFORE SOARING TO HEAVEN.
A BIT LIKE MOHAMMED ON HIS HORSE.

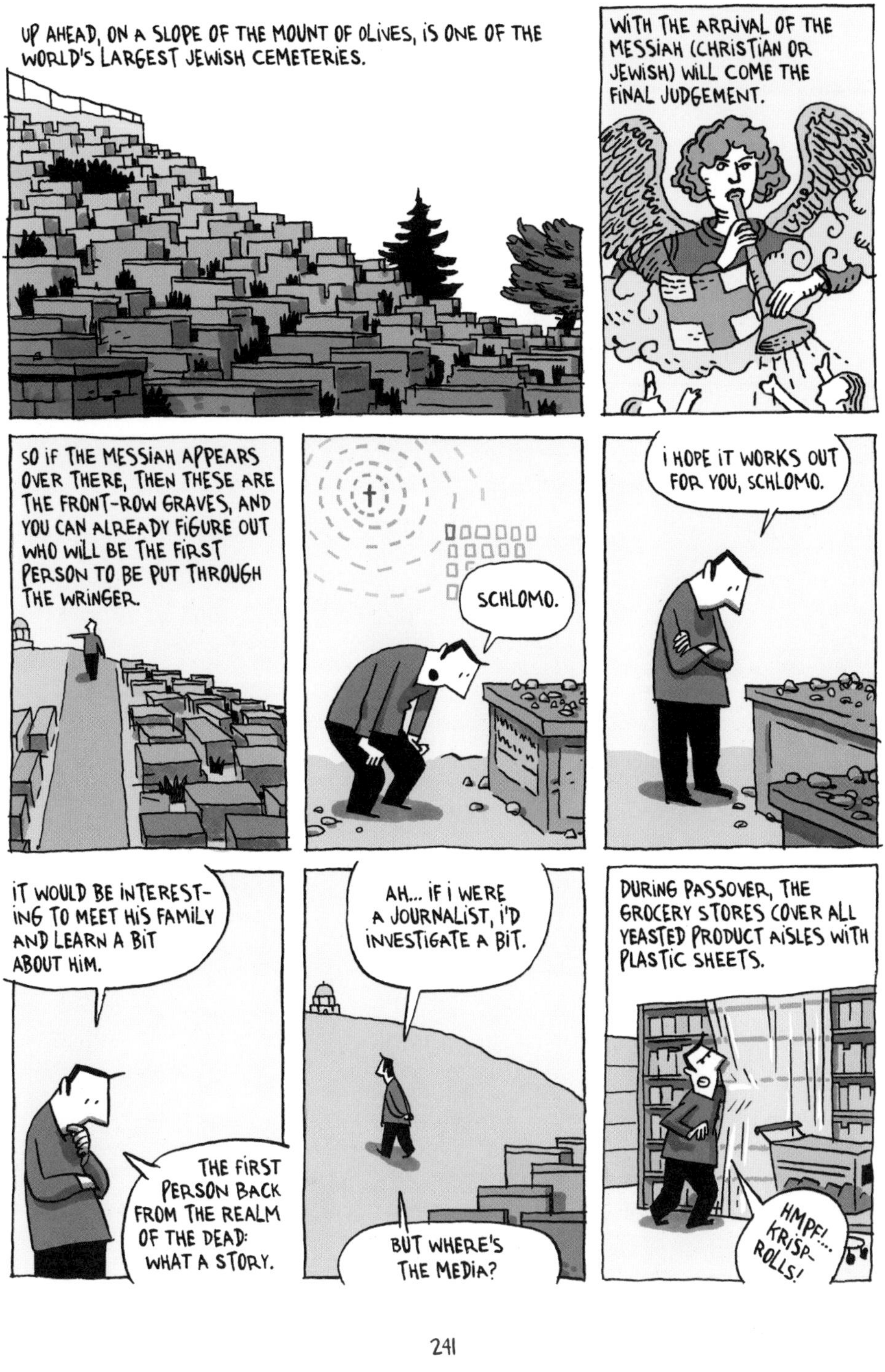
UP AHEAD, ON A SLOPE OF THE MOUNT OF OLIVES, IS ONE OF THE WORLD'S LARGEST JEWISH CEMETERIES.
WITH THE ARRIVAL OF THE MESSIAH (CHRISTIAN OR JEWISH) WILL COME THE FINAL JUDGEMENT.
SO IF THE MESSIAH APPEARS OVER THERE, THEN THESE ARE THE FRONT-ROW GRAVES, AND YOU CAN ALREADY FIGURE OUT WHO WILL BE THE FIRST PERSON TO BE PUT THROUGH THE WRINGER.
SCHLOMO.
I HOPE IT WORKS OUT FOR YOU, SCHLOMO.
IT WOULD BE INTEREST-ING TO MEET HIS FAMILY AND LEARN A BIT ABOUT HIM.
THE FIRST PERSON BACK FROM THE REALM OF THE DEAD: WHAT A STORY.
AH... IF I WERE A JOURNALIST, I'D INVESTIGATE A BIT.
BUT WHERE'S THE MEDIA?
DURING PASSOVER, THE GROCERY STORES COVER ALL YEASTED PRODUCT AISLES WITH PLASTIC SHEETS.
HMPF!... KRISP-ROLLS!

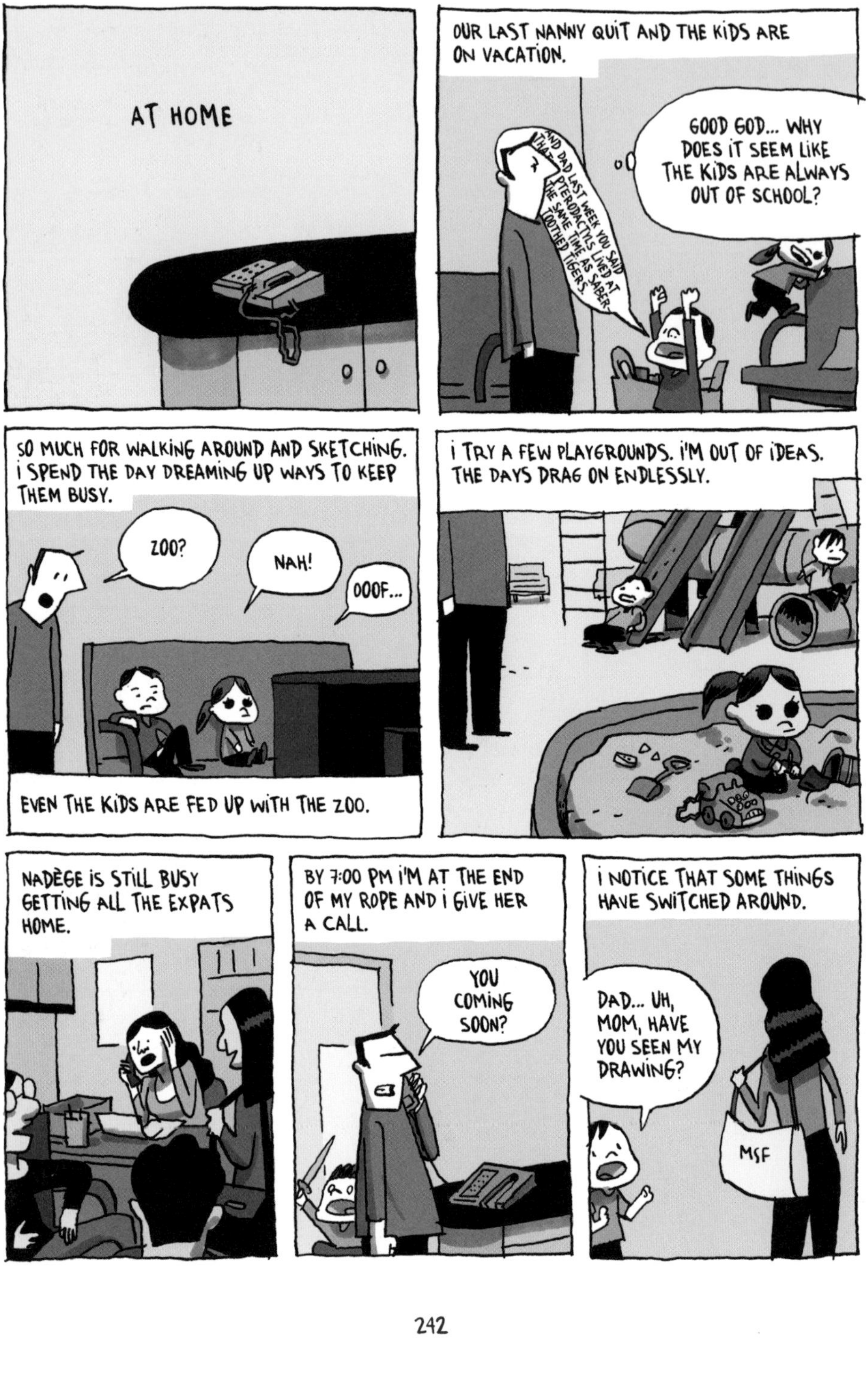
AT HOME
OUR LAST NANNY QUIT AND THE KIDS ARE ON VACATION.
AND DAD LAST WEEK YOU SAID THAT PTERODACTYLS LIVED AT THE SAME TIME AS SABER-TOOTHED TIGERS.
GOOD GOD... WHY DOES IT SEEM LIKE THE KIDS ARE ALWAYS OUT OF SCHOOL?
SO MUCH FOR WALKING AROUND AND SKETCHING. I SPEND THE DAY DREAMING UP WAYS TO KEEP THEM BUSY.
ZOO?
NAH!
OOOF...
EVEN THE KIDS ARE FED UP WITH THE ZOO.
I TRY A FEW PLAYGROUNDS. I'M OUT OF IDEAS. THE DAYS DRAG ON ENDLESSLY.
NADÈGE IS STILL BUSY GETTING ALL THE EXPATS HOME.
BY 7:00 PM I'M AT THE END OF MY ROPE AND I GIVE HER A CALL.
YOU COMING SOON?
I NOTICE THAT SOME THINGS HAVE SWITCHED AROUND.
DAD... UH, MOM, HAVE YOU SEEN MY DRAWING?
MSF

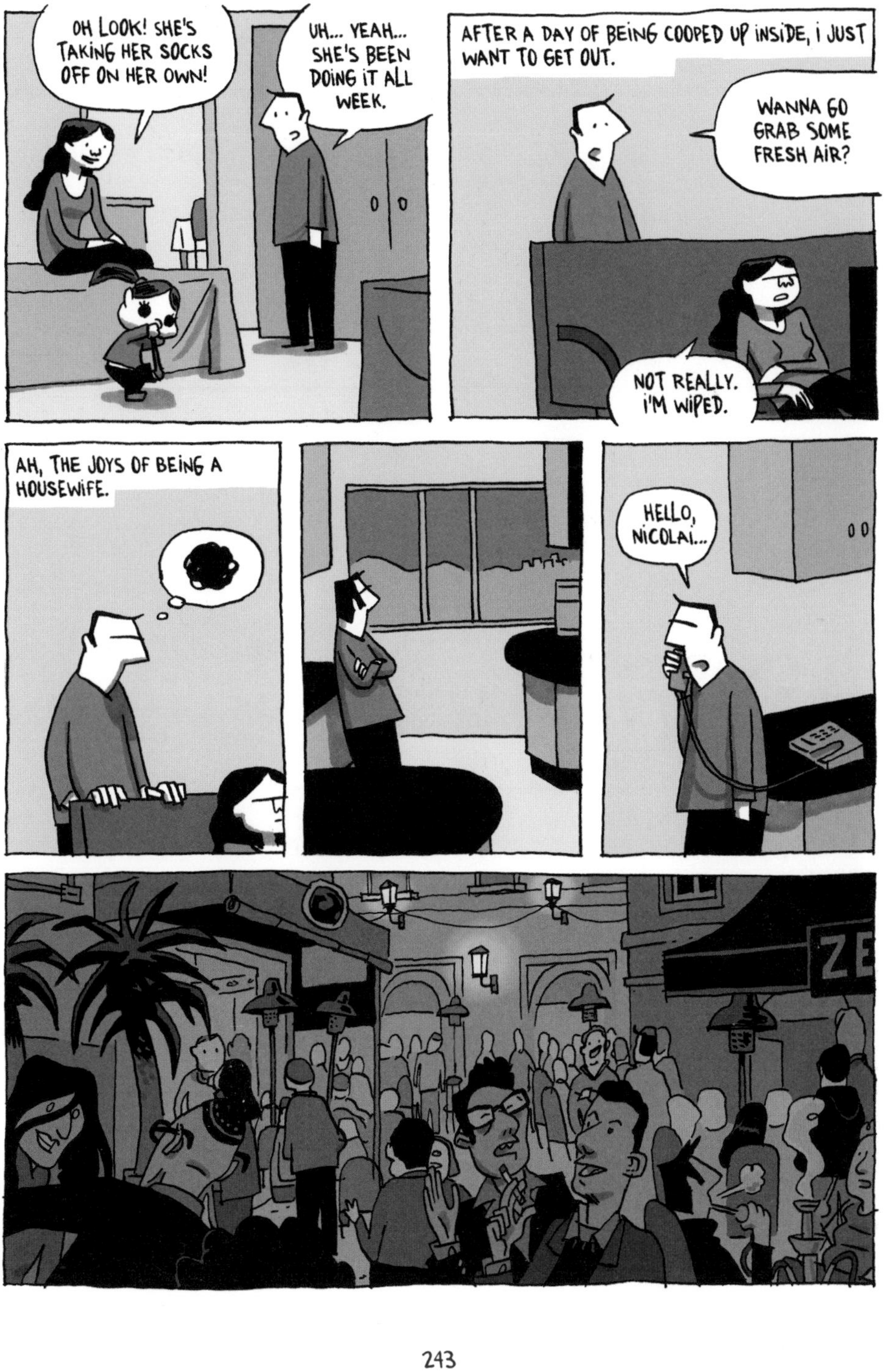
OH LOOK! SHE'S TAKING HER SOCKS OFF ON HER OWN!
UH... YEAH... SHE'S BEEN DOING IT ALL WEEK.
AFTER A DAY OF BEING COOPED UP INSIDE, I JUST WANT TO GET OUT.
WANNA GO GRAB SOME FRESH AIR?
NOT REALLY. I'M WIPED.
AH, THE JOYS OF BEING A HOUSEWIFE.
HELLO, NICOLAI...
ZE

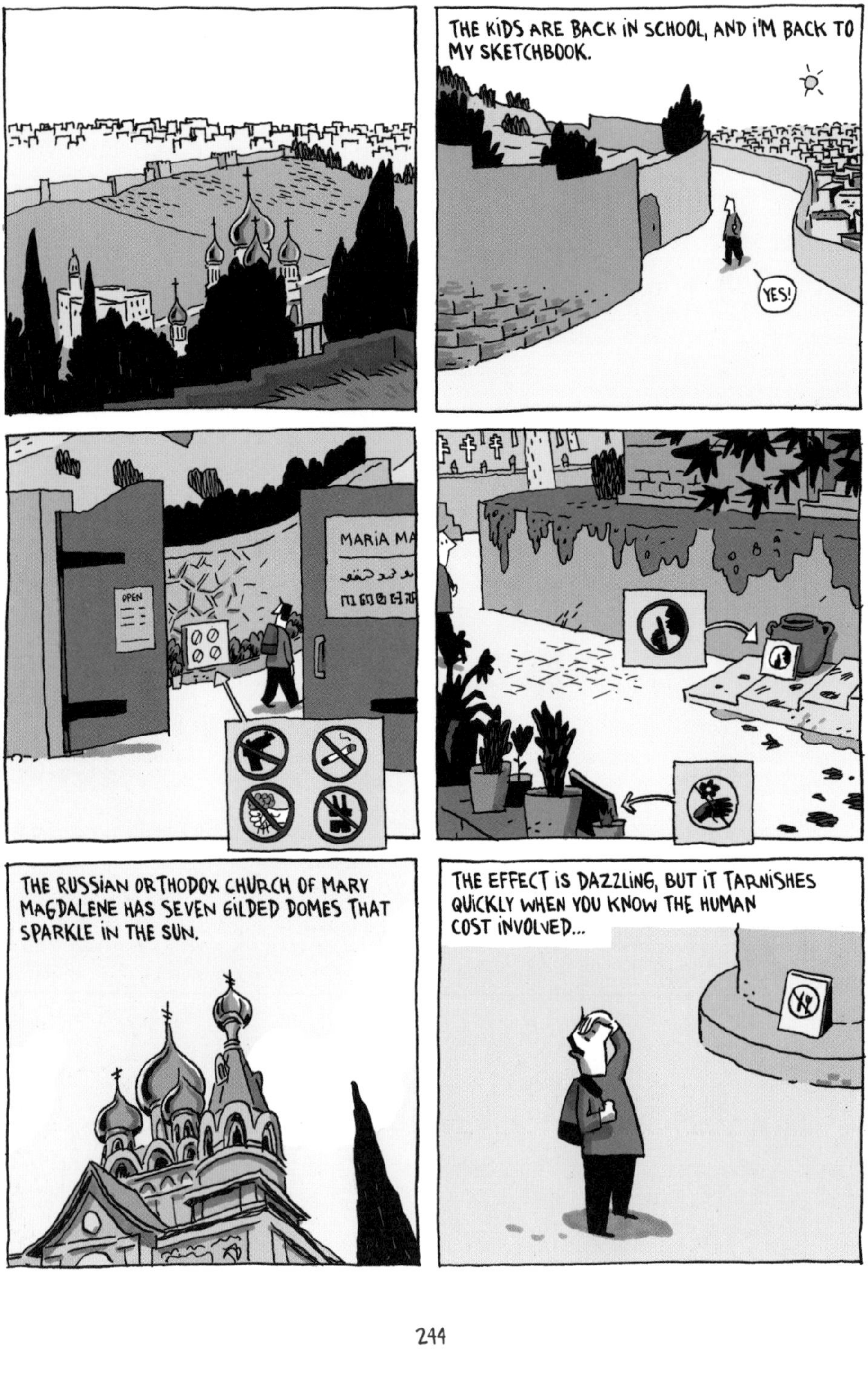
THE KIDS ARE BACK IN SCHOOL, AND I'M BACK TO MY SKETCHBOOK.
YES!
MARIA MA
OPEN
THE RUSSIAN ORTHODOX CHURCH OF MARY MAGDALENE HAS SEVEN GILDED DOMES THAT SPARKLE IN THE SUN.
THE EFFECT IS DAZZLING, BUT IT TARNISHES QUICKLY WHEN YOU KNOW THE HUMAN COST INVOLVED...

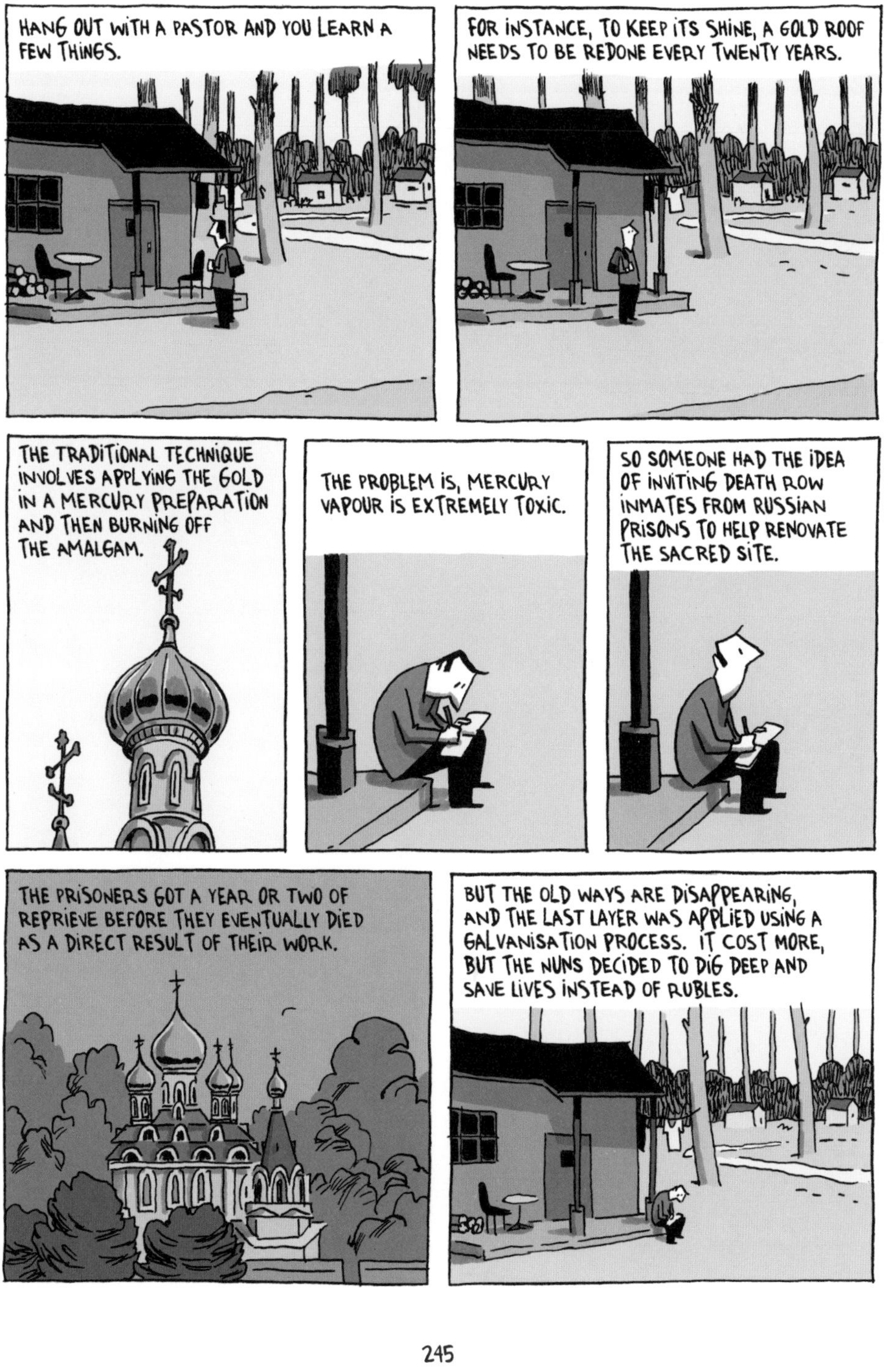
HANG OUT WITH A PASTOR AND YOU LEARN A FEW THINGS.
FOR INSTANCE, TO KEEP ITS SHINE, A GOLD ROOF NEEDS TO BE REDONE EVERY TWENTY YEARS.
THE TRADITIONAL TECHNIQUE INVOLVES APPLYING THE GOLD IN A MERCURY PREPARATION AND THEN BURNING OFF THE AMALGAM.
THE PROBLEM IS, MERCURY VAPOUR IS EXTREMELY TOXIC.
SO SOMEONE HAD THE IDEA OF INVITING DEATH ROW INMATES FROM RUSSIAN PRISONS TO HELP RENOVATE THE SACRED SITE.
THE PRISONERS GOT A YEAR OR TWO OF REPRIEVE BEFORE THEY EVENTUALLY DIED AS A DIRECT RESULT OF THEIR WORK.
BUT THE OLD WAYS ARE DISAPPEARING, AND THE LAST LAYER WAS APPLIED USING A GALVANISATION PROCESS. IT COST MORE, BUT THE NUNS DECIDED TO DIG DEEP AND SAVE LIVES INSTEAD OF RUBLES.

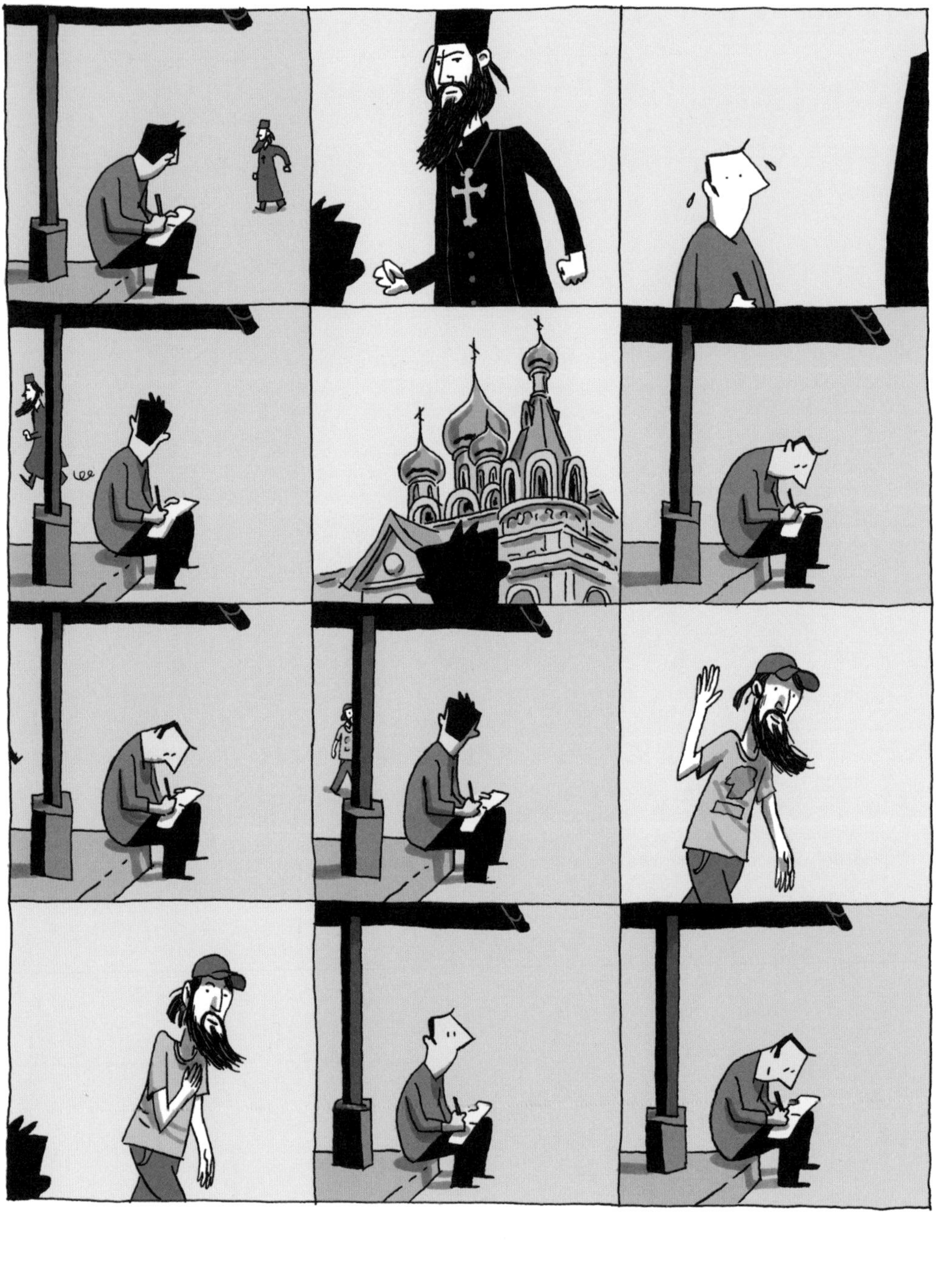

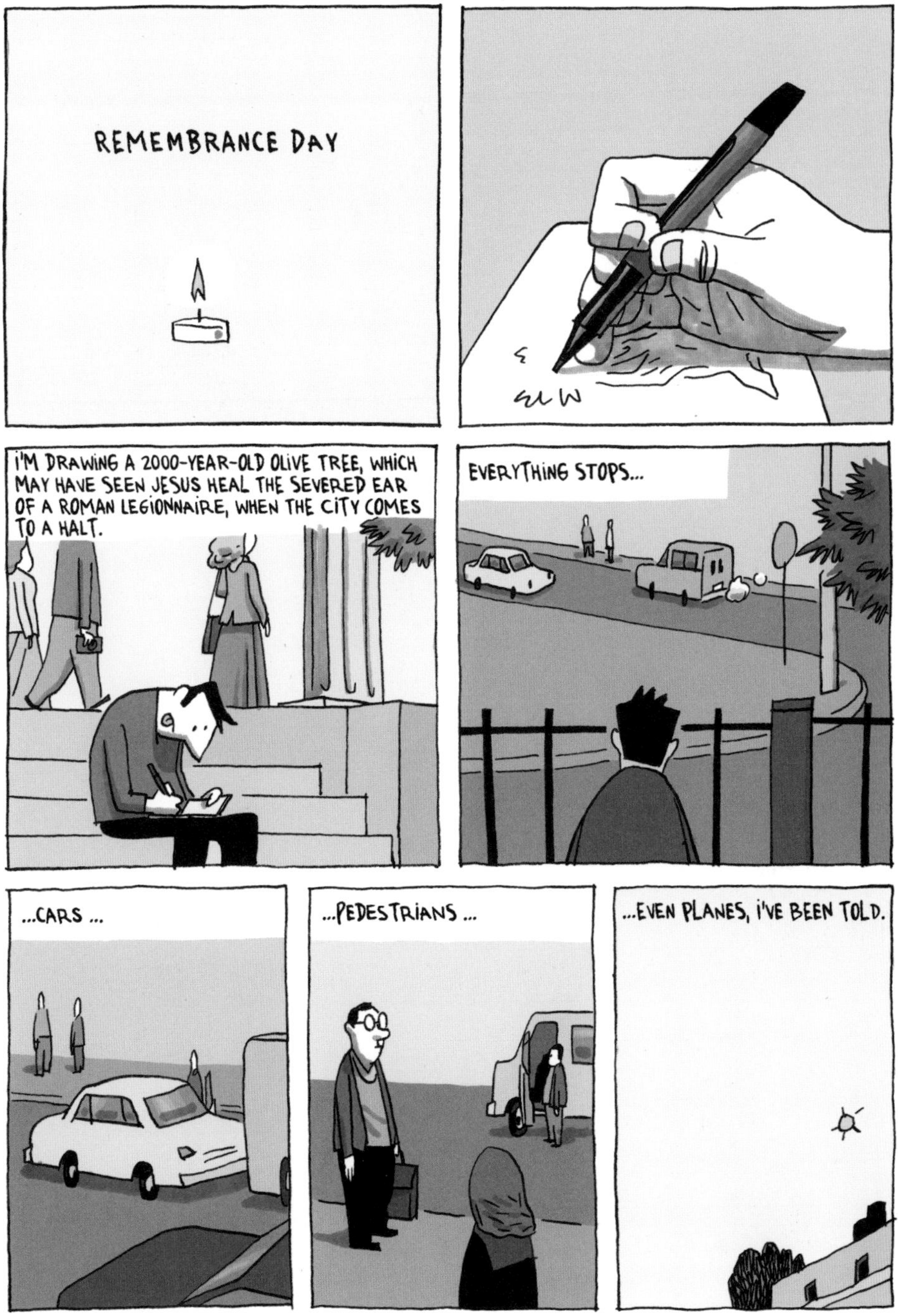
REMEMBRANCE DAY
I'M DRAWING A 2000-YEAR-OLD OLIVE TREE, WHICH MAY HAVE SEEN JESUS HEAL THE SEVERED EAR OF A ROMAN LEGIONNAIRE, WHEN THE CITY COMES TO A HALT.
EVERYTHING STOPS...
...CARS ...
...PEDESTRIANS ...
...EVEN PLANES, I'VE BEEN TOLD.

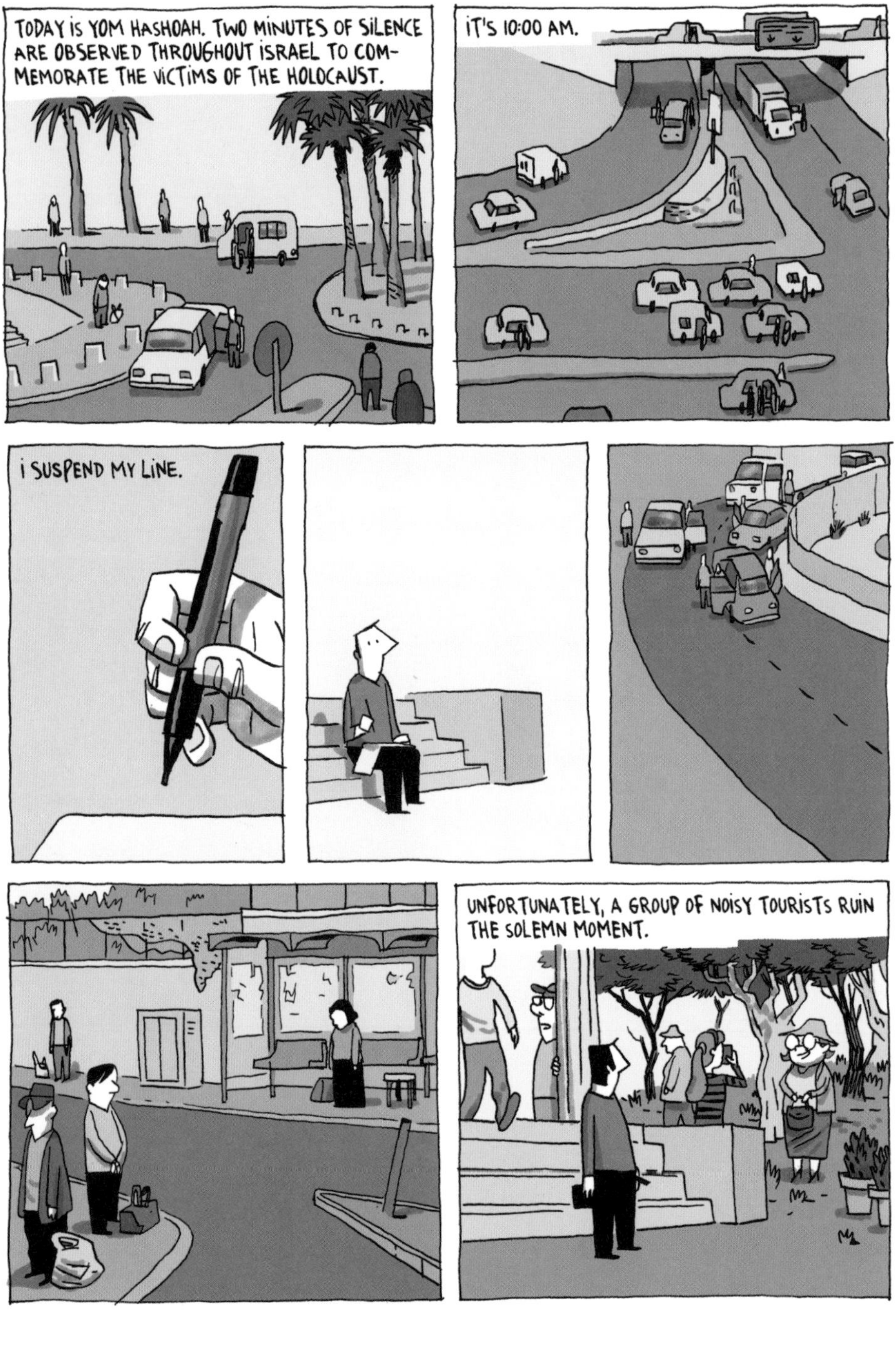
TODAY IS YOM HASHOAH. TWO MINUTES OF SILENCE ARE OBSERVED THROUGHOUT ISRAEL TO COMMEMORATE THE VICTIMS OF THE HOLOCAUST.
IT'S 10:00 AM.
I SUSPEND MY LINE.
UNFORTUNATELY, A GROUP OF NOISY TOURISTS RUIN THE SOLEMN MOMENT.

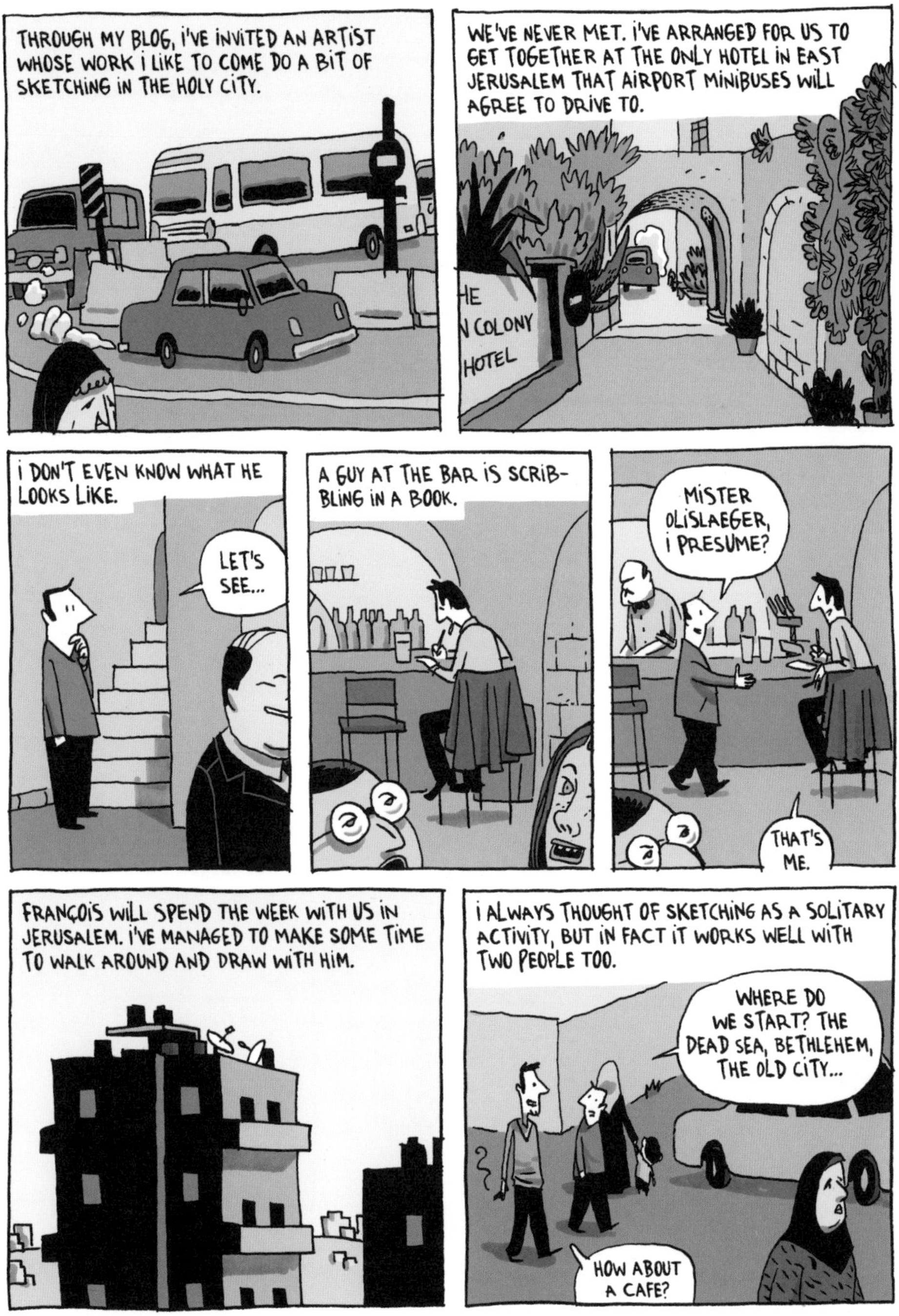
THROUGH MY BLOG, I'VE INVITED AN ARTIST WHOSE WORK I LIKE TO COME DO A BIT OF SKETCHING IN THE HOLY CITY.
WE'VE NEVER MET. I'VE ARRANGED FOR US TO GET TOGETHER AT THE ONLY HOTEL IN EAST JERUSALEM THAT AIRPORT MINIBUSES WILL AGREE TO DRIVE TO.
HE
N COLONY
HOTEL
I DON'T EVEN KNOW WHAT HE LOOKS LIKE.
LET'S SEE...
A GUY AT THE BAR IS SCRIBBLING IN A BOOK.
MISTER OLISLAEGER, I PRESUME?
THAT'S ME.
FRANÇOIS WILL SPEND THE WEEK WITH US IN JERUSALEM. I'VE MANAGED TO MAKE SOME TIME TO WALK AROUND AND DRAW WITH HIM.
I ALWAYS THOUGHT OF SKETCHING AS A SOLITARY ACTIVITY, BUT IN FACT IT WORKS WELL WITH TWO PEOPLE TOO.
WHERE DO WE START? THE DEAD SEA, BETHLEHEM, THE OLD CITY...
HOW ABOUT A CAFE?

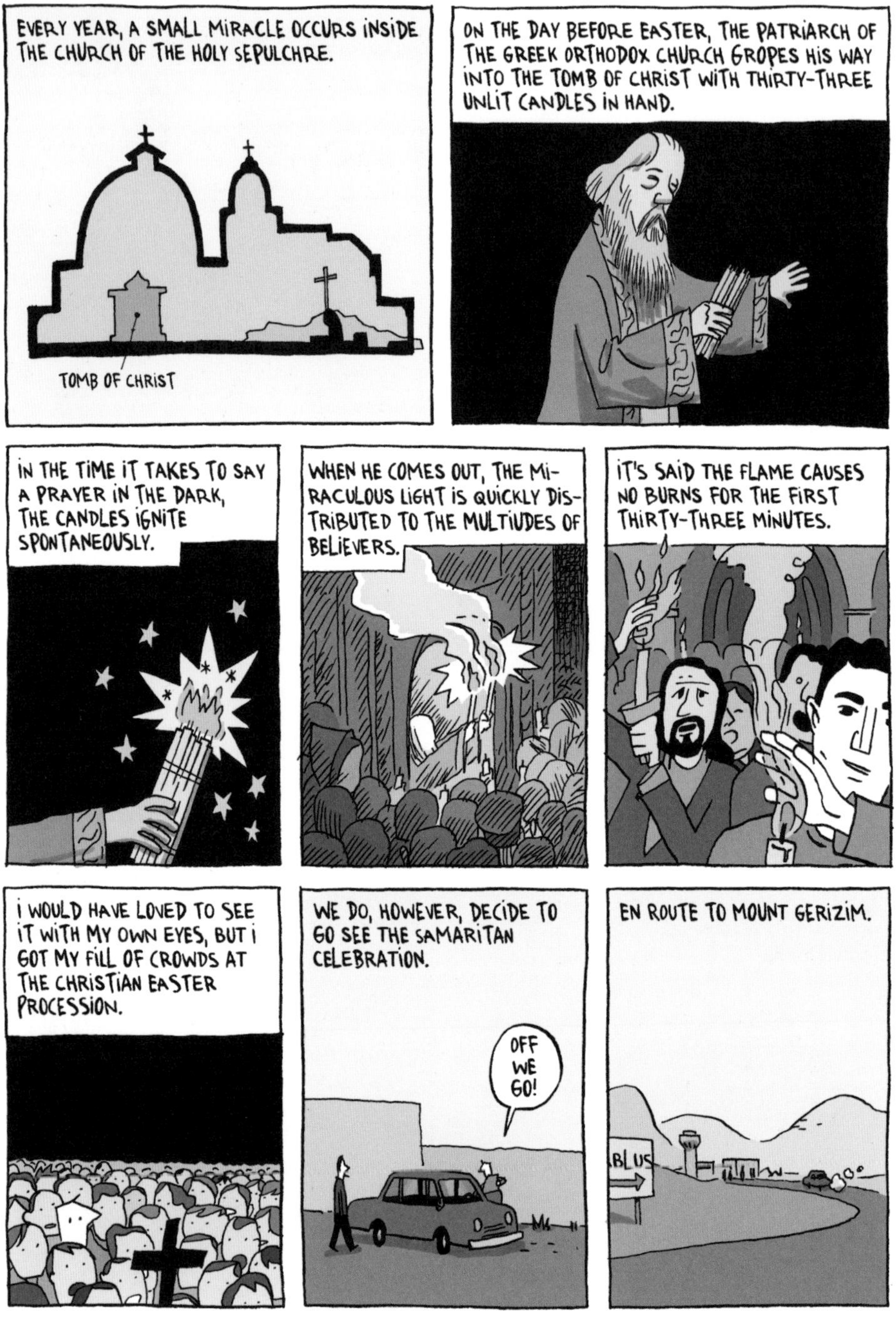

EVERY YEAR, A SMALL MIRACLE OCCURS INSIDE THE CHURCH OF THE HOLY SEPULCHRE.
TOMB OF CHRIST
ON THE DAY BEFORE EASTER, THE PATRIARCH OF THE GREEK ORTHODOX CHURCH GROPES HIS WAY INTO THE TOMB OF CHRIST WITH THIRTY-THREE UNLIT CANDLES IN HAND.
IN THE TIME IT TAKES TO SAY A PRAYER IN THE DARK, THE CANDLES IGNITE SPONTANEOUSLY.
WHEN HE COMES OUT, THE MIRACULOUS LIGHT IS QUICKLY DISTRIBUTED TO THE MULTIUDES OF BELIEVERS.
IT'S SAID THE FLAME CAUSES NO BURNS FOR THE FIRST THIRTY-THREE MINUTES.
I WOULD HAVE LOVED TO SEE IT WITH MY OWN EYES, BUT I GOT MY FILL OF CROWDS AT THE CHRISTIAN EASTER PROCESSION.
WE DO, HOWEVER, DECIDE TO GO SEE THE SAMARITAN CELEBRATION.
OFF WE GO!
EN ROUTE TO MOUNT GERIZIM.

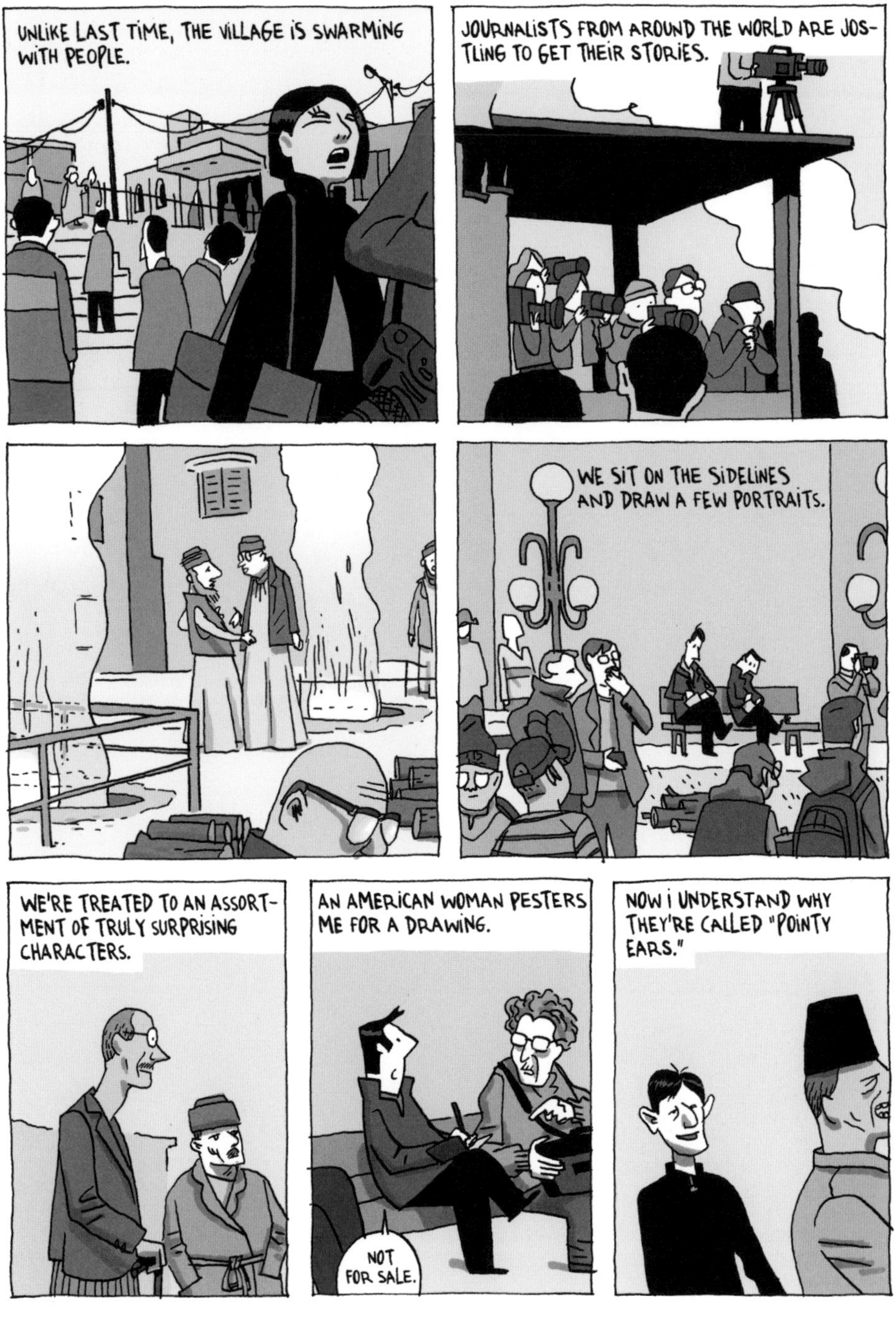
UNLIKE LAST TIME, THE VILLAGE IS SWARMING WITH PEOPLE.
JOURNALISTS FROM AROUND THE WORLD ARE JOSTLING TO GET THEIR STORIES.
WE SIT ON THE SIDELINES AND DRAW A FEW PORTRAITS.
WE'RE TREATED TO AN ASSORTMENT OF TRULY SURPRISING CHARACTERS.
AN AMERICAN WOMAN PESTERS ME FOR A DRAWING.
NOT FOR SALE.
NOW I UNDERSTAND WHY THEY'RE CALLED "POINTY EARS."

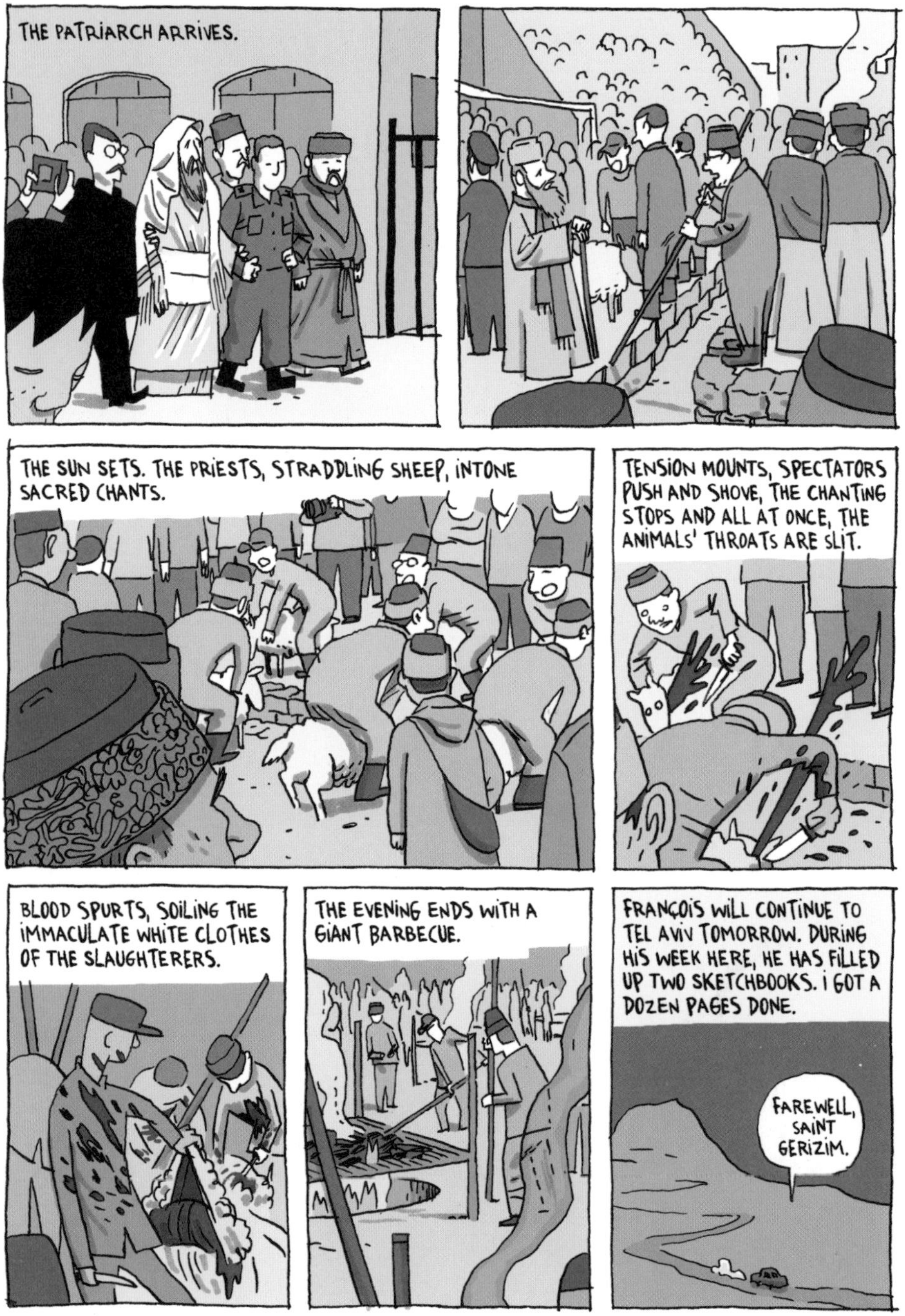
THE PATRIARCH ARRIVES.
THE SUN SETS. THE PRIESTS, STRADDLING SHEEP, INTONE SACRED CHANTS.
TENSION MOUNTS, SPECTATORS PUSH AND SHOVE, THE CHANTING STOPS AND ALL AT ONCE, THE ANIMALS' THROATS ARE SLIT.
BLOOD SPURTS, SOILING THE IMMACULATE WHITE CLOTHES OF THE SLAUGHTERERS.
THE EVENING ENDS WITH A GIANT BARBECUE.
FRANÇOIS WILL CONTINUE TO TEL AVIV TOMORROW. DURING HIS WEEK HERE, HE HAS FILLED UP TWO SKETCHBOOKS. I GOT A DOZEN PAGES DONE.
FAREWELL, SAINT GERIZIM.

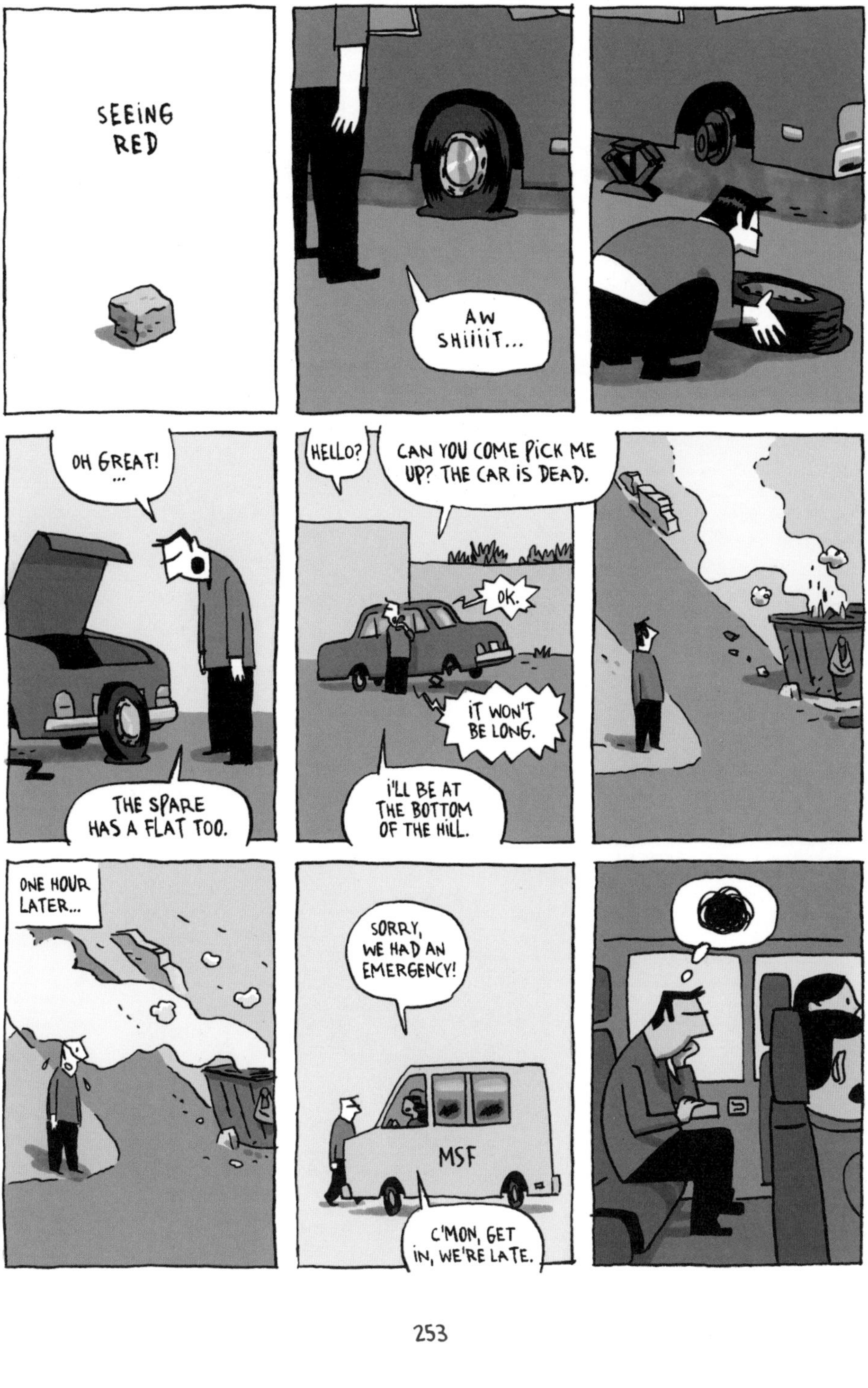
SEEING RED
AW SHIIIIT...
OH GREAT! ...
THE SPARE HAS A FLAT TOO.
HELLO?
CAN YOU COME PICK ME UP? THE CAR IS DEAD.
OK.
IT WON'T BE LONG.
I'LL BE AT THE BOTTOM OF THE HILL.
ONE HOUR LATER...
SORRY, WE HAD AN EMERGENCY!
MSF
C'MON, GET IN, WE'RE LATE.

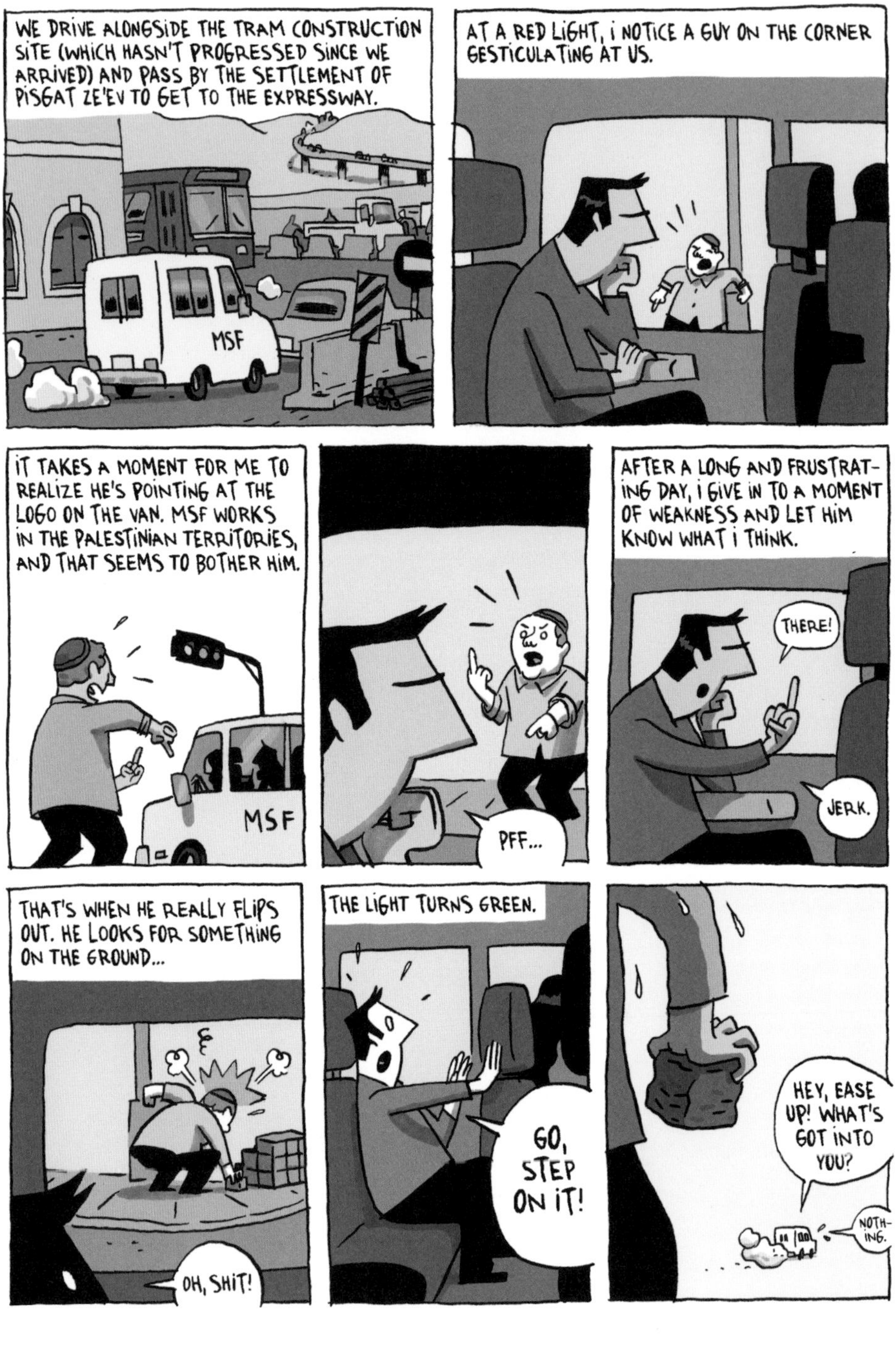
WE DRIVE ALONGSIDE THE TRAM CONSTRUCTION SITE (WHICH HASN'T PROGRESSED SINCE WE ARRIVED) AND PASS BY THE SETTLEMENT OF PISGAT ZE'EV TO GET TO THE EXPRESSWAY.
MSF
AT A RED LIGHT, I NOTICE A GUY ON THE CORNER GESTICULATING AT US.
IT TAKES A MOMENT FOR ME TO REALIZE HE'S POINTING AT THE LOGO ON THE VAN. MSF WORKS IN THE PALESTINIAN TERRITORIES, AND THAT SEEMS TO BOTHER HIM.
MSF
PFF...
AFTER A LONG AND FRUSTRATING DAY, I GIVE IN TO A MOMENT OF WEAKNESS AND LET HIM KNOW WHAT I THINK.
THERE!
JERK.
THAT'S WHEN HE REALLY FLIPS OUT. HE LOOKS FOR SOMETHING ON THE GROUND...
OH, SHIT!
THE LIGHT TURNS GREEN.
GO, STEP ON IT!
HEY, EASE UP! WHAT'S GOT INTO YOU?
NOTHING.

MAY

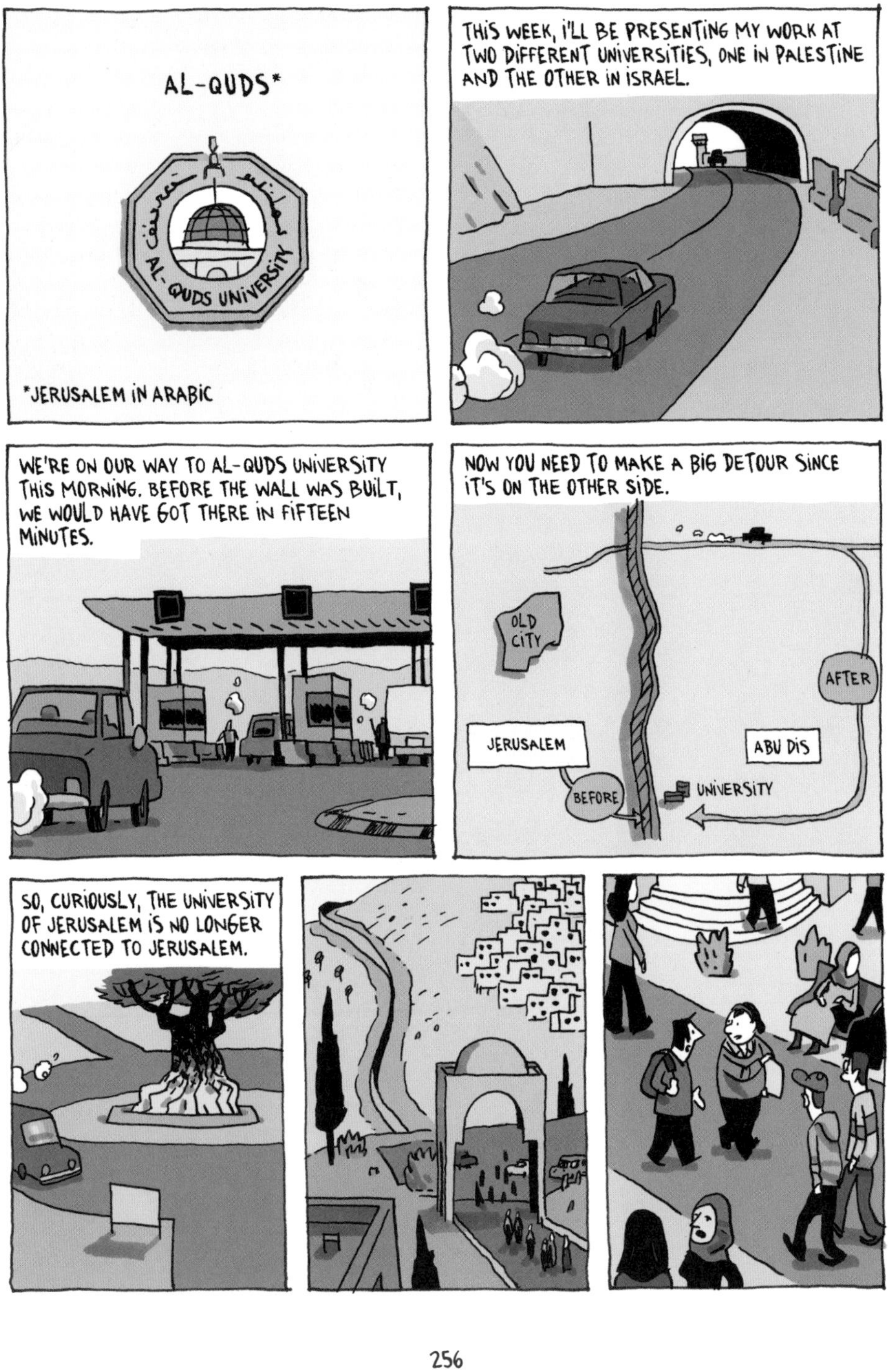
AL-QUDS*
AL-QUDS UNIVERSITY
*JERUSALEM IN ARABIC
THIS WEEK, I'LL BE PRESENTING MY WORK AT TWO DIFFERENT UNIVERSITIES, ONE IN PALESTINE AND THE OTHER IN ISRAEL.
WE'RE ON OUR WAY TO AL-QUDS UNIVERSITY THIS MORNING. BEFORE THE WALL WAS BUILT, WE WOULD HAVE GOT THERE IN FIFTEEN MINUTES.
NOW YOU NEED TO MAKE A BIG DETOUR SINCE IT'S ON THE OTHER SIDE.
OLD CITY
AFTER
JERUSALEM
ABU DIS
BEFORE
UNIVERSITY
SO, CURIOUSLY, THE UNIVERSITY OF JERUSALEM IS NO LONGER CONNECTED TO JERUSALEM.

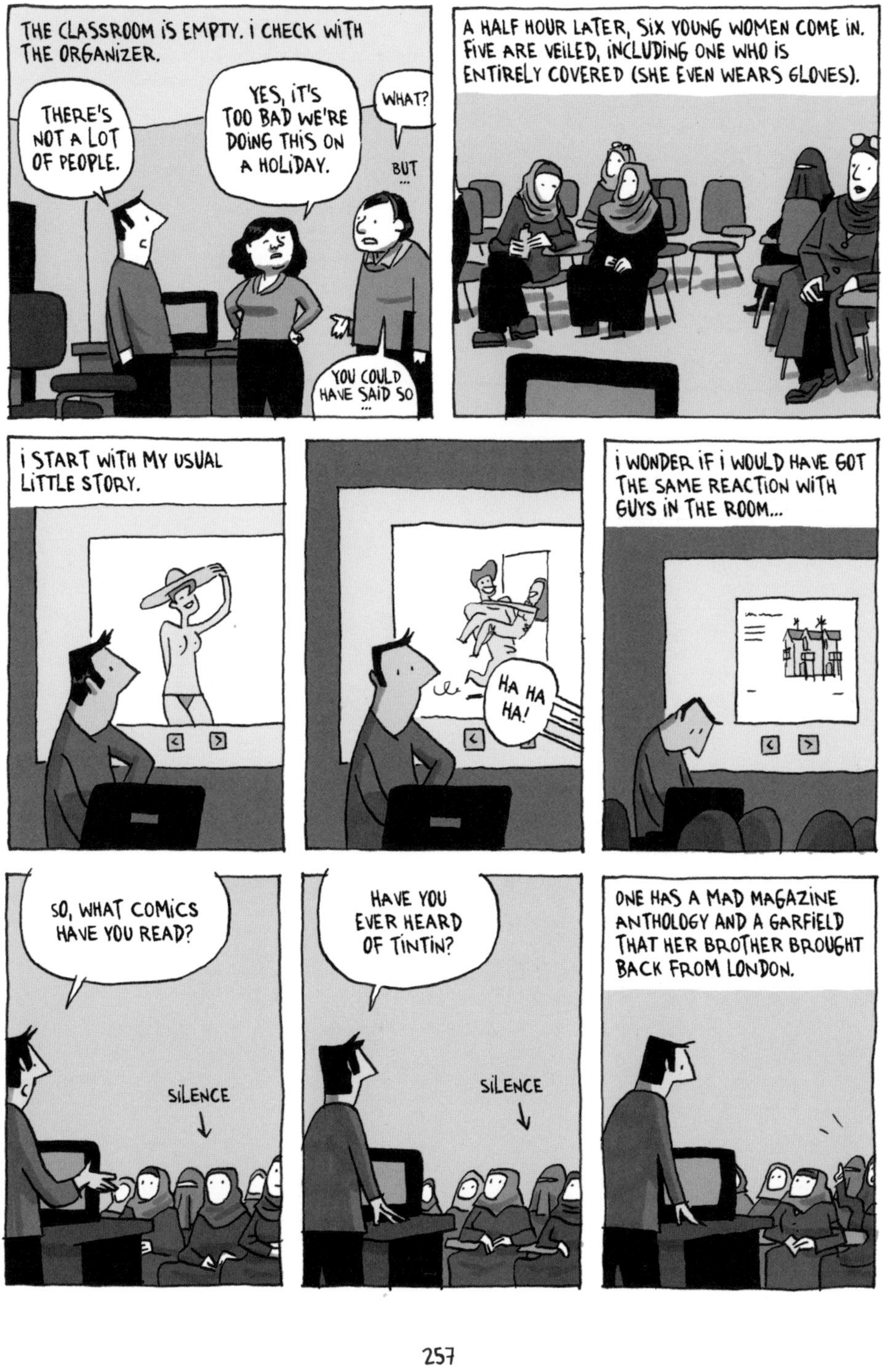
THE CLASSROOM IS EMPTY. I CHECK WITH THE ORGANIZER.
THERE'S NOT A LOT OF PEOPLE.
YES, IT'S TOO BAD WE'RE DOING THIS ON A HOLIDAY.
WHAT?
BUT ...
YOU COULD HAVE SAID SO ...
A HALF HOUR LATER, SIX YOUNG WOMEN COME IN. FIVE ARE VEILED, INCLUDING ONE WHO IS ENTIRELY COVERED (SHE EVEN WEARS GLOVES).
I START WITH MY USUAL LITTLE STORY.
HA HA HA!
I WONDER IF I WOULD HAVE GOT THE SAME REACTION WITH GUYS IN THE ROOM...
SO, WHAT COMICS HAVE YOU READ?
SILENCE
HAVE YOU EVER HEARD OF TINTIN?
SILENCE
ONE HAS A MAD MAGAZINE ANTHOLOGY AND A GARFIELD THAT HER BROTHER BROUGHT BACK FROM LONDON.

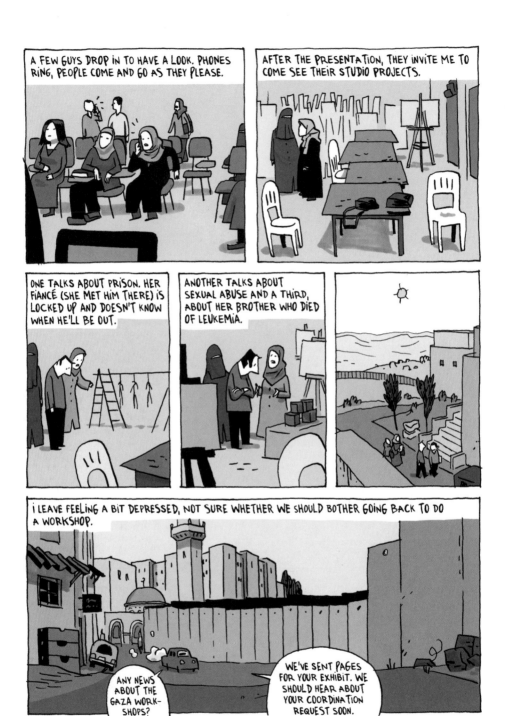

A FEW GUYS DROP IN TO HAVE A LOOK. PHONES RING, PEOPLE COME AND GO AS THEY PLEASE.

AFTER THE PRESENTATION, THEY INVITE ME TO COME SEE THEIR STUDIO PROJECTS.

ONE TALKS ABOUT PRISON. HER FIANCÉ (SHE MET HIM THERE) IS LOCKED UP AND DOESN'T KNOW WHEN HE'LL BE OUT.

ANOTHER TALKS ABOUT SEXUAL ABUSE AND A THIRD, ABOUT HER BROTHER WHO DIED OF LEUKEMIA.

I LEAVE FEELING A BIT DEPRESSED, NOT SURE WHETHER WE SHOULD BOTHER GOING BACK TO DO A WORKSHOP.

ANY NEWS ABOUT THE GAZA WORKSHOPS?

WE'VE SENT PAGES FOR YOUR EXHIBIT. WE SHOULD HEAR ABOUT YOUR COORDINATION REQUEST SOON.

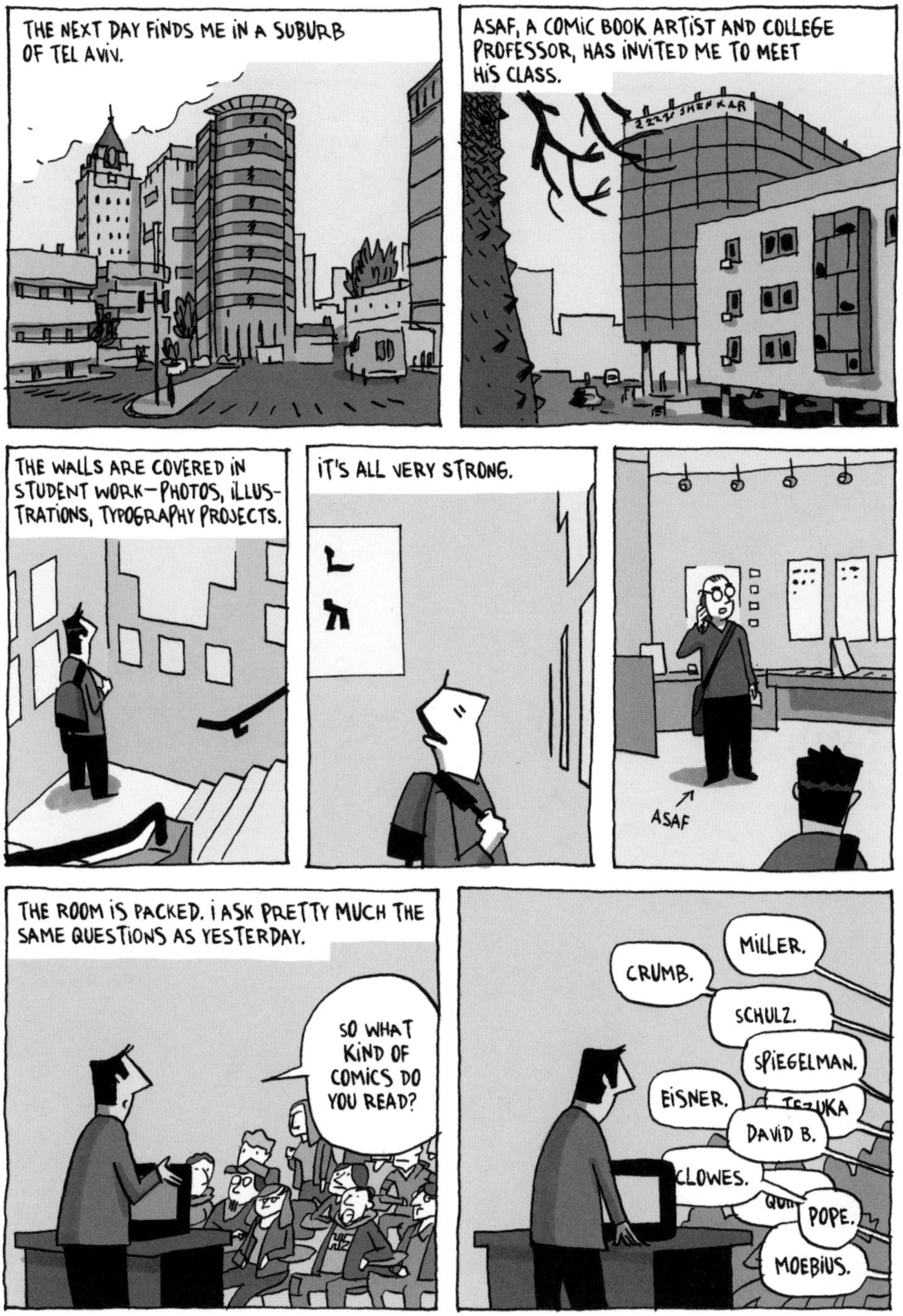
THE NEXT DAY FINDS ME IN A SUBURB OF TEL AVIV.
ASAF, A COMIC BOOK ARTIST AND COLLEGE PROFESSOR, HAS INVITED ME TO MEET HIS CLASS.
SHENKAR
THE WALLS ARE COVERED IN STUDENT WORK—PHOTOS, ILLUSTRATIONS, TYPOGRAPHY PROJECTS.
IT'S ALL VERY STRONG.
ASAF
THE ROOM IS PACKED. I ASK PRETTY MUCH THE SAME QUESTIONS AS YESTERDAY.
SO WHAT KIND OF COMICS DO YOU READ?
CRUMB.
MILLER.
SCHULZ.
SPIEGELMAN.
EISNER.
DAVID B.
CLOWES.
POPE.
MOEBIUS.

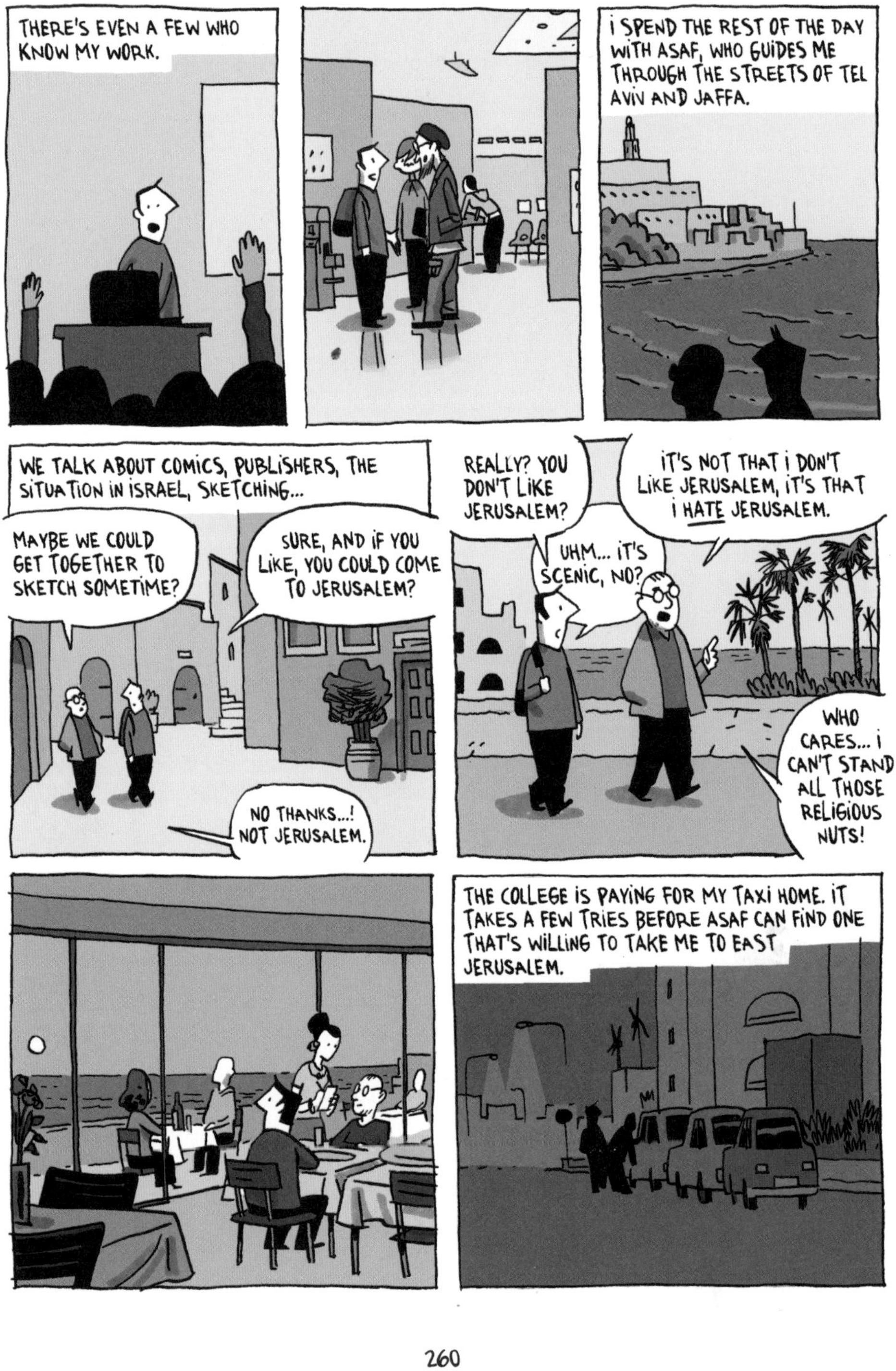

THERE'S EVEN A FEW WHO KNOW MY WORK.
I SPEND THE REST OF THE DAY WITH ASAF, WHO GUIDES ME THROUGH THE STREETS OF TEL AVIV AND JAFFA.
WE TALK ABOUT COMICS, PUBLISHERS, THE SITUATION IN ISRAEL, SKETCHING...
MAYBE WE COULD GET TOGETHER TO SKETCH SOMETIME?
SURE, AND IF YOU LIKE, YOU COULD COME TO JERUSALEM?
NO THANKS...! NOT JERUSALEM.
REALLY? YOU DON'T LIKE JERUSALEM?
IT'S NOT THAT I DON'T LIKE JERUSALEM, IT'S THAT I HATE JERUSALEM.
UHM... IT'S SCENIC, NO?
WHO CARES... I CAN'T STAND ALL THOSE RELIGIOUS NUTS!
THE COLLEGE IS PAYING FOR MY TAXI HOME. IT TAKES A FEW TRIES BEFORE ASAF CAN FIND ONE THAT'S WILLING TO TAKE ME TO EAST JERUSALEM.

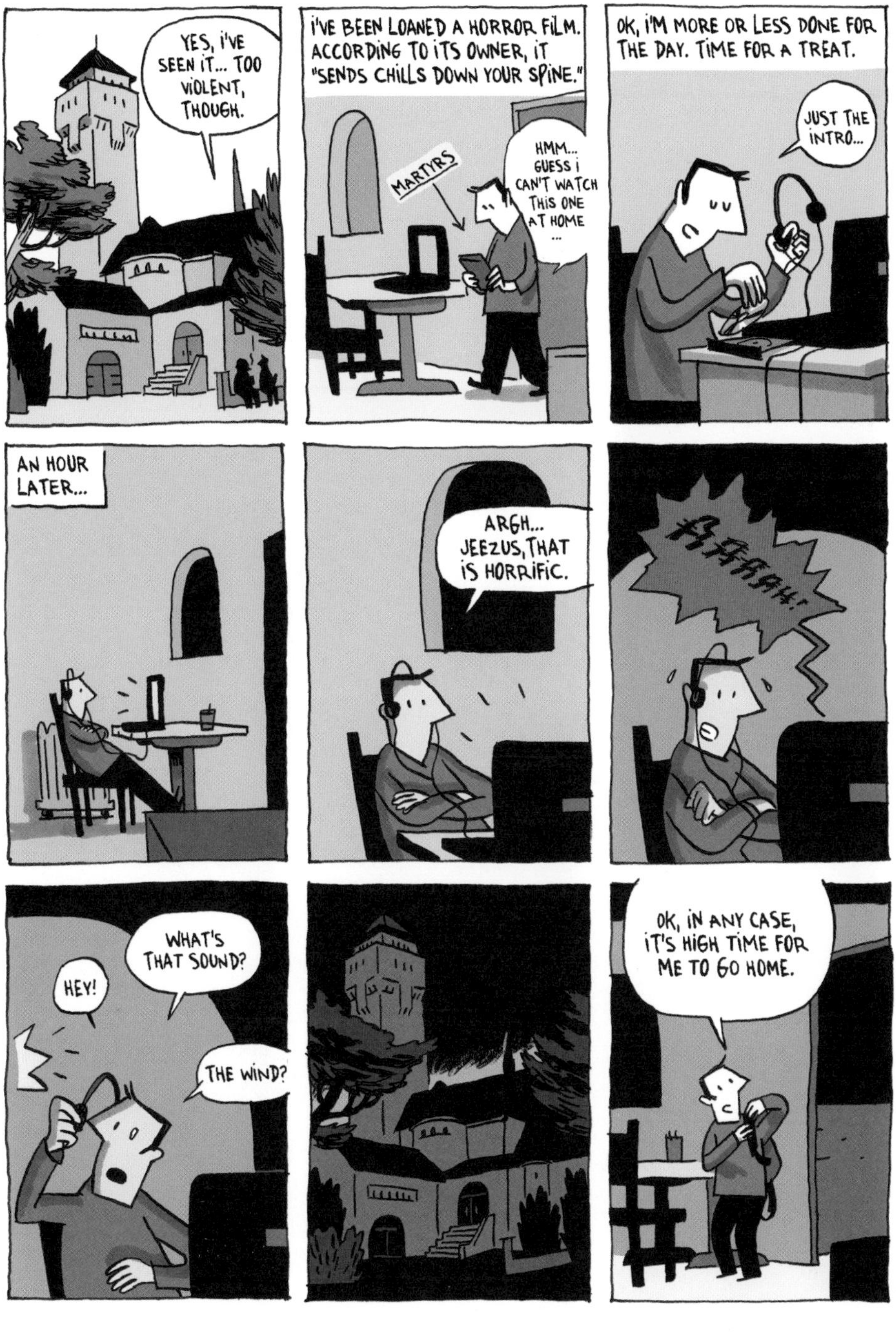
YES, I'VE SEEN IT... TOO VIOLENT, THOUGH.
I'VE BEEN LOANED A HORROR FILM. ACCORDING TO ITS OWNER, IT "SENDS CHILLS DOWN YOUR SPINE."
MARTYRS
HMM... GUESS I CAN'T WATCH THIS ONE AT HOME ...
OK, I'M MORE OR LESS DONE FOR THE DAY. TIME FOR A TREAT.
JUST THE INTRO...
AN HOUR LATER...
ARGH... JEEZUS, THAT IS HORRIFIC.
AAAAAH!
WHAT'S THAT SOUND?
HEY!
THE WIND?
OK, IN ANY CASE, IT'S HIGH TIME FOR ME TO GO HOME.

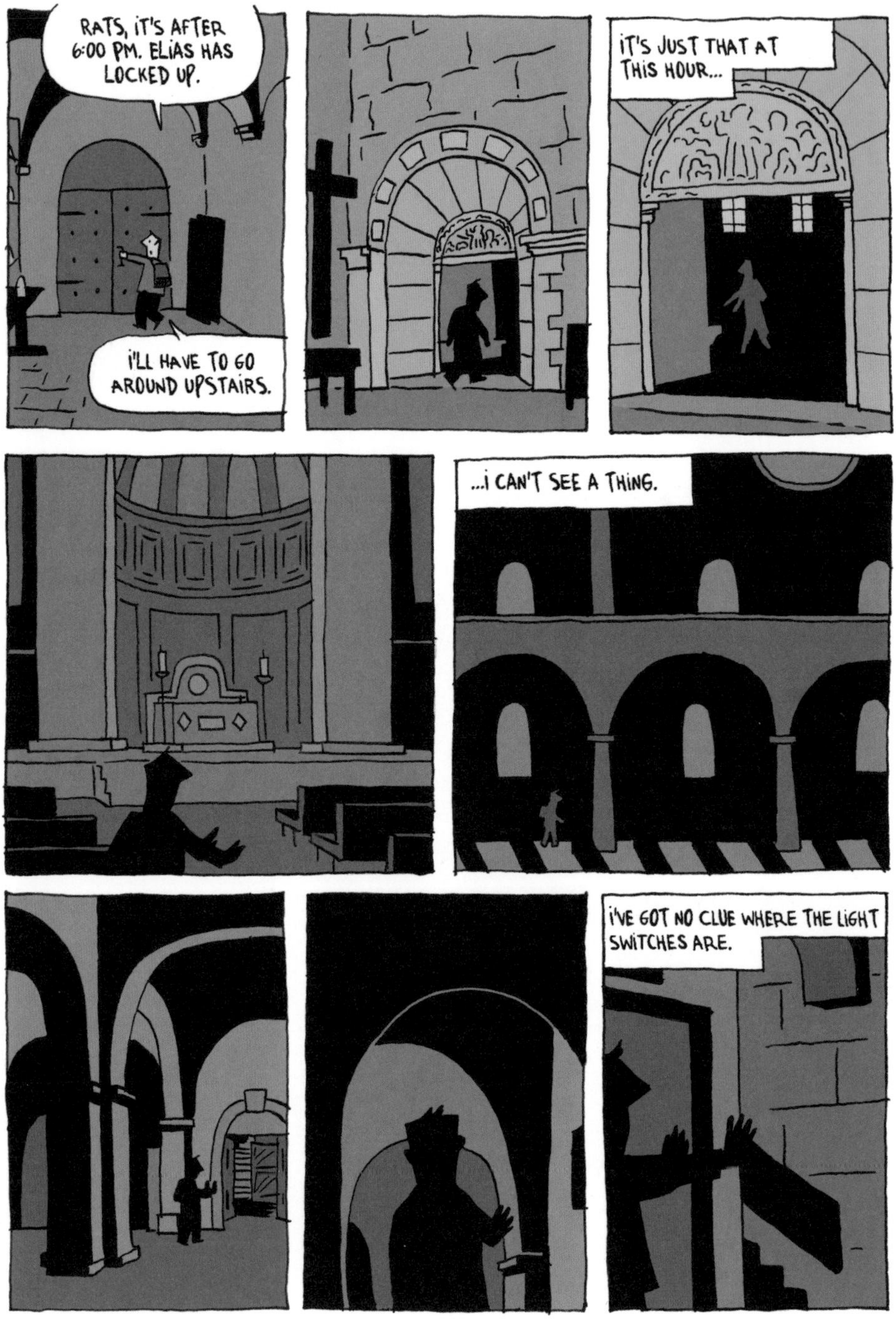
RATS, IT'S AFTER 6:00 PM. ELIAS HAS LOCKED UP.
I'LL HAVE TO GO AROUND UPSTAIRS.
IT'S JUST THAT AT THIS HOUR...
...I CAN'T SEE A THING.
I'VE GOT NO CLUE WHERE THE LIGHT SWITCHES ARE.

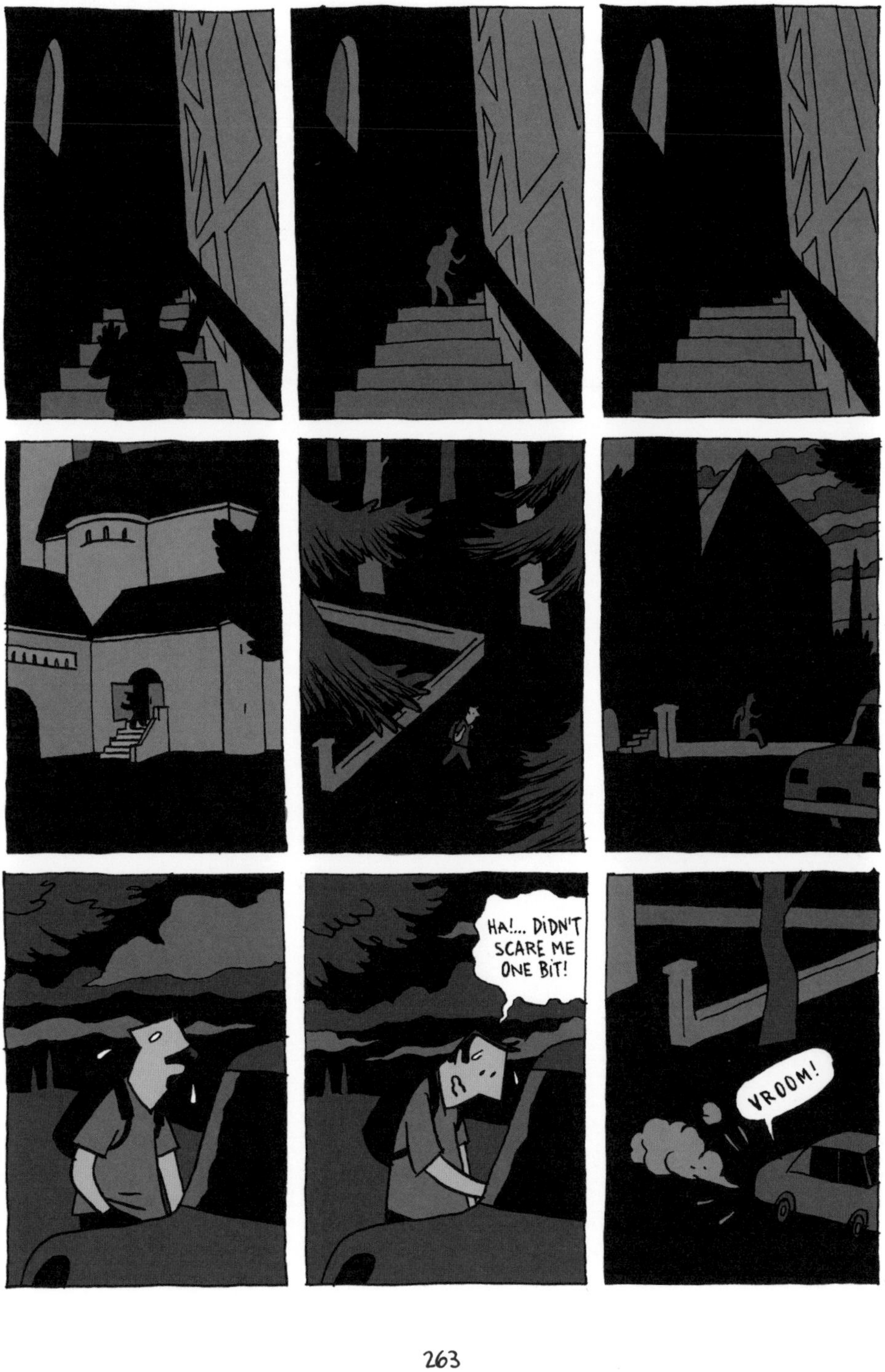
HA!... DIDN'T SCARE ME ONE BIT!
VROOM!

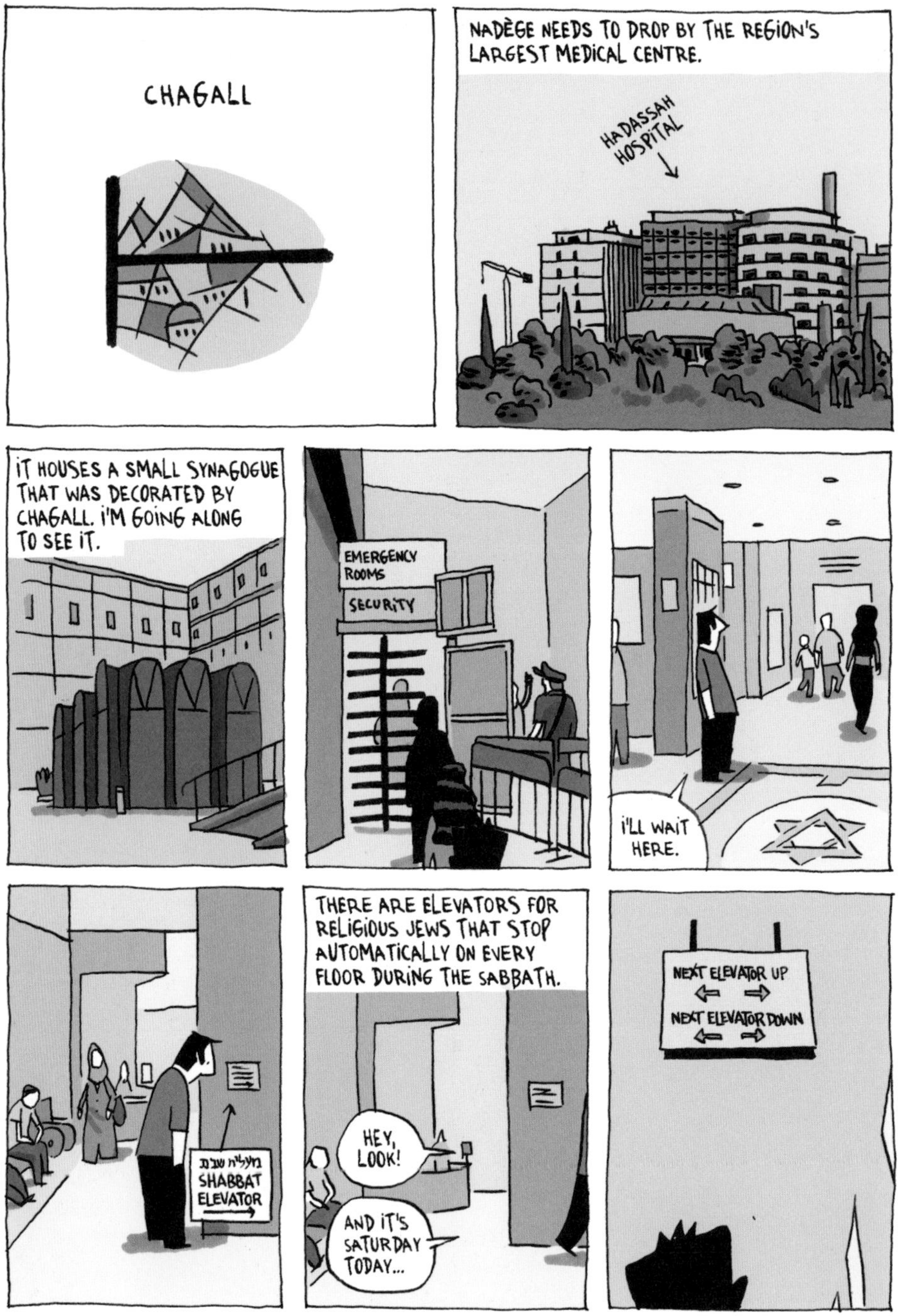
CHAGALL
NADÈGE NEEDS TO DROP BY THE REGION'S LARGEST MEDICAL CENTRE.
HADASSAH HOSPITAL
IT HOUSES A SMALL SYNAGOGUE THAT WAS DECORATED BY CHAGALL. I'M GOING ALONG TO SEE IT.
EMERGENCY ROOMS
SECURITY
I'LL WAIT HERE.
מעלית שבת
SHABBAT ELEVATOR
THERE ARE ELEVATORS FOR RELIGIOUS JEWS THAT STOP AUTOMATICALLY ON EVERY FLOOR DURING THE SABBATH.
HEY, LOOK!
AND IT'S SATURDAY TODAY...
NEXT ELEVATOR UP
NEXT ELEVATOR DOWN

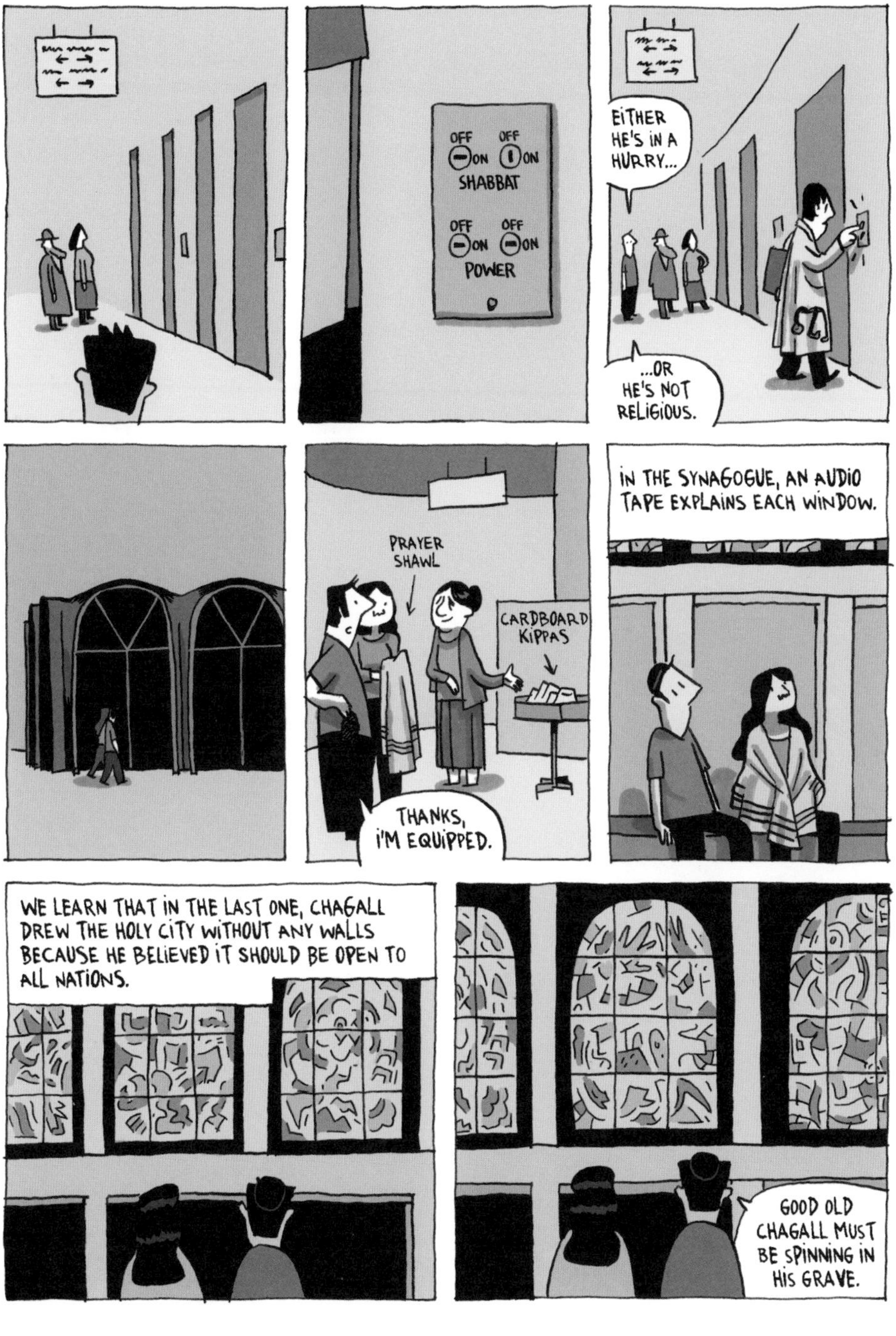
OFF OFF
ON ON
SHABBAT
OFF OFF
ON ON
POWER
EITHER HE'S IN A HURRY...
...OR HE'S NOT RELIGIOUS.
PRAYER SHAWL
CARDBOARD KIPPAS
THANKS, I'M EQUIPPED.
IN THE SYNAGOGUE, AN AUDIO TAPE EXPLAINS EACH WINDOW.
WE LEARN THAT IN THE LAST ONE, CHAGALL DREW THE HOLY CITY WITHOUT ANY WALLS BECAUSE HE BELIEVED IT SHOULD BE OPEN TO ALL NATIONS.
GOOD OLD CHAGALL MUST BE SPINNING IN HIS GRAVE.

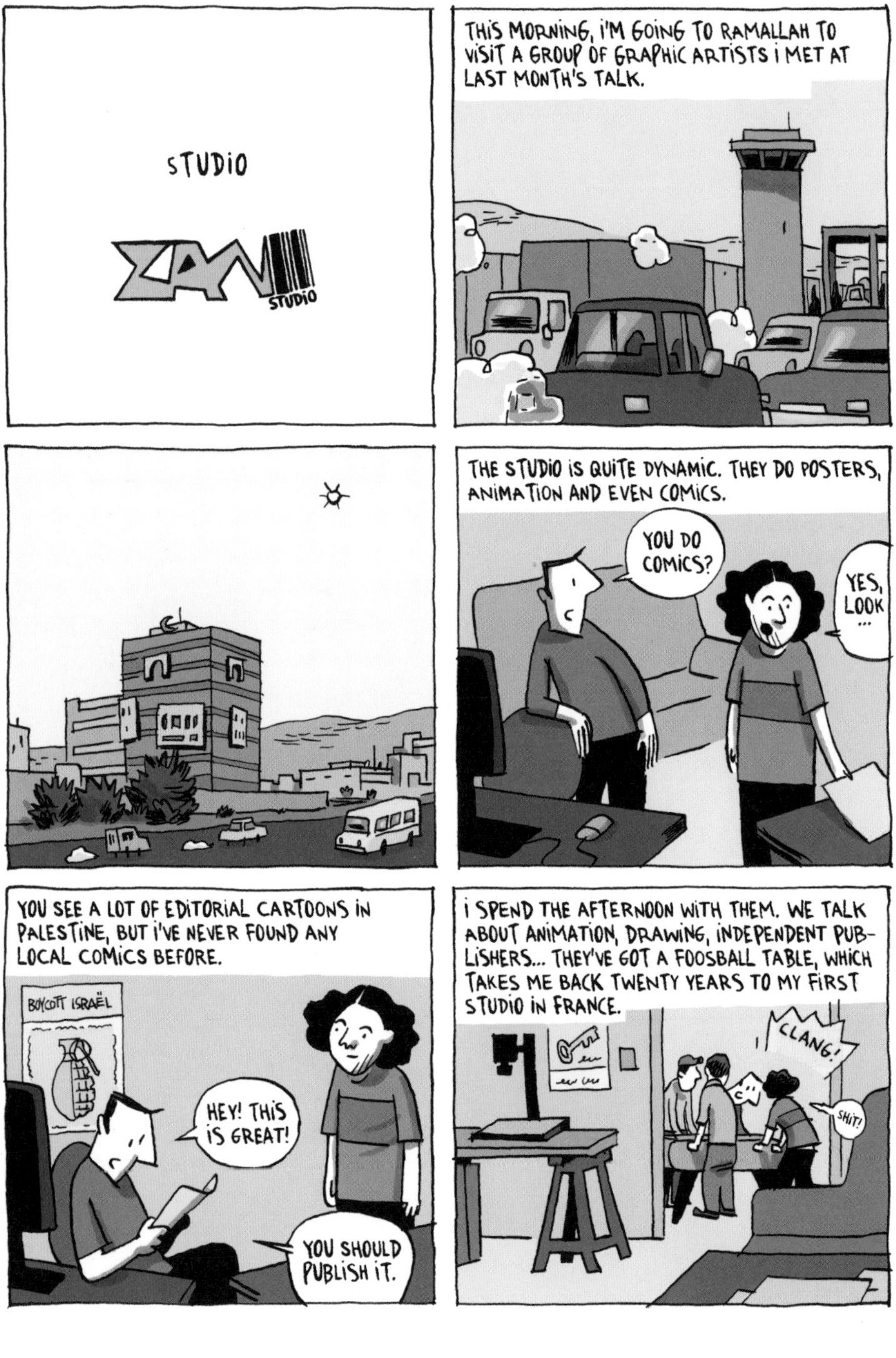
STUDIO
STUDIO
THIS MORNING, I'M GOING TO RAMALLAH TO VISIT A GROUP OF GRAPHIC ARTISTS I MET AT LAST MONTH'S TALK.
THE STUDIO IS QUITE DYNAMIC. THEY DO POSTERS, ANIMATION AND EVEN COMICS.
YOU DO COMICS?
YES, LOOK ...
YOU SEE A LOT OF EDITORIAL CARTOONS IN PALESTINE, BUT I'VE NEVER FOUND ANY LOCAL COMICS BEFORE.
BOYCOTT ISRAËL
HEY! THIS IS GREAT!
YOU SHOULD PUBLISH IT.
I SPEND THE AFTERNOON WITH THEM. WE TALK ABOUT ANIMATION, DRAWING, INDEPENDENT PUBLISHERS... THEY'VE GOT A FOOSBALL TABLE, WHICH TAKES ME BACK TWENTY YEARS TO MY FIRST STUDIO IN FRANCE.
CLANG!
SHIT!

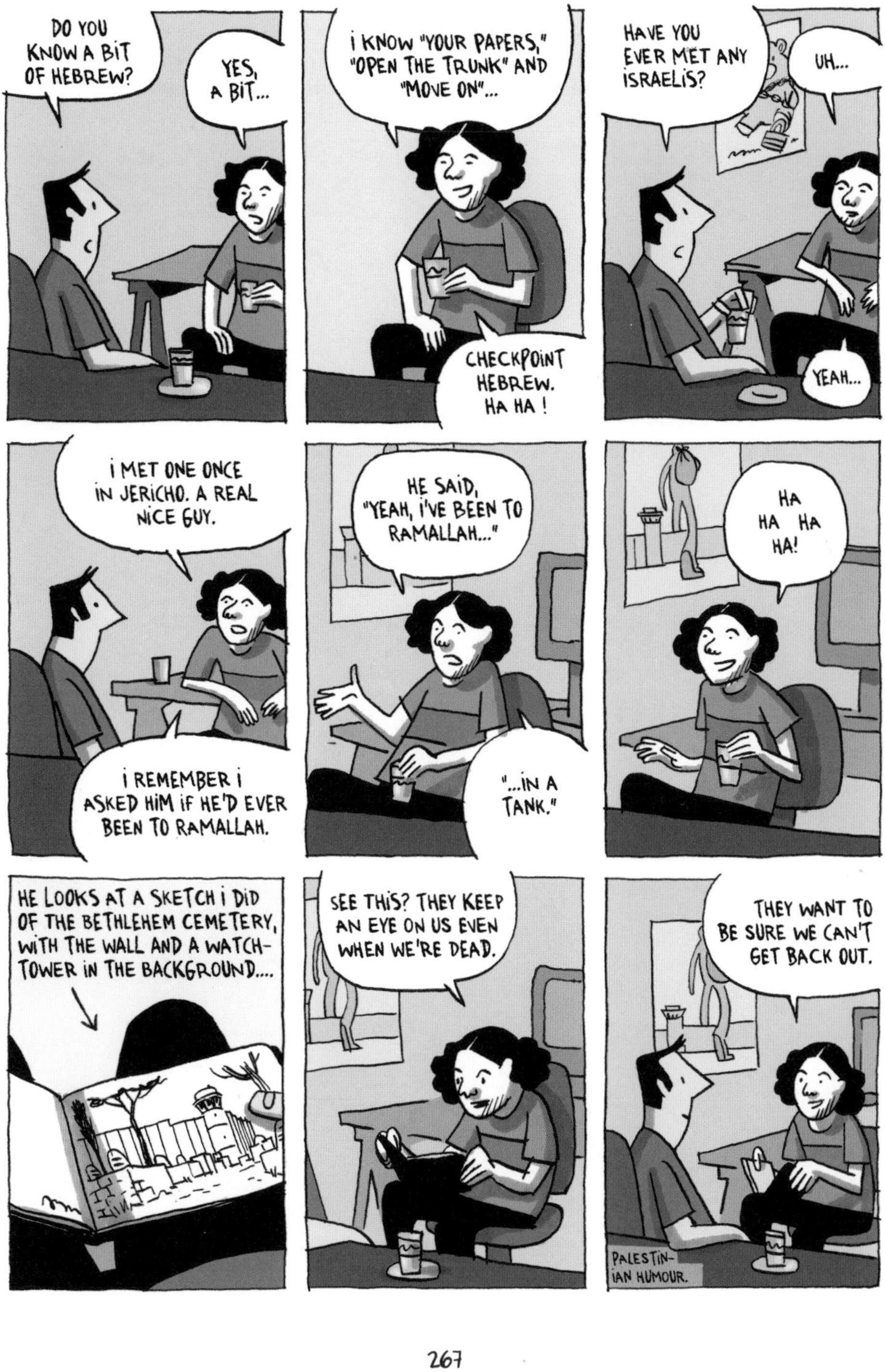
DO YOU KNOW A BIT OF HEBREW?
YES, A BIT...
I KNOW "YOUR PAPERS," "OPEN THE TRUNK" AND "MOVE ON"...
CHECKPOINT HEBREW. HA HA !
HAVE YOU EVER MET ANY ISRAELIS?
UH...
YEAH...
I MET ONE ONCE IN JERICHO. A REAL NICE GUY.
I REMEMBER I ASKED HIM IF HE'D EVER BEEN TO RAMALLAH.
HE SAID, "YEAH, I'VE BEEN TO RAMALLAH..."
"...IN A TANK."
HA HA HA HA!
HE LOOKS AT A SKETCH I DID OF THE BETHLEHEM CEMETERY, WITH THE WALL AND A WATCH-TOWER IN THE BACKGROUND....
SEE THIS? THEY KEEP AN EYE ON US EVEN WHEN WE'RE DEAD.
THEY WANT TO BE SURE WE CAN'T GET BACK OUT.
PALESTIN-IAN HUMOUR.

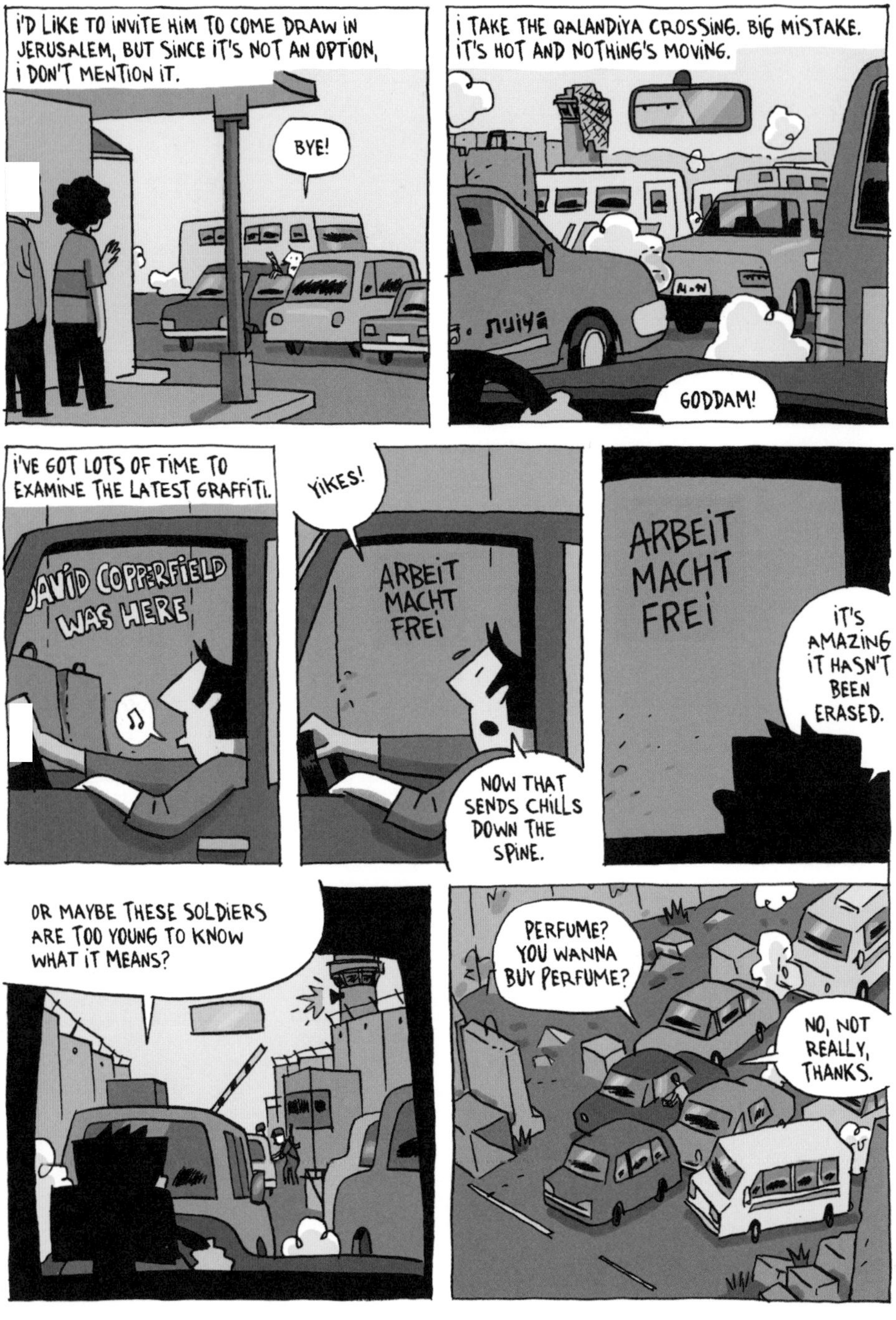
I'D LIKE TO INVITE HIM TO COME DRAW IN JERUSALEM, BUT SINCE IT'S NOT AN OPTION, I DON'T MENTION IT.
BYE!
I TAKE THE QALANDIYA CROSSING. BIG MISTAKE. IT'S HOT AND NOTHING'S MOVING.
GODDAM!
I'VE GOT LOTS OF TIME TO EXAMINE THE LATEST GRAFFITI.
DAVID COPPERFIELD WAS HERE
YIKES!
ARBEIT MACHT FREI
NOW THAT SENDS CHILLS DOWN THE SPINE.
ARBEIT MACHT FREI
IT'S AMAZING IT HASN'T BEEN ERASED.
OR MAYBE THESE SOLDIERS ARE TOO YOUNG TO KNOW WHAT IT MEANS?
PERFUME? YOU WANNA BUY PERFUME?
NO, NOT REALLY, THANKS.

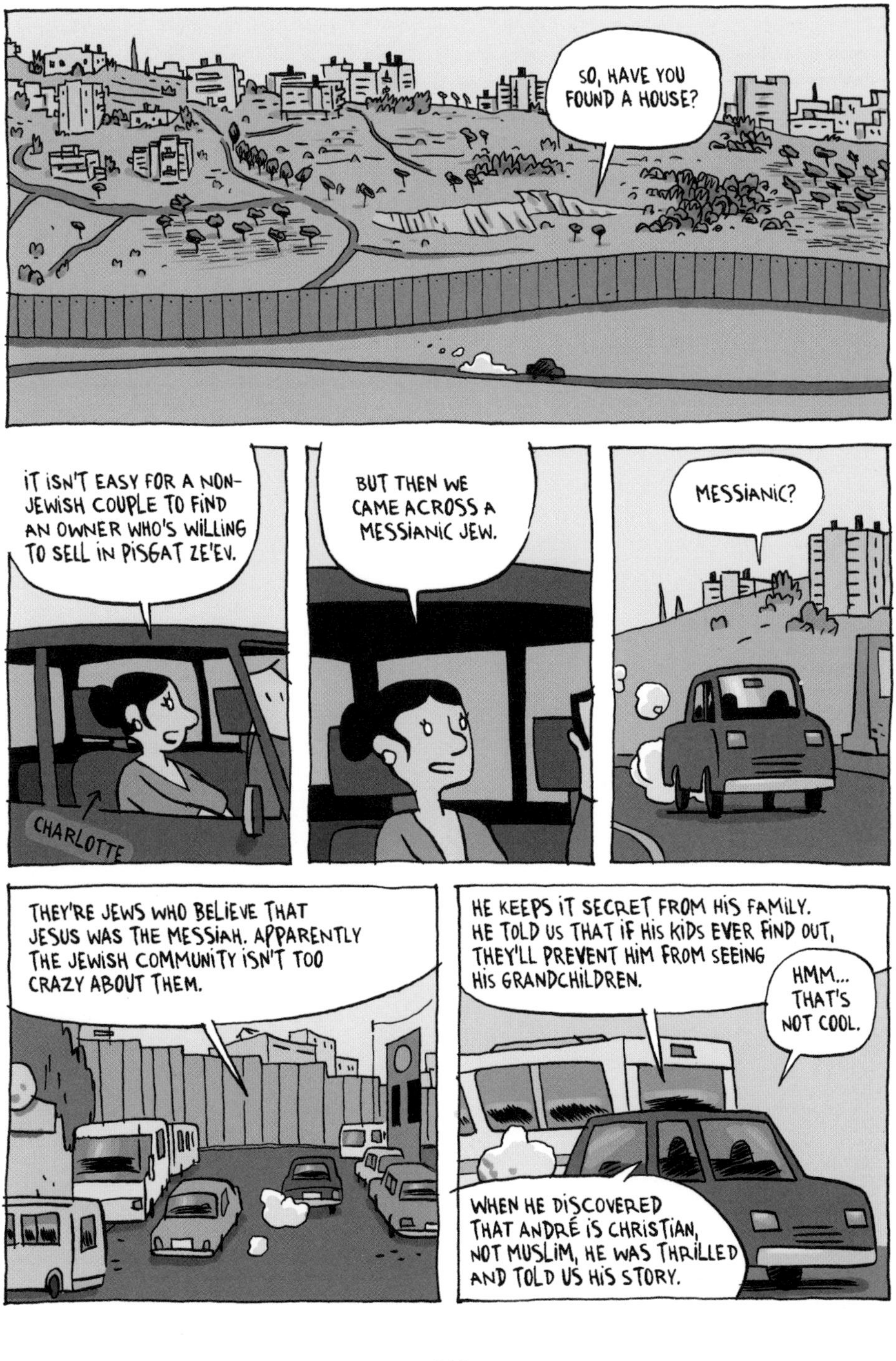
SO, HAVE YOU FOUND A HOUSE?
IT ISN'T EASY FOR A NON-JEWISH COUPLE TO FIND AN OWNER WHO'S WILLING TO SELL IN PISGAT ZE'EV.
CHARLOTTE
BUT THEN WE CAME ACROSS A MESSIANIC JEW.
MESSIANIC?
THEY'RE JEWS WHO BELIEVE THAT JESUS WAS THE MESSIAH. APPARENTLY THE JEWISH COMMUNITY ISN'T TOO CRAZY ABOUT THEM.
HE KEEPS IT SECRET FROM HIS FAMILY. HE TOLD US THAT IF HIS KIDS EVER FIND OUT, THEY'LL PREVENT HIM FROM SEEING HIS GRANDCHILDREN.
HMM... THAT'S NOT COOL.
WHEN HE DISCOVERED THAT ANDRÉ IS CHRISTIAN, NOT MUSLIM, HE WAS THRILLED AND TOLD US HIS STORY.

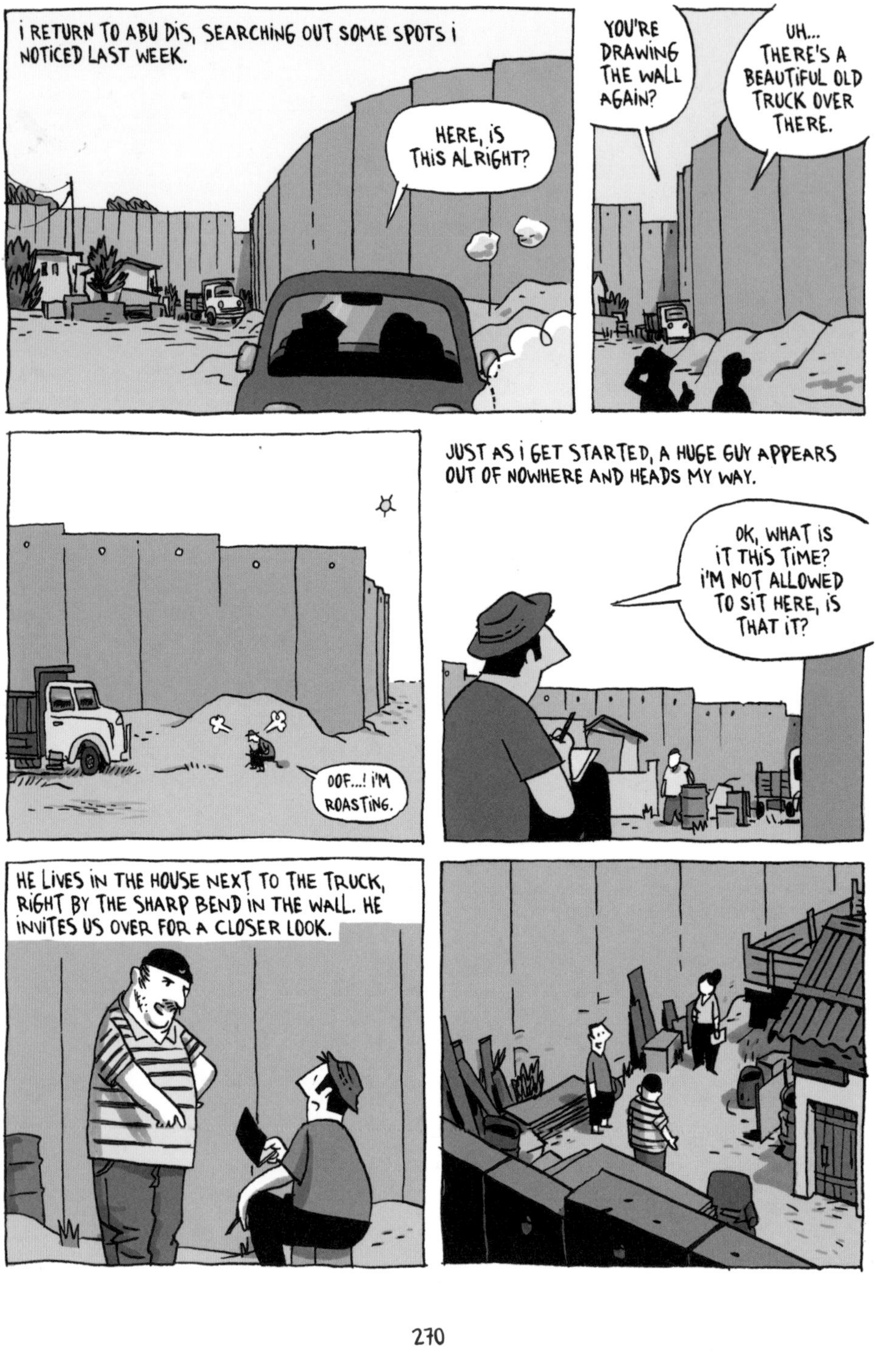

i RETURN TO ABU DiS, SEARCHiNG OUT SOME SPOTS i NOTICED LAST WEEK.
HERE, iS THIS ALRiGHT?
YOU'RE DRAWiNG THE WALL AGAiN?
UH... THERE'S A BEAUTiFUL OLD TRUCK OVER THERE.
OOF...! i'M ROASTiNG.
JUST AS i GET STARTED, A HUGE GUY APPEARS OUT OF NOWHERE AND HEADS MY WAY.
OK, WHAT iS iT THiS TiME? i'M NOT ALLOWED TO SiT HERE, iS THAT iT?
HE LiVES iN THE HOUSE NEXT TO THE TRUCK, RiGHT BY THE SHARP BEND iN THE WALL. HE iNViTES US OVER FOR A CLOSER LOOK.

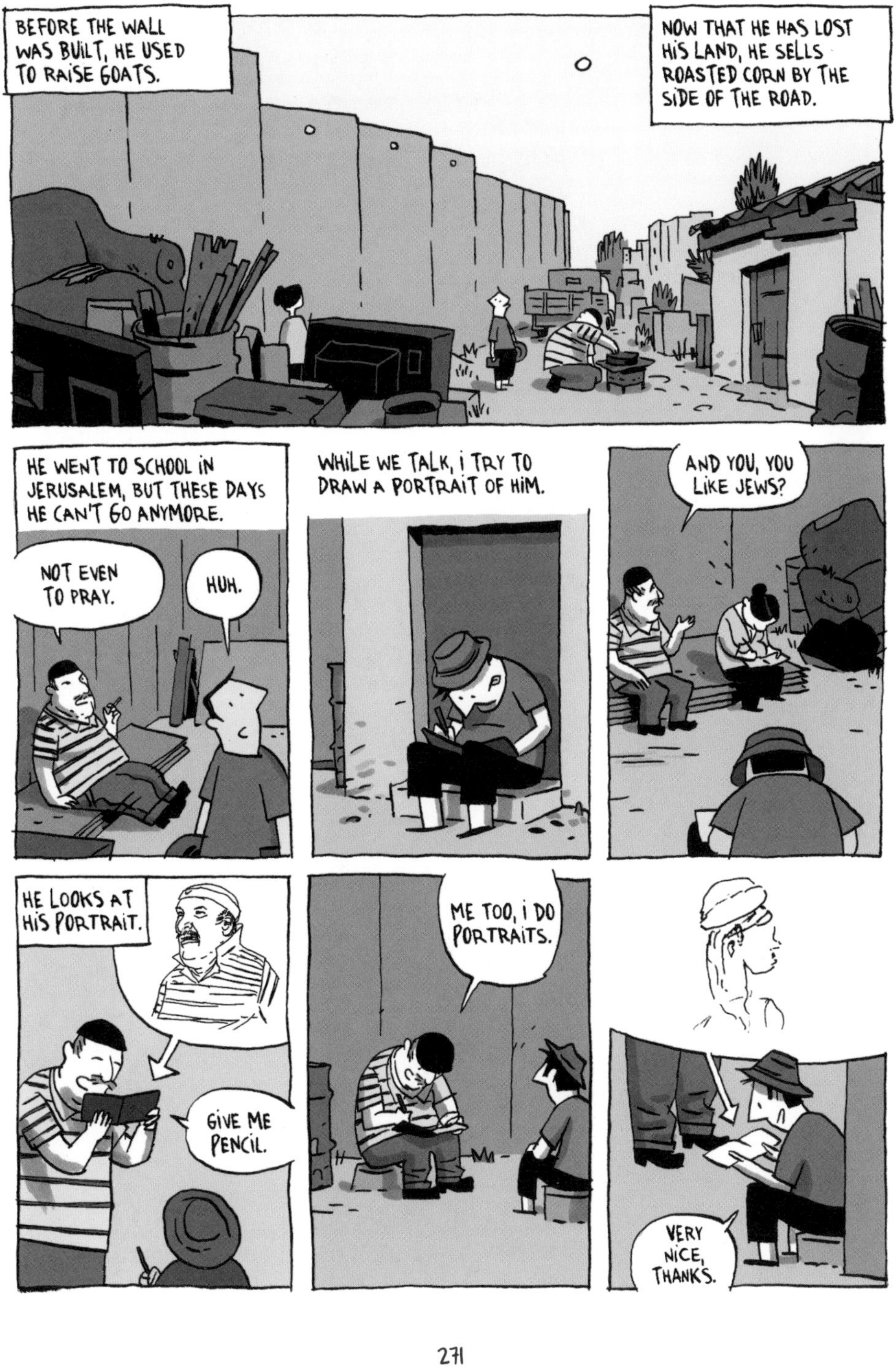

BEFORE THE WALL WAS BUILT, HE USED TO RAISE GOATS.
NOW THAT HE HAS LOST HIS LAND, HE SELLS ROASTED CORN BY THE SIDE OF THE ROAD.
HE WENT TO SCHOOL IN JERUSALEM, BUT THESE DAYS HE CAN'T GO ANYMORE.
NOT EVEN TO PRAY.
HUH.
WHILE WE TALK, I TRY TO DRAW A PORTRAIT OF HIM.
AND YOU, YOU LIKE JEWS?
HE LOOKS AT HIS PORTRAIT.
GIVE ME PENCIL.
ME TOO, I DO PORTRAITS.
VERY NICE, THANKS.

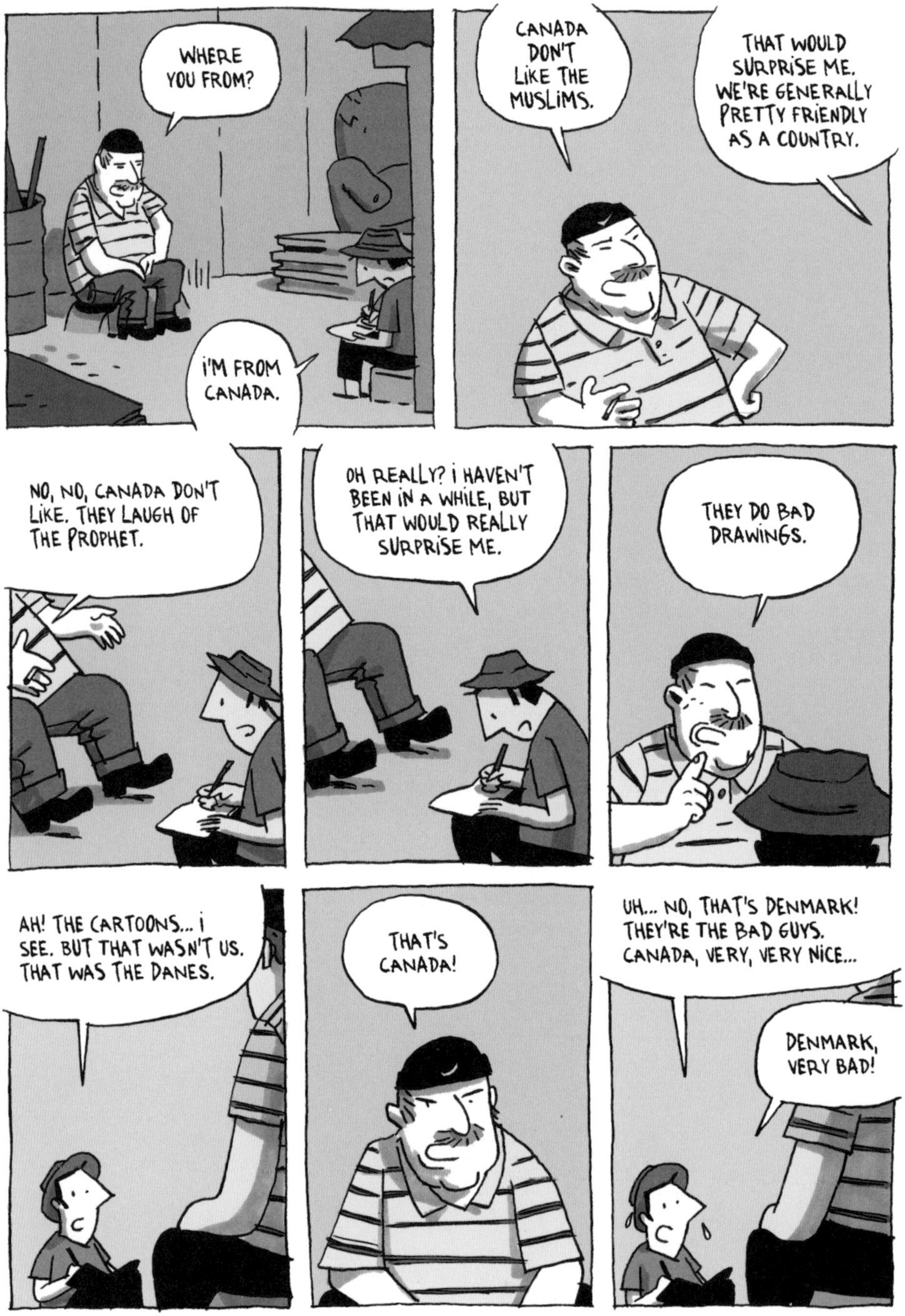
WHERE YOU FROM?
I'M FROM CANADA.
CANADA DON'T LIKE THE MUSLIMS.
THAT WOULD SURPRISE ME. WE'RE GENERALLY PRETTY FRIENDLY AS A COUNTRY.
NO, NO, CANADA DON'T LIKE. THEY LAUGH OF THE PROPHET.
OH REALLY? I HAVEN'T BEEN IN A WHILE, BUT THAT WOULD REALLY SURPRISE ME.
THEY DO BAD DRAWINGS.
AH! THE CARTOONS... I SEE. BUT THAT WASN'T US. THAT WAS THE DANES.
THAT'S CANADA!
UH... NO, THAT'S DENMARK! THEY'RE THE BAD GUYS. CANADA, VERY, VERY NICE...
DENMARK, VERY BAD!

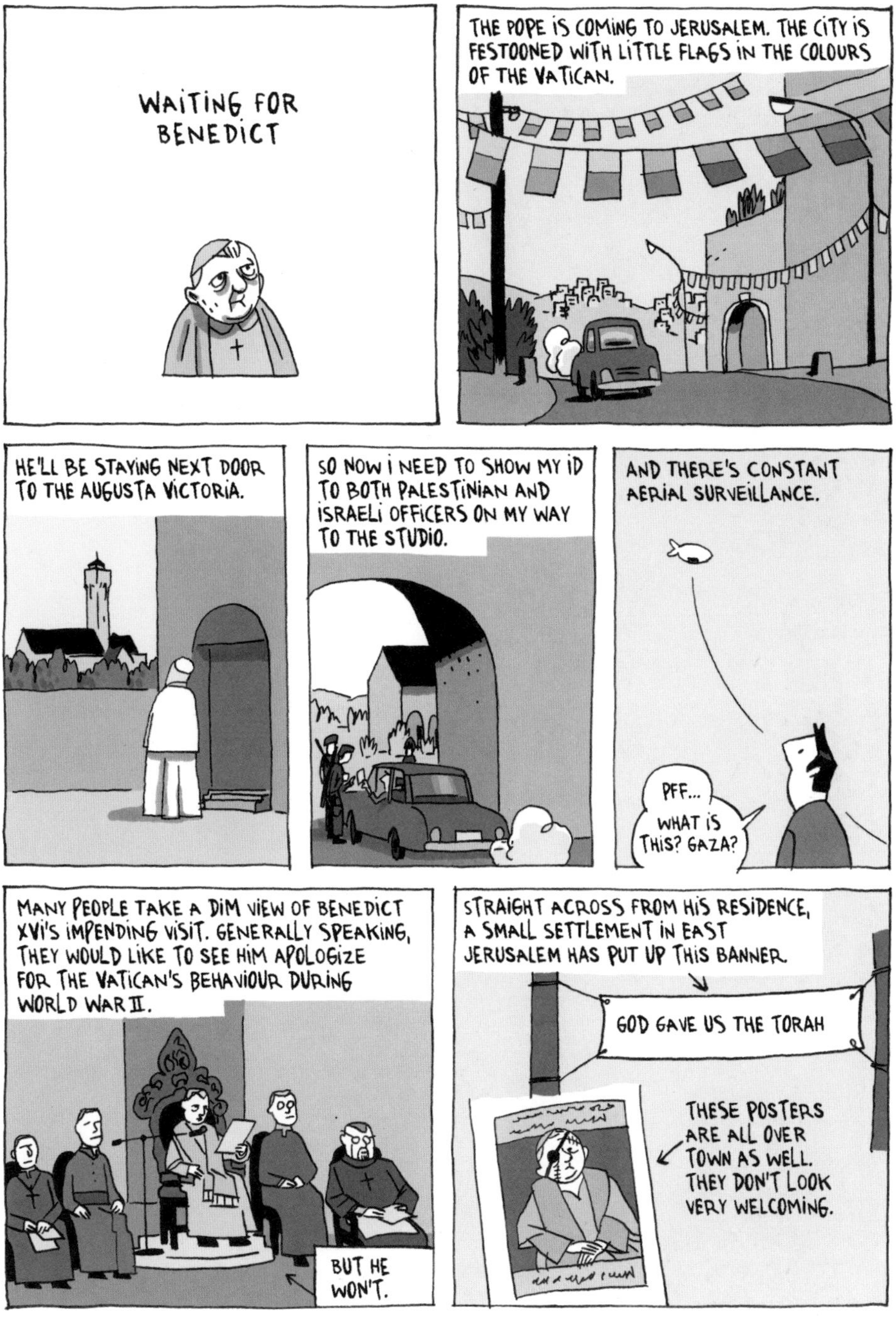
WAITING FOR BENEDICT
THE POPE IS COMING TO JERUSALEM. THE CITY IS FESTOONED WITH LITTLE FLAGS IN THE COLOURS OF THE VATICAN.
HE'LL BE STAYING NEXT DOOR TO THE AUGUSTA VICTORIA.
SO NOW I NEED TO SHOW MY ID TO BOTH PALESTINIAN AND ISRAELI OFFICERS ON MY WAY TO THE STUDIO.
AND THERE'S CONSTANT AERIAL SURVEILLANCE.
PFF... WHAT IS THIS? GAZA?
MANY PEOPLE TAKE A DIM VIEW OF BENEDICT XVI'S IMPENDING VISIT. GENERALLY SPEAKING, THEY WOULD LIKE TO SEE HIM APOLOGIZE FOR THE VATICAN'S BEHAVIOUR DURING WORLD WAR II.
BUT HE WON'T.
STRAIGHT ACROSS FROM HIS RESIDENCE, A SMALL SETTLEMENT IN EAST JERUSALEM HAS PUT UP THIS BANNER.
GOD GAVE US THE TORAH
THESE POSTERS ARE ALL OVER TOWN AS WELL. THEY DON'T LOOK VERY WELCOMING.

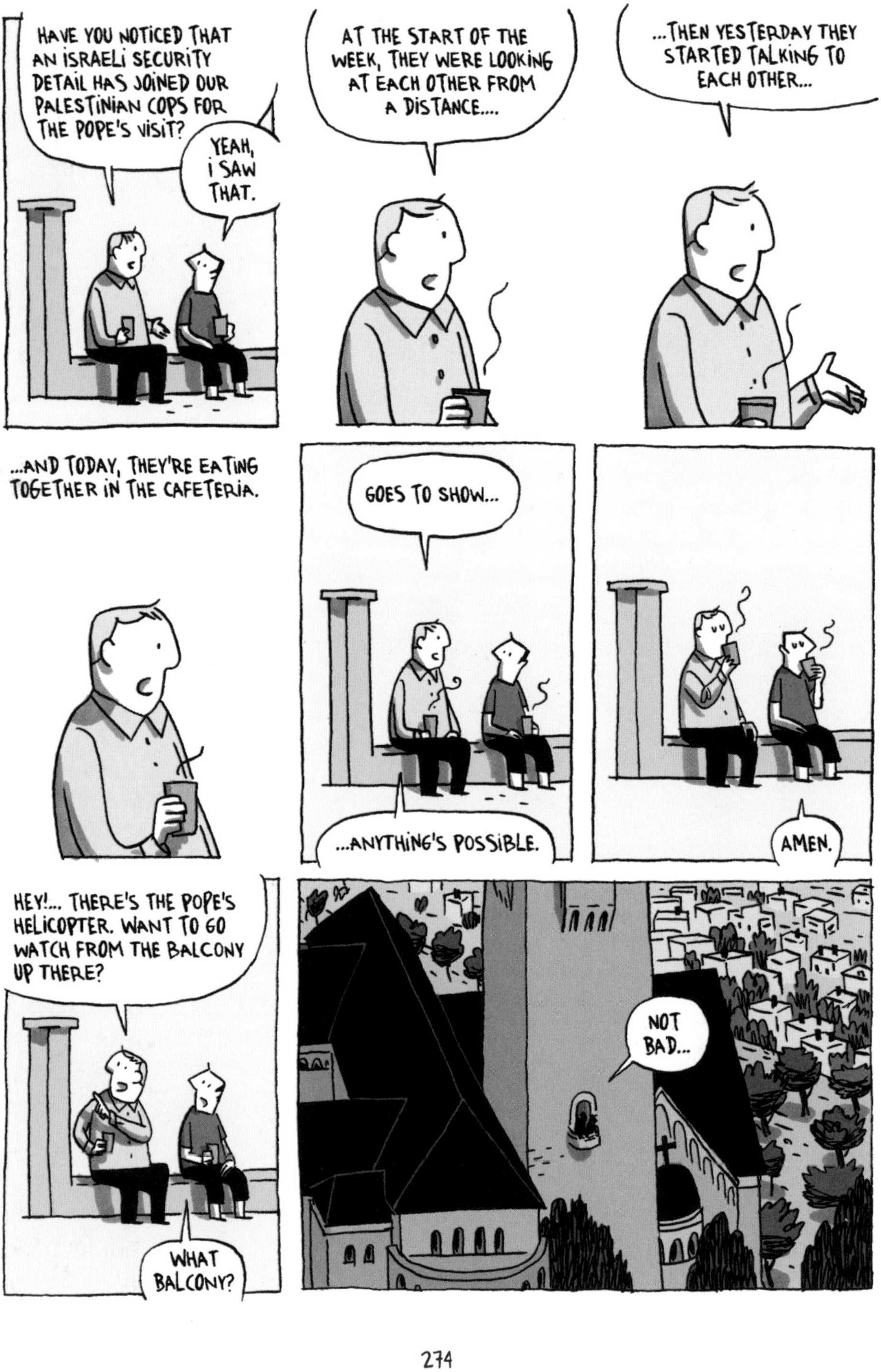
HAVE YOU NOTICED THAT AN ISRAELI SECURITY DETAIL HAS JOINED OUR PALESTINIAN COPS FOR THE POPE'S VISIT?
YEAH, I SAW THAT.
AT THE START OF THE WEEK, THEY WERE LOOKING AT EACH OTHER FROM A DISTANCE....
...THEN YESTERDAY THEY STARTED TALKING TO EACH OTHER...
...AND TODAY, THEY'RE EATING TOGETHER IN THE CAFETERIA.
GOES TO SHOW...
...ANYTHING'S POSSIBLE.
AMEN.
HEY!... THERE'S THE POPE'S HELICOPTER. WANT TO GO WATCH FROM THE BALCONY UP THERE?
WHAT BALCONY?
NOT BAD...

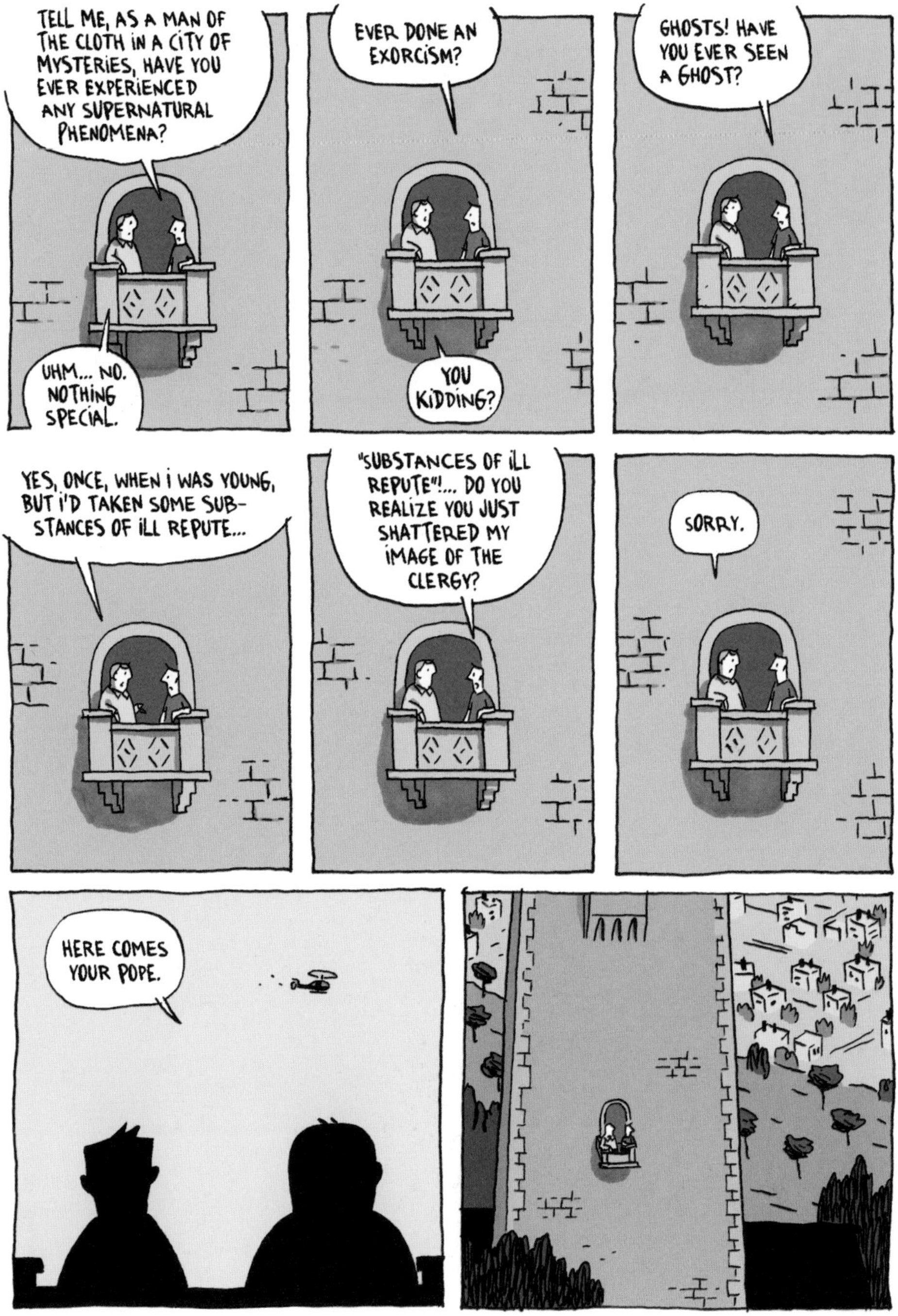
TELL ME, AS A MAN OF THE CLOTH IN A CITY OF MYSTERIES, HAVE YOU EVER EXPERIENCED ANY SUPERNATURAL PHENOMENA?
UHM... NO. NOTHING SPECIAL.
EVER DONE AN EXORCISM?
YOU KIDDING?
GHOSTS! HAVE YOU EVER SEEN A GHOST?
YES, ONCE, WHEN I WAS YOUNG, BUT I'D TAKEN SOME SUB-STANCES OF ILL REPUTE...
"SUBSTANCES OF ILL REPUTE"!... DO YOU REALIZE YOU JUST SHATTERED MY IMAGE OF THE CLERGY?
SORRY.
HERE COMES YOUR POPE.

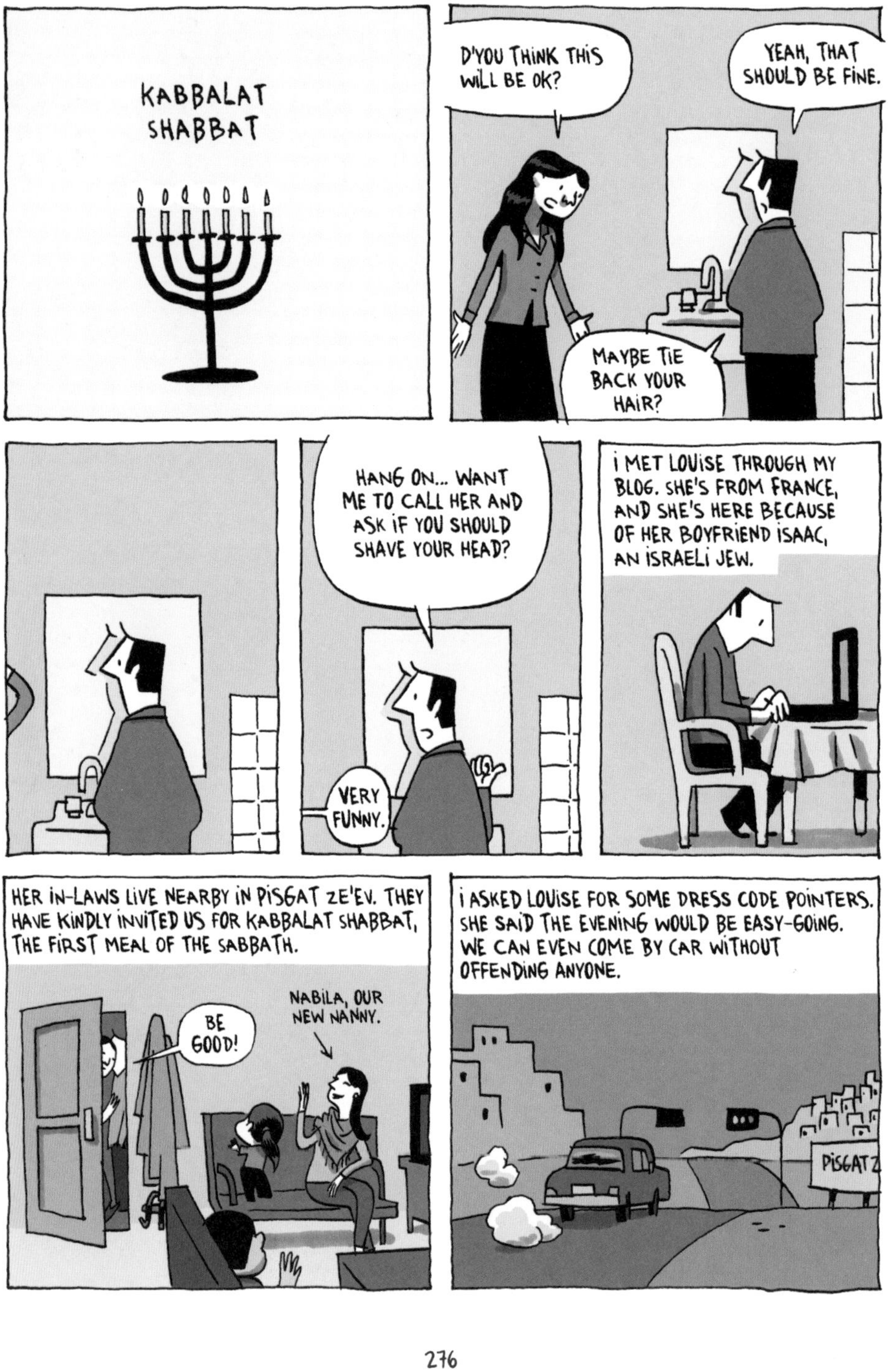
KABBALAT SHABBAT
D'YOU THINK THIS WILL BE OK?
YEAH, THAT SHOULD BE FINE.
MAYBE TIE BACK YOUR HAIR?
HANG ON... WANT ME TO CALL HER AND ASK IF YOU SHOULD SHAVE YOUR HEAD?
VERY FUNNY.
I MET LOUISE THROUGH MY BLOG. SHE'S FROM FRANCE, AND SHE'S HERE BECAUSE OF HER BOYFRIEND ISAAC, AN ISRAELI JEW.
HER IN-LAWS LIVE NEARBY IN PISGAT ZE'EV. THEY HAVE KINDLY INVITED US FOR KABBALAT SHABBAT, THE FIRST MEAL OF THE SABBATH.
BE GOOD!
NABILA, OUR NEW NANNY.
I ASKED LOUISE FOR SOME DRESS CODE POINTERS. SHE SAID THE EVENING WOULD BE EASY-GOING. WE CAN EVEN COME BY CAR WITHOUT OFFENDING ANYONE.
PISGAT Z

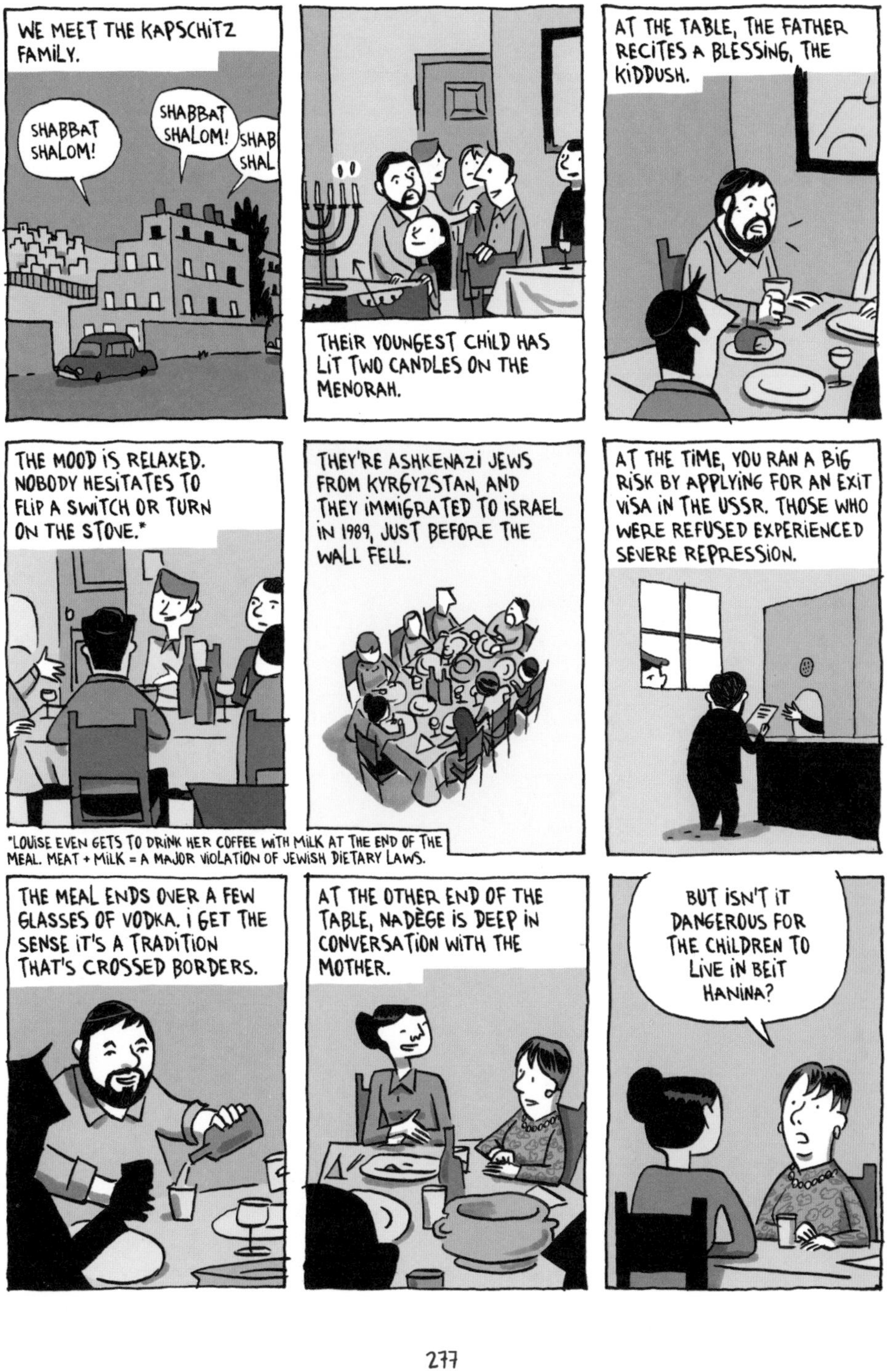
WE MEET THE KAPSCHITZ FAMILY.
SHABBAT SHALOM!
SHABBAT SHALOM!
SHAB SHAL
THEIR YOUNGEST CHILD HAS LIT TWO CANDLES ON THE MENORAH.
AT THE TABLE, THE FATHER RECITES A BLESSING, THE KIDDUSH.
THE MOOD IS RELAXED. NOBODY HESITATES TO FLIP A SWITCH OR TURN ON THE STOVE.*
THEY'RE ASHKENAZI JEWS FROM KYRGYZSTAN, AND THEY IMMIGRATED TO ISRAEL IN 1989, JUST BEFORE THE WALL FELL.
AT THE TIME, YOU RAN A BIG RISK BY APPLYING FOR AN EXIT VISA IN THE USSR. THOSE WHO WERE REFUSED EXPERIENCED SEVERE REPRESSION.
*LOUISE EVEN GETS TO DRINK HER COFFEE WITH MILK AT THE END OF THE MEAL. MEAT + MILK = A MAJOR VIOLATION OF JEWISH DIETARY LAWS.
THE MEAL ENDS OVER A FEW GLASSES OF VODKA. I GET THE SENSE IT'S A TRADITION THAT'S CROSSED BORDERS.
AT THE OTHER END OF THE TABLE, NADÈGE IS DEEP IN CONVERSATION WITH THE MOTHER.
BUT ISN'T IT DANGEROUS FOR THE CHILDREN TO LIVE IN BEIT HANINA?

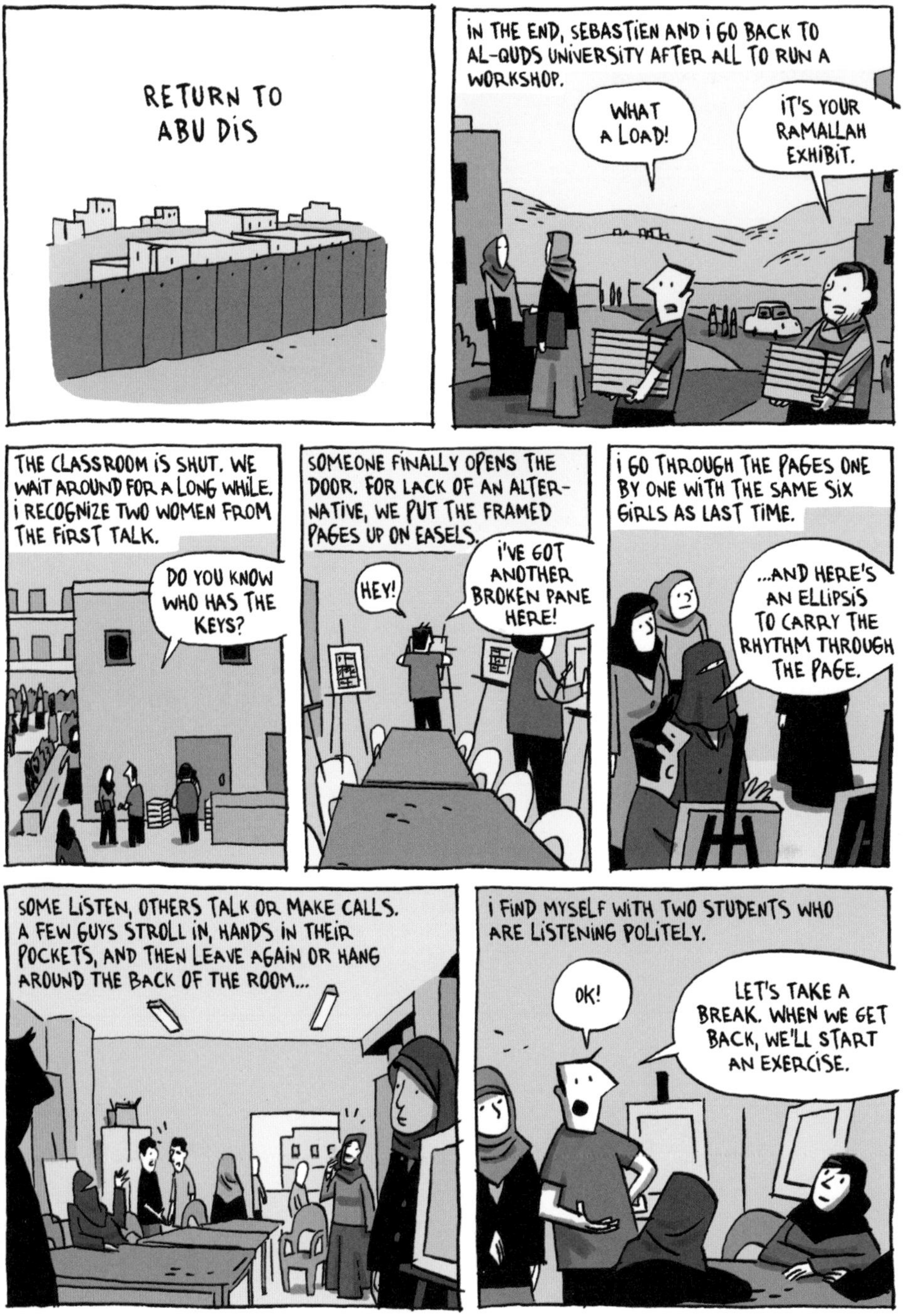
RETURN TO ABU DIS
IN THE END, SEBASTIEN AND I GO BACK TO AL-QUDS UNIVERSITY AFTER ALL TO RUN A WORKSHOP.
WHAT A LOAD!
IT'S YOUR RAMALLAH EXHIBIT.
THE CLASSROOM IS SHUT. WE WAIT AROUND FOR A LONG WHILE. I RECOGNIZE TWO WOMEN FROM THE FIRST TALK.
DO YOU KNOW WHO HAS THE KEYS?
SOMEONE FINALLY OPENS THE DOOR. FOR LACK OF AN ALTERNATIVE, WE PUT THE FRAMED PAGES UP ON EASELS.
HEY!
I'VE GOT ANOTHER BROKEN PANE HERE!
I GO THROUGH THE PAGES ONE BY ONE WITH THE SAME SIX GIRLS AS LAST TIME.
...AND HERE'S AN ELLIPSIS TO CARRY THE RHYTHM THROUGH THE PAGE.
SOME LISTEN, OTHERS TALK OR MAKE CALLS. A FEW GUYS STROLL IN, HANDS IN THEIR POCKETS, AND THEN LEAVE AGAIN OR HANG AROUND THE BACK OF THE ROOM...
I FIND MYSELF WITH TWO STUDENTS WHO ARE LISTENING POLITELY.
OK!
LET'S TAKE A BREAK. WHEN WE GET BACK, WE'LL START AN EXERCISE.

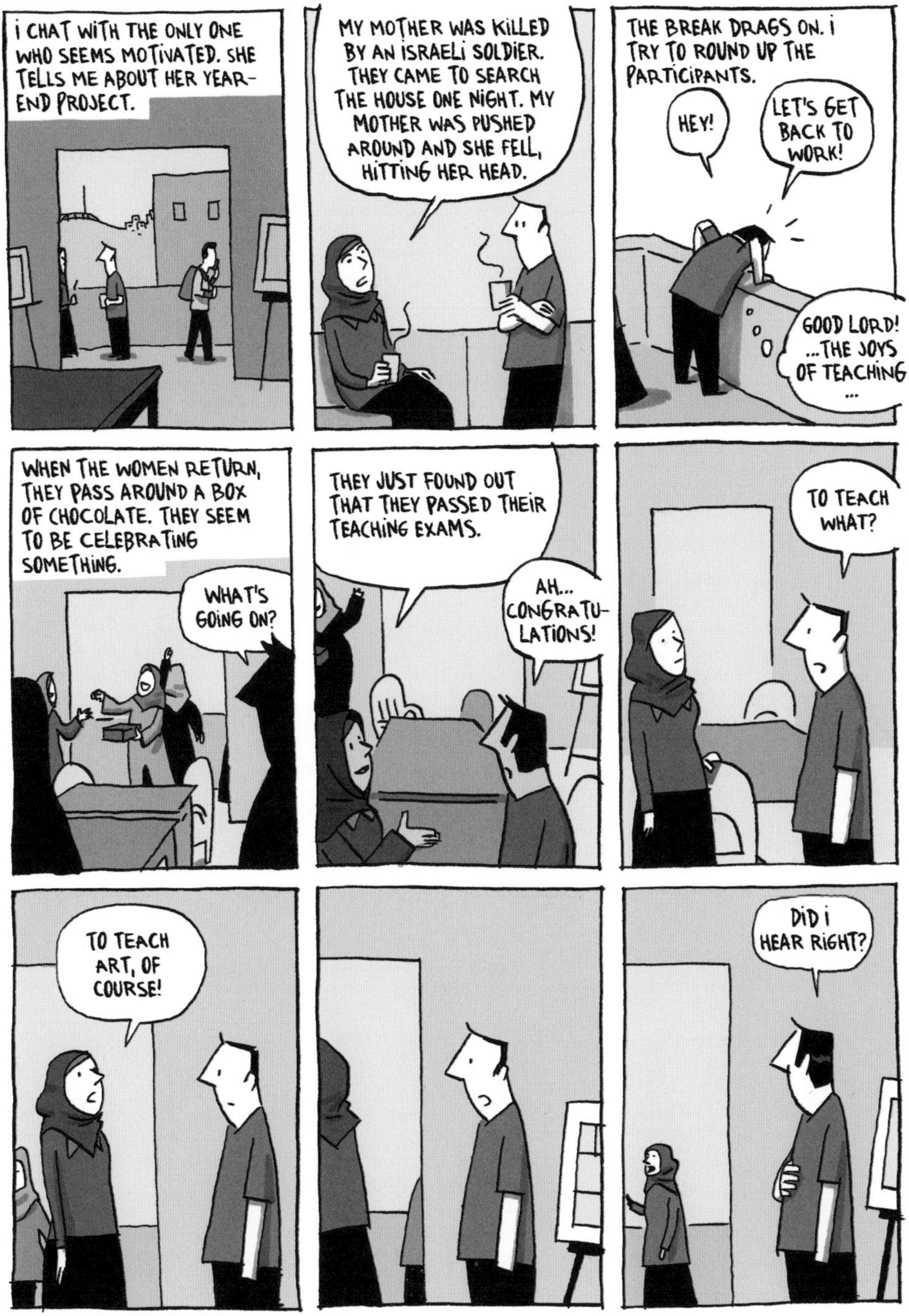
I CHAT WITH THE ONLY ONE WHO SEEMS MOTIVATED. SHE TELLS ME ABOUT HER YEAR-END PROJECT.
MY MOTHER WAS KILLED BY AN ISRAELI SOLDIER. THEY CAME TO SEARCH THE HOUSE ONE NIGHT. MY MOTHER WAS PUSHED AROUND AND SHE FELL, HITTING HER HEAD.
THE BREAK DRAGS ON. I TRY TO ROUND UP THE PARTICIPANTS.
HEY!
LET'S GET BACK TO WORK!
GOOD LORD! ...THE JOYS OF TEACHING ...
WHEN THE WOMEN RETURN, THEY PASS AROUND A BOX OF CHOCOLATE. THEY SEEM TO BE CELEBRATING SOMETHING.
WHAT'S GOING ON?
THEY JUST FOUND OUT THAT THEY PASSED THEIR TEACHING EXAMS.
AH... CONGRATU-LATIONS!
TO TEACH WHAT?
TO TEACH ART, OF COURSE!
DID I HEAR RIGHT?

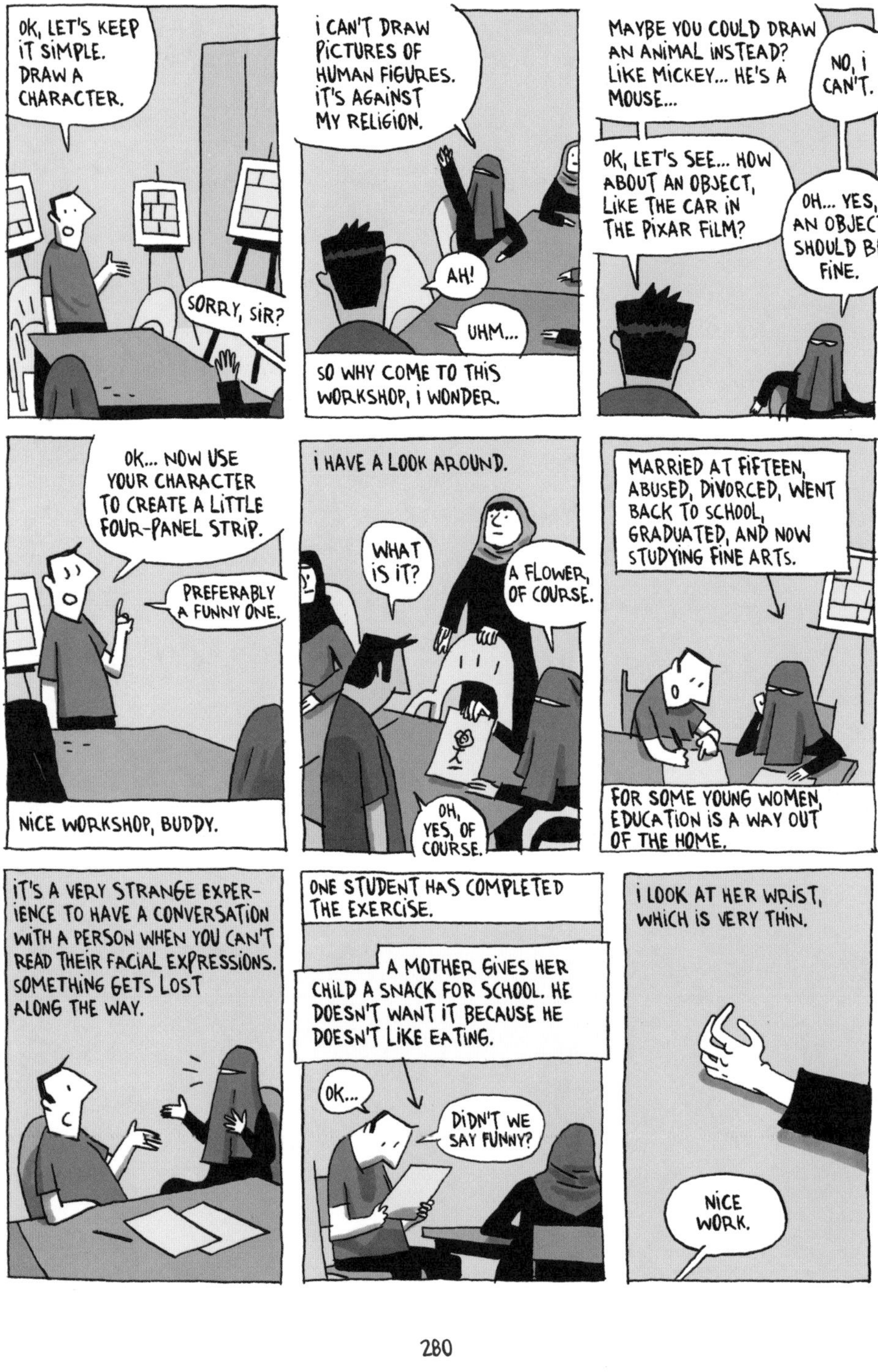
OK, LET'S KEEP IT SIMPLE. DRAW A CHARACTER.
SORRY, SIR?
I CAN'T DRAW PICTURES OF HUMAN FIGURES. IT'S AGAINST MY RELIGION.
AH!
UHM...
SO WHY COME TO THIS WORKSHOP, I WONDER.
MAYBE YOU COULD DRAW AN ANIMAL INSTEAD? LIKE MICKEY... HE'S A MOUSE...
NO, I CAN'T.
OK, LET'S SEE... HOW ABOUT AN OBJECT, LIKE THE CAR IN THE PIXAR FILM?
OH... YES, AN OBJECT SHOULD BE FINE.
OK... NOW USE YOUR CHARACTER TO CREATE A LITTLE FOUR-PANEL STRIP.
PREFERABLY A FUNNY ONE.
NICE WORKSHOP, BUDDY.
I HAVE A LOOK AROUND.
WHAT IS IT?
A FLOWER, OF COURSE.
OH, YES, OF COURSE.
MARRIED AT FIFTEEN, ABUSED, DIVORCED, WENT BACK TO SCHOOL, GRADUATED, AND NOW STUDYING FINE ARTS.
FOR SOME YOUNG WOMEN, EDUCATION IS A WAY OUT OF THE HOME.
IT'S A VERY STRANGE EXPERIENCE TO HAVE A CONVERSATION WITH A PERSON WHEN YOU CAN'T READ THEIR FACIAL EXPRESSIONS. SOMETHING GETS LOST ALONG THE WAY.
ONE STUDENT HAS COMPLETED THE EXERCISE.
A MOTHER GIVES HER CHILD A SNACK FOR SCHOOL. HE DOESN'T WANT IT BECAUSE HE DOESN'T LIKE EATING.
OK...
DIDN'T WE SAY FUNNY?
I LOOK AT HER WRIST, WHICH IS VERY THIN.
NICE WORK.

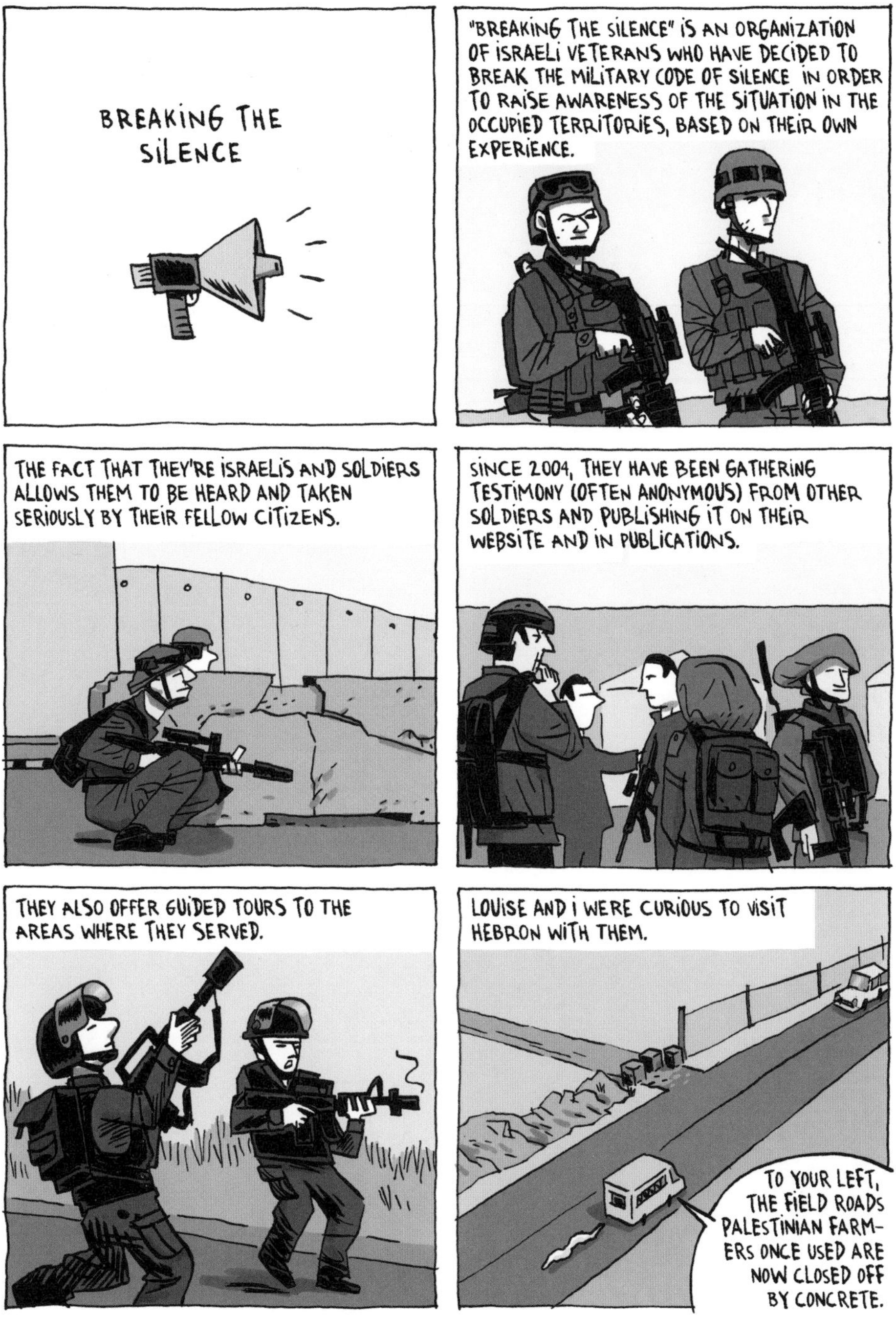
BREAKING THE SILENCE
"BREAKING THE SILENCE" IS AN ORGANIZATION OF ISRAELI VETERANS WHO HAVE DECIDED TO BREAK THE MILITARY CODE OF SILENCE IN ORDER TO RAISE AWARENESS OF THE SITUATION IN THE OCCUPIED TERRITORIES, BASED ON THEIR OWN EXPERIENCE.
THE FACT THAT THEY'RE ISRAELIS AND SOLDIERS ALLOWS THEM TO BE HEARD AND TAKEN SERIOUSLY BY THEIR FELLOW CITIZENS.
SINCE 2004, THEY HAVE BEEN GATHERING TESTIMONY (OFTEN ANONYMOUS) FROM OTHER SOLDIERS AND PUBLISHING IT ON THEIR WEBSITE AND IN PUBLICATIONS.
THEY ALSO OFFER GUIDED TOURS TO THE AREAS WHERE THEY SERVED.
LOUISE AND I WERE CURIOUS TO VISIT HEBRON WITH THEM.
TO YOUR LEFT, THE FIELD ROADS PALESTINIAN FARMERS ONCE USED ARE NOW CLOSED OFF BY CONCRETE.

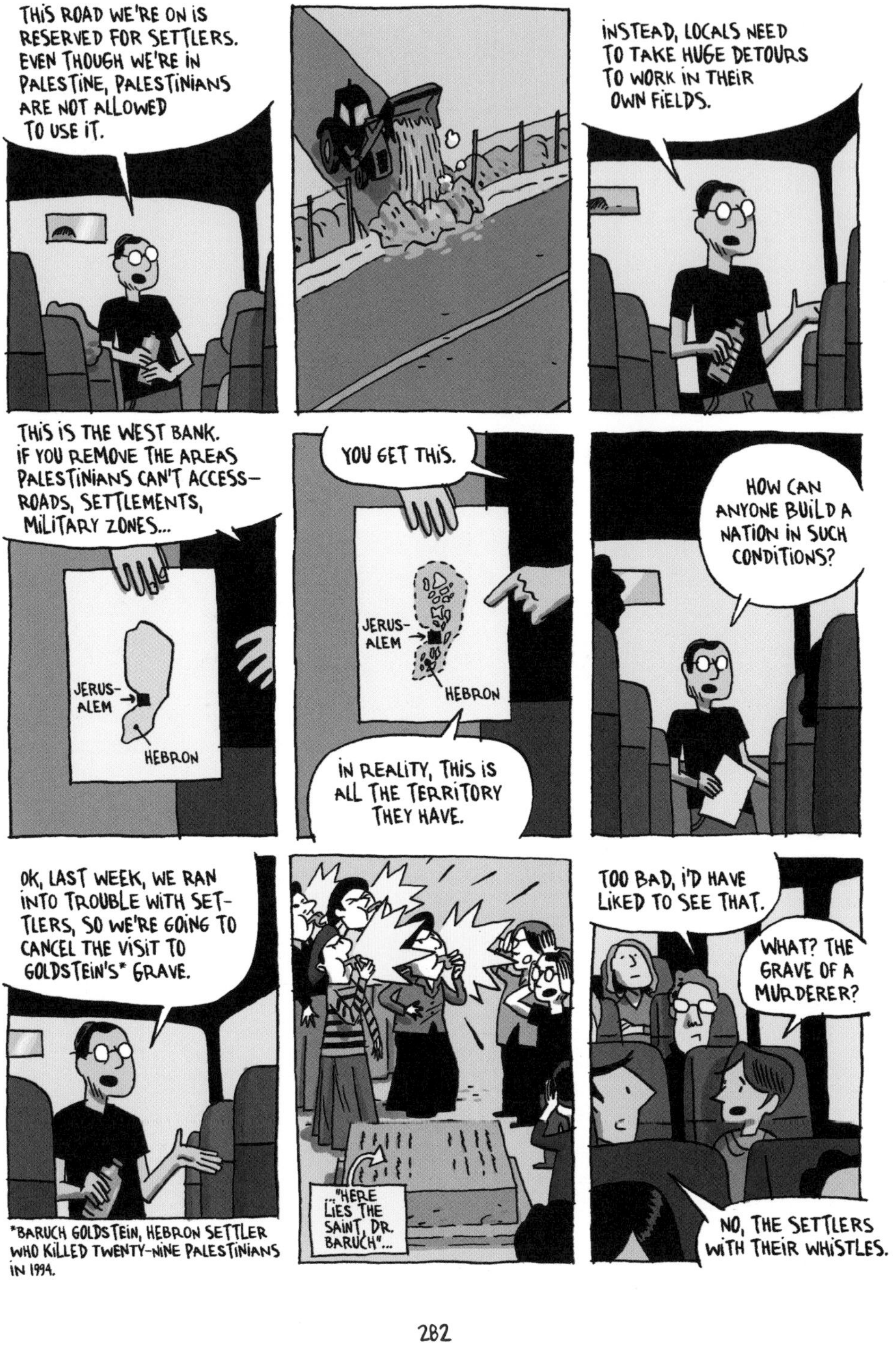
THIS ROAD WE'RE ON IS RESERVED FOR SETTLERS. EVEN THOUGH WE'RE IN PALESTINE, PALESTINIANS ARE NOT ALLOWED TO USE IT.
INSTEAD, LOCALS NEED TO TAKE HUGE DETOURS TO WORK IN THEIR OWN FIELDS.
THIS IS THE WEST BANK. IF YOU REMOVE THE AREAS PALESTINIANS CAN'T ACCESS–ROADS, SETTLEMENTS, MILITARY ZONES...
JERUS-ALEM
HEBRON
YOU GET THIS.
JERUS-ALEM
HEBRON
IN REALITY, THIS IS ALL THE TERRITORY THEY HAVE.
HOW CAN ANYONE BUILD A NATION IN SUCH CONDITIONS?
OK, LAST WEEK, WE RAN INTO TROUBLE WITH SET-TLERS, SO WE'RE GOING TO CANCEL THE VISIT TO GOLDSTEIN'S* GRAVE.
*BARUCH GOLDSTEIN, HEBRON SETTLER WHO KILLED TWENTY-NINE PALESTINIANS IN 1994.
..."HERE LIES THE SAINT, DR. BARUCH"...
TOO BAD, I'D HAVE LIKED TO SEE THAT.
WHAT? THE GRAVE OF A MURDERER?
NO, THE SETTLERS WITH THEIR WHISTLES.

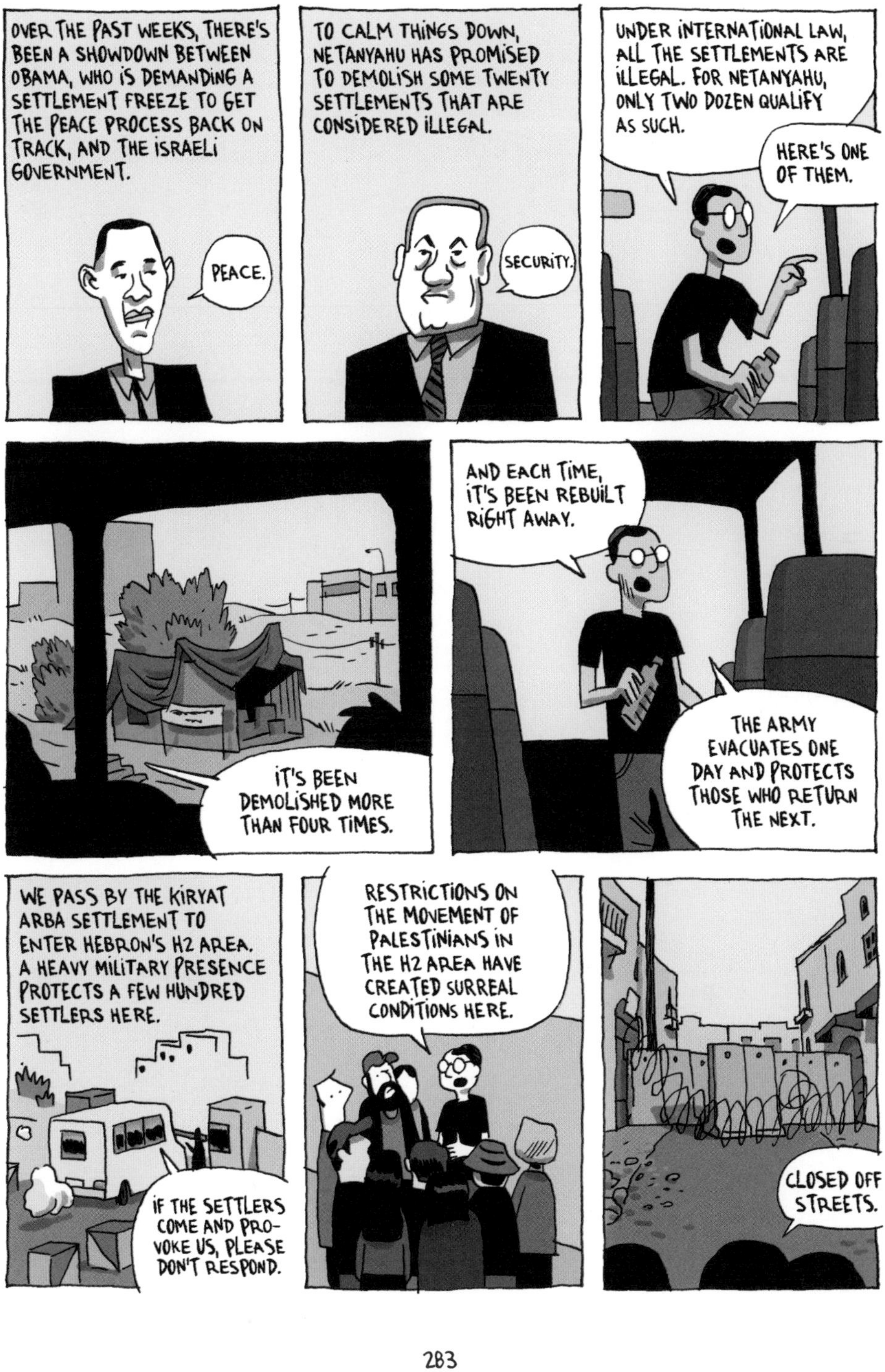
OVER THE PAST WEEKS, THERE'S BEEN A SHOWDOWN BETWEEN OBAMA, WHO IS DEMANDING A SETTLEMENT FREEZE TO GET THE PEACE PROCESS BACK ON TRACK, AND THE ISRAELI GOVERNMENT.
PEACE.
TO CALM THINGS DOWN, NETANYAHU HAS PROMISED TO DEMOLISH SOME TWENTY SETTLEMENTS THAT ARE CONSIDERED ILLEGAL.
SECURITY.
UNDER INTERNATIONAL LAW, ALL THE SETTLEMENTS ARE ILLEGAL. FOR NETANYAHU, ONLY TWO DOZEN QUALIFY AS SUCH.
HERE'S ONE OF THEM.
IT'S BEEN DEMOLISHED MORE THAN FOUR TIMES.
AND EACH TIME, IT'S BEEN REBUILT RIGHT AWAY.
THE ARMY EVACUATES ONE DAY AND PROTECTS THOSE WHO RETURN THE NEXT.
WE PASS BY THE KIRYAT ARBA SETTLEMENT TO ENTER HEBRON'S H2 AREA. A HEAVY MILITARY PRESENCE PROTECTS A FEW HUNDRED SETTLERS HERE.
IF THE SETTLERS COME AND PRO-VOKE US, PLEASE DON'T RESPOND.
RESTRICTIONS ON THE MOVEMENT OF PALESTINIANS IN THE H2 AREA HAVE CREATED SURREAL CONDITIONS HERE.
CLOSED OFF STREETS.

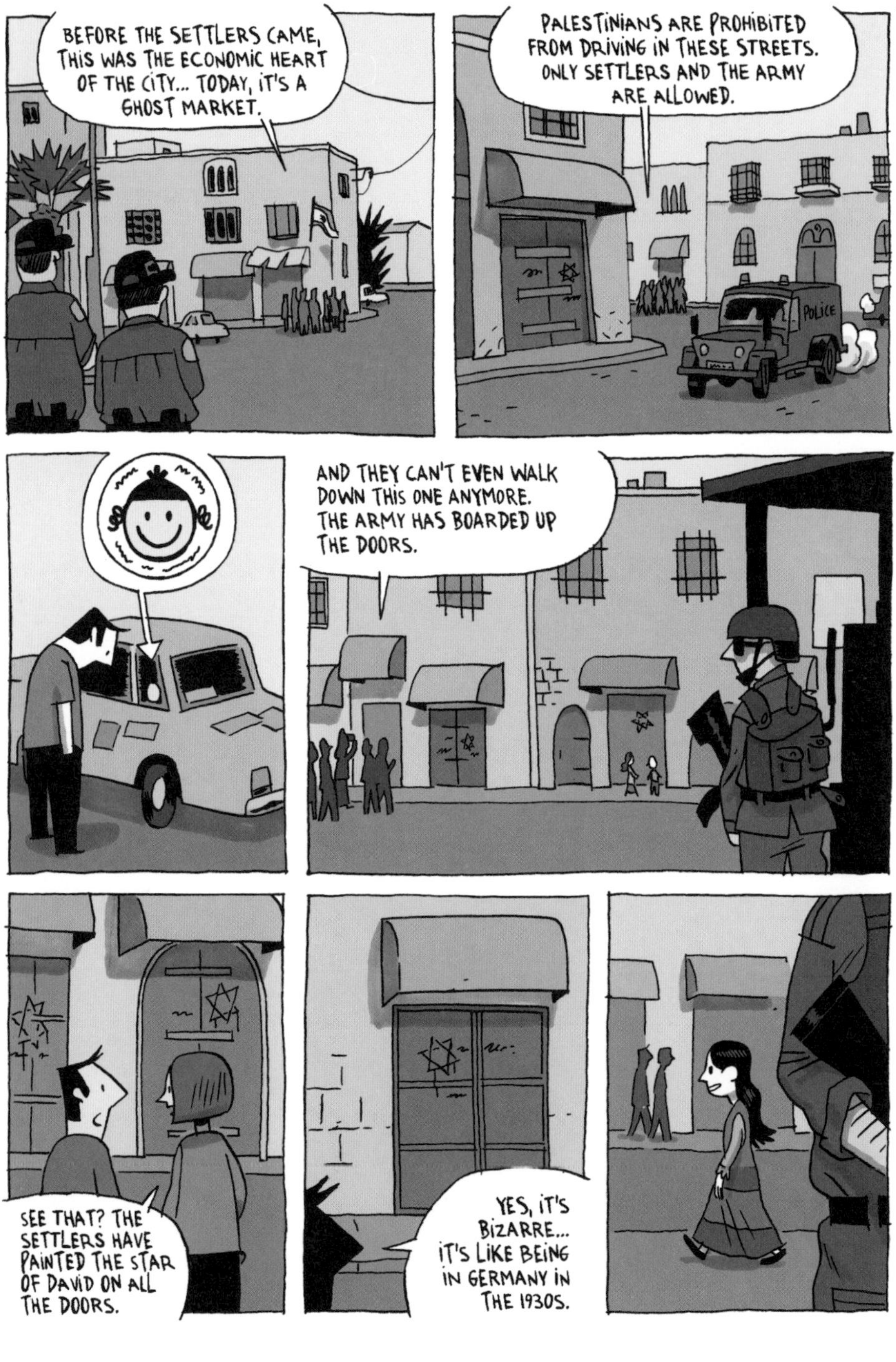
BEFORE THE SETTLERS CAME, THIS WAS THE ECONOMIC HEART OF THE CITY... TODAY, IT'S A GHOST MARKET.
PALESTINIANS ARE PROHIBITED FROM DRIVING IN THESE STREETS. ONLY SETTLERS AND THE ARMY ARE ALLOWED.
POLICE
AND THEY CAN'T EVEN WALK DOWN THIS ONE ANYMORE. THE ARMY HAS BOARDED UP THE DOORS.
SEE THAT? THE SETTLERS HAVE PAINTED THE STAR OF DAVID ON ALL THE DOORS.
YES, IT'S BIZARRE... IT'S LIKE BEING IN GERMANY IN THE 1930S.

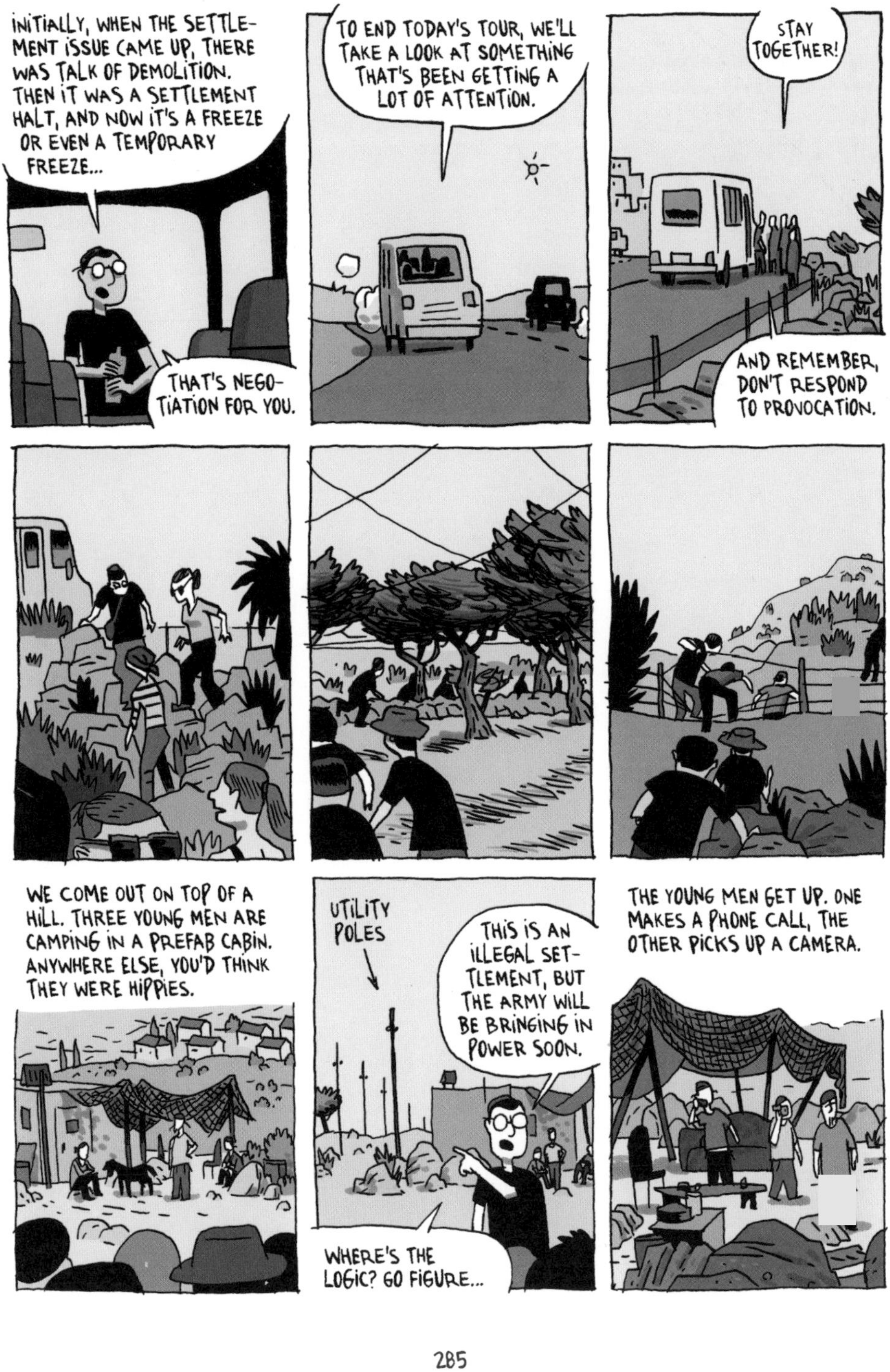

INITIALLY, WHEN THE SETTLEMENT ISSUE CAME UP, THERE WAS TALK OF DEMOLITION. THEN IT WAS A SETTLEMENT HALT, AND NOW IT'S A FREEZE OR EVEN A TEMPORARY FREEZE...
THAT'S NEGOTIATION FOR YOU.
TO END TODAY'S TOUR, WE'LL TAKE A LOOK AT SOMETHING THAT'S BEEN GETTING A LOT OF ATTENTION.
STAY TOGETHER!
AND REMEMBER, DON'T RESPOND TO PROVOCATION.
WE COME OUT ON TOP OF A HILL. THREE YOUNG MEN ARE CAMPING IN A PREFAB CABIN. ANYWHERE ELSE, YOU'D THINK THEY WERE HIPPIES.
UTILITY POLES
THIS IS AN ILLEGAL SETTLEMENT, BUT THE ARMY WILL BE BRINGING IN POWER SOON.
WHERE'S THE LOGIC? GO FIGURE...
THE YOUNG MEN GET UP. ONE MAKES A PHONE CALL, THE OTHER PICKS UP A CAMERA.

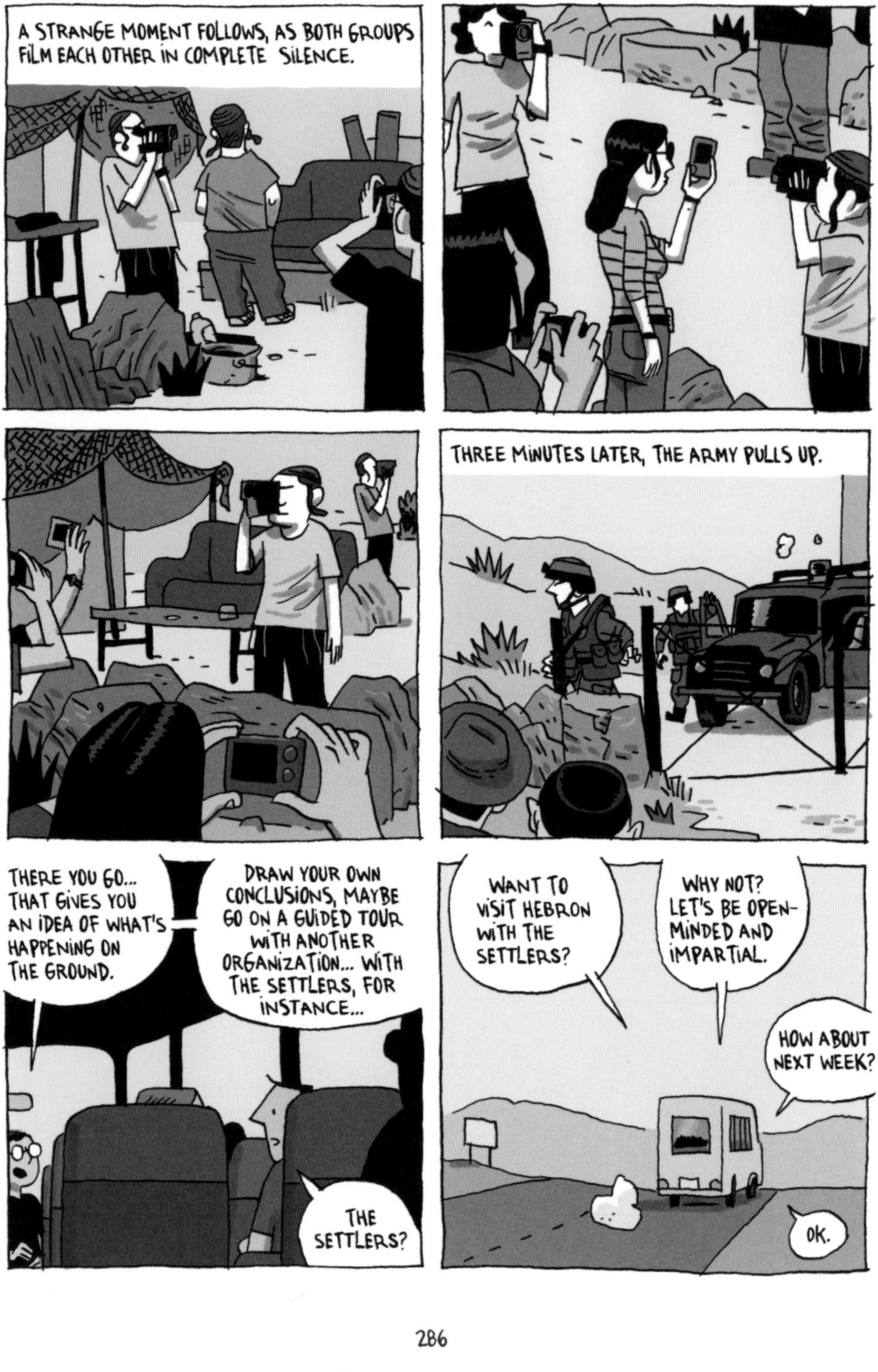
A STRANGE MOMENT FOLLOWS, AS BOTH GROUPS FILM EACH OTHER IN COMPLETE SILENCE.
THREE MINUTES LATER, THE ARMY PULLS UP.
THERE YOU GO... THAT GIVES YOU AN IDEA OF WHAT'S HAPPENING ON THE GROUND.
DRAW YOUR OWN CONCLUSIONS, MAYBE GO ON A GUIDED TOUR WITH ANOTHER ORGANIZATION... WITH THE SETTLERS, FOR INSTANCE...
THE SETTLERS?
WANT TO VISIT HEBRON WITH THE SETTLERS?
WHY NOT? LET'S BE OPEN-MINDED AND IMPARTIAL.
HOW ABOUT NEXT WEEK?
OK.

JUNE

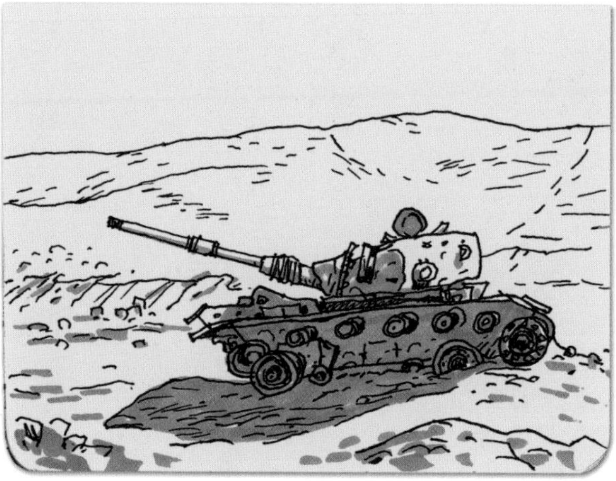

THE MONASTERY

MY FAVOURITE MOMENT IN THE WEEK IS WHEN I TAKE THE CAR OUT TO LOOK FOR SOMETHING TO DRAW.

NOW THAT WE'VE FOUND NABILA (WHO SPEAKS ENGLISH FLUENTLY), I GET TO INDULGE MORE OFTEN.

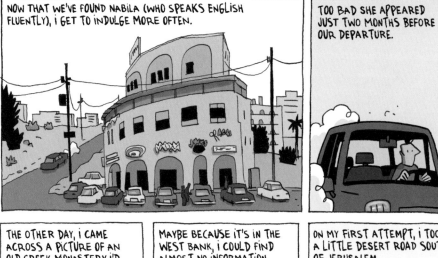

TOO BAD SHE APPEARED JUST TWO MONTHS BEFORE OUR DEPARTURE.

THE OTHER DAY, I CAME ACROSS A PICTURE OF AN OLD GREEK MONASTERY I'D NEVER HEARD OF.

MAYBE BECAUSE IT'S IN THE WEST BANK, I COULD FIND ALMOST NO INFORMATION ABOUT IT.

ON MY FIRST ATTEMPT, I TOOK A LITTLE DESERT ROAD SOUTH OF JERUSALEM.

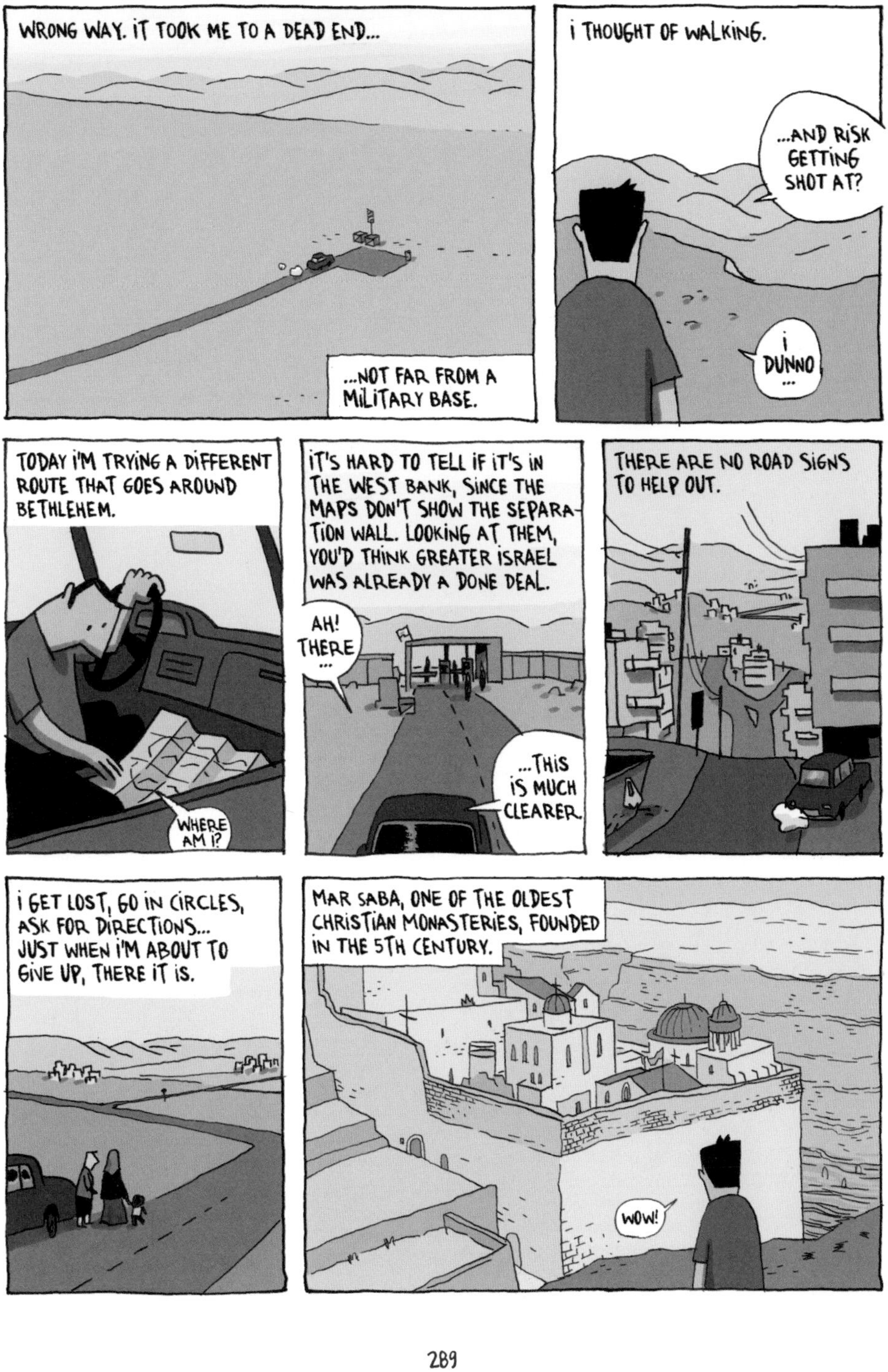
WRONG WAY. IT TOOK ME TO A DEAD END...
...NOT FAR FROM A MILITARY BASE.
I THOUGHT OF WALKING.
...AND RISK GETTING SHOT AT?
I DUNNO...
TODAY I'M TRYING A DIFFERENT ROUTE THAT GOES AROUND BETHLEHEM.
WHERE AM I?
IT'S HARD TO TELL IF IT'S IN THE WEST BANK, SINCE THE MAPS DON'T SHOW THE SEPARATION WALL. LOOKING AT THEM, YOU'D THINK GREATER ISRAEL WAS ALREADY A DONE DEAL.
AH! THERE...
...THIS IS MUCH CLEARER.
THERE ARE NO ROAD SIGNS TO HELP OUT.
I GET LOST, GO IN CIRCLES, ASK FOR DIRECTIONS... JUST WHEN I'M ABOUT TO GIVE UP, THERE IT IS.
MAR SABA, ONE OF THE OLDEST CHRISTIAN MONASTERIES, FOUNDED IN THE 5TH CENTURY.
WOW!

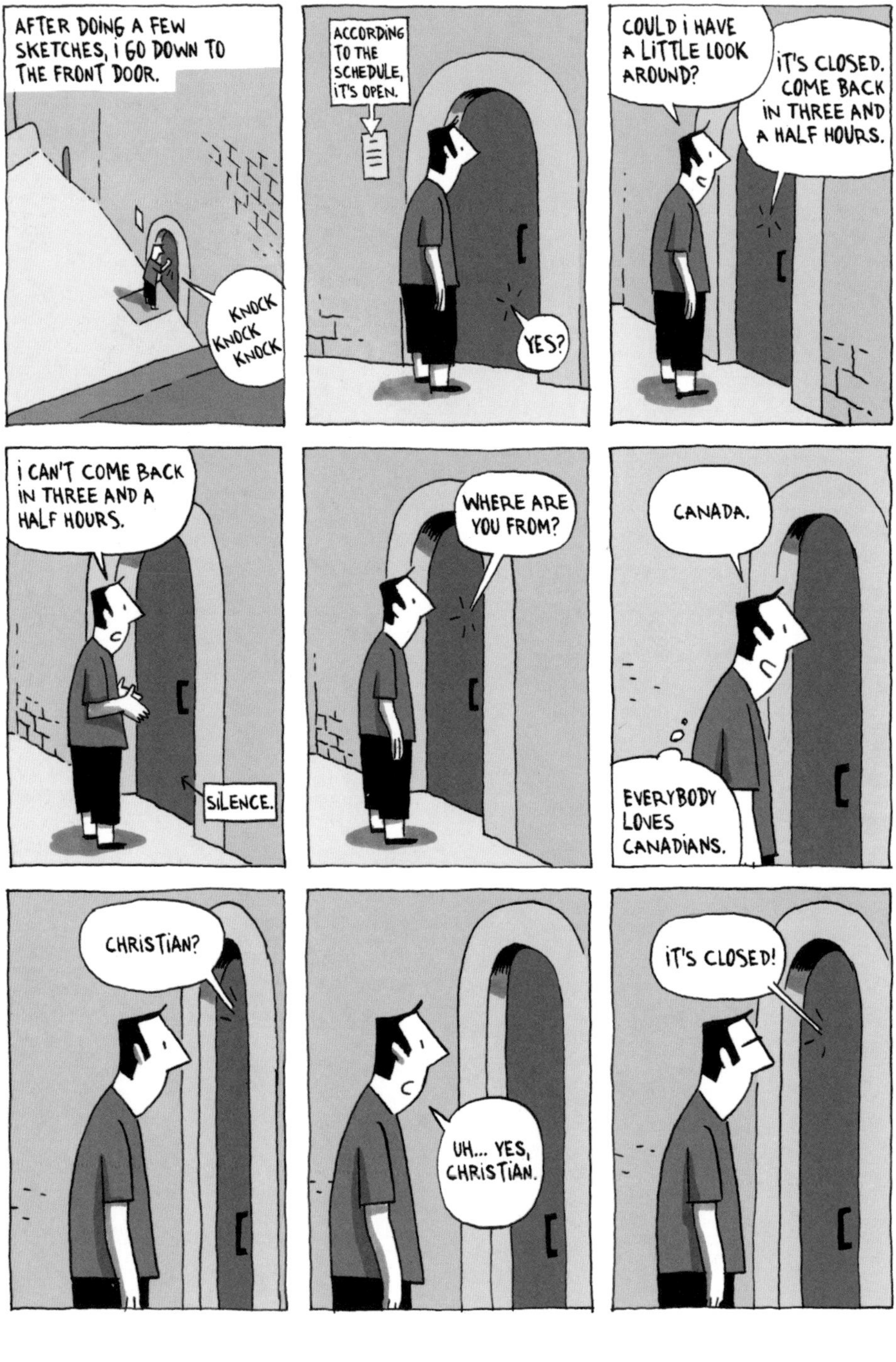
AFTER DOING A FEW SKETCHES, I GO DOWN TO THE FRONT DOOR.
KNOCK KNOCK KNOCK
ACCORDING TO THE SCHEDULE, IT'S OPEN.
YES?
COULD I HAVE A LITTLE LOOK AROUND?
IT'S CLOSED. COME BACK IN THREE AND A HALF HOURS.
I CAN'T COME BACK IN THREE AND A HALF HOURS.
SILENCE.
WHERE ARE YOU FROM?
CANADA.
EVERYBODY LOVES CANADIANS.
CHRISTIAN?
UH... YES, CHRISTIAN.
IT'S CLOSED!

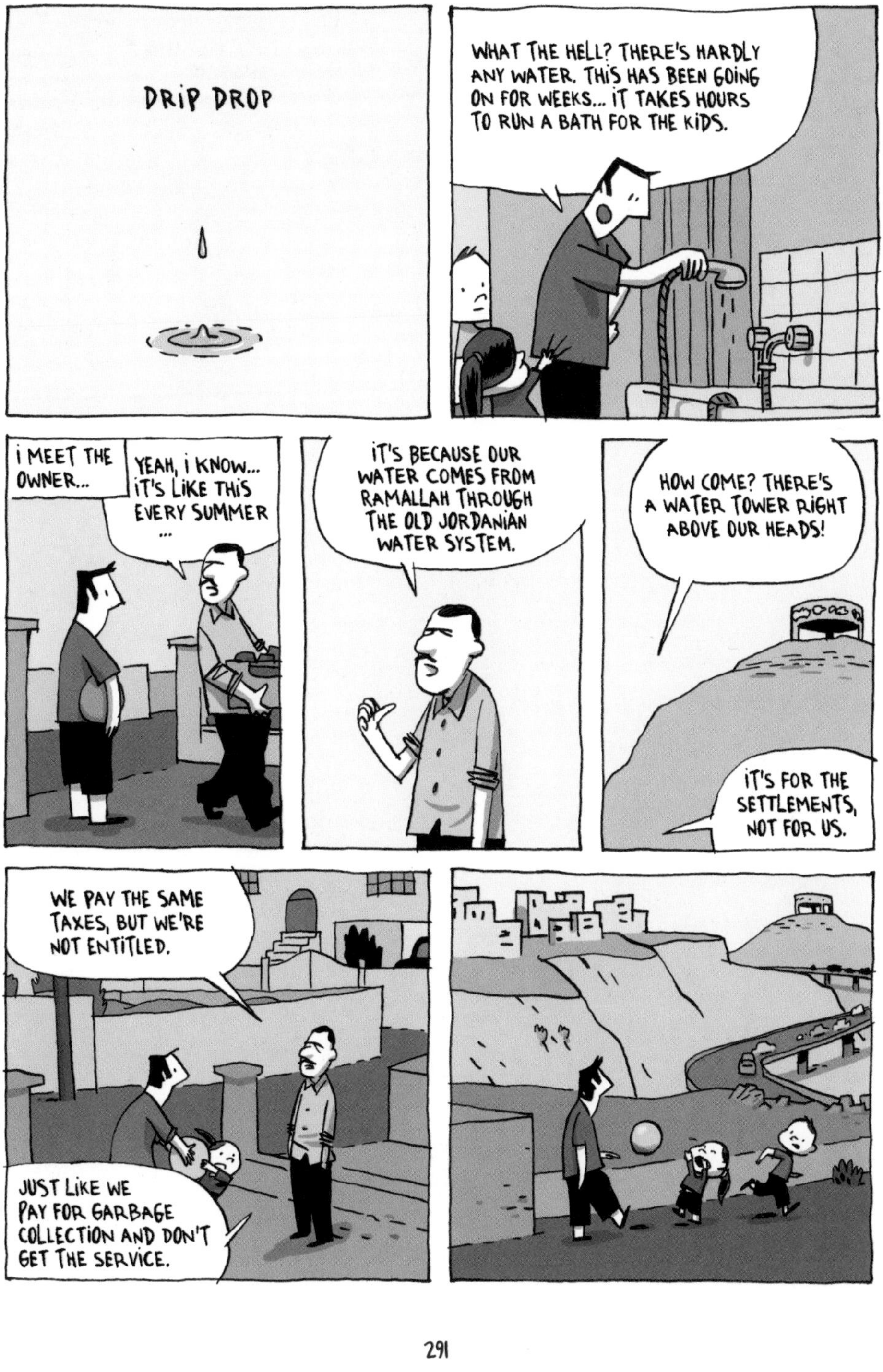
DRIP DROP
WHAT THE HELL? THERE'S HARDLY ANY WATER. THIS HAS BEEN GOING ON FOR WEEKS... IT TAKES HOURS TO RUN A BATH FOR THE KIDS.
I MEET THE OWNER...
YEAH, I KNOW... IT'S LIKE THIS EVERY SUMMER ...
IT'S BECAUSE OUR WATER COMES FROM RAMALLAH THROUGH THE OLD JORDANIAN WATER SYSTEM.
HOW COME? THERE'S A WATER TOWER RIGHT ABOVE OUR HEADS!
IT'S FOR THE SETTLEMENTS, NOT FOR US.
WE PAY THE SAME TAXES, BUT WE'RE NOT ENTITLED.
JUST LIKE WE PAY FOR GARBAGE COLLECTION AND DON'T GET THE SERVICE.

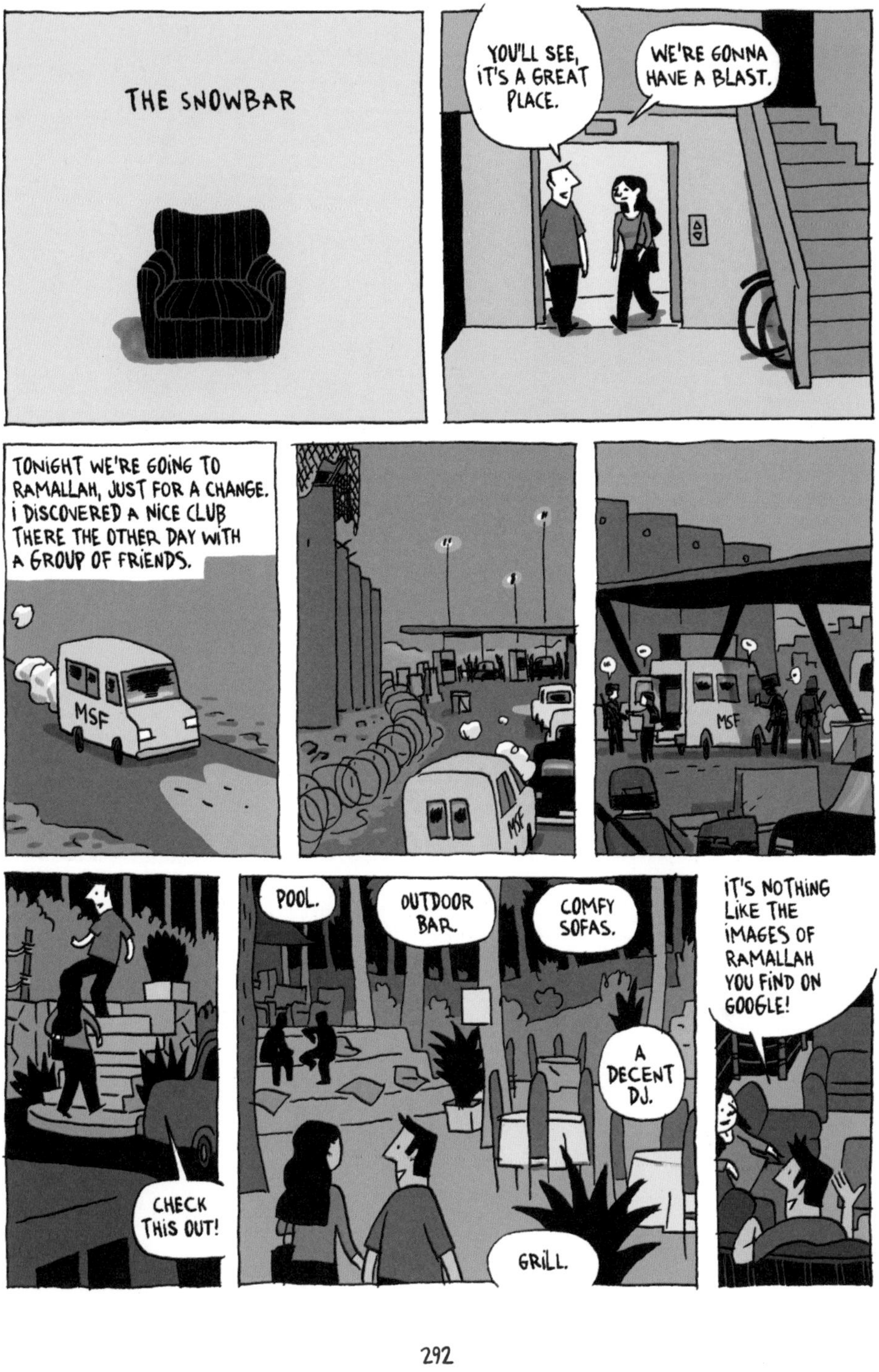
THE SNOWBAR
YOU'LL SEE, IT'S A GREAT PLACE.
WE'RE GONNA HAVE A BLAST.
TONIGHT WE'RE GOING TO RAMALLAH, JUST FOR A CHANGE. I DISCOVERED A NICE CLUB THERE THE OTHER DAY WITH A GROUP OF FRIENDS.
MSF
MSF
MSF
CHECK THIS OUT!
POOL.
OUTDOOR BAR.
COMFY SOFAS.
A DECENT DJ.
GRILL.
IT'S NOTHING LIKE THE IMAGES OF RAMALLAH YOU FIND ON GOOGLE!

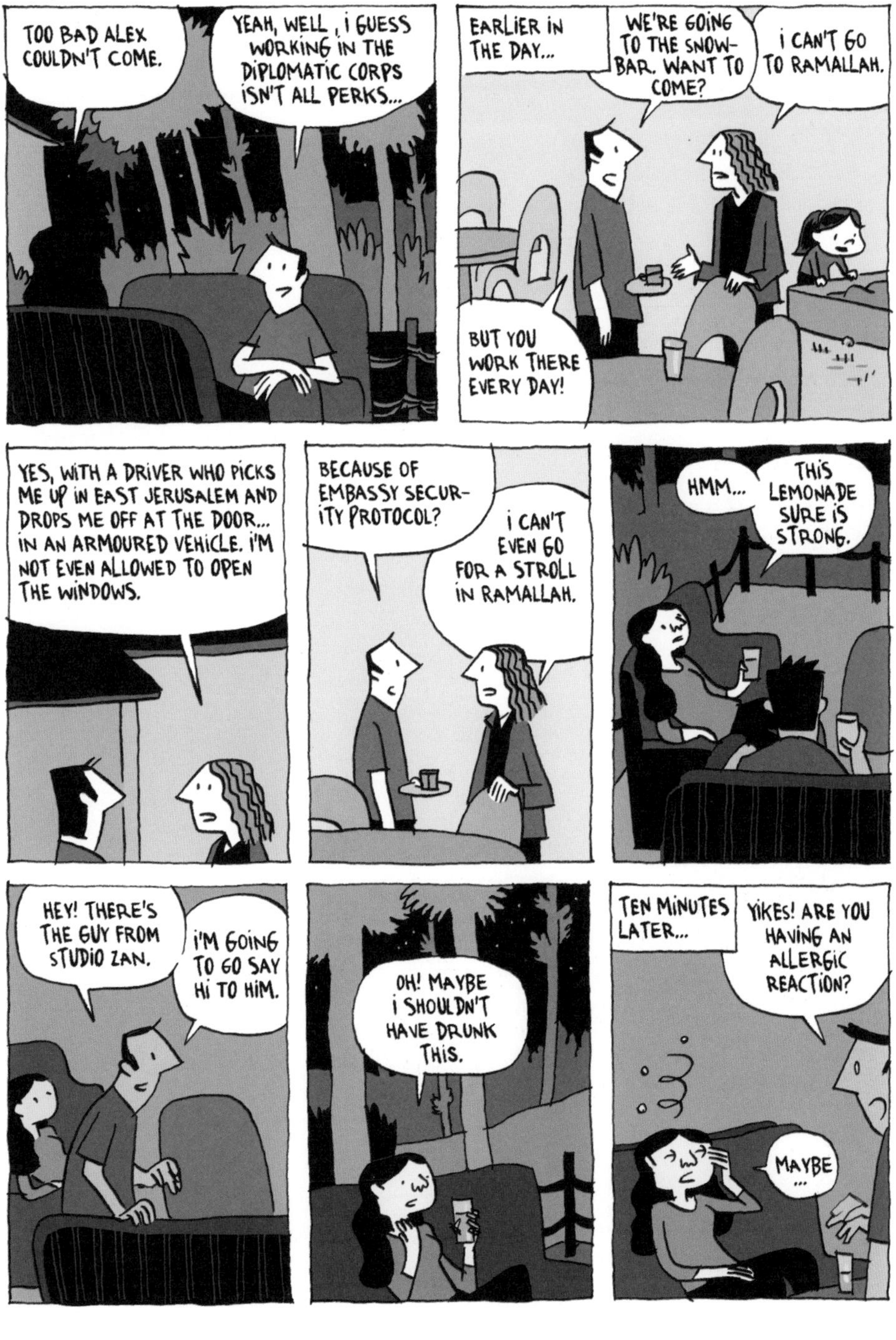
TOO BAD ALEX COULDN'T COME.
YEAH, WELL, I GUESS WORKING IN THE DIPLOMATIC CORPS ISN'T ALL PERKS...
EARLIER IN THE DAY...
WE'RE GOING TO THE SNOW-BAR. WANT TO COME?
I CAN'T GO TO RAMALLAH.
BUT YOU WORK THERE EVERY DAY!
YES, WITH A DRIVER WHO PICKS ME UP IN EAST JERUSALEM AND DROPS ME OFF AT THE DOOR... IN AN ARMOURED VEHICLE. I'M NOT EVEN ALLOWED TO OPEN THE WINDOWS.
BECAUSE OF EMBASSY SECURITY PROTOCOL?
I CAN'T EVEN GO FOR A STROLL IN RAMALLAH.
HMM...
THIS LEMONADE SURE IS STRONG.
HEY! THERE'S THE GUY FROM STUDIO ZAN.
I'M GOING TO GO SAY HI TO HIM.
OH! MAYBE I SHOULDN'T HAVE DRUNK THIS.
TEN MINUTES LATER...
YIKES! ARE YOU HAVING AN ALLERGIC REACTION?
MAYBE ...

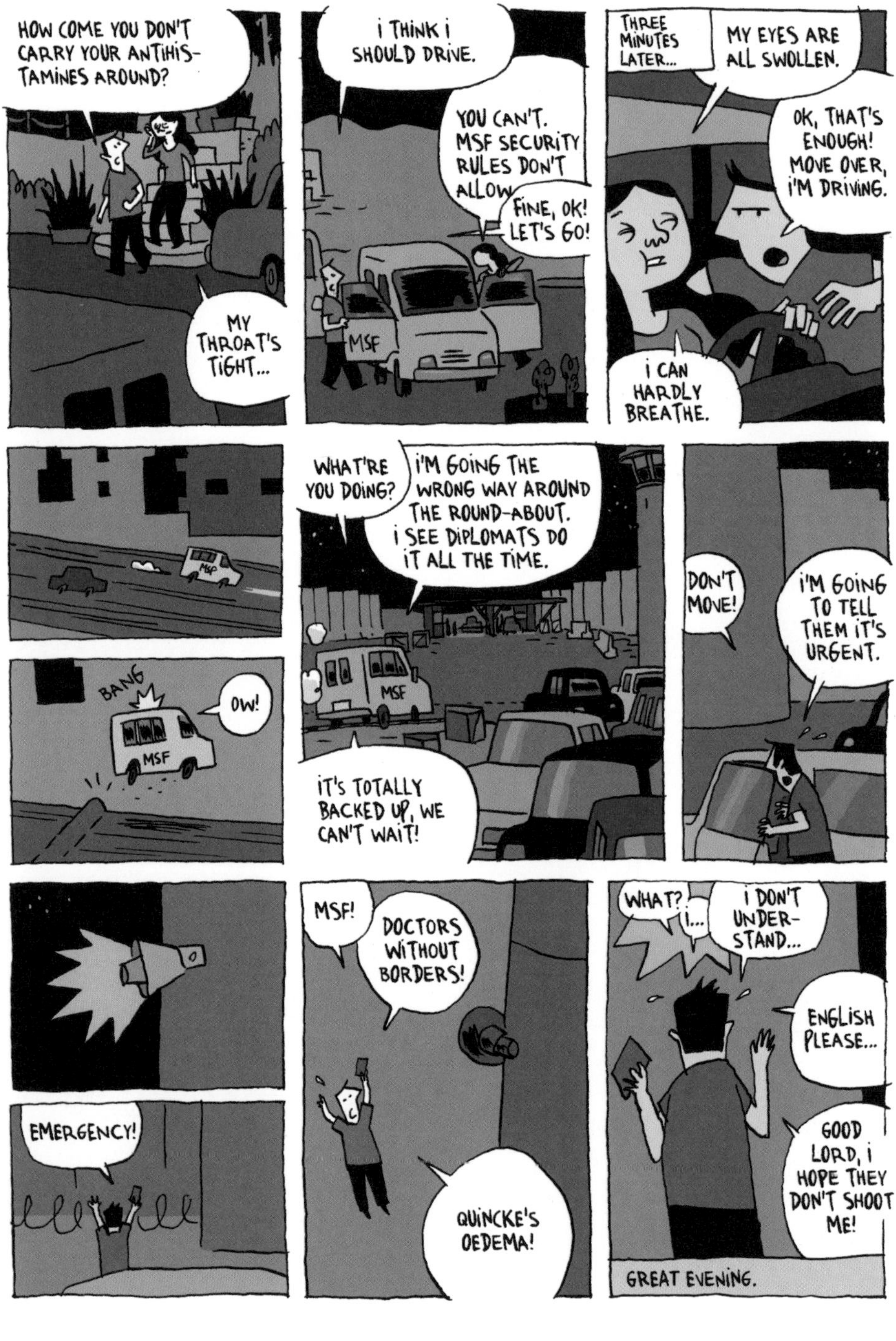
HOW COME YOU DON'T CARRY YOUR ANTIHIS-TAMINES AROUND?
MY THROAT'S TIGHT...
I THINK I SHOULD DRIVE.
YOU CAN'T. MSF SECURITY RULES DON'T ALLOW
FINE, OK! LET'S GO!
MSF
THREE MINUTES LATER...
MY EYES ARE ALL SWOLLEN.
OK, THAT'S ENOUGH! MOVE OVER, I'M DRIVING.
I CAN HARDLY BREATHE.
MSF
BANG
OW!
MSF
WHAT'RE YOU DOING?
I'M GOING THE WRONG WAY AROUND THE ROUND-ABOUT. I SEE DIPLOMATS DO IT ALL THE TIME.
MSF
IT'S TOTALLY BACKED UP, WE CAN'T WAIT!
DON'T MOVE!
I'M GOING TO TELL THEM IT'S URGENT.
EMERGENCY!
MSF!
DOCTORS WITHOUT BORDERS!
QUINCKE'S OEDEMA!
WHAT?
I...
I DON'T UNDER-STAND...
ENGLISH PLEASE...
GOOD LORD, I HOPE THEY DON'T SHOOT ME!
GREAT EVENING.

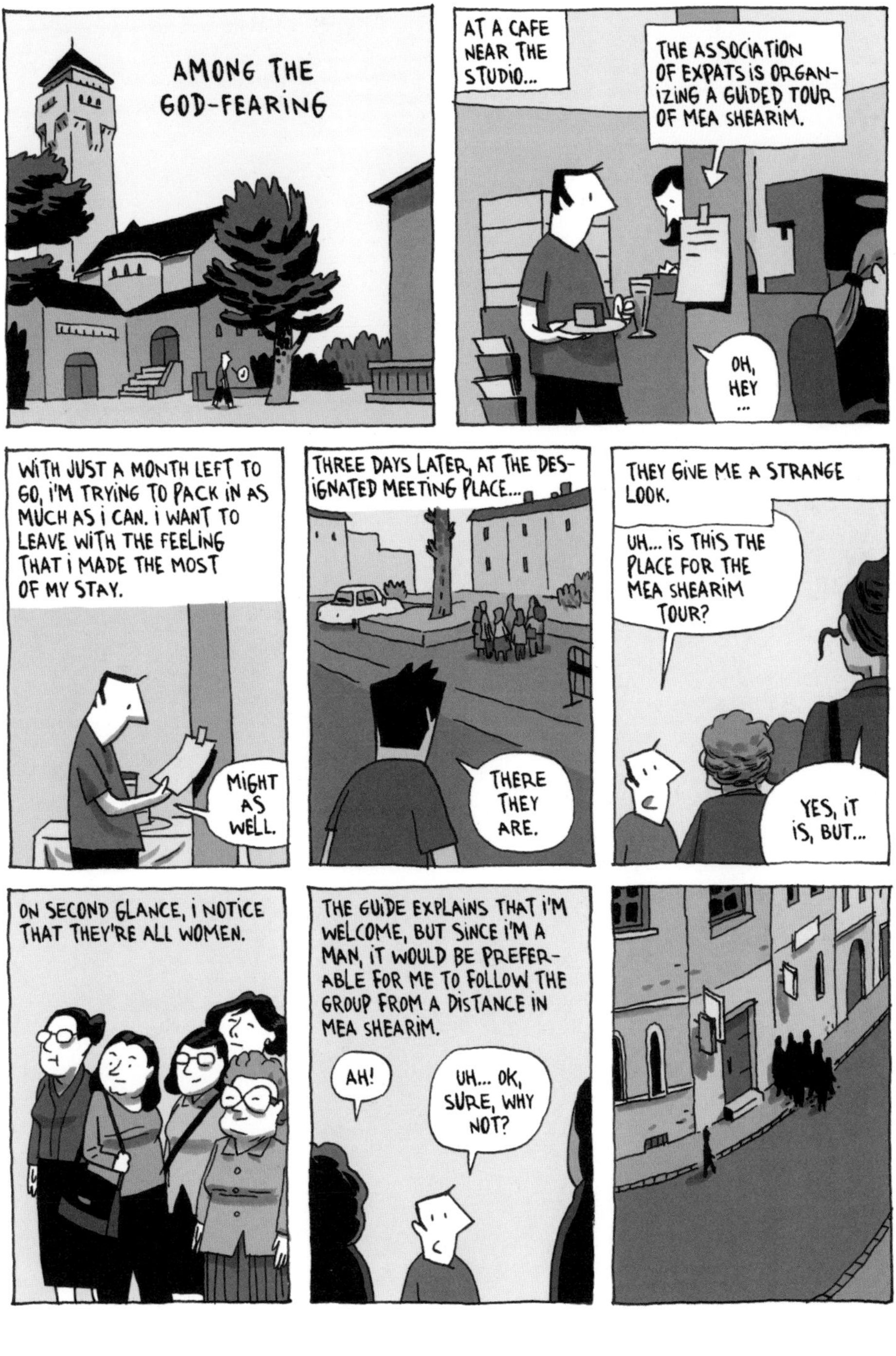
AMONG THE GOD-FEARING
AT A CAFE NEAR THE STUDIO...
THE ASSOCIATION OF EXPATS IS ORGANIZING A GUIDED TOUR OF MEA SHEARIM.
OH, HEY ...
WITH JUST A MONTH LEFT TO GO, I'M TRYING TO PACK IN AS MUCH AS I CAN. I WANT TO LEAVE WITH THE FEELING THAT I MADE THE MOST OF MY STAY.
MIGHT AS WELL.
THREE DAYS LATER, AT THE DESIGNATED MEETING PLACE...
THERE THEY ARE.
THEY GIVE ME A STRANGE LOOK.
UH... IS THIS THE PLACE FOR THE MEA SHEARIM TOUR?
YES, IT IS, BUT...
ON SECOND GLANCE, I NOTICE THAT THEY'RE ALL WOMEN.
THE GUIDE EXPLAINS THAT I'M WELCOME, BUT SINCE I'M A MAN, IT WOULD BE PREFERABLE FOR ME TO FOLLOW THE GROUP FROM A DISTANCE IN MEA SHEARIM.
AH!
UH... OK, SURE, WHY NOT?

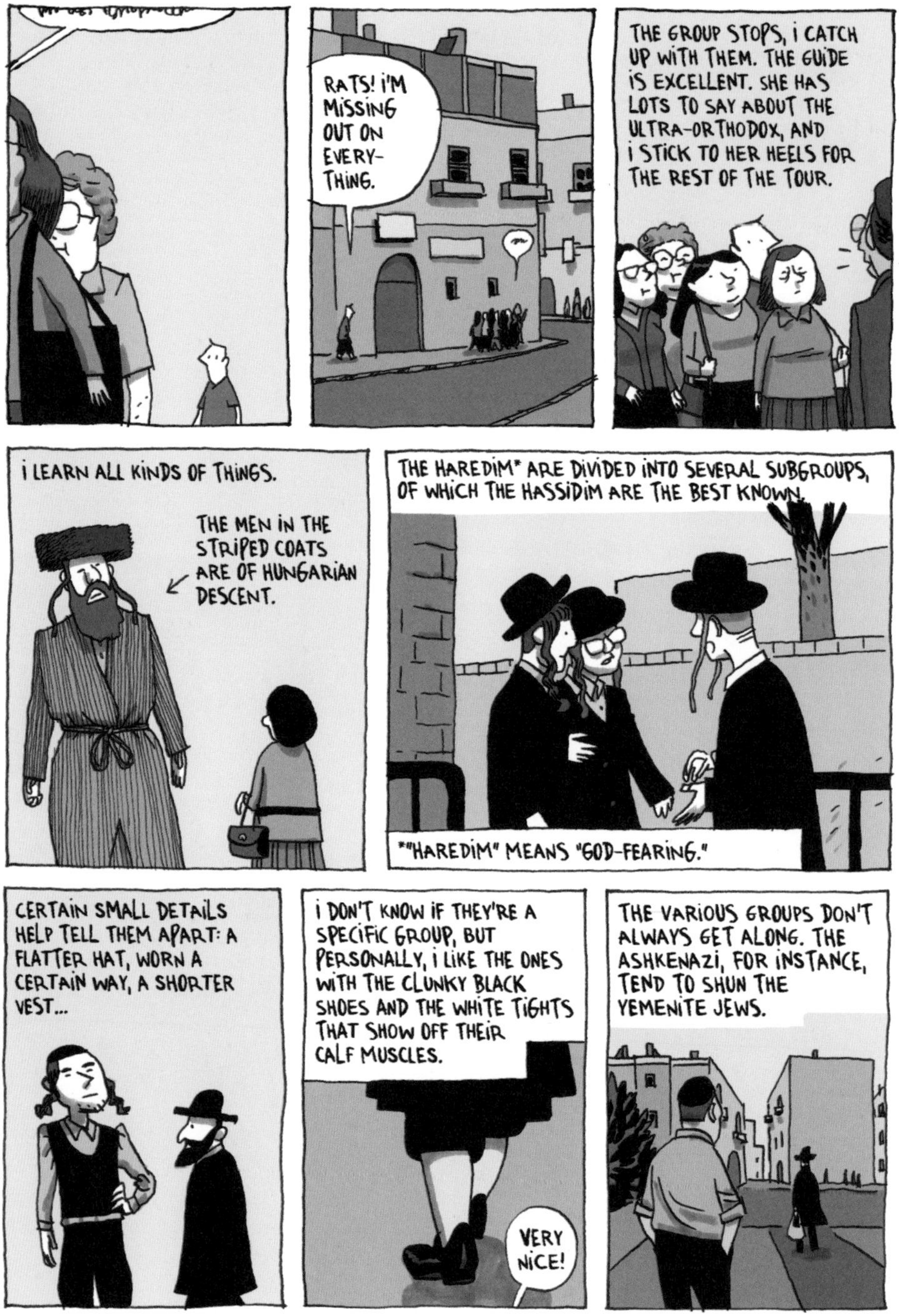

RATS! I'M MISSING OUT ON EVERY-THING.
THE GROUP STOPS, I CATCH UP WITH THEM. THE GUIDE IS EXCELLENT. SHE HAS LOTS TO SAY ABOUT THE ULTRA-ORTHODOX, AND I STICK TO HER HEELS FOR THE REST OF THE TOUR.
I LEARN ALL KINDS OF THINGS.
THE MEN IN THE STRIPED COATS ARE OF HUNGARIAN DESCENT.
THE HAREDIM* ARE DIVIDED INTO SEVERAL SUBGROUPS, OF WHICH THE HASSIDIM ARE THE BEST KNOWN.
*"HAREDIM" MEANS "GOD-FEARING."
CERTAIN SMALL DETAILS HELP TELL THEM APART: A FLATTER HAT, WORN A CERTAIN WAY, A SHORTER VEST...
I DON'T KNOW IF THEY'RE A SPECIFIC GROUP, BUT PERSONALLY, I LIKE THE ONES WITH THE CLUNKY BLACK SHOES AND THE WHITE TIGHTS THAT SHOW OFF THEIR CALF MUSCLES.
VERY NICE!
THE VARIOUS GROUPS DON'T ALWAYS GET ALONG. THE ASHKENAZI, FOR INSTANCE, TEND TO SHUN THE YEMENITE JEWS.

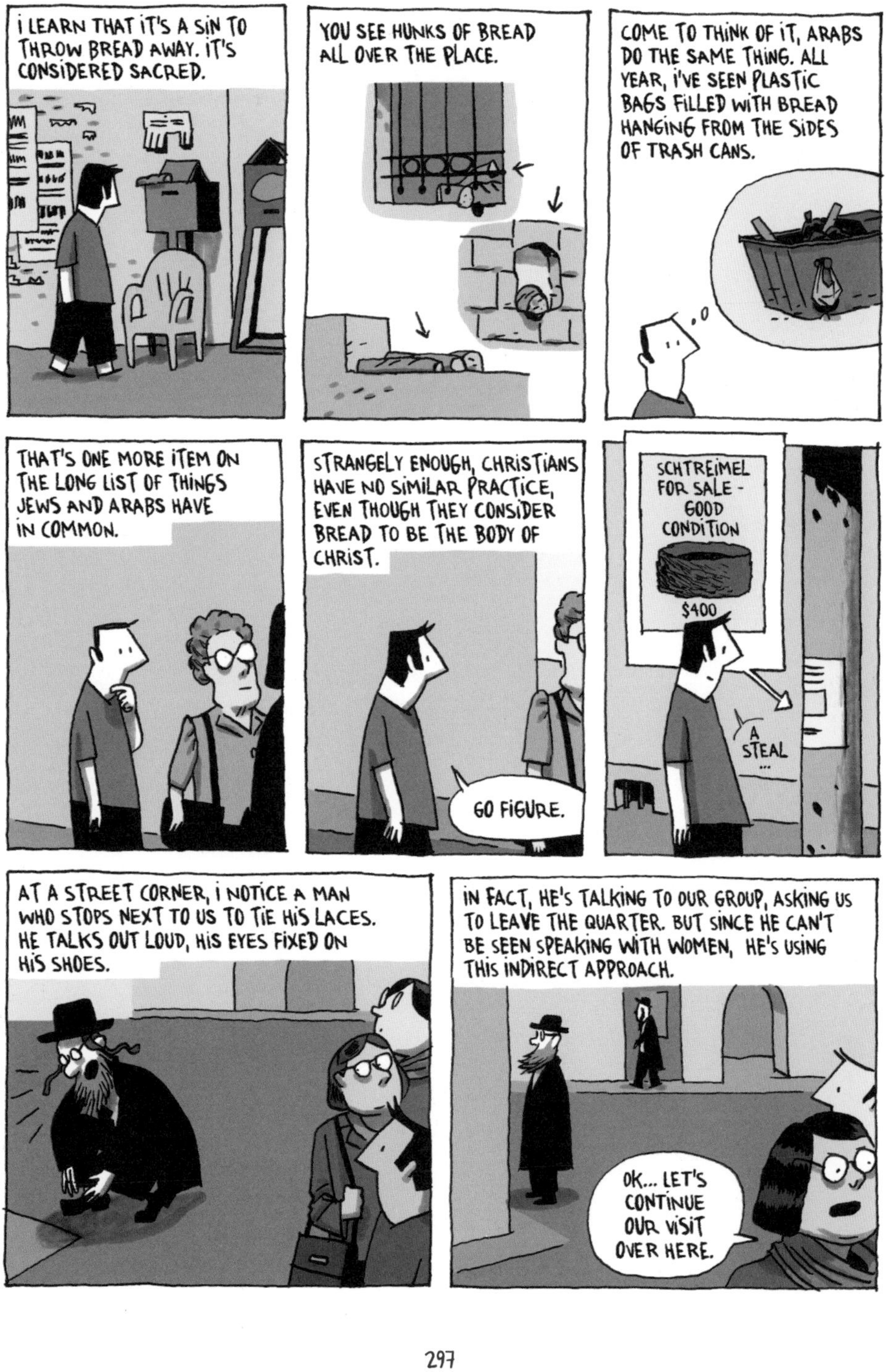
I LEARN THAT IT'S A SIN TO THROW BREAD AWAY. IT'S CONSIDERED SACRED.
YOU SEE HUNKS OF BREAD ALL OVER THE PLACE.
COME TO THINK OF IT, ARABS DO THE SAME THING. ALL YEAR, I'VE SEEN PLASTIC BAGS FILLED WITH BREAD HANGING FROM THE SIDES OF TRASH CANS.
THAT'S ONE MORE ITEM ON THE LONG LIST OF THINGS JEWS AND ARABS HAVE IN COMMON.
STRANGELY ENOUGH, CHRISTIANS HAVE NO SIMILAR PRACTICE, EVEN THOUGH THEY CONSIDER BREAD TO BE THE BODY OF CHRIST.
GO FIGURE.
SCHTREIMEL FOR SALE - GOOD CONDITION
$400
A STEAL...
AT A STREET CORNER, I NOTICE A MAN WHO STOPS NEXT TO US TO TIE HIS LACES. HE TALKS OUT LOUD, HIS EYES FIXED ON HIS SHOES.
IN FACT, HE'S TALKING TO OUR GROUP, ASKING US TO LEAVE THE QUARTER. BUT SINCE HE CAN'T BE SEEN SPEAKING WITH WOMEN, HE'S USING THIS INDIRECT APPROACH.
OK... LET'S CONTINUE OUR VISIT OVER HERE.

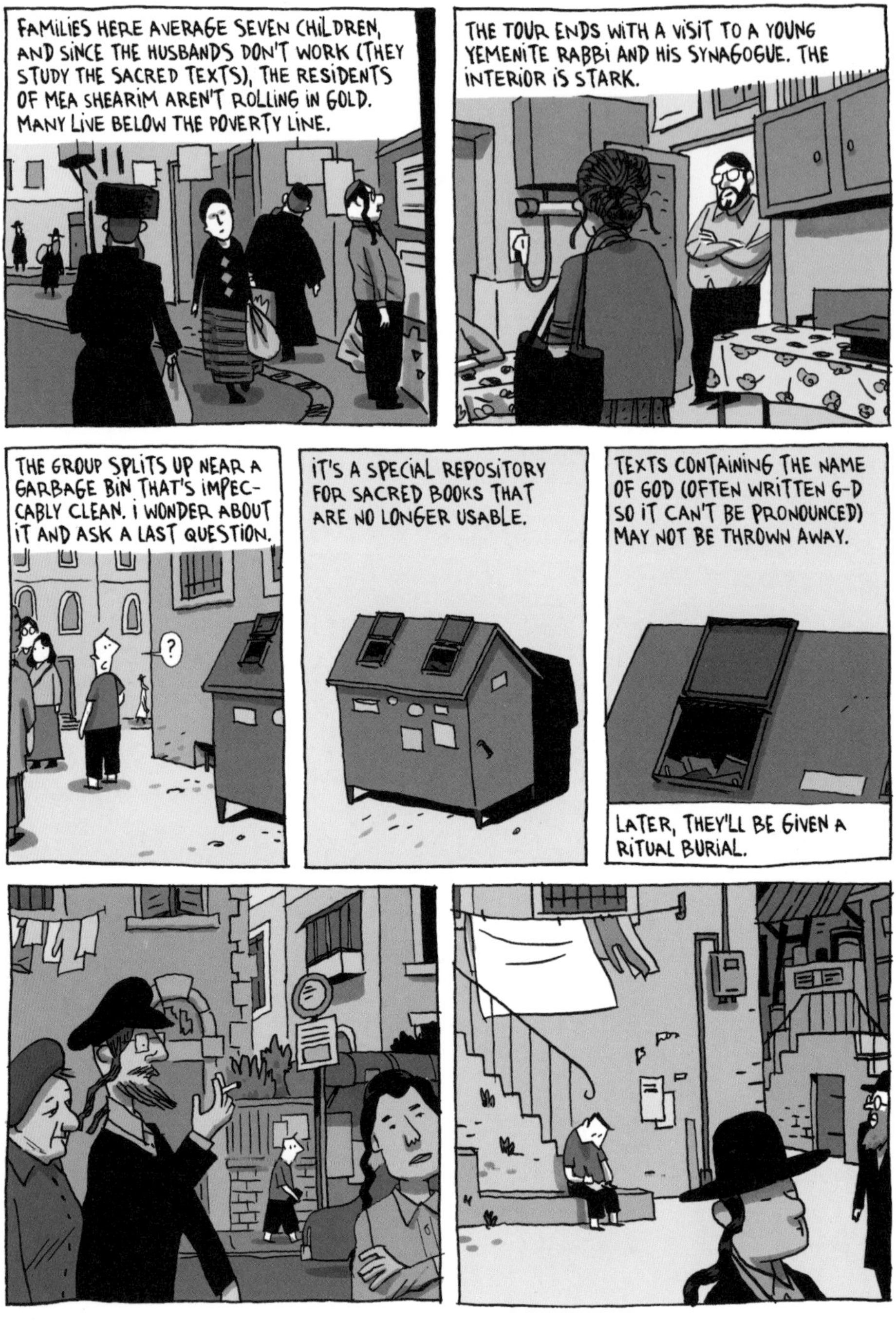
FAMILIES HERE AVERAGE SEVEN CHILDREN, AND SINCE THE HUSBANDS DON'T WORK (THEY STUDY THE SACRED TEXTS), THE RESIDENTS OF MEA SHEARIM AREN'T ROLLING IN GOLD. MANY LIVE BELOW THE POVERTY LINE.
THE TOUR ENDS WITH A VISIT TO A YOUNG YEMENITE RABBI AND HIS SYNAGOGUE. THE INTERIOR IS STARK.
THE GROUP SPLITS UP NEAR A GARBAGE BIN THAT'S IMPECCABLY CLEAN. I WONDER ABOUT IT AND ASK A LAST QUESTION.
?
IT'S A SPECIAL REPOSITORY FOR SACRED BOOKS THAT ARE NO LONGER USABLE.
TEXTS CONTAINING THE NAME OF GOD (OFTEN WRITTEN G-D SO IT CAN'T BE PRONOUNCED) MAY NOT BE THROWN AWAY.
LATER, THEY'LL BE GIVEN A RITUAL BURIAL.

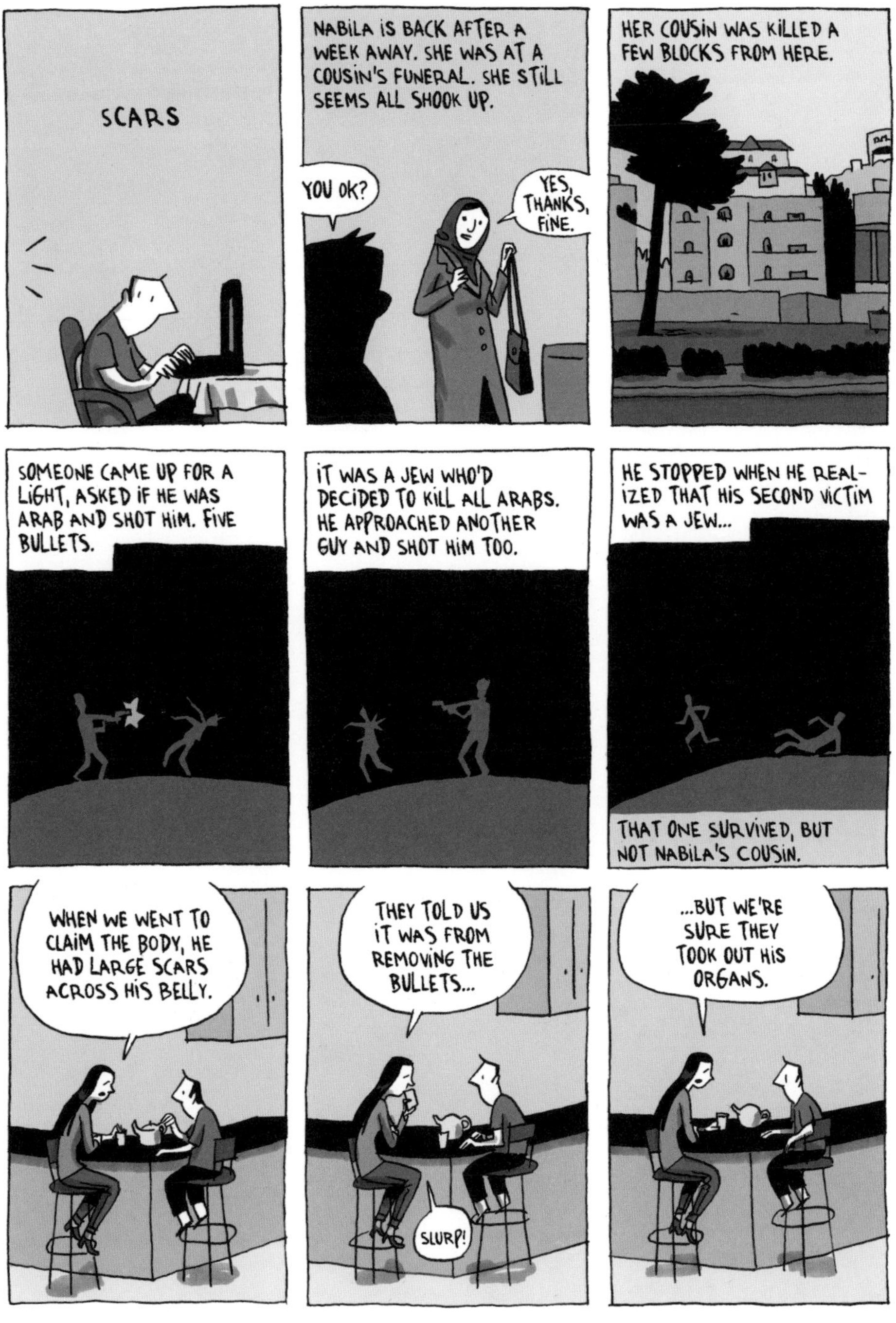
SCARS
NABILA IS BACK AFTER A WEEK AWAY. SHE WAS AT A COUSIN'S FUNERAL. SHE STILL SEEMS ALL SHOOK UP.
YOU OK?
YES, THANKS, FINE.
HER COUSIN WAS KILLED A FEW BLOCKS FROM HERE.
SOMEONE CAME UP FOR A LIGHT, ASKED IF HE WAS ARAB AND SHOT HIM. FIVE BULLETS.
IT WAS A JEW WHO'D DECIDED TO KILL ALL ARABS. HE APPROACHED ANOTHER GUY AND SHOT HIM TOO.
HE STOPPED WHEN HE REALIZED THAT HIS SECOND VICTIM WAS A JEW...
THAT ONE SURVIVED, BUT NOT NABILA'S COUSIN.
WHEN WE WENT TO CLAIM THE BODY, HE HAD LARGE SCARS ACROSS HIS BELLY.
THEY TOLD US IT WAS FROM REMOVING THE BULLETS...
SLURP!
...BUT WE'RE SURE THEY TOOK OUT HIS ORGANS.

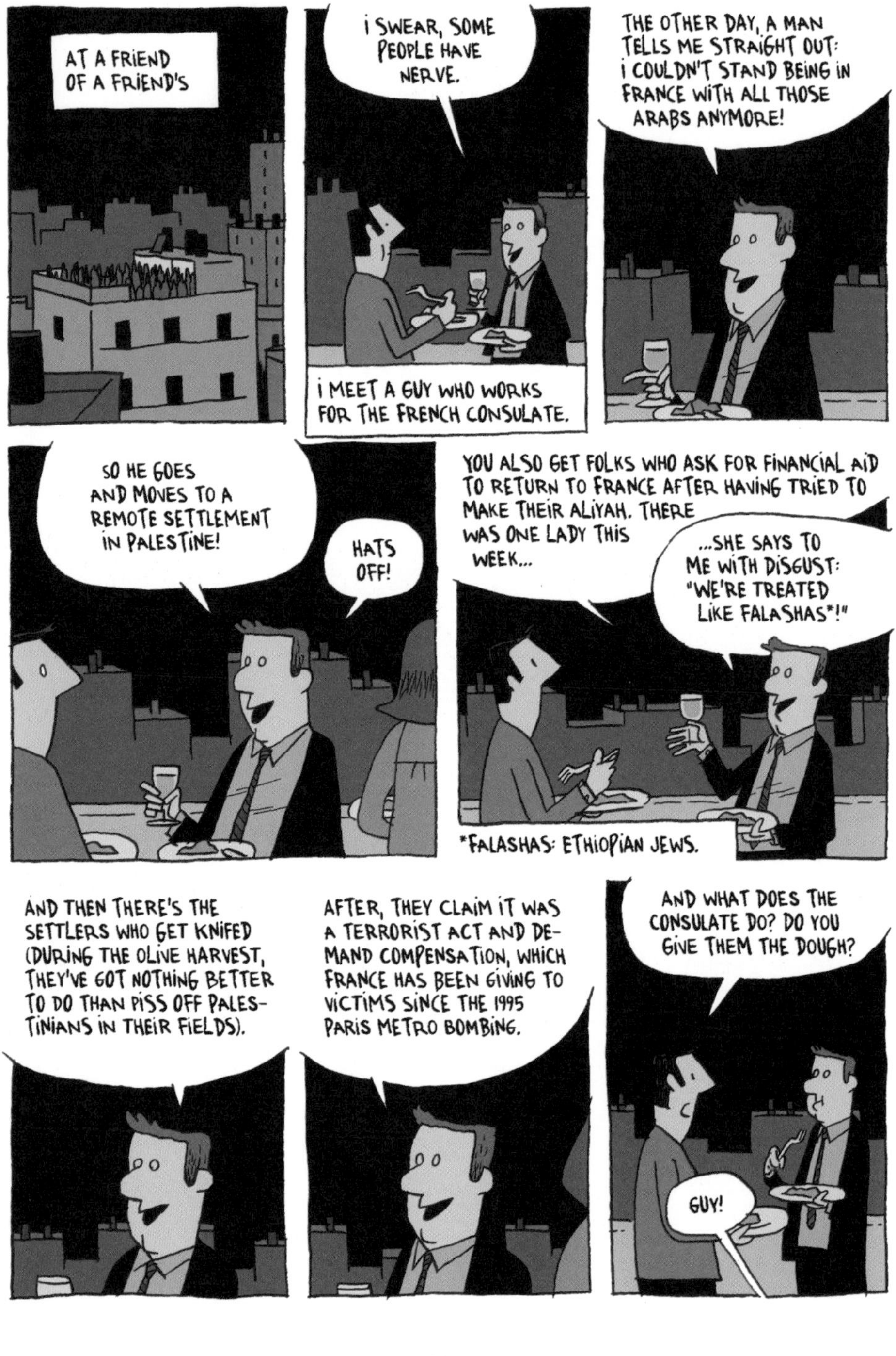

AT A FRIEND OF A FRIEND'S
I SWEAR, SOME PEOPLE HAVE NERVE.
I MEET A GUY WHO WORKS FOR THE FRENCH CONSULATE.
THE OTHER DAY, A MAN TELLS ME STRAIGHT OUT: I COULDN'T STAND BEING IN FRANCE WITH ALL THOSE ARABS ANYMORE!
SO HE GOES AND MOVES TO A REMOTE SETTLEMENT IN PALESTINE!
HATS OFF!
YOU ALSO GET FOLKS WHO ASK FOR FINANCIAL AID TO RETURN TO FRANCE AFTER HAVING TRIED TO MAKE THEIR ALIYAH. THERE WAS ONE LADY THIS WEEK...
...SHE SAYS TO ME WITH DISGUST: "WE'RE TREATED LIKE FALASHAS*!"
*FALASHAS: ETHIOPIAN JEWS.
AND THEN THERE'S THE SETTLERS WHO GET KNIFED (DURING THE OLIVE HARVEST, THEY'VE GOT NOTHING BETTER TO DO THAN PISS OFF PALESTINIANS IN THEIR FIELDS).
AFTER, THEY CLAIM IT WAS A TERRORIST ACT AND DEMAND COMPENSATION, WHICH FRANCE HAS BEEN GIVING TO VICTIMS SINCE THE 1995 PARIS METRO BOMBING.
AND WHAT DOES THE CONSULATE DO? DO YOU GIVE THEM THE DOUGH?
GUY!

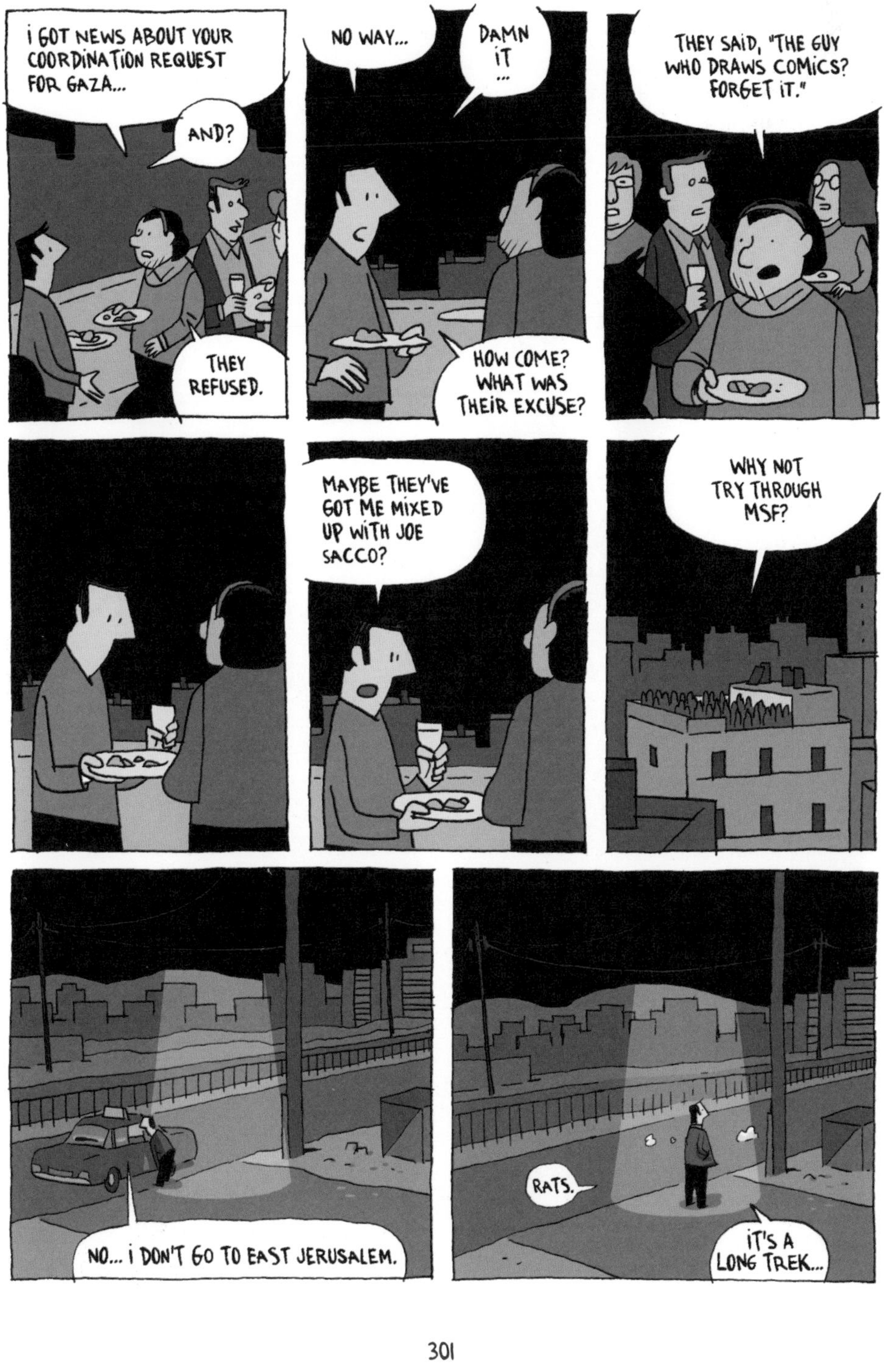
I GOT NEWS ABOUT YOUR COORDINATION REQUEST FOR GAZA...
AND?
THEY REFUSED.
NO WAY...
DAMN IT ...
HOW COME? WHAT WAS THEIR EXCUSE?
THEY SAID, "THE GUY WHO DRAWS COMICS? FORGET IT."
MAYBE THEY'VE GOT ME MIXED UP WITH JOE SACCO?
WHY NOT TRY THROUGH MSF?
NO... I DON'T GO TO EAST JERUSALEM.
RATS.
IT'S A LONG TREK...

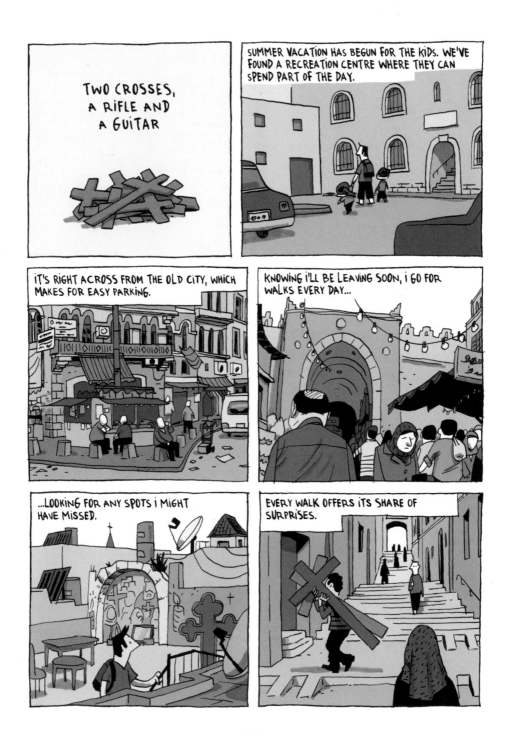

TWO CROSSES,
A RIFLE AND
A GUITAR

SUMMER VACATION HAS BEGUN FOR THE KIDS. WE'VE FOUND A RECREATION CENTRE WHERE THEY CAN SPEND PART OF THE DAY.

IT'S RIGHT ACROSS FROM THE OLD CITY, WHICH MAKES FOR EASY PARKING.

KNOWING I'LL BE LEAVING SOON, I GO FOR WALKS EVERY DAY...

...LOOKING FOR ANY SPOTS I MIGHT HAVE MISSED.

EVERY WALK OFFERS ITS SHARE OF SURPRISES.

302

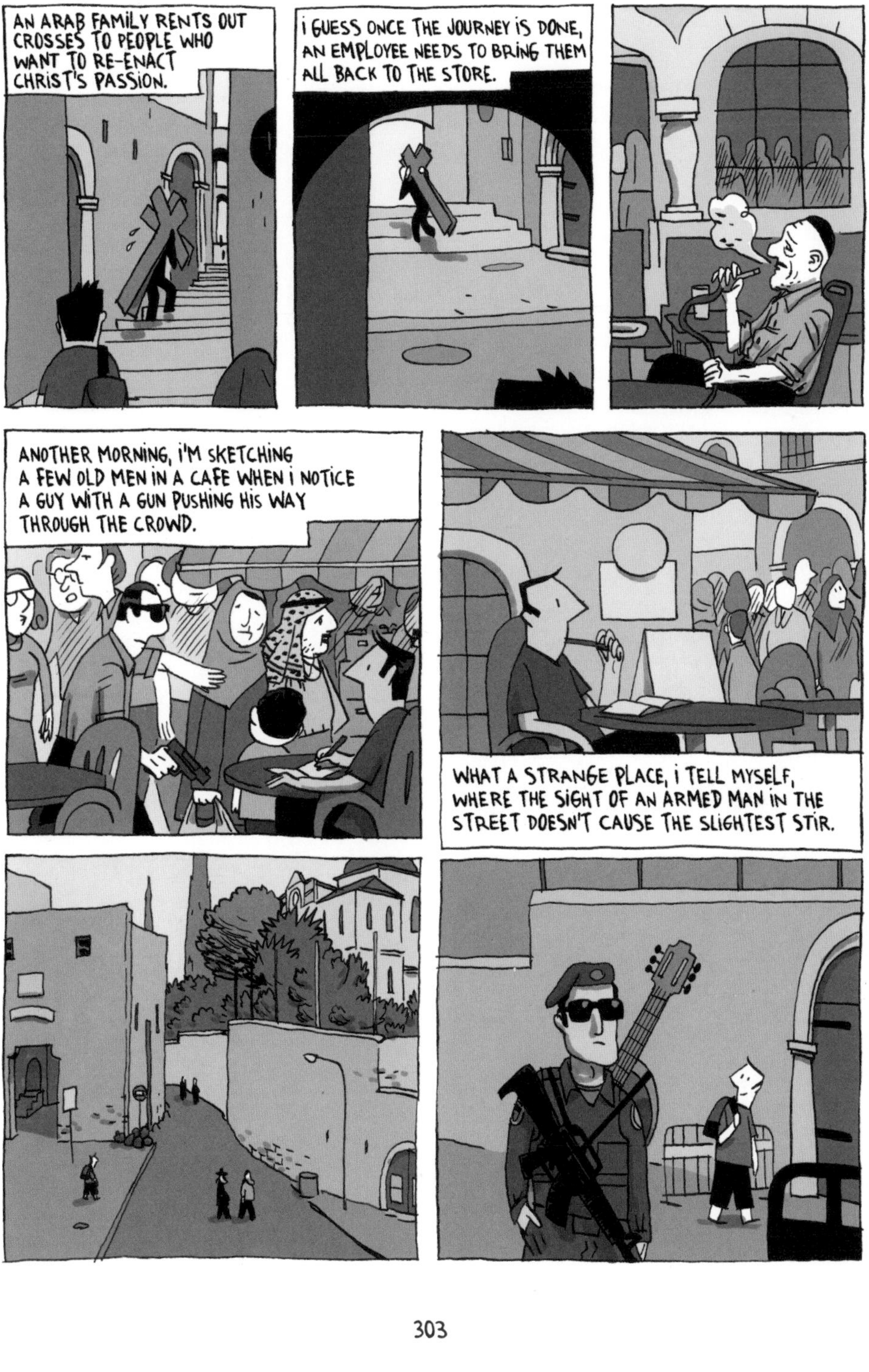
AN ARAB FAMILY RENTS OUT CROSSES TO PEOPLE WHO WANT TO RE-ENACT CHRIST'S PASSION.
I GUESS ONCE THE JOURNEY IS DONE, AN EMPLOYEE NEEDS TO BRING THEM ALL BACK TO THE STORE.
ANOTHER MORNING, I'M SKETCHING A FEW OLD MEN IN A CAFE WHEN I NOTICE A GUY WITH A GUN PUSHING HIS WAY THROUGH THE CROWD.
WHAT A STRANGE PLACE, I TELL MYSELF, WHERE THE SIGHT OF AN ARMED MAN IN THE STREET DOESN'T CAUSE THE SLIGHTEST STIR.

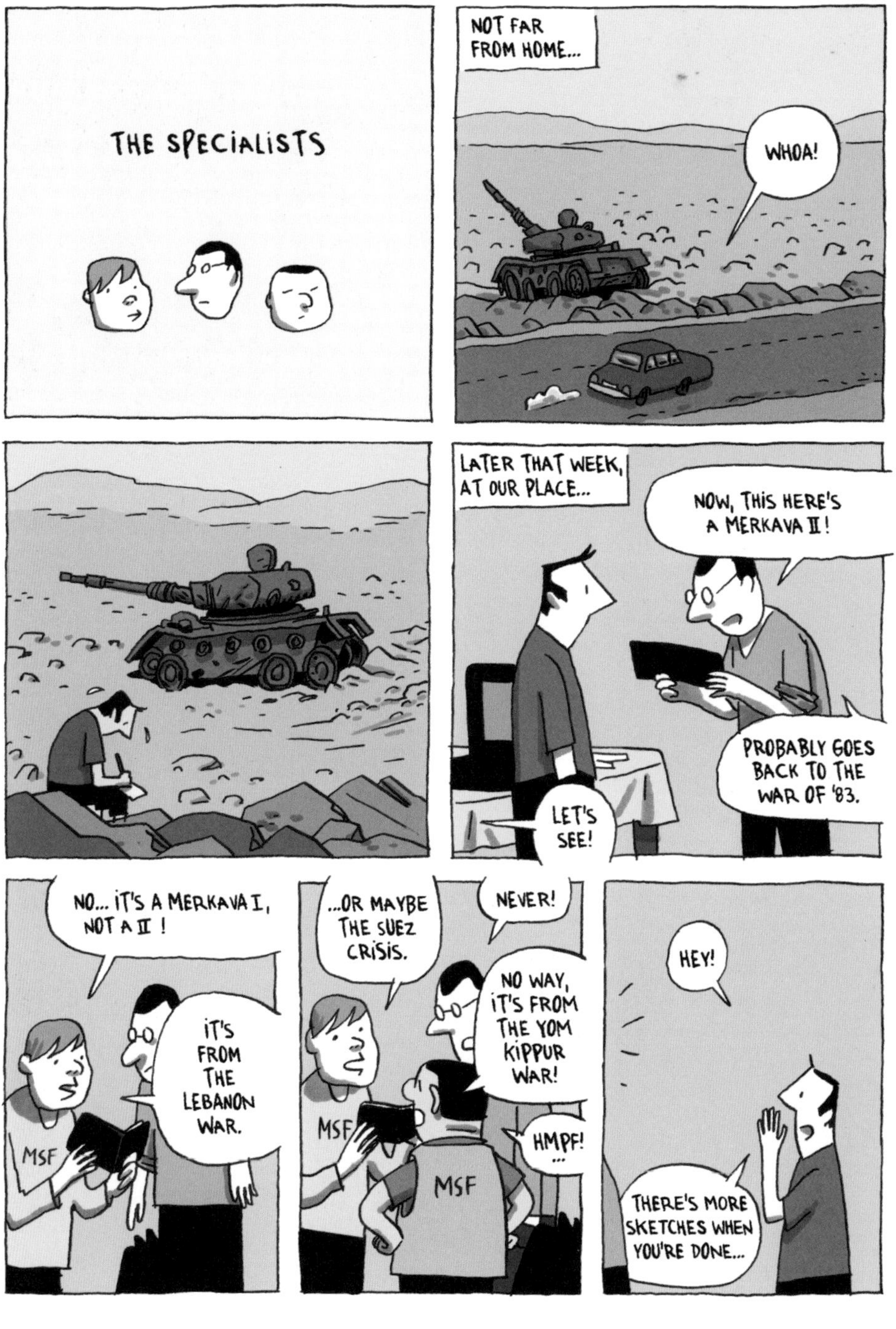
THE SPECIALISTS
NOT FAR FROM HOME...
WHOA!
LATER THAT WEEK, AT OUR PLACE...
NOW, THIS HERE'S A MERKAVA II!
PROBABLY GOES BACK TO THE WAR OF '83.
LET'S SEE!
NO... IT'S A MERKAVA I, NOT A II !
IT'S FROM THE LEBANON WAR.
...OR MAYBE THE SUEZ CRISIS.
NEVER!
NO WAY, IT'S FROM THE YOM KIPPUR WAR!
HMPF! ...
HEY!
THERE'S MORE SKETCHES WHEN YOU'RE DONE...

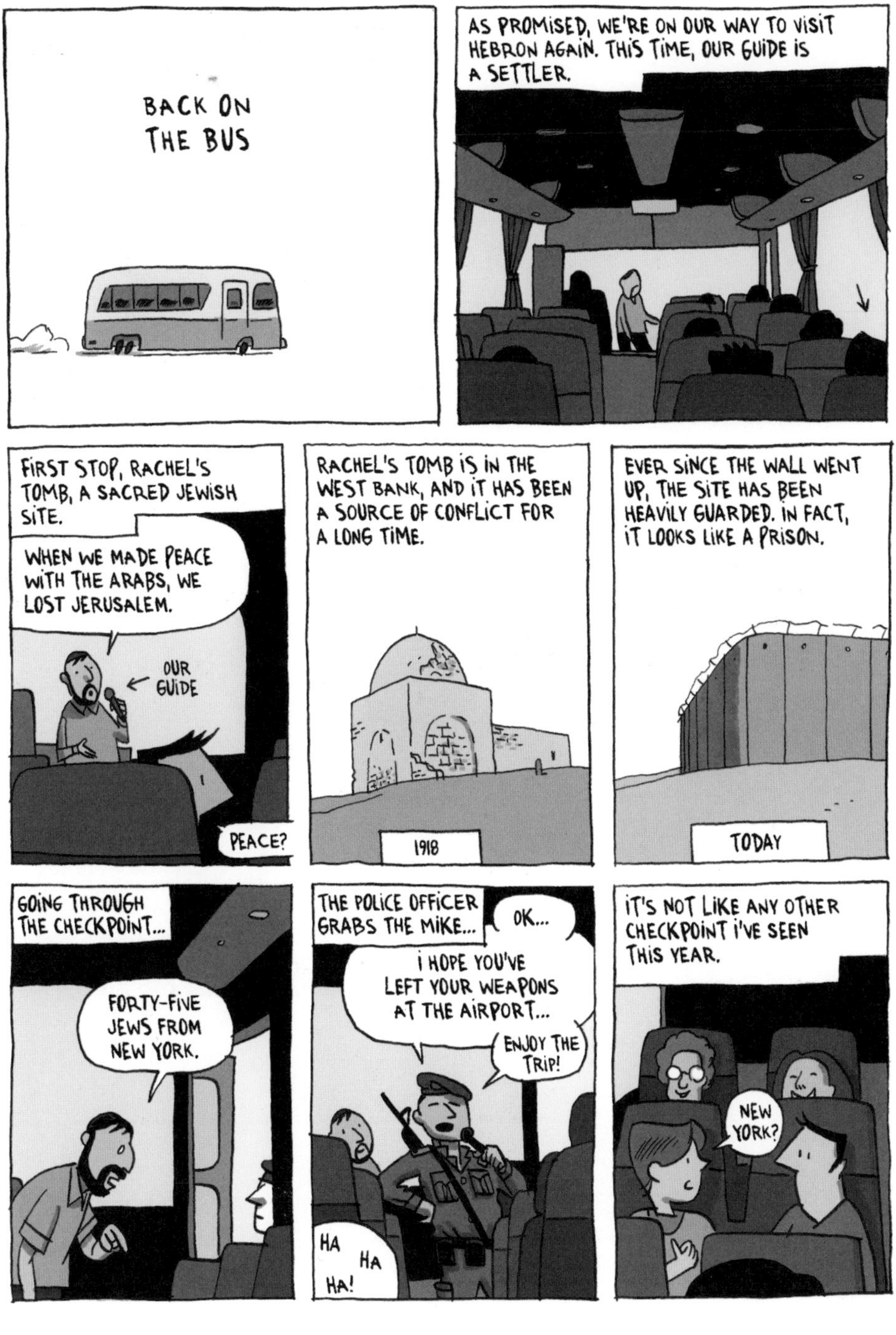
BACK ON THE BUS
AS PROMISED, WE'RE ON OUR WAY TO VISIT HEBRON AGAIN. THIS TIME, OUR GUIDE IS A SETTLER.
FIRST STOP, RACHEL'S TOMB, A SACRED JEWISH SITE.
WHEN WE MADE PEACE WITH THE ARABS, WE LOST JERUSALEM.
OUR GUIDE
PEACE?
RACHEL'S TOMB IS IN THE WEST BANK, AND IT HAS BEEN A SOURCE OF CONFLICT FOR A LONG TIME.
1918
EVER SINCE THE WALL WENT UP, THE SITE HAS BEEN HEAVILY GUARDED. IN FACT, IT LOOKS LIKE A PRISON.
TODAY
GOING THROUGH THE CHECKPOINT...
FORTY-FIVE JEWS FROM NEW YORK.
THE POLICE OFFICER GRABS THE MIKE...
OK...
I HOPE YOU'VE LEFT YOUR WEAPONS AT THE AIRPORT...
ENJOY THE TRIP!
HA HA HA!
IT'S NOT LIKE ANY OTHER CHECKPOINT I'VE SEEN THIS YEAR.
NEW YORK?

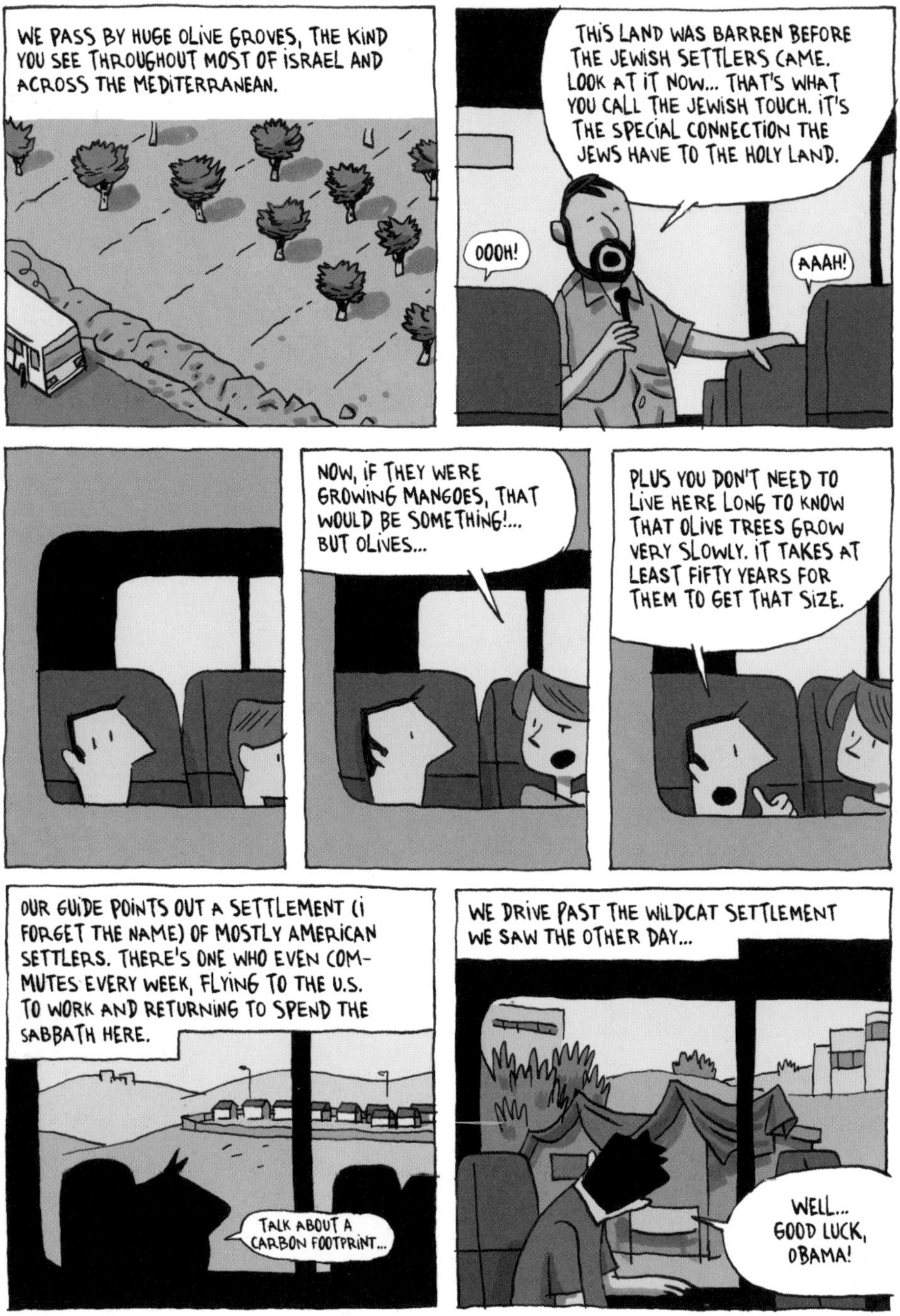
WE PASS BY HUGE OLIVE GROVES, THE KIND YOU SEE THROUGHOUT MOST OF ISRAEL AND ACROSS THE MEDITERRANEAN.
THIS LAND WAS BARREN BEFORE THE JEWISH SETTLERS CAME. LOOK AT IT NOW... THAT'S WHAT YOU CALL THE JEWISH TOUCH. IT'S THE SPECIAL CONNECTION THE JEWS HAVE TO THE HOLY LAND.
OOOH!
AAAH!
NOW, IF THEY WERE GROWING MANGOES, THAT WOULD BE SOMETHING!... BUT OLIVES...
PLUS YOU DON'T NEED TO LIVE HERE LONG TO KNOW THAT OLIVE TREES GROW VERY SLOWLY. IT TAKES AT LEAST FIFTY YEARS FOR THEM TO GET THAT SIZE.
OUR GUIDE POINTS OUT A SETTLEMENT (I FORGET THE NAME) OF MOSTLY AMERICAN SETTLERS. THERE'S ONE WHO EVEN COMMUTES EVERY WEEK, FLYING TO THE U.S. TO WORK AND RETURNING TO SPEND THE SABBATH HERE.
TALK ABOUT A CARBON FOOTPRINT...
WE DRIVE PAST THE WILDCAT SETTLEMENT WE SAW THE OTHER DAY...
WELL... GOOD LUCK, OBAMA!

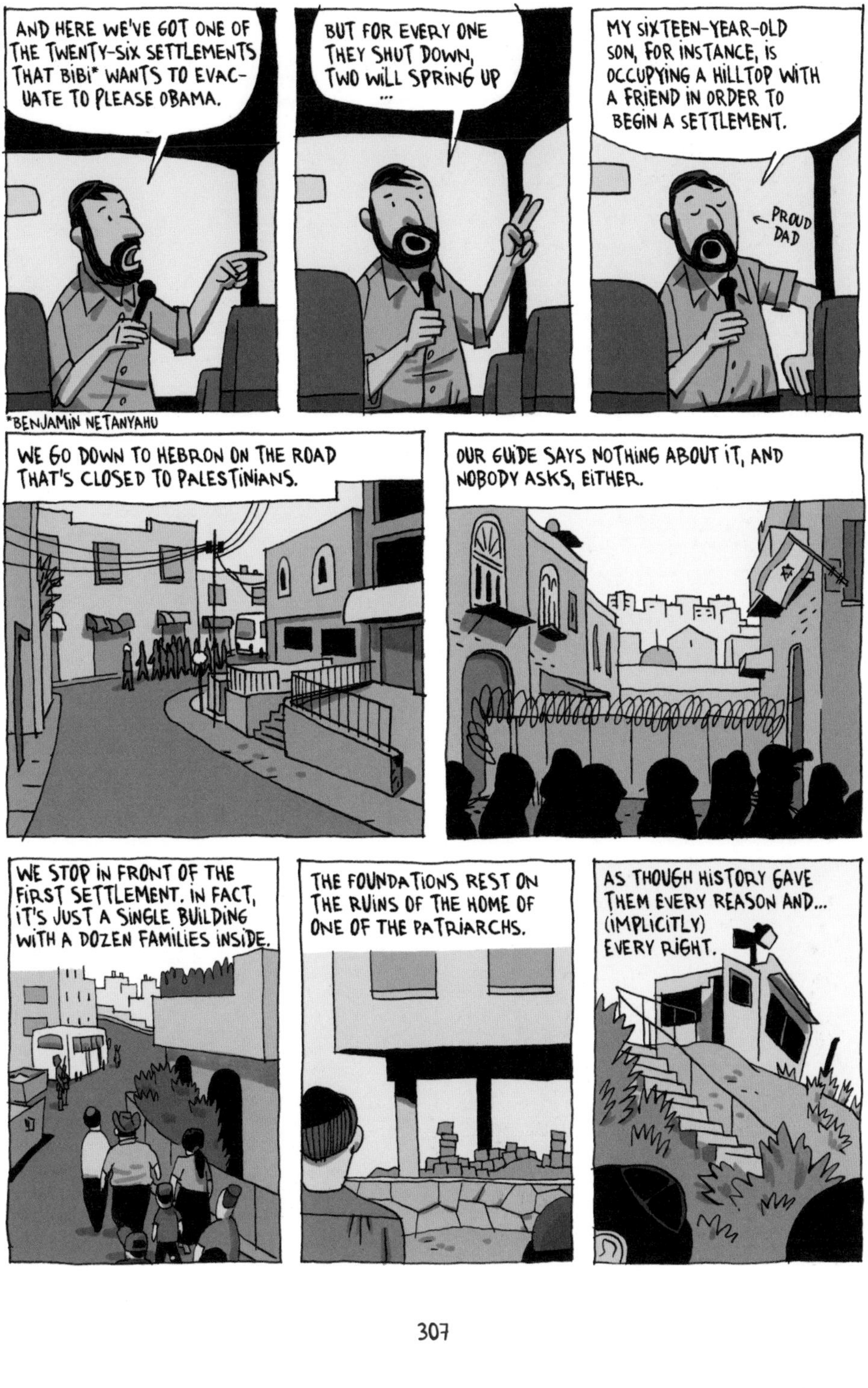
AND HERE WE'VE GOT ONE OF THE TWENTY-SIX SETTLEMENTS THAT BIBI* WANTS TO EVACUATE TO PLEASE OBAMA.
BUT FOR EVERY ONE THEY SHUT DOWN, TWO WILL SPRING UP ...
MY SIXTEEN-YEAR-OLD SON, FOR INSTANCE, IS OCCUPYING A HILLTOP WITH A FRIEND IN ORDER TO BEGIN A SETTLEMENT.
← PROUD DAD
*BENJAMIN NETANYAHU
WE GO DOWN TO HEBRON ON THE ROAD THAT'S CLOSED TO PALESTINIANS.
OUR GUIDE SAYS NOTHING ABOUT IT, AND NOBODY ASKS, EITHER.
WE STOP IN FRONT OF THE FIRST SETTLEMENT. IN FACT, IT'S JUST A SINGLE BUILDING WITH A DOZEN FAMILIES INSIDE.
THE FOUNDATIONS REST ON THE RUINS OF THE HOME OF ONE OF THE PATRIARCHS.
AS THOUGH HISTORY GAVE THEM EVERY REASON AND... (IMPLICITLY) EVERY RIGHT.

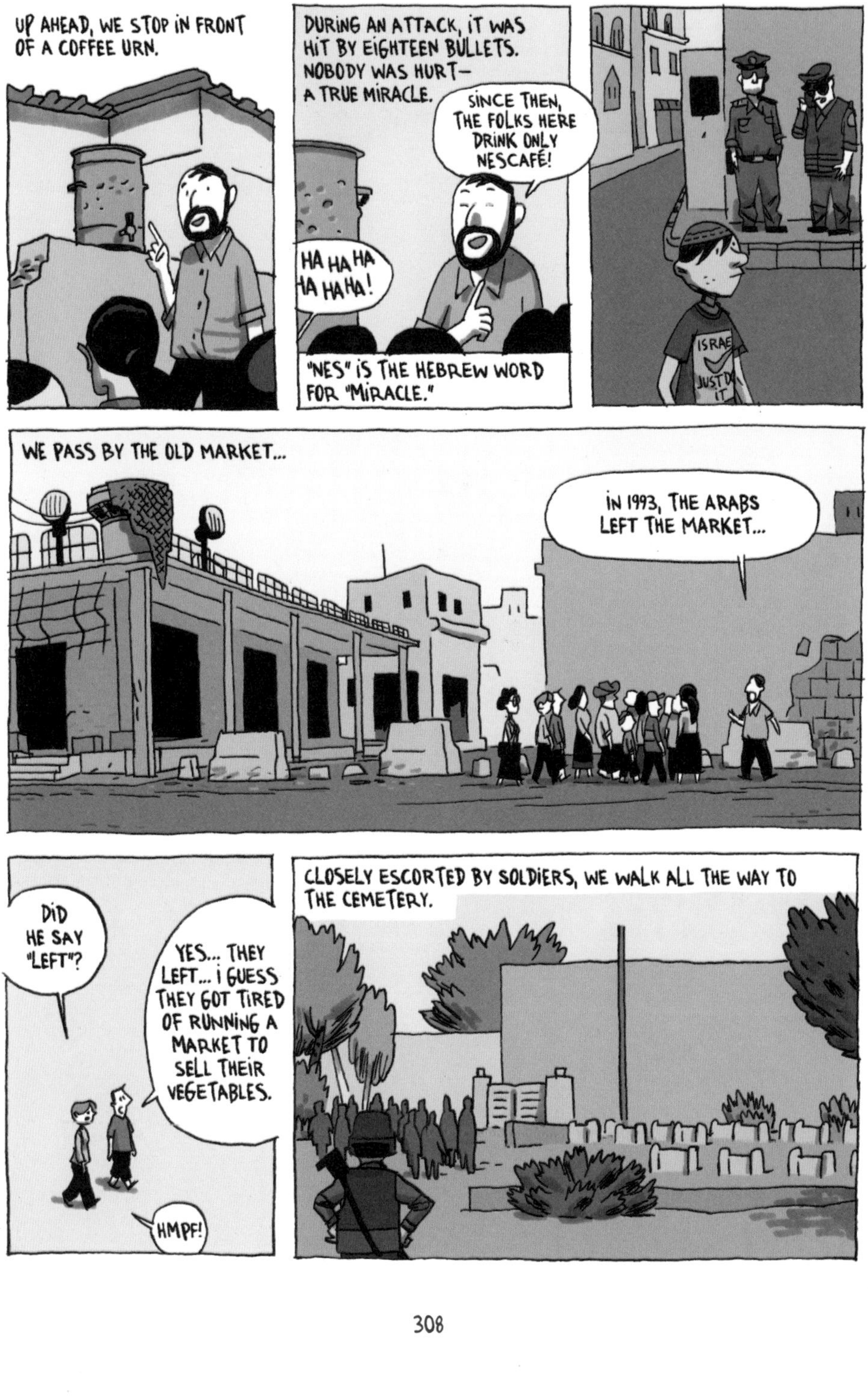
UP AHEAD, WE STOP IN FRONT OF A COFFEE URN.
DURING AN ATTACK, IT WAS HIT BY EIGHTEEN BULLETS. NOBODY WAS HURT— A TRUE MIRACLE.
SINCE THEN, THE FOLKS HERE DRINK ONLY NESCAFÉ!
HA HA HA HA HA HA!
"NES" IS THE HEBREW WORD FOR "MIRACLE."
WE PASS BY THE OLD MARKET...
IN 1993, THE ARABS LEFT THE MARKET...
DID HE SAY "LEFT"?
YES... THEY LEFT... I GUESS THEY GOT TIRED OF RUNNING A MARKET TO SELL THEIR VEGETABLES.
HMPF!
CLOSELY ESCORTED BY SOLDIERS, WE WALK ALL THE WAY TO THE CEMETERY.

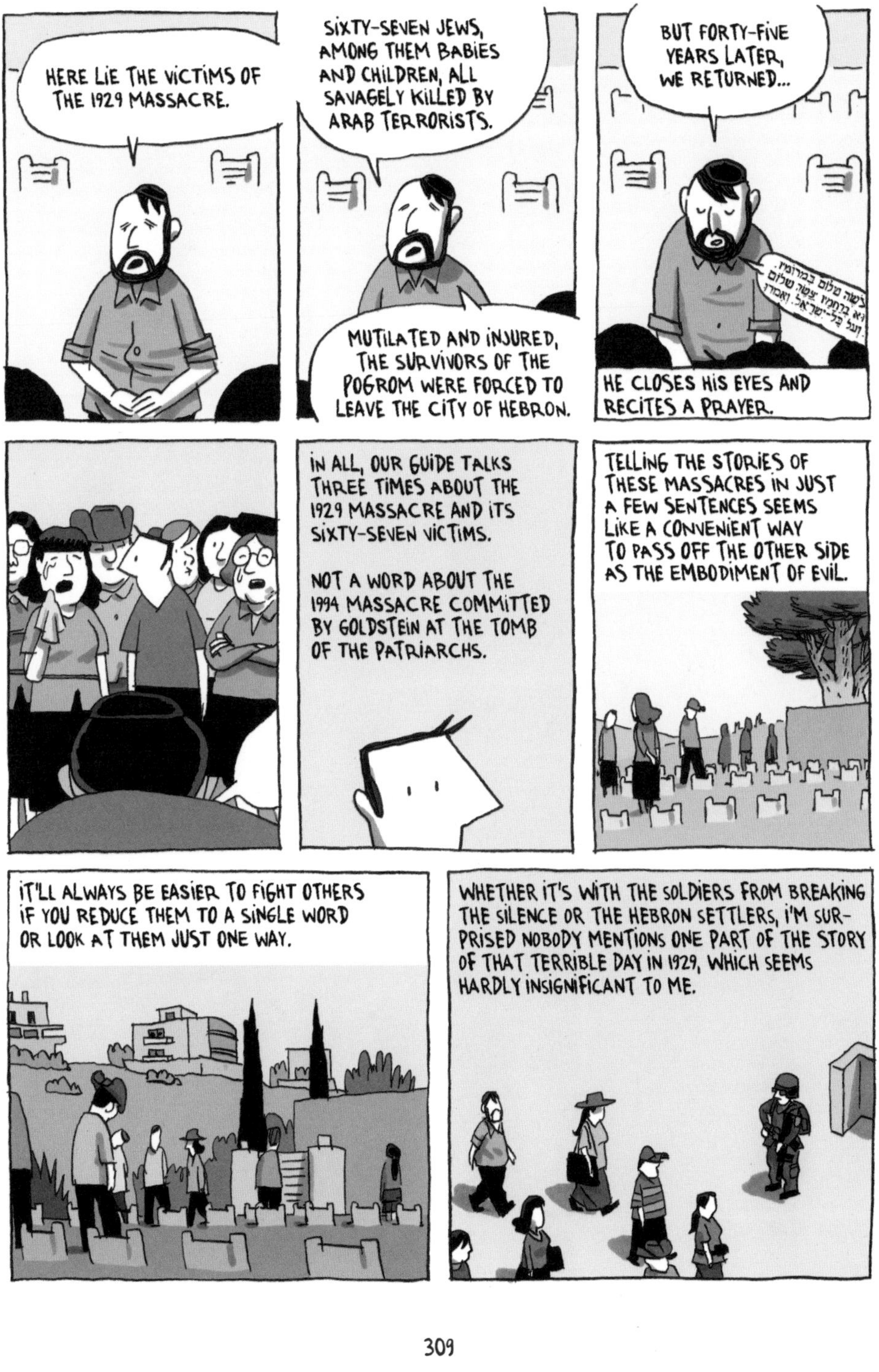
HERE LIE THE VICTIMS OF THE 1929 MASSACRE.
SIXTY-SEVEN JEWS, AMONG THEM BABIES AND CHILDREN, ALL SAVAGELY KILLED BY ARAB TERRORISTS.
MUTILATED AND INJURED, THE SURVIVORS OF THE POGROM WERE FORCED TO LEAVE THE CITY OF HEBRON.
BUT FORTY-FIVE YEARS LATER, WE RETURNED...
HE CLOSES HIS EYES AND RECITES A PRAYER.
IN ALL, OUR GUIDE TALKS THREE TIMES ABOUT THE 1929 MASSACRE AND ITS SIXTY-SEVEN VICTIMS.
NOT A WORD ABOUT THE 1994 MASSACRE COMMITTED BY GOLDSTEIN AT THE TOMB OF THE PATRIARCHS.
TELLING THE STORIES OF THESE MASSACRES IN JUST A FEW SENTENCES SEEMS LIKE A CONVENIENT WAY TO PASS OFF THE OTHER SIDE AS THE EMBODIMENT OF EVIL.
IT'LL ALWAYS BE EASIER TO FIGHT OTHERS IF YOU REDUCE THEM TO A SINGLE WORD OR LOOK AT THEM JUST ONE WAY.
WHETHER IT'S WITH THE SOLDIERS FROM BREAKING THE SILENCE OR THE HEBRON SETTLERS, I'M SURPRISED NOBODY MENTIONS ONE PART OF THE STORY OF THAT TERRIBLE DAY IN 1929, WHICH SEEMS HARDLY INSIGNIFICANT TO ME.

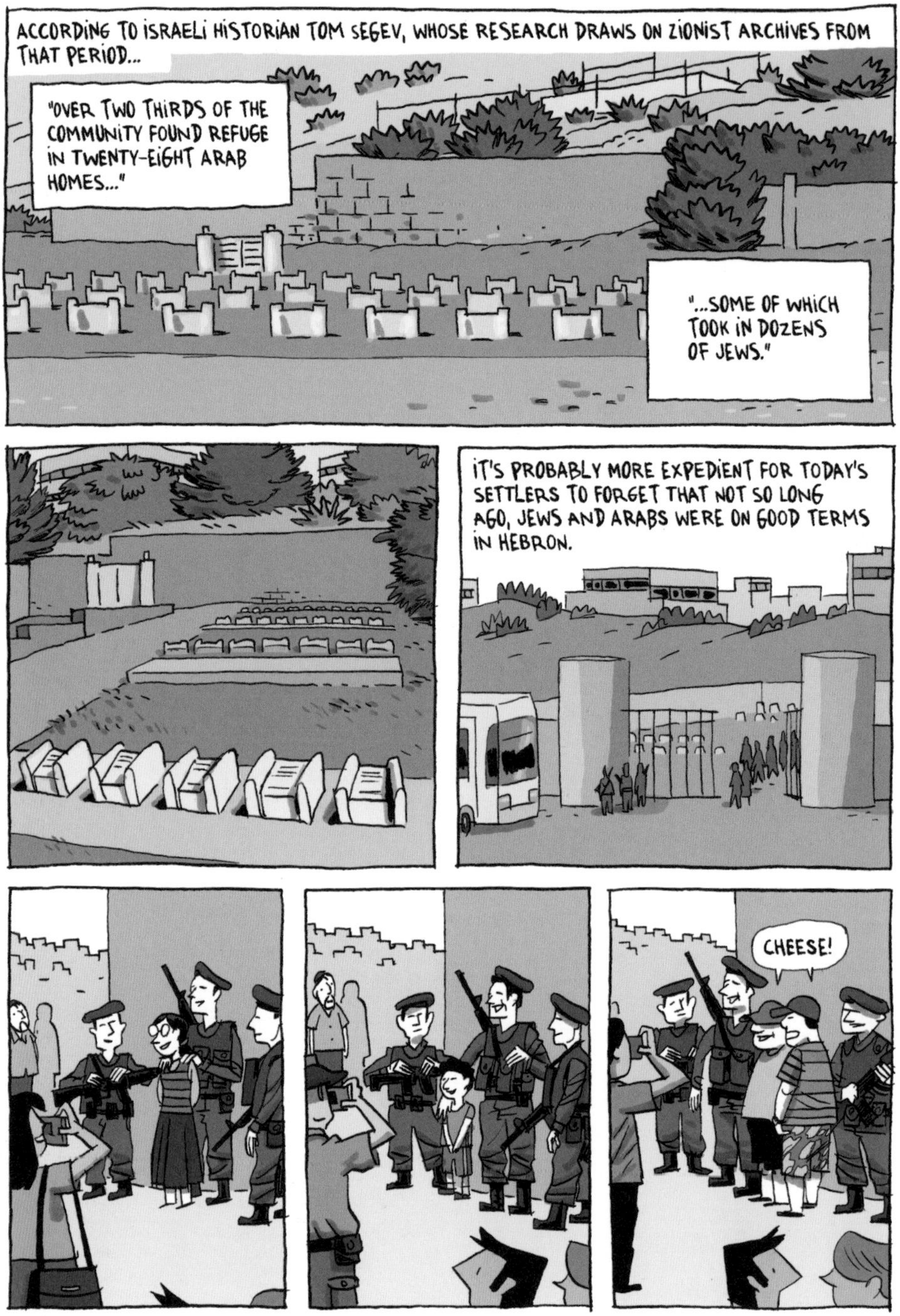
ACCORDING TO ISRAELI HISTORIAN TOM SEGEV, WHOSE RESEARCH DRAWS ON ZIONIST ARCHIVES FROM THAT PERIOD...
"OVER TWO THIRDS OF THE COMMUNITY FOUND REFUGE IN TWENTY-EIGHT ARAB HOMES..."
"...SOME OF WHICH TOOK IN DOZENS OF JEWS."
IT'S PROBABLY MORE EXPEDIENT FOR TODAY'S SETTLERS TO FORGET THAT NOT SO LONG AGO, JEWS AND ARABS WERE ON GOOD TERMS IN HEBRON.
CHEESE!

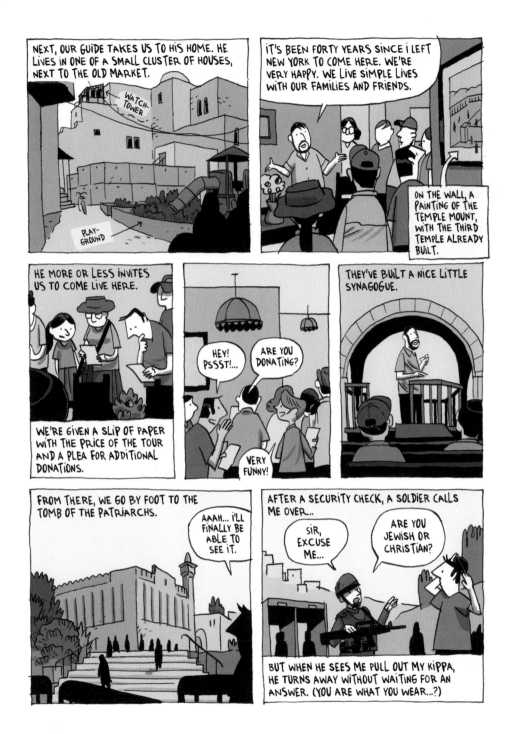

NEXT, OUR GUIDE TAKES US TO HIS HOME. HE LIVES IN ONE OF A SMALL CLUSTER OF HOUSES, NEXT TO THE OLD MARKET.

WATCH-TOWER

PLAY-GROUND

IT'S BEEN FORTY YEARS SINCE I LEFT NEW YORK TO COME HERE. WE'RE VERY HAPPY. WE LIVE SIMPLE LIVES WITH OUR FAMILIES AND FRIENDS.

ON THE WALL, A PAINTING OF THE TEMPLE MOUNT, WITH THE THIRD TEMPLE ALREADY BUILT.

HE MORE OR LESS INVITES US TO COME LIVE HERE.

WE'RE GIVEN A SLIP OF PAPER WITH THE PRICE OF THE TOUR AND A PLEA FOR ADDITIONAL DONATIONS.

HEY! PSSST!...

ARE YOU DONATING?

VERY FUNNY!

THEY'VE BUILT A NICE LITTLE SYNAGOGUE.

FROM THERE, WE GO BY FOOT TO THE TOMB OF THE PATRIARCHS.

AAAH... I'LL FINALLY BE ABLE TO SEE IT.

AFTER A SECURITY CHECK, A SOLDIER CALLS ME OVER...

SIR, EXCUSE ME...

ARE YOU JEWISH OR CHRISTIAN?

BUT WHEN HE SEES ME PULL OUT MY KIPPA, HE TURNS AWAY WITHOUT WAITING FOR AN ANSWER. (YOU ARE WHAT YOU WEAR...?)

311

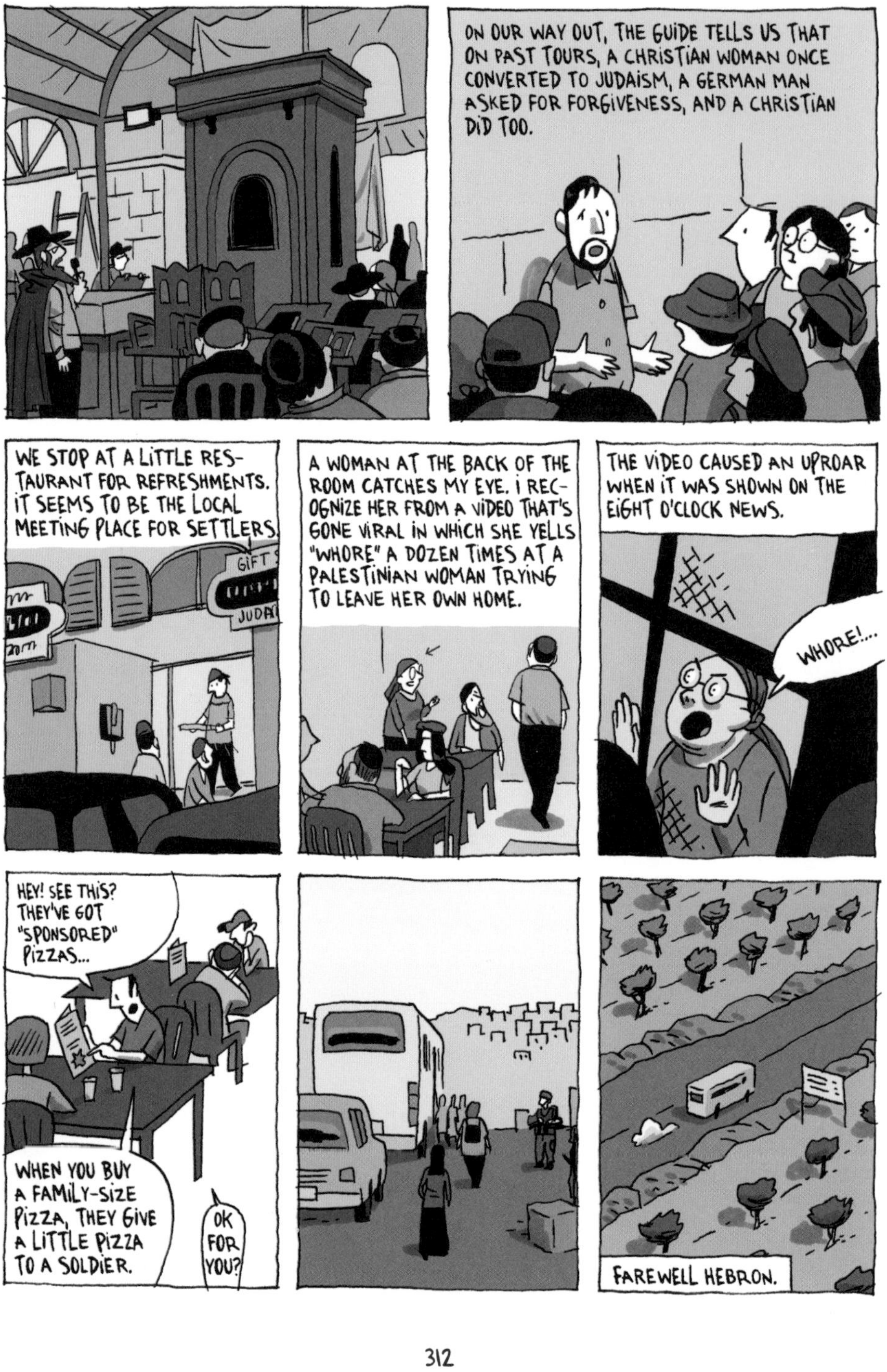
ON OUR WAY OUT, THE GUIDE TELLS US THAT ON PAST TOURS, A CHRISTIAN WOMAN ONCE CONVERTED TO JUDAISM, A GERMAN MAN ASKED FOR FORGIVENESS, AND A CHRISTIAN DID TOO.
WE STOP AT A LITTLE RESTAURANT FOR REFRESHMENTS. IT SEEMS TO BE THE LOCAL MEETING PLACE FOR SETTLERS.
GIFT S
JUDA
A WOMAN AT THE BACK OF THE ROOM CATCHES MY EYE. I RECOGNIZE HER FROM A VIDEO THAT'S GONE VIRAL IN WHICH SHE YELLS "WHORE" A DOZEN TIMES AT A PALESTINIAN WOMAN TRYING TO LEAVE HER OWN HOME.
THE VIDEO CAUSED AN UPROAR WHEN IT WAS SHOWN ON THE EIGHT O'CLOCK NEWS.
WHORE!...
HEY! SEE THIS? THEY'VE GOT "SPONSORED" PIZZAS...
WHEN YOU BUY A FAMILY-SIZE PIZZA, THEY GIVE A LITTLE PIZZA TO A SOLDIER.
OK FOR YOU?
FAREWELL HEBRON.

JULY

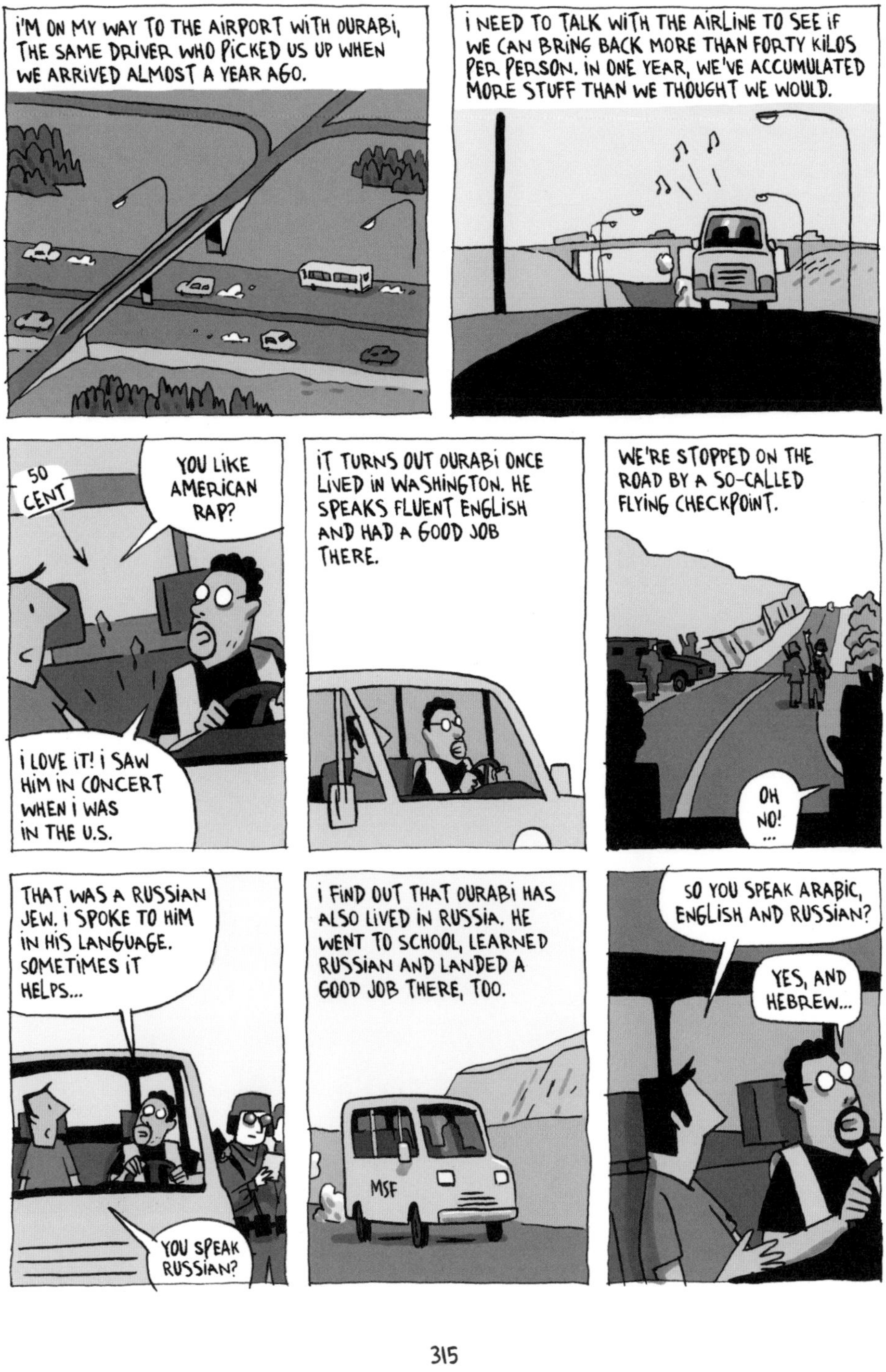

I'M ON MY WAY TO THE AIRPORT WITH OURABI, THE SAME DRIVER WHO PICKED US UP WHEN WE ARRIVED ALMOST A YEAR AGO.
I NEED TO TALK WITH THE AIRLINE TO SEE IF WE CAN BRING BACK MORE THAN FORTY KILOS PER PERSON. IN ONE YEAR, WE'VE ACCUMULATED MORE STUFF THAN WE THOUGHT WE WOULD.
50 CENT
YOU LIKE AMERICAN RAP?
I LOVE IT! I SAW HIM IN CONCERT WHEN I WAS IN THE U.S.
IT TURNS OUT OURABI ONCE LIVED IN WASHINGTON. HE SPEAKS FLUENT ENGLISH AND HAD A GOOD JOB THERE.
WE'RE STOPPED ON THE ROAD BY A SO-CALLED FLYING CHECKPOINT.
OH NO! ...
THAT WAS A RUSSIAN JEW. I SPOKE TO HIM IN HIS LANGUAGE. SOMETIMES IT HELPS...
YOU SPEAK RUSSIAN?
I FIND OUT THAT OURABI HAS ALSO LIVED IN RUSSIA. HE WENT TO SCHOOL, LEARNED RUSSIAN AND LANDED A GOOD JOB THERE, TOO.
MSF
SO YOU SPEAK ARABIC, ENGLISH AND RUSSIAN?
YES, AND HEBREW...

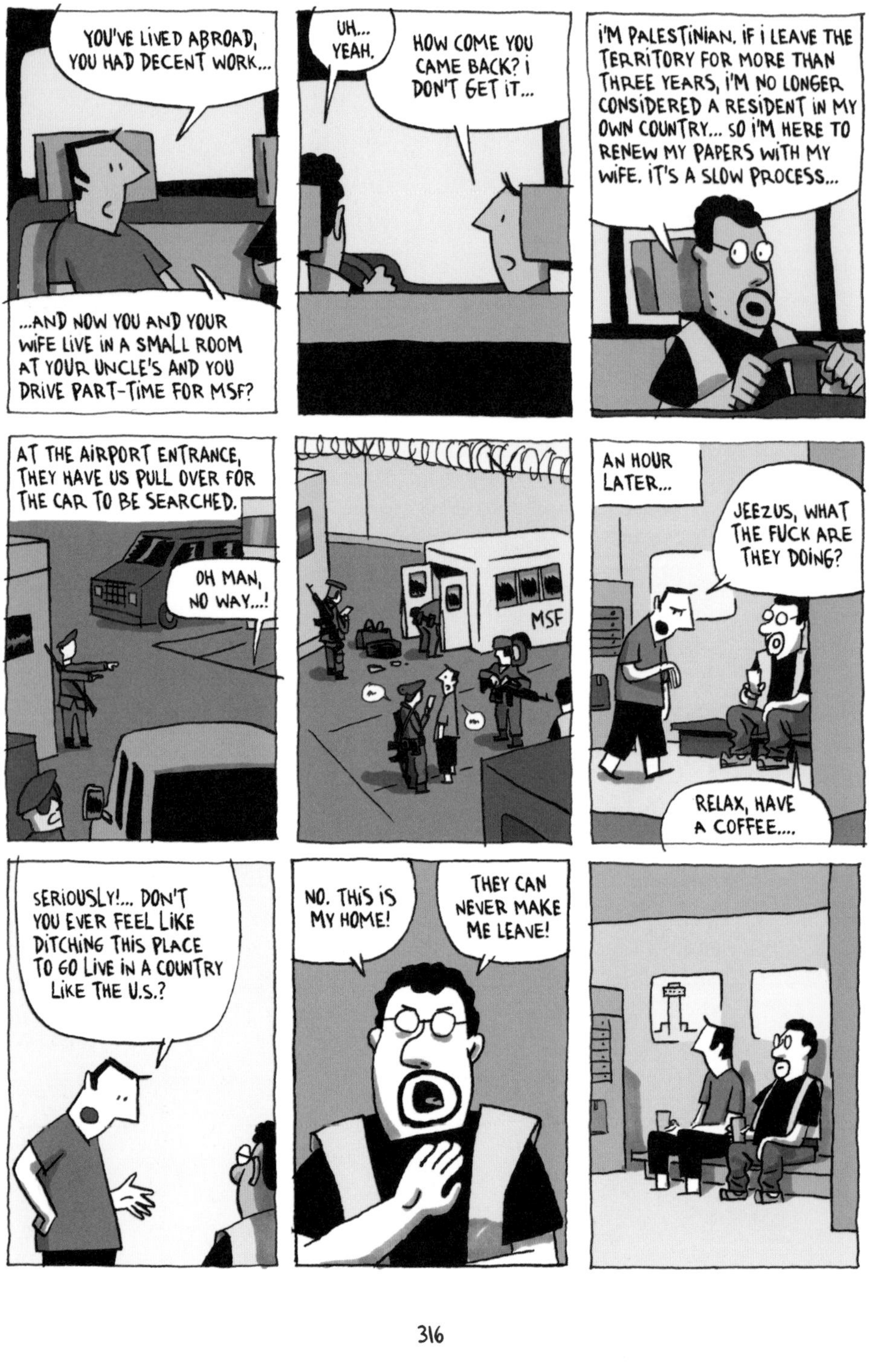
YOU'VE LIVED ABROAD, YOU HAD DECENT WORK...
...AND NOW YOU AND YOUR WIFE LIVE IN A SMALL ROOM AT YOUR UNCLE'S AND YOU DRIVE PART-TIME FOR MSF?
UH... YEAH.
HOW COME YOU CAME BACK? I DON'T GET IT...
I'M PALESTINIAN. IF I LEAVE THE TERRITORY FOR MORE THAN THREE YEARS, I'M NO LONGER CONSIDERED A RESIDENT IN MY OWN COUNTRY... SO I'M HERE TO RENEW MY PAPERS WITH MY WIFE. IT'S A SLOW PROCESS...
AT THE AIRPORT ENTRANCE, THEY HAVE US PULL OVER FOR THE CAR TO BE SEARCHED.
OH MAN, NO WAY...!
MSF
AN HOUR LATER...
JEEZUS, WHAT THE FUCK ARE THEY DOING?
RELAX, HAVE A COFFEE....
SERIOUSLY!... DON'T YOU EVER FEEL LIKE DITCHING THIS PLACE TO GO LIVE IN A COUNTRY LIKE THE U.S.?
NO. THIS IS MY HOME!
THEY CAN NEVER MAKE ME LEAVE!

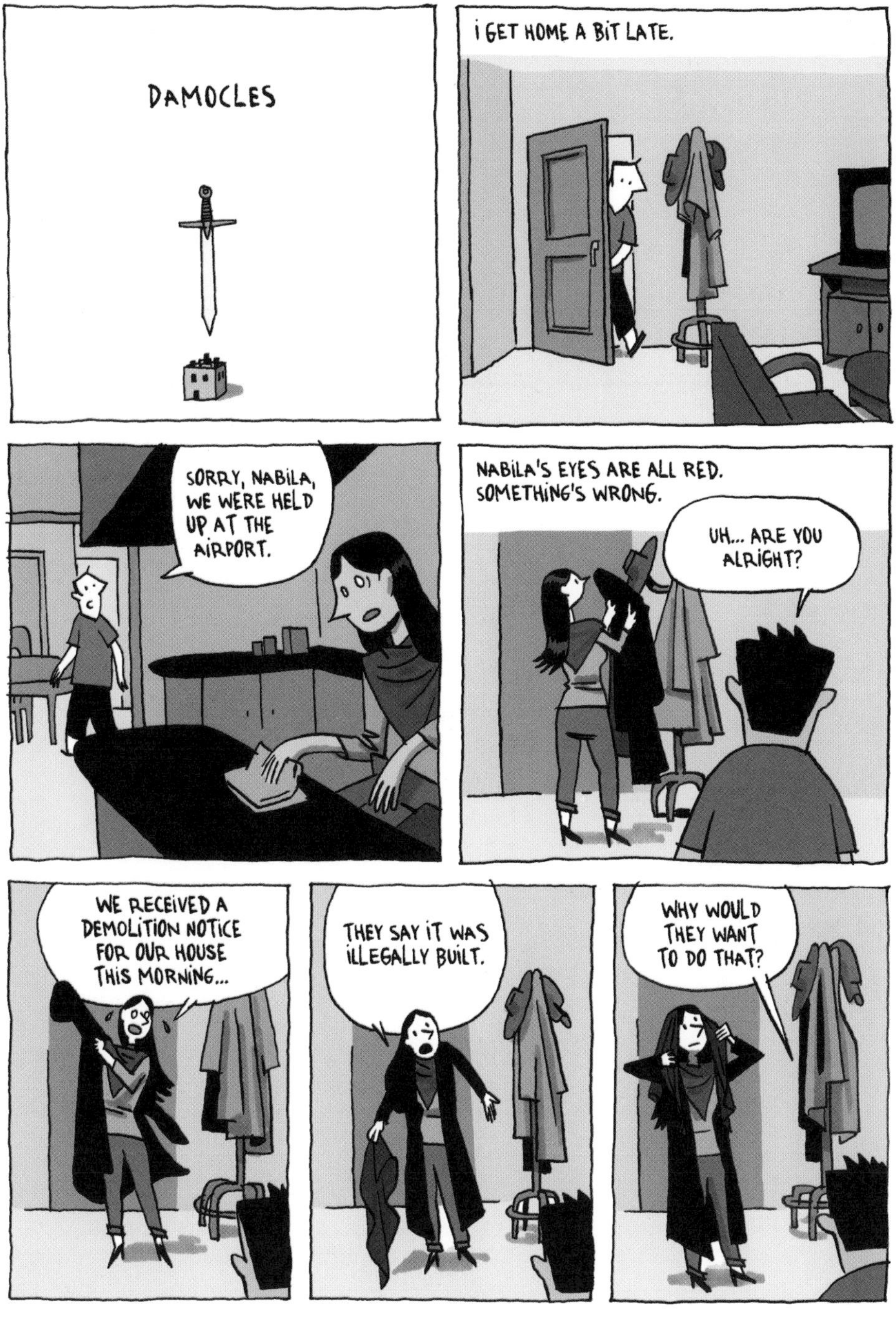
DAMOCLES
I GET HOME A BIT LATE.
SORRY, NABILA, WE WERE HELD UP AT THE AIRPORT.
NABILA'S EYES ARE ALL RED. SOMETHING'S WRONG.
UH... ARE YOU ALRIGHT?
WE RECEIVED A DEMOLITION NOTICE FOR OUR HOUSE THIS MORNING...
THEY SAY IT WAS ILLEGALLY BUILT.
WHY WOULD THEY WANT TO DO THAT?

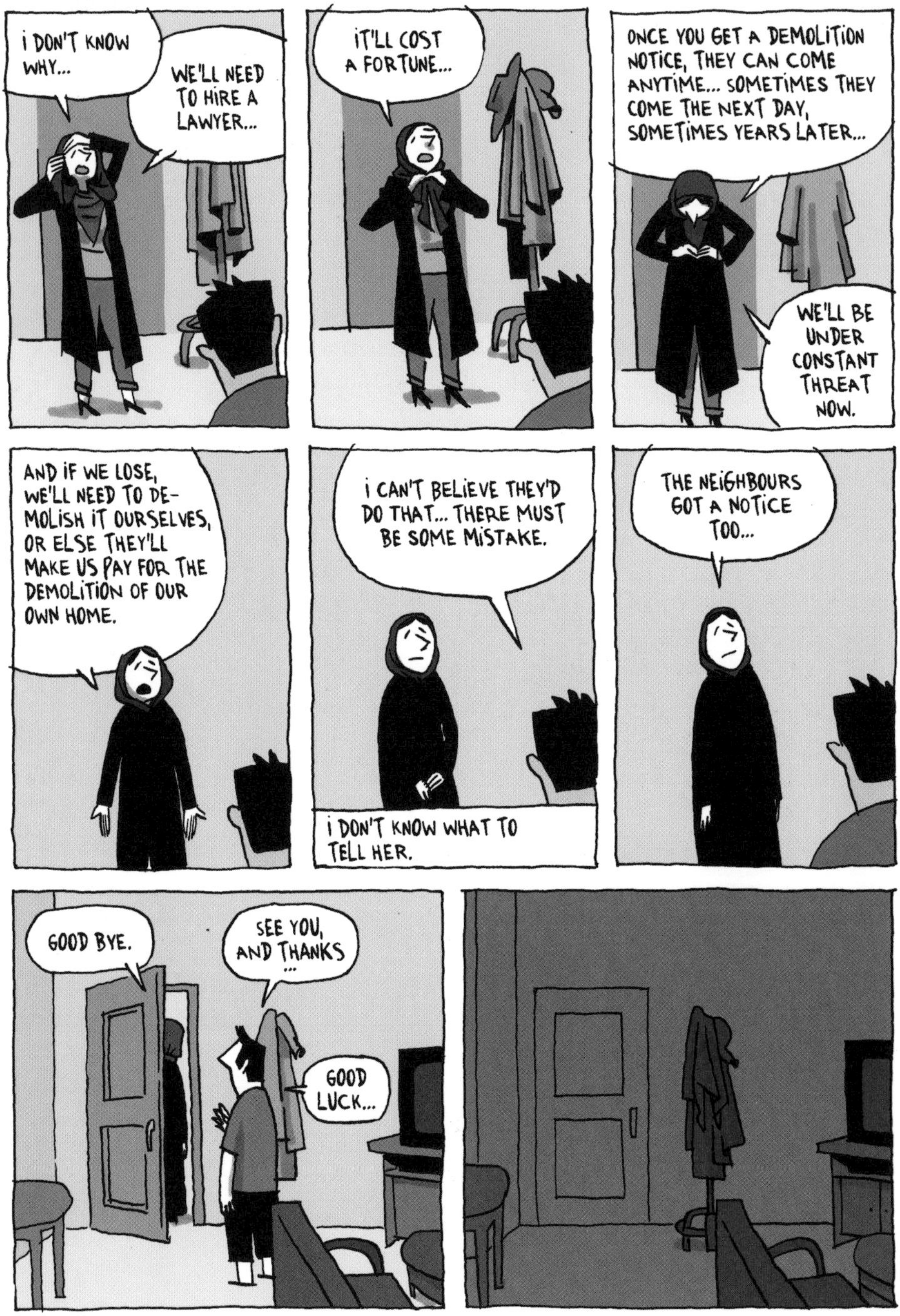
I DON'T KNOW WHY...
WE'LL NEED TO HIRE A LAWYER...
IT'LL COST A FORTUNE...
ONCE YOU GET A DEMOLITION NOTICE, THEY CAN COME ANYTIME... SOMETIMES THEY COME THE NEXT DAY, SOMETIMES YEARS LATER...
WE'LL BE UNDER CONSTANT THREAT NOW.
AND IF WE LOSE, WE'LL NEED TO DE-MOLISH IT OURSELVES, OR ELSE THEY'LL MAKE US PAY FOR THE DEMOLITION OF OUR OWN HOME.
I CAN'T BELIEVE THEY'D DO THAT... THERE MUST BE SOME MISTAKE.
I DON'T KNOW WHAT TO TELL HER.
THE NEIGHBOURS GOT A NOTICE TOO...
GOOD BYE.
SEE YOU, AND THANKS ...
GOOD LUCK...

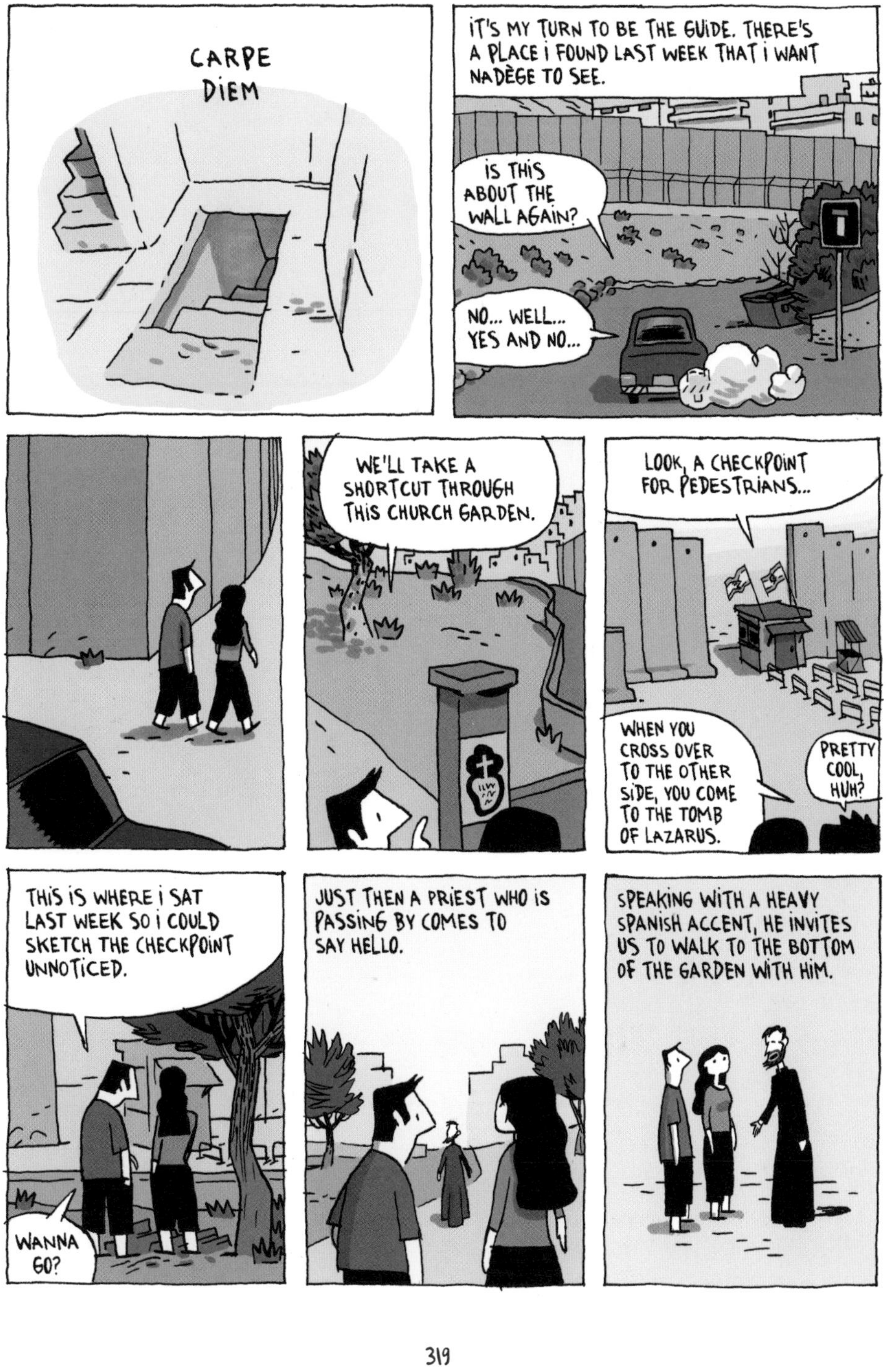
CARPE DIEM
IT'S MY TURN TO BE THE GUIDE. THERE'S A PLACE I FOUND LAST WEEK THAT I WANT NADÈGE TO SEE.
IS THIS ABOUT THE WALL AGAIN?
NO... WELL... YES AND NO...
WE'LL TAKE A SHORTCUT THROUGH THIS CHURCH GARDEN.
LOOK, A CHECKPOINT FOR PEDESTRIANS...
WHEN YOU CROSS OVER TO THE OTHER SIDE, YOU COME TO THE TOMB OF LAZARUS.
PRETTY COOL, HUH?
THIS IS WHERE I SAT LAST WEEK SO I COULD SKETCH THE CHECKPOINT UNNOTICED.
WANNA GO?
JUST THEN A PRIEST WHO IS PASSING BY COMES TO SAY HELLO.
SPEAKING WITH A HEAVY SPANISH ACCENT, HE INVITES US TO WALK TO THE BOTTOM OF THE GARDEN WITH HIM.

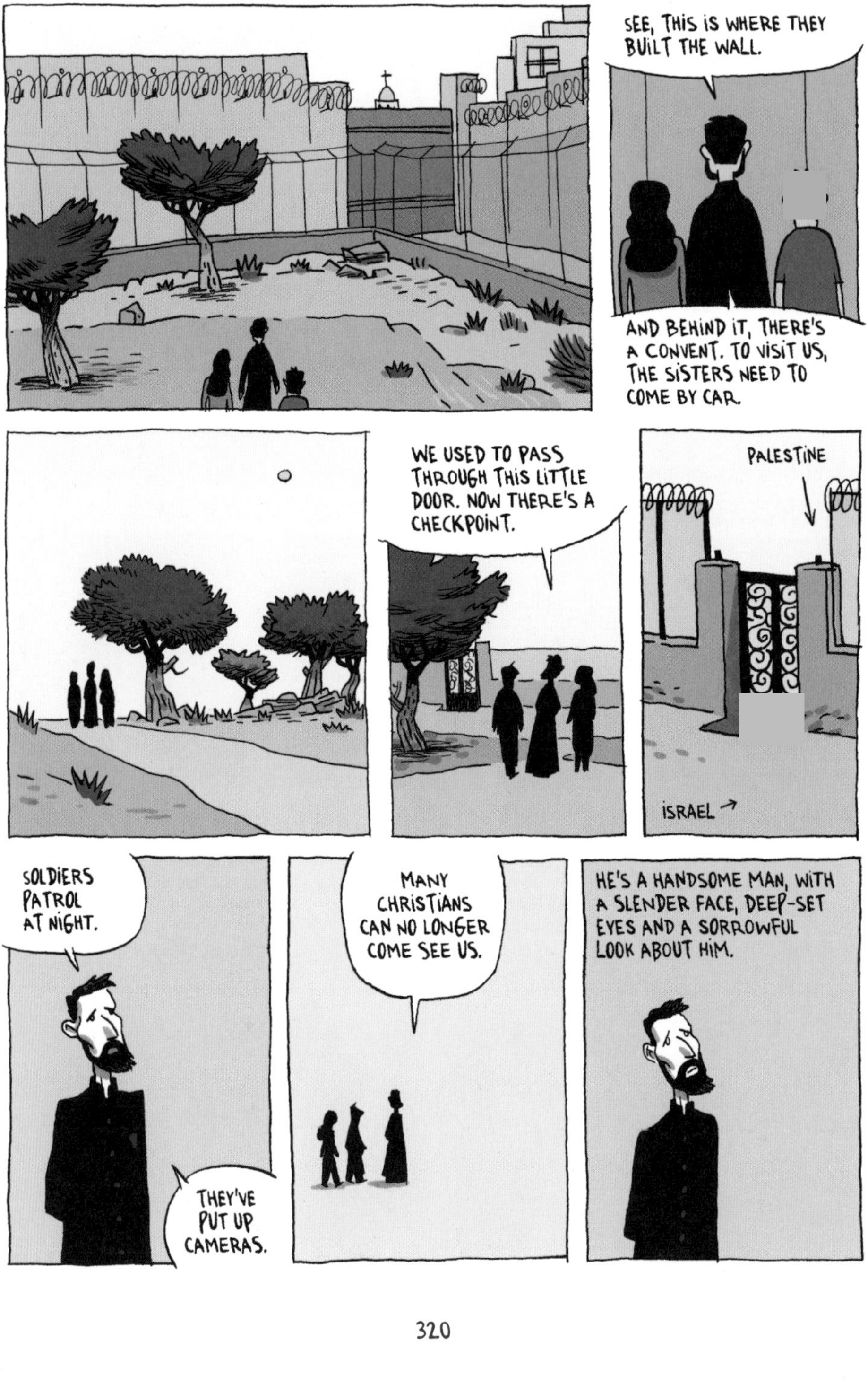

SEE, THIS IS WHERE THEY BUILT THE WALL.
AND BEHIND IT, THERE'S A CONVENT. TO VISIT US, THE SISTERS NEED TO COME BY CAR.
WE USED TO PASS THROUGH THIS LITTLE DOOR. NOW THERE'S A CHECKPOINT.
PALESTINE
ISRAEL
SOLDIERS PATROL AT NIGHT.
THEY'VE PUT UP CAMERAS.
MANY CHRISTIANS CAN NO LONGER COME SEE US.
HE'S A HANDSOME MAN, WITH A SLENDER FACE, DEEP-SET EYES AND A SORROWFUL LOOK ABOUT HIM.

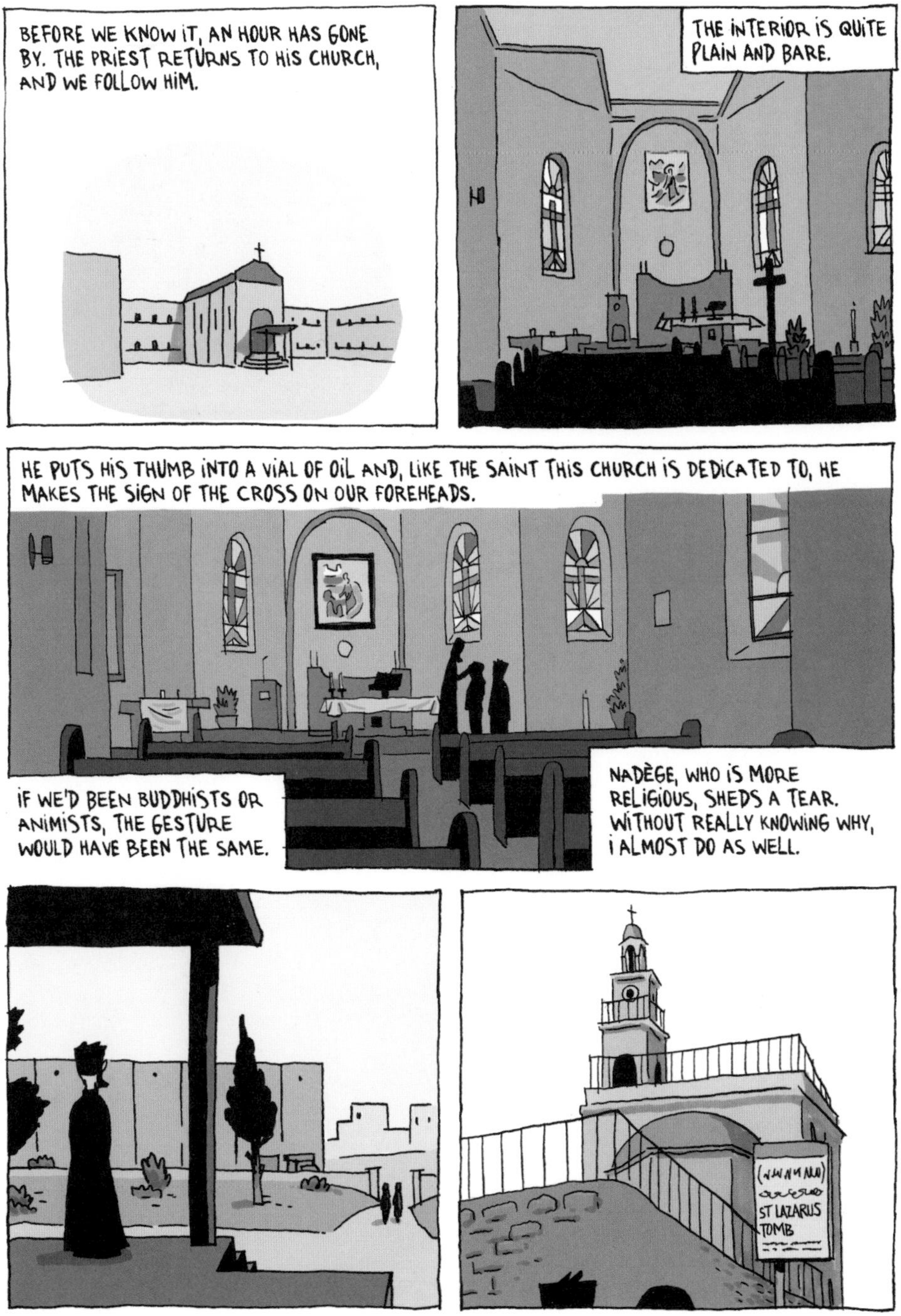
BEFORE WE KNOW IT, AN HOUR HAS GONE BY. THE PRIEST RETURNS TO HIS CHURCH, AND WE FOLLOW HIM.
THE INTERIOR IS QUITE PLAIN AND BARE.
HE PUTS HIS THUMB INTO A VIAL OF OIL AND, LIKE THE SAINT THIS CHURCH IS DEDICATED TO, HE MAKES THE SIGN OF THE CROSS ON OUR FOREHEADS.
IF WE'D BEEN BUDDHISTS OR ANIMISTS, THE GESTURE WOULD HAVE BEEN THE SAME.
NADÈGE, WHO IS MORE RELIGIOUS, SHEDS A TEAR. WITHOUT REALLY KNOWING WHY, I ALMOST DO AS WELL.
ST LAZARUS
TOMB

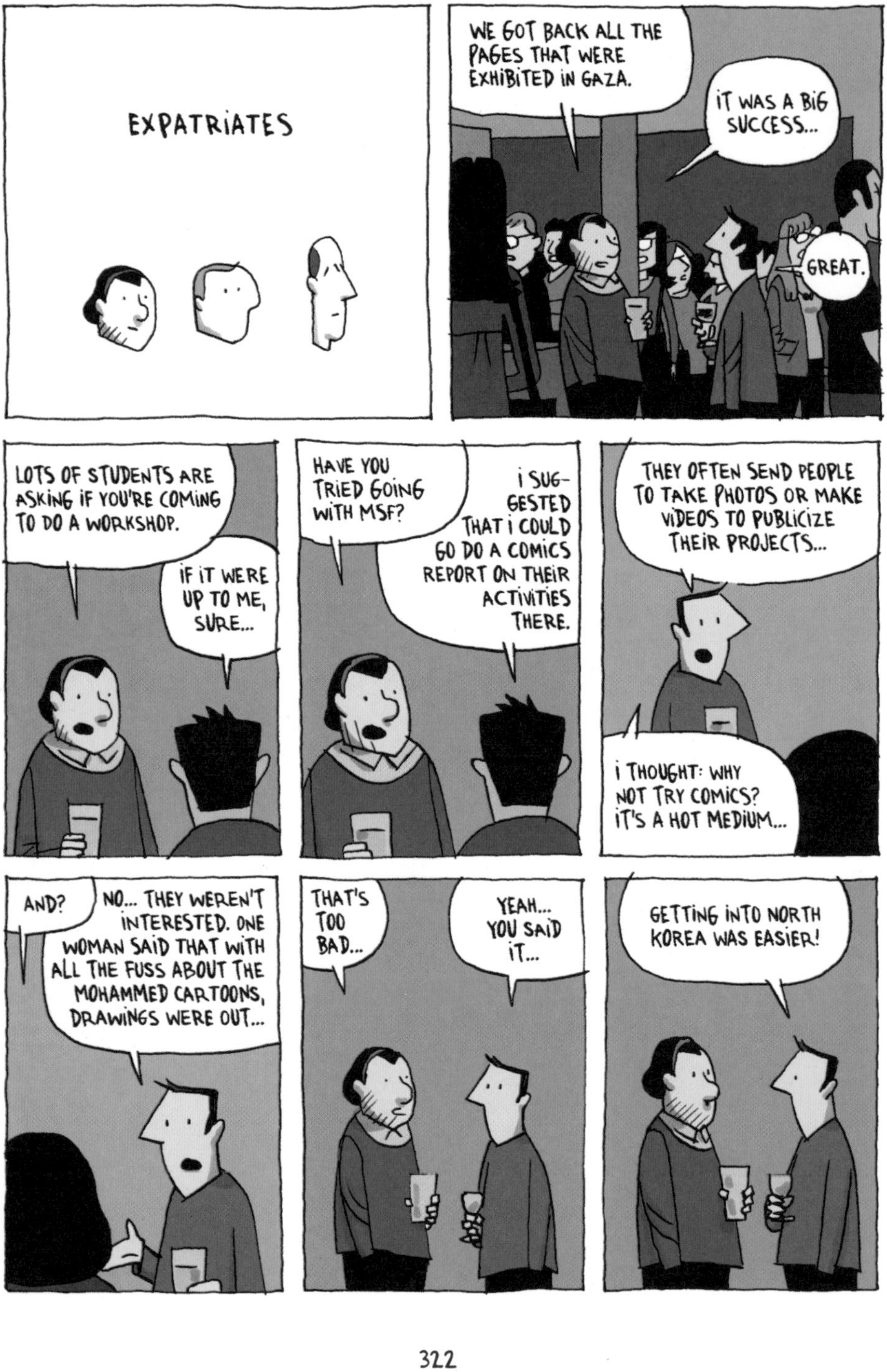
EXPATRIATES
WE GOT BACK ALL THE PAGES THAT WERE EXHIBITED IN GAZA.
IT WAS A BIG SUCCESS...
GREAT.
LOTS OF STUDENTS ARE ASKING IF YOU'RE COMING TO DO A WORKSHOP.
IF IT WERE UP TO ME, SURE...
HAVE YOU TRIED GOING WITH MSF?
I SUG-GESTED THAT I COULD GO DO A COMICS REPORT ON THEIR ACTIVITIES THERE.
THEY OFTEN SEND PEOPLE TO TAKE PHOTOS OR MAKE VIDEOS TO PUBLICIZE THEIR PROJECTS...
I THOUGHT: WHY NOT TRY COMICS? IT'S A HOT MEDIUM...
AND?
NO... THEY WEREN'T INTERESTED. ONE WOMAN SAID THAT WITH ALL THE FUSS ABOUT THE MOHAMMED CARTOONS, DRAWINGS WERE OUT...
THAT'S TOO BAD...
YEAH... YOU SAID IT...
GETTING INTO NORTH KOREA WAS EASIER!

IT'S ALWAYS SURPRISING WHO YOU MEET AT THESE EXPAT EVENINGS. THERE'S BASICALLY THREE CATEGORIES: JOURNALISTS, AID WORKERS AND DIPLOMATS.

i MEET A SCOTSMAN WHO WORKS FOR THE MIDEAST QUARTET.

THE QUARTET INCLUDES:

	POPULATION IN MILLIONS
○ THE UNITED STATES....	300
○ RUSSIA.............................	140
○ THE EUROPEAN UNION...	500
○ THE UNITED NATIONS..	7000

THEY COOPERATE ON EFFORTS TO ADVANCE THE PEACE PROCESS BETWEEN:

ISRAEL...............................	7
AND PALESTINE..................	5

SINCE 2007, TONY BLAIR HAS BEEN ITS OFFICIAL ENVOY.

SO, HERE'S A GUY WHO'S HIGH UP ON THE POLITICAL AND DIPLOMATIC LADDER.

AND... UH... HOW TO PUT THIS...

THIS IS MY ONE CHANCE TO GET SOME FIRSTHAND INFORMATION.

WHAT'S YOUR WORK LIKE ON A DAILY BASIS?... ARE THERE OPTIMISTIC MOMENTS ONCE IN A WHILE, OR DO THINGS LOOK PRETTY BAD MOST OF THE TIME?

i FIGURE HE'LL PROBABLY ELABORATE...

THINGS LOOK PRETTY BAD MOST OF THE TIME...

AH!...

AND HOW'S TONY?

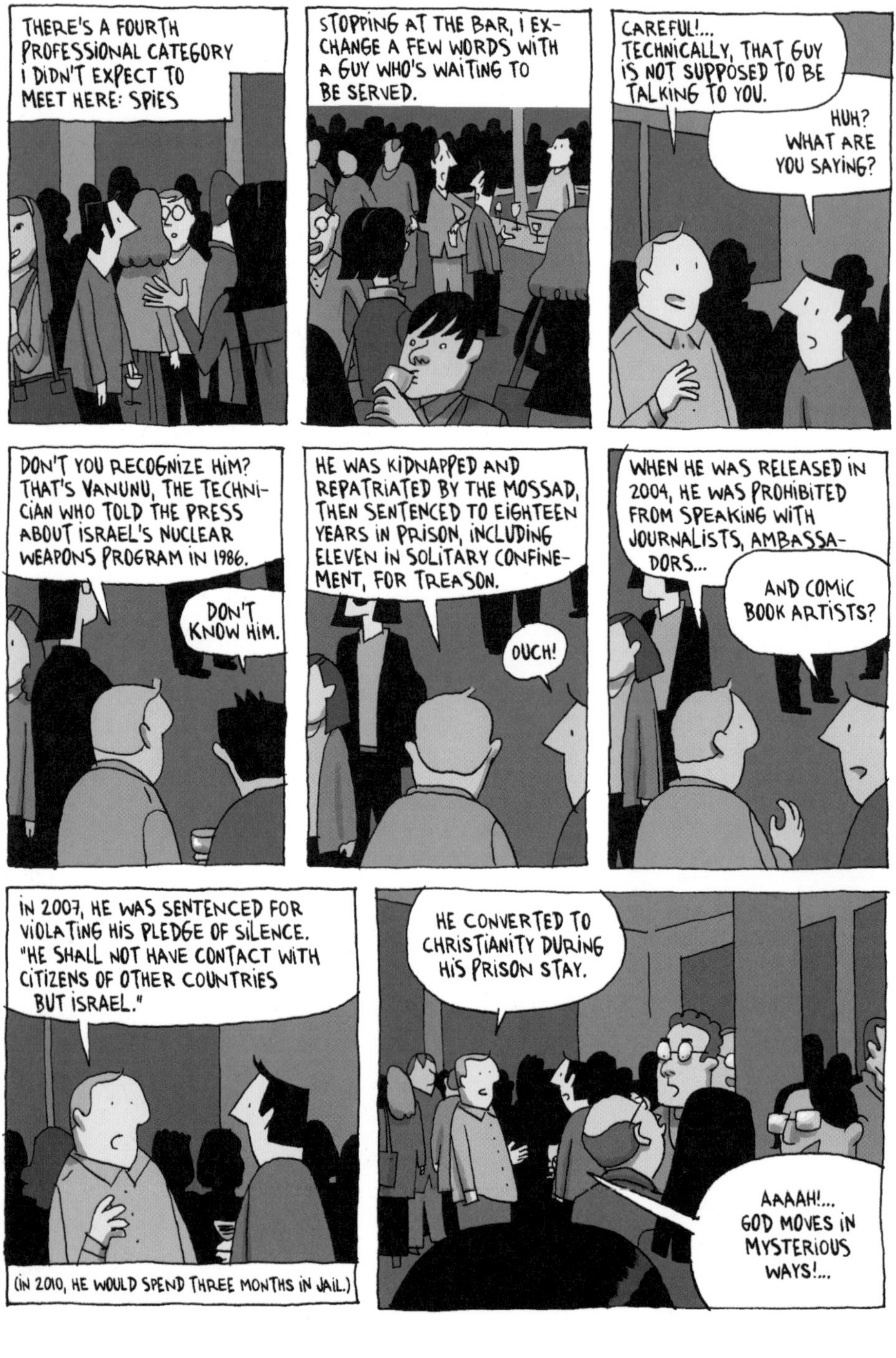
THERE'S A FOURTH PROFESSIONAL CATEGORY I DIDN'T EXPECT TO MEET HERE: SPIES
STOPPING AT THE BAR, I EXCHANGE A FEW WORDS WITH A GUY WHO'S WAITING TO BE SERVED.
CAREFUL!... TECHNICALLY, THAT GUY IS NOT SUPPOSED TO BE TALKING TO YOU.
HUH? WHAT ARE YOU SAYING?
DON'T YOU RECOGNIZE HIM? THAT'S VANUNU, THE TECHNICIAN WHO TOLD THE PRESS ABOUT ISRAEL'S NUCLEAR WEAPONS PROGRAM IN 1986.
DON'T KNOW HIM.
HE WAS KIDNAPPED AND REPATRIATED BY THE MOSSAD, THEN SENTENCED TO EIGHTEEN YEARS IN PRISON, INCLUDING ELEVEN IN SOLITARY CONFINEMENT, FOR TREASON.
OUCH!
WHEN HE WAS RELEASED IN 2004, HE WAS PROHIBITED FROM SPEAKING WITH JOURNALISTS, AMBASSADORS...
AND COMIC BOOK ARTISTS?
IN 2007, HE WAS SENTENCED FOR VIOLATING HIS PLEDGE OF SILENCE. "HE SHALL NOT HAVE CONTACT WITH CITIZENS OF OTHER COUNTRIES BUT ISRAEL."
(IN 2010, HE WOULD SPEND THREE MONTHS IN JAIL.)
HE CONVERTED TO CHRISTIANITY DURING HIS PRISON STAY.
AAAAH!... GOD MOVES IN MYSTERIOUS WAYS!...

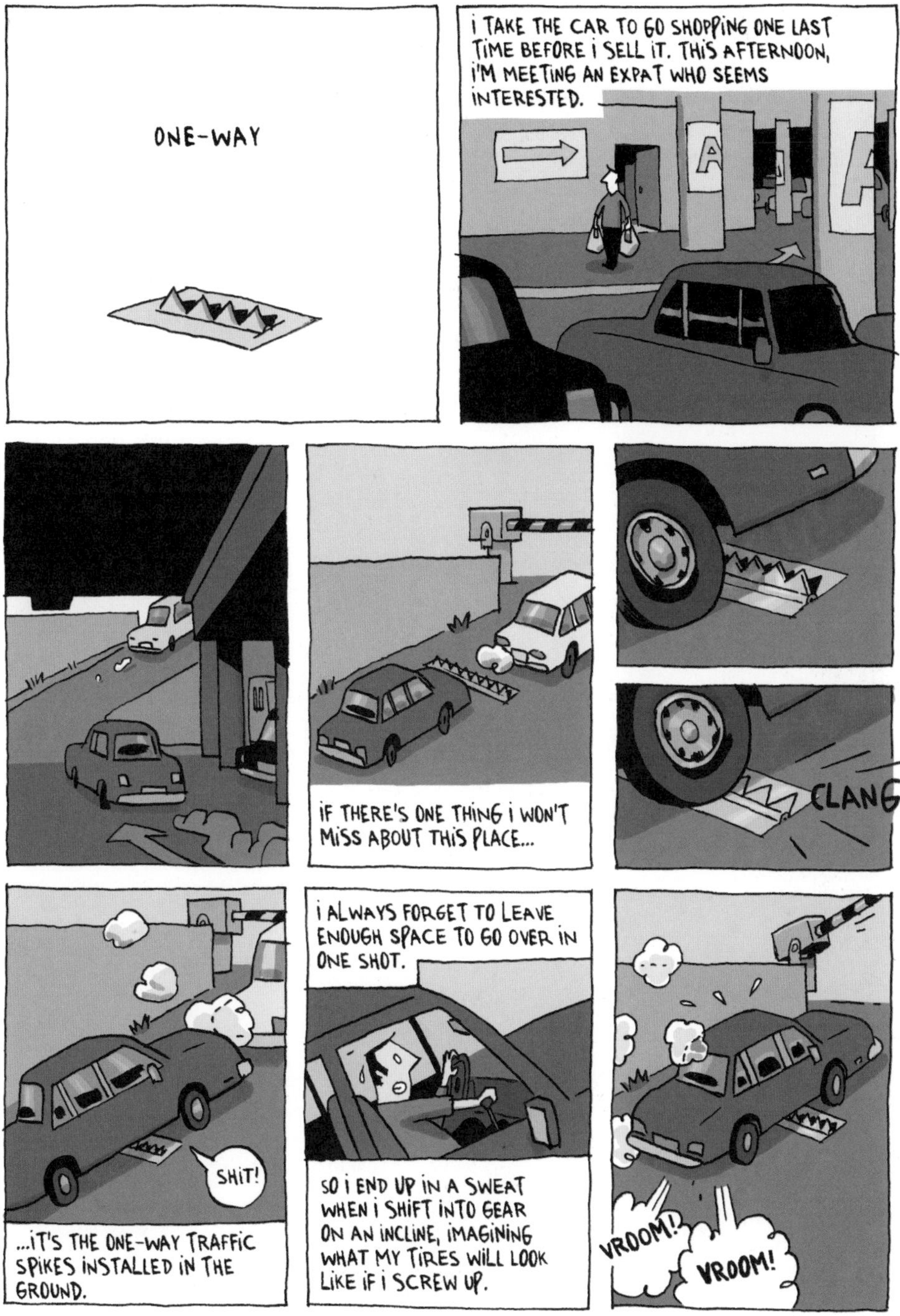
ONE-WAY
I TAKE THE CAR TO GO SHOPPING ONE LAST TIME BEFORE I SELL IT. THIS AFTERNOON, I'M MEETING AN EXPAT WHO SEEMS INTERESTED.
IF THERE'S ONE THING I WON'T MISS ABOUT THIS PLACE...
CLANG!
SHIT!
...IT'S THE ONE-WAY TRAFFIC SPIKES INSTALLED IN THE GROUND.
I ALWAYS FORGET TO LEAVE ENOUGH SPACE TO GO OVER IN ONE SHOT.
SO I END UP IN A SWEAT WHEN I SHIFT INTO GEAR ON AN INCLINE, IMAGINING WHAT MY TIRES WILL LOOK LIKE IF I SCREW UP.
VROOM!
VROOM!

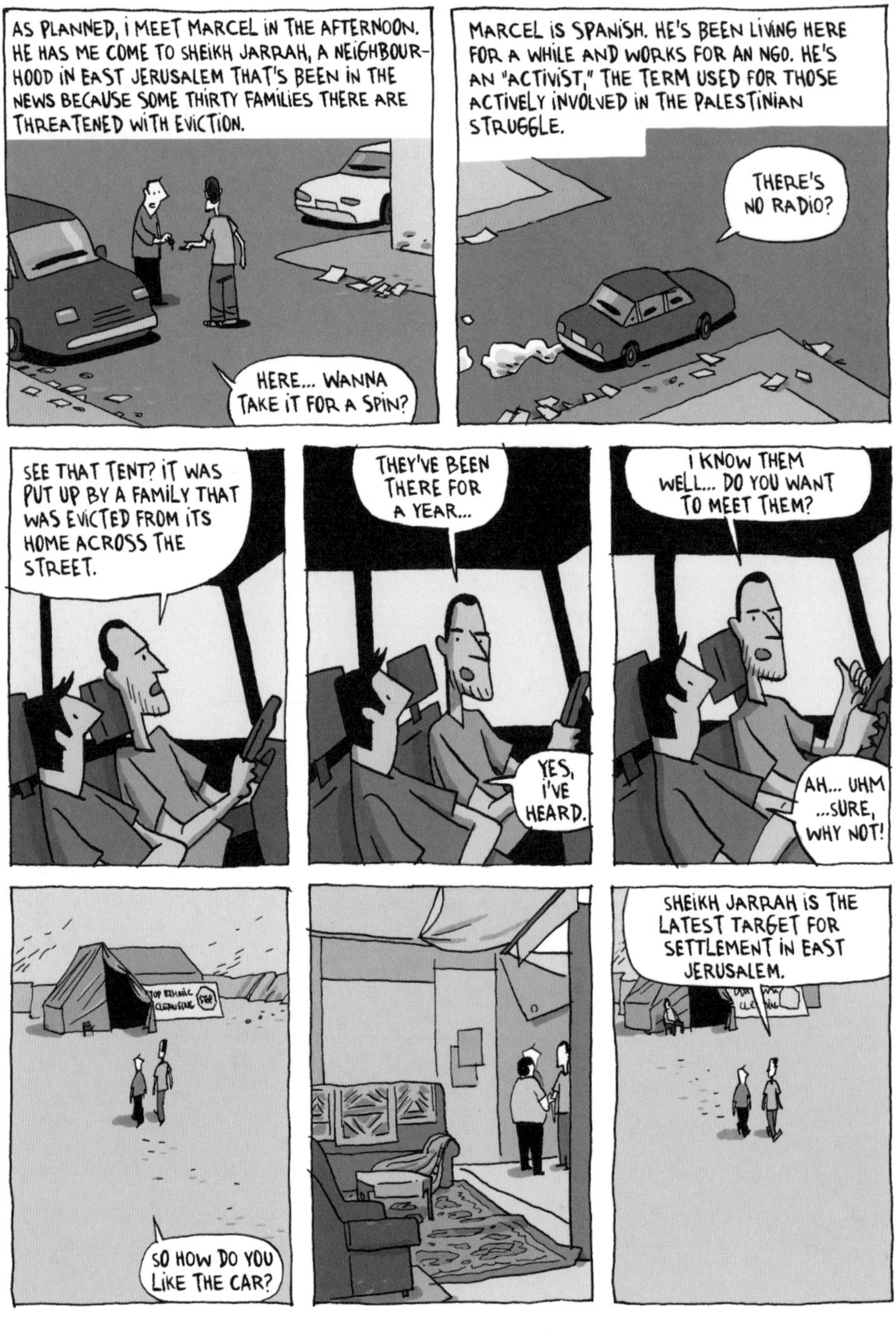
AS PLANNED, I MEET MARCEL IN THE AFTERNOON. HE HAS ME COME TO SHEIKH JARRAH, A NEIGHBOURHOOD IN EAST JERUSALEM THAT'S BEEN IN THE NEWS BECAUSE SOME THIRTY FAMILIES THERE ARE THREATENED WITH EVICTION.
HERE... WANNA TAKE IT FOR A SPIN?
MARCEL IS SPANISH. HE'S BEEN LIVING HERE FOR A WHILE AND WORKS FOR AN NGO. HE'S AN "ACTIVIST," THE TERM USED FOR THOSE ACTIVELY INVOLVED IN THE PALESTINIAN STRUGGLE.
THERE'S NO RADIO?
SEE THAT TENT? IT WAS PUT UP BY A FAMILY THAT WAS EVICTED FROM ITS HOME ACROSS THE STREET.
THEY'VE BEEN THERE FOR A YEAR...
YES, I'VE HEARD.
I KNOW THEM WELL... DO YOU WANT TO MEET THEM?
AH... UHM ...SURE, WHY NOT!
SO HOW DO YOU LIKE THE CAR?
SHEIKH JARRAH IS THE LATEST TARGET FOR SETTLEMENT IN EAST JERUSALEM.

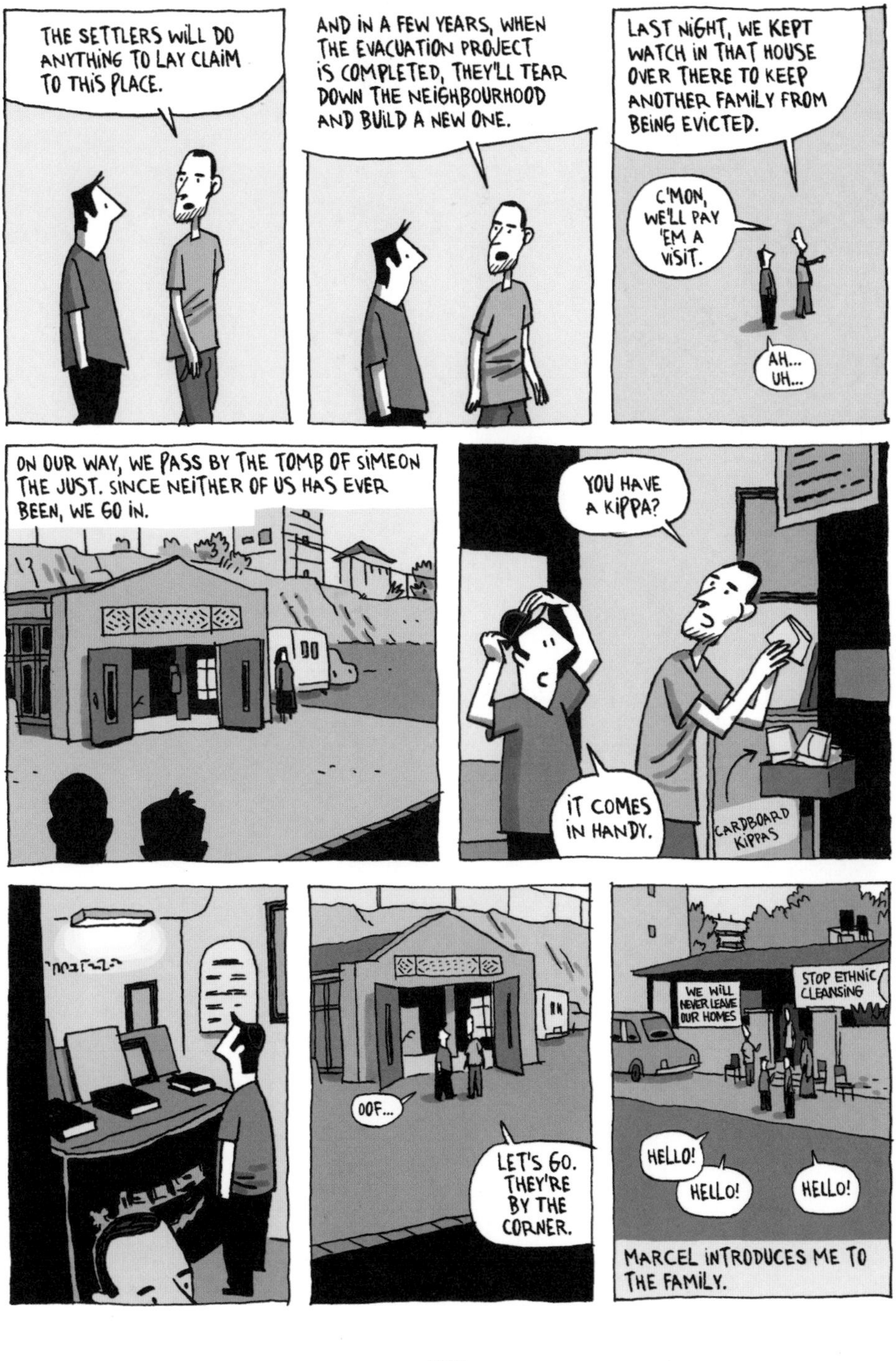

THE SETTLERS WILL DO ANYTHING TO LAY CLAIM TO THIS PLACE.
AND IN A FEW YEARS, WHEN THE EVACUATION PROJECT IS COMPLETED, THEY'LL TEAR DOWN THE NEIGHBOURHOOD AND BUILD A NEW ONE.
LAST NIGHT, WE KEPT WATCH IN THAT HOUSE OVER THERE TO KEEP ANOTHER FAMILY FROM BEING EVICTED.
C'MON, WE'LL PAY 'EM A VISIT.
AH... UH...
ON OUR WAY, WE PASS BY THE TOMB OF SIMEON THE JUST. SINCE NEITHER OF US HAS EVER BEEN, WE GO IN.
YOU HAVE A KIPPA?
IT COMES IN HANDY.
CARDBOARD KIPPAS
OOF...
LET'S GO. THEY'RE BY THE CORNER.
WE WILL NEVER LEAVE OUR HOMES
STOP ETHNIC CLEANSING
HELLO!
HELLO!
HELLO!
MARCEL INTRODUCES ME TO THE FAMILY.

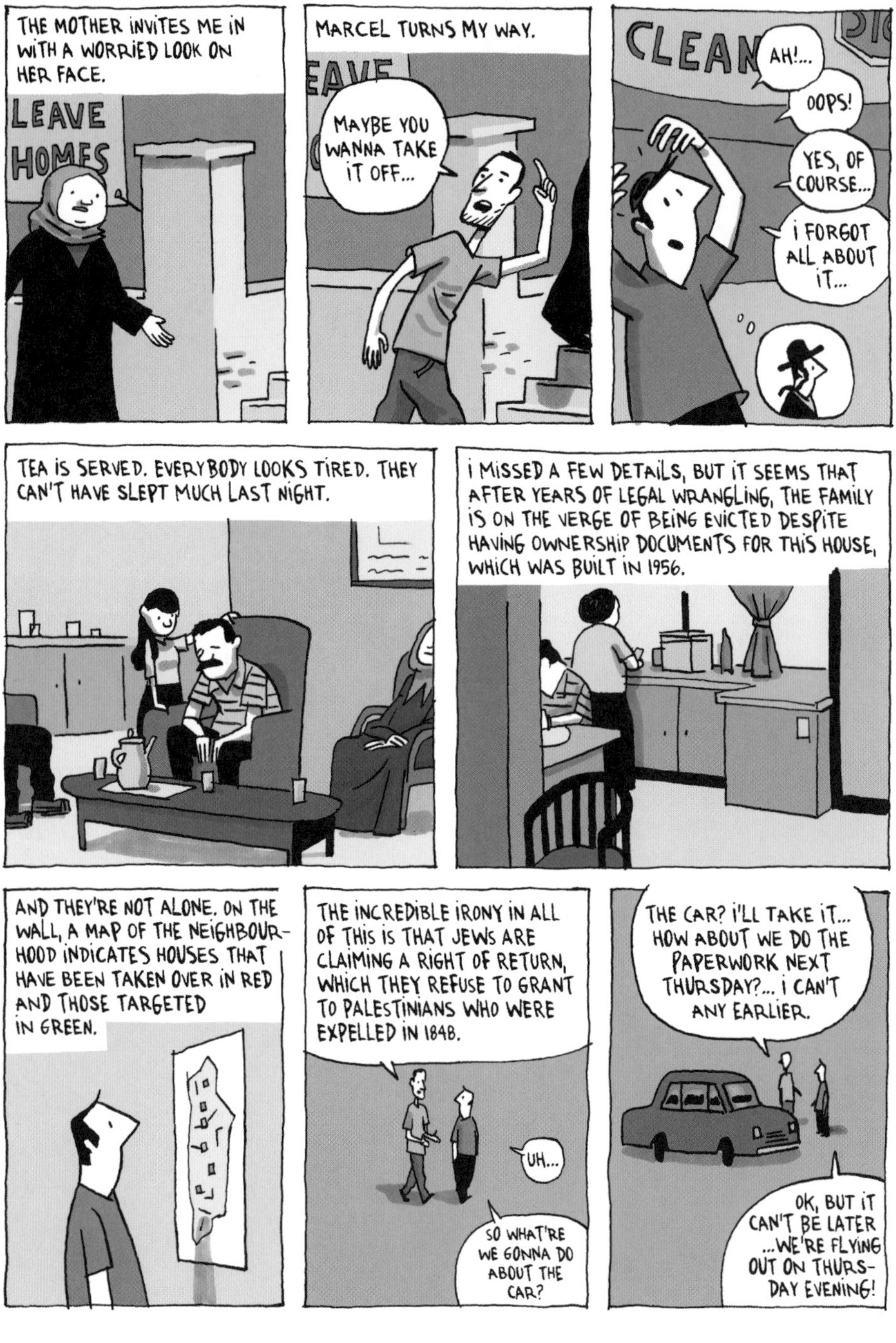
THE MOTHER INVITES ME IN WITH A WORRIED LOOK ON HER FACE.
LEAVE HOMES
MARCEL TURNS MY WAY.
MAYBE YOU WANNA TAKE IT OFF...
CLEAN
AH!...
OOPS!
YES, OF COURSE...
I FORGOT ALL ABOUT IT...
TEA IS SERVED. EVERYBODY LOOKS TIRED. THEY CAN'T HAVE SLEPT MUCH LAST NIGHT.
I MISSED A FEW DETAILS, BUT IT SEEMS THAT AFTER YEARS OF LEGAL WRANGLING, THE FAMILY IS ON THE VERGE OF BEING EVICTED DESPITE HAVING OWNERSHIP DOCUMENTS FOR THIS HOUSE, WHICH WAS BUILT IN 1956.
AND THEY'RE NOT ALONE. ON THE WALL, A MAP OF THE NEIGHBOURHOOD INDICATES HOUSES THAT HAVE BEEN TAKEN OVER IN RED AND THOSE TARGETED IN GREEN.
THE INCREDIBLE IRONY IN ALL OF THIS IS THAT JEWS ARE CLAIMING A RIGHT OF RETURN, WHICH THEY REFUSE TO GRANT TO PALESTINIANS WHO WERE EXPELLED IN 1848.
UH...
SO WHAT'RE WE GONNA DO ABOUT THE CAR?
THE CAR? I'LL TAKE IT... HOW ABOUT WE DO THE PAPERWORK NEXT THURSDAY?... I CAN'T ANY EARLIER.
OK, BUT IT CAN'T BE LATER ...WE'RE FLYING OUT ON THURSDAY EVENING!

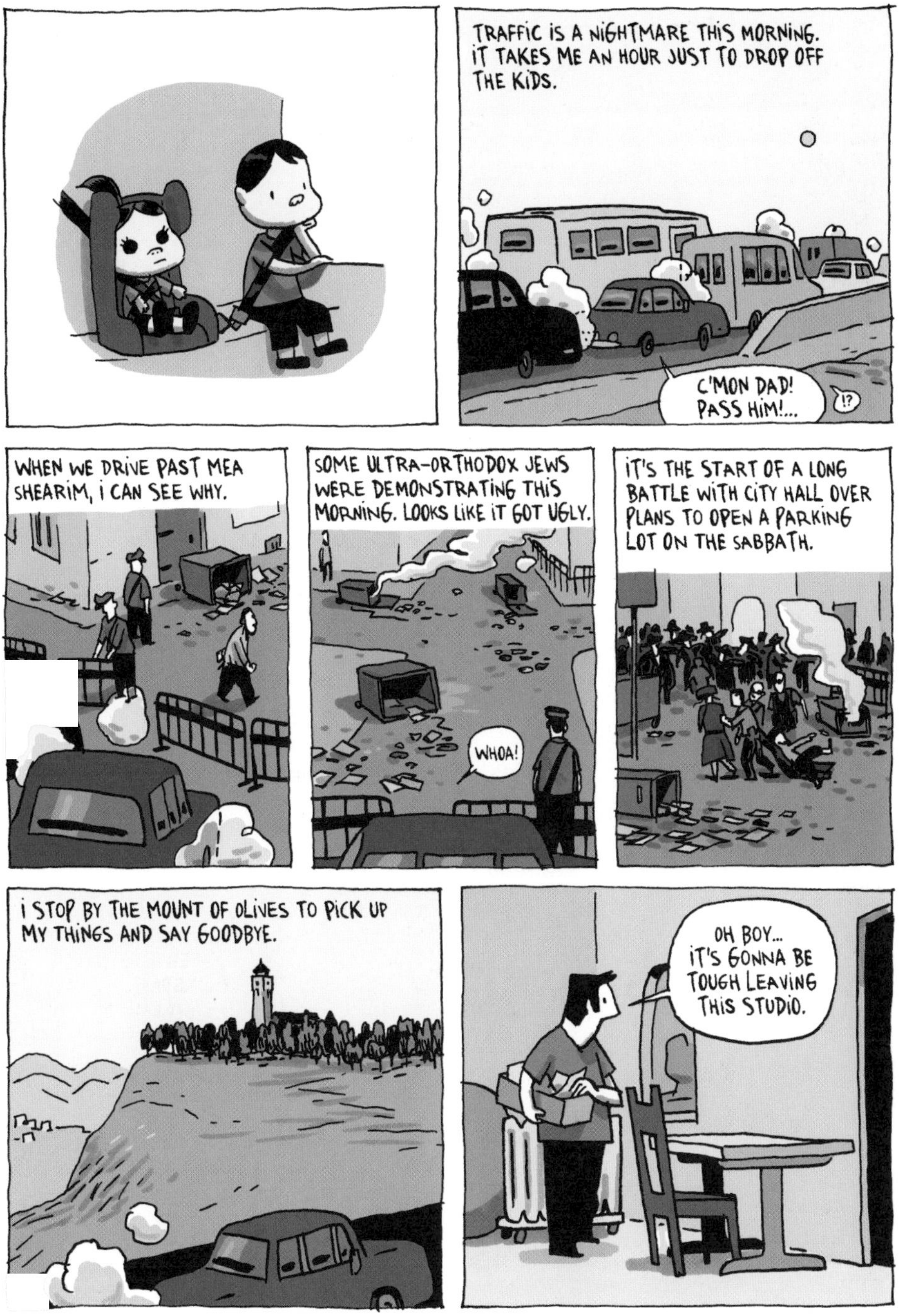
TRAFFIC IS A NIGHTMARE THIS MORNING. IT TAKES ME AN HOUR JUST TO DROP OFF THE KIDS.
C'MON DAD! PASS HIM!...
!?
WHEN WE DRIVE PAST MEA SHEARIM, I CAN SEE WHY.
SOME ULTRA-ORTHODOX JEWS WERE DEMONSTRATING THIS MORNING. LOOKS LIKE IT GOT UGLY.
WHOA!
IT'S THE START OF A LONG BATTLE WITH CITY HALL OVER PLANS TO OPEN A PARKING LOT ON THE SABBATH.
I STOP BY THE MOUNT OF OLIVES TO PICK UP MY THINGS AND SAY GOODBYE.
OH BOY... IT'S GONNA BE TOUGH LEAVING THIS STUDIO.

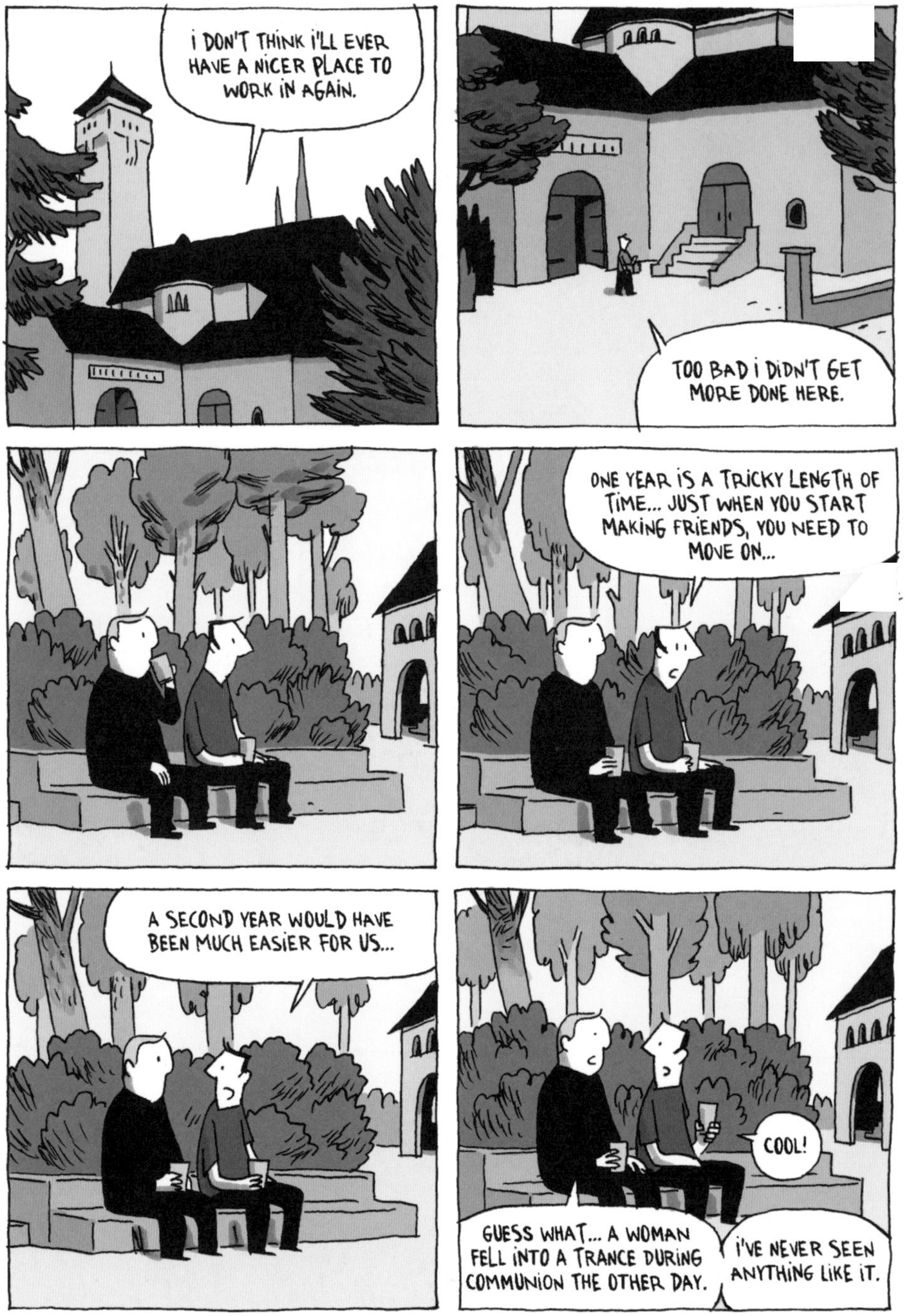
I DON'T THINK I'LL EVER HAVE A NICER PLACE TO WORK IN AGAIN.
TOO BAD I DIDN'T GET MORE DONE HERE.
ONE YEAR IS A TRICKY LENGTH OF TIME... JUST WHEN YOU START MAKING FRIENDS, YOU NEED TO MOVE ON...
A SECOND YEAR WOULD HAVE BEEN MUCH EASIER FOR US...
GUESS WHAT... A WOMAN FELL INTO A TRANCE DURING COMMUNION THE OTHER DAY.
I'VE NEVER SEEN ANYTHING LIKE IT.
COOL!

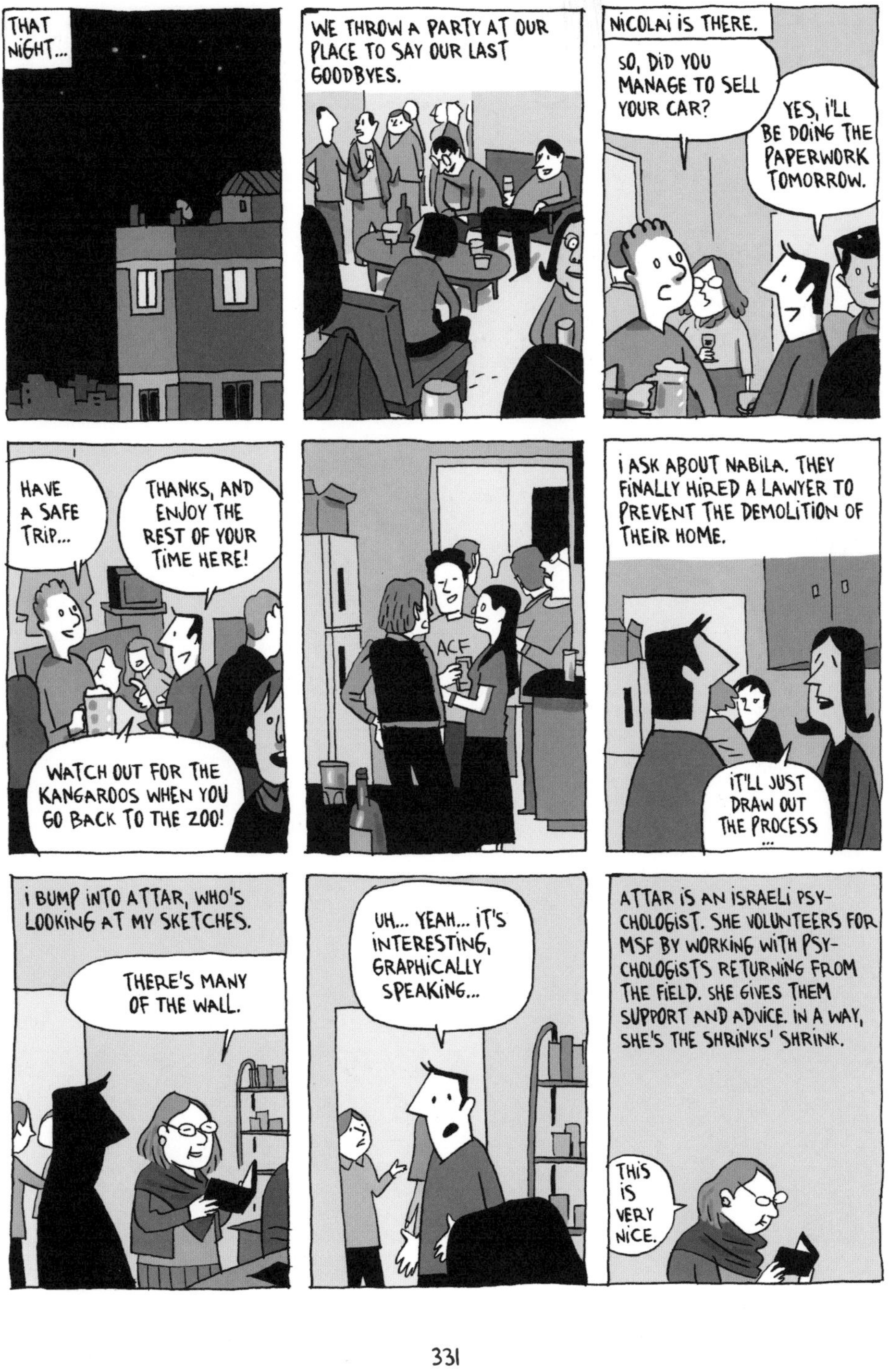
THAT NIGHT...
WE THROW A PARTY AT OUR PLACE TO SAY OUR LAST GOODBYES.
NICOLAI IS THERE.
SO, DID YOU MANAGE TO SELL YOUR CAR?
YES, I'LL BE DOING THE PAPERWORK TOMORROW.
HAVE A SAFE TRIP...
THANKS, AND ENJOY THE REST OF YOUR TIME HERE!
WATCH OUT FOR THE KANGAROOS WHEN YOU GO BACK TO THE ZOO!
ACF
I ASK ABOUT NABILA. THEY FINALLY HIRED A LAWYER TO PREVENT THE DEMOLITION OF THEIR HOME.
IT'LL JUST DRAW OUT THE PROCESS ...
I BUMP INTO ATTAR, WHO'S LOOKING AT MY SKETCHES.
THERE'S MANY OF THE WALL.
UH... YEAH... IT'S INTERESTING, GRAPHICALLY SPEAKING...
ATTAR IS AN ISRAELI PSY-CHOLOGIST. SHE VOLUNTEERS FOR MSF BY WORKING WITH PSY-CHOLOGISTS RETURNING FROM THE FIELD. SHE GIVES THEM SUPPORT AND ADVICE. IN A WAY, SHE'S THE SHRINKS' SHRINK.
THIS IS VERY NICE.

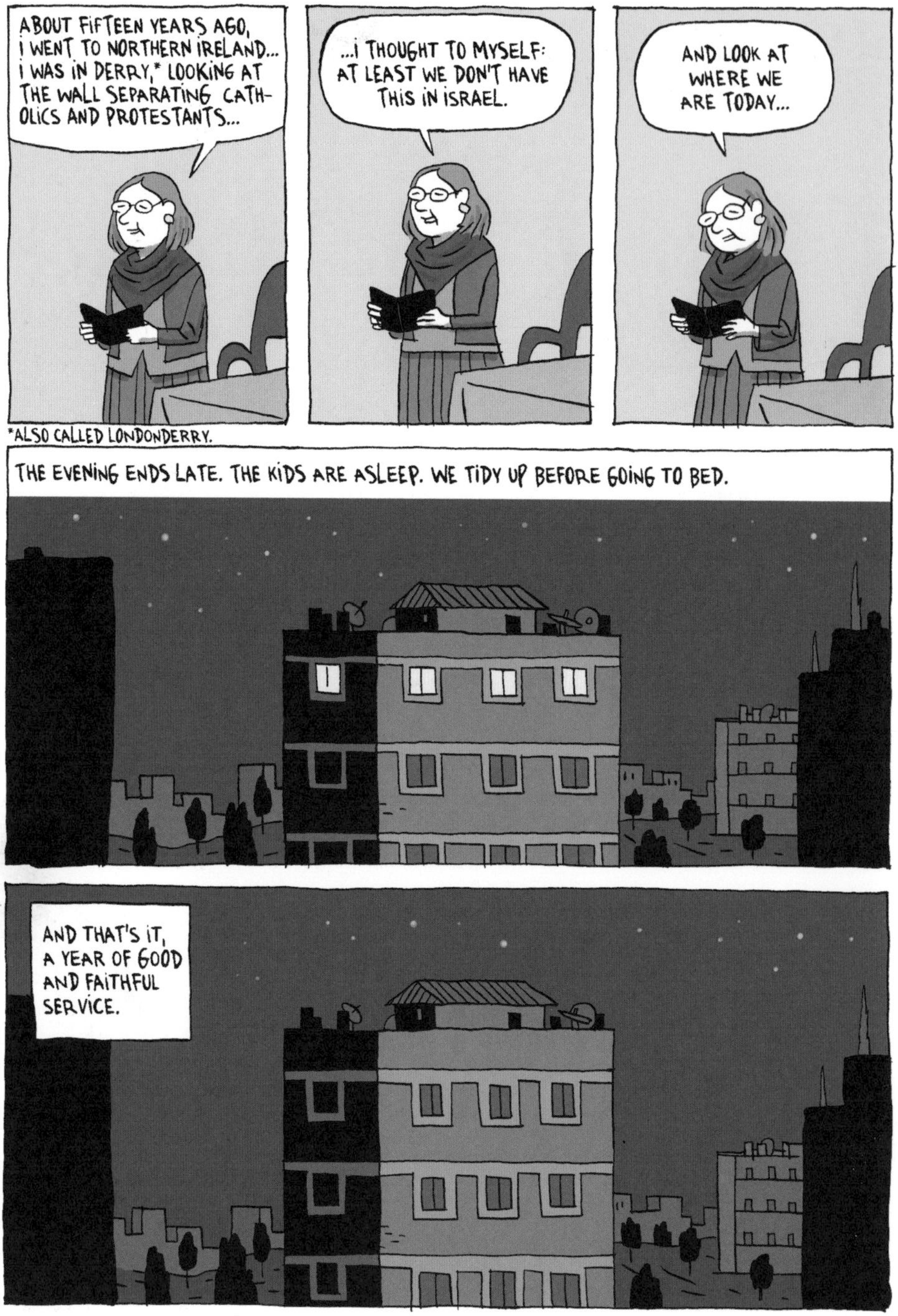
ABOUT FIFTEEN YEARS AGO, I WENT TO NORTHERN IRELAND... I WAS IN DERRY,* LOOKING AT THE WALL SEPARATING CATH-OLICS AND PROTESTANTS...
...I THOUGHT TO MYSELF: AT LEAST WE DON'T HAVE THIS IN ISRAEL.
AND LOOK AT WHERE WE ARE TODAY...
*ALSO CALLED LONDONDERRY.
THE EVENING ENDS LATE. THE KIDS ARE ASLEEP. WE TIDY UP BEFORE GOING TO BED.
AND THAT'S IT, A YEAR OF GOOD AND FAITHFUL SERVICE.

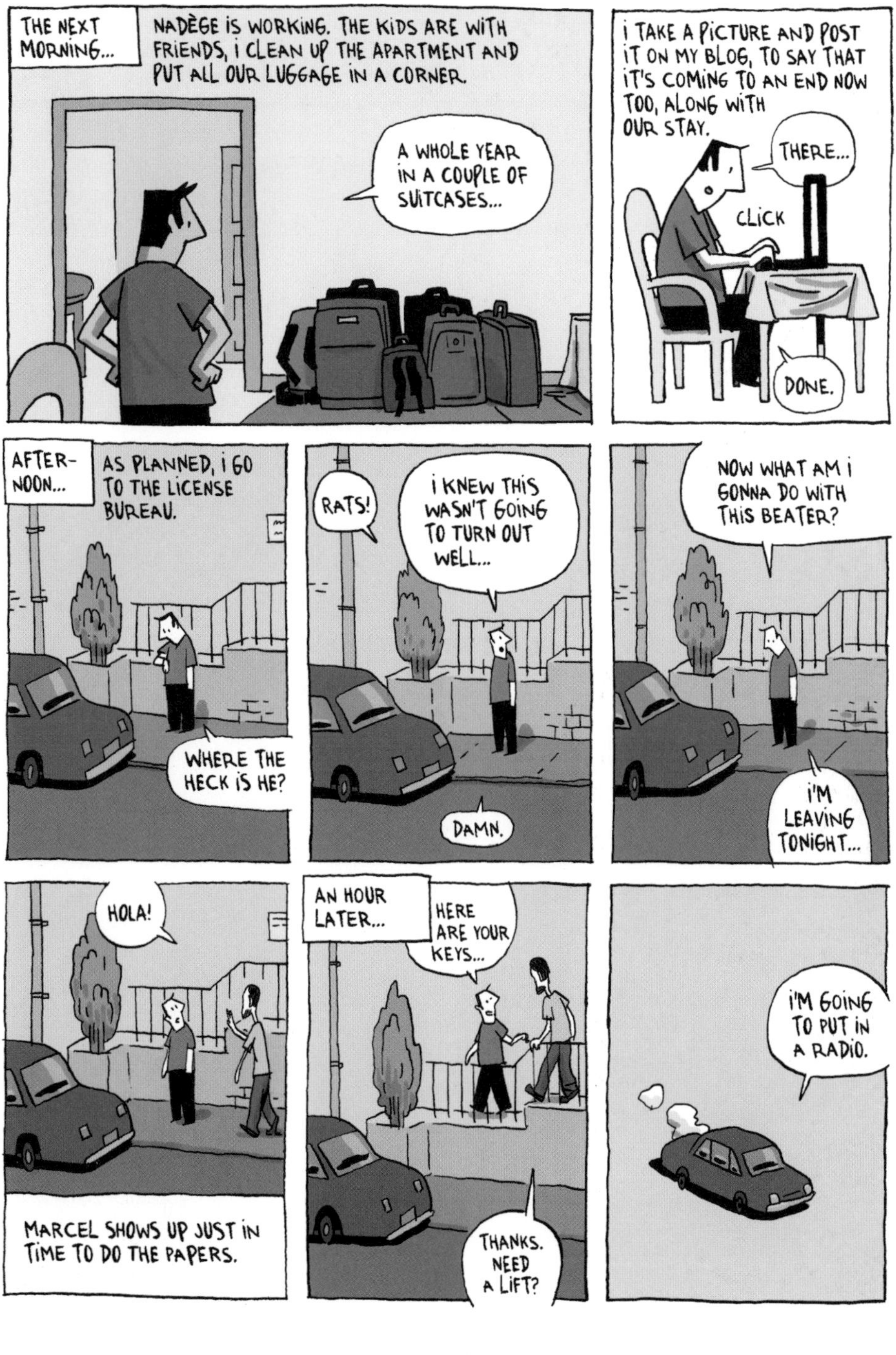
THE NEXT MORNING...
NADÈGE IS WORKING. THE KIDS ARE WITH FRIENDS, I CLEAN UP THE APARTMENT AND PUT ALL OUR LUGGAGE IN A CORNER.
A WHOLE YEAR IN A COUPLE OF SUITCASES...
I TAKE A PICTURE AND POST IT ON MY BLOG, TO SAY THAT IT'S COMING TO AN END NOW TOO, ALONG WITH OUR STAY.
THERE...
CLICK
DONE.
AFTER-NOON...
AS PLANNED, I GO TO THE LICENSE BUREAU.
WHERE THE HECK IS HE?
RATS!
I KNEW THIS WASN'T GOING TO TURN OUT WELL...
DAMN.
NOW WHAT AM I GONNA DO WITH THIS BEATER?
I'M LEAVING TONIGHT...
HOLA!
MARCEL SHOWS UP JUST IN TIME TO DO THE PAPERS.
AN HOUR LATER...
HERE ARE YOUR KEYS...
THANKS. NEED A LIFT?
I'M GOING TO PUT IN A RADIO.

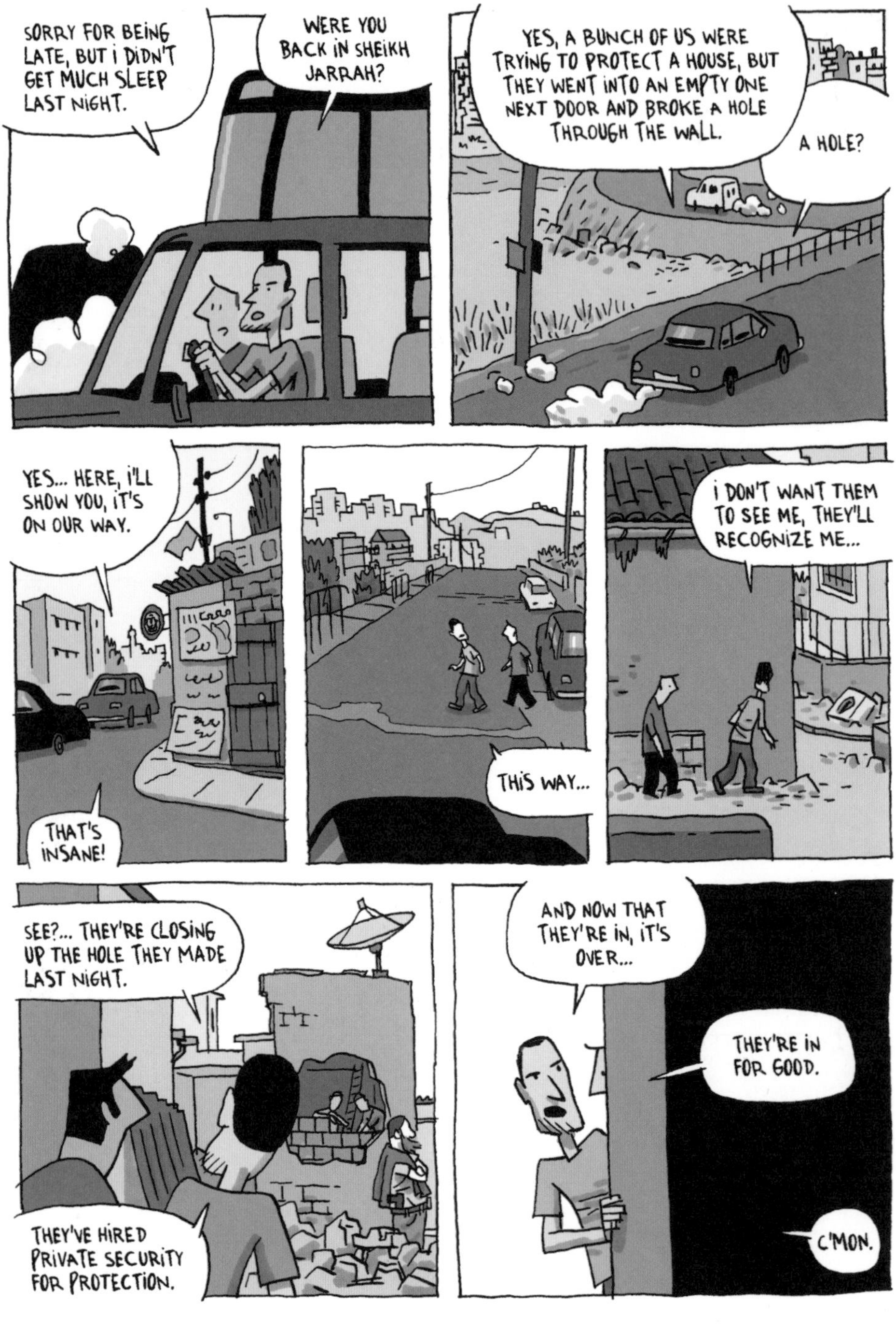
SORRY FOR BEING LATE, BUT I DIDN'T GET MUCH SLEEP LAST NIGHT.
WERE YOU BACK IN SHEIKH JARRAH?
YES, A BUNCH OF US WERE TRYING TO PROTECT A HOUSE, BUT THEY WENT INTO AN EMPTY ONE NEXT DOOR AND BROKE A HOLE THROUGH THE WALL.
A HOLE?
YES... HERE, I'LL SHOW YOU, IT'S ON OUR WAY.
THAT'S INSANE!
THIS WAY...
I DON'T WANT THEM TO SEE ME, THEY'LL RECOGNIZE ME...
SEE?... THEY'RE CLOSING UP THE HOLE THEY MADE LAST NIGHT.
THEY'VE HIRED PRIVATE SECURITY FOR PROTECTION.
AND NOW THAT THEY'RE IN, IT'S OVER...
THEY'RE IN FOR GOOD.
C'MON.

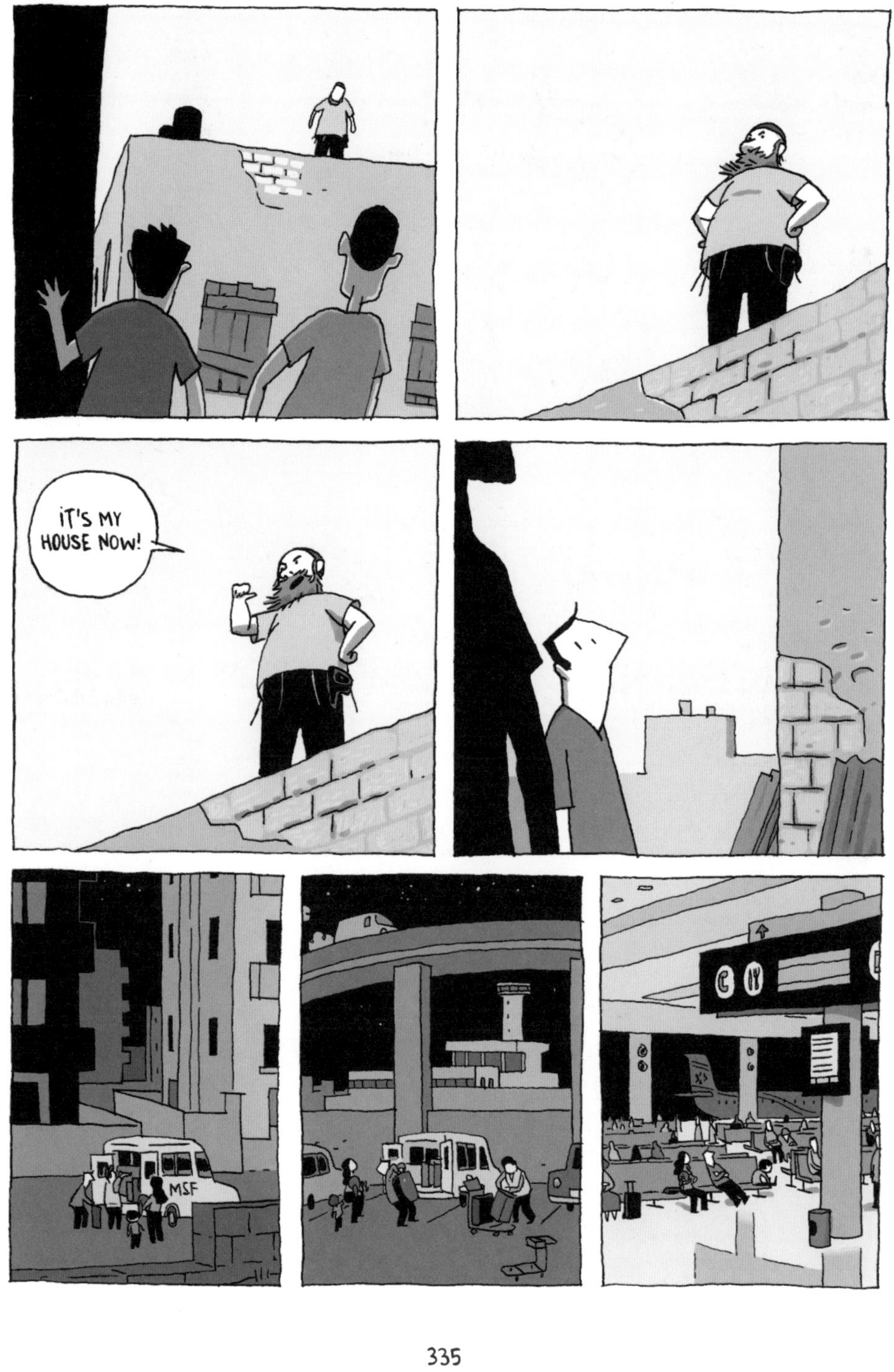
IT'S MY HOUSE NOW!
MSF

DELISLE 2011